Lincoln Christian College

W9-CBP-010

LANGUAGE LOYALTY IN THE UNITED STATES

JANUA LINGUARUM

STUDIA MEMORIAE
NICOLAI VAN WIJK DEDICATA

edenda curat

CORNELIS H. VAN SCHOONEVELD
STANFORD UNIVERSITY

SERIES MAIOR
XXI

1966
MOUTON & CO.
LONDON · THE HAGUE · PARIS

LANGUAGE LOYALTY
IN THE UNITED STATES

The Maintenance and Perpetuation
of Non-English Mother Tongues
by American Ethnic and Religious Groups

by

JOSHUA A. FISHMAN

YESHIVA UNIVERSITY

and

Vladimir C. Nahirny, John E. Hofman, Robert G. Hayden

with the assistance of
Mary E. Warshauer, Heinz Kloss, Herve B. Lemaire,
Chester C. and Jane Christian, and Nathan Glazer

and with an Introduction by
Einar Haugen
Harvard University

1966
MOUTON & CO.
LONDON · THE HAGUE · PARIS

© Copyright 1966 Mouton & Co., Publishers, The Hague, The Netherlands.

No part of this book may be translated or reproduced in any form, by print, photoprint, microfilm, or any other means, without written permission from the publishers.

Printed in The Netherlands by Mouton & Co., Printers, The Hague.

409.73
F53

34085

Dedicated to the memory
of my father, for whom the trials
and treasures of language maintenance
represented the very core of existence.

"... for a man to speak one language rather than another is a ritual act, it is a statement about one's personal status; to speak the same language as one's neighbours expresses solidarity with those neighbours, to speak a different language from one's neighbours expresses social distance or even hostility."

E. R. Leach, "Political Systems of Highland Burma", 1954

"Now the question no longer is: how shall we learn English so that we may take part in the social life of America and partake of her benefits; the big question is: how can we preserve the language of our ancestors here, in a strange environment, and pass on to our descendents the treasures which it contains?"

Trond Bothne, Professor at Luther College, 1898

INTRODUCTION

EINAR HAUGEN

The pioneer is one of the folk heroes of American life. The very word calls forth images of energy and resourcefulness, of daring and high adventure. The word immigrant has no such connotations, in spite of the fact that virtually all Americans are immigrants or the descendants of immigrants, and that every immigrant was also a pioneer. He broke out of the settled folkways of his childhood home, emerged from the sheltering womb of his old world, and went forth to conquer a new one. The tears which he or his kinsmen shed on this occasion were his farewell to the past. Whether he liked it or not, his eyes were now turned to the future, scanning the horizon for opportunities that might in fact never materialize.

His first shock was the realization that he was an "immigrant", by popular conception an uprooted, homeless, displaced person, assigned a position at or near the bottom of the social ladder. The immigrant was a greenhorn, an ignoramus, raw material for the future American, only the rudiment of a human being. It is hard for Americans to remove this cliche from their vocabulary or their thinking. The huddled, the homeless, the dispossessed – these are the categories that involuntarily attach themselves to the word "immigrant".

Joshua Fishman has done us all a great service in building up a more positive image of the immigrant in this book. He has brought to light a facet of the immigrant's life in this country which has remained unknown and unheralded even by most historians of immigration, let alone historians of America. He has demonstrated the importance of seeing the immigrant as one who brought with him in his native language a pearl of great price. He has portrayed the efforts of immigrants to maintain their linguistic identity against overwhelming odds. He has documented the cost to each immigrant group of the loss which they endured when their children or their children's children refused to speak the old language. Many capitulated without a struggle, but some trait of stubborn self-assertion, some streak of pride, made many others rally to their language and wage a fight which would have been called heroic had others been there to witness it. Against indifference and contempt even the gods fight in vain, but these fighters for a doomed ethnic medium have at least been given belated recognition through the vast and patient research effort of Professor Fishman and his associates.

When, a decade ago, I outlined in some detail the history of the Norwegian language in America, I was struck by the utter apathy of most Americans to the problem of immigrant languages. I wrote then: "Americans have tended to take it for granted that 'foreigners' should acquire English, and that a failure to do so was evidence by implication of a kind of disloyalty to the basic principles of American life... It has seldom been recognized that the bilingual might have problems of adjustment which called on the best efforts of students and scholars for their solution." It is highly gratifying to see this response to my complaint: a statistically and conceptually sophisticated analysis of the problem on a national scale. In trying to assess the Norwegian development, I noted that it was impossible to evaluate its significance without seeing it against the entire background of linguistic assimilation in our country. "The facts on which such an evaluation could be based are not yet available." This statement no longer applies, thanks to the present volume.

Dr. Fishman and his associates have given many of us a new concept to consider in "ethnicity", and have applied it in a keen analysis of American nationalism. They have shown how the immigrant responded to the threatening loss of ethnic identity from the moment of immigration to the last of his ethnically conscious descendants. They have explored the role of the grandparents in immigrant life, and have critically examined Marcus Lee Hansen's concept of "third-generation interest". They have given us overall statistics on language maintenance, where these exist. They have scrutinized in detail certain large linguistic groups and have set up cross-group hypotheses of great interest. They have cast a searching look at the role of the church, of secular societies, and of the neighborhood in either maintaining or discouraging language loyalty.

By bringing us thus far along the road to understanding, they have opened the way to further studies which cry out to be done. Every language group has its hitherto unrecognized linguistic profile, its unsung heroes of language maintenance and language shift, and its contribution to make to the total picture of ethnic America. The studies here collected can now be enriched by further research in depth into the linguistic experiences of the immigrants, especially their piecemeal adjustment to American thinking by the adoption of English words and values. There is still much to be said concerning the beauty and the truth embodied in immigrant literatures, and their often worm's-eye view of American life. We are only at the threshold of such studies, but deeply sensible of the great forward step which has here been taken.

Dr. Fishman has pointed out two not unrelated vistas which are opened up by his studies. One is pragmatic: that there may still be time to salvage some of these resources for general American life, that indeed the success of our foreign policy may depend on our doing so. In a thoughtful but provocatively inciting semi-final chapter he urges certain policies which can hardly check the inevitable, but which might possibly channel these forces in a productive way. The other vista is theoretical; in an even more closely reasoned appendix he beckons the scholar into the green pastures of future sociolinguistic research. He makes the point that the American development has a world setting and a long perspective. Language shifts and the resistance to them have been going on and are still going on wherever languages impinge on one another. Through studies of our problem we may cast light on the problems of the world.

Bloomington, Indiana
July 20, 1964

TABLE OF CONTENTS

This is a study of the self-maintenance efforts, rationales, and accomplishments of non-English speaking immigrants on American shores. It is not a study of the assimilation of American immigrants and of the resultant formation of the supra-ethnic American nation. The two processes – de-ethnization and Americanization, on the one hand, and cultural-linguistic self-maintenance, on the other – are equally ubiquitous throughout all of American history. They are neither necessarily opposite sides of the same coin nor conflicting processes. Frequently the same individuals and groups have been simultaneously devoted to both in different domains of behavior. However, as a nation we have paid infinitely more attention to the Americanization process than to the self-maintenance process. As a result, we have tended to be insulated from some of the most stirring cognitive and emotional processes within ourselves and throughout the rest of the world. This study represents an all too preliminary attempt to redress this imbalance in attention. Such redress would seem to be particularly appropriate at the present time when non-English language skills have been recognized as scarce and vital commodities in the conduct of our nation's international relations. Is it possible that we have appreciable but as yet unrecognized resources of these scarce commodities? Is it possible that these resources are being wasted as a result of apathy and ignorance? It is unfortunate that these questions were not asked and answered years ago.

What do we – citizens and social scientists – know about culture and language maintenance efforts in the United States? Very little indeed. How many of us, even among professional historians or students of religion in America, know that a Polish National Catholic Church grew up on *our* shores, rather than in Poland proper, because so many Polish-Americans were distressed by the policy of American Catholic leaders toward language and culture maintenance? Or that a similar state of affairs almost came into being among Franco-Americans in New England? How many of us know about the language problems that convulsed several German and Norwegian Lutheran denominations for well over half a century, or of the language issues that have influenced Jewish ethnic, religious, and intellectual life in America? Certainly, few serious students of American mass media know that the nearly defunct German press of today is a vestigial remnant of hundreds of periodic publications that appeared as recently as sixty years ago and that once represented a major force in American journalism. Few serious students of American education are aware of the bilingual *public* elementary schools that existed in several states until quite recent years. One purpose of this study is to introduce such information into the mainstream of American awareness.

What do we know in terms of basic social bookkeeping in the area of culture and language maintenance? No accurate records have been kept concerning the non-English language press or non-English broadcasting. No systematic or accurate data are available concerning the ethnic group schools, camps, choruses, research institutes, or other educational, cultural, and fraternal efforts proceeding by means of or on behalf of languages other than English. Even the mother tongue data of the United States Bureau of the Census have been collected irregularly, reluctantly, and inappropriately. Silence and disinterest have conspired to make us ignorant of our own past and present. Even worse, they have conspired to make it difficult, if not impossible, for us ever to become fully informed. Appropriate records have never been kept, nor are such records being kept today. Many researchers have come to take for granted the huge establishments which supply us with data (inadequate though these data, too, may be) on births and deaths, immigration and housing, family size and divorce, crime, income, and so on. The researcher interested in topics not blessed by similarly consistent and exhaustive bookkeeping is painfully aware of what is missing and of gaps that can never be entirely filled. Another purpose of this report is to supply some basic descriptive information in a number of pitifully ignored fields.

Most basically, however, this study is an attempt to explore the current *extent* and *status* of culture and language maintenance efforts. In some chapters this is done by means of trend analyses. In others it is done by contrasting separate cultural and linguistic groups. In still others the approach is that of internal comparisons, i.e., of contrasting maintenance-oriented and maintenance-opposed units within particular groups or within a particular domain of cultural activity. The relevance of language maintenance and language shift phenomena in the United States for a broader understanding of similar phenomena in other (including less-developed nations) throughout the world is also pointed to, as is the relevance of the latter for a deeper understanding of the former.

This study was conceived and conducted as an exploratory, hypotheses-generating venture into a field that had hitherto received so little attention that even its major subdivisions were as yet unknown. As a result, a large number of parameters have received attention, more in an effort to establish their location or amenability to further research than to determine their relative importance or their detailed characteristics. Focused attempts to attain methodological rigor or innovation, linguistic, psychological and sociological interrelation, or theoretical sophistication were postponed for future occasions when grosser sociological and historical dimensions would be more recognizable. Thus, rather than run the risk of prematurely imposing a single theoretical model on all chapters, the risks of proceeding without such a model were accepted. Varying theoretical approaches (as well as starkly atheoretical ones) were equally encouraged. Furthermore, some topics were pursued by staff members working together or aware of each other's approaches, whereas others were studied by individuals who were not in contact with each other's work. This pattern was adopted in order to determine whether consistent findings and interpretations would present themselves independently of agreement in advance on theoretical matters. Finally, as investigators worked on subsequent topics, various formulations they had merely glimpsed in prior work ultimately became more fully integrated and more consciously developed. I hope that the report produced as a result of these permissive approaches nevertheless leaves the field of inquiry somewhat more organized than it was when my associates and I initially encountered it.

Chapter 1 presents the questions, assumptions, and self-imposed limitations that guided our efforts to uncover and study the non-English language resources of the United States as of approximately 1960.

Chapters 2 through 6 deal primarily with the enumerative aspects of formal language maintenance resources and institutions. The size, generational structure, and other socio-demographic characteristics of the immigrant-derived non-English mother tongue population are examined. Similarly, non-English periodic publications, radio broadcasts, schools and parishes are examined in turn, with attention being given to their number, distribution, functional characteristics, changes over time, and prospects with respect to the future.

Chapters 7 and 8 focus upon interacting language maintenance contexts and processes. The ethnic family, the ethnic community, the ethnic organization, and the organizational and cultural leadership are examined to determine the extent and circumstances of positive or negative language maintenance views and behaviors.

Chapters 9 through 12 are integrative essays each of which deals with the speakers of a particular language. Of the six languages originally studied in this fashion, four are discussed in this volume. Three have long been major prestige languages on the world scene. Their firm roots on the North American continent are found in early colonial days before the United States itself arose as a political entity. The remaining language accorded similarly detailed attention contrasts significantly with the former three in world-wide prestige, in number of speakers, in recency of immigrant status in the United States, and in other respects. The availability of these several contrasts permits a consideration of their importance in conjunction with current language maintenance status and prospects. In addition, these four essays facilitate a reconsideration of empirical relationships and theoretical propositions advanced in the topical chapters that precede them.

Chapters 13 through 15 and Appendix B present summaries, recommendations, and conclusions. They indicate the distance covered by the current study as well as the much greater distance still to be travelled if language maintenance and language shift are to be adequately understood, not to mention appropriately controlled. Chapter 13 deserves particular mention since it represents an independent attempt to integrate and interpret our data on the part of a well known student of American ethnic groups who was not otherwise involved in our inquiries. As such it may serve both as a stimulant to further efforts and as a reliability-validity check on our own work.

My ability to undertake this study, to pursue it, and to complete it was crucially dependent upon the continued assistance and encouragement of a number of individuals and institutions. First among these is obviously the Language Research Section of the United States Office of Education. I am particularly grateful to Dr. A. Bruce Gaarder, then Director of the Section, for his encouragement, constant support, and remarkable understanding. The staff and associates of the Language Resources Project unquestionably deserve greater recognition than the mere listing of their names next to the titles of the studies with which they were most intimately involved. Their tasks were frequently far more difficult than any of them had bargained for. Their performance in response to these difficulties was far above and beyond "the call of duty". Since her name is not otherwise listed in this report, I want to acknowledge my particular debt to Mrs. Rebecca Joseph. She served the Language Resources Project for three and a half years as senior secretary and office manager. Crowning the several minor miracles which she performed throughout this period was the major miracle of typing, duplicating, and collating the original 1800 page, three volume version of this study[1] in a thoroughly expert manner at a time when I was 3,000 miles away.

From the very first, a distinguished group of scholars regularly offered me their wisdom, their time, and their encouragement. Since they asked for no recognition or compensation in this connection, I am all the more eager to list their names at this time: Professor Theodore Andersson, Chairman, Department of Romance Languages, University of Texas; Professor John B. Carroll, Director, Laboratory of Research in Instruction, Harvard University Graduate School of Education; Professor Einar Haugen, then Chairman, Department of Scandinavian, University of Wisconsin (now at Harvard University); Read Lewis, Executive Director, American Council for Nationalities Service, New York; the late Professor Irving D. Lorge, Director, Institute of Psychological Research, Teachers College, Columbia University; Professor Howard Lee Nostrand, Chairman, Department of Romance Languages and Literatures, University of Washington; and Professor Uriel Weinreich, Chairman, Department of General and Comparative Linguistics, Columbia University. Their genuine (rather than pro forma) interest and their incisive criticism redounded to my decided benefit.

---

[1] The original report to the Language Research Section ("Language Loyalty in the United States", New York, Yeshiva University, 1964, 3 volumes, mimeo.) is in many respects a more intensive and extensive treatment than the current published version and will be referred to as a primary source on several occasions throughout this presentation, particularly in connection with empirical and methodological details. Copies of the original report are available upon request from the Language Research Section or on inter-library loan from the Yeshiva University Graduate Center Library.

A large number of other consultants, readers, and critics assisted in connection with one or more of the studies included in this report. Their names are far too numerous to mention here. My hope is that my indebtedness to them is accurately acknowledged in the original report.

When this study was initially commissioned I was a faculty member in the Departments of Psychology and Human Relations at the University of Pennsylvania. However, very soon thereafter, I accepted an appointment as Dean of the Graduate School of Education and as a faculty member in the Department of Psychology at Yeshiva University. I am, therefore, substantially indebted to members of the faculty and administration of both these institutions. At the University of Pennsylvania my debt is greatest to Professor Martin P. Chworowsky, Director, Albert M. Greenfield Center for Human Relations and Chairman, Department of Human Relations. He was a truly stimulating and helpful friend throughout my association with the University and has remained thus. At Yeshiva University I am indebted to Associate Dean Abraham J. Tannenbaum and to Assistant Dean Adelaide Jablonsky to an almost unconscionable degree. They took upon themselves heavy administrative burdens so that I might more easily find the time and the peace of mind required for research. I can never sufficiently acknowledge nor return their kindness.

My indebtedness to my wife and my children can easily be imagined. What is less easily imagined is their capacity to understand, to forgive, and to love.

Finally, I owe acknowledgement and gratitude to the Center for Advanced Study in the Behavioral Sciences. The peace, the stimulation, and the comradeship provided by the Center during the 1963-64 academic year were unsurpassable for the purposes of preparing, first, the final text of my report to the Language Research Section, subsequently for preparing the current abridged version for publication; and finally, for preparing myself for future work in the sociology and social psychology of language. Each of the Fellows and staff members of the Center assisted and stimulated me in many important ways. Miriam Gallaher, who painstakingly edited my original report and greatly improved its organization and presentation deserves particular thanks and recognition, as does Mary Tye who expertly retyped the entire manuscript.

It is my fond hope to return to this topic-area in the future to pursue each of the three kinds of initial studies that "might have been", but which were postponed until later: (a) a study giving explicit attention to language proficiency and to formal characteristics of language performance under varying conditions of language maintenance and language shift; (b) a study giving explicit attention to the social-psychological processes and problems of language maintenance and language shift at the level of individual behavior; (c) a presentation of the story of language maintenance and language shift in the United States for the average "lay" reader.

All in all, my work on the study reported in this volume has provided me with a great deal of satisfaction over a period of many months. I am grateful to have had the opportunity to examine language maintenance and language shift at a time when questions of culture continuity and culture change are of increasing concern to the United States, to its neighbors, and to much of the world. While this growing interest has enabled me to study a socially meaningful topic, I am also grateful to all those enumerated above for enabling me to do so without undue pressure and with some intellectual detachment and perspective. Without being overly proud of the *product* of my labors, I complete them with a very real sense of satisfaction with the *process*.

Stanford, California   JOSHUA A. FISHMAN
June 12, 1964

1. THE HISTORICAL AND SOCIAL CONTEXTS OF AN INQUIRY INTO LANGUAGE MAINTENANCE EFFORTS

JOSHUA A. FISHMAN

The cultural and linguistic self-maintenance efforts of American minority groups are surrounded by towering mountains of ignorance and vast oceans of apathy. The average American citizen, the political leader, the intellectual, and the minority group member himself have, at least, these bonds of ignorance and apathy to unite them. These are strange bonds in a "nation of immigrants", a "citadel of democracy", and a "leader of the free world". To the extent that they have been aware of ethnic minorities at all, laymen and social scientists alike have most frequently been concerned with "disappearance phenomena", i.e., the processes by which these groups of immigrant or indigenous origin become assimilated into American core society and the rapidity with which they become culturally indistinguishable, if not un-distinguished. The lack of attention – indeed the repression of awareness – that characterizes our reaction to "maintenance phenomena", the efforts of minority cultural groups to maintain and develop their particular heritages as vibrant (rather than as ossified or makeshift) lifeways, is undoubtedly related to the unusual position of immigrants and of minorities in the relatively brief period of American national and cultural existence. Only recently has a change of heart and a change of mind become noticeable. It is an open question whether this change represents an instance of "better late than never" or of "too little and too late".

While admitting the centrality of de-ethnization and acculturation in American history and in American national awareness, it must be pointed out that its opposite has also been a part of the continental American scene from the very beginning. Although American core society has usually been ignorant of the efforts of ethnic minorities to maintain themselves in its midst, such efforts have always been underway. Furthermore, from the very first, these efforts have been expressed within a broad context of religious, cultural, and value differences. Language maintenance, prompted by one or another variety of language loyalty, has frequently been a component – and, at times, a catalyst – in these efforts. And it is with language maintenance – sometimes in relation to culture maintenance and sometimes in its own right – that this study is primarily concerned.

Once the fact of language maintenance is recognized, its persistence acknowledged, its relationship to our national needs and to our cultural growth considered, a host of questions arise to confront the investigator. What is the current "state of health" of the various non-English languages spoken natively (or reasonably so) by segments of the American population? What factors are responsible or co-responsible (and to what extent) for the better health of some and the poorer health of others? What characteristics differentiate linguistically more retentive from less retentive individuals, organizations, and communities of similar ethnic background? What rationales are currently advanced on behalf of (or in opposition to) language maintenance, and how do they differ from those advanced a generation or more ago? How does language maintenance compare with – and how is it related to – the maintenance of non-linguistic components of life-style and world-view among minority culture groups in the United States? How hopeful are language maintenance activists today, and how realistic do their hopes seem to be? These and countless other, more detailed, questions stream in one upon the other. They are a reflection of our current ignorance and our past neglect. Indeed, we are ignorant of the extent to which these are really separate questions, as well as of the extent to which they require separate answers for separate languages, as opposed to theoretically integratable and common questions and answers for all languages or for clusters of languages. We hope in the course of our study to open up much of this realm of inquiry for further study and, in so doing, to provide tentative answers to some of the above mentioned questions.

THE LANGUAGES OF THE UNITED STATES

The non-English languages of the continental United States are commonly classified into three groups: (a) indigenous or native languages, (b) colonial languages, and (c) immigrant languages (Haugen 1946).

Indigenous Languages

The indigenous languages are those formerly or currently spoken by various Indian tribes. Today, the Indian population of the United States is estimated to be as great as or even somewhat greater than what it was when European colonization began in earnest. Nevertheless, many of the original tribes have disappeared entirely (as a result of warfare, disease, or assimilation), and all but a few have been relocated on reservations far from their ancestral lands. Since the second half of the 19th century, the federal government has vacillated between policies oriented toward forced de-tribalization and tribal autonomy. This on-again, off-again treatment has greatly weakened the ability and interest of Indian tribes to retain their languages. Almost all American Indians now speak English; a substantial number are still bilingual; only a minor fraction (primarily individuals of advanced age) are monolingual in one or another Indian language.

Of the nearly 300 recognizably separate American Indian languages and dialects still extant, only roughly 40% have more than one hundred speakers (Chafe 1962).

In the case of approximately 55% of these languages, the remaining speakers are of advanced age. Both of these facts imply that many American Indian languages are destined to disappear with the death of their current speakers, barring the unlikely development of major revitalization movements with linguistic emphases (Linton 1943; Wallace 1956). Currently, concerted efforts are once more underway on the part of American Indian organizations and their intellectual allies among professional anthropologists, to safeguard Indian tribal lands and to strengthen tribal autonomy (Tax 1958). These efforts reflect a desire for continued culture maintenance and a demand for greater economic certainty. However, they do not include specific linguistic emphases in their programs. Although the language maintenance efforts of American Indians are not included within the scope of the present study, their current status and their prospects provide us with perspective concerning language maintenance efforts on behalf of colonial and immigrant languages in the United States.

Colonial Languages

The colonial languages are those initially spoken by 16th, 17th, and 18th century European colonizers of territories that later became the continental United States. The colonial languages are English, Spanish, French, German, Russian, Swedish, and Dutch. The last three did not survive as colonial languages (except in a few isolated pockets) for any appreciable length of time after the mother countries involved lost control of their colonial holdings, although they do continue to be spoken in the United States today as a result of their subsequent reintroduction with immigrant status.

Of the four colonial languages that have maintained uninterrupted continuity on American soil, English has become the recognized language of the nation and its public and governmental institutions. No other language currently has official, national sanction although, on occasion, other languages are employed by public or private agencies of a non-ethnic character seeking to direct messages to population groups not sufficiently familiar or comfortable with the English language.[1]

Of the other colonial languages, Spanish continues to have the greatest number of speakers. These are largely concentrated in the southwestern states of Texas, New Mexico, Colorado, Utah, Arizona, Nevada, and California. The majority of Spanish speakers are not themselves of European-Spanish ancestry (since the Spanish colonial empire was supported largely by troops and clergymen rather than by settlers in the English or French manner), but of Mexican-Indian origin (Burma 1954; Kloss 1940, 1942). As a result of centuries of Spanish rule, Spanish became the language of large indigenous populations (just as Catholicism became their religion) and continues as

---

[1] During brief periods of continental American history, both German and Spanish gained local recognition as permissible languages for certain public functions above and beyond that of translation. Spanish currently enjoys co-official status in Puerto Rico. Language maintenance efforts in Puerto Rico, Hawaii, and Alaska are outside the scope of this study.

such to this day. In recent years this population has been joined by other Spanish speakers emigrating from outside the continental United States. Large contingents of Spanish-speaking American citizens from Puerto Rico have migrated to New York and to other urban centers in search of economic advancement, leaving an environment in which Spanish is culturally and legally protected for one where their own status and that of their language are similar to those of immigrants from afar. Indeed, the influx of Puerto Ricans and of Spanish speakers from Mexico, Cuba, and other quota-free Latin American countries exemplifies the conversion to dual colonial-immigrant status that other major colonial languages have also experienced.

The situation of French as a colonial language superficially resembles that of Spanish. Again we encounter a continuous history spanning centuries, huge language islands, and two separate centers of concentration: a large one in New England, a smaller one in Louisiana. Once more immigrants have been added to the original colonial base. However, by far the greater proportion of Franco-Americans may be considered as immigrant stock, inasmuch as their forebears entered the United States in post-colonial days in response to the lures of booming New England mill towns.

Although introduced on a large scale during colonial days, German was not the language of a colonial power on the American continent. In this sense, it represents an even greater amalgam of colonial and immigrant statuses. A great variety of German dialects were employed in colonial days. Yet it is only through several non-standard and non-prestige variants – commonly referred to as "Pennsylvania Dutch" – that linguistic continuity with the colonial German period is still maintained. The vast majority of German speakers who can be located in the United States today, and the millions of German speakers who left their imprint on 19th and early 20th century American history, have been of post-colonial immigrant origin. Nevertheless, the very early and large post-colonial population concentrations that developed gave German a base which long seemed to be every bit as powerful as those of other languages that more fully meet the technical qualifications of "colonial" status.

About Spanish, French, and German language maintenance efforts alike, we know pitifully and surprisingly little. By any reasonable standards these three languages are now and have long been among the most important and the most prestigeful in the Western world – indeed, in the entire world. Yet they, their speakers, and the cultures they represent have existed in our very midst for two centuries or longer without much awareness on our part of their existence, their struggles, or their prospects. Certainly such parochialism must seem strange even to those who recognize it as a commonplace of American life.

Immigrant Languages

Any over-all consideration of language maintenance in the United States must stress the immigrant languages, for these are the most numerous and their speakers and adherents have been exposed to the assimilative currents of American life for the shortest periods of time. Mass immigration to the United States lasted from approximately 1880 to 1920. During these forty years, millions of speakers of scores of languages arrived in the United States, adding to our population many linguistic and cultural ingredients that had hitherto been only meagerly represented. Moreover, the bearers of immigrant languages varied greatly among themselves. Peasants and townsmen, illiterates and literati, speakers of prestigeful and speakers of officially unrecognized tongues, avowed language loyalists and those who had no particular awareness of their language, localists, nationalists and internationalists, political refugees and economic immigrants, temporary and permanent immigrants – all these and more were represented in their midst. This internal diversity may have been no greater than that of the earlier immigrants of colonial days; yet its recency makes it all the more striking. The diversity is particularly inviting for the student of language maintenance for it both prompts him and enables him to ask whether any of these factors have made a difference in language maintenance outcomes. The immigrant languages raise other questions as well. How have they fared since the cessation of mass immigration? How have they fared in comparison with the colonial languages? What has been the impact upon them of post-World War II immigrants, most of whom differ so greatly from their predecessors of one or two generations earlier?

All in all, an inquiry into language maintenance in the United States is blessed (or complicated) by a surfeit of questions. Moreover, the phenomena under study can be examined in a great variety of widely differing American contexts. Most of the circumstances influencing minority group language maintenance efforts throughout the modern world are available for study within the continental limits of the United States, drawing on experiences over the past two centuries. In some instances, historical research is called for; in others, what is needed is social-psychological, sociological, and demographic research on current conditions and processes. Because language maintenance efforts in the United States are so little known, their initial illumination calls for truly interdisciplinary efforts on both an extensive and an intensive scale.

THE IMMIGRANT ROOTS OF LANGUAGE MAINTENANCE IN AMERICA

The history of organized language consciousness, language loyalty, and language maintenance on behalf of vernaculars in the Western world dates back some five centuries or more (Weisgerber 1948), although its origins may be traced back much further (Jakobson 1945). Like most histories, this one, too, is full of pain and glory. It reveals many instances of popular democratic triumphs in which submerged and deprecated tongues threw off the social and intellectual shackles of superimposed languages and became languages of governments, languages of education for the people as well as for elites, languages of culture, of commerce, and of diplomacy. It also reveals instances of hitherto lowly languages becoming hard taskmasters – indeed, oppressors – of other tongues after their own liberation and recognition had been secured. The history of organized language consciousness in the West is part of the history of the Renaissance, the Reformation, the growth of nationalism and the consolidation of nation-states, the rise of industrialization and of the city, the spread of colonialism and of post-colonial internationalisms, neo-colonialisms, and independence movements. The printing press and universal literacy, religious and political liberty, a world made "safe for democracy", and the self-determination of peoples – these are all intertwined with the rise of successive "lower" languages, beginning in western and proceeding throughout successively more eastern European and non-European territories (Deutsch 1953; Harrison 1957; Jakobson 1945; Rundle 1946). There are many instances in which language loyalty provided the momentum, the unity, and the devotion which carried libertarian movements of an avowedly socio-political nature to their successful conclusions (Hertzler 1953-54; Kohn 1952; Lewis 1948). Granting this, one must also grant that religious and temporal wars, expansionism as well as Balkanization, irridentism and animosities, genocide and cultural subjugation have also been associated with language loyalty. It would be strange, indeed, if this were not so. As language interpenetrates every aspect of modern life, so it must follow modern man to his brightest heights as well as his darkest depths.

Language loyalty in the United States could not but be related to its European origins and to the tenor of American-European relations. At times it was undoubtedly fanned by, and contributed to, the perpetuation on our shores of Old World rivalries and tensions. However, the American immigrant population was too varied and too scattered, American social and economic realities were too novel and too inviting, and Old World governments and treaties changed too rapidly and too basically, for this aspect of language maintenance to maintain firm footing even within the ranks of immigrants themselves. Yet the very fact of immigrant status highlighted several other, more positive features of linguistic and cultural continuity.

Those who come to a new land do not begin their lives there as *tabulae rasae*. There are joys and tears, births and deaths, seasons of the year and seasons of man. There are events for which individual attention will suffice, but there are others for which group attention is more fitting and more traditional. In a nation of immigrants, millions face problems they never faced before; indeed, millions face problems of the same kind at the same time and are, therefore, more likely to seek joint solutions to them. Among the problems of life in a new country – a country where almost everyone and everything is new – is the absence of the old, the familiar, the traditional. The opportunity to begin afresh, to turn over a new leaf, may or may not be entirely welcomed. For all these reasons – reasons of habit and of conviction and of wisdom – the songs and the stories, the customs and the celebrations, the religious beliefs and the literary treasures, the foods, the values, and the memories of the "old country" were not and could not be scrapped. There is no way of adjusting to the new but through the old. Thus the languages and traditions of immigrants – colonial and post-colonial – were established on American soil both because they were valued in and of themselves, and because they provided sympathetic companions for the journey of adaptation to America.

So much for history. One must be as careful to distinguish between history and people as to relate the two. As certain as it is that organized language consciousness, language loyalty, and language maintenance have played a major role during the last five centuries of European history, so is it equally certain that many, if not most, European immigrants to America arrived here with only the most meager familiarity with the events and movements to which these processes contributed. The slogans, the anthems, the banners, the crusades, the poets, the saints – the entire fiery sword and flaming ideology of political and cultural nationalism – apparently made little, if any, permanent impression on millions who left Europe to come to the United States. The peasants, small land holders, and urban poor, who were most likely to stream to the United States, were less caught up in these movements than were the intelligentsia, the middle class, and working class elements that more frequently remained behind. Thus, while the United States was born, grew up, and came of age during the two centuries in which nationalism reached hitherto unsurpassed heights in Western history (Kohn 1955; Kohn 1962), and though part of American history itself can only be properly understood in terms of reactions to European nationalism, millions of immigrants to the United States remained basically unmoved by nationalistic sentiments or ideologies. Ethnicity of a traditional, particularistic, and non-ideological character – rather than nationalism in its strident and symbolically elaborated manifestations – was the general rule. The languages spoken were related to the countless acts of everyday life rather than to "causes" or ideologies. Most usually it was only *after* immigration that group maintenance became a conscious goal. In some instances, indeed, it was only in America that many immigrants *became aware of their "groupness"*, i.e., of their common origin and their common past, as well as of their common current problems. Thus it was that only *after* immigration did language loyalty and language maintenance become aspects of consciousness for many.

As their seemingly primordial ways of life crumbled – ways of life that had protected the mother tongue and had been protected by it in turn – novel institutions and organizations came to be established that had been unknown in the "old country". Voluntary organizations and schools and newspapers and other consciously directed media of segmented urban-industrial existence were formed by and for populations that had little or no prior experience with them. While certain relics of ethnicity remained, and at times attained far greater prominence than they had originally enjoyed (various ethnic costumes, foods, celebrations), others were substantially altered while many were lost entirely. It is in this context of overriding social change, of a grasping for continuity at the same time new means and new ends were being pursued, that language loyalty and language maintenance efforts most frequently came into play.

There were always some immigrants, at least since the early German sects, who did view themselves quite explicitly as the preservers and even the saviors of their old country languages and heritages. At times such individuals and groups espoused separatist and non-participationist philosophies. In other instances, the more highly intellectualized and symbolically elaborated concepts of nationalism were employed. In still other (and much later) instances, pluralistic rationales were advanced. These loyalists founded political groups, schools, children's camps, choral and dramatic societies, and literary and scholarly associations. They established publications at an intellectual level substantially higher than that of the mass immigrant press or the mass English-speaking press. They organized societies, institutes, and congresses for the very purpose of linguistic and cultural self-maintenance. They often served as conscience-prickers, arousing widespread – even if temporary – concern for re-tentivism among their less conscientious and less intellectual countrymen. Their long-term impact on most immigrant groups arriving before the Second World War was probably negligible. Nevertheless, each succeeding wave of immigration since colonial days brought some number of this ilk. As a result, the tradition of struggling for linguistic and cultural self-maintenance is an old one on American shores (Read 1937), even if not a particularly successful or officially recognized one.

The relative proportions of retentivists and non-retentivists, of nationalists and ethnicists, of rural and urban dwellers that obtained among pre-World War II immigrants do not apply to those arriving in post-World War II days. Several factors distinguish these latter immigrants, particularly those coming from "behind the Iron Curtain", from their earlier counterparts. To begin with, more of them possess formal education in their mother tongue – with disciplined study of the literary standard and of its literature. Second, more of them came with strong and conscious national sentiments – with a knowledge of national history, national creativity, and national aspirations. Finally, more of them had a diaspora consciousness and, there-fore, a clearly retentivist mission. With their homelands under anti-religious and often anti-national control, they saw themselves (and other countrymen in the diaspora) as the only ones at liberty to preserve and perpetuate the "true culture" during the period of "foreign" domination. Such characteristics and sentiments usually have immediate positive consequences for language loyalty and language maintenance. Do they actually have such consequences in the United States today? Or is it possible that the more advanced educational, social, and cultural status of post-World War II immigrants enables them to undergo even more rapid and painless Americanization than that which was possible for their predecessors (Kent 1953)? The fact that this question needs to be asked with respect to very recent immigrants indicates that immigrational recency cannot of itself fully account for language loyalty.

It may be that not only are the roots of language maintenance far more varied than European nationalism alone would imply, but that they are also far more native, since they are ultimately an accommodation to American circumstances. One of the purposes of this study is to determine whether the varied roots of language maintenance have actually yielded varied harvests. Another is to determine how roots and harvests alike have been influenced by the circumstances of American life.

THE AMERICAN IMPACT ON LANGUAGE MAINTENANCE

Part of the national consciousness of all Americans is the awareness that successive waves of immigrants have been "digested" and have become integral parts of the body politic. Since "Americans" have no ethnic roots in past millenia, as do many other peoples of the world, the Americanizing process itself takes on a central role in the formation of national identity and the national self-concept of most Americans. The "naturalization" of immigrants has gone on throughout history all over the world. Yet in only a few instances have new nations and new cultures been created "from scratch" in the process. To question the wisdom or the necessity or the naturalness of the de-ethnization of immigrant populations strikes many as questioning the very legitimacy or the very possibility of America's national and cultural existence. Both the *fact* and the *expectation* of de-ethnization have affected language maintenance in the United States, and both have probably done so in a cumulative and accelerating fashion.

Nevertheless, a double anomaly is hidden in this phenomenon. The first anomaly is that so many could be de-ethnicized so easily. The second is that having, apparently, been de-ethnicized, they have not become even more indistinguishable than they have. The first anomaly has always received the lion's share of scholarly and popular attention (e.g., Drachsler 1920; Glazer 1956; Handlin 1951; Ross 1914; Wittke 1939, and many others). The Americanization of immigrants has been explained on the basis of: the irresistible attractiveness of American mass-culture; the destruction of immigrant folkways under the impact of rapid American industrialization and urbanization; the openness and ampleness of the American reward system through public education to social mobility; the geographic mobility of a highly diversified population which worked *against* the entrenchment of regional traditionalism and *for* a lingua franca and other shifting but common cultural denominators; the emphases on childhood and youth, and the outdating of adult values and patterns, whether ethnic or non-ethnic; and even an "Old World weariness" which immigrants purportedly carried with them at a subconscious level. All of these explanations are undoubtedly true – in part, at times, and for some immigrants. If it is at all desirable to add to this overly long list, perhaps it would be permissible to observe that American "nationalism" has been non-ethnic from the very first. From the days of the Pilgrim fathers to our own days, American leaders have ideologized morality, opportunity, or freedom. "Foreign" ethnicity has normally been taboo only because it has been considered irrelevant to the higher mission and the greater opportunity envisioned by American nationalism. There was no apparent logical opposition between the ethnicity of incoming immigrants and the ideology of America. Individually and collectively immigrants could accept the latter without consciously denying the former. However, once they accepted the goals and values of Americans the immigrants were already on the road to accepting their life-styles, their customs, and their language.

Similar observations may be made concerning the role of the English language in American nationalism. Just as there is hardly any ethnic foundation to American nationalism, so there is no special language awareness in the use of English. The English language – as a symbol, as a cause, as a supreme good – does not figure prominently in the scheme of values, loyalties, and traditions by which Americans define themselves as "American". English is spoken because it is the accepted medium of communication rather than because it is beautiful, divine, or indivisible from American traditions. Americans have no particular regard for English, no particular pride in English as an exquisite instrument, no particular concern for its purity, subtlety, or correctness. Even the fact that so few Americans command any other language than English – if, indeed, they can be said to command English itself – is largely a result of educational failure, cultural provincialism, and the absence of pragmatic utility for bilingualism. Given such endemic indifference to ethnic and linguistic values, the linguistic facility and interest of immigrants steadily diminishes or atrophies once they have consciously or unconsciously accepted the American dream.

Only rarely has America taken steps to hasten the linguistic and cultural enfeeblement of its immigrant groups. Anti-foreigner movements (at times, more narrowly anti-Catholic ones) and anti-immigration sentiments usually have assumed noticeably active and sizable proportions only during periods of social and economic dislocation (Billington 1952; Higham 1955; Kohn 1961; Solomon 1956). Such movements and the immigration restrictions related to them undoubtedly have exerted pressure on all minority groups to dissolve their separatist bonds. Thus the two World Wars gave adherents of German language and culture in America two very direct and severe blows, such as have never been experienced by bearers of any other Old World heritage. However, these instances of specific pressure are historical exceptions related to unusual circumstances on the national and international scenes. More normal by far is the unplanned attrition of minority cultures that has come to pass in a reasonably open society which usually has needed and welcomed all newcomers into its schools, its industries, its businesses, and its organizations. By and large, more linguistic and cultural treasures have been buried and eroded due to permissiveness and apathy than would ever have been the case had repression and opposition been attempted. Immigrant minorities were never forbidden to organize and maintain their own communities, organizations, schools, or publications. In fact, it is only in relatively recent years that most state education departments have thought to *require* instruction in English in all private schools purporting to function within the compulsory education laws (Kloss 1940, 1942). The examples of American life and of American ideology which immigrants encountered all around have themselves usually been sufficient to weaken and overcome any sentiments or habits of separateness and retentivism harbored by particular groups or particular elites.

Yet, once more we must distinguish between people and history. Just as immigrants were far from perfect guardians of the ideologies of their homelands, so Americans have not been perfect guardians of the American dream. Here we come to the second anomaly. Ethnic groups and ethnicity, language loyalty and language maintenance, still exist on the American scene. Even Americans of western European origin (German, Norwegian, Swedish, Irish, etc.) continue to this very day to recognize their ancestry and to partially define themselves in accord with it (Glazer and Moynihan 1963; Hansen 1940; Haugen 1953). For reasons that are not really well understood, these groups have not lost themselves entirely within their American surroundings even after three, four, and more generations, although they have had every opportunity to do so. Do the much-touted social permissiveness and economic mobility of America nevertheless retain certain limits which ethnics – particularly non-Anglo-Saxon and non-Protestant ethnics – cannot easily transcend? Have the recurring anti-foreigner sentiments elicited protective withdrawal reactions in their targets? Is the absence of ethnicity and traditionalism in the American milieu so conducive to anomie and to alienation that the retention of ethnicity of some kind performs an orienting and a stabilizing function? We know very little about the anomalous half-life of ethnicity in present-day America. We know even less about which (if any) current expressions of ethnicity are conducive to language maintenance.

WHAT WE WOULD KNOW AND WHY

The very idea of ethnicity and of language maintenance in America should be of some interest to all Americans. That third and subsequent generations frequently continue to think of themselves in partially ethnic terms and frequently maintain positive attitudes and interests with respect to the heritages of their grandparents is a significant fact in American life. Why these ethnic overtones persist is something that social research on American life could well seek to understand. Theoretically, the American melting pot should have been more successful – considering the rapid social mobility which it holds out as an explicit reward, the forces of urbanization and industrialization that support it, and the absence of well-defined or deeply-rooted American cultural patterns which might have conflicted with contrasting immigrant cultures. At the same time this very lack of a substantive and traditional core culture may also conduce to a partial failure of the melting pot. It may be that ethnicity is one of the strongest unrecognized facets of American life – in politics, in religion, in consumer behavior, in life-styles and in self-concepts (Gans 1962; Glazer and Moynihan 1963; Lieberson 1963). In a peculiarly American way, ethnicity may have found a place for itself in American life by becoming partner to a compact which requires that it not be formally recognized, at least not recognized as such.

It has sometimes been said that Americans cannot understand the rest of the world because they are so different from the rest of the world. How can the United States understand traditional or cultured societies if it has neither traditions nor culture? How can it understand extreme and hopeless poverty if it has never experienced it itself? Or ethnicity and ethnic-nationalism if it contains neither of these attributes in its own life? Or the attraction of substantive ideologies or religions if its own are purely procedural and formal? Actually, these questions (and the views that they imply) represent a misreading of American life – a misreading that the United States itself has, unfortunately, abetted. If this country cannot understand the rest of the world, nor make itself in turn understood, it is not because it lacks any of the above characteristics nor a multitude of other common ties with the rest of mankind. If Americans cannot understand the rest of the world, it is largely due to the fact that they have not sufficiently come to understand themselves, to recognize themselves, or to accept themselves.

Today, scores of nations – new and old, developed and developing – have problems of language and ethnicity, of unity and diversity (Deutsch and Foltz 1963; Ferguson 1962; Foster 1962; Harrison 1957). Europe and Africa, Asia and Oceania, North America and South America – all reveal current and recurring problems of this kind. Social scientists can discover in language and ethnicity new perspectives for the study of socialization, social change, religion, nation building, language planning, and international relations (Hertzler 1953-54). Language loyalists throughout the world can discover on the American scene almost the entire range of circumstances and outcomes that pertain to their own goals and problems. An intelligent citizenry can discover within this domain vital information required for a more thorough appreciation of both internal and foreign affairs and, as a result, knowledge appropriate for a more constructive role in respect to their own responsibilities.

Since so precious little systematic information is now available about language maintenance and language loyalty in the United States, this study primarily represents an attempt to provide basic data and to review integrative concepts. Its levels of analysis are necessarily diverse as it spans the continuum from historical depth through descriptive and demographic rates to current social and psychological dynamics. Although its methods are frequently crude and its findings tentative, they are presented in the hope that others will be attracted to this same area of study. If it poses more questions than answers for the careful reader, he is invited to join in the search.

REFERENCES

Billington, R. A., *The Protestant Crusade: 1800-1860; A Study of the Origins of American Nativism* (New York, Rinehart, 1952).

Burma, J., *Spanish-Speaking Groups in the United States* (Durham, Duke Univ. Press, 1954).

Chafe, W. L., "Estimates regarding the present speakers of North American Indian languages", *International Journal of American Linguistics*, 28 (1962), 162-171.

Deutsch, K. W., *Nationalism and Social Communication: An Inquiry into the Foundations of Nationality* (New York, Wiley, 1953).

——, and Foltz, W. J. (eds.), *Nation-Building* (New York, Atherton, 1963).

Drachsler, J., *Democracy and Assimilation* (New York, Macmillan, 1920).

Ferguson, C. A., "The Language Factor in National Development", *Anthropological Linguistics*, 4 (1962) 23-27.

Foster, G. M., *Traditional Cultures and the Impact of Technological Change* (New York, Harper, 1962).

Gans, H. S., *The Urban Villagers* (New York, Free Press, 1962).

Glazer, N., "The Integration of American Immigrants", *Law and Contemporary Problems*, 21 (1956), 256-269.

——, and Moynihan, D. P., *Beyond the Melting Pot* (Cambridge, M.I.T. and Harvard Univ. Press, 1963).

Handlin, O., *The Uprooted: The Epic Story of the Great Migrations That Made the American People* (Boston, Little, Brown, 1951).

Hansen, M. L., *The Immigrant in American History*, Arthur M. Schlesinger, ed. (Cambridge, Harvard Univ. Press, 1940).

Harrison, S. S., *The Most Dangerous Decades: An Introduction to the Comparative Study of Language Policy in Multi-Lingual States* (New York, Columbia Univ. Press, 1957).

Haugen, E., *Bilingualism in the Americas: A Bibliography and Research Guide* (University, Ala., American Dialect Society, 1946).

——, *The Norwegian Language in America*, 2 volumes (Phila., Univ. of Penna. Press, 1953).

Hertzler, J. O., "Toward a sociology of language", *Social Forces*, 32 (1953-54), 109-119.

Higham, J., *Strangers in the Land; Patterns of American Nativism, 1860-1925* (New Brunswick, Rutgers Univ. Press, 1955).

Jakobson, R., "The Beginnings of National Self-determination in Europe", *Review of Politics*, 7 (1945), 29-42.

Kent, D. P., *The Refugee Intellectual* (New York, Columbia Univ. Press, 1953).

Kloss, H., *Volksgruppenrecht in den Vereinigten Staaten von Amerika* (Essen, Essener Verlagsanstalt, I: 1940; II: 1942). (Also his more recent *Das Nationalitätenrecht der Vereinigten Staaten von Amerika*, Vienna and Stuttgart, Wilhelm Braumuller, 1963.)

Kohn, H., *Prophets and Peoples: Studies in Nineteenth Century Nationalism* (New York, Macmillan, 1952).

——, *Nationalism: Its Meaning and History* (Princeton, Van Nostrand, 1955).

——, *American Nationalism* (New York, Collier, 1961).

——, *The Age of Nationalism* (New York, Harper & Bros., 1962).

Lewis, M. M., *Language in Society; The Linguistic Revolution and Social Change* (New York, Social Sciences Publishers, 1948).

Lieberson, S., *Ethnic Patterns in American Cities* (New York, Free Press, 1963).

Linton, R., "Nativistic Movements", *Amer. Anthrop.*, 45 (1943), 230-240.

Read, A. W., "Bilingualism in the Middle Colonies, 1725-1775", *American Speech*, 12 (1937), 93-100.

Ross, E. A., *The Old World in the New; The Significance of Past and Present Immigration to the American People* (New York, Century, 1914).

Rundle, S., *Language as a Social and Political Factor in Europe* (London, Faber and Faber, 1946).

Solomon, Barbara M., *Ancestors and Immigrants* (Cambridge, Harvard Univ. Press, 1956).

Tax, S., *Federal Indian Policy and the N.C.A.I.* (Washington, National Congress of American Indians, 1958).

Wallace, A. F. C., "Revitalization Movements", *Amer. Anthrop.*, 58 (1956), 264-81.

Weisgerber, J. L., *Die Entdeckung der Muttersprache im europäischen Denken* (Luneberg, Heiland, 1948).

Wittke, C., *We Who Built America: The Saga of the Immigrant* (New York, Prentice-Hall, 1939).

2. MOTHER TONGUE AND NATIVITY IN THE AMERICAN POPULATION

JOSHUA A. FISHMAN AND JOHN E. HOFMAN

The only official data on non-English mother tongues in the United States are those that have been collected and reported by the Bureau of the Census. Census reports on mother tongues have appeared in 1910, 1920, 1930, 1940, and 1960. These reports are a natural starting place for the student of language maintenance in the United States, and on the basis of them we will seek to reveal trends of growth or decline in the frequency with which specified languages have been claimed as mother tongues. In addition, we will estimate non-English mother tongue figures for the *native* born as of 1960, since the 1960 Census itself provides no mother tongue data for either the native-of-foreign-parentage or the native-of-native-parentage. Finally, we will seek to utilize these data to construct a composite index of language maintenance, potential and to relate this index to indices of other relevant social characteristics.

It should be stressed at the outset that we are dealing here primarily with self-reported mother tongue claims rather than with indicators of current language use. These two variables are undoubtedly related to each other, although the exact nature or consistency of the relationship is still unknown. Nevertheless the mere act of claiming a particular mother tongue is of substantial interest to students of language maintenance and language shift.

GROWTH AND DECLINE OF NON-ENGLISH MOTHER TONGUES

The total number of foreign born in the American population reached its twentieth century apex of 13,983,405 in 1930. At that time the total white population of the United States was 108,864,207 and the foreign-born white constituted 12.8% of this total. By 1960, the absolute number of foreign born had decreased appreciably, whereas the total population of the country had grown greatly. As a result, the 9,738,143 foreign born in 1960 constituted only 5.4% of the total American population of 179,325,671.

It may be that the decline in proportion as well as in absolute numbers of foreign born is in some way responsible for the decline in proportion of foreign born who claim a non-English mother tongue. This proportion was never before as low as the 73.7% figure for 1960. At the same time, the "not reported" figure has grown tremendously from less than 1 % in 1910, 1920, and 1930 to a point where it accounts for 7.3 % of all foreign born in 1960. These two data considered together lead us to suspect that as the foreign born population Americanizes (culturally) and diminishes (numerically), an increasing proportion may prefer not to claim a non-English mother tongue. This may well be a basic datum of language maintenance and language displacement in the United States.

THE FOREIGN BORN ("FIRST GENERATION")

Few explanatory principles need be invoked in order to explain or summarize the trends for non-English mother tongues among foreign born claimants (Table 2.1). Decade of major immigration to the United States, the age distribution (known or estimated) of foreign-born claimants of a particular mother tongue at a particular time, the existence or non-existence of an immigration quota since the early 1920's – these usually seem to be the "big three" factors involved.

Since 1930 most languages have consistently revealed declining numbers of claimants. Even the few departures from this general rule usually require no additional explanatory concepts. For example, in some cases the decline becomes apparent in 1920, although mass immigration was still underway during the previous decade. Thus Norwegian, Swedish, French, and German were less frequently claimed as mother tongues by foreign-born individuals in 1920 than in 1910. This is understandable in terms of the relatively early northern and western European immigrations which brought speakers of these languages to the United States. During the second decade of the present century and even before, these early immigrants who had arrived in large numbers between 1840 and 1860 were dying out. Mother tongue data for 1910 and 1920 undoubtedly reflect this natural generational turnover in the case of northern and western European languages.[1]

Overall, the figures for other mother tongues increased through 1920. However, by the time 1930 data on mother tongue were collected, mass immigration to the United States had ceased and a more restrictive as well as discriminatory immigration policy had been instituted. Since then, more foreign-born individuals have died or departed than have entered the United States during each census interval. The general decline in the number of non-English mother tongue claimants since 1930 among the foreign born is directly attributable to this fact.

But every rule has its exceptions. Spanish and Portuguese speakers have quite regularly registered increases, inasmuch as the usual quota limitations do not apply to immigrants from Latin America and from the Azores.[2] French speakers hold a

---

[1] Some proportion of the German decrease must also be attributed to postwar reluctance to claim German as a mother tongue.

[2] The Spanish increase since 1930 is somewhat exaggerated due to the reclassification of Mexicans under whites in that year. In 1930, 85.6 % of the foreign born claiming Spanish as their mother tongue claimed Mexico as their country of origin.

TABLE 2.1

*Mother Tongue of the Foreign Born, for the United States,
Urban and Rural, 1960, and of the Foreign-Born White
for Conterminous United States, 1910 to 1940*[a]

Mother tongue	United States – Total foreign born, 1960				Conterminous United States Foreign-born white			
	Total	Urban	Rural nonfarm	Rural farm	1940	1930	1920	1910
Total	9,738,143	8,510,152	1,007,621	220,370	11,109,620	13,983,405	13,712,754	13,345,545
English	1,852,992	1,614,686	213,976	24,330	2,506,420	3,097,021	3,007,932	3,363,792
Norwegian	140,774	107,902	24,332	8,540	232,820	345,522	362,199	402,587
Swedish	211,597	171,062	31,897	8,638	423,200	615,465	643,203	683,218
Danish	79,619	61,035	13,331	5,253	122,180	178,944	189,531	186,345
Dutch[b]	123,613	97,686	17,394	8,533	102,700	133,142	136,540	126,045
French	330,220	278,125	45,533	6,562	359,520	523,297	466,956	528,842
German	1,278,772	1,073,961	160,244	44,567	1,589,040	2,188,006	2,267,128	2,759,032
Polish	581,936	527,678	43,233	11,025	801,680	965,899	1,077,392	943,781
Czech	91,711	73,886	12,427	5,398	159,640	201,138	234,564	228,738
Slovak	125,000	103,954	17,881	3,165	171,580	240,196	274,948	166,474
Hungarian	213,114	192,561	17,360	3,193	241,220	250,393	268,112	229,094
Serbo-Croatian	88,094	77,744	8,782	1,568	70,600	109,923	125,844	105,669
Slovenian	32,108	26,521	4,680	907	75,560	77,671	102,744	123,631
Russian	276,834	258,640	14,639	3,555	356,940	315,721	392,049	57,926
Ukrainian	106,974	97,565	7,314	2,095	35,540	58,685	c	d
Lithuanian[e]	99,043	89,227	8,080	1,736	122,660	165,053	182,227	140,963
Finnish[f]	53,168	35,704	14,284	3,180	97,080	124,994	133,567	120,086
Rumanian	38,019	35,827	1,657	535	43,120	56,964	62,336	42,277
Yiddish	503,605	497,270	4,837	1,498	924,440	1,222,658	1,091,820	1,051,767
Greek	173,031	165,202	6,895	934	165,220	189,066	174,658	118,379
Italian	1,226,141	1,145,410	69,711	11,020	1,561,100	1,808,289	1,624,998	1,365,110
Spanish	766,961	653,858	90,135	22,968	428,360	743,286	556,111	258,131
Portuguese	87,109	73,157	8,966	4,986	83,780	110,197	105,895	72,649
Japanese	95,027	75,103	15,674	4,250	g	g	g	g
Chinese	89,609	86,221	3,042	346	g	g	g	g
Arabic	49,908	47,282	2,350	276	50,940	67,830	57,557	32,868
All other	314,293	271,925	36,113	6,256	135,780	151,812	167,277	121,869
Not reported	708,871	570,960	112,855	25,056	248,500	42,233	7,166	116,272

a   Table derived from *U.S. Census of Population 1960*: General Social and Economic Characteristics, United States Summary. Final Report PC(1)-1C, Table 70 (Washington, D.C., U.S. Government Printing Office, 1962). Population figures for 1910 to 1940 apply to whites only.

b   Includes Flemish in 1960 and Frisian in 1910 and 1920.

c   1920 figure not reported in 1960. Reported as 55,672 (including Ruthenian) in 1920.

d   1910 figure not reported in 1960. Reported as 25,131 (including Ruthenian) in 1910.

e   Includes Lettish (1910-1920).

f   Includes Lappish (1910-1930) and Estonian (1910-1920).

g   Not available.

favored position because of the absence of a Canadian quota, a fact which enabled large numbers of French Canadians to enter the United States during the prosperity decade. Unusual circumstances underlie the 1960 gains for Serbo-Croatian, Ukrainian, and Greek. In these cases, as well as in those of the very minor losses for Hungarian and Rumanian, substantial post World-War II Displaced Persons immigration – often on a special quota basis – has prevailed. A few other exceptions to the rule may be of interest to the student of language maintenance and language displacement. A 1930 increase for Yiddish cannot be explained entirely on the basis of "last minute" immigration before the quota bias was fully fastened in the mid-20's. It is doubtless true that Jewish immigration to the United States continued at high tide somewhat longer during the 20's than that of coterritorial Eastern European populations, for Jews quickly appeared as still disadvantaged minorities in the new Versailles and Trianon inspired states, whereas Poles, Baltics, and others were caught up in the dramas of building their own nation states. These dramas doubtless also enticed many former Poles, Czechs, Slovaks, Hungarians, Serbs, Russians, and others to return to their homelands during the post-war decade. It is also likely that many Jews who had previously claimed either Russian or Polish mother tongues began to claim Yiddish in 1930. This was the period of highest prestige and most rapid growth for Yiddish culture in Eastern Europe and to some extent in the United States and abroad. The gains for Ukrainian since 1940 also represent, in part, a similar growth in language consciousness and language pride among individuals who had previously claimed a variety of other mother tongues.

Nevertheless, the few unexpected increases here and there (e.g., Russian in 1940, "Dutch"[3] in 1960) do not balance out the heavy losses that have regularly occurred. Almost all of the decade reflected by the 1940 figures passed under the shadow of the great American depression. Many immigrants returned to their homelands during these years as a result of failure to attain the primarily economic goals that had initially brought most of them to the United States. This process of return to the homeland certainly affected the mother tongue figures of 1940. Moreover, the last part of the decade was marked by gathering war clouds. Many individuals of foreign birth may not have reported their non-English mother tongues (cases of mother tongue not reported, although few in number, increased by 488.4% from 1930 to 1940). Yet the fact that the total reservoir of foreign born decreased by 20.6%, and that even the foreign born claiming English as their mother tongue decreased by 19.1%, indicate that the 30's also represent a decade of significant generational turnover.

Twenty- and thirty-year-old immigrants who had arrived in the United States during the mass immigration decades at the end of the 19th and the beginning of the 20th century became 60, 70, and 80 years old during the 1930's. This decade un-

---

[3] The Pennsylvania Dutch frequently claim Dutch (rather than German) as their mother tongue, or Dutch is entered for them by census takers. The quotation marks here and elsewhere are intended to remind the reader of this.

TABLE 2.2

Mother Tongue of the Native White of Foreign or Mixed Parentage,
1940, 1920, and 1910; and Mother Tongue of the Native White
of Native Parentage, 1940, for the United States[a]

(1940 statistics are based on a 5-percent sample. 1940 figures have been revised to include Mexicans
who were classified with "Other races" in earlier reports).

Mother Tongue	Native White of Foreign or Mixed Parentage			Native White of Native parentage: 1940
	1940	1920	1910	
Total	23,157,580	[b]22,686,204	18,897,837	84,124,840
Northwestern Europe:				
English	12,181,040	6,721,433	6,673,628	78,352,180
Norwegian	344,240	658,589	607,267	81,160
Swedish	374,040	841,859	762,651	33,660
Danish	95,460	274,150	257,524	9,100
Dutch	103,240	233,959	198,885	61,200
Flemish	17,840	42,194	19,026	4,600
French	533,760	823,154	828,327	518,780
Central Europe:				
German	2,435,700	5,896,983	6,058,239	925,040
Polish	1,428,820	1,359,503	763,859	185,820
Czech	279,040	388,232	310,654	81,760
Slovak	283,520	344,918	117,970	29,260
Magyar (Hungarian)	198,600	205,426	91,799	13,180
Serbian	18,300	16,074	3,424	1,280
Croatian	58,980	58,503	20,161	3,920
Slovenian	97,300	105,808	59,800	5,780
Eastern Europe:				
Russian	214,160	339,900	37,211	13,980
Ukrainian	45,280	[c]39,786	[c]10,228	2,780
Armenian	26,440	15,193	6,083	1,880
Lithuanian	140,620	[d]154,373	[d]70,272	9,400
Finnish	118,460	[e]131,905	[e]80,602	14,880
Rumanian	20,340	29,347	8,847	2,060
Yiddish	773,680	951,793	624,995	52,980
Southern Europe:				
Greek	102,140	47,110	12,000	6,160
Italian	2,080,680	1,740,866	786,312	125,040
Spanish	714,060	294,737	190,067	718,980
Portuguese	120,500	109,833	68,619	11,380
All other:				
Arabic	52,760	46,582	13,859	3,720
All other	34,520	9,766	18,756	11,080
Not reported	264,060	13,170	196,772	2,843,600

doubtedly marked the passing from the scene of large contingents of "old timers" who had, in many cases, laid the foundations of language maintenance institutions – organizations, press, schools, etc. – in the United States. This had happened earlier in the case of the northern and western European mother tongues, at the turn of the century. However, in their case the first large contingents of "old timers" (those who arrived in the 1840's through 1860's) were subsequently replenished – at least in part – by sizable new contingents. In the case of most eastern and southern European mother tongues, the "old timers" arriving between 1880 and 1920 were the last sizable contingents to arrive on American shores. The 1930's, therefore, marked the beginning of an unmistakable and seemingly irreversible downward trend for most southern and eastern European mother tongues.

The average age of the foreign born in 1940 was roughly twice that of the American population as a whole. These 1940 figures foretold a rapid decline in non-English mother tongues, if maintenance of these tongues were to depend primarily on the foreign born and if American immigration policy were to continue essentially unchanged. The next twenty years revealed the general accuracy of this projection. World War II came and went, and the "normal" immigration bars were both reinforced and weakened by the war and its aftermath. During the war itself, immigration dropped to a trickle as only the very fortunate managed to leave the Old World and arrive in the New. Still, the post-war period saw some increased immigration opportunities in response to pressures to absorb Displaced Persons and to utilize the unused quota allotments of the war years. But these increases were paltry in comparison to the clamor for admission and to the continued high death rate in the American foreign-born population. Relative to 1940 the total number of foreign born in the United States in 1960 had decreased by an additional 12.35% to a total of 9,738,143, its lowest point in 50 years. At this rate of decrease, foreign-born speakers of some of the mother tongues would be virtually non-existent by 1970.

THE NATIVE BORN OF FOREIGN OR MIXED PARENTAGE
("SECOND GENERATION")

Mother tongue data on natives of foreign or mixed parentage are available only for

---

[a]   Table derived from *U.S. Census of Population: 1940*, "*Mother Tongue*", Table 1, p. 7. Note that prior to 1940, mother tongue of the foreign born was defined as the language of customary speech in the homes of the immigrants prior to immigration. Natives of foreign or mixed parentage were classified as of the language of customary speech in the homes of their immigrant parents prior to immigration. In 1940, however, mother tongue was formally defined as the principal language spoken in the home of the person in his earliest childhood. This definition was frequently interpreted as referring to the language spoken by the person himself.
[b]   Includes 791,058 person classified in 1920 as of "Mixed mother tongue" for whom a more detailed classification is not available.
[c]   Includes Ruthenian.
[d]   Includes Lettish.
[e]   Includes Estonian and Lappish.

1910, 1920, and 1940 (Table 2.2). Once again the major demographic factors may be conscripted to render yeoman's service in accounting for trends. Decade of immigration on the part of the first generation, age distribution and birth rate among these parents, and, on occasion, repatriation to the parental homeland seem to be the standard variables. On the other hand, at least two non-demographic factors also merit attention, particularly in 1940, namely, (a) the varying prestige of the "mother tongue", both among its own speakers and among "Americans in general", and (b) the social mobility experienced by the second generation. Where the prestige of a particular mother tongue was low and where the social mobility of its prospective claimants was high, it is likely the language less frequently *became* the mother tongue of American-born ("second generation") offspring and was even less frequently claimed as such. Unfortunately, no census-type data are available on either of these variables and it has been necessary to study them by other means.

Most mother tongues showed increasing numbers of native-of-foreign claimants through to 1920. Of course, the percentages of increase between 1910 and 1920 vary significantly from one language-grouping to another. The mother tongues of northwestern Europe show a relatively slight increase. Most immigrants from these countries had arrived sufficiently long ago that relatively few were still within the usual child-bearing span in the 1910-1920 decade. Increases are greater for second-generation claimants of central and southern European mother tongues, and greatest of all for claimants of eastern European mother tongues. The relative recency of mass immigration of foreign-born individuals with the latter mother tongues and the relative youth of these immigrants go far to explain the second generation increases and the differences in rate of increase.

Socio-political and socio-psychological factors also may be noted in at least a few cases. Certainly, the drop in 1920 of second-generation claimants of German mother tongue must be attributed in part to anti-German sentiments fostered by World War I. In contrast, the tenfold increase in second-generation claimants of Russian may be attributed in part to enthusiasm for the Russian revolution, which affected not only the foreign born (and attracted claimants who on subsequent occasions more accurately reported Yiddish, Ukrainian, Polish, and other mother tongues) but their American-born children as well. The 1910-1920 increases for Serbian and Ukrainian are also considerably larger than demographic factors alone can explain. The rise of a Serbian-dominated Yugoslavia and the new recognition of Ukrainian as a language (briefly in an independent Ukraine, and subsequently under Soviet rule) most likely played a role.

By 1940 the decline that had earlier set in among the foreign born was fully evident in respect to the native-of-foreign parentage as well. Among these second-generation claimants of non-English mother tongues the decline was sharpest and most consistent for northwestern European languages and for German, less for central and eastern European languages, and temporarily absent for southern European languages. But the drop in general, as well as the fact that noted increases are so few and so small, must be considered indicative of a 1940 tendency for the second generation *not to learn* or *not to claim* the non-English mother tongue to which it was exposed and which *would* have been learned and *would* have been claimed under other socio-linguistic conditions.

THE NATIVE BORN OF NATIVE PARENTAGE ("THIRD GENERATION")

Only once in recent years (1940) has the U.S. Bureau of the Census inquired as to the mother tongue of those Americans whose parents were themselves American born (Table 2.2). As a result, no trend analysis of native-of-native mother tongue data is possible. In most instances there was, in 1940, a precipitous drop from the number of second- to the number of third-generation claimants. Only French and Spanish stand out as exceptions. For most other mother tongues, the number of native-of-native claimants was appreciably *less* than the number of native-of-foreign claimants; for French and Spanish, the number of native-of-native claimants was slightly *greater* than the number of native-of-foreign claimants. Even in the latter case a passing familiarity with birth-rate statistics will suffice to show that only a small proportion of third- or subsequent-generation individuals whose second generation parents spoke Spanish or French claimed these languages as their mother tongue in 1940.

In 1940 the average age of the second generation of individuals of "new immigrant" backgrounds claiming eastern and southern European mother tongues was in the early or middle twenties.[4] Thus, most second-generation individuals whose parents belonged to "new immigrant" groups were still too young to have produced many children by 1940. This factor certainly resulted in a smaller number of third-generation claimants of the "new immigrant" mother tongues in 1940 than might otherwise have been the case. Some substantiation for the above argument is in fact found in the 1940 data. Second generation claimants of Czech mother tongue had the highest median age (34.24 years) among "new immigrant" groups in that year. They also had the highest proportion of third-generation claimants relative to the number of second-generation claimants. This may be due to the fact that more second-generation Czech claimants had produced children by 1940 than had claimants of the other "new immigrant" mother tongues.

All in all, 1940 is too early a date for a rigorous determination from U.S. Census data as to whether most non-English mother tongues were being underclaimed by individuals from third and subsequent generations. It is certainly too early a date to be used in determining whether "new immigrant" mother tongues were being under-claimed to any lesser or greater extent than were "old immigrant" mother tongues which were already seriously underclaimed by that time. It may, nevertheless, be justifiable to say that the languages in the strongest position vis-a-vis native-of-native speakers in 1940 were those that had succeeded, at least to some extent, in freeing themselves of dependence on immigration and in establishing their own language

[4] *U.S. Census of Population: 1940*, "Mother Tongue", Table 5, p. 38.

TABLE 2.3

Summary of Census Data and Estimates for Three Generations of
Claimants of Non-English Mother Tongues, 1960
(Estimates in round numbers)

Language	1st Generation Claimants	2nd Generation Claimants	3rd Generation Claimants	Totals
Norwegian	140,774	141,000	40,000	321,774
Swedish	211,597	187,000	17,000	415,597
Danish	79,619	62,000	6,000	147,619
Dutch/Flemish	123,613	124,000	74,000	321,613
French	330,220	330,000	383,000	1,043,220
German	1,278,772	1,279,000	588,000	3,145,772
Polish	581,936	1,516,000	87,000	2,184,936
Czech	91,711	92,000	34,000	217,771
Slovak	125,000	125,000	10,000	260,000
Hungarian	213,114	175,000	16,000	404,114
Serbo-Croatian	88,094	89,000	7,000	184,094
Slovenian	32,108	32,000	3,000	67,208
Russian	276,834	166,000	18,000	460,834
Ukrainian	106,974	136,000	10,000	252,974
Lithuanian	99,043	99,000	8,000	206,043
Finnish	53,168	53,000	4,000	110,168
Rumanian	38,019	18,000	2,000	58,019
Yiddish	503,605	422,000	39,000	964,605
Greek	173,031	107,000	12,000	292,031
Italian	1,226,141	2,300,000	147,000	3,673,141
Spanish	766,961	1,278,000	1,291,000	3,335,961
Portuguese	87,109	87,000	7,000	181,109
Arabic	49,908	50,000	4,000	103,908
Total	6,677,351	8,868,000	2,807,000	18,352,351

islands outside of metropolitan centers: Spanish, French, "Dutch", Norwegian, and German. The importance of 1960 data on native-of-native claimants is quite obvious if the above impression is to be checked out. Unfortunately, the U.S. Census did not provide such data and estimates must be resorted to.

1960 ESTIMATES FOR SECOND AND THIRD GENERATION CLAIMANTS

The methodological problems of estimating the numbers of second- and third-generation claimants of non-English mother tongues in 1960 are many and difficult.[5] The solutions to these problems involve varying assumptions which produce alter-

---

[5] For a detailed discussion as well as references to other pertinent attempts, see Fishman, J. A. and Hofman, J. E., "Non-English mother tongues in the United States of America", in Fishman, J. A., et al., *Language Loyalty in the United States* (New York, Yeshiva University, 1964, Ch. 2, pp. 19-35. (Mimeo.)

native results and require compromise decisions. The most plausible estimates arrived at are those shown in Table 2.3.

If we compare our most plausible second generation estimates for 1960 with 1940 census data on the second generation (Table 2.2), we find that several clusters of mother tongues appear.

a. *Sharp Losses:* Losses of 50% or more occurred for second-generation claimants of Norwegian, Swedish, German, Czech, Slovak, Slovenian, and Finnish.
b. *Moderate Losses:* Losses of lesser relative severity were suffered by Danish, French, Hungarian, Russian, Lithuanian, Rumanian, Yiddish, and Portuguese.
c. *Moderate Gains:* Slight gains were registered by Dutch, Polish, Serbo-Croatian, Italian, and Arabic.
d. *Sharp Gains:* Gains of 100% or more occurred for Ukrainian, Greek, and Spanish.

Obviously, estimated losses between 1940 and 1960 have been far more widespread and of greater magnitude than estimated gains. The number of second-generation claimants has decreased not only for all of the "old immigrant" mother tongues (with the exception of "Dutch") but for most of the "new immigrant" mother tongues as well. Primarily those that have experienced substantial post-war immigration show gains or minor losses. Decreases in the number of second-generation claimants seem to be tied more closely to the size, recency, and fecundity of the *first generation* than to any goals or processes embedded in the second generation itself. This is not as "natural" or obvious a phenomenon as one might expect at first blush. If generations are removed from each other in age by a 20-25 year gap, there is no obvious demographic reason why the second generation should immediately decrease as the first dies off. On the other hand, when most immigrants are in their early adult years, it is quite likely that the second generation will quickly increase as the number of immigrants increases. Thus, the second generation's losses are more readily influenced by socio-psychological factors than are its gains. The passing of the first generation accelerates the Americanization of the second and, therefore, increases the prevalence of under-claiming in that generation and in subsequent ones as well. Indeed, claiming and underclaiming by the third generation would seem to be especially subject to socio-psychological factors, for their demographic link to the old first generation is indirect whereas any link to more recent immigrants is entirely mediated by social and psychological factors.

On purely demographic grounds both the number and proportion of third-generation claimants should have increased between 1940 and 1960, particularly in connection with eastern and southern European mother tongues. A comparison between Table 2.2 and Table 2.3 indicates that our estimation methods were such as to make both these expectations inoperative except in a very few cases. In sum, two facts appear quite clearly: one, that the estimated number of second-generation claimants of mother tongues in 1960 is only slightly larger than the reported number of aging first-generation claimants in that year, and two, that the estimated number of third-generation claimants in 1960 has decreased rather than increased since 1940. These figures clearly indicate a serious erosion of the manpower base upon which language maintenance may well depend, particularly in the case of urban immigrants.

TOTAL 1940-1960 COMPARISONS

The passage of 20 years has brought about significant changes in the numerical status of most non-English mother tongues (Table 2.4). Four patterns are recognizable in this connection:

a. *Sharp Losses*: Characterized by sharp losses in most generations (or by a sharp loss in at least one generation, and moderate losses in the others) are Norwegian Swedish, Czech, Slovak, Slovenian, Finnish, German, Danish, and Yiddish. These

TABLE 2.4

1940-1960 Totals for 23 Languages

Language	1940 Total	1960 Total	Total Change	
			n	%
Norwegian	658,220	321,774	−336,446	−51.1%
Swedish	830,900	415,597	−415,303	−50.0%
Danish	226,740	147,619	−79,121	−65.1%
Dutch/Flemish	289,580	321,613	+32,033	+11.1%
French	1,412,060	1,043,220	−368,840	−26.1%
German	4,949,780	3,145,772	−1,804,008	−36.4%
Polish	2,416,320	2,184,936	−231,384	−9.6%
Czech	520,440	217,771	−302,669	−58.2%
Slovak	484,360	260,000	−224,360	−46.3%
Hungarian	453,000	404,114	−48,886	−10.8%
Serbo-Croatian	153,080	184,094	+31,014	+20.3%
Slovenian	178,640	67,108	−111,532	−62.4%
Russian	585,080	460,834	−124,246	−21.2%
Ukrainian	83,600	252,974	+169,374	+202.6%
Lithuanian	272,680	206,043	−66,637	−24.4%
Finnish	230,420	110,168	−120,252	−52.2%
Rumanian	65,520	58,019	−7,501	−11.4%
Yiddish	1,751,100	964,605	−786,495	−44.9%
Greek	273,520	292,031	+18,511	+6.8%
Italian	3,766,820	3,673,141	−93,679	−2.5%
Spanish	1,861,400	3,335,961	+1,474,561	+79.2%
Portuguese	215,660	181,109	−34,551	−16.0%
Arabic	107,420	103,908	−3,512	−3.3%
Total	21,786,540	18,352,351	−3,434,189	−15.8%

mother tongues would seem to require unusually large immigration and revitalization movements if their further decline is to be stemmed.

b. *Moderate Losses*: Characterized by moderate losses in most generations (but by sharp losses in none) are French, Lithuanian, Rumanian, Polish, Hungarian, Russian, and Portuguese. Continued sizable immigration and/or effective language maintenance movements would seem to be required if they are not to slip into the sharp loss category during the next decade. Three quarters of all mother tongues are in one or another of these first two categories.

c. *Moderate Gains*: Four mother tongues experiencing moderate gains in at least two generations (and neither sharp losses nor sharp gains in any) are "Dutch", Italian, Arabic, and Serbo-Croatian. They might be able to withstand serious erosion without special maintenance efforts during the next decade. Given such efforts, their position might even be appreciably reinforced.

d. *Sharp Gains*: Three mother tongues experiencing sharp gains in at least two generations (and at least moderate gains in the other) are Greek, Ukrainian, and Spanish. While these languages would seem to be in no immediate danger of numerical decimation in the near future, their creative maintenance cannot be assured on this basis alone.

In 1940 the numerically strongest mother tongues in the United States were German, Italian, Polish, Spanish, Yiddish, and French, in that order. Each of these languages was claimed by approximately a million and a half or more individuals. In 1960 these same languages remained the "big six" although their order had changed to Italian, Spanish, German, Polish, French, and Yiddish. Among them, only Spanish registered gains (and substantial gains at that) in this 20-year interval. The losses among the "big six" varied from a low of 2.5% for Italian to a high of 44.9% for Yiddish. The only other languages to gain in overall number of claimants during this period (disregarding the generational distribution of such gains) were Ukrainian, Serbo-Croatian, "Dutch"/Flemish, and Greek. The greatest gain of all was that of Ukrainian (202.6%!). Most mother tongues, including five of the "big six", suffered substantial losses during this period, the sharpest being that of Danish (65.1%). All in all, the 23 non-English mother tongues for which a 1940-1960 comparison is possible lost approximately one-sixth of their claimants during this interval. Yet the total number of claimants of non-English mother tongues in the United States is still quite substantial, encompassing nearly 11% of the total 1960 population (and an appreciably higher proportion of the white population).[6]

[6] The 1940 and 1960 totals shown in Table 2.4 must not be taken as the totals for *all* non-English mother tongue claimants in those years. Figures for Armenian were reported in 1940 but not in 1960. Figures for Chinese and Japanese were reported in 1960 but not in 1940. Total figures for "All other" languages were reported in both years. None of these inconsistent or non-specific listings are included in Table 2.4. Adding in these figures, as well as the necessary generational estimates based upon them, the two totals would become 1940: 22,036,240; 1960: 19,381,786.

NUMERICAL PROSPECTS FOR LANGUAGE MAINTENANCE

While intergenerational comparisons undoubtedly provide the best evidence derivable from census data, a single overall ranking also may be of some value in considering the prospects of language maintenance. The overall ranking shown in the last column of Table 2.5 is a composite of four rankings for particular generations. Two of these rankings pertain to the first generation, with the second and third generations each

TABLE 2.5

Overall Ranking of Mother Tongue Maintenance Prospects

First Generation		Second Generation	Third Generation	"Overall"
Languages ranked by number of claimants, 1960	Languages ranked by increase, 1940-1960	Languages ranked by the most plausible estimate, 1960	Languages ranked by the most plausible estimate, 1960	Languages ranked by averaging 4 previous rankings
1. German	1. Ukrainian	1. Italian	1. Spanish	1. Spanish
2. Italian	2. Spanish	2. Polish	2. German	2. German
3. Spanish	3. Serbo-Croatian	3. German	3. French	3. Italian
4. Polish	4. Dutch/Flemish	4. Spanish	4. Italian	4. French
5. Yiddish	5. Greek	5. Yiddish	5. Polish	5. Polish
6. French	6. Portuguese	6. French	6. Dutch/Flemish	6. Dutch/Flemish
7. Russian	7. Arabic	7. Swedish	7. Norwegian	7. Hungarian
8. Hungarian	8. French	8. Hungarian	8. Yiddish	8. Yiddish
9. Swedish	9. Hungarian	9. Russian	9. Czech	9.5. {Ukrainian {Russian
10. Greek	10. Rumanian	10. Norwegian	10. Russian	
11. Norwegian	11. Lithuanian	11. Ukrainian	11. Swedish	11. Greek
12. Slovak	12. German	12. Slovak	12. Hungarian	12. Norwegian
13. Dutch/Flemish	13. Italian	13. Dutch/Flemish	13. Greek	13. Swedish
14. Ukrainian	14. Russian	14. Greek	14. Ukrainian	14.5. {Slovak {Slovenian
15. Lithuanian	15. Slovak	15. Lithuanian	15. Slovak	
16. Czech	16. Polish	16. Czech	16. Lithuanian	16. Serbo-Croatian
17. Serbo-Croatian	17. Danish	17. Serbo-Croatian	17. Portuguese	17. Lithuanian
18. Portuguese	18. Norwegian	18. Portuguese	18. Serbo-Croatian	18. Portuguese
19. Danish	19. Czech	19. Danish	19. Danish	19. Czech
20. Finnish	20. Finnish	20. Finnish	20. Finnish	20. Arabic
21. Arabic	21. Yiddish	21. Arabic	21. Arabic	21. Danish
22. Rumanian	22. Swedish	22. Slovenian	22. Slovenian	22. Rumanian
23. Slovenian	23. Slovenian	23. Rumanian	23. Rumanian	23. Finnish

represented by only one ranking, in view of the likelihood that language maintenance in the United States will continue, in the case of most mother tongues, to depend primarily on the numerical strangth of the first generation. Although Table 2.5 represents quite a reasonable approach to the construction of a composite predictive ranking, it must be added that certain additional quantifiable factors (such as population concentration, intermarriage rates, social mobility, and fertility) are not directly represented. As a result the present ranking is primarily a reflection of the magnitudes of manpower pools available for the several mother tongues, rather than an indication of how loyal or how able the individuals in these pools are with respect to language maintenance.

The ability of America's non-English mother tongue groups to preserve their language may indeed depend to a very significant degree on the *number* of claimants involved. If the number of such individuals drops too low, then formal institutions of language maintenance (press, schools, organizations) cannot be maintained and creative potential must soon disappear. Relatively small groups may be able to preserve themselves linguistically if they maintain geographic concentration in addition to substantial physical, economic, and cultural separation from surrounding populations. However, separatist groups are very few in number in the United States and weak in impact on the total language maintenance constellation. Given the urban nature of most Americans of foreign stock and given their extensive social, occupational, and cultural interaction with American "core society", the numerical size of mother tongue groups (with some attention to recency of influx) probably becomes a far more crucial component of language maintenance than might otherwise be the case.

The composite ranking of languages places Spanish, German, Italian, French, Polish, and "Dutch" at the head of the list. These include almost all of the large immigrant groups that have appeared on American shores (with the notable exception of eastern European Jews), although the languages of several smaller, recent immigrant groups (Hungarian, Ukrainian) are represented high on the list as well. Not only do we find relatively recent and large immigrant groups near the top but we also find there all of the larger old groups that have achieved semi-indigenous stature by virtue of their colonial and early-post colonial impact on specific geographic regions (Spanish, German, French, and "Dutch"). Our composite ranking thus seems to make sense – at least, common sense – within the limitations of simple enumerative data. This being the case, we proceed to correlate this ranking with a number of others in an effort to suggest the major modifiers or concomitants of numerical potential for language maintenance.

SOME CORRELATES OF COMPOSITE LANGUAGE MAINTENANCE RANKING

Census data on population concentration reveal that *internal concentration* of first-generation mother tongue claimants is unrelated to the composite ranking (Table 2.6). The highest ranking mother tongue groups do *not* tend to be concentrated in fewer states than are the numerically weakest mother tongue groups. Indeed, no more than five states (and usually no more than four) are required in order to account for 50% of the first-generation claimants of any major non-English mother tongue. On the other hand, *external concentration* of first-generation claimants (the only claimants for which the 1960 census provides concentration data) does reveal a substantial relationship to the composite ranking. The highest ranking mother tongue groups do tend to constitute relatively greater proportions of the populations of the states in which most

TABLE 2.6

External Concentration (in Selected States), Internal Concentration and Urbanness (in the United States) of Foreign Born Claimants of 23 Non-English Mother Tongues

Composite Ranking of Language	Foreign Born Claimants in selected States: 1960	Total Population in selected States: 1960	"External" Concentration	Rank	% Urban	Rank	"Internal" Concentration: No. of States
Spanish	467,147	25,296,881	.01846	2	.848	12	2
German	694,824	53,900,032	.01196	3	.837	13	4
Italian	692,155	34,168,452	.02026	1	.932	5	3
French	173,775	40,183,320	.00432	6	.836	14	4
Polish	340,347	46,006,022	.00739	5	.905	8	4
Dutch/Flemish	72,823	46,389,484	.00157	15	.787	20	4
Hungarian	110,170	32,555,483	.00338	8	.900	9	3
Yiddish	295,308	16,782,304	.00760	4	.982	1	1
Ukrainian	58,678	34,168,452	.00172	14	.910	7	3
Russian	157,917	43,818,874	.00360	7	.927	6	3
Greek	89,429	47,729,244	.00185	13	.944	2	4
Norwegian	76,492	38,766,586	.00197	11	.765	21	4
Swedish	109,102	45,994,530	.00237	10	.806	17	4
Slovak	85,925	43,874,849	.00196	12	.831	16	4
Slovenian	16,692	31,106,921	.00054	21	.825	18	3
Serbo-Croatian	47,577	46,824,125	.00102	17	.880	11	4
Lithuanian	60,203	43,331,406	.00139	16	.899	10	4
Portuguese	56,257	20,865,782	.00270	9	.834	15	2
Czech	45,376	52,287,063	.00087	18	.803	19	4
Arabic	26,630	55,177,677	.00048	22	.937	4	5
Danish	37,415	45,338,203	.00083	19	.764	22	4
Rumanian	12,946	33,246,795	.00039	23	.739	3	3
Finnish	32,242	48,838,144	.00066	20	.669	23	5
			U.S.A.		.699		

of their claimants reside. The rank order correlation between external concentration (i.e., concentration relative to the total population rather than to the total number of claimants of a particular mother tongue) and the composite ranking is +.853, a value which is much too high to be attributable to chance or artifactual considerations alone. Clearly there is no necessity for the groups that are numerically strongest also to represent *relatively sizable concentrations* in a few states. Nor is there any reason why these same groups should not also be absolutely (internally) concentrated in a fewer number of states than the numerically smaller groups. This state of affairs seems to be a peculiarly American-immigrational language maintenance condition. The groups that rank highest on numerical potential *do* account for relatively more of the total populations of the states in which they are concentrated, but they are not concentrated in markedly fewer states.

That external concentration is of greater importance than internal concentration suggests that certain constants in American majority-minority relations, rather than

TABLE 2.7

Formal Education of Foreign Born Claimants of Eight Mother Tongues in 1960, Ages 50-74[a]

Mother Tongue	Formal Education					Overall Maintenance Rank
	None	Elementary	High School	College	Educ. Rank	
"Scandinavian"	3%	63%	30%	3%	3	8
French	—	83	17	—	5	4
German	2	65	32	2	2	2
Polish	31	59	6	3	7	5
Russian	25	29	21	25	1	7
Yiddish	39	29	15	17	4	6
Italian	20	74	6	—	8	3
Spanish	20	64	16	—	6	1
					R = .– 43	

[a] Data from punched cards on a representative .001 sample of the U.S. population, 1960, released by the Bureau of the Census.

internal minority group variations, may be the predominant forces influencing language maintenance in the United States.

Several earlier studies have pointed to rurality-urbanness as an important factor in explaining language maintenance differentials *within* particular mother tongue groups. The question still remains open as to whether this factor has any overall significance *between* groups. Table 2.6 indicates that only a minor relationship exists between rurality-urbanness and the composite ranking. Some languages in a very strong quantitative position are quite urban (e.g., Italian) whereas others are much less so (e.g., French, "Dutch"). All in all, the correlation between urbanness and the composite ranking is but +.251. In part this is due to the generally high urbanness of the foreign born in the United States (84%) relative to the national rate (70%). Only one group of mother tongue claimants (Finnish) has a lower rate of urbanness (67%) than the national average. All others score quite a bit higher in this respect, to such an extent that for some languages (Yiddish, Greek, Rumanian, Arabic, Italian, Russian, Ukrainian, Polish, and Hungarian) it can be said that nearly all their foreign born claimants are urban residents. If national trends are of any significance, this must be even more true of second- and third-generation claimants. Thus language maintenance in the United States is increasingly and overridingly an urban affair.[7]

Since the majority of immigrants, particularly those arriving before and soon after the First World War, have been primarily of rural origin it is reasonable to suspect that life in American urban industrial centers may have posed uniformly serious problems for their language and culture maintenance. Life in such centers presents

[7] Interestingly enough, the "prestige cluster" — French, Spanish, and German — is not encountered among the most urbanized languages reported in Table 2.6.

several maximal contrasts to life in traditional ethnic communities. Occupational, associational, and generational patterns are the primary features of urban behavior as contrasted with the traditions and values of the family and the immediate neighborhood. Social mobility, socio-cultural change, and mass culture are particularly pervasive in these settings and it becomes increasingly difficult to maintain family or neighborhood uniquenesses in the absence of determined separatism. Little wonder, then, that a single factor such as extent of formal education among 50-74 year old foreign born claimants of eight mother tongues correlates —.43 with the composite ranking of numerical potential (Table 2.7).[8] Given the well-known accelerated rate of social mobility within generations and in successive generations over time, particularly in our urban centers, we need not wonder that large and periodically replenished concentrations of claimants figure so prominently among the requirements of language maintenance in the United States.

---

[8]　These eight mother tongues are the only ones for which educational cross-tabulations were derivable from the .001 sample punched cards released by the Bureau of the Census.

3. THE NON-ENGLISH AND THE ETHNIC GROUP PRESS, 1910-1960

JOSHUA A. FISHMAN, ROBERT G. HAYDEN AND MARY E. WARSHAUER

The demise of the American non-English press has been documented and predicted frequently. Social scientists on the one hand, and the very readers and writers of non-English publications on the other, have held out little or no hope for its survival. Nevertheless the non-English press, which traces its origins back to Ben Franklin's *Die Philadelphische Zeitung* of 1732, still boasts an overall circulation of approximately four million today, and would seem to have more lives than the proverbial cat. If we add to the above figure the circulation of those ethnic publications (as distinguished from scholarly publications for non-ethnic readers) which publish sections of each issue in a non-English "ethnic mother tongue" the total circulation rises to approximately five and a half million. This figure is certainly still large enough, and implies a sufficiently high incidence of subscriptions among the seven million foreign-born claimants of non-English mother tongues in the U.S. in 1960, to imply that the disappearance of the non-English press is a long way off, if foreseeable at all. What we do find, if we differentiate between the various kinds of non-English publications currently published in the United States, is that some kinds are becoming unmistakably weaker while others are becoming unmistakably stronger. In addition, there has developed a huge press directed toward readers of various ethnic backgrounds but published entirely in English. The non-English and ethnic group press in America is a topic that merits attention on the part of those interested in American social and cultural developments, whether in conjunction with the mass media, language maintenance, cultural pluralism, or all three. Heretofore, little systematic attention has been devoted to this topic. The present chapter seeks to supply (i) basic trend data on the *number* and the *circulation* of various categories of non-English and ethnic group publications and (ii) attitudinal data concerning the current plans, purposes, and prospects of these publications.

TREND DATA, 1910-1960

Non-English (Mother Tongue) Publications

Dailies. – Ayer's *Directory* (N. W. Ayer and Son's, etc.) lists 61 non-English dailies in 1960 (Table 3.1).[1] This number represents a 53% decline since 1910 (when mass immi-

[1] Although both Directory and "Language Resources Project" (LRP) data are availabe for that

TABLE 3.1

Number of Mother Tongue Dailies, 1910-1960

Languages	1910	1920	1930	1940	1950	1960	1960 LRP	Percent Increase or Decrease		
								1910-1930	1930-1960	1950-1960
French	9	10	7	6	2	1	1	−22%	−86%	−50%
Spanish	1	5	10	8	8	6	6	+900	−40	−25
German	70	29	22	13	7	4	4	−68	−82	−43
Yiddish	7	11	11	10	6	5	5	+57	−54	−17
Hungarian	3	3	3	3	3	2	2	0	−33	−33
Ukrainian	—	1	2	2	2	2	2	—	0	0
Italian	12	11	10	10	5	5	5	−17	−50	0
Polish	9	15	16	10	9	7	6	+78	−56	−22
Greek	2	2	5	2	2	2	2	+150	−60	0
Czech	7	9	8	7	5	2	2	+14	−75	−60
Other Slavic	1	16	15	12	9	7	10	+1400	−53	−22
Scandinavian	2	2	2	—	—	—	—	0	−100	—
Other Germanic	—	—	—	—	—	—	—	—	—	—
Other Romance	—	1	3	1	1	1	1	—	67	0
Near Eastern	1	4	6	2	4	1	1	+500	−83	−75
Far Eastern	5	9	10	10	12	9	10	+100	−10	−25
All Other	—	12	12	10	11	7	7	—	−42	−36
Total	129	140	142	106	86	61	64	+10	−57	−29

gration to the United States was still under way) and a 57% decline since 1930 (when non-English dailies were at their 20th century peak). The decline has not been uniform for all languages, although none shows an increase since 1930. Ukrainian dailies have not decreased in number since their first appearance in the United States. This is undoubtedly due to the large increase in foreign-born Ukrainian speakers between 1940 (35,540) and 1960 (106, 974). Italian, Greek, and "Other Romance" (Portuguese, Rumanian) dailies have not decreased in number since 1950, although they experienced sharp decreases during the 1930-1950 period. The sharpest declines since 1930 have occurred among Scandinavian (Norwegian, Swedish, Danish), French, Near Eastern (Arabic), German, and Czech dailies, all of which have lost three-quarters or more of their 1930 dailies, the Scandinavian dailies disappearing entirely.[2]

The linguistic distribution of non-English dailies has changed considerably since 1910. At that time 54% were published in German alone. By 1960 German dailies accounted for only 7% of the total! This sharp decline is noticeable as early as 1920

---

year, only *Directory* data for 1960 are referred to in trend analyses (e.g. 1930-1960, 1950-1960, etc.), so as to maintain a consistent base for comparisons.

[2]   A steady decline has also occurred in the number of non-ethnic dailies. Ayer reports 2,015 English-language dailies in 1940; 1,894 in 1950; and 1,854 in 1960. The decline since 1940 is 8%. Liebling indicates that 837 English-language dailies were discontinued between 1909 and 1961 (Liebling 1961). This represents a decline of 31%.

TABLE 3.2

Circulation of Mother Tongue Dailies, 1910-1960

Languages	1910	1920	1930	1940	1950	1960	1960 LRP	Percent Increase or Decrease		
								1910-1930	1930-1960	1950-1960
French	(7)[a] 43[b]	(8) 41	(6) 32	(6) 25	(2) 8	(1) 3	(1) 3	−26%	−91%	−62%
Spanish	— —	(2) 15	(7) 56	(8) 74	(7) 70	(6) 114	(6) 135	—	+104	+63
German	(64) 935	(14) 239	(20) 354	(12) 261	(5) 69	(4) 74	(4) 74	−62	−79	+7
Yiddish	(5) 261	(11) 507	(10) 558	(9) 424	(6) 238	(4) 140	(4) 166	+114	−75	−41
Hungarian	(3) 27	(2) 72	(3) 98	(3) 98	(3) 52	(2) 43	(2) 43	+263	−56	−17
Ukrainian	—	—	(2) 31	(2) 46	(2) 27	(2) 30	(2) 30	—	−3	+11
Italian	(4) 57	(11) 330	(10) 348	(8) 217	(5) 149	(4) 136	(4) 133	+511	−61	−9
Polish	(6) 63	(13) 239	(15) 345	(10) 261	(9) 238	(7) 184	(6) 152	+448	−47	−23
Greek	(1) 4	(2) 65	(3) 37	(2) 26	(2) 34	(2) 34	(2) 32	+825	−8	0
Czech	(6) 75	(9) 113	(7) 156	(5) 145	(4) 135	(2) 64	(2) 61	+108	−59	−53
Other Slavic	—	(12) 184	(13) 254	(11) 200	(8) 101	(6) 74	(9) 84	—	−71	−27
Scandinavian	(2) 28	(2) 31	(1) 12	—	—	—	—	−57	—	—
Other Germanic	—	(1) 11	(3) 33	(1) 10	(1) 10	(1) 9	(1) 9	—	−73	−10
Other Romance	—	(2) 88	(5) 17	(1) 5	(4) 23	(1) 3	(1) 3	—	−82	−87
Near Eastern	(1) 3	(8) 33	(7) 46	(8) 73	(11) 74	(9) 61	(10) 66	+1433	+33	−18
All Other	—	(11) 95	(11) 158	(8) 128	(11) 168	(7) 127	(7) 127	—	−20	−24
Total	(99) 1499	(108) 1990	(123) 2542	(94) 2000	(80) 1402	(58) 1103	(61) 1125	+70	−57	−16

[a] Number of dailies for which circulation figures are available.
[b] Last three digits have been dropped in all circulation figures.

(when dailies in most other languages were still increasing in number) and can be attributed, in large part, to anti-German sentiments that were widespread during World War I and subsequently. Dailies published in Slavic languages – Ukrainian, Polish, Czech, and "Other Slavic" (Russian, Serbo-Croatian, Slovak, and Slovenian) – accounted for only 13 % of the 1910 total but rose to 33 % in 1960. The lesser overall decline of Slavic dailies (and, therefore, their proportional increase) is largely attributable to absolute increases in the numbers of foreign-born speakers of Slavic languages since the end of World War II.

Circulation trends for non-English dailies show parallels to the trends noted above (Table 3.2). Circulation, too, rose from 1910 to 1930 and has decreased regularly since then as both mortality and Americanization have taken their tolls in the foreign-born population. Nevertheless, there are some interesting differences between the trends for number and circulation.[3] During the period 1910-1930 circulation rose *more* rapidly than did the number of dailies. Moreover, circulation has fallen off *less* rapidly since 1950 (or even since 1910) than has the number of dailies. Such differences indicate some lack of articulation between circulation changes and changes in the number of dailies. The publishers did not rush to establish new publications when circulation was on the upgrade, but quickly discontinued them when circulation turned to the downgrade. Perhaps we might refer to this as a "cautious bias". Some dailies consolidate even when circulation is on the increase, as, for example, the Spanish dailies which enjoyed a 63 % *increase in circulation* and a 25 % *decrease in number* in the 1950-1960 period. German dailies are another example. Although their number and circulation dropped precipitously during and immediately after both World Wars, a slight recouping of lost circulation occurred about a decade later in both instances while the numbers of dailies continued to decline. The average circulation of non-English dailies in 1960 was 18,442.

Weeklies. – Ayer reports that 188 non-English weeklies were published in 1960 (Table 3.3). This number represents a decline of 76 % relative to 1910 and of 63 % relative to 1930. A decrease of 34 % occurred during the 1950-1960 decade alone. Each of these declines is appreciably greater than those noted earlier for the dailies. There was no 1930 spurt in the number of weeklies, as there was for dailies. Every decade since 1910 hass witnessed a decline in the total number of weeklies. For the period 1910-1930 this was primarily due to the precipitous decline in the number of German and Scandinavian weeklies, which was so sharp as to mask increases in the number of weeklies in most other languages during this period. As in the case of dailies, the relative positions of German and Slavic weeklies were reversed from 1910 to 1960. In 1910 German weeklies accounted for 56 % of non-English weeklies, and by 1960

[3]   Ayer reports the following divergence between aggregate circulation and number of publications for American non-ethnic dailies; *1940*: 39,434,382 for 2,015 dailies; *1950*: 52,270,718 for 1,894 dailies; *1960*: 57,611,477 for 1,854 dailies. The average circulation for non-ethnic dailies in *1960* was 31,074.

TABLE 3.3

Number of Mother Tongue Weeklies, 1910-1960
(including publications appearing twice and three times per week)

Languages	1910	1920	1930	1940	1950	1960	1960 LRP	Percent Increase or Decrease		
								1910-1930	1930-1960	1950-1960
French	18	17	18	14	13	8	8	0%	−55%	−38%
Spanish	30	39	39	18	18	10	12	+30	−74	−44
German	433	172	106	68	35	29	30	−76	−73	−17
Yiddish	8	16	7	3	8	2	3	−12	−71	−75
Hungarian	7	16	28	25	26	19	19	+300	−32	−27
Ukrainian	1	5	3	2	3	2	3	+200	−33	−33
Italian	48	66	73	29	28	12	12	+52	−84	−57
Polish	37	54	64	43	35	18	22	+73	−72	−49
Greek	5	8	6	7	6	3	3	+20	−50	−50
Czech	34	29	27	28	12	9	9	−21	−67	−25
Other Slavic	11	31	28	22	26	20	17	+155	−29	−23
Scandinavian	94	73	51	32	26	14	15	−46	−73	−46
Other Germanic	16	13	11	8	3	1	1	−31	−91	−67
Other Romance	8	12	12	10	6	4	5	+50	−75	−33
Near Eastern	5	6	2	1	6	8	9	−60	+300	+33
Far Eastern	4	5	8	3	5	3	3	+100	−62	−40
All Other	17	32	28	24	29	26	27	+65	−7	−10
Total	776	594	511	337	285	188	198	−34	−63	−34

for only 15%. In 1910 weeklies published in Slavic languages accounted for 11% of the total, and in 1960 for 26%.

During the period 1930-1960, only in Near Eastern languages did the number of weeklies increase – by 300%; from 1950 to 1960 alone they increased by 33%. All other languages show rather sharp and regular decreases. The most precipitous decreases from 1930 to 1960 occurred among weeklies published in "Other Germanic (Dutch)", Italian, "Other Romance", Spanish, German, Polish, Scandinavian, and Yiddish. In each case the decrease has been of the order of 70% or more. Of these eight languages (or language groupings) only two also experienced sharp decreases in the number of dailies during the same period. This implies that the fortuntes of these two types of publication are not interlocked. It may be that weeklies represent an "unstable state" for non-English language publications. Some dailies may "slip" to become weeklies; in this case, as well as in the case of publications initiated as weeklies, continued circulation losses may lead to rapid discontinuation or to a further slip to the status of monthlies.

Like the dailies, the non-English weeklies reached their circulation peak in 1930 (Table 3.4). However, whereas the 1930 peak for dailies represents a 70% increase over the 1910 circulation, the 1930 peak for weeklies represents only a 6% gain. More-

TABLE 3.4

Circulation of Mother Tongue Weeklies, 1910-1960
(including publications appearing twice and three times per week)

Languages	1910		1920		1930		1940		1950		1960		1960 LRP		Percent Increase or Decrease		
															1910-1930	1930-1960	1950-1960
French	(13)[a]	60[b]	(13)	46	(13)	71	(8)	44	(9)	33	(7)	21	(7)	36	+18%	−70%	−36%
Spanish	(18)	35	(25)	86	(24)	143	(9)	29	(12)	52	(8)	30	(9)	43	+309	−79	−42
German	(383)	2092	(119)	831	(72)	832	(49)	481	(25)	137	(26)	133	(28)	165	−60	−84	−3
Yiddish	(3)	60	(11)	236	(5)	178	(2)	86	(5)	74	(2)	21	(3)	34	+197	−88	−72
Hungarian	(5)	23	(9)	92	(17)	95	(19)	209	(22)	109	(19)	109	(19)	101	+313	+15	0
Ukrainian	(1)	11	(3)	27	(2)	19	(1)	6	(2)	8	(1)	2	(2)	7	+73	−89	−75
Italian	(24)	187	(29)	253	(31)	264	(15)	146	(22)	152	(11)	84	(11)	108	+41	−68	−45
Polish	(20)	126	(33)	666	(37)	558	(22)	627	(27)	302	(17)	146	(21)	203	+342	−74	−52
Greek	(1)	6	(3)	12	(4)	26	(5)	23	(4)	14	(2)	8	(2)	8	+333	−69	−43
Czech	(25)	243	(23)	263	(21)	279	(20)	233	(11)	99	(9)	122	(9)	124	+15	−56	+23
Other Slavic	(4)	21	(17)	157	(22)	455	(19)	414	(22)	164	(16)	75	(16)	84	+2067	−84	−54
Scandinavian	(78)	795	(58)	758	(35)	532	(24)	267	(19)	185	(14)	114	(15)	116	−33	−79	−43
Other Germanic	(12)	33	(13)	47	(5)	22	(7)	23	(3)	9	(1)	4	(1)	4	−33	−82	−55
Other Romance	(5)	6	(4)	14	(9)	97	(6)	43	(5)	25	(3)	7	(4)	17	+1517	−93	−72
Near Eastern	(2)	10	(2)	7	(1)	21	(1)	2	(3)	4	(6)	17	(7)	22	+110	−19	+325
Far Eastern	(2)	5	(3)	14	(2)	300	—		(4)	18	(2)	5	(2)	4	+5900	−98	−72
All Other	(10)	49	(18)	91	(16)	116	(16)	130	(22)	121	(23)	104	(25)	115	+137	−10	−14
Total	(606)	3769	(383)	3608	(316)	4014	(223)	2769	(216)	1512	(167)	1010	(181)	1198	+6	−75	−33

[a] Number of weeklies for which circulation are available.
[b] Last three digits have been dropped in all circulation figures.

over, the subsequent circulation losses for weeklies were greater than those for dailies; for dailies they were 57% from 1930 to 1960 and 16% from 1950 to 1960, but they were 75% and 33% respectively for weeklies. Indeed, while *circulation* losses for dailies have lagged somewhat behind the decrease in the *number* of dailies, circulation losses for weeklies exceed their losses in numbers. If publishers of non-English dailies exhibit a "cautious bias", then the publishers of weeklies may be said to exhibit an "amateur bias". The average circulation of non-English weeklies in 1960 (6,619) was only one-third the average circulation of non-English dailies. The position of the weeklies, overall, seems less secure than that of the dailies.

TABLE 3.5

Number of Mother Tongue Monthlies, 1910-1960
(including publications appearing twice a month and every other week)

| Languages | 1910 | 1920 | 1930 | 1940 | 1950 | 1960 | 1960 LRP | Percent Increase or Decrease | | |
								1910-1930	1930-1960	1950-1960
French	1	2	3	2	4	4	1	+200%	+33%	0%
Spanish	3	12	9	—	5	11	18	+200	+22	+120
German	49	31	17	9	8	8	15	−65	−53	0
Yiddish	2	1	2	3	8	6	7	0	+200	−25
Hungarian	1	5	3	—	6	11	17	+200	+267	+83
Ukrainian	—	2	1	1	2	6	12	—	+500	+200
Italian	1	2	2	3	3	3	6	+100	+50	0
Polish	4	2	4	1	8	10	11	0	+150	+25
Greek	—	3	4	1	2	4	4	—	0	+100
Czech	7	11	9	5	8	7	10	+29	−22	−12
Other Slavic	17	5	10	4	8	16	26	−41	+60	+100
Scandinavian	27	20	9	5	5	4	7	−67	−56	−20
Other Germanic	4	1	2	—	—	—	—	−50	—	—
Other Romance	1	4	—	—	—	1	1	—	—	—
Near Eastern	—	1	—	—	—	1	1	—	—	—
Far Eastern	1	1	—	—	—	—	—	—	—	—
All Other	14	6	4	3	8	14	21	−71	+250	+75
Total	132	109	79	37	75	106	157	−40	+34	+41

Monthlies. – Ayer reports that 106 non-English monthlies were published in the United States in 1960 (Table 3.5). This number represents a 20% decrease relative to 1910 but a 34% increase relative to 1930. Indeed, monthlies (and even less frequent publications) represent the only growing segment of the non-English language press. Their ranks increased by 41% from 1950 to 1960 alone! Certainly, this is a far different picture from that of dailies and weeklies.

The entire developmental pattern for monthlies is unique. Their apex came in

TABLE 3.6

Circulation of Mother Tongue Monthlies, 1910-1960
(including publications appearing twice a month and every other week)

Languages	1910	1920	1930	1940	1950	1960	1960 LRP	Percent Increase or Decrease		
								1910-1930	1930-1960	1950-1960
French	—	(2) 31	(1) 48	(2) 46	(3) 51	(4) 92	(14) 141	—	+92%	+80%
Spanish	(2)ᵃ 28ᵇ	(5) 133	(5) 88	—	(2) 8	(8) 109	(15) 88	+214%	+24	+1262
German	(40) 361	(19) 240	(8) 168	(6) 89	(3) 79	(8) 73	—	−53	−57	−8
Yiddish	—	(1) 65	(1) 37	—	(4) 48	(3) 16	(6) 25	—	−57	−67
Hungarian	—	(2) 21	(3) 38	—	(6) 58	(6) 46	(13) 66	—	+21	−21
Ukrainian	—	(1) 20	—	—	(1) 1	(5) 11	(11) 18	—	—	+1000
Italian	(2) 22	—	—	(2) 5	(1) 45	(2) 41	(5) 50	—	—	−9
Polish	—	—	(2) 95	(1) 3	(5) 96	(10) 341	(11) 349	+332	+259	+255
Greek	—	(1) 25	(1) 10	—	(2) 12	(3) 22	(4) 26	—	+120	+83
Czech	(4) 51	(7) 67	(8) 77	(3) 52	(5) 91	(6) 83	(9) 88	+51	+8	−9
Other Slavic	(9) 75	(1) 12	(7) 20	(1) 3	(3) 18	(10) 65	(22) 80	−73	+225	+261
Scandinavian	(16) 99	(14) 134	(6) 36	(5) 67	(3) 8	(2) 5	(6) 39	−64	−86	−38
Other Germanic	(4) 48	—	—	—	—	—	—	—	—	—
Other Romance	—	(1) ᶜ	—	—	—	(1) 7	(1) 3	—	—	—
Near Eastern	—	—	—	—	—	(1) 16	(1) 16	—	—	—
Far Eastern	—	—	—	—	—	—	—	—	—	—
All Other	(10) 59	(4) 22	(3) 21	(3) 4	(6) 14	(11) 19	(19) 27	−64	−10	+36
Total	(87) 747	(58) 756	(45) 643	(23) 272	(44) 534	(80) 952	(137) 1023	−14	+48	+78

ᵃ Number of monthlies for which circulation figures are available.
ᵇ Last three digits have been dropped in all circulation figures.
ᶜ Less than 1000.

1910 (or perhaps earlier), their nadir in 1940, and they have been growing in number ever since. The largest increases have been registered by Ukrainian, Hungarian, "Other Slavic", Polish, Spanish, and Greek. These are languages that have experienced proportionately great post-World War II reinforcement through immigration. Recent immigrants speaking these languages have tended to gravitate more toward specialized monthlies than toward mass appeal dailies. This may be due to the higher educational level of these immigrants, as a result of which they often found their own monthlies rather than depend as completely on dailies as have their predecessors (Zubrzycki 1958).

Circulation trends for monthlies differ from trends with respect to number (Table 3.6). While the circulation nadir, like the numbers nadir, occurred in 1940, the apex in circulation occurred in 1960. This is another indication of the continued growth of non-English monthlies. During 1910-1930 they decreased less in circulation than in number and, subsequently, have increased more in circulation than in number. Thus they, like the dailies, reveal a "cautious bias" on the part of publishers. The important difference between dailies and monthlies is that the former are in a downward circulation trend, and the latter in an upward trend. It may be that the circulation increases for monthlies have recouped some of the recent losses in daily and weekly circulations

TABLE 3.7

Total Number of Mother Tongue Publications, 1910-1960
(including periodicals appearing less frequently than monthly)

Languages	1910	1920	1930	1940	1950	1960	1960 LRP	Percent Increase or Decrease		
								1910-1930	1930-1960	1950-1960
French	28	29	28	23	20	13	15	0%	−54%	−35%
Spanish	35	58	61	28	35	31	49	+74	−49	−11
German	554	234	146	90	50	41	54	−74	−72	−18
Yiddish	17	28	20	16	23	15	22	+18	−20	−35
Hungarian	11	24	35	28	35	32	40	+218	−9	−9
Ukrainian	1	8	6	5	7	14	25	+500	+113	+100
Italian	61	79	85	42	36	21	26	+39	−75	−42
Polish	50	71	84	54	52	37	43	+68	−56	−29
Greek	7	13	15	10	10	9	10	+114	−40	−10
Czech	48	49	44	40	25	19	24	−8	−57	−24
Other Slavic	31	52	53	38	44	46	64	+71	−13	+5
Scandinavian	123	96	62	37	31	20	23	−50	−68	−29
Other Germanic	20	14	13	8	3	1	1	−35	−92	−67
Other Romance	9	17	15	11	7	7	9	+67	−53	0
Near Eastern	6	11	8	3	10	10	16	+33	+25	0
Far Eastern	10	15	18	13	17	12	14	+80	−33	−29
All Other	32	50	44	37	48	49	82	+38	+11	+2
Total	1043	848	737	483	453	377	517	−29	−49	−17

TABLE 3.8

Circulation of Mother Tongue Publications, 1910-1960
(including periodicals appearing less frequently than monthly)

Languages	1910		1920		1930		1940		1950		1960		1960 LRP		Percent Increase or Decrease		
															1910-1930	1930-1960	1950-1960
French	(20)[a]	104[b]	(23)	119	(20)	151	(16)	116	(14)	93	(12)	118	(13)	87	+45%	−22%	+17%
Spanish	(21)	74	(33)	256	(39)	298	(18)	114	(24)	147	(25)	268	(40)	507	+303	−10	+82
German	(488)	3391	(152)	1311	(100)	1354	(67)	832	(33)	286	(38)	281	(52)	343	−60	−79	−2
Yiddish	(8)	321	(23)	808	(16)	775	(11)	510	(16)	401	(9)	179	(18)	239	+141	−77	−55
Hungarian	(8)	50	(13)	186	(24)	238	(22)	308	(31)	219	(27)	198	(36)	214	+376	−17	−10
Ukrainian	(1)	11	(4)	29	(4)	51	(3)	52	(5)	38	(12)	47	(23)	66	+364	−8	+24
Italian	(28)	245	(40)	584	(41)	613	(25)	369	(28)	346	(18)	270	(23)	298	+150	−56	−22
Polish	(28)	212	(46)	906	(54)	999	(33)	892	(41)	637	(36)	690	(42)	739	+371	−31	+8
Greek	(2)	10	(6)	102	(8)	74	(7)	49	(8)	60	(7)	65	(9)	68	+640	−12	+8
Czech	(35)	371	(39)	444	(36)	513	(28)	431	(20)	326	(18)	274	(23)	288	+38	−47	−16
Other Slavic	(14)	99	(30)	353	(42)	730	(31)	618	(33)	284	(33)	216	(57)	261	+637	−70	+24
Scandinavian	(96)	922	(75)	925	(42)	580	(29)	334	(22)	193	(17)	120	(22)	157	−37	−79	−38
Other Germanic	(16)	82	(13)	47	(5)	22	(7)	23	(2)	9	(1)	4	(1)	4	−73	−82	−56
Other Romance	(5)	6	(6)	26	(12)	130	(7)	54	(6)	36	(6)	25	(8)	58	+2117	−81	−17
Near Eastern	(2)	10	(4)	16	(6)	38	(2)	7	(7)	27	(8)	37	(14)	44	+280	−3	+37
Far Eastern	(3)	8	(11)	47	(9)	346	(8)	73	(15)	92	(11)	67	(13)	72	+4225	−81	−27
All Other	(20)	108	(33)	210	(30)	296	(27)	262	(39)	305	(42)	253	(77)	308	+174	−15	−17
Total	(795)	6029	(551)	6378	(488)	7216	(341)	5052	(344)	3506	(320)	3118	(471)	3759	+20	−57	−11

[a] Number of publications for which circulation figures are available.
[b] Last three digits have been dropped in all circulation figures.

noted earlier. The average circulation of monthlies is 7,467. This figure is larger than that of weeklies but still quite a bit smaller than that of dailies.

Total non-English publications. – All in all, 377 non-English publications were listed in Ayer's *Directory* for 1960 (Table 3.7). The Language Resources Project located 140 additional publications for a grand total of 517. The combined circulation for 471 of these (no circulation figures being available for the remaining 46) was slightly in excess of three and three-quarter million (Table 3.8), yielding an average circulation of 7,983 for non-English publications in 1960. Assuming that the publications were largely intended for and read by the slightly more than seven million foreign-born claimants of non-English mother tongues reported by the 1960 census, we obtain a ratio of circulation to claimants of 1:2. Actually, not all claimants are sufficiently interested in or fluent in their claimed non-English mother tongues to warrant subscribing to non-English publications. On the other hand, the non-English press has a sizable "pass-along" readership. This latter group of non-subscribing or non-purchasing readers is likely to be as great as or greater than the claimants of non-English mother tongues who have lost facility or interest in their mother tongues. As a result, the 1:2 ratio between circulation and claimants may still be said to hold.[4]

The 1:2 ratio does not hold equally well, of course, for all non-English mother tongue groups. In some instances, the ratio is far lower, particularly for "Other Germanic", Italian, French, German, Scandinavian, and Greek. These groups may be characterized either as having little in the way of a publication-reading tradition (e.g., Italian, Greek, and particularly "Other Germanic", which includes a large proportion of Pennsylvania Dutch) or as having Americanized beyond the point of major interest in non-English publications (e.g., French, German, and Scandinavian). Groups in which the ratio of circulation to claimants is much above the average include Czech, Polish, Hungarian, and Near Eastern languages (primarily Arabic). In those instances we encounter ratios of 1:1 or better. Wherever we encounter a larger circulation than the number of mother tongue claimants, it is reasonable to surmise (a) automatic distribution of publications on the basis of organizational membership or (b) frequent multiple subscriptions.[5] Both circumstances are likely in the case of recent immigrant groups such as those listed above.

Obviously the more numerous the speakers of a particular language, the greater the theoretical circulation potential for publications in that language. The actual relationship between these two variables confirms the theoretical expectation. The rank order correlation between number of foreign-born claimants of various non-English

---

[4] No strictly comparable data are available for the American non-ethnic press. The aggregate circulation of all the 1,854 English-language dailies published in 1960 was 57,611,477. This figure would yield a circulation-to-population ratio of 1:3 in 1960. The circulation-to-claimants ratio for non-English *dailies* alone was 1:7 in 1960.

[5] Another possible explanation would be circulation among second, third, and subsequent generations of American born readers. There is very little evidence of many such readers of the non-English press in the United States at this time.

mother tongues in 1960 and the combined 1960 circulation of publications in these languages yields a coefficient of $+.80$. A strong positive relationship also exists between the number of claimants and the total number of publications, the rank order correlation coefficient being $+.64$. However, the relationship between the number of claimants of various non-English mother tongues in 1960 and the circulation-to claimant ratios is a *negative* one, yielding a rank order coefficient of $-.21$; i.e., many *larger* mother tongue groups have *smaller* circulation-to-claimant ratios and many *smaller* mother tongue groups have *larger* circulation-to-claimant ratios. Some insight into this phenomenon is gained by examining the specific groups in question. Among the largest groups of non-English mother tongue claimants (German, Italian, Spanish, Scandinavian, French) we find both those who are now most Americanized as a result of earlier mass immigration and those who have greatest access to publications originating in their ethnic homelands. On the other hand, among the smallest groups of non-English mother tongue claimants (Near Eastern, Czech, Ukrainian, Hungarian) the opposite situations obtain. Thus, it is not the size of the mother tongue groups which leads to variations in circulation-to-claimant ratios but the different pre-immigration and post-immigration circumstances that characterize the groups.

Mixed (*English and Mother Tongue*) *Publications*

Periodic ethnic publications that combine English and non-English features are certainly at least a century old on the American scene and probably much older (Chyz 1959). Ayer reports a total of 107 such publications in 1960 (Table 3.9), including dailies, weeklies, monthlies, and publications of lesser frequency. This number represents a 32% increase since 1910, when mass immigration was still underway and when most immigrant groups supported publications appearing entirely in the ethnic mother tongue. In 1910 mixed publications were largely limited to German-Americans and Scandinavian-Americans, who were among out earliest non-English-speaking mass immigrants. By 1910 their Americanization had progressed to a point where non-English publications alone could not suffice if American-born offspring were to be kept within the ethnic-religious fold. The mixed publication represented and still represents an attempt to reach Anglified ethnics along with linguistically retentive ethnics by means of a single medium. It was and is an attempt to bridge the linguistic and cultural cleavage that often develops between immigrants to the United States and their children or grandchildren. However, it has frequently been an unstable solution to the problem of inter-generational continuity. As a result of financial rather than ideological considerations, English slowly but surely pushes the ethnic mother tongue out of the mixed publication. Moreover, the linguistically Anglified ethnic is a less faithful subscriber than the linguistically retentive one. Consequently, mixed publications have tended toward a shorter life span than all-mother-tongue or all-English-language ethnic publications, and have frequently made a subsequent transition to all-English, or have been discontinued entirely. Nevertheless, both their num-

TABLE 3.9

Number of Mixed Publications, 1910-1930

Languages	1910	1920	1930	1940	1950	1960	1960 LRP	Percent Increase or Decrease		
								1910-1930	1930-1960	1950-1960
French	3	5	6	7	6	3	3	−100%	−50%	−50%
Spanish	10	11	9	18	17	13	14	−10	−44	−24
German	29	22	22	16	10	9	16	−24	−59	−10
Yiddish	—	7	13	10	6	4	6	—	−69	−33
Hungarian	—	2	4	5	4	1	3	—	−75	−75
Ukrainian	—	1	1	1	2	3	5	—	+200	+50
Italian	10	18	38	39	37	20	27	+280	−47	−46
Polish	1	3	2	5	3	2	10	+100	0	−33
Greek	1	2	4	3	4	5	12	+300	+25	+25
Czech	—	—	1	1	2	4	6	—	+300	+100
Other Slavic	3	8	14	18	18	19	32	+367	+36	+6
Scandinavian	13	17	17	14	9	5	11	+31	−71	−44
Other Germanic	3	4	5	3	3	2	4	+67	−60	−33
Other Romance	—	—	1	—	2	1	7	—	0	−50
Near Eastern	1	—	—	1	2	1	7	—	—	−50
Far Eastern	4	6	6	7	8	8	9	+50	+33	0
All Others	3	4	6	5	7	7	15	+100	+17	0
Total	81	111	149	153	140	107	187	+84	−28	−24

bers and their circulations indicate they have played and continue to play an important *transitional* role.

The number of mixed publications increased regularly to 1940 and has decreased since then. Within the last decade alone they have decreased by 24%, a greater decline than that of the entire non-English press in the same period. Today, mixed publications for German and Scandinavian readers represent only 13% of the mixed press whereas they constituted 52% of the mixed press in 1910. Yet certain recent immigrant groups that previously had few or no mixed publications registered increases during this time (e.g., Czech, Ukrainian, Greek, "Other Slavic", etc.).

In 1960 the average circulation of the mixed press was 6,926. This figure is less by a thousand than the average circulation of mother tongue publications in the same year. The circulation of mixed publications has continued to rise since 1910 as Anglification reached first the old immigrant groups and then ever larger proportions of the new immigrant groups (Table 3.10). While a total increase in circulation of 96% has occurred since 1910, the rate of increase slowed up considerably during the latter part of this period. Thus, circulation increased 68% from 1910 to 1930, 50% from 1930 to 1960, and only 7% from 1950 to 1960. It would appear that by the last decade the mixed press was finding it difficult to serve its customary transitional role, its many erstwhile readers having passed into non-ethnic statuses or having switched to ethnic

TABLE 3.10

Circulation of Mixed Publications, 1910-1930

Languages	1910	1920	1930	1940	1950	1960	1960 LRP	Percent Increase or Decrease		
								1910-1930	1930-1960	1950-1960
French	(3)[a] 3[b]	(3) 5	(3) 10	(5) 21	(3) 8	(2) 5	(2) 14	+233%	-50%	-38%
Spanish	(4) 4	(6) 7	(4) 3	(14) 17	(12) 113	(9) 54	(10) 55	-25	+1700	-52
German	(21) 206	(14) 101	(12) 65	(10) 94	(9) 155	(9) 146	(16) 157	-68	+125	-6
Yiddish	—	(2) 14	(8) 34	(6) 33	(2) 6	(2) 63	(6) 75	—	+85	+950
Hungarian	—	(1) 7	(2) 9	(5) 48	(4) 27	(1) 4	(3) 11	—	-56	-85
Ukrainian	—	(1) 6	—	(1) 10	(2) 12	(3) 27	(5) 27	—	—	+125
Italian	(3) 15	(10) 59	(20) 114	(26) 174	(25) 132	(17) 164	(27) 251	+660	+44	-24
Polish	(1) 9	(2) 19	(2) 23	(5) 37	(3) 31	(2) 9	(8) 36	+155	-61	-71
Greek	(1) 8	—	(1) 12	(3) 20	(3) 17	(4) 15	(9) 39	+50	+25	-12
Czech	—	—	—	(1) 7	(2) 9	(4) 17	(6) 25	—	—	+89
Other Slavic	(1) 5	(5) 98	(10) 167	(10) 219	(12) 218	(16) 243	(32) 272	+3240	+46	+11
Scandinavian	(11) 58	(11) 58	(11) 82	(11) 52	(7) 36	(5) 40	(11) 69	+24	-51	+11
Other Germanic	(3) 9	(2) 9	(3) 16	(2) 11	(3) 23	(2) 15	(4) 36	+78	-6	-35
Other Romance	—	—	—	—	(1) 2	(1) 4	(7) 31	—	—	+100
Near Eastern	—	—	—	—	(1) [a]	(1) 6	(7) 23	—	—	+600
Far Eastern	(3) 20	(4) 34	(5) 52	(5) 42	(5) 23	(8) 45	(9) 54	+160	-13	+96
All Others	(2) 12	(1) 1	(1) 7	(2) 3	(5) 9	(5) 26	(15) 51	-42	+271	+189
Total	(53) 352	(62) 422	(82) 591	(106) 793	(99) 829	(91) 889	(177) 1226	+68	+50	+7

[a] Number of publications for which circulation figures are available.
[b] Last three digits have been dropped in all circulation figures.

publications appearing entirely in English. From the point of view of safeguarding its own continuity, the mixed press may have been more successful as a transitional institution than it intended to be.

English Language Publications for Ethnic Group Members

Ayer's *Directory* reports 214 English language publications in 1960 intended for readers of specific ethnic backgrounds (Table 3.11). The number of such publications

TABLE 3.11

Number of English-Language Publications Directed Toward Various Ethnic Groups, 1910-1960

Ethnic Groups	1910	1920	1930	1940	1950	1960	1960 LRP	Percent Increase or Decrease		
								1910-1930	1930-1960	1950-1960
French	1	1	1	1	1	1	1	0%	0%	0%
Spanish	2	3	5	5	4	4	4	+150	−20	0
German	91	92	78	57	49	60	77	−14	−23	+22
Jewish	30	47	62	75	92	85	122	+107	+37	−8
Hungarian	—	—	—	—	1	1	1	—	—	0
Ukrainian	—	—	—	1	1	2	4	—	—	+100
Italian	—	—	2	5	6	5	5	—	+150	−17
Polish	—	2	2	2	2	4	8	—	+100	+100
Greek	—	—	2	2	3	5	7	—	+150	+67
Czech	—	1	—	—	—	—	—	—	—	—
Other Slavic	5	3	—	2	2	3	5	—	—	+50
Scandinavian	7	11	19	18	25	21	37	+171	+22	−16
Other Germanic	—	6	5	3	5	10	13	—	+100	+100
Other Romance	—	—	—	—	1	—	—	—	—	—
Near Eastern	—	—	1	2	3	5	6	—	+400	+67
Far Eastern	—	2	3	1	1	1	2	—	−67	0
All Others	—	1	1	2	6	7	12	—	+600	+17
Total	136	169	181	176	202	214	305	+33	+18	+6

has increased consistently since 1910, although the rate of increase has slowed down considerably in recent years. From 1910 to 1930, English-language publications increased by 33%; from 1930 to 1960, by 18%; from 1950 to 1960, by only 6%.

From the very first, only three groups have displayed any great affinity for an English-language press: Germans, Jews, and Scandinavians. These three groups accounted for 94% of all English-language ethnic publications in 1910, and in 1960 for slightly more than three-quarters. Although publications in English for Jews and Scandinavian-Americans decreased slightly during the decade 1950-1960, at a time when such publications for readers of most other ethnic backgrounds were increasing,

TABLE 3.12

Circulation of English-Language Publications Directed Toward Ethnic Groups, 1910-1960

Ethnic Groups	1910	1920	1930	1940	1950	1960	1960 LRP	Percent Increase or Decrease		
								1910-1930	1930-1960	1950-1960
French	(1)[a] [b]	(1) 1	— —	(1) [b]	(1) 1	— —	— —	—	—	—
Spanish	(1) [b]	(2) 2	(3) 3	(4) 4	(4) 5	(4) 7	(4) 7	—	+133%	+44%
German	(72) 701[c]	(68) 847	(42) 598	(43) 704	(41) 634	(52) 2274	(69) 2450	—	+280	+306
Jewish	(18) 205	(28) 372	(26) 264	(47) 794	(54) 1321	(62) 1826	(106) 2228	+29%	+592	+38
Hungarian	— —	— —	— —	— —	(1) 5	(1) 6	(1) 6	—	—	+20
Ukrainian	— —	— —	— —	— —	— —	(1) 2	(3) 3	—	—	—
Italian	— —	— —	(2) 16	(4) 27	(4) 41	(4) 47	(4) 47	—	+194	+15
Polish	— —	(2) 31	(2) 15	(2) 14	(2) 9	(3) 18	(7) 50	—	+20	+100
Greek	— —	— —	(2) 10	(2) 20	— —	(3) 24	(6) 112	—	+140	—
Czech	— —	(1) 5	— —	— —	— —	— —	(1) 3	—	—	—
Other Slavic	(3) 10	(1) 12	(16) 93	(1) 2	(1) 5	(3) 17	(5) 20	+830	−82	+240
Scandinavian	(7) 25	(10) 39	(3) 21	(11) 76	(23) 192	(20) 303	(35) 520	−16	+1343	+58
Other Germanic	— —	(4) 13	— —	(3) 46	(4) 124	(10) 216	(13) 250	—	—	+74
Other Romance	— —	— —	— —	— —	— —	— —	— —	—	—	—
Near Eastern	— —	— —	— —	(2) 28	(3) 16	(3) 11	(4) 14	—	—	−31
Far Eastern	— —	— —	— —	(1) 11	— —	(1) 6	(2) 9	—	—	—
All Others	— —	— —	— —	(1) 25	(4) 5	(7) 20	(12) 51	—	—	+300
Total	(102) 943	(117) 1325	(95) 1023	(176) 1723	(142) 2358	(174) 4784	(272) 5776	+8	+368	+103

[a] Number of publications for which circulation figures are available.
[b] Less then 1000.
[c] Last three digits have been dropped in all circulation figures.

the original "big three" of the English-language ethnic press still have unchallenged leadership.

The "big three" loom even larger in respect to circulation of such publications than they do in respect to number. In 1910 they accounted for 99% of the total circulation; in 1960, for 90%. Except for a single reversal from 1920 to 1930 (due primarily to temporary circulation losses in the ranks of the "big three"), the total circulation of English-language publications has increased regularly since 1910 (Table 3.12). The major growth in circulation occurred between 1930 and 1960 (368%), but even the last decade (1950-1960) witnessed an increase of over 100%. The average 1960 circulation of English publications in the "big three" was 24,752 (for publications directed toward German-Americans: 35,507; Jews: 21,018; Scandinavian-Americans: 14,857). The average circulation of all other English-ethnic publications was 9,322. Although the last figure is much smaller than the three that preceed it, it should be recognized that it is, nevertheless, larger than the average circulation for either non-English or mixed publications.

The English-language press provides a third way-station in the process of immigrant-ethnic accommodation to American life. Whereas recent immigrant groups under-standably arrive at the third way-station later than others, not all old immigrant groups have gravitated toward this way-station alike. The meager representation of Franco-American and Spanish-American English-language publications exemplifies this. It may well be that the English-language ethnic press is not merely a third way-station but also the last ethnic way-station, or even an escape-hatch from ethnicity itself, for many Americans of diverse immigrant-ethnic backgrounds. Thus for many ethnic groups, an English-language press is self-defeating. Its linguistically assimilated readers are also orientationally and behaviorally assimilated to the extent that they come to have little need for an ethnic press. Indeed for many ethnic groups, no stable English-language press has ever developed. Germans and Scandinavians, on the one hand, and Jews on the other, therefore represent special and atypical cases.

To understand the German and Scandinavian development of an extensive English-language press, one might well compare it with the absence of such a press among French- and Spanish-Americans. In all these groups, huge language islands existed and to some extent continue to this very day. A close relationship between language and religion has also obtained in all these cases. Therefore, neither concentration of population, emphasis on parochial schools, priority of settlement, nor other related factors can explain the presence of a large English-language press in some instances and its absence in others.

Certainly the de-ethnization of the American Catholic church when compared to the relatively greater continuing ethnicity of the German (Missouri) and Scandinavian Lutheran Synods is a difference of primary importance in this connection. English-language religious publications specifically for French or Spanish (or Polish, Italian) Catholics hardly exist. Rather, "all-Catholic" (non-ethnic) publications have risen in their stead (Deedy 1963). The originally German and Scandinavian Lutheran churches, on the other hand, are still largely composed of members of their original ethnic groups and their English-language publications still reach millions of readers. No other major Protestant denominations have been similarly protective of a non-English ethnic origin (Marty 1963).

Education may be another differentiating variable. Among foreign-born claimants of French and Spanish mother tongues aged 50-74, 17% and 16% respectively have received high school education or higher. Among foreign-born claimants of German and Scandinavian mother tongues in the same age range, the percentages are 33% and 34% respectively. This relative educational advantage results in a greater propensity to read and support the press in the parental as well as in the younger generations, who also possess relative educational advantages. Thus, an extensive English-language press may be said to develop among groups that possess educational advantages in addition to such reinforcements of ethnicity as early and concentrated settlement, religious homogeneity, religiously protected ethnicity, and religiously based educational separatism.

While the huge Anglo-Jewish press may also be largely explained in these terms (Silverman 1963), Jews have the additional advantage of being able to fluctuate between the ethnic and the religious aspects of their group identity. It is obviously simpler to retain a meaningful Jewish identity in the United States without Yiddish and other Jewish-ethnic customs (Soltes 1923), than to retain a Franco-American identity without French and Franco-American customs. The Catholic religion does not continue to reinforce Franco-American identification for Anglified Franco-Americans, whereas the Jewish religion does reinforce Jewish-ethnic identification for many Anglified American Jews. To a large extent the German and Scandinavian Lutheran Synods perform a similar function. In the latter two populations, an additional self-maintaining factor is the greater concentration in small urban units in a relatively traditional region of the United States.

PROPORTIONS OF MOTHER TONGUE, MIXED, AND ENGLISH-LANGUAGE PUBLICATIONS

The total number of publications directed toward members of (religio-) ethnic groups decreased by 35% between 1930 and 1960 (Table 3.13), while the combined circulation of these publications remained virtually constant (Table 3.14). Yet underneath this overall constancy in circulation, and above and beyond the change in number of publications, it is clear that the non-English, mixed, and English components of the ethnic press fared very differently during this 30-year period. We have already noted that non-English and mixed publications decreased in number whereas English-language publications increased. As a result, non-English publications constituted only 54% of the total number of publications in 1960 instead of the 69% of 1930. At the same time, English-language publications increased from 17% to 31%. Hardly any change occurred in the overall proportion of mixed publications during this period.

TABLE 3.13

Proportions of Types of Publication, 1930 and 1960
Number

Ethnic Groups	1930 Mother Tongue		1930 Mixed		1930 English		1930 Total	1960 Mother Tongue		1960 Mixed		1960 English		1960 Total
	n	%	n	%	n	%	n	n	%	n	%	n	%	n
French	28	80	6	17	1	3	35	13	76	3	18	1	6	17
Spanish	61	81	9	12	5	7	75	31	65	13	27	4	8	48
German	146	59	22	9	78	32	246	41	37	9	8	60	55	110
Jewish	20	21	13	14	62	65	95	15	14	4	4	85	82	104
Hungarian	35	90	4	10	0	0	39	32	94	1	3	1	3	34
Ukrainian	6	86	1	14	0	0	7	14	74	3	16	2	10	19
Italian	85	68	38	30	2	2	125	21	16	20	43	5	11	46
Polish	84	95	2	2	2	2	88	37	86	2	5	4	9	43
Greek	15	71	4	19	2	10	21	9	47	5	26	5	26	19
Czech	44	98	1	2	0	0	45	19	83	4	17	0	0	23
Other Slavic	53	79	14	21	0	0	67	46	68	19	28	3	4	68
Scandinavian	62	63	17	17	19	19	98	20	43	5	11	21	46	46
Other Germanic	13	56	5	22	5	22	23	1	8	2	15	10	77	13
Other Romance	15	94	1	6	0	0	16	7	88	1	12	0	0	8
Near Eastern	8	89	0	0	1	11	9	10	63	1	6	5	31	16
Far Eastern	18	67	6	22	3	11	27	12	57	8	38	1	5	21
All Others	44	86	6	12	1	2	51	49	78	7	11	7	11	63
Total	737	69	149	14	181	17	1067	377	54	107	15	214	31	698

The proportional decline in the number of non-English publications affected all ethnic (-religious) groups but one, the Hungarian. The proportional increase in the number of English-language publications affected all groups but three – Czech and "Other Romance", which continued to have no publications in English, and Far Eastern, where a decline in the number and proportion of such publications occurred. In those few groups in which the proportion of mixed publications declined, non-English publications also declined (Jewish, Scandinavian, "Other Germanic"), while the proportion of English-language publications generally increased sharply. It thus seems that the English-language press grew proportionally at the expense of both the non-English and the mixed press, whereas the mixed press grew proportionally only at the expense of the non-English press, not only overall but in the case of almost every group.

In 1930, non-English publications constituted a majority in all groups except the Jewish, which had a decided majority of English-language publications even then. By 1960, English-language publications had come into the majority among Americans of German and "Other Germanic" backgrounds (Dutch, Pennsylvania German). Among Scandinavians, English-language publications constituted a plurality. Non-English publications still constituted pluralities among Italians and Greeks, but had

JOSHUA A. FISHMAN, ROBERT G. HAYDEN, MARY E. WARSHAUER

TABLE 3.14
Proportions of Types of Publications, 1930 and 1960
Circulation

Ethnic Groups	1930 Mother Tongue		1930 Mixed		1930 English		1930 Total	1960 Mother Tongue		1960 Mixed		1960 English		1960 Total
	n	%	n	%	n	%	n	n	%	n	%	n	%	n
French	151[a]	94	10	6	—	—	161	118[a]	96	5	4	—	—	123
Spanish	298	98	3	1	3	1	304	268	81	54	16	7	2	329
German	1354	67	65	3	598	30	2017	281	10	146	5	2274	84	2701
Jewish	775	72	34	3	264	25	1073	179	9	63	3	1826	88	2068
Hungarian	238	96	9	4	0	0	247	198	95	4	2	6	3	208
Ukrainian	51	100	—	—	0	0	51	47	62	27	36	2	2	76
Italian	613	83	114	15	16	2	743	270	56	164	34	47	10	481
Polish	999	96	23	2	15	1	1037	690	96	9	1	18	2	717
Greek	74	77	12	12	10	10	96	65	62	15	14	24	23	104
Czech	513	100	—	—	0	—	513	274	94	17	6	0	0	291
Other Slavic	730	74	167	17	93	9	990	216	45	243	51	17	4	476
Scandinavian	580	85	82	12	21	3	683	120	26	40	9	303	65	463
Other Germanic	22	58	16	42	—	—	38	4	2	15	6	216	92	235
Other Romance	130	100	—	—	0	0	130	25	86	4	4	0	0	29
Near Eastern	38	100	0	0	—	—	38	37	69	6	11	11	20	54
Far Eastern	346	87	52	13	—	—	398	67	57	45	38	6	5	118
All Others	296	98	7	2	—	—	303	253	85	26	9	20	7	299
Total	7216	82	591	7	1023	12	8830	3118	35	889	10	4784	54	8791

[a] Last three digits have been dropped in all circulation figures.

lost their majority position as the result of increases in mixed and English-language publications. In only seven groups did the non-English press in 1960 constitute at least three-quarters of all publications: French, Hungarian, Ukrainian, Polish, Czech, "Other Romance", and "All Others".

Mixed publications have never been the most numerous in any group. In 1960 they constituted 43% of all publications for Italo-Americans, 38% for Far Eastern readers, and 26% for "Other Slavic" readers. They were much less important in all other groups – particularly the German, Jewish, Hungarian, Polish, and Near Eastern – and accounted for only 15% of the general total.

In 1960, the English-language press was of considerable importance among the "big three" and "Other Germanic", Near Eastern, and Greek ethnics, but of very little importance to most other groups. Although still growing in 1960, in almost all groups, it will not likely achieve major importance in many of them since separate ethnic identity on English linguistic foundations is difficult to imagine for large numbers of individuals of most ethnic backgrounds. Even the English-language press for people of German and Scandinavian, (as well as "Other Germanic", Greek, and Near Eastern) backgrounds may begin to shrink in the not too distant future as church mergers with their non-ethnic American counterparts continue and accelerate.

Although the circulation of the total ethnic press remained virtually unchanged from 1930 to 1960, the linguistic distribution within this total changed dramatically. Non-English publications accounted for 82% of the total circulation in 1930; in 1960, for only 35%. The mixed and English-language press represented 7% and 12% of the total circulation in 1930; by 1960 they had increased to 10% and 54%. Whereas the non-English press accounted for a greater proportion of the circulation than of the number of publications in 1930 (82% vs. 69%), this situation was reversed in 1960 (35% vs. 54%). All in all, circulation data fully corroborate a directional sequence from non-English to mixed to English-only publications.

ATTITUDES, PURPOSES, AND PLANS OF THE ETHNIC PRESS

Among the publications currently constituting the American ethnic press, non-English publications more often claim primarily ethnic purposes and proportionately fewer commercial or other purposes than do the mixed and, particularly, the English-language publications. Nevertheless, fully 46% of responding English-language publications claimed primarily ethnic purposes. Although this percentage may be somewhat inflated (as a result of elimination of non-respondents and of probable response bias), it is nevertheless appropriate to conclude that a goodly proportion of English-language publications consider themselves to be serving primarily ethnic purposes.

Language maintenance should obviously be of concern to non-English publications. However, many mixed and English-language publications also claim language maintenance interests, even if they rationalize them somewhat differently than do non-English publications. These interests may be expressed via specific *content* (articles encouraging language maintenance, language instruction, etc.) or via *activities* organized or supported by the publication (contests, schools, courses, camps, publication and sale of books, etc.). The typical English-language publication engages in no language maintenance effort, through either content or activities. The typical non-English publication engages in specific language maintenance efforts through its content but not through activities. At least a quarter of them are involved in no language maintenance efforts of any kind. Some are oriented toward recent arrivals, many of whom are more interested in learning English than in language maintenance. Some aim at readers who have no *ideological* interest in language maintenance and who remain loyal to a mother tongue publication on purely traditional and habitual grounds. Mixed publications appear most frequently involved in language maintenance efforts of one kind or other, probably because they purportedly serve generationally mixed audiences and seek to provide an intergenerational transition for ethnicity, and perhaps also because of the instability of mixed publications. Their efforts can be viewed, in part, as a kind of self-serving attempt to hold the line.

In view of the more frequent ethnic orientation of non-English publications – and in view of the declining numbers and circulation of these publications as ethnicity itself becomes ever more diluted in American life – how do non-English publications compare with the others in terms of perceived success? Surprisingly enough, it is they who most frequently claim "complete success" and least frequently claim "some" or "little or no" success. In contrast, English-language publications, while riding the creast of increasing numbers and circulation, claim "complete" success least frequently and "some" or "little or no" success most frequently. Such a response pattern may be due to differing levels of aspiration. Merely to continue publication may seem to be "complete" success for many non-English publications. Not to be able to expand more rapidly may seem to be merely "some" success for many English-language publications.

Responding non-English publications view their future more darkly than their present, whereas responding mixed publications view their future more brightly. The average non-English publication expects to have a smaller circulation by 1970 than does the average mixed, while the average English-language publication expects to continue to have a larger circulation than either of the others. These expectations are consistent with current trends. Their predictive accuracy will depend on the ability of mixed and English-language publications to attract and hold those readers who leave the non-English publications, and/or their Americanized (not necessarily American born) and linguistically Anglified children. Without such attracting and holding power on their part – at least on a temporary basis – it remains possible for the non-English press, which deals with a more conservative public, to once more emerge as the strongest branch of the American ethnic press, as it was in 1930 and earlier. In an environment marked by great and increasing de-ethnization, conservative groups are much more likely to preserve their identity than are those which embark on paths of novelty or compromise.

Although relatively few ethnic publications admit to commercial goals as their "primary purpose", they are inevitably influenced by commercial considerations in gauging their own success. It is frequently claimed that the ethnic press (particularly the non-English press) is more altruistic than the general American press, that it is more genuinely concerned with the welfare of its readers, that it maintains a more intimate tie with them, and that it is a reflection of gemeinschaft ties (Soltes 1923; Wittke 1957). This may well be. Nevertheless, no publications can indefinitely substitute sentiment for substance. The ethnic press, therefore, must measure its success by the practical criteria of co-territorial American society.

As already noted, non-English publications more frequently claim success. They also more frequently devote 40% or more of their space to material dealing with their ethnic mother country. These two findings might lead us to expect that self-perceived success and the amount of space devoted to material on the mother country would be appreciably related. This is not so. Those non-English publications perceived as being a complete success are frequently among those devoting *least* space to materials on the mother country, while those perceived as having little or no success are likely to be devoting the most. It may well be that publications in all three language categories will come to view the minimization of materials concerning the mother country as one means of achieving greater success. Instead, ethnic publications may stress materials pertaining to group maintenance in the United States. Or, they may come to stress general, non-ethnic material even though such material is presented in the non-English mother tongue. To the extent that the latter path is followed (a path which the general news and feature services render simple and inexpensive), the ethnic press may be inadvertently preparing its readers for a more rapid transition to the general press.

All in all, we find considerable ambivalence in the ethnic press – particularly among its non-English constituents. Many of the latter neither claim ethnic goals nor engage in language maintenance efforts. Though eager, perhaps over-eager, to claim success they also expect less growth in circulation in the next ten years than either their mixed or their English-language competitors. The non-English press is at a peculiar disadvantage. It can seek greater success in the normal, practical sense only by becoming less ethnic. However, by becoming less ethnic it abandons its special mission and its special audience and hastens its own demise. For there may be even less loyalty toward a *non-ethnic* "ethnic" press than to its somewhat anachronistic but less compromising predecessors.

The ethnic press reflects all the characteristics and difficulties of ethnicity in the United States in the latter half of the 20th century (Fishman, Hayden and Warschauer 1964). Just as ethnicity is straining toward a redefinition along religious lines – perhaps toward a religiously sanctified demise – so the ethnic press is straining in the direction of de-ethnization along increasingly religious lines. The press has sought to follow the immigrant, his children and grandchildren from their original non-English and primarily traditional ethnicity through successive stages of increasing biculturism, decreasing language maintenance and ethnicity, to the final stage of completely Anglified ethnicity. Indeed, while "de-ethnicized ethnicity" may be a contradiction in terms it is nonetheless a reality of current American life.

Although de-ethnicized ethnicity may have the greatest appeal for the greatest numbers, it hardly provides a stable or creative basis for group existence. It differs so little from non-ethnicity that this is its inevitable consequence. As such, it cannot support either the traditions or the organized media of group life – among these, a separate press. Thus, while mixed and English-ethnic publications continue to grow in circulation they are not as successful as are non-English publications in retaining their "differentness" or their *raisons d'être*. Their readers may find it painless indeed to transfer from them to entirely non-ethnic publications in the future. It remains to be seen whether the English-ethnic press and the increasingly Anglified mixed press can learn the secret that ethnicity itself has learned in the United States: to exist and yet not to exist, to be needed and yet to be unimportant, to be different and yet to be the same, to be integrated and yet to be separate.

REFERENCES

Chyz, Y. J., *225 Years of the U.S. Foreign Language Press* (New York, American Council for Nationalities Service, 1959).

Deedy, J. G., Jr., "The Catholic Press: The Why and the Wherefore", in Marty, M. E., et al., *The Religious Press in America* (New York, Holt, Rinehart and Winston, 1963), pp. 65-121.

Fishman, J. A., et al., "The non-English and ethnic group press in the United States, 1910-1960", in *Language Loyalty in the United States* (New York, Yeshiva Univ., 1964), Chapter 3. (Mimeo.)

Liebling, A. J., *The Press* (New York, Ballantine Books, 1961).

Marty, M. E., "The Prostestant Press: Limitations and Possibilities", in Marty, M. E., et al., *The Religious Press in America* (New York, Holt, Rinehart and Winston, 1963), pp. 3-63.

N. W. Ayer and Sons's (Annual) Directory, Newspapers and Periodicals. (Formerly: *American Newspaper Annual and Directory*) (Philadelphia, N. W. Ayer and Son, Inc.), 1910, 1920, 1930, 1940, 1950, 1960.

Silverman, D. W., "The Jewish Press: a Quadrilingual Phenomenon", in Marty, M. E., et al., *The Religious Press in America* (New York, Holt, Rinehart and Winston, 1963), pp. 123-171.

Soltes, M., *The Yiddish Press: an Americanizing Agency* (New York, Teachers College, Columbia University, 1923).

Zubrzycki, J., "The role of the foreign language press in immigrant integration", *Population Studies*, 12 (1958), 73-82.

4. FOREIGN LANGUAGE BROADCASTING

MARY ELLEN WARSHAUER

There are a number of quantitative and qualitative aspects of foreign language broadcasting (FLB) in the United States. The present chapter attempts to answer such questions as the following: To what extent has FLB increased or decreased in recent years? Are there any differences among ethnic mother tongue groups with respect to increases or decreases noted? Do the various language groups differ in the type, length, and perceived success of their programs? Do they view these programs as positive avenues of language and culture maintenance? Do the programs find themselves confronted with problems due to their use of a non-English language, and, if so, do the problems vary from one language group to another? Do the various ethnic groups expect increases or decreases in their broadcast time in the near future and are their goals in this connection compatible with past and existing trends?

Radio broadcasting, in general, has long been viewed as a convenient and successful medium of communication for all the diverse segments composing American society. As of 1958, it was observed that "Radio is now in virtually every home in America, in two-thirds of the 54,000,000 passenger cars on the road, and in 10,000,000 public places" (Bogart 1960). The relatively low purchase cost and operating expense of a radio set have rendered this medium available to the lowest income groups, recent immigrants very often being among these.

Given the widespread availability of radio, it is not surprising that foreign language broadcasting has been developed and supported by various ethnic-linguistic groups. Carl Wittke's remarks about the foreign language press are equally applicable to radio. He points out that the foreign language press performs two functions: "... it is concerned with preserving the cultural ties of the immigrant with the land of his origin, promoting the activities of the group in its new home, and keeping the mother tongue alive as long as possible.... [Secondly, it serves] to initiate the immigrant into his new environment and to interpret for him, in words which he can understand, the political, economic and social pattern of America" (Wittke 1957). However, besides serving as a link to the "Old Country" and reducing the isolation and disorientation of minorities in a new environment, FLB is also an important avenue of entertainment, cultural exposure, and relaxation for linguistic minorities. It is capable, moreover, of reaching those members of linguistic minorities who are illiterate in their mother tongue and for whom the foreign language press is not accessible.

With the decline of mass immigration to the United States, the function of FLB has begun to change. As older immigrant groups have become more Americanized, and as the second and third generations have become less familiar with their parents' and grandparents' language and culture – and, in many cases, have rejected both completely – foreign language broadcasting has experienced increasing difficulties. These have been augmented by the advent of television. The last decade has witnessed a sharp increase in television viewing and a corresponding decrease in redio listening (Table 4.1). Since radio listening, as a whole, has declined, it is not unreasonable to assume that foreign language radio listening, which is only a small proportion of the former, has also decreased.

TABLE 4.1

Radio and Television Use per Day Compared, for an Average Home[a]

Year	Radio	Television
1950	4 hrs. 19 mins.	0 hrs. 35 mins.
1955	2:27	3:39
1959	1:54	5:29

[a] From Wilbur Schramm, ed., *Mass Communications* (Urbana, University of Illinois Press, 1960), p. 458.

In 1956 the American Council for Nationalities Service (ACNS) reported 1,005 foreign language radio "stations"[1] in the continental United States broadcasting a total of 5,442.08 hours per week for an average of 5.42 hours/week per station.[2] In 1960 a total of 6,214.70 hours were broadcast over 1,340 "stations" for an average of 4.64 hours per week (Table 4.2). Thus, in terms of average hours of broadcasting per week, FLB experienced a decrease of 14.4% from 1956 to 1960 even though the total number of "stations"increased by 33% and the total hours of FLB by 14%. When 1960 Language Resources Project information is juxtaposed with 1956 ACNS data, a decrease in hours/week per station, although not as great, still obtains. According to LRP information for 1960, a total of 6,804.70 hours were broadcast over 1,291 "stations" for an average of 5.27 hours per week (Table 4.3). This represents a decrease of 2.8% in average hours/week per "station", but an increase of 28% in the total number of stations and an increase of 25% in the total hours of FLB. A closer

---

[1] Throughout this report "*station*" is used to designate "language per station", i.e., if a station broadcasts in three languages, it is counted as three "stations". When station is used in the conventional sense, the quotation marks will *not* appear. "Station" is used instead of "program" since if a station has three different programs in the same language, it is counted as one unit, the hours being summed.

[2] Actually, more foreign language "stations" were reported than this figure indicates, but since no data on hours of broadcasting were given for some "stations" they could not be used in our computations. All our tables will present both the *total number of* "*stations*" and the *number of* "*stations*" *for which information is available*. The latter alone will be discussed in this report.

TABLE 4.2

Hours and "Stations" of Foreign Language Broadcasting per week (according to ACNS) for 1956 and 1960, by Language

Languages and Language Groupings	ACNS 1956				ACNS 1960				% I or D in Aver. Hours
	Total Hours	"Stations"			Total Hours	"Stations"			
		Total	with Info.	Average Hours		Total	with Info.	Average Hours	
Romance	4231.51	599	485	8.72	4774.70	730	642	7.44	− 14.7%
French	160.75	73	56	2.87	225.50	83	76	2.97	+ 3.5%
Italian	522.84	194	148	3.53	608.95	229	194	3.14	− 11.0%
Spanish	3419.42	284	246	13.90	3802.50	363	324	11.74	− 15.5%
Portuguese	126.50	43	31	4.08	132.25	48	43	3.08	− 24.5%
Rumanian	2.00	5	4	.50	5.50	7	5	1.10	+120.0%
Slavic	671.83	359	248	2.71	705.00	392	307	2.30	− 15.1%
Polish	526.58	188	151	3.49	509.00	203	174	2.93	− 16.0%
Ukrainian	41.25	39	27	1.53	28.75	32	21	1.37	− 10.5%
Russian	8.25	12	5	1.65	41.75	28	23	1.82	+ 10.3%
Other[a]	95.75	120	65	1.47	125.50	129	89	1.41	− 4.2%
Scandinavian[b]	35.00	55	31	1.13	43.00	66	42	1.02	− 9.7%
Greek	64.00	65	44	1.45	90.50	86	71	1.27	− 12.4%
Germanic	161.25	84	64	2.52	292.50	138	117	2.50	− .8%
German	152.25	78	60	2.54	275.75	129	108	2.55	+ .4%
Other[c]	9.00	6	4	2.25	16.75	9	9	1.86	− 17.3%
Near East[d]	6.50	13	10	.65	8.00	17	12	.67	+ 3.1%
Far East[e]	6.75	11	6	1.13	33.75	17	15	2.25	+ 99.1%
Yiddish	167.25	46	28	5.97	142.75	42	29	4.92	− 17.6%
Finnish, Hung., Turkish	59.00	71	52	1.13	60.50	72	57	1.06	− 6.2%
Hungarian	43.50	48	36	1.21	38.25	43	37	1.03	− 14.9%
Other	15.50	23	16	.97	22.25	29	20	1.11	+ 14.4%
Miscellaneous[f]	39.00	51	37	1.05	64.00	62	48	1.33	+ 26.7%
Total	5442.08	1354	1005	5.42	6214.70	1622	1340	4.64	− 14.4%

[a] Includes Croatian, Serbian, Slovene, Czech and Slovak.
[b] Includes Norwegian, Swedish, Danish and "combined" Scandinavian.
[c] Includes Dutch, Swiss-German, Pennsylvania German (Pennsylvania Dutch).
[d] Includes Lebanese, Syrian and Egyptian Arabic.
[e] Includes Chinese, Japanese and Hindustani.
[f] Includes Lithuanian, Estonian, Latvian, Armenian, Albanian, Maltese, Basque and Filipino languages.
(These language groupings apply to all tables that follow.)

examination of the 1956 and 1960 ACNS data shows that the overall decline of FLB in terms of average hours/week per station was not uniform for all mother tongue groups. Of the broader language groupings, average broadcast time per week increased for those stations presenting programs in the Near Eastern languages (+3.1%), the Far

TABLE 4.3

Hours and "Stations" of Foreign Language Broadcasting per week
(according to LRP data) for 1960 by Language

Languages and Language Groupings	"Stations"				% I or D in Average Hours to ACNS 1956
	Total Hours	Total	with Info.	Average Hours	
Romance	5447.44	659	607	8.97	+ 2.9%
French	248.00	77	73	3.40	+ 18.5%
Italian	582.42	196	181	3.22	− 8.8%
Spanish	4498.82	338	308	14.61	+ 5.1%
Portuguese	111.70	42	39	2.86	− 29.9%
Rumanian	6.50	6	6	1.08	+116.0%
Slavic	629.41	331	299	2.11	− 22.1%
Polish	437.66	177	163	2.69	− 22.9%
Ukrainian	33.00	28	22	1.50	− 2.0%
Russian	24.00	21	20	1.20	− 27.3%
Other	134.75	105	94	1.43	− 2.7%
Scandinavian	48.60	62	43	1.13	0%
Greek	120.25	73	66	1.82	+ 25.5%
Germanic	229.25	115	105	2.18	− 13.5%
German	215.00	104	97	2.22	− 12.60%
Other	14.25	11	8	1.78	− 20.9%
Near East	12.75	22	17	.75	+ 15.4%
Far East	54.75	18	17	3.22	+185.0%
Yiddish	129.25	34	32	4.04	− 32.3%
Finish, Hung., Turkish	56.50	64	49	1.15	+ 1.8%
Hungarian	40.25	41	34	1.18	− 2.5%
Other	16.25	23	15	1.08	+ 11.3%
Miscellaneous	76.50	61	56	1.37	+ 30.5%
Total	6804.70	1439	1291	5.27	− 2.8%

Eastern languages (+99.1%), and in the miscellaneous grouping (+26.7%). All remaining language groups showed decreases ranging from a high of 17.6% for Yiddish to a low of .8% for Germanic languages. Individual languages showing an increase in average per week broadcast time were: French (3.5%), German (.4%), Russian (10.3%), Rumanian (120.0%), and Finnish and Turkish combined (14.4%).

While an increase was noted in French language broadcasting, the number of French mother tongue claimants decreased from 1940-1960.[3] Moreover, the increase in French broadcasting is mainly in the west (58.0%) and the south (19.9%) (Table 4.4), rather than in the New England area adjacent to French-Canada. The increase in the west seems due, in large part, to the small number of "stations" and hours existing as a 1956 base. However, the increase in the south may be explained by a recent expansion

---

[3]　Chapter 2, p. 36.

TABLE 4.4

Percent Increase or Decrease of Average Hours per week of
FLB From 1956-1060 by Area[a]

	Increase or Decrease Area					
	MA	NE	ENC	WNC	West	South
Romance	− 44.0	− 33.1	+ 10.5	+ 20.6	− 4.4	− 10.4
French	− 4.0	− 5.7	− 33.0	—	+ 58.0	+ 19.9
Italian	− 17.6	− 42.6	+ 54.5	+ 33.3	+ 22.3	− 36.1
Spanish	− 60.3	− 41.3	− 16.9	+ 16.7	− 4.8	− 10.1
Portuguese	—	− 5.47	—	—	− 8.2	—
Rumanian	—	—	+120.0	—	—	—
Slavic	− 38.5	− 27.7	+ 29.6	+ 83.1	+ 32.2	− 15.6
Polish	− 39.3	− 25.6	+ 33.3	+130.1	+166.0	+ 17.2
Ukrainian	− 20.9	—	+ 12.2	0	—	—
Russian	− 4.7	+100.0	− 33.3	—	0	—
Other	− 57.1	—	+ 30.3	+ 68.3	0	− 28.0
Scandinavian	− 2.8	− 37.3	− 20.9	− 1.0	− 16.7	0
Greek	− 15.2	− 14.2	+ 16.9	—	+ 44.0	− 14.1
Germanic	+ 7.1	+ 26.0	− 8.2	− 12.0	+ 92.1	− 31.1
German	+ 5.8	+ 26.0	− 4.7	− 12.0	+ 65.1	− 24.7
Other	− 44.0	—	− 23.2	—	+100.0	+100.0
Near East	b	+ 1.6	+ 34.0	—	—	+ 50.0
Far East	b	—	—	—	+ 75.2	—
Yiddish	11.7	− 71.1	− 11.1	—	− 43.8	− 38.7
Finnish, Hung.,						
Turkish	− 10.3	− 32.9	+ 9.2	− 21.9	0	− 12.0
Hungarian	− 19.3	− 50.0	− 4.2	+100.0	0	− 33.3
Other	−100.0	− 19.2	+ 45.0	− 24.8	0	+ 66.0
Miscellaneous	− 22.9	+ 6.9	+ 67.3	+ 31.6	− 7.3	+100.0
Total	− 31.0	− 33.5	+ 21.2	+ 7.4	− 9.5	− 16.7

[a] Based on ACNS data for 1956 and 1960, Average Hours by Area.
[b] Percentage of I or D cannot be determined owing to the presence of "stations' with no information for one of the years.

of French programs in Louisiana, which has a large French-speaking population. The small increase in "stations" in this area and the large increase in hours per week supports this conclusion. Additional confirmation is provided by J. L. Tisch, who writes (Tisch 1959):

At their recent annual conventions, the Southern Baptists have voted hundreds of thousands of dollars to work for the conversion of the French-Catholics of Louisiana, which they call 'the greatest missionary field' for the Baptist Church. They have at least one French radio program every day. These programs are geared to affect the mentality of our French people who prefer something in their own language as long as 'il parle du Bon Dieu'. The aggressive Baptist radio campaign in French has awakened large numbers of Catholics to the need

TABLE 4.5

*Proportion of Total FLB Accounted for by Major Languages or
Language Groupings in 1956 and in 1060*

Language	ACNS 1956	ACNS 1960	LRP 1960
Romance	77.8%	76.8%	80.0%
French	(3.0)	(3.6)	(3.6)
Italian	(9.6)	(9.8)	(8.6)
Spanish	(62.8)	(61.2)	(66.1)
Slavic	12.3	11.3	9.2
Polish	(9.7)	(8.2)	(6.4)
Scandinavian	.6	.7	.7
Greek	1.2	1.4	1.8
Germanic	3.0	4.7	3.4
German	(2.8)	(4.4)	(3.2)
Near Eastern	.1	.1	.2
Far Eastern	.1	.5	.8
Yiddish	3.1	2.3	1.9
Finn., Hung., Turk.	1.1	1.0	.8
Miscellaneous	.7	1.0	1.1
Total	100%	100%	100%

for French language radio broadcasts. There are now four separate Catholic programs in French in the Diocese of Lafayette and one in the Diocese of Alexandria.

The only marked discrepancies between ACNS and LRP data for 1960 are in respect to German, Russian, Spanish, and Greek broadcasting. In the later two instances ACNS data show a decrease of 15.5% and 12.4% respectively, while LRP information shows increases of 5.1% and 25.5%. The positive LRP trend can be justified by supplementary information. Both Spanish and Greek mother tongue claimants have increased from 1940-1960[4] and, hence, an increase in FLB seems plausible. Moreover, the constant flow of Puerto Rican, Mexican, Cuban, and other Latin American immigrants into the United States would lead one to expect an increase in Spanish FLB in the west and south – the only two areas in LRP data that actually do show an increase. Thus the LRP data concerning Spanish and Greek FLB are given some support, though the trends must be accepted with caution.

In relative and descriptive terms, the period 1956 to 1960 is marked by considerable consistency even though a number of minor but interesting changes occurred. The lion's share of FLB continued to be in the Romance languages – 76.8% or 80.0% of the 1960 total hours (depending on the source of 1960 data) – with Spanish alone accounting for nearly two-thirds of all FLB hours (Table 4.5). The Slavic languages (Polish foremost among them) continued to hold undisputed claim to second place in total hours, although their 11.3% or 9.2% is puny in comparison with Spanish alone. Spanish, Italian, Polish, German, and French constituted "the big five" in

[4]   Ch. 2, p. 36.

FLB in 1960, their claims to this distinction remaining essentially the same as in 1956.[5]

Neither the prominence nor the rank order of "the big five" is readily explainable on the basis of non-English mother tongue data alone, regardless of the number of generations referred to (Table 4.6). Spanish broadcasting accounts for a far greater

TABLE 4.6

1960 Mother Tongue Claimants, 1960 Press Circulation, and
1960 Total Hours of Broadcasting for the "Big Five"
Languages in FLB

Language	1st Gen. Claimants[a]	1st, 2nd, 3rd Gen. Claim.[a]	Press Circulation[b]	Total Hours/wk. of FLB (LRP)
Spanish	766,961 (10.7%)	3,335,961 (18.3%)	268,000 (8.6%)	4498.82 (66.1%)
Italian	1,226,141 (17.1%)	2,979,141 (16.4%)	270,000 (8.7%)	582.42 (8.6%)
Polish	581,936 (8.1%)	2,184,936 (12.0%)	690,000 (22.1%)	437.66 (6.4%)
German	1,278,772 (17.8%)	3,145,772 (17.3%)	281,000 (9.0%)	215.00 (3.2%)
French	320,220 (4.6%)	1,043,220 (5.7%)	118,000 (3.8%)	248.00 (3.6%)
	(58.3%)	(69.7%)	(52.2%)	(87.9%)
Total	7,176,280	18,157,280	3,118,000	

[a] Ch. 2, Table 2.3.
[b] Ch. 3, Table 3.14.

proportion of all FLB hours than we would expect from the proportion of Spanish speakers among all claimants of non-English mother tongues in the United States. On the other hand, Italian, Polish, and German broadcasting account for much smaller proportions than we would expect on this same basis. The contrast between foreign language press data and FLB data may be instructive here. Broadcasting seems to be much more popular than the mother tongue press among speakers of Spanish. The opposite seems to be true among speakers of Polish, and German. It may be that the mother tongue *press* is relatively more popular among those groups whose speakers have experienced great upward educational and economic mobility while mother tongue *broadcasting* may remain more popular among those whose mobility has been low.

All in all, most foreign languages have experienced decreases in average per week broadcast time from 1956 to 1960. Those languages which record increases are, for the most part, mother tongues of relatively small ethnic groups for which FLB data are least reliable. The only substantially reliable increases in average hours of broadcasting per week are those reported for Far Eastern languages, and French, Spanish, and Greek.

If we remove the Spanish speaking from consideration, FLB is distributed regionally in proportions similar to those obtaining for the foreign stock. Here we see most

[5] Yiddish, rather than German, may have been one of the "big five" in 1956, but both sources of 1960 data indicate that it has decreased sharply in total hours of broadcasting.

TABLE 4.7

Percent Distribution of FLB[a] in 1960 Within Regions

Language	MA	NE	ENC	WNC	West	South
Romance	61.7	67.3	34.9	19.0	94.8	96.4
French	.7	25.2	.2	.7	.2	6.4
Italian	18.7	33.8	11.4	2.3	5.0	.9
Spanish	42.3	1.3	22.9	16.0	86.0	89.1
Portuguese	—	7.1	—	—	3.4	—
Rumanian	—	—	.5	—	.1	—
Slavic	17.9	16.1	35.8	30.3	.4	1.6
Polish	13.7	15.8	24.5	15.7	b	.2
Ukranian	1.7	—	1.7	—	b	—
Russian	1.8	.2	.3	—	b	—
Other	.8	—	9.3	14.7	.3	1.4
Scandinavian	.8	.5	1.9	24.0	.2	—
Greek	2.9	6.4	4.1	—	.8	.5
Germanic	5.3	1.4	13.7	19.0	.8	.9
German	5.2	1.4	12.3	19.0	.8	.9
Other	.1	—	1.4	—	b	b
Near East	.1	2.0	.3	—	—	b
Far East	.4	—	—	—	2.1	—
Yiddish	9.4	1.8	1.0	—	.3	.3
Finnish, Hung.,						
Turkish	.7	.9	4.0	7.0	.1	.2
Hungarian	.7	.5	3.0	1.3	.1	.1
Other	—	.4	1.0	5.7	—	.1
Miscellaneous	.8	3.6	4.3	.7	.6	.1
Total	100.0%	100.0%	100.0%	100.0%	100.0%	100.0%
N	1096.01	419.92	836.92	75.00	2380.51	1996.34

[a] Based on 1960 LRP Total Hours.
[b] Less than .1%.

clearly the dependence of FLB upon immigrants. Most FLB occurs in the Middle Atlantic region – where the foreign stock population is largest – and the least occurs in the West-North-Central region – where the foreign stock population is smallest. Indeed, not only is the magnitude of immigration crucial for FLB, but its recency is even more crucial. Thus, only in the East-North-Central region, where Slavic, Germanic, Baltic, and other post-World War II immigrants have settled in large numbers, has FLB increased appreciably in recent years.

The East- and West-North Central regions[6] are the only ones in which Romance languages did not predominate in FLB in 1960 (Table 4.7). Whereas broadcast time in Romance languages accounted for 96.4% of all FLB in the South, 94.8% in the

[6] All regions are defined in accordance with U.S. census usage.

TABLE 4.8

Percent Distribution of FLB[a] in 1960 Across Regions

Language	MA	NE	ENC	WNC	West	South	Total	N
Romance	12.5	5.2	5.4	.3	41.4	35.3	100%	5447.44
French	3.1	42.6	.6	.2	1.9	51.5	100%	248.00
Italian	35.2	24.3	16.4	.3	20.6	3.2	100%	582.42
Spanish	10.3	.1	4.3	.3	45.5	39.5	100%	4498.82
Portuguese	—	26.6	—	—	73.4	—	100%	111.70
Rumanian	—	—	61.5	—	38.5	—	100%	6.50
Slavic	31.2	10.7	47.7	3.6	1.7	5.1	100%	129.41
Polish	34.2	15.2	46.8	2.7	.2	.9	100%	437.66
Ukrainian	56.1	—	42.4	—	1.5	—	100%	33.00
Russian	81.3	4.2	10.4	—	4.2	—	100%	24.00
Other	6.5	—	58.3	8.2	5.9	21.1	100%	134.75
Scandinavian	18.7	4.1	32.4	37.0	7.7	—	100%	48.60
Greek	26.2	22.5	28.7	—	13.7	8.9	100%	120.25
Germanic	25.2	2.6	49.8	6.2	8.3	7.9	100%	229.25
German	26.3	2.8	47.8	6.6	8.4	8.1	100%	215.00
Other	8.8	—	80.7	—	7.0	3.5	100%	14.25
Near East	7.8	66.7	19.6	—	—	5.9	100%	12.75
Far East	7.3	—	—	—	92.7	—	100%	54.75
Yiddish	79.5	5.8	6.2	—	4.6	3.9	100%	129.25
Finnish, Hung., Turkish	14.6	6.6	59.3	9.3	3.5	6.6	100%	56.50
Hungarian	20.5	5.0	62.7	2.5	5.0	4.3	100%	40.25
Other	—	10.8	50.8	26.2	—	12.3	100%	16.25
Miscellaneous	11.8	19.6	47.4	.7	19.3	1.3	100%	76.50
Total	16.1	6.2	12.3	1.1	35.0	29.3	100%	6804.70

[a] Based on 1960 LRP data.

West, 67.3% in New England, and 61.7% in the Middle Atlantic states, the East- and West-North-Central regions showed only 34.9% and 19.0% of their broadcast time in this language category. In these two regions the Slavic languages predominated, accounting for 35.8% of the East-North-Central's and 30.3% of the West-North-Central's FLB. It is also significant that the percent distribution of total FLB across the six regions shows that the East-North-Central region accounts for the largest proportion of Slavic broadcasting (Table 4.8). There is ample evidence of increased Slavic cultural activity in the East-North-Central region and in the midwest more generally in recent years.[7] The increase – of which FLB is only one indication – is attributed to post-war immigration of Ukrainians and other Slavs into this area. It is unlikely, however, that increased FLB in the East-North-Central region can con-

[7] See e.g., Ch. 12.

TABLE 4.9

% I or D of Average Hours of FLB[a] from 1956-1960 by Community Size

	25,000 or under	250,000-500,000	500,000-750,000	750,000-1,000,000	1 mill.
Romance	− 11.9	+ 64.7	− 15.2	− 35.1	− 22.7
French	+ 5.7	+100.00	+ 34.0	—	− 33.3
Italian	+ 7.6	− 21.1	− 74.2	− 33.6	− 15.8
Spanish	− 14.4	+ 58.4	+ 17.9	b	− 18.1
Portuguese	− 26.0	+ 20.0	0	—	b
Rumanian	+300.0	—	—	0	0
Slavic	− 13.4	− 19.0	− 40.1	− 11.0	+ 9.8
Polish	− 11.8	− 13.2	+ 28.2	− 2.4	− 5.3
Ukrainian	− 8.2	0	0	− 20.6	− 27.3
Russian	+184.1	—	—	—	− 14.2
Other	− 17.2	− 16.0	− 13.0	− 21.0	+ 80.5
Scandinavian	− 3.7	b	—	—	− 45.4
Greek	0	b	− 9.1	+ 49.3	− 15.7
Germanic	− 9.6	+ 9.4	− 37.5	− 3.6	+ 82.7
German	− 10.8	+ 9.4	− 40.7	− 3.6	+ 82.7
Other	+ 2.0	—	—	—	—
Near East	+ 5.2	+ 50.0	—	—	+ 20.5
Far East	+ 75.6	− 50.0	+100.0	—	b
Yiddish	− 29.7	− 33.5	− 78.5	+ 12.3	− .8
Finnish, Hung., Turkish	− 6.4	− 14.5	− 16.7	− 14.0	+ 22.1
Hungarian	− 16.8	− 14.5	− 16.7	− 14.0	− 2.8
Other	+ 3.7	—	—	—	−100.0
Miscellaneous	+ 42.9	b	− 28.6	− 25.4	+ 8.6
Total	− 13.9	+ 36.6	− 20.2	− 13.4	− 4.3

[a] Based on 1956 and 1960 ACNS Data.
[b] Percentage of I or D cannot be determined due to the presence of "stations" with no information for one of the years.

siderably affect the trends for the country as a whole. The region accounts for only 11.8% of total FLB hours for 1960. In comparison, the West, South, and Middle Atlantic regions accounted for 33.7%, 30.2%, and 17.7% respectively. As long as the latter three regions (accounting for approximately 80% of total FLB) continue to register declines, it is doubtful that an increase in the East-North-Central region will overcome the general downward trend of average FLB time in the future.

Language maintenance has usually been found to be most successful in the smaller and the very largest communities. In view of this, it is interesting to note that all but one of the community-size categories employed in our analysis show decreases in average hours per week of FLB, ranging from a loss of 4.3% in the million plus category to a loss of 20.2% in the 500,000-750,000 category (Table 4.9). An increase, of 36.6%, is registered only in the 250,000-500,000 bracket. An explanation for this

increase in the latter size-category may be found in the percent distribution of total
FLB within the various size-categories (Table 4.10). This distribution shows that
89.2% of all FLB in the 250,000-500,000 category is in the Spanish language. In no
other community-size category is such a large proportion of total FLB time accounted
for by a single foreign language.

TABLE 4.10

Percent Distribution of Total FLB[a] in 1960 within Community Size

	250,000 or under	250,000- 500,000	500,000- 750,000	750,000- 1,000,000	1 mill. or more
Romance	83.5	93.3	76.1	20.2	72.0
French	5.8	.1	.4	—	.2
Spanish	68.0	89.2	57.0	3.3	61.3
Portuguese	2.6	.5	.2	—	b
Rumanian	.1	.1	—	.7	.1
Slavic	8.8	2.8	8.9	36.1	10.6
Polish	6.4	2.2	6.1	10.2	7.7
Ukrainian	.4	.2	. 7	.7	.7
Russian	.4	—	.1	—	.4
Other	1.5	.3	2.0	25.1	1.8
Scandinavian	.9	.8	—	—	.6
Greek	1.2	.5	5.3	9.1	1.9
Germanic	2.3	1.1	5.2	17.9	5.2
German	2.1	1.1	4.4	17.9	5.2
Other	.2	—	.8	—	—
Near East	.1	.1	.7	.4	.1
Far East	.9	b	1.8	—	.5
Yiddish	.4	.7	.9	3.3	7.2
Finnish, Hung., Turkish	.7	.4	.2	11.7	.5
Hungarian	.3	.4	.2	11.7	.5
Other	.4	—	—	—	—
Miscellaneous	1.2	.3	.8	1.5	1.4
N	100.0%	100.0%	100%	100.2%	100.1%
Total	4194.20	532.50	537.50	137.25	1403.25

a   Based on 1960 LRP data.

b   Less than 1%.

When one takes note of the languages which contribute to the overall increment of
FLB in communities of population 250,000-500,000 (a very small number to begin
with), it becomes evident that Spanish FLB accounts for most of the increase. Although
there was an increase of only one "station" between 1956 and 1960, the total number of
hours broadcast in Spanish expanded from 249.25 in 1956 to 418.00 in 1960. In contrast to Spanish, the very small absolute increases registered by a few other languages

in this size-category can be attributed almost completely to the addition of "stations" not listed in 1956. Since such increases are of more questionable validity, the increment of FLB in this size-category should be thought of, on the whole, as an expansion of one language – Spanish.

That Spanish alone accounts for two-thirds of all FLB in the United States today is a phenomenon that could not have been predicted on the basis of either the number of Spanish mother tongue claimants in the American population or the circulation of the Spanish press. It is a sign that radio broadcasting (and, presumably, radio listening) must be studied in its own right for it follows laws of its own. The huge indigenous, semi-indigenous, and immigrant Spanish-speaking populations of the American southwest and south are much more oriented toward radio than toward publications or other formal means of language maintenance and culture expression. In this respect they differ greatly from the primarily immigrant-based groups with non-English mother tongues in the Middle Atlantic states and in other regions. This difference suggests other far-reaching differences in educational level, in economic mobility, and, indeed, in the entire cultural orientation toward American industrial and urban values as well as toward less transmuted ethnic values and behaviors.

There is a strong tendency in America to predict and expect the discontinuance of the most overt signs of "foreign" ethnicity. Such expectations have both subjective and objective origins as well as subjective and objective consequences. Indeed, this concern with discontinuance has often obscured all other curiosity and has long paralyzed inquiry into phenomena at the very heart of American existence. Joseph S. Roucek's comments concerning FLB, penned a generation ago, merit re-examination at this time (Roucek 1945):

Over the long years the problem of foreign language broadcasts will disappear. Data presented throughout this volume indicate the rapid decrease in the familiarity of second and third generation foreign born with the language of their forbears. In the interim, broadcasts in the mother tongue will be an important channel of communication to the foreign born and a means of maintaining in the youth an appreciation of the language and culture of their elders.

Our data for 1956-1960 may suggest to many that the interim period mentioned by Roucek is drawing to a close. Of the languages accounting for the lion's share of FLB (Spanish, Italian, Polish, French, and German) the only one that shows an increase in average hours (both in ACNS and in LRP data) during this period is French. Yet predicting the demise of FLB is like predicting the demise of the foreign language press and of non-English mother tongues more generally – it is fraught with many risks and exposes prophets to the charge of wishful thinking, particularly when a span of only four years is considered.

The number of stations engaged in FLB continues to rise at a rate commensurate with that of American broadcasting in general. The overall decline in average hours of FLB has been slight and may be quite consistent with that for all American broadcasting. The total number of hours of FLB has increased during the four years 1956-

1960 as the result of addition of new "stations". It might, therefore, be appropriate to dwell less on the declines observed in average FLB time per "station" and to pay greater attention to more qualitative aspects of FLB.

SOME QUALITATIVE ASPECTS OF FLB

One of the first questions that must be answered concerns the extent to which foreign language programs (FLPs) are actually perceived as avenues of language and culture maintenance, rather than as means toward commercial or de-ethnicizing goals. Our data indicate that among "the big five", at least, language and culture maintenance goals are recognized and predominant (Table 4.11). This is most clearly the case with respect to German and French programs and least clearly for the Italian, Spanish, and Polish.

TABLE 4.11

Primary Goals of FLP

Language	Language and Culture Maintenance	Other[a]	NA	Total
Spanish	59.0	32.8	8.2	100%
Polish	60.0	30.0	10.0	100%
Italian	50.0	26.3	23.7	100%
German	67.9	17.9	14.3	100%
French	60.0	25.0	15.0	100%

[a] Commercial, "Americanization", etc.

Polish and Italian broadcasts are aimed at relatively recent immigrant populations. Most claimants of these mother tongues are concentrated in American metropoli, with the industrialized Middle Atlantic states accounting for a major share of their numbers. First generation speakers of these languages were almost exclusively the carriers of their respective ethnic "little traditions". These traditions have largely crumbled under the impact of American urban industrialized life and no "high traditions" of transmuted ethnicity have arisen to replace them. As a result, language and culture maintenance are less frequently recognized goals within these populations, and are also less frequently claimed goals for the broadcasts beamed at them.

German and French broadcasting are aimed at populations of less recent immigrant extraction. More claimants of these mother tongues are outside the Middle Atlantic metropolitan-industrial complex. Indeed, although few German or French speakers can properly be classified as rural, more of them are residents of smaller cities and towns than is the case for Polish and Italian speakers. They are also regionally concentrated and have achieved semi-indigenous status by virtue of their large numbers over several generations within the same regions. These languages are more frequently associated with "high culture" and their speakers are more aware of the "great traditions" associated with their languages. Thus, their "little traditions" have less frequently been entirely demolished than they have for Polish and Italian speakers, and their "great traditions" are more recognized – internally and externally. As a result, language and culture maintenance are frequently recognized goals, and are frequently claimed goals for the broadcasts beamed at them.

Spanish broadcasting constitutes a unique case. It is the only non-English language in the United States whose broadcasts currently command entire stations and entire broadcasting days. Many of its speakers are indigenous or semi-indigenous. Not only are they regionally concentrated and encountered in appreciable numbers outside the major metropoli, but their numbers are large and increasing while their educational and social mobility remains low. "Little tradition" predominates among Spanish speakers and remains intact more frequently than is the case for most other language groups in the United States. As a result, language and culture maintenance do not need to be conscious goals for Spanish broadcasting.

In general the languages with the largest number of hours and stations are relatively more attractive for commercial sponsors, while languages with far smaller audiences have a greater proportion of educational and cultural sponsors. Although we have no direct evidence on this, the extent to which the ethnic mother tongue is used exclusively in FLPs (as contrasted with the extended use of English or the alternating use of English and the mother tongue in the same program) may be an oblique indication of the implementation of proclaimed language maintenance goals. The high proportion of programs utilizing the mother tongue only (Table 4.12) implies that the stated goals

TABLE 4.12

Utilization of Mother Tongue in FLP

Language	Mother Tongue only	Both Mother Tongue and Eng.	English only	Total
Spanish	83.6	14.8	1.6	100.0%
Polish	55.0	35.0	10.0	100.0%
Italian	68.4	26.3	5.3	100.0%
German	64.3	32.1	3.6	100.0%
French	85.0	15.0	—	100.0%

are more than just convenient rationalizations or attempts to say the "right thing". Nevertheless, there are different approaches to language and culture maintenance goals (as there are to commercial and "Americanization" goals), and degree of utilization of the mother tongue cannot be considered a uniform indicator in this respect. Many German programs use English in conjuncion with culture maintenance goals, while French programs do so less frequently. On the other hand, many Spanish and Italian programs use the mother tongue on behalf of commercial and "Americanizing" goals, whereas Polish programs do so less frequently. The variations are, in fact, related to the differences in *content* of the programs. German-American listeners are offered many religious programs, conducted in English, the goal being perceived as primarily that of culture maintenance. Spanish-American and Italian-American listeners are offered many musical programs conducted in the mother tongue, the goals being primarily commercial and "Americanizing". Polish-American listeners are offered the largest diet of musical programs, but most of these are conducted largely in English and unconcerned with either language or culture maintenance.

The relatively high proportion of FLPs which broadcast entirely in the mother tongue leads to the question whether reliance on a non-English language poses special problems for the stations or program managers. Such problems are, indeed, quite frequently mentioned, with Italian, German, and French programs more frequently mentioning "problems" than "no problems". The most frequently mentioned problems are: (1) getting sponsors or backers; (2) securing personnel with adequate knowledge of the language; (3) difficulties in scheduling, and (4) loss of audience as a result of the indifference of younger generations and the weakening of ethnic interests among old and young alike. While many of the Polish "music only" or "Polka" programs are directed primarily to listeners of Polish origin, they are, in reality, not as ethnically based as most other FLPs. Since they are often enjoyed by some of the non-ethnic population, it is not surprising that the problems mentioned by the other FLPs would have less applicability to the Polish case.

Spanish programs are least beset by problems. This is, no doubt, the result of two complementary factors: the recent flow of Puerto Rican, Mexican, and Cuban immigrants to the U.S., replenishing the prior Spanish-language radio audience; and the "throughout the day" nature of Spanish broadcasting. With the exception of Spanish, almost all FLB in the United States occurs for specified periods of time (usually of short duration) over primarily "English language" stations. Radio stations sometimes hesitate to offer FLPs because such programs are thought to serve only a small audience and, at the same time, perhaps to be irritating or non-prestigeful as regards potential non-ethnic listeners.[8] To a large extent Spanish FLB escapes these problems, since in view of the size and concentration of the audience many radio stations in the United States broadcase primarily or completely in Spanish.

---

[8]   This view is even held by some staff members of the Federal Communications Commission. In a recent decision concerning the awarding of a television station in Buffalo, the Examiner, in a preliminary report, stated that "[applicant's] proposal to present 5.8% of its programming in foreign languages was less calculated to serve the public interest than were the proposals of [a competing applicant] which would present a lesser amount of foreign language programming, and [still another applicant] which would broadcast all of its programs in English" (Federal Communications Commission Report: *FCC 58-734 61564*, p. 63). Although this opinion was not accepted by the rest of the FCC sitting on this case, the fact that many directors of radio stations and some FCC officials hold this view intensifies the problems facing FLP in securing sponsors, in obtaining desirable time spots, or, in fact, in obtaining time at all. For another recent instance of FCC preference for English rather than non-English broadcasting see FCC Report 63D-46 34441.

One might expect, then, that Spanish and Polish programs would more frequently classify themselves as successful in achieving their goals than would the problem-ridden programs in other languages. Our data, however, fail to give this expectation very strong support. Most programs in all of the "big five" languages claim "complete" or "great" success in connection with their efforts. Although the more problem-ridden and more language-maintenance oriented German and French programs do claim "complete" or "great" success somewhat less frequently they nevertheless claim such success more often than one would expect. This finding suggests that perceived success and language-maintenance orientation may interact with each other. Language-maintenance goals may result in a lower threshold for perceived success. In addition, language maintenance advocates may feel threatened by data gathering and efforts at evaluation. As a result they may tend to overclaim success as a self-protective device. If this is in truth the case, one would expect that those programs whose primary goals are in the direction of language and culture maintenance (regardless of the language involved) would claim success more frequently than those directed along commercial or "Americanizing" lines. On the whole, our data support this expectation. Of those programs which classify themselves as being a "complete" or "great" success, a majority are positively oriented toward language and culture maintenance. This is true for all of the "big five", Conversely, in most of the language groups, a majority of programs comprising the least successful category ("some, little or none") are those directed primarily along commercial or "Americanizing" lines. The very fact that Spanish programs fail to show such a relationship between claims of success and language-maintenance goals suggests a lesser need to "justify" or "protect" themselves in view of their large and faithful audience for whom language maintenance is, for the most part, not yet a problem. The only programs which appear to refute the justification hypothesis are those in French, which are anomalous in several other ways. Only in the case of French are more programs considered "unsuccessful" ("some, little or none") than "completely" successful. However, their recent increase in average hours of broadcasting (cf. Table 4.2) may permit French program directors to admit lack of success, even those pursuing primarily language-maintenance goals. Like the Spanish, many French programs have less need to protect themselves.

Which of the two cognitive-emotional states is predominant in guiding current and and future planning? If problem consciousness predominates over success consciousness, the best that can be hoped for is to retain current levels of programming. A large majority of the programs in each language (ranging from 60.7% in Spanish to 67.9% in German) do indicate an anticipation of keeping their broadcasting time at the same level as in 1960. However, the more language- and culture-maintenance oriented (German and French) may be more likely to seek ways of overcoming their problems and more hopeful of increasing their hours of broadcasting than are programs guided primarily by commercial or "Americanizing" goals (Polish and Italian) – even though the latter are less problem-ridden. Spanish broadcasting excepted, language and culture maintenance seems to be a much stronger motivating and rallying goal than any other available to foreign language programs in the United States today (Warshauer, 1964).

Yet language and culture maintenance on the one hand and the younger generation on the other have in the past rarely been found to be combinable in the United States. Neither FLB nor the non-English press (nor – as we will see – the major ethnic organizations, nor the mother tongue schools) has really succeeded in such an attempt, nor have they usually seemed to recognize the changes in content and level that such an attempt requires. Certainly a greater emphasis on "high tradition" than on the vanishing "low tradition" is only part – but a vital part – of the effort that FLB must make if it expects to protect its own future and become more than a vestigial relic of an ethnicity that existed long ago and far away.

REFERENCES

Bogart, Leo, "The Growth of Television", in *Mass Communications*, Wilbur Schramm, ed. (Urbana, University of Illinois Press, 1960), p. 101.

Radio Stations in the United States Broadcasting Foreign Language Programs (New York, American Council for Nationalities Service, 1956 and 1960).

Roucek, Joseph. C., "Foreign Language Broadcasts", in *One America*, Francis J. Brown and Joseph C. Roucek, eds. (New York, Prentice-Hall, 1945), p. 391.

Tisch, Joseph LeSage, *French in Louisiana* (New Orleans, A. F. Laborde and Sons, 1959).

Warshauer, Mary E., "Foreign Language Broadcasting in the United States", in Fishman, J. A., et al., *Language Loyalty in the United States* (New York, Yeshiva University, 1964), Chapter 4. (Mimeo.)

Wittke, Carl, *The German Language Press in America* (Kentucky, University of Kentucky Press, 1957), p. 2.

5. THE ETHNIC GROUP SCHOOL AND MOTHER TONGUE MAINTENANCE

JOSHUA A. FISHMAN AND VLADIMIR C. NAHIRNY

Inquiries and discussions dealing with education in the United States rarely mention the continued educational efforts of almost all immigrant-based ethnic groups on American shores. Most educational scholars and educational commentators are probably as unaware of these efforts as is the public in general. Similarly, students of American ethnic groups have themselves only rarely focused attention on the schools of the groups they have studied. As a result, the ethnic group school in the United States is largely terra incognita. This is regrettable, not only because these schools represent an important chapter in American social and educational history but because they provide provocative data for the testing of hypotheses of concern both to the sociology of education and to the study of ethnicity.

The ethnic group school in the United States is faced by the general dilemma of immigrants and their children with respect to the retention or denial of their original identity and its associated cultural forms. Studying the ethnic school within the context of a larger inquiry into non-English language maintenance among American ethnic groups enables us to observe extreme as well as many intermediate behavioral and philosophical solutions to this dilemma, on which other social scientists have recently commented (Glazer and Moynihan 1963; Gordon 1961). Thus, this chapter serves a twofold purpose. It seeks to sketch some of the general characteristics of the schools sponsored by or on behalf of ethnic groups in the United States: their size, auspices, faculty, student body, curricula, and activists. At the same time, it seeks to derive the language maintenance implications of this descriptive information as well as to present data pertaining directly to the language maintenance efforts of ethnic schools.

By and large, the ethnic school is a product of dislocation wherever it is encountered throughout the world. Most folk cultures in which ethnicity thrives do not provide for formal schooling since literacy is either unknown or restricted, and ethnicity itself is unconcerned with either formal occupational training or formal ideological indoctrination. Most late 19th and early 20th century American immigrants, particularly those from southern and eastern Europe, knew neither schools nor schooling in the peasant ethnic communities which they left behind. The extended family was itself the primary school and the timeless traditions of daily life constituted this school's curriculum. The priest was frequently the only formal teacher and the church the only formal school (as well as the only formal institution) in the village, and both priest and church stood at least partially outside the bounds of ethnicity.

The very existence of ethnic schools in the United States is an indication of far going change in the primordial constellation of ethnicity. Immigrants have rarely succeeded in preserving an entirely ethnic life-space in America. Non-ethnic components of American mass culture have intruded to dominate or influence the area of work, of dress, of food, of entertainment and so on. Schools, as well as other formal ethnic institutions, became necessary because the complete ethnic pattern no longer functioned and automatic inculturation of the young via exposure to the daily activities of the family could no longer be counted upon to ensure ethnic continuity. But the ethnic group school taught *about* ethnicity, whereas ethnicity consists of *living* ethnically. In the school, ethnicity became self-conscious. It was something to be "studied", "valued", "appreciated" and "believed in". It became a "cause". As it was raised to the level of ideology, belief system, national symbolism, or selective sentimentality it also ceased being ethnic in the original and authentic sense.

The ethnic school is therefore one product of the encounter between ethnic immigrants and urban, industrial American mass culture. It not only represents a means or mechanism novel (and, perhaps, inappropriate) to ethnicity, it also is a means toward an end which is strange for ethnicity. However, the failure of most immigrants to re-establish self-contained ethnic communities after immigration to the United States quickly made the school into an unusually crucial venture. Only specifically designed institutions and organizations could preserve the scattered seeds of ethnicity among immigrants who had lost their traditional way of life and its natural cohesion.

Schools require teachers, administrators, students, and funds. Frequently, the supply of one or another of these "commodities" is insufficient or at least problematic. Inasmuch as general American education faces similar problems or uncertainties, we might anticipate that such would be even more true of ethnic schools with their far more limited command of manpower, means, and sanctions. Nevertheless, thousands of such schools continue to function.

SCHOOL TYPES

Ethnically affiliated schools in the United States comprise three major "structural types" based upon frequency of instruction and total number of instructional hours per week.

a. *All Day Schools* offer complete educational programs that fulfill the requirements of compulsory education laws enacted by state and local educational authorities. The pupils attending these schools do not attend general American public schools. All Day Schools are frequently and popularly referred to as "parochial schools" in view of the fact that most of them are maintained by Catholic parishes of both Latin and Byzantine rites. This usage is not followed here because a number of All Day Schools are conducted by non-Catholic groups that are not organized on a parish basis (Jewish, Protestant, Orthodox) as well as by organizations or individuals entirely independent of official religious supervision. Most All Day Schools in our current sample, nevertheless, are affiliated with Catholic ethnic parishes serving French, Polish, Italian, Spanish (including Latin American), and Slovak parishioners.

For our purposes it is important to underscore that many ethnically affiliated All Day Schools provide instruction in the religious, cultural, and linguistic heritages of particular ethnic groups. Such instruction is given during the regular school day and is over and above the general curricular requirements of American education law. In some instances, this "dual program" of general plus ethnic-religious studies requires a somewhat extended school day. In any case, the All Day School provides an opportunity for a more intensive and prolonged ethnic education of the young than is available to American ethnic groups by any other formal means. Whether this opportunity is utilized on behalf of ethnicity or language maintenance and whether it is effective when so utilized is one of the questions we have sought to examine.

b. *Weekday Afternoon Schools* are supplementary schools in the sense that their pupils also attend general American public schools during the regular school day. They are usually under Jewish or Eastern Orthodox sponsorship and are in session during two or more weekday afternoons throughout the usual school year.

c. *Weekend Schools* normally meet either on Saturdays or on Sundays. They usually offer fewer hours of instruction per academic year than do the Weekday Afternoon Schools. Their pupils attend general American public schools (rather than All Day Schools) on weekdays during the usual school year. Weekend Schools for the most part serve recent Baltic, eastern and central European immigrant groups and afford the least intensive program of the three major structural types of ethnic schools.

In addition to these three types there is also an "Other" category composed of summer schools, evening classes, and special classes in schools or community centers, which meet less frequently than once a week during the usual school year.

Our best estimates indicate that approximately 2000 ethnically affiliated schools were operating in the continental United States in 1960 (Fishman and Nahirny 1964(a)). The Language Resources Project succeeded in compiling a name and address list of 1885 such schools, 943 of which responded to an initial brief questionnaire. Of these, 339 subsequently provided much more exhaustive data. These data, as well as those provided independently by 316 mother tongue teachers in ethnic schools, constitute the basis of this report.

SCHOOL CHARACTERISTICS

The ethnically affiliated All Day School is substantially different from the others not only in structure but in human resources and instructional emphases. Besides being the only non-supplementary ethnic school type, its units are quite a bit older, larger,

TABLE 5.1

School Types and Mother Tongue Instruction

School Type	Mother Tongue Instruction		
	Yes	No	Total
All Day	47%	53%	100% (194)
Weekday	70%	30%	100% (92)
Weekend	62%	38%	100% (34)
"Other"	58%	42%	100% (19)
Total	55%	45%	100% (339)

TABLE 5.2

Median Number of Grades and Hours/Week of Instruction by School Type

	All Day	Weekday Afternoon	Weekend	Other
Highest Mdn. Grade	8	6	6	8
Hrs./Wk.	10+	3-5	3-5	3-5
Lowest Mdn. Grade of MTI[a]	4	1	1	1
Hrs./Wk.	2	3	2	1
Highest Mdn. Grade of MTI[a]	8	5	6	8
Hrs./Wk.	3	3	2	2
Lowest Mdn. Grade of OES[b]	5	1	2	1
Hrs./Wk.	4	2	1	2
Highest Mdn. Grade of OES[b]	8	5	6	4
Hrs./Wk.	4	1	1	2
Mdn. Yrs. of MT Instruction	5	5	6	8

[a] Mother Tongue Instruction.
[b] Other Ethnic Subjects.

and wealthier than units of the other types. It is different in human resources in that its teachers, pupils, and activists are most Americanized and have been so for the longest time, and in instructional emphases for it least frequently offers mother tongue instruction (Table 5.1) and devotes relatively less time to it or to any other ethnic instruction even when offered (Table 5.2). By every available index the All Day School is far less embedded in ethnicity, and, therefore, far less concerned with language maintenance, than any other type of ethnically affiliated school.[1] As the school

[1] In this connection see Francis Bolek, *The Polish American School System* (New York, Columbia Press Corp., 1948); J. A. Burns, *The Growth and Development of the Catholic School System in the United States* (New York, Benziger, 1912); Natalie A. Czuba, *History of the Ukrainian Catholic Parochial Schools in the United States* (Chicago, De Paul Univ., 1956); Joseph H. Fichter, *Parochial School* (Notre Dame, Ind., Univ. of Notre Dame Press, 1958); Sister M. L. Kaiser, *The Development of the Concept and Function of the Catholic Elementary School in the American Parish* (Washington, Catholic Univ. of America Press, 1955); Peter H. Rossi and Alice S. Rossi, "Some Effects of Parochial-School Education in America", *Daedalus*, Spring 1961, 300-328. Also, note the section on "Complications of Language and Tradition", in Thomas T. McAvoy (ed.), *Roman Catholicism and the American Way of Life* (Notre Dame, Univ. of Notre Dame Press, 1960).

type with the greatest theoretical potential for *intensive* culture and language maintenance programs and for a leadership role in this connection within American ethnic
communities, All Day Schools by no means typically offer such programs or undertake
this role. On the contrary, their reluctant and vestigial ethnicity may be said to have
a dampening, discouraging and weakening effect on the language maintenance interests and capacities of the communities they serve, as well as upon other schools and
ethnic groups that cannot but be impressed by the greater size and strength of the All
Day Schools and their firm institutional base in major Church bodies.

In sharpest contrast to the All Day School is the Weedday Afternoon School.
Although it too is usually under religious auspices, it most frequently offers mother
tongue instruction, its curriculum is most language-centered, its teachers are most
frequently active in ethnic organizations and are most often readers of (as well as
contributors to) the ethnic press, and its mother tongue teachers have most frequently
received training for their current assignments. By comparison, the Weekend School
is far less frequently under religious auspices, far less frequently employs trained
mother tongue teachers, and more often involves foreign born or second generation
teachers, parents, and pupils. With their fewer hours of instruction and their more
frequent foreign born personnel the Weekend Schools are intermediate in language
maintenance emphases.

The various types of ethnic school differ least in their human resources, and these
resources are far less "foreign" than is usually assumed. Pupils, teachers, and parents
are now most commonly American born and very frequently "native of native" –
regardless of school type or of language maintenance orientation. Nevertheless the
ethnicity of the schools – even when it is of a minor and marginal, organizationally
sustained, and ritualized variety – continues to have some meaning, some value, some
value, some role, even when it does not have the meanings, values, or roles for those
now involved that it had in previous years. The continued staying power of marginal
ethnicity is the result of three interacting influences: the inertia of tradition; the
institutionalization of the schools under religious and organizational auspices which
protect marginal ethnicity at the same time as they tend toward de-ethnization; the
lack in American national life-ways of substitutes for "little tradition" ethnicity once
such ethnicity has reached a minimal and non-abrasive level.

Neither ethnic schools as such nor their curricular emphases seem to require a strong
immigrant-ethnic base. While this may not continue to be the case indefinitely, it does
provide us with some insight into the possible variations of ethnic functioning in the
United States. Although the ethnicity of the ethnic school has become increasingly
marginal in many instances, the fact that its existence continues to be institutionally
protected and that its role remains a meaningful one may both be *a result* of the increasing marginality of ethnicity. Just as active ethnicity required an organized institutional base in the United States, so does marginal ethnicity that is still above a certain
threshold. Language itself provides many examples of the drift from active to successively more marginal ethnicity. Thus, what was originally a functional mother tongue

in many domains of everyday life for the first generation becomes a cultural "ethnic mother tongue" learned in school and heard in church for the second or third generation. Ethnicity, whatever it is, is not an all-or-none proposition in the United States. Even when it becomes marginal to the central concerns of many individuals and groups it still continues – even as marginal ethnicity – to fulfill some functions for them.[2]

INSTITUTIONAL BASES AND LANGUAGE MAINTENANCE

That ethnically affiliated All Day Schools are least likely to offer mother tongue instruction, when coupled with the fact that such schools are so frequently under religious auspices, leads one to question whether religious auspices per se are likely to be antithetical to language maintenance. Available evidence indicates that, at present, most major religious bodies in America are powerful de-ethnicizing forces, although there is considerable evidence that in former days religion served as a strong force on behalf of ethnic and linguistic continuity among American immigrants and their children. Greek Catholic, Greek Orthodox, and many smaller Protestant bodies still function in this way. Today most ethnic schools in the United States (81 %) are under religious sponsorship. Except for the relatively minor category of "Other" schools the majority of school units of each structural type claim such sponsorship. This is particularly true of All Day and Weekday Afternoon Schools. Although the Weekend Schools are also primarily under religious auspices, a sizable proportion report non-religious organizational auspices. Finally, in the case of "Other" schools we find a plurality of units under organizational auspices and a sizable number under private or other unaffiliated sponsorship. Thus it might seem that the more "intensive" types of ethnically affiliated schools are almost exclusively under religious sponsorship, whereas the least intensive types are frequently under non-religious organizational or private sponsorship. This may well imply that only religious bodies are sufficiently interested in ethnic and language maintenance to sponsor intensive schools on behalf of these goals. It may be, however, that the most intensive schools are actually under the least hospitable auspices for language maintenance and that religious auspices merely reflect the greater wealth and organizational strength required for the operation and support of intensive schools for religious indoctrination.

Mother tongue instruction might be much more common in certain predominantly Catholic ethnic groups today if the language loyalists among them were strong enough to maintain schools under other than Church auspices. Conversely, mother tongue instruction might be far less common among recent immigrants from Baltic and Eastern European homelands if the language loyalists among them were unable to

---

[2] See Joshua A. Fishman, "Childhood Indoctrination for Minority Group Membership", *Daedalus*, Spring 1961, 329-349, and Einar Haugen, *The Norwegian Language in America*,Vol. I (Philadelphia, Univ. of Pennsylvania Press, 1953).

maintain schools under non-religious auspices. Because the religious components of ethnicity have always been partially outside ethnicity (i.e., most immigrant religions were and are supra-ethnic rather than completely particularistic as was and is ethnicity per se), immigrant religions established themselves more firmly in America and lost less numerical strength under the impact of Americanization than did other components of ethnicity. As a result, the Americanization of immigrant religions must, in the long run, be conducive to their organizational (institutional) strength and antithetical to immigrant-based ethnicity and its cultural or linguistic continuity.

Other institutional characteristics are likewise suggestive. The age of responding schools differs markedly in association with structural type. All Day Schools have the most advanced average age, approximately half of them going back at least to World War I years. Weekend Schools stand at the opposite pole, two thirds of them going back only to 1950, with Weekday Afternoon Schools standing between these two extremes. The relationship between mother tongue instruction and date of school establishment is an interesting one. In all the major school types those units offering mother tongue instruction tend to be "younger" than those not offering such instruction. This finding does not necessarily fly in the face of the general view that language maintenance as a goal has less attraction for the more recent foreign stock than it had for immigrants and their children in earlier years. As the total number of ethnic group schools (and other distinctive ethnic group institutions) decreases over time due to attrition and adaptation, the percentage of recently founded institutions with culture maintenance goals may remain high (or even increase), even though early 20th century immigrants may well have been initially more retentive than their most recent counterparts.

The dynamics of discontinuance of mother tongue instruction may differ greatly from one school type to another. All Day and Weekday Afternoon Schools alike report units established in all decades since before the turn of the century. However, while no Weekday Afternoon School in our sample has discontinued teaching the mother tongue since 1929 (although several have been established entirely without that goal), among All Day Schools we find not only the constant establishment of new schools that do not teach the mother tongue but also continued cessation of mother tongue instruction. Thus, language transition within the same school unit may be an adaptive device for All Day Schools, whereas such does not seem to be the case for Weekday Afternoon Schools. In the former, Church support may be strong enough to enable weathering the crisis of language transition (even though – or precisely because – the schools still remain nominally ethnic). In the latter, language transition crises may result more frequently in the closing of an old school which had language maintenance goals and in the opening of a new school which does not have such goals, rather than in a transition within the same unit. Religious support for the ethnically affiliated Catholic All Day Schools may provide a powerful superordinate authority which can cushion or manipulate generational cleavages and generational turnover within specific school units, while religious support for the ethnically affiliated Weekday Afternoon Schools (largely Jewish or Greek Orthodox) may provide less super-ordinate authority for bridging the crises that develop.

The retention of mother tongue instruction in All Day Schools has been greatest in small towns. This apparently is a result of proportionately fewer discontinuances rather than the establishment of proportionately fewer schools that have not taught the mother tongue from the very outset. Whereas only 31% of ethnically affiliated Catholic All Day Schools in towns of less than 50,000 population have discontinued mother tongue instruction, discontinuance has occurred in 59% of such schools in cities with a population between 750,000 and one million. All Day Schools in large communities have discontinued mother tongue instruction not only more frequently but more rapidly. In recently established ethnic parishes mother tongue instruction in All Day Schools has been discontinued much more quickly than in schools attached to older ethnic parishes. Among parishes established before 1923, only 29% discontinued mother tongue instruction within twenty years of the date of their establishment. By contrast, among ethnic parishes established since 1923, fully 80% discontinued such instruction within twenty years. This difference may be due, in part, to the decrease in immigration after 1923. As a result of this decrease, ethnic parishes established after that date may have had a smaller membership to begin with. However, above and beyond this possibility is the further fact that newer Catholic immigrants have shown a greater tendency to settle in larger cities and metropoli and to be less linguistically retentive, so that mother tongue instruction in 1960 was less common in All Day Schools in new ethnic parishes than in old ones. Thus we come face to face with an important "reality" of mother tongue instruction in ethnically affiliated All Day Schools today: such instruction is most frequently associated with schools established for the recent foreign stock; at the same time it is more quickly discontinued in the schools serving the recent foreign stock.

This finding has several implications. It implies that mother tongue instruction in All Day Schools of ethnic parishes is, at best, offered on demand rather than as a matter of language maintenance interest on the part of the Church. Older Catholic immigrants who settled in the small towns have maintained this demand longer than have newer Catholic immigrants, who settled in larger cities. The former, of course, constituted a larger proportion of the total population in their place of residence. They could more nearly control the entire environment and establish their language and customs within it. Moreover, older Catholic immigrants were more truly ethnic to begin with than are recent Catholic immigrants, most of whom have come from de-ethnicized urban centers in their homelands. In the small town the ethnic mother tongue has lingered on in the All Day School, as it has in the town itself, because populations have changed less and life has changed less.

THE ETHNIC COMMUNITY AND THE SCHOOL

The ethnic group school represents a focal point at which a population of pupils, contributors, and active supporters meet and interact.[3] How do these various sub-populations differ from each other? Do they differ, or are they basically similar, when comparing schools that *do* offer instruction in a mother tongue with schools that are not, or when comparing schools of various structural types? What language maintenance implications can be derived from these characteristics? Differences between the "manpower" involved in various types of ethnic schools are of interest not only because of their general orientational significance with respect to an understanding of ethnic group schools, but also because of their importance for an understanding of ethnicity in the United States. Consistent "manpower" differences between school types or between instructional types would indicate appreciable ideological-adaptational differences between the populations they serve. On the other hand, if pupils, contributors, and activists in the various school types differ little and inconsistently from each other, then the existence of several types of schools may be due to vested organizational operations rather than to curricular differences between the schools themselves or to ideological-adaptational differences between the populations they serve.

It is clear that the overwhelming majority of pupils in all school types are American born. This is particularly true in the more "intensive" school types. Only 3% to 5% of All Day, Weekday Afternoon, and "Other" Schools report a majority of foreign born students, whereas 15% of the Weekend Schools report such a majority. Schools with a majority of foreign born students almost always teach the mother tongue. Nevertheless, so few are the schools in which foreign born pupils are in the majority that the lion's share, by far, of all schools offering mother tongue instruction have a majority of American born students.

The above findings should not be interpreted as indicating that All Day Schools and Weekday Schools do not attract children of recent immigrants – for they do. However, only rarely do such children become predominant in their student bodies. This may be due to the fact that these schools usually are neither neighborhood schools nor exclusively ethnic schools. As a result, they may not only draw students from a large geographic area but may also attract students of non-ethnic (or of inappropriate ethnic) but appropriate religious backgrounds. Only 48% of All Day Schools and 40% of Weekday Afternoon Schools indicate that most of their students are of an ethnic background (whether foreign born or not) appropriate to the ethnic sponsorship of the school. On the other hand, 68% of Weekend Schools and 74% of "Other" Schools claim that a majority of their students are of appropriate ethnic background. The implication of these sizable differences for language maintenance seems clear enough.[4]

---

[3] The teachers too, of course, form a part of this interacting community, and will be treated separately later in the chapter.
[4] The differences between school types may be even greater than these figures imply. All Day Schools may tend to consider children of ethnically mixed backgrounds as still being of "appropriate" background as long as at least one parent is of appropriate background. Proportionately fewer

Schools offering instruction in the mother tongue are "purer" or more homogeneous with respect to the ethnicity of their pupils. Within every school type, more of the schools offering such instruction claim that a majority of their pupils are of the appropriate ethnic background than do schools not offering such instruction. To some extent this may be due to school policy, such that only ethnically appropriate students are admitted. In addition, self-selection on the part of the pupils (actually, on the part of their parents) must also be involved. Schools with active mother tongue programs may not be as attractive to those of inappropriate ethnic background even where a common religious affiliation is involved. Finally, such schools may more frequently be located in ethnically homogeneous neighborhoods.

The "inappropriate" ethnicity reported by many schools is not always as inappropriate – particularly for the schools offering mother tongue instruction – as might appear at first glance. Changes in generational composition (usually an increase in third generation students who do not come with any mother tongue facility) are frequently considered "inappropriate" since they involve pedagogical and curricular problems of de-ethnization. Most All Day Schools seem to have gone through major de- ethnicizing changes some time ago. Their organizational base has helped them make the transition. Many Weekday Afternoon Schools seemed to be in the throes of the most serious changes at the very time of the study, while many Weekend Schools were just moving into the kinds of changes in ethnic composition which other school-types had faced before – some of these being conducive to ethnic retentionism rather than detracting from it. Whether the Weekday Afternoon and Weekend Schools can weather the changes previously experienced by the All Day Schools is problematic. All Day Schools may be able to continue on a nominally ethnic basis for a longer time than others having a less powerful organizational base. It should also be noted that schools offering language maintenance programs are less affected than others by *changes* in ethnic composition, and receive infusions of new immigrants more frequently. Both these factors help them retain their linguistic emphases even as their ranks grow thinner.

Ethnic group schools rely to a considerable extent on voluntary contributors and activists who provide the funds and the hands to keep the schools running. Most of these schools – particularly those under organizational auspices (whether religious or non-religious) – are ostensibly conducted by a school board or school committee of interested laymen (activists). The members of this board or committee have a wide variety of responsibilities: they determine the school budget, engage in fund-raising activities, help arrange school celebrations for pupils and parents, seek to interest more parents in the school's work, recruit pupils, plan cultural programs or courses for parents, and so on. Less commonly, they may be responsible for hiring the teaching staff and may also be concerned with curriculum definition and evaluation. Whether

---

children of ethnically mixed backgrounds attend Weekend Schools and, therefore, their estimates are not inflated in this manner.

Lincoln Christian College

or not all of these responsibilities are within its province the school board represents a vital link between the school and the ethnic community it serves. Not only is the board frequently concerned with finding funds and getting things done, it is also the adjusting mechanism which regulates the ethnicity of the school relative to the ethnicity of its clientele.

Weekend Schools present the highest proportions of foreign born contributors and activists. On the whole, the major contributors and activists tend to be foreign born more frequently in schools that offer mother tongue instruction than in schools that do not. The major contributors are much more frequently foreign born than are the major activists, this being particularly so for All Day and for Weekday Afternoon Schools. Major contributors are almost exclusively males; major activists are usually males but not nearly as frequently as are the major contributors. Weekday Afternoon Schools have particularly high proportions of males among their major contributors and activists. This is of interest to us in view of the common assumption that religio-ethnic concerns have been predominantly delegated (or relegated) to females after the early post-immigration period. Contributors tend to be older than activists, but this overall trend is due entirely to the distributions reported for the All Day and Weekday Afternoon Schools. Weekend and "Other" Schools tend to have particularly youthful contributors. All Day Schools tend to have particularly youthful activists. No consistent differences appear between schools that do and those that do not teach the ethnic mother tongue with respect to either the sex or the age of their major contributors and activists.

Our survey of pupils, contributors, and activists rarely disclosed any significant difference between schools that do and schools that do not teach the ethnic mother tongue, suggesting a basic contextual and operational similarity between these two instructional subtypes. The differences noted *between school types* are often much sharper than those noted *within school types*, i.e., between schools offering and those not offering instruction in the mother tongue. However, of possibly greater importance for a fundamental understanding of American ethnic group schools today are the similarities which characterize the various types. As already noted, few schools report a majority of foreign born pupils; the percentage of such schools (5%) is roughly equivalent to the percentage of foreign born in the general American population as of 1960 (5.4%). The proportion of foreign born activists (24%) is also quite low. Highest of all is the proportion of foreign born contributors (44%), but even this proportion is smaller than half. Thus it would seem that ethnic schools are now making the transition from first to second generation contributors, having already shifted (with the exception of Weekend Schools) from second to third (or subsequent) generation pupils and from first to second generation activists.

The data presented in this section reinforce our impression of the distinctive nature of the All Day School. In addition, they imply that the developmental path traversed by most All Day Schools (in the direction of de-ethnization, supra-ethnic religious convergence, and Americanization) is one toward which other school types are tending, with the Weekend School being farthest away from that developmental status. In the absence of further mass immigration in the immediate future, it would seem that ethnic schools will tend to become increasingly similar with respect to the minimality and non-particularity of their ethnicity and that, as a result, their religious particularities will remain the major distinction between them. This may well pose an additionally severe problem for Weekend Schools, many of which are religiously unaffiliated.

INSTRUCTIONAL AND CURRICULAR EMPHASES

That ethnic group schools may officially continue as such even after the mother tongue is no longer taught implies that such schools can and do have other bonds with their constituencies besides those forged by language. Nevertheless, it is interesting to inquire as to how ethnic schools that no longer teach their respective mother tongues explain the discontinuance of such instruction. Our returns for All Day Schools may be considered quite typical in this connection. The most frequently reported explanation (or rationalization) is that *parents and children are indifferent to the mother tongue and have no interest in seeing it taught* (30%). A somewhat smaller percentage of schools indicate that parents of parishioners are actually *opposed to further teaching of the mother tongue* (21%). These two reasons alone account for half of those given. Other reasons much less frequently mentioned include: overcrowded curriculum (11%), mother tongue unimportant in United States (10%), students of different national backgrounds enrolled in the school (9%), anti-mother tongue pressures inspired by World War I and World War II (9%), lack of competent teachers (6%), and discontinuance demanded by Church authorities (4%).

Professional educational reasons (teachers, curriculum) are thus rarely mentioned. Large-scale developments manifestly beyond the school's control (enrollment of students of different nationalities, World Wars I and II, Church authorities opposed) are more frequently cited. The frequency with which pressures from parishioners are reported suggests that these may be important forces leading to the eventual discontinuance of ethnic mother tongues in many Catholic All Day Schools. Given the hierarchical nature of the Church and its curricular control, it is at least noteworthy that there has been no insistence "from above" on behalf of language maintenance. Active and passive guidance from "Americanists" in the Church have resulted in neutral directives at best and in hostile directives at worst toward mother tongue instruction in All Day Schools. Opposition from second generation parishioners, "patriotic" public hostility, and diverse pupil backgrounds are all factors that Church authorities have successfully coped with when defending other components of All Day School programs. Obviously, mother tongue instruction has no deep doctrinal or ritual significance (except in Byzantine Rite parishes) and so has been judged to be expendable or undesirable by leading churchmen in the United States (De Marco 1960).

Two current major tenets of instruction in foreign languages are: (a) that instruction begin as early as possible in the learner's development and (b) that it continue as intensively and over as long a period as possible. Although mother tongue instruction in American ethnic schools is not entirely the same as "foreign language" instruction, it is nevertheless increasingly of this order. Even were we to assume that most pupils enter these schools with some familiarity with their ethnic mother tongue, however latent or non-functional this might at times be, the above tenets would still deserve attention since they seem to be appropriate to the maintenance of most minority group languages in the context of modern American society.

Within all four school types, those units that do offer mother tongue instruction typically begin it in the very first year. This is particularly true in Weekday Afternoon and in "Other" Schools, where approximately three quarters of all units offering mother tongue instruction begin with the first year. All Day Schools are most remiss in this respect; only 58 % of those that teach it at all begin instruction in the first year. Indeed, 15 % of them do not begin until the 6th grade or later!

One general conclusion might be drawn from the fact that mother tongue instruction does not always begin in the first year (as well as that it is not always continued through to the highest year). It would seem to imply a view toward the mother tongue, apparently common even in many schools which offer instruction in it, that it is a desirable flourish or adornment in the education of the ethnic group child. It is needed for letter writing, for newspaper reading, for ties with older family members, and for group sentiments. Elementary education would be incomplete without it. Yet these peripheral components of both "little" and "great" tradition are not considered sufficiently basic (to either "little" or "great" tradition) as to be absolutely necessary in every year of the curriculum. A frequent rationale for this underlying (and often unverbalized) view is that the ethnic mother tongue is "too difficult" for young children to begin studying in their very first year in school without "losing" them or "antagonizing" their parents. Then too, it either yields "too little progress' for advanced instruction in the upper grades, or "sufficient progress" has already been made in it by that time. As a result, many schools that are ambivalent toward ethnic mother tongue instruction tend to concentrate it in the middle elementary grades and to assign it to teachers who can integrate it with other ethnically related subjects taught at that time. Such a view might stem from a natural and intact "little" tradition in which language as a separate ingredient is rarely appreciated. On the other hand, it might stem from a decaying "great" tradition or from a "great" tradition that has been interfered with by another. In the case of most ethnic schools currently functioning in the United States, the latter circumstance seems to obtain more frequently than the former.

As for hours per week of ethnic mother tongue instruction, we find that All Day Schools again seem to represent a minimalist position – certainly so in comparison to the total number of hours per week theoretically available to them for ethnic instruction. No involved explanation is called for as to why the average Weekend or "Other" School unit devotes but one or two hours per week to mother tongue instruction; the total instructional time available in these school types is usually no more than three to five hours per week. But All Day Schools, with 10-15 hours per week available, for ethnic instruction, likewise usually devote only one or two hours per week to mother tongue instruction. The typical Weekday Afternoon School offers *three or four hours of mother tongue instruction per week* out of a total of 3 to 5 hours of instructional time. This is not only the greatest amount of time in *absolute* terms, it is also greatest *relative* to the total number of hours devoted to ethnic instruction.

Thus Weekday Afternoon Schools clearly appear as the most language centered, both in their greater readiness to begin mother tongue instruction earlier and in greater willingness to devote more hours to it in absolute as well as in relative terms, while All Day Schools are the least language centered, according to both of these indices. Weekend and "Other" Schools occupy an intermediate position but, in general, stand relatively closer to the pattern of the Weekday Afternoon School than to that of the All Day School.

Language maintenance within ethnic schools may be either furthered by or replaced by "other ethnic subjects". History, religious studies, singing, dramatics, and holiday celebrations may also involve mother tongue materials and these may contribute substantially to language maintenance even when no formal instruction in the mother tongue is offered. It is possible, of course, that language maintenance is in such a healthy state in certain ethnic groups that their schools can concentrate entirely on "other ethnic subjects" rather than take time to teach the mother tongue directly. On the other hand, "other ethnic subjects" need not involve language maintenance at all. They may be taught entirely in English and may actually displace mother tongue instruction.

Our data indicate that if "other ethnic subjects" make any significant contribution to language maintenance, this is likely to be the case only in those schools that also offer instruction in the mother tongue. In every school type, "other ethnic subjects" utilizing the mother tongue are offered far more frequently by schools that do give mother tongue instruction than by those that do not. This finding not only vitiates the notion of indirect or latent language learning as a major current alternative route to language maintenance, it also suggests the probable chronology of discontinuance of instruction in the mother tongue and in "other ethnic subjects". Initially, the ethnic school offers holistic instruction (not unlike the core curriculum so popular in former days in American schools) in which language and other ethnic subjects are fully and continuously interrelated. At this stage schools may indicate that they offer either mother tongue instruction or "other ethnic instruction" or both. Subsequently, as both language competence and ethnic traditions deteriorate among pupils and their parents alike, these two ingredients are separated out from each other. It is often not noticed that ethnicity has retreated from being a behavioral system in this process. (This is the stage at which many ethnic schools serving urbanized, secularized, and nationalistically oriented immigrants begin their functioning, and it is important to realize that it represents a retreat from ethnicity at the very outset.) A further step toward de-ethnization is taken when mother tongue instruction is progressively lessened and finally discontinued while certain "other ethnic subjects" are retained. At this stage rationales are advanced and defended which champion group-identification on an English language base. Ethnicity now avowedly becomes an object of sentiment and of study rather than a pattern of behavior. Over time, the "other ethnic subjects" too are slowly reinterpreted and then discontinued; a predominantly religious curriculum obtains which includes only minor historical and festive references to ethnicity. The several types of ethnic schools tend to cluster at various points along this chronological continuum (although there are undeniable variations within each type), with Weekend Schools closer to the earlier and All Day Schools to the later of these stages.

In support of this reconstructed developmental progression one might point out that among schools *not* offering mother tongue instruction hardly any All Day Schools offer instruction in "other ethnic subjects", whereas over a quarter of Weekday Afternoon and Weekend Schools still do so. Thus we may question the language and group maintenance concerns of most All Day Schools even more strongly than we have already, while reaffirming those of the remaining school types, particularly the Weekday Afternoon Schools.

Whether or not a school offers instruction in the ethnic mother tongue usually determines the language of instruction of ethnically related subjects. Nevertheless there is a slight tendency for religion-history-culture to be taught in English even in schools that do offer mother tongue instruction and an opposite tendency to teach art-music-dance (the folk arts) in the mother tongue, even in schools that do not offer formal mother tongue instruction. Thus, in teaching those subjects that deal with theoretically and symbolically elaborated or transmuted ethnicity – subjects that require extensive discussion, explanation, and reading rather than behavioral incorporation – English is more frequently employed. In teaching subjects that involve traditional pursuits – folk singing, folk dancing, and folk arts – the mother tongue is more frequently employed. This distinction between symbolic-intellectual-cultural subjects and traditional-festive subjects tends to cross the lines of school type and instructional type. It implies a relegation of the ethnic mother tongue and of ethnicity more generally to a delimited segment of life and to a delimited segment of the curriculum. Few schools, indeed, currently correspond to an integrated ethnic way of life. Transmuted ethnicity is behaviorally de-ethnicized and linguistically enfeebled.

Ethnic schools that exert effort on behalf of mother tongue instruction face many difficulties. Basically, they face a host society and a cultural context in which language maintenance is atypical and is either viewed as an unnecessary goal or immersed entirely in a sea of ignorance and apathy. Given the urban, participationist setting of most American ethnic groups, the orientation of co-territorial non-ethnic populations has very definite, direct, and continuous consequences within the ethnic communities themselves. As a result, the communities served by language maintenance oriented schools frequently lack firm and vigorous ideological commitments to language maintenance. Language loyalists are rare and language-based ideological movements are weak or non-existent. The non-ideological momentum of tradition is usually the strongest force on behalf of language maintenance, but this force is constantly eroded by the passing of older members and by the ongoing linguistic and cultural Americanization of old and young alike. What little ideological-symbolic retentivism may exist is counteracted by the lack of ideology in American life and by the tendency – among ethnics and non-ethnics alike – to view nationalistic ideologies as un-American or anti American.

Given this array of difficulties to overcome, the adherents of language maintenance can attribute their trials and reverses to outside factors (i.e., to public opinion, to general American hostility or indifference, to unsatisfactory environmental circumstances), or they can turn their disappointment upon themselves and blame in-group circumstances. Data from various parts of the Language Resources Project indicate that the latter path is chosen far more frequently than the former. On the whole, there seems to be an implication by School officials that if parents and children were more concerned with language maintenance, more conscious and appreciative of its importance, other problems (such as staff, time, materials and finances) would be more readily solvable. Of least importance, as reported, are more "distant" factors such as public opinion, Church authorities, and curricular emphases (which frequently are established by outside authorities). Perhaps their impact is not felt as constantly or as directly as that of the parents and children with whom school officials are in daily contact.

How disinterested in or how opposed to ethnic mother tongue instruction are the parents and pupils? What forms do their disinterest and opposition take? Are there recognizable subgroups of parents and pupils who are more favorable inclined (or less unfavorably disposed)? At this point we can only say that there seems to be a direct relationship between the prevalence of parent and pupil difficulties and the prevalence of second generation, third generation, and non-ethnic, mixed ethnic or other ethnic pupils in the various school types. Thus, parents and pupils constitute 60% of the "major difficulties in mother tongue instruction" in All Day Schools, but only 48% and 28% in Weekday Afternoon and Weekend Schools respectively. Therefore it would seem that the significance of parent-pupil opposition to mother tongue instruction must be interpreted differently for different school types.

By and large, schools claim little more for such instruction than that their pupils learn to speak, read, and write the ethnic mother tongue with at least minimal fluency. Whereas approximately half the units in each type claim that their major accomplishment is in this area, far fewer claim such accomplishments as "following church services in the mother tongue" or "love for the ethnic culture", and few indeed claim "closer relationships with parents and grandparents" or "strong interest in ethnic art, music, and dance". Thus it would seem that language maintenance efforts attain limited and narrowly linguistic goals *at best*, and that the broader culture maintenance and intergenerational continuity goals frequently advanced as the ultimate justifications for language maintenance are rarely attained.

The dysfunctional relationship between hierarchical goals is an outcome of culture change frequently noted by anthropologists in societies that have come under the impact of Western technology and ideology. However, it is also an aspect of culture change and of acculturation more generally. Formerly interlocking goals first cease to dovetail. Immediate goals then receive greater stress and ultimate goals less stress than has been the case traditionally. Finally, the ultimate goals are abandoned as being unattainable or unimportant and the immediate goals are reinterpreted. Mother tongue instruction in American ethnic schools is at various stages of this transitional sequence, depending on the size, immigrational recency, concentration, and language consciousness of the groups involved. Most of our respondents seem to be either well along in the second stage or into the third stage of the transitional sequence.

The responses of school principals concerning their "future plans with respect to mother tongue instruction" for the most part indicate an intent to continue current practices. However, 38% of all school units do intend some change and hardly any of these indicate an intention to discontinue or to decrease mother tongue instruction (Table 5.3). Indeed, nearly a third of all units not now offering it indicate that they

TABLE 5.3

Future Plans with Respect to Mother Tongue Instruction by School Type and Current Mother Tongue Instruction

School Type	M.T. Instr.	Future Plans			
		As Currently	Intensify-Improve, Introduce	Decrease-Discont.	Total
All Day	Yes	69%	30%	1%	(100%) 91
	No	84%	16%		(100%) 102
Weekday	Yes	33%	66%	1%	(100%) 64
	No	22%	78%		(100%) 27
Weekend	Yes	48%	48%	4%	(100%) 21
	No	50%	50%		(100%) 12
"Other"	Yes	73%	27%		(100%) 11
	No	88%	12%		(100%) 8
Total		62%	37%	1%	(100%) 336

plan to do so in the future. This percentage is unusually high among Weekday Afternoon and Weekend Schools, where 78% and 50% of the units not now offering such instruction indicate an intention to do so. In All Day Schools and in "Other" Schools, where mother tongue instruction is already a less frequent occurrence, plans to introduce such instruction are far less frequently reported. Of the units that are currently offering mother tongue instruction, 44% plan to intensify or improve such instruction in the future. However, in Weekday Afternoon and Weekend Schools these percentages are 66% and 48% respectively, whereas in All Day and "Other" Schools they are only 30% and 27%. It is possible that many of these plans to introduce, improve, or intensify mother tongue instruction will never materialize, that they are pious wishes at best and "replies to please the researcher" at worst. Nevertheless, they may also be indicative of behavioral tendencies in response to conflicting values; that is, they may reflect behavioral tendencies for conflict resolution. As language maintenance becomes more and more problematic and even dysfunctional with respect to ultimate goals, some schools may seek to overcome the strains in the situation by redoubling their efforts on behalf of language maintenance; others may escape from the strains by slackening their efforts (devaluing the goal). The school types reporting an intent to increase their efforts are the very ones that are already making the greatest efforts or the very ones serving groups for whom language maintenance is still most important.[5] Language maintenance efforts in American ethnic schools are, therefore, likely to become increasingly concentrated in certain school types serving certain ethnic groups.

Even among schools that do offer mother tongue instruction, language mastery remains only one of a number of ultimate goals. Among these, group maintenance is usually far more fundamental than language maintenance. In the primordial ethnic community these two goals were indistinguishable. Under the de-ethnicizing impact of urban mass culture, however, the two have become increasingly unraveled. What, for example, is a school to do if suitable children's literature in the etnic mother tongue becomes increasingly unavailable? Those schools least interested in either language or group maintenance (predominantly All Day Schools) simply discontinue expanding or revising their holdings in the area of ethnicity. The schools most concerned with group maintenance are finally forced to make another compromise. If suitable children's literature in the ethnic mother tongue is unavailable, it seems to them more desirable to provide pupils with English books on ethnic themes – ultimately on ethnic-religious themes – than to lose pupil reading interests entirely. Thus language maintenance itself must often step aside for more ultimate goals (the group, the Church), and it must do so *most* frequently in the future in the very schools in which it has done so *least* frequently in the past. The above mentioned redoubling of effort with respect to language maintenance, if it is to come about at all, must be considered in relation to the entire hierarchy of goals recognized by ethnic groups and by their schools in the United States.

THE ETHNIC SCHOOL TEACHER

The teacher's role in the United States is one that commands little respect. It is more

---

[5] In some cases, mother tongue instruction previously integrated with other ethnic subjects is "broken out" as a separate identifiable subject when language maintenance begins to slip badly. This may explain some of the future instructional plans of schools not currently claiming mother tongue instruction.

frequently associated with economic failure than with positive individual attributes or societal goals. Teaching attracts a large number of young novices who view it as an avenue to immediate income without overly difficult entrance requirements. On the other hand, the lack of prestige and lack of substantial income associated with teaching leads to a constant withdrawal of younger members into marriage (on the part of woman) or into more lucrative and prestigeful fields (on the part of men).

In comparison with the age distribution of teachers in American public schools, that of mother tongue teachers in ethnic schools is five to seven years higher, the median age being in the late forties as compared to 41.5 years for American public school teachers.[6] The most advanced age distribution is that of All Day School teachers, whose median age is in the early 50's, while the youngest is that of Weekday Afternoon School teachers, whose median age is in the early 40's, with teachers in "Other" and Weekend Schools being quite similar to the latter.

Whereas mother tongue teachers in all of the other school types are predominantly foreign born (from 56% to 68%), this is true of only 28% of mother tongue teachers in All Day Schools. It seems that several years ago – perhaps at a time when they were more concerned with language maintenance than they are today – All Day Schools were successful in recruiting and training a large contingent of American born mother tongue teachers. As language maintenance has receded in importance in All Day Schools, very few additional (and, therefore, very few younger) mother tongue teachers have been added. As a result, the largely American born student bodies of ethnically associated All Day Schools receive their mother tongue instruction from American born teachers who are, nevertheless, older than the largely foreign born teachers to whom the largely American born student bodies of other school types are exposed for such instruction. Interesting differences in classroom socio-linguistic dynamics may result under these two different confrontational settings. Pupils in Weekday Afternoon Schools, for example, may identify mother tongue instruction and language maintenance efforts with the homelands of their parents and teachers (and, as a result, with matters that are foreign), while pupils in All Day Schools might be more likely to identify mother tongue instruction and language maintenance efforts with the homelands of their grandparents (and, as a result, with matters that are not only foreign but also old-fashioned and outdated). It is a moot point as to who is psychologically more distant from American born pupils – a young foreign born teacher or an old native born teacher. Given the secular and urban nature of recent immigrants, and given the fact that most mother tongue teachers in All Day Schools are sisters in religious orders, it may well be that the latter are more distant than the former.

Most foreign born mother tongue teachers have arrived in the United States since the Second Warld War. This is particularly true of those who are teaching in other than All Day Schools, since it is only in this latter type that we encounter an appreciable proportion (68%) of currently employed foreign born mother tongue teachers

[6] "Interesting Facts and Figures on American Education", *NEA Research Bulletin*, 41 (1963), No. 1, pp. 3-9.

who arrived during the '30's or earlier. Indeed, foreign born mother tongue teachers in Weekday Afternoon Schools include a very large contingent (37%) that have arrived in the United States as recently as the post-war decade of the 50's. Indications are that all school types are largely dependent on foreign supply for their recruitment of younger mother tongue teachers. American born mother tongue teachers have by no means been as easy to recruit as other teachers in ethnic schools; 50% of all mother tongue teachers are foreign born compared to only 24% of all teachers in ethnic schools.

An overwhelming majority of mother tongue teachers in each school type has received at least some higher education. In most instances this higher education has been pursued in the United States and, therefore, has required the prior mastery of English. Only among mother tongue teachers in Weekend Schools do we encounter a sizable proportion (55%) who have received their education – including their higher education – outside the United States and in countries in which the vernacular is identical with the ethnic mother tongue of the school in which the teacher is currently teaching. In all school types, the proportions of mother tongue teachers formally educated in the United States are greater than the proportions that are American born. Whereas education abroad might indicate greater facility in the mother tongue, education in the United States may mean greater educational and psychological similarity to the largely American born student bodies with which these teachers must interact. Even mother tongue teachers in Weekend Schools, most of whom have been educated abroad, have very frequently studied English before coming to the United States and have mastered it thoroughly soon after their arrival here. In both these respects they are similar to many other post-World War II immigrants and quite dissimilar from their pre-World War I predecessors.

Teacher background characteristics have indirect implications for language maintenance and for teaching proficiency. In all school types the percentage of foreign born teachers is appreciably greater than the percentage of foreign born pupils. Ethnic schools either seek foreign born teachers or fail to attract American born teachers suitable for their programs. The meager financial reward for teaching in such schools is no doubt partially responsible for the relative scarcity of American born teachers on their faculties. In addition, schools that are more strongly oriented toward culture and language maintenance may be unable to locate American born teachers who can adequately present their curricular emphases. Finally, a larger proportion of foreign born teachers than pupils obtains if only because of the generational distinction between these two populations. Nevertheless the proportion of American born teachers in ethnic schools is larger than one might suppose from the facile equation of ethnicity with foreign birth. Somewhat more than three quarters of all teachers employed in these schools in 1960-61 were American born and in no school type does the proportion of American born teachers fall below 44%. The proportion of foreign born teachers among mother tongue teachers in ethnic schools is understandably larger.

Foreign born teachers are most frequently encountered in Weekend Schools and least frequently in All Day Schools – the former being the least Americanized and the latter the most, regardless of whether mother tongue instruction is offered. Nevertheless, in view of the fact that Weekend Schools are so frequently affiliated with recent immigrant groups, the proportion of foreign born teachers in these schools is surprisingly low. The low proportion throughout once again suggests that ethnic schools no longer require a firm foreign born population base and that they engage in many non-ethnic activities for which American born personnel are both more available and more suitable. Marginal ethnicity *does* continue, sometimes for more than one generation beyond the generation of immigrant forebears. In addition, as the marginality of ethnicity grows so do the non-ethnic components of school and organizational programs. In all cases non-ethnic religious curricular material tends to force out non-religious ethnic material. Awareness of this trend once more raises the question: "What is 'ethnic' about ethnic group schools in the United States?"

Just as the high proportion of American born teachers in ethnic schools may be surprising, so may the low proportion of teachers who speak the "mother tongue" only. In all school types, and regardless of whether the mother tongue is or is not taught, this percentage is exceedingly small, varying between 1 and 3 percent. On the other hand, while three quarters of all teachers are American born, only one quarter are reported as speaking "English only". Obviously a substantial number of American born teachers – as many as two thirds – have learned to speak the ethnic mother tongue. Although their degree of mother tongue fluency is not reported and probably varies considerably, it appears that ethnic schools require an appreciable number of teachers who have some grasp of both ethnic and general American linguistic and cultural patterns. They are neither paragons of assimilation nor paragons of retentivism. By and large they are mixtures of both.

Overall, in all types of ethnic schools, about a quarter of the teachers speak only English and the remainder speak both English and the mother tongue. The distribution of languages spoken by teachers – particularly by teachers in schools with language maintenance programs – is, however, more than merely an interesting background variable. The very model of language maintenance depends, to some extent, on which teachers know which languages. If language maintenance consciously or unconsciously functions as a component of separatism, then it would be both quite acceptable and reasonable for many teachers in ethnic schools, particularly mother tongue teachers, to speak only the mother tongue. If, on the other hand, participationism is either the desired or the necessary major approach to current language maintenance in the United States, then it becomes necessary for teachers in these schools to know both English and the mother tongue. Bilingualism – in teacher and pupil – may well be the maximal obtainable goal, as well as the optimal goal, for language maintenance adherents in American ethnic groups today. Indeed, it may be necessary to differentiate between language maintenance *dedication* and language maintenance *effectiveness* among teachers in those ethnic schools that do pursue language maintenance goals.

Given the nativity distribution of pupils attending ethnic schools – and, more important, given their general cultural orientation – the teacher who does not know English would seem to be too distant psychologically from the pupils in attendance. An overly zealous champion of the ethnic mother tongue may antagonize pupils by his inflexible insistence on using the mother tongue; without a mastery of American English and of American ways the teacher may be unable to communicate to his pupils the very devotion that characterizes and inspires him; he may succeed in doing nothing more than identifying language maintenance in the minds of his pupils with "foreignness" rather than with a point of view or a mode of behavior that can find roots and prosper on American soil. Finally, attendance at ethnic schools is entirely "at the pleasure" of pupils and their parents. A teacher who is "too foreign" (or, in rare cases, too American) may elicit protests and even dropouts. Currently, an American born teacher with a less-than-native command of the mother tongue, if properly oriented and motivated, may accomplish more for language maintenance and ethnic self-identification among the predominantly American born pupils of ethnic schools than can foreign born teachers in general and non-English speaking teachers in particular. Currently, the best compromise easily available to schools concerned with language maintenance is the foreign born teacher who knows both English and the mother tongue. Ultimately, since the supply of such teachers is constantly diminishing, the language maintenance function of the school will depend on its ability to train, attract, and retain American born teachers who have the necessary attitudinal and linguistic characteristics that make the pursuit of language maintenance possible.

The current distribution of languages spoken by teachers in ethnic schools – namely, a high proportion of bilingual, American born teachers (many of whom are not mother tongue teachers) – augurs well for participationist language maintenance, provided this is the genuine desire of the groups involved and provided that ability to speak the mother tongue is not too carelessly (minimally) defined. Certainly, corps of dedicated American born teachers who adequately master their respective non-English mother tongues would constitute very powerful models and influences on behalf of positive language maintenance attitudes and skills among pupils in ethnic schools. Indeed, the preparation of just such teachers might very well represent an appropriate goal for those schools in which language maintenance continues to be a serious concern.

In the United States as a whole a majority of teachers – particularly those at the elementary level – currently hold no more than undergraduate degrees. There is a growing tendency to require a master's degree – particularly for teachers at the secondary education level – from those teachers who desire permanent certification by state or local educational authorities.[7] This tendency will be reinforced by the continued conversion of state teachers colleges into liberal arts colleges and by the progressive

---

[7]   See: "Interesting Facts and Figures on American Education", *NEA Research Bulletin*, 41 (1963), No. 1, pp. 3-9. Forty-three states and the District of Columbia require the bachelor's degree for "regular certification" of beginning elementary school teachers. The remaining states have lower requirements.

displacement of professional teacher-training from the undergraduate into the graduate level. The general academic credentials of mother tongue teachers in ethnic schools are slightly inferior to those of elementary and secondary teachers in American public schools. Whereas 12% of mother tongue teachers have received no higher education (these being largely concentrated in other than All Day Schools), only 4% of American public school teachers had received no higher education at all as of 1956-57.[8] Because the total amount of time devoted to professional teacher training usually amounts to no more than a year or two, the vast majority of American teachers *have* received such professional training. However, whereas 88% of mother tongue teachers have obtained some higher education, almost half (47%) have obtained no formal teacher training in the process. Inasmuch as the *functional significance* of teacher training for teacher effectiveness is still a moot point on the American educational scene (Conant 1963), it is not possible to conclude whether the absence of such training is actually detrimental to the teaching effectiveness of mother tongue teachers. Nevertheless, the relative deficiency in such training among mother tongue teachers when compared to public school teachers is likely to be known to parents and pupils and may contribute to an overall negative image. Yet mother tongue teachers are an intellectual elite among teachers in ethnic schools, inasmuch as they have more frequently obtained both higher education and teacher training than have the other teachers. It would be interesting to determine whether this too is known by parents and pupils.

How actively involved are mother tongue teachers in the daily life and formal activities of the ethnic group whose language they teach? Although newspapers and organizations may have played little or no role in pre-immigration ethnicity, such formal and purposive devices are basic to communal cohesion in American cities. Therefore, it is useful to inquire whether mother tongue teachers are really "insiders" in ethnic associational society – psychologically, socially and culturally – or whether they are "peripheralists" (Lewin 1948) whose orientation is outward, away from the ethnic group, and for whom mother tongue teaching is a conflicted status. We have only a few, indirect indices pertaining to this area of inquiry but their implications are far-reaching.

The ethnic group press – including both newspapers and journals – has been considered an avenue through which strong group ties are expressed and reinforced among immigrants living in the midst of an urban society. It becomes a visible link between scattered readers. Its loyalists staunchly extol its group maintenance virtues: ethnic group news, features, editorials, and advertisements not carried by the general press. Its detractors – whose ethnic backgrounds may be equally immediate – charge that the news carried by the ethnic press is usually a day or more late, that it is copied from the English press, that its contents and emphases are archaic and stodgy, that its uniqueness is inconsequential, etc. (Fishman 1960). Obviously, both these views are arrived at on the basis of equally selective perception and interpretation. Our problem is to

[8]   U.S. Office of Education, *Circular*, No. 644 (1961).

determine the points, relative to these two extreme views, that best characterize mother tongue teachers in various school types.

Our data reveal that the great majority of mother tongue teachers in all school types regularly read one or more ethnic newspapers or journals, not all of which are necessarily in the mother tongue. In this relatively passive and private sense, at least, they are embedded in the ethnic world whose mother tongue they teach. Nevertheless, there are interesting differences in this respect between the four structural contexts of mother tongue teaching. The ethnic newspapers and journals regularly read by mother tongue teachers in All Day Schools are subscribed for by their schools or parishes, are published by the orders to which teachers belong (or by allied religious organizations), are more accurately characterizable as religious rather than ethnic publications, and are more frequently in English than are the ethnic publications read by mother tongue teachers in other school types. Thus, mother tongue teachers in All Day Schools may more accurately be said to be concerned with the de-ethnicizing institutional press than concerned with the ethnic press (or through it, with the ethnic community). Very few mother tongue teachers write for the ethnic press in the mother tongue, only some 18% of all mother tongue teachers claiming to do so. Another 3% claim to write for the ethnic group press in English. Almost all of those in either of these categories are attached to weekday afternoon or weekend schools. In summary, the ethnic press preferences of most mother tongue teachers in All Day Schools are largely of a religious nature, expressed through "official" English media, and institutionally rather than individually patterned; the preferences of most mother tongue teachers in the other major school types seem to be much more ethnic, and are more often individually arranged and expressed through non-English media.

Mother tongue teachers in All Day Schools are least frequently affiliated with ethnic organizations (16%), while even those few who are affiliated have least frequently been officers of these organizations (53%). Once again, we find that mother tongue teachers in Weekday Afternoon Schools stand at the other extreme; they are most frequently affiliated with ethnic organizations (76%) and those who are affiliated have most frequently been officers as well (also 76%). Mother tongue teachers in Weekend Schools and in "Other" schools stand close to the affiliational pattern of their counterparts in Weekday Afternoon Schools, but in the office-holding pattern they stand closer to those in All Day Schools. Their overall interaction with ethnic organizations may be said to be intermediate between the two delineated extremes.

Our two indices of ethnic group embeddedness – inadequate though they are – indicate such involvement for between half and three-quarters of mother tongue teachers in three school types – Weekday Afternoon, Weekend, and "Other" – while implying that such involvement is quite rare (15 to 20%) among mother tongue teachers in All Day Schools. American nativity, more advanced age, enrollment in religious orders, and lack of special training for the mother tongue teacher role may all be involved in the latter's low participation. Indeed, it would seem that the typical mother tongue teacher in All Day Schools is an "outsider" from the point of view of ethnic group life.

To our prior evidence that ethnically related All Day Schools tend to be least linguistically retentive and least ethnically oriented, we can now add evidence that mother tongue teachers functioning within these schools are also characterizable in similar terms.

TEACHER ESTIMATES OF MOTHER TONGUE KNOWLEDGE AND ATTITUDES OF THEIR PUPILS

Important though they doubtless are, the most desirable teacher characteristics are not sufficient for the achievement of language mastery, let alone language maintenance. There are other realities to cope with and among these the most immediate and the most painful is the pupil. The primordial ethnic collectivity usually knew neither official pupil nor official teacher, although it did differentiate skilled and unskilled, novice and expert. The classical mother tongue teacher who was accepted into this non-purposive and traditional society, even though he was the bearer of formal associationism and functional differentiation, was accepted largely because he was willing to begin by identifying with tradition. A bond of mutual affection – almost Emile-like, if we are to believe personal recollections and literary recreations – grew up between teachers and pupils. As the teacher accepted the concreteness and the particularism of local village traditions and symbols, his pupils drew closer to the more general and more abstract symbols (transcending local attachments and local loyalties) of the consciously evolved and transmuted traditions represented by the teacher. Thus, an affinity and unity of pupils and teachers were at the base of the classical mother tongue teacher's "methodology". Later, during the accelerating breakdown of the ethnic community under the impact of 20th century nationalism, industrialization, and urbanization, the mother tongue teacher's success depended largely on the accelerated surrender of "little" tradition to "great" tradition and on the material gain and social status which the latter alone could provide in a mobile secular society. Under these circumstances the mother tongue teacher may have been less loved (for education now became compulsory) but he was clearly the bringer of light. As such, a common purposive bond still united pupils and teachers.

On the American educational scene many commentators have noted a slow falling away of initially positive attitudes toward school-learning as pupils proceed into successively higher grades. It is as if the school neutralized or antagonized an initial reservoir of naive good feeling deposited in advance to its credit. For whatever set of complex reasons, the American school tends to lose favor even with pupils who initially are favorably disposed to it, and elicits a feeling of growing resentment toward formal learning (Friedenburg 1962; Friedenburg 1963). As a result, adolescent culture within the American high school and college frequently incorporates substantial anti-intellectual or, at best, non-intellectual overtones (Becker et al. 1962; Coleman 1961; Tannenbaum 1962). Given the above set of circumstances in American society at large, it is probably less surprising than it might otherwise be to observe that students in ethnic group schools show a decline in favorable attitudes toward the mother tongue, from 74% to 47%, from the first to the second half of the elementary program (Table 5.4). Nevertheless, there are interesting differences between school types in this respect.

TABLE 5.4

*Mother Tongue Teacher Estimates of Language Attitudes of Pupils
at the Beginning and at the End of the Elementary School Program
in Various School Types*

School Type	Language Attitudes						
	First Half of Elementary School Program				Second Half of Elementary School Program		
	Fav.	Neut.	Unfav.	Total	Fav.	Neut.	Unfav.
All Day	40%	53%	7%	100% (120)	49%	47%	4%
Weekday	74%	21%	5%	100% (73)	48%	51%	1%
Weekend	65%	34%	1%	100% (86)	43%	57%	—
Other	78%	19%	3%	100% (37)	43%	54%	3%
Total	74%	21%	5%	100% (316)	47%	51%	2%

During the first half of the elementary school program we find mother tongue teachers in All Day Schools standing apart – as they do in so many other respects. Less than half (40%) report favorable student attitudes toward the mother tongue, whereas in other school types two thirds to three fourths of all mother tongue teachers make this claim. The relative infrequency of favorable pupil attitudes during the first half of the elementary All Day School program may be related to the fact that somewhat fewer All Day School pupils begin formal study of the ethnic mother tongue during this period. Not only are many mother tongue teachers in these schools likely to be less familiar with early pupil attitudes but, in addition, they are likely to interpret the lack of formal mother tongue instruction during the early elementary years as being indicative of a lack of positive pupil attitudes; certainly, when Church and school authorities have been called upon to explain the absence of mother tongue instruction in All Day Schools, they have frequently done so in terms of disinterest or opposition on the part of parents and pupils. The greater representation of other-ethnic and non-ethnic children among All Day School pupils may also contribute to the lesser frequency of positive attitudes toward the mother tongue. Finally, the weaker language maintenance interests and the more marginal ethnicity of mother tongue teachers in All Day Schools would help to explain the difference.

By the second half of the elementary program, we find that roughly half the mother tongue teachers in all school types claim favorable attitudes on the part of pupils. Although this yields a 9% increase for All Day School teachers, it represents a decrease for teachers in all other school types. The reasons for this falling off of pupil interest are many. Awareness that non-English language mastery is frequently viewed as an indication of "hyphenated Americanism" rather than as a valuable attribute develops during this period (ages 10-14). At the same time, the ethnic group child begins to "outgrow" fragmentary ethnicity and to "unlearn" the mother tongue as he draws closer to the occupationally integrated and functionally differentiated American society and its mobile mass culture – a society and culture for which neither his family nor his ethnic school can prepare him adequately. Thus, the language attitudes of pupils change as the role and the centrality of their ethnicity continues to change from early childhood through advancing adolescence. Whereas the ethnic school, the ethnic church, the ethnic youth organization, and the ethnic family can frequently fill the lives of younger pupils, it becomes progressively harder for them to do so as these children mature and come increasingly under the influence of non-ethnic media, value systems, and behavior patterns. While some may follow the classical "second genera-tion" pattern of totally rejecting ethnicity, most currently follow the more selective "third generation" pattern of choosing and idealizing those aspects of ethnicity which are least incongruent and competitive with dominant, non-ethnic modes of behavior and systems of values. In the latter case, we would expect certain ethnic subjects to rise in the estimation of pupils in ethnic group schools as others fall. This is precisely what we find. That the mother tongue is one of those experiencing a sharp drop indi-cates the dependence of language maintenance on either a well articulated and all encompassing way of life or a similarly powerful *weltanschauung*, two desiderata which most ethnic groups lose after (and even during) their first generation in American urban centers.

Finally, instructional factors also enter into the decreasing popularity of the mother tongue as children enter adolescence. The inevitable lack of even and continued pro-gress in language learning during the earlier years ("inevitable" in that 1-3 hours per week are really not sufficient for progressive mastery of a language not reinforced outside the ethnic school and a very few other ethnic group settings) exacts its own toll in pupil interest by the time pupils enter the second half of the elementary school program. They find that they are frequently still studying the same texts, reviewing the same grammatical rules, and becoming increasingly unable to express their more complex and mature thoughts in the mother tongue at the very same time they are beginning to wonder why they "need" to learn "that language" anyway, what "use" it can possibly be to them, and what "others" will think of them for knowing it.

Mother tongue teachers are practically unanimous in attributing the positive mother tongue attitudes of their pupils primarily to positive attitudes on the part of the parents of these pupils. Nearly 75% of all reasons advanced for positive pupil attitudes fall into this single category. Use of the mother tongue at home is viewed as not enough in itself, since use is often accompanied by attitudinal neutrality or even by negativeness. Nor is the influence of the Church, of the teachers themselves, or of grandparents frequently referred to. Negative attitudes are attributed to a somewhat greater variety of sources and reveal greater differences between mother tongue teachers in the various school types. Once again, parental attitudes (indifference and hostility) are considered to be the primary source of negative pupil attitudes, but this time only about 60% of all reasons advanced fall into this category. Parental ignorance of the mother tongue is quite frequently referred to by teachers in All Day Schools. This is undoubtedly a reflection of the more Americanized and "other ethnic" character of parents whose children attend All Day Schools. Lack of sufficient time in the school program is frequently mentioned by teachers in Weekday Afternoon Schools, and the "drive toward Amesicanization" by teachers in Weekend Schools.

The reasons advanced by mother tongue teachers are, to be sure, oversimplified and primarily derived from their own immediate environments. That the "drive toward Americanization" was so rarely advanced as a reason for negative pupil attitudes indicates that conceptual-analytic reasons were rarely employed by these teachers. Rather, the pupil's home environment was readily seized upon for major blame or praise. Mother tongue teachers appear convinced that given the backing of a home environment positively disposed toward the mother tongue, teachers would still have some opportunity for attaining the language attitude goals they desire. Lacking such conscientious support from the home, they feel they have little hope of eliciting positive attitudes in their pupils.

Reading appears to be the aspect of language "mastery" most frequently attained, followed by "understanding" (which often may be limited to understanding the teacher's carefully simplified communications). The two most active forms of language mastery – writing and speaking – are the very ones in which fluency is least frequently claimed (Table 5.5). Nevertheless, a decided increase in claimed speaking fluency is evidenced between the first and last grades of mother tongue instruction. The report by mother tongue teachers that their pupils more frequently attain proficiency in the

TABLE 5.5

Typical Mother Tongue Knowledge of Pupils upon completing Highest Grade of Instruction as estimated by Mother Tongue Teachers in Various School Types

School Type	Aspects of Language Mastery								
	Understanding		Reading		Writing		Speaking		Total n
	Fair	Fluent	Fair	Fluent	Fair	Fluent	Fair	Fluent	
All Day	36%	22%	33%	28%	37%	14%	36%	13%	120
Weekday	32%	45%	18%	62%	41%	34%	55%	19%	73
Weekend	23%	40%	23%	40%	41%	17%	27%	30%	86
Other	35%	32%	11%	57%	27%	38%	22%	30%	37
Total	31%	33%	24%	42%	38%	22%	36%	21%	316

passive than in *active* aspects of language mastery is similar to many reports of general foreign language instruction in the United States. It may well be that the mother tongue proficiency levels attained by pupils in ethnic schools are quite similar to those attained by students in many American secondary schools after similar periods of instruction (Mustard 1962). It should be pointed out, however, that in the former such proficiency is usually reached earlier and under much less favorable learning circumstances.

Mother tongue teachers in ethnic schools at most levels of instruction agree that the mother tongue is not the most popular ethnic subject among their pupils. The popularity of other ethnic subjects tends to rise as that of the mother tongue wanes with successive years of study. Although a great variety of other ethnic subjects are reported as "favorites", the ethnic arts (music, singing, dancing, graphic arts) are named most frequently. If it is true that the arts are preferred to the mother tongue, this must be viewed not merely as a "childish preference for the colorful and dramatic" but as a preference for idealized and selected aspects of ethnicity over either its daily behavioral oral or its symbolic-idealogical implementation. Mother tongue fluency fails to lead ethnic adolescents in the direction of any kind of meaningful ethnicity, while at the same time it is often perceived as threatening several highly desirable goals and interactions which depend upon acceptance by American core society. The ethnic arts, on the other hand, carry quite different implications. Unlike the mother tongue they have lost their former association with daily ethnicity – whether at the "little" or the "great" culture level – and have become associated with special "occasions" or "events". For the young, the concerts, pageants, fairs, exhibitions, and celebrations with which the ethnic arts are associated represent a highly selected, rewarding, and non-threatening link with the associational ethnicity of the adult world as well as an acceptable direction to their own striving for an ethnicity which is purified and minimal. The proficiency and the pleasure gained through the ethnic arts remain a link which is frequently activated during parenthood when these former pupils have their own children to direct.

Is the mother tongue teacher himself a "true believer", a devoted protagonist of language maintenance? We have largely assumed thus far that such is the case for most mother tongue teachers. This assumption is justifiable to the extent that most people make some emotional investment in their life work even when it is by and large regarded as a "job of work". Moreover, most people tend to become increasingly convinced by the roles and positions they take even if they were not initially in full rapport with them. However, the degree and singleness of commitment are at issue here, for it is only if we know about these that we can fully appreciate the difficulties and dilemmas of mother tongue teachers, and the hopes and aspirations they may bring to their work. The classical mother tongue teacher was peculiarly a man of ideals and of idealism. These characteristics not only prompted him to undertake the more difficult life "among the people", rather than to pursue a career of greater personal advantage, but also strengthened and directed him in the face of reverses. The mother tongue teacher in the United States, however, is not the "influential" that his predecessor was. Is it possible for him to be the same kind of loyalist?

Conceived of in the most general sense, two broad and separate categories of goals are currently available to mother tongue teachers. One, it is possible to aim at functional bilingualism as a component of functional ethnicity, i.e., ethnicity that is oriented primarily toward the level of modified "little" tradition. Two, it is possible to aim at cultural bilingualism as a component of biculturality, i.e., ethnicity that is oriented primarily toward the level of modified "great" tradition. The first approach to language maintenance concentrates on speaking facility, the second on psychological justification. The first approach emphasizes ethnic *behavior*, in language as in other ethnic domains; the second, ethnic *appreciations*. While it is possible to artfully combine these goals, given a very able and sophisticated teacher, just as it is possible to artlessly subvert them both to a sterile professionalism, most usually one or the other of them is clearly preferred.

By far the most frequent complaint registered by mother tongue teachers is that their pupils do not speak the ethnic mother tongue by the time they reach the highest year of instruction. This might be taken to indicate that mother tongue teachers primarily pursue the first approach to language maintenance, that of behavioral rather than appreciational ethnicity. They almost unanimously attribute their instructional difficulties to parental indifference or opposition. They appear to sense a basic disparity between themselves and the parents and children they wish to serve or influence. Whereas many mother tongue teachers still retain a dedication to a goal and a value which the entire ethnic community once shared and reinforced, they are now increasingly in the position of holding onto something which others have abandoned.

ATTITUDINAL DETERMINANTS AMONG MOTHER TONGUE TEACHERS

When asked to name the two most respected "foreign languages" in the United States, mother tongue teachers again reacted with great unanimity. In all school types French and Spanish are considered to be by far the most respected. German, while it rates a poor third, is mentioned many times more frequently than any of the mother tongues of non-European or of eastern or southern European ethnic groups. In general, four clusters of languages appear in connection with the "respect" nominations of mother tongue teachers.

a. *Mother tongues not nominated by any of their own teachers or by any teachers of other languages*: Armenian, Chinese, Czech, Estonian, Hungarian, Latvian, Rumanian, Slovak, Slovene, Yiddish, and Ruthenian. These are all either non-European or eastern and southern European languages.
b. *Mother tongues nominated by only a small percentage of their own teachers and not nominated by any others*: Croatian, Greek, Hebrew, Italian, Lithuanian, Polish,

and Ukrainian. Once again we note only eastern and southern European or non-European languages.

c. *Mother tongues nominated by all or most of their own teachers as well as by many others*: French, Spanish, and German.

d. *Finally, two languages which were nominated although there were no teachers of these languages in our sample*: Russian and Latin. Here we find one language which currently has great political and scientific prestige, and one which is not a mother tongue but has firmly established religious and cultural significance.

This categorization into untouchable, unenviable, enviable, and holy languages is one that probably a large portion of the American public would accept. For our present interest, however, the classification reveals that many teachers do not consider the mother tongue they are teaching to be among the most respected. Only 21% of all responding teachers nominated their own mother tongue. If we remove the mother tongue teachers of French, Spanish, and German from further consideration, we find that hardly any others nominated their own mother tongues as being among the two most respected. These latter teachers are fully aware that the language to which they are devoted enjoys little or no respect in the United States. Indeed, even French and Spanish may be significantly more respected in theory – i.e., in regions of the United States where they are not frequently employed by large numbers of ethnic speakers – than in practice (viz., French in New England, Spanish in the Southwest).

Awareness that the "apple of one's eye" is not even respected by most others, let alone adored, may be painful indeed. Nonetheless, most of us experience something to this effect during our lives – and recover without permanent disability. Mother tongue teachers of non-prestige languages continue to function appropriately and acceptably, in ethnic as well as in non-ethnic milieus. Yet just as a tinge of disaffection characterizes many of their relationships with the students and parents they interact with, so a tinge of alienation may mark their relationship with American society at large. The long-term impact on their work and on their convictions is perhaps particularly important with respect to mother tongue teachers in Weekday Afternoon and Weekend Schools, the overwhelming majority of whom are associated with languages they believe to be "unenviable" or "untouchable". Insufficiency of respect may either galvanize or depress mother tongue teachers, depending upon their pre-existing and concurrent orientations.

The most common explanation advanced by teachers for the lack of respect encountered by their mother tongue is that it is not sufficiently taught in American (i.e., non-ethnic) schools or colleges. Teachers of "untouchable" and "unenviable" tongues are frequently embarrassed by the utilitarian approach to language learning of their own pupils and countrymen. With the decline of ethnicity, many come to believe that if language X is not even recognized by "American" high schools, and if "American" colleges will grant no entrance credit for having mastered it, then what is the use of learning language X and what kind of language can it possibly be? Thus, for minority group members standards of evaluation (in language as in most other matters) often come from "outside" their own group. Mother tongue teachers are by no means immune to such influences. If the "outside" school does not show respect for language X by offering it as a language of instruction, then how can "insiders", particularly the young, grow up to respect it? This line of reasoning may go far to explain the eagerness of several smaller, non-prestigeful language groups to endow a chair for their language at various major American universities. It is as much (if not more) a means of endowing "respect" for the mother tongue as it is of preparing additional scholars or speakers.

Other frequently reported explanations for insufficiency of respect are: negative "American" attitudes toward the mother country (particularly in All Day Schools and primarily among Polish mother tongue teachers); most nationals speak their mother tongue poorly or not at all (particularly in Weekday Afternoon Schools and primarily among Greek and Yiddish mother tongue teachers); few high status Americans speak or know about the mother tongue (particularly in Weekend Schools and primarily among Latvian mother tongue teachers). The loci of "sufficient" respect are, generally speaking, inverse images of the loci of insufficient respect. Thus, sufficient respect is most frequently explained on the basis of positive "American" attitudes toward the home country, and the fact that the mother tongue is well and frequently taught in "American" schools. Here again, the predominant forces leading to respect are "outside" forces, far removed from the cotrol of mother tongue teachers themselves, as well as from the control of ethnic communities, parents, or pupils.

Apparently, mother tongue teachers differentiate almost completely between the loci of their instructional successes and failures and the loci of their mother tongue's prestige. On the one hand, they attribute responsibility in instructional matters to "ingroup" factors – primarily to the parents and homes of their pupils. On the other hand, they attribute responsibility in matters of language prestige to "outgroup" factors – primarily of a general political and educational variety. Mother tongue teachers do not refer to language prestige as a factor influencing their instructional outcomes.

All in all, mother tongue teachers in ethnic group schools do not view themselves as powerful factors in language maintenance. They do not believe that their pupils accomplish overly much – particularly in the more active domains of language mastery. They also report that as their pupils grow older and advance through the grades they become decreasingly interested in mother tongue instruction (also note Lambert et al. 1958). Mother tongue teachers attribute this and other instructional difficulties to parental apathy or opposition to the mother tongue. They most frequently view their language as not being among the most prestigeful in the United States, and attribute this to general American rather than to ethnic group factors. As a result of these many internal, external, and personal pressures most mother tongue teachers either have ceased being believers in language maintenance or they are hanging onto this belief in the face of discouraging evidence and even more discouraging odds.

Mother tongue teachers in All Day Schools – the same teachers who are themselves least ethnically embedded, who make the most minimal claims concerning the language mastery of their pupils, and who consistently seem to be less characterizable as language maintenance centered – more frequently claim that group continuity *is impossible* without continuity of the mother tongue than do the appreciable more language maintenance oriented mother tongue teachers in Weekday Afternoon Schools. Thus, we have a seeming incongruence of attitude to cope with (Table 5.6). Moreover,

TABLE 5.6

Attitudes of Mother Tongue Teachers in various School Types Concerning Possibility of Group Continuity in the U.S. without Mother Tongue

School Type	Can Group Continue in U.S. without Mother Tongue?			
	Yes	No	N.R.	Total
All Day	58%	39%	3%	100% (120)
Weekday Afternoon	81%	19%	—	100% (73)
Weekend	55%	44%	1%	100% (86)
Other	65%	30%	5%	100% (37)
Total	63%	35%	2%	100% (316)

while the language oriented mother tongue teachers of Weekday Afternoon Schools stand out in their readiness to claim that group continuity *is possible* without language maintenance, Weekend and All Day School teachers – so far apart on all other language maintenance indices – now stand closer together by more frequently implying that group continuity without language continuity *is impossible*. How can this incongruence be explained? Three patterns seem to be involved here.

All Day School mother tongue teachers who claim that without the mother tongue their ethnic group cannot continue to exist also seem to be as eager for the Americanization of their ethnic group as they are minimalistic with respect to language maintenance. Their language maintenance pessimism not only has its counterpart in group maintenance pessimism but they do not even consider group maintenance to be a desired goal. The interest of the Catholic Church in becoming an "American Church" (i.e., a non-ethnic church) may influence the group maintenance attitudes of mother tongue teachers in All Day Schools (Rossi and Rossi 1961) just as much as it influences their language maintenance goals. Thus, mother tongue teachers in All Day Schools may be neither disappointed nor broken in spirit, but, rather, reluctant servants who long ago were assigned to tasks which they find distasteful and toward which they are frequently unsympathetic.

On the other hand, the secular mother tongue teachers in Weekend Schools are bruised but unbowed. Most of them think that their ethnic group cannot continue to exist without language maintenance and, therefore, they are oriented toward redoubling their efforts on its behalf. In their case, the total integrated constellation of ethnicity, religion, and language has not yet lost its holistic appearance. The elements constituting the "whole" are considered inseparable and equally valuable.

Finally, the mother tongue teachers in Weekday Afternoon Schools – many of them under religious auspices – are broken and bowed, but by no means unconcerned. As vibrant language maintenance seems to become an ever more impossible goal, they have by and large withdrawn to a more fundamental goal: group maintenance. Religion, culture, tradition, etc. – all the things that language maintenance is initially believed to be inseparable from and conducive to – are ultimately seen as salvageable even without language maintenance. When a cultural constellation breaks, certain elements disappear more quickly than others. The Weekday Afternoon Schools hold onto the non-linguistic relics of their ethnicity. Since religious institutions are the strongest among these fragments, their ethnicity too has become a matter of identification and belief rather than of daily life.

Cognitive dissonance theory leads us to predict that when two values are in conflict some change in their relative valuation will occur (Festinger 1957). The two values under consideration here are language maintenance and group maintenance. Our respondents were asked to choose between them as if they were incompatible. Mother tongue teachers in All Day Schools seem to have surrendered on both scores. For them neither of the values has great attraction and they are both incompatible with a third and more basic loyalty: the Church. Mother tongue teachers in Weekday Afternoon Schools also revert to a more basic value, group maintenance, when language maintenance is seen as unattainable. Mother tongue teachers in Weekend Schools (where teachers, parents, and pupils alike have more recent immigrant roots) indicate that they are not yet ready to withdraw from language maintenance, for without it they see no hope for group maintenance.

There is a continuum of intersecting devotions when two interrelated loyalties are under stress so that one is made to appear incompatible with the other. At one extreme both values may be reinforced so that the conflicted choice point is not below the motivational level.[9] At another extreme both values may be abandoned. The intermediate position is that in which one value gives way to another which is more fundamental or central in an individual's or group's scheme of values. In the context of participationism in American core society, and given a constant diminution of the percentage as well as the absolute number of foreign born, this "continuum of devotion" may represent different stages of withdrawal from the struggle for ethnic and linguistic continuity. Initially, when the conflict first appears, the "true believers" are young, strong and hopeful enough to reject the conflict and to hold out staunchly for

[9] See Robert F. Weiss, "Defection from Social Movements and Subsequent Recruitment to New Movements", *Sociometry*, 28 (1963), 1-20, for a recent application of psychological conflict theory to socio-ideological movements.

both goals. Group maintenance is not seen as possible without language maintenance and, therefore, the latter is not expendable. Subsequently, with continued attrition and reverses, the more ultimate goal – group maintenance – is protected and language maintenance is reluctantly abandoned or, at least, declaired unlikely. Group maintenance is viewed as still possible, even after language maintenance is no longer feasible. The latter is expendable whereas the former is not. Finally, after further reverses and ideological readjustments, both goals become expendable. Although the interrelatedness of the two goals is still acknowledged, both goals are no longer sufficiently prized to merit the struggle. Indeed, both goals may be declared thankless and ultimately rejected (Fishman and Nahirny 1964b). Mother tongue teachers in Weekend, Weekday Afternoon and Allday ethnic schools tend to reflect these three sequential positions at the present time.

REFERENCES

Becker, H. S., Blanche Geer, E. C. Hughes, and A. L. Strauss, *Boys in White* (Chicago, University of Chicago Press, 1962).

Coleman, J. S., *The Adolescent Society* (New York, Free Press, 1961).

Conant, J., *The Education of American Teachers* (New York, McGraw-Hill, 1963).

DeMarco, A. A., *The Church of Rome and the Problem of the Vernacular Versus the Liturgical Language* (Washington, D.C., Catholic Univ. of America Press, 1960).

Festinger, L., *A Theory of Cognitive Dissonance* (Stanford, Stanford Univ. Press, 1957).

Fishman, J. A., "New York's Non-English Dailies and the Deliveryman's Strike", *Journalism Quarterly*, 37 (1960), 241-254.

——, and Nahirny, V. C., "The Ethnic Group School in the United States", in Fishman, J. A., et al., *Language Loyalty in the United States* (New York, Yeshiva University, 1962a). Chapter 6. (Mimeo.)

——, and Nahirny, V. C., "The Mother Tongue Teacher in Ethnic Group Schools in the United States", in Fishman, J. A., et al., *Language Loyalty in the United States* (New York, Yeshiva University, 1962b), Chapter 7. (Mimeo.)

Friedenburg, E. Z., Review of J. S. Coleman's *The Adolescent Society*, in *Commentary*, 32 (1962), No. 5, 445-447.

——, "The Social Role of the High Schools", *College Board Review*, No. 49 (1963), 30-36.

Glazer, N., and D. P. Moynihan, *Beyond the Melting Pot* (Cambridge, The M.I.T. Press and Harvard University Press, 1963).

Gordon, M. M., "Assimilation in America: Theory and Reality", *Daedalus*, Spring 1961, pp. 263-285.

——, *Assimilation in American Life* (New York-Oxford, 1964).

Lambert, W. E., J. Havelka, and C. Crosby, "The Influence of Language Acquisition Contexts on Bilingualism", *Journal of Abnormal and Social Psychology*, 56 (1958), 239-244.

Lewin, K., "Self Hatred among Jews", in *Resolving Social Conflicts*, G. W. Lewin, ed. (New York, Harper, 1948).

Mustard, Helen M., "A Survey of Language Schools not under Academic Auspices", in *Reports of Surveys and Studies in the Teaching of Modern Foreign Languages* (New York, Modern Language Association, 1962 (?)), 187-196.

Rossi, P. H., and Alice S. Rossi, "Some Effects of Parochial-school Education in America", *Daedalus*, Spring 1961, 300-328.

Tannenbaum, A. J., *Adolescent Attitudes toward Academic Brilliance* (New York, Teachers College, Columbia University, 1962).

6. MOTHER TONGUE RETENTIVENESS IN ETHNIC PARISHES

JOHN E. HOFMAN

"Ethnic parishes" were originally organized by or on behalf of those who, for varying reasons, felt it necessary or desirable to utilize and preserve their non-English language and other ethnic traditions in Church-related activities. In the Catholic Church the ethnic ("national") parish became a form of organization enjoying official recognition. Similar units were also organized by various Protestant and other churches catering to individuals of immigrant or semi-indigenous ethnic background. The ethnic parish may be contrasted with the more prevalent form of parish organization, the territorial parish, which draws its membership from the area in which it is located, regardless of the ethnic origin or composition of its constituents.

CATHOLIC AND ORTHODOX PARISHES

Language maintenance (or its absence) is reflected, as are so many things, at two different levels of behavior: (a) what people do and (b) how they feel about what they do. The questions directed at ethnic parishes by the Language Resources Project sought to gather information at both these levels. The extent to which ethnic mother tongues continue to be used in religious services, in the schools sponsored by the ethnic parish, and in the organizations affiliated with it were subjects of inquiry, as well as the attitudes of parish members, as perceived by responding pastors, and the attitudes of the pastors themselves toward the future prospects of language maintenance. Table 6.1 reports the current frequency of mother tongue use in sermons (this being the most thoroughly reported and apparently the most reliable index of language maintenance in the ethnic parish) and the current frequency of mother tongue instruction in Roman Catholic, Greek Catholic and Eastern Orthodox ethnic parishes and parish-affiliated schools of all types. In addition, the interest expressed by pastors in the continued use of the mother tongue in these two contexts is shown.

Our data reveal widespread *interest* (77.5%) in the continued *use* of non-English mother tongues in the sermons of Catholic and Orthodox ethnic parishes. In addition, if we may use the sermon as an appropriate index of language maintenance in ethnic parishes – and we shall presently justify the use of that index – we find that in 75.4% of these parishes at least some sermons are still preached in the mother tongue. How-

TABLE 6.1

Language Maintenance Characteristics of Ethnic Parish Sample

a. Mother Tongue in Sermons

Actual Use			Interest in Continuation		
	N	%		N	%
Mother Tongue only	213	14.8	Interested	1118	77.5
More Mother Tongue	139	9.6	Not Int.	302	20.9
Half and Half	511	35.4	No Answer	22	1.6
More English	225	15.6 75.4%			
English only	323	22.4			
No Answer	31	2.2 24.6%			
Total Parishes	1442	100.0	Total Parishes	1442	100.0

b. Mother Tongue in Parish Schools of All Types

Actually Taught			Interest in Continuation		
	N	%		N	%
Through 1961	439	30.4	Interested	539	37.4
No Longer Taught	141	9.8	Not Int.	20	1.4
No Answer	862	59.8	No Answer	883	61.2
Total Parishes	1442	100.0	Total Parishes	1442	100.0

ever, when we turn to mother tongue instruction in parish schools, only 37.4% of ethnic parishes appear to favor this form of language maintenance, while only 30.4% still practiced it as of 1961.

On the most general level, then, we note that *interest* in the preservation of the mother tongue is slightly more prevalent than *practice*. More important is the fact that both interest and practice are much higher in connection with sermons (largely directed at first-generation adults) than with instruction (largely directed at second- or third-generation children and adolescents). The difference between these percentages invites us to speculate concerning the image of the future of language maintenance held by most pastors of ethnic parishes. Language maintenance is still frequently desired – but "in its place", viz., in connection with appropriate activities for older members. Too great and too all-inclusive an emphasis on language maintenance may lose or irritate the younger generations. Thus, language maintenance practices and attitudes may vary from one area of ethnic parish activity to another.

Ethnic parishes that favor language maintenance may have widely differing reasons for doing so. Some may be engaged in a conscious policy of language maintenance, although such a policy may be motivated either by national or religious ideology (conviction) or by non-ideological traditionalism (habit). Other parishes may merely be accommodating their older members, or in a few cases immigrants, until the time is reached when this is no longer necessary. Even this latter approach may be variously defined or rationalized. Thus, if we may view *conviction* and *habit* as representing somewhat different guides to behavior, we may examine the reasons given for language maintenance with respect to the prevalence of these two modes. Also, if we can keep the ethnic and the religious aspects of tradition separate, we may be able to arrive at a somewhat better understanding of the content of these modes.

In connection with mother tongue use in church sermons, most reasons advanced appear to reflect *habit* rather than *conviction* (Table 6.2, items 1 through 4, totaling

TABLE 6.2

Reasons for Use of Mother Tongue in Church Sermons

Reason	Frequency	
	N	%[a]
Arrival of new immigrants	140	9.2
Parishioners' mother tongue	474	31.3
Older folks prefer it	388	25.6
Used traditionally	320	21.1
Church authorities require	96	6.4
Other	97	6.4
Total	1515	100.00

[a] Percentages are based upon total responses rather than upon total parishes in view of multiple responses given by some parishes.

87% of all responses). Only one reason listed, that church authorities require the use of the mother tongue, shows an element of ideology or conviction. More difficult to determine is whether ethnic or religious motives dominate. The first three reasons strongly point to ethnicity (65% of all responses), while the fourth and fifth point toward religion. However, it is necessary to keep in mind that the ethnic and religious points of view are highly interwoven in the "little traditions" in which most American immigrants have their roots. All in all, in would seem that the rationales for language maintenance efforts with respect to *sermons* are clearly more traditional than ideological and somewhat more ethnic than religious. This is all the more striking when viewed in the context of parish (i.e., religious) behavior. Indeed, these findings may provide partial answers to the (at best) lukewarm attitude of many religious leaders toward language maintenance in the organizations under their jurisdiction. They view it as a factor which is unrelated to religion as they understand it, and as one which appeals to deep, unconscious, and potentially divisive sentiments. Thus, from their original post-immigrational position as "keepers of the faith", non-English languages have increasingly been redefined as unrelated to or detracting from the faith, particularly as faith itself has become increasingly de-ethnicized and secularized in America.

When we turn our attention to other parish activities somewhat less infused than the sermon with the aura of "formal religion", we find that habit and ethnicity come even more to the fore. In connection with mother tongue use in Church-sponsored organizations, we find hardly any reasons that reflect either conviction or religion

TABLE 6.3

Reasons for Use of Mother Tongue in Church-sponsored Organizations

Reason	Frequency	
	N	%[a]
Organization of "old folks"	229	36.1
New immigrants	68	10.7
Parishioners enjoy it	126	19.8
Church choir	58	9.1
Other	154	24.3
Total	635	100.0

[a]   See note Table 6.2.

(Table 6.3). A kind of "natural traditionalism" seems to pervade the reasons advanced: parishioners speak the languages they have always spoken and enjoyed speaking without much reflection, deliberateness, or formulated purpose.

But what is natural, traditional, and habitual for adults of the first generation is frequently far from being such for their second- and third-generation children and grandchildren. Adults may not be particularly reflective about their own habitual behavior and yet be quite reflective about the appropriateness of similar behaviors for their children – particularly when generational cleavages, cultural discontinuities, and social change become exceedingly obvious. On each of these counts, therefore, we

TABLE 6.4

Reasons for Teaching Mother Tongue in Church-sponsored Schools

Reason	Frequency	
	N	%[a]
Parishioners approve	55	4.9
Parents desire it	108	9.7
Children are interested	16	1.4
Cultural advantage of bilingualism	361	32.5
Follow services in mother tongue	196	17.6
"To preserve the ethnic heritage"	321	28.9
Other	55	5.0
Total	1112	100.0

[a]   See note Table 6.2.

would expect the reasons advanced for language maintenance by means of Church-sponsored schools to be appreciably more reflective, purposeful, and conviction-oriented than those encountered with respect to adult behavior. Our data tend to confirm this expectation (Table 6.4). Conviction is clearly dominant over tradition, while religious motives, though still secondary, are more prominent than in the other activities. Some of the reasons advanced are derived neither from ethnicity nor from religion. Indeed, a third guide for behavior – functional utility for personal advantage – becomes evident in the value put on bilingualism. Thus, not only is language mainte-nance less frequently practiced and advocated in connection with parish activities addressed to the young (Table 6.1), but it is differently rationalized. For the old, the basis of language maintenance in habit and ethnicity is clearly derivable from the "little" traditions of folk cultures rather than from the "great" traditions of religion, nationalism, or cultural creativity. For the young, language maintenance is rational-ized at a more purposive level, although neither religion nor ethnicity are as dominant as the functionalization of knowledge. The rationalization reflects many things simul-taneously. It reflects the absence of habitual mother tongue use and of habitual ethnicity in the younger generation, and the disruptive impact of American non-ethnic urban values upon two erstwhile major guides of human behavior: ethnicity and religion. In general, the parish school has become the clearest repository of purposeful, conviction-directed, ideological language maintenance in ethnic parishes but, at the same time, school-based language maintenance has also come to be championed for neither ethnic-oriented nor religious-oriented purposes.

REASONS FOR DISCONTINUANCE OF MOTHER TONGUE

Adult language maintenance based on habitual ethnicity succumbs to the extinction of ethnic habits – whether as a result of generational turnover or as a result of inexorable de-ethnization (Table 6.5). The lack of ideological mainsprings for mother tongue maintenance among adults in the ethnic parish is fully paralleled by the lack of ideolog-ical or purposeful mainsprings for discontinuance. Almost all of the language pressures that parishes yield to, both internal and external, may be considered func-tional. The purpose of the parish is to meet the religious needs of its parishioners; and when these needs are best served in English, the mother tongue is dropped. The process of mother tongue discontinuance appears infrequently to be planned or direc-ted. It is rarely the result of organized and rationalized opposition. It happens "naturally", and expressions of either regret or satisfaction are few and far between.

In ethnic parish schools, on the other hand, just as we found that language mainte-nance efforts directed toward children were more frequently idologized, purposeful, and conviction-oriented, so we find that the discontinuance of mother tongue instruc-tion more frequently reveals these same characteristics (Table 6.6). The opposition of parents, the greater importance of other curricular content, the independence of

TABLE 6.5

*Reasons for Discontinuing the Use of Mother Tongue
in Church Sermons*

Reason	Frequency	
	N	%[a]
Old immigrants dying out	39	15.3
American – born prefer English	83	32.4
No understanding of mother tongue	58	22.6
Ethnic composition changed	14	5.5
Parishioners are opposed	7	2.7
Church authorities demand it	9	3.5
Pressures of World War I, II	11	4.3
Loss of membership	6	2.3
Other	29	11.4
Total	256	100.0

[a] See note Table 6.2.

TABLE 6.6

*Reasons for Discontinuing the Use of the Mother Tongue
in Church-affiliated Schools*

Reason	Frequency	
	N	%[a]
Parishioners and parents opposed	24	5.8
Parents and children indifferent	97	23.5
No competent teachers	37	9.0
Overcrowded curriculum	18	4.4
Mixed ethnicity of students	15	3.6
WW I and II pressures	4	1.0
Church authorities opposed	5	1.2
M.T. not used in U.S. – waste of time	45	10.9
Children should master English instead	26	6.3
Religion can be taught in any language	25	6.1
Other	102	24.8
Generally negative	14	3.4
Total	412	100.0

[a] See note, Table 6.2.

religion from language, and other, less frequent indications of concerted, organized opposition account for more than a third of all responses. Obviously, the parish school is an arena of conscious and conviction-centered planning because it is an arena in which action must be taken rather than postponed (Fichter 1958; Brady 1956). Segregated sermons, services, and organizations in the mother tongue for "old timers" can be continued for a few more years until the natural course of events makes them unnecessary. However, "the natural course of events" has already run out with respect to language maintenance at the child level. Overt decisions are called for and must be rationalized. Even so, the most frequent explicitly mentioned reason for discontinuance of mother tongue instruction is merely indifference, while other practical-functional reasons are also in ample evidence. Thus, even in the parish school the path of Anglification is frequently taken for no other reason than that it requires the least effort and results in the most favorable practical outcomes (Fichter 1958).

PREDICTORS OF LANGUAGE MAINTENANCE

Parishes may be viewed in different ways for different purposes. One well-known student of the American Catholic parish (Fichter 1952) has suggested the following possible approaches: parishes may be conceived of as legal corporations, as super-imposed associations, as institutionalized associations, as communal groupings, as clusters of sub-groupings within communities, as series of statistical categories, as systems of kinship groupings, etc. Each conceptualization of the parish blurs certain characteristics of intra-parish dynamics and accentuates others. For the purpose of clarifying and predicting language maintenance, the three latter approaches to the ethnic parish would seem to be more revealing than the others. Therefore, the variables that are to be considered here are: religious denomination, ethnic group, size of community, ethnic homogencity, and rate of interethnic marriage.

Use of the mother tongue in church sermons seems to be the most meaningful index of language maintenance because the sermon is probably most sensitive to the linguistic needs and preferences of the congregation as a whole. Other parts of the church service may retain the mother tongue or another non-English language for purely ritual reasons, while the linguistic habits of parishioners in their social organizations may relate to largely segregated subgroupings of the congregation. In Table 6.7 language maintenance as reflected through use of mother tongue in sermons has been related to religious denomination for the three largest denominations in our sample: Latin Rite Catholic, Eastern Rite Catholic (mostly Ukrainian), and Eastern Orthodox. Obviously parishes observing either of the two Eastern rites are much more retentive of non-English mother tongues in their church services than are parishes observing the Roman Catholic (Latin) rite. The two factors most likely to be involved in the differences are the greater immigrational recency and the mutual reinforcement between mother tongues and Church languages which obtain in the case of parishioners affiliated with the Eastern churches (Auvray et al. 1960). The phenomenon of ritual reinforcement of a vernacular exists in the American Jewish community as well. There the sacred Hebrew of the services leads to the study (if not the mastery) of modern Hebrew in synagogue schools, while non-ritualized Yiddish falls into disuse even among the ultra-Orthodox who are ideologically and traditionally most bound to it.

TABLE 6.7

Language Maintenance and Religious Denomination[a]

Denomination	M.T. Always	M.T. more than English	Half and Half	More English	Always English	Total
Latin Rite Catholic	87 (12.5%)	47 (6.7%)	246 (35.2%)	157 (22.5%)	161 (23.1%)	698 (100.0%)
Eastern Rite Catholic	42 (17.0%)	22 (8.9%)	138 (55.9%)	15 (6.1%)	30 (12.1%)	247 (100.0%)
Eastern Orthodox	36 (14.6%)	45 (18.2%)	84 (34.0%)	32 (13.0%)	50 (20.2%)	247 (100.0%)

[a] Eliminating Data for parishes of the Polish National Catholic Church, other "national" catholic churches, and ethnically mixed parishes.

Thus even though the Church language of Eastern Rite Catholic Ukrainians and Ruthenians and that of Eastern Orthodox Greeks, Armenians, and Russians are not identical with the vernaculars utilized in sermons or in other activities of their ethnic parishes, the two nonetheless bear more similarity than Latin does to any of the modern Romance languages. The sacred tongues of the Eastern Churches undoubtedly reinforce the use of their secular offspring more directly than is possible in the case of Catholic churches of the Latin rite.

When parishes are classified by ethnic groups rather than by denominations, clear differences again appear with respect to language maintenance. In order to render such intergroup comparisons possible, the thirteen ethnic groups represented by the largest number of parishes in our sample were rank-ordered for language maintenance by dividing the total number of parishes in each group into the number of parishes using the mother tongue in at least half of their sermons (Table 6.8). The ethnic groups at the top of the maintenance score list are distinguished from the others by a somewhat more recent immigrational pattern and by the significant role which an older variant of the mother tongue plays in the Church ritual. Nevertheless, the relatively low position of Russians (whose language is ritually reinforced) as contrasted with the relatively high position of Poles (whose language is not triually reinforced) implies that of the two predictors, immigrational recency and ritual reinforcement, the former is the more important. The high standing of Lithuanians and Spanish speakers – both characterized by immigrational recency but not by ritual reinforcement of their mother tongues – and the low standing of Carpatho-Russians – characterized by such ritual reinforcement but not by immigrational recency – provide similar evidence. Language maintenance in the parish is most certain when both immigrational recency and ritual reinforcement are present. It is least certain when both are absent. However, it is more certain when only immigrational recency is present than when only ritual reinforcement is present. Once again, ethnicity is dominant over religion as a reinforcer of language maintenance – even within a parish setting.

TABLE 6.8

Language Maintenance Scores of 13 Ethnic Groups

Rank	Group	Maintenance Score
1	Armenian (27)[a]	.93
2	Greek (175)	.92
3	Ukrainian (93)	.86
4	Lithuanian (44)	.80
5	Spanish (39)	.77
6	Polish (227)	.73
7	French (51)	.61
8	Russian (96)	.60
9	Hungarian (24)	.58
10	Slovak (68)	.54
11	Italian (118)	.35
12	Carpatho-Russian (67)	.30
13	German (128)	.13

[a] Figures in parentheses indicate the number of responding parishes providing information on which maintenance scores are based.

On the whole, we find that language maintenance in sermons is more common in larger cities than in small cities and towns. In this connection Oscar Handlin's observations are of interest (Handlin 1962):

... American Catholics are an urban people. Fully 80% of them live in cities, perhaps one-third of the total in the eight largest alone.... For a long time, any tendency toward dispersal was a danger. Catholics who moved out of the city to the isolated rural West lost the shelter of the Church.

While urban concentration may well have been a necessity for the survival of the Catholic Church in America, we found in our study of Lutheran parishes, to be dealt with later in the chapter, that urbanness was *negatively* related to language maintenance. Perhaps we must sharply distinguish between Catholic (and probably Orthodox) and Protestant experiences in American cities. The Catholic Church built its strength in the city because this is where its immigrant members concentrated. Language maintenance among Catholic and Orthodox immigrants had its greatest chance of survival where there were the greatest concentrations of like-minded and like-tongued people. German and Scandinavian Protestant denominations established such concentrations in smaller towns and rural areas. Thus, it might actually be that language maintenance is related to relative ethnic-denominational concentration rather than to urbanity-rurality itself. Yet the urban industrialized metropolis undoubtedly poses particular problems for language maintenance based upon "little ethnic traditions". The greater de-ethnization of metropolitan life – based as it is upon an occupation-integrated and functionally differentiated associational mode of existence, with the greater mixture and mobility of its populations and the greater volume of mass communication and mass culture – must have a particularly disruptive influence on language maintenance, in ways that still require definitive study.

Ethnic homogeneity as a feature of parish membership composition has considerable influence on language maintenance. There is much evidence that the older and larger urban parish, in contrast to the older and larger rural parish, is gradually infiltrated by diverse elements for whom the English language represents the only common denominator of worship and communication. As long as the ethnic parish has no special ideological or traditional link to the linguistic status quo, Anglification of its services is bound to occur in time. The more non-ethnic or other-ethnic members in parishes still officially designated as pertaining to particular groups, the greater the share of English in the services of these parishes. However, homogeneity of membership does not seem to be sufficient, in and of itself, to guarantee language maintenance. The Italians present an obvious case in point. The homogeneity of their parishes is high, and yet their language maintenance is low indeed. The paradox of ethnic homogeneity coexisting with linguistic indulgence may find its explanation in particular historical circumstances. Most Italian immigrants to the United States came from the southern part of Italy where feelings about the Italian nation and the "official language" (originally a Tuscan dialect) are ambivalent to this very day. That many brought with them some of their regional indifference to or dislike for standard Italian is illustrated repeatedly in the pages of "Il Progresso Italo-Americano", of New York, which alternately reflects pride and embarrassment with respect to the southern dialect and southern localism in its columns and in its letters to the editor. Many Italo-Americans have obviously surrendered Italian without, at the same time, renouncing the strong kinship ties carried over from the "old country". Thus the point should be made that ethnicity can express itself in several ways which need not be highly correlated. Language maintenance is only one such expression.

A parish may become ethnically heterogeneous in two ways: by the influx of other-ethnic members and, more romantically, by inter-ethnic marriages. The influx of-other-ethnics through marriage may be more powerful in its effects on language maintenance than the general expansion of membership. A new member-by-marriage may, in many cases, move right into the social nucleus of the parish and exert direct influence on opinion leaders and their families (Fichter 1951). Italian parishes, however, are much more likely to perform marriages between individuals of Italian background than to offer sermons in Italian. Italian ethnicity, as previously noted, expresses itself much more vigorously through kinship ties. An opposite tendency is noted on the part of Lithuanians. Lithuanians, who are on the whole more recent immigrants, still use in church the language most familiar to them, but their young intermarry with persons of other ethnic groups with greater frequency.

The way in which institutional variables are related to language maintenance suggests two general forces pulling in opposite directions. Parishes of ethnic origin tend to relinquish the use of the mother tongue in their sermons as the composition of the parish becomes ethnically or genei ationally more heterogeneous. They incline to persevere in the use of the mother tongue in their sermons to the extent that the mother tongue has religious significance. In short, heterogeneity in the parish or in its surrounding environment works against the use of the mother tongue, while ritual reinforcement works in its favor.

In examining the first of these forces, we may say that heterogeneity of membership increases as the direct result of opportunity for such heterogeneity. The older an urban ethnic parish, the longer and greater is its exposure to outgroup contacts and the greater are the Anglifying tendencies of its native-born members. A parish that once nestled securely in all-Polish Hamtramck, gradually finds itself in a community of changing ethnic character. Whether the parish remains in its original area or moves to the suburbs, in one way or another it will sooner or later be confronted with a choice of losing strength or of taking in non-ethnic or other-ethnic members. The ethnic tongue will have to yield to the need for reaching these new members, unless it happens to be an integral part of the religious observance, as in the case of Greeks, Ukrainians, and a few other ethnic groups associated with Eastern churches. Such factors as size of membership or size of community exercise potent negative influences on language maintenance only insofar as they lead to changes (primarily to greater heterogeneity) in the composition of the membership. Any process that leads to heterogeneity in the composition of the membership is at one and the same time a process that brings about the Anglification of the church service. The factors favoring heterogeneity and Anglification can be analyzed into primary and secondary contributors. The primary factors such as interethnic marriages, generational turnover, and the admission of non-ethnics (or other-ethnics) to membership inevitably and immediately pull in the direction of diversity or de-ethnization. Secondary, indirect factors such as size and heterogeneity of the surrounding population or the growth rate of the parish may but do not necessarily lead to greater heterogeneity within the parish.

In the face of primary and secondary forces leading toward heterogeneity and change, the presence of ritual reinforcement of the mother tongue may be expected to counteract Anglification at least temporarily.[1] Eventually, under the pressure of competition for the loyalty of Anglified parishioners, church authorities and parishioners alike may come to seek the Anglification of successive elements of the church service. This has happened in church after church in which the vernaculars of immigrants to the United States initially enjoyed direct ritual reinforcement. It may be expected to happen as well in those churches where indirect ritual reinforcement is mediated through a sacred language related to but not identical with the vernacular still obtains.

---

[1] The recent liberalization (summer 1964) of Roman Catholic policy with respect to the use of vernaculars in various parts of the service probably comes too late to be of major importance for language maintance among most Catholics of ethnic stock in the United States except in the case of the Spanish speaking in the Southwestern states, Florida, and a few other large concentrations.

THE CLERGYMAN AND LANGUAGE MAINTENANCE

The clergyman is often the mediator of language transition in the ethnic parish. Janus-like, he must face both his hierarchical superiors and his flock. This becomes a problem only where the interests of the hierarchy conflict with those of the parishioners. The language area is one in which such a conflict has frequently arisen. On the whole, church authorities may be expected to be guided by religious rather than by ethnic considerations whenever the two are perceived to be contradictory. There is much evidence, outside the scope of this paper, that more than an occasional Catholic parish has become Anglified as a result of desire on the part of the hierarchy, rather than the flock, to accommodate greater numbers and to strengthen the operational efficiency and effectiveness of the church as an organization. It is true of other denominations as well that ethnicity and language have been forced to yield when the growth of the church was perceived to be sufficiently endangered or handicapped by their retention. Examples may be found in almost all the Lutheran denominations, whether their background is German, Norwegian, Finnish, or Swedish. At one time or another they have reached the point where they had to decide between the interests of non-institutionalized ethnicity and institutionalized religion. In each case the latter ultimately won out over the former. The church's loyalty to itself and to its own future "along American lines", abetted by second and third generation Anglification and drift toward marginal ethnicity, have made English the language of one immigrant church after another. Where a religion is limited to a particular ethnic-linguistic group, as in the Armenian, Greek, or Ukrainian churches, and where the vernacular of the group receives direct or indirect ritual reinforcement, the problem of accommodating English speakers may not arise before the third generation of "same-ethnics". The influx of "other ethnics" and "non-ethnics" is largely limited to cases of membership by marriage. In addition, these churches make particularly strenuous efforts to transmit their languages to the young. Nevertheless, if they remain exposed to heterogeneity of membership – if only through involvement in society on a large scale – church-based language maintenance must first weaken and then vanish.

Not only does the church change in its goals and its composition, but the pastors, too, are slowly changed. Foreign-born and same-ethnic pastors are replaced by American-born and non-ethnic (or other-ethnic) pastors – not only to reinforce the Americanizing policy of the church and not only to gratify the more marginally ethnic second and third generation membership, but also because international political and cultural developments block the supply of foreign pastors or render them truly "foreign" even to first-generation members of ethnic parishes in the United States.

Currently, only a third of the clergymen directing Roman Catholic, Eastern Catholic and Eastern Orthodox ethnic parishes are foreign born (Table 6.9) – a percentage which is almost identical with the percentage of foreign-born parishioners in these parishes. However, very few of these clergymen are encountered in parishes in which the mother tongue is used in less than half of all sermons. Furthermore, while foreign-

TABLE 6.9

*Language Maintenance and the Distribution of Foreign Born
and Native Born Clergymen*

| | Use of Mother Tongue in Sermon | | | | | | | |
| | At Least Half | | | | Less Than Half | | | |
Nativity of Clergyman	Always	More M.T.	Half and Half	Sub-Total	Less M.T. than Eng.	Never M.T.	Sub-Total	Total
Foreign	192	110	371	673 (73.1%) (46.8%)	134	114	248 (26.9%) (27.0%)	921
Native	120	113	531	764 (53.2%) (53.2%)	293	378	671 (46.8%) (73.0%)	1435
Total Responding Clergymen				1437			919	2356

born clergymen are clearly concentrated in ethnic parishes that emphasize use of the mother tongue in sermons, more than half of such parishes are now staffed by American-born pastors. While many of the latter have learned the ethnic mother tongues of their parishioners, most have not. Thus, the pastor himself inevitably becomes a factor in language maintenance and language transition within the ethnic parish.

On the whole, the clergyman is not an activist on behalf of language maintenance. He is somewhat more indulgent of the mother tongue than the rapid "Americanizers" would prefer. He is somewhat less devoted to it than the staunch retentivists would prefer. He seeks to retain the interest of old and young alike. He accommodates to the forces that shape language maintenance rather than attempting to shape them. A foreign-born pastor or a pastor sympathetic to ethnicity in general and to language maintenance in particular may delay the process of Anglification. An American-born pastor or a pastor who is unsympathetic to ethnicity and to language maintenance may accelerate the process. But the process as such would seem to be much too interwoven with large-scale and continual social and cultural change for any man or group of men to control, even were they inclined to do so (Schuyler 1957).

LUTHERAN ETHNIC PARISHES

From the time of the Protestant Reformation, Lutheran churches had been "national" in character, and the meeting of mother tongue and faith proved mutually reinforcing. It was, therefore, natural that many Scandinavians and Germans should continue the use of Norwegian, Swedish, Danish, and German in their newly-founded American parishes. E. Haugen writes: "In the case of the Norwegians, as apparently among most immigrants, the church is the primary institution which provides the immigrants with a justification for the use of the language" (Haugen 1953, p. 238). Time and the total environment, however, were on the side of Anglification. Gradually the use of English entered the church services of these immigrant Lutherans, and the ethnic mother tongue retreated surely and inexorably. Yet the transition has been far from even in different places and at different times.

The general trend toward gradual Anglification is well illustrated by such indices as the relative use of ethnic- and English-language church publications.[2] Table 6.10

TABLE 6.10

Circulation in % of Church Publications in Missouri Synod,
between 1923 and 1947

Year	Lutheraner	Witness	Kinder und Jugendblatt	Young Lutherans Magazine	Amerikanischer Kalender	Lutheran Annual
	(German)	(English)	(German)	(English)	(German)	(English)
1923	52	48	50	50	63	37
1925	51	49	44	56	60	40
1927	51	49	44	56	60	40
1929	51	49	44	56	60	40
1931	51	49	44	56	60	40
1933	39	61	44	56	60	40
1935	25	75	36	64	44	56
1937	23	77			35	65
1940					35	65
1945					21	79
1947	7	93				

Source: Adapted from *Statistical Yearbook of Missouri Synod*. Missing data unavailable.

compares the circulation of three types of English- and German-language organs read in The Lutheran Church-Missouri Synod. Here we see clearly the steady advance of the English media. Of special interest is the comparatively steep decline of German in the 30's. Whether this is due to a turnover of generations twenty-five to thirty years after the end of mass immigration, to political factors such as a revulsion again German during the rise of Hitler, to a natural breakthrough of English, or to a combination of all of these and other factors remains open to question.

The relatively greater decline of the *Lutheraner* as compared to the children's *Kinder und Jugendblatt* and the *Kalender* invites speculation. It is reasonable to

[2] The main source of our data is the *Statistical Yearbook of the Missouri Synod* of the Lutheran Church published by the Concordia Publishing Co. in St. Louis. Similar material has been gleaned from publications of the Wisconsin Synod and the Norwegian Lutheran bodies. Information on ethnic and religious concentrations was taken form publications of the U.S. Census Bureau.

assume that the children's magazine continued to be ordered by the Lutheran Day Schools of the Synod, which persisted in using German in the 30's for reading instruction. The *Kalender*, which incidentally became bilingual in the 30's, may have enjoyed similar institutional favors.

Table 6.11 summarizes the information available on parochial schools during a twelve-year period. Clearly, while some use of German continued to be made in the 30's within the schools, especially in reading instruction, the language was rapidly yielding to English.

TABLE 6.11

The Use of Language in Lutheran Day Schools of the Missouri Synod, between 1923 and 1935

	In Religious Instruction			In Reading Instruction	
Year	German %	English-German %	English %	English-German %	English %
1923	17	38	45	59	41
1925	—	—	—	—	—
1927	4.7	34.8	60.5	47.5	52.5
1929	3.7	29.1	67.2	43.3	56.7
1931	2.2	24.4	73.4	37.7	62.3
1933	0.8	20.1	79.1	31.4	68.6
1935	1.7	15.7	82.6	27.6	72.4

Note: No data available for 1925.
Source: Adapted from *Statistical Yearbook of Missouri Synod*, 1923, 1925, 1927, 1929, 1931, 1933, 1935.

TABLE 6.12

Immigration of Germans and Norwegians between the years 1880 and 1960

Years	German Immigrants	% of Total (1871-1960)	Norwegian Immigrants	% of Total (1871-1960)
1871-1880	718,182	16.9	95,323	13.2
1881-1890	1,452,970	34.3	176,586	24.5
1891-1900	505,152	11.9	95,015	13.2
1901-1910	341,498	8.1	190,505	26.4
1911-1920	143,945	3.4	66,395	9.2
1921-1930	412,202	9.7	68,531	9.5
1931-1940	114,058	2.7	4,740	.7
1941-1950	226,578	5.3	10,100	1.4
1951-1960	326,423	7.7	13,607	1.8
Total	4,241,008	100.0	720,802	100.0

Source: Adapted from the *Statistical Abstracts of the U.S.*, 1940 and 1960.

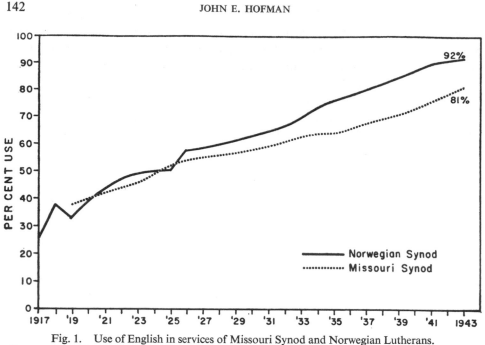

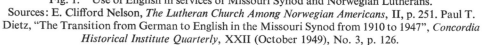

Fig. 1.   Use of English in services of Missouri Synod and Norwegian Lutherans.
Sources: E. Clifford Nelson, *The Lutheran Church Among Norwegian Americans*, II, p. 251. Paul T.
Dietz, "The Transition from German to English in the Missouri Synod from 1910 to 1947", *Concordia
Historical Institute Quarterly*, XXII (October 1949), No. 3, p. 126.

In Figure 1, the general trends for German and Norwegian show a close similarity in
the curves of language transition. It is interesting that the use of Norwegian in church
services underwent an unusually sharp decline at the onset of World War I. Evidently,
the political currents engendered by the war with Germany forced a "premature"
rise in the use of English which subsided with the return of normal times. After 1925
the Anglification of the Norwegian church proceeded at a faster pace than that of the
Missouri Synod, and the notion of a greater conservatism in the German-speaking
denomination could easily suggest itself. But here care should be exercised against
drawing any hasty conclusions. An inspection of immigration data may throw some
light on the question of why German showed greater retentiveness. Table 6.12, which
presents comparisons of the immigration of German and Norwegian settlers into the
United States, shows that the German immigration began earlier, remained more sustained for a longer period, and was always much larger numerically. This indicates
that the most crucial variable in the relatively greater persistence of German may well
be the greater numerical concentration of Germans. More German was heard by
more Germans in more places. Conservatism is an unnecessary assumption in order
to account for the somewhat greater retentiveness of German.

Not only was the persistence of German as a vehicle of instruction somewhat
greater than that of Norwegian, but the enrollment in Missouri Synod schools was
larger than that in the Norwegian Lutheran Church of America. "The three Synods

which united to form the Norwegian Lutheran Church in America in 1917 reported that week-day or vacation instruction was being given by 1,796 teachers to 41,716 children" (Haugen 1953, p. 101). In 1920, the elementary schools of the Missouri Synod reported enrollment of 73,063 students (Report of Board 1961, Cumulative Tables, Table I). Nevertheless the language transition in these two Lutheran churches has been monotonously steady in the direction of Anglification as both German and Norwegian have gradually yielded to the constant environmental pressure exerted upon them.

REGIONAL TRENDS

Our study of regional differences in the language transition utilizes data of the Missouri Synod exclusively. The districts can be roughly grouped as follows (see Figure 2):

1. *Most heavily shaded*: Those at or near 30% Anglification in 1920 (base line) and reaching the vicinity of 70% (1940 ceiling), representing an annual increase of 2% These districts comprise Minnesota, Wisconsin, Michigan, northern and southern Illinois, North Dakota, Texas, Kansas, and northern Nebraska.
2. *Less heavily shaded*: Districts which resemble the first group in most respects except that their base line and ceiling are about 5% to 10% higher, comprising Iowa, southern Nebraska, southern Dakota, and central Illinois. The districts in these first two groupings constitute the "heartland" of the Missouri Synod.
3. *Least heavily shaded*: Districts whose 1920 base line is near 50% use of English and whose 1940 ceiling is near or above 75%. In this group are the Western, Atlantic, Central, Eastern, Oregon-Washington, California-Nevada, Oklahoma, and Colorado districts. All except Central are at the periphery of the "heartland". They are, generally, areas of secondary migration and considerably more exposed to the inroads of Anglification than is the "heartland".
4. *Not included in Figure*: Districts outside the United States, viz., the Canadian districts of Alberta, Ontario, British Columbia, and Manitoba-Saskatchewan. The development in Canada appears to have been different from that in the United States.
5. *Not shaded in Figure*: The Southern District, high in Anglification from the start, and almost completely Anglified by 1950.

The geographic aspect of differences in the language transition becomes immediately apparent. It follows then, that differences in the institutional retentiveness of the ethnic language are a function of varying situations as they have come about in different localities. Most German Lutherans settled originally in certain Midwestern states where, at least till the 30's, they maintained their greatest relative ethnic, religious, and occupational continuity. Hence, their linguistic "retentiveness". In the more peripheral Western regions, the greater mobility and heterogeneity of the population

JOHN E. HOFMAN

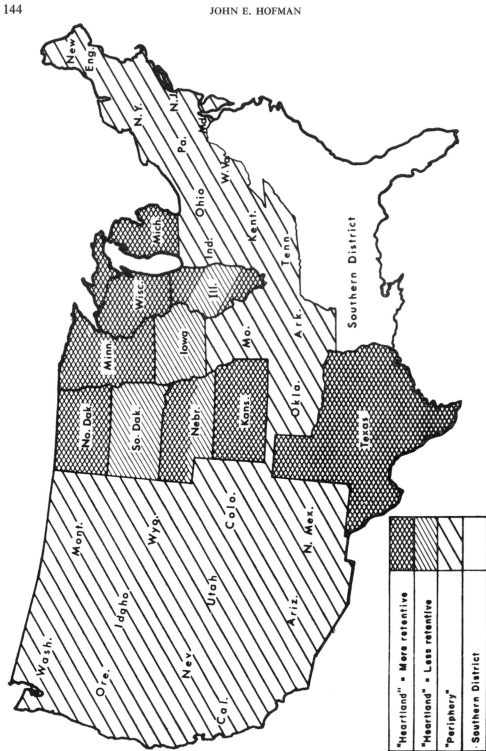

Fig. 2. Linguistic retentiveness in U.S.A. "Heartland" of Missouri Synod, 1940.

TABLE 6.13

Distribution of German and English Services in Lutheran Church,
Missouri Synod between 1923 and 1941

Year	District	All German	More German	Half and Half	More English	All English	Total
1923	Minnesota	46	120	100	27	58	351
1925	,,	37	109	117	39	81	383
1927	,,	21	97	119	50	77	364
1929	,,	17	84	137	46	123	407
1931	,,	15	60	147	60	134	416
1933	,,	9	43	148	63	151	414
1935	,	6	30	127	90	147	400
1937	,,	1	22	114	94	165	396
1939	,,	2	12	113	106	179	412
1941	,,	4	9	95	93	192	393
1923	North Dakota and Montana	42	30	54	14	48	188
1925	,,	36	29	54	20	51	190
1927	,,	20	23	61	17	51	172
1929	,,	32	22	67	29	63	213
1931	,,	26	16	61	32	69	204
1933	,,	25	10	58	36	72	201
1935	,	26	8	46	38	84	202
1937	,	15	11	44	38	91	199
1939	,,	17	12	38	39	102	208
1941	,,	15	10	37	39	113	214

Source: *Stat. Yearbook of the Evangelical Lutheran Synod of Missouri, Ohio, and other States* (St. Louis, Mo., Concordia Publishing House).

made the task of preserving the ethnic mother tongue quite difficult, regardless of intention. Hence, a more rapid pace of Anglification.[3] We may thus advance the hypothesis that *whenever religio-ethnic concentrations coincide with other factors, such as occupational and residential stability and a traditional frame of reference, a situation is created which enhances the ideological climate suitable for the retentiveness of the ethnic mother tongue in the religious service.* In our discussion of certain Minnesota

[3] Haugen anticipated these observations in his analysis of the language situation in the Norwegian Lutheran Church services: "As late as in 1930 there was still a wide variation between different districts. In Canada there were 70.6% Norwegian services in 1930 compared to only 12.3 in the Rocky Mts. district. In the latter area the Norwegians were scattered and largely urban, while in Canada they lived in compact rural settlements in the prairie provinces. The farming areas of North Dakota and Northern Minnesota were also notably higher in their retention than South Dakota and Southern Minnesota. East Coast and West Coast show almost identical distributions, close to the national average. The so-called Eastern district included such Midwestern States as Wisconsin and Illinois, but also urban communities like Chicago and Brooklyn. As the years passed, however, the difference between the districts was rapidly disappearing. Norwegian appeared to be approaching extinction at about the same time everywhere (Haugen 1953, p. 268).

TABLE 6.14

Distribution of German and English Services in Lutheran Church,
Missouri Synod between 1923 and 1941

Canada

Year	District Alberta and	All German	More German	Half and Half	More English	All English	Total
1923	British Columbia	57	2	20	1	27	107
1925	,,	49	6	16	4	62	137
1927	,	47	5	25	4	63	144
1929	,,	48	4	30	11	51	144
1931	,,	55	11	36	3	53	158
1933	,,	58	12	36	5	58	169
1935	,,	46	11	32	5	58	152
1937	,,	51	9	36	9	75	180
1939	,,	37	23	23	11	101	195
1941	,,	29	14	21	9	108	181
1923	Manitoba and Saskatchewan	57	13	17	8	27	122
1925	,,	58	16	15	5	13	107
1927	,,	68	12	13	3	22	115
1929	,,	63	16	17	7	39	142
1931	,,	75	18	22	7	42	164
1933	,,	63	18	24	7	53	165
1935	,,	52	25	24	27	50	178
1937	,,	52	21	29	6	60	168
1939	,,	39	21	32	4	61	157
1941	,,	38	20	34	6	87	185

Source: Stat. Yearbook of the Evangelical Lutheran Synod of Missouri, Ohio, and other States (St. Louis, Mo., Concordia Publishing House).

counties, we shall try to adduce further evidence for the plausibility of such situational factors underlying linguistic retentiveness.

Tables 6.13 and 6.14 illustrate the presence of both similarities and differences in regional development. The linguistic transition in Minnesota, like that in North Dakota-Montana on the one hand and in Manitoba-Sasketchawan on the other, points to the overall advance of the use of English in church services. But, differences are readily seen. The existence of hundreds of parishes in Minnesota probably favored a great variety of solutions as reflected in the prominence of the part-German, part-English approach. Such compromise solutions were practical only in the larger, better organized parishes of the Missouri Synod, and do not seem to have been as readily adopted in Canada or North Dakota-Montana. These latter communities were apparently forced into "either-or" alternatives. For them, the presence of older members in a parish may have prolonged the retention of "German-only" beyond the point of usefulness with younger members. Then, since the parish was too weak to try a bilingual solution, a switch to "English-only" became inevitable. The fact that these states lagged behind the national average in membership increase may have been in part a consequence of this organizational weakness.

It is within the local community, however, that we must look for the interplay of forces making for one linguistic solution or another. Thus in examining our hypothesis that whenever religio-ethnic concentrations and certain other factors coincide, a situation is created which enhances the ideological climate suitable to retentiveness of the ethnic mother tongue, we are led to seek confirmation on the local level.

LOCAL FACTORS IN LINGUISTIC RETENTIVENESS

First, let us briefly trace the process of linguistic concentration. In Figures 3, 4, and 5,

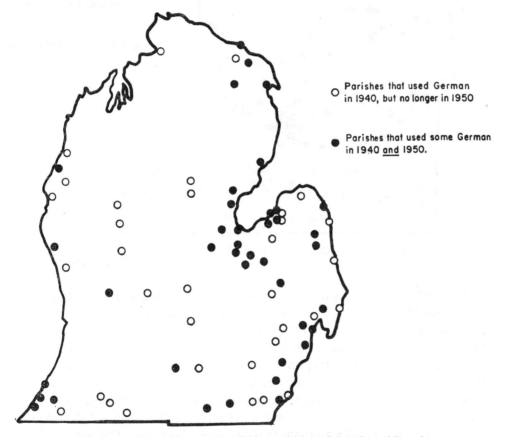

○ Parishes that used German in 1940, but no longer in 1950

● Parishes that used some German in 1940 and 1950.

Fig. 3. The use of German in Michigan Parishes of the Missouri Synod.
Source: Adapted from *Statistical Yearbooks of Missouri Synod*, 1940, 1950.

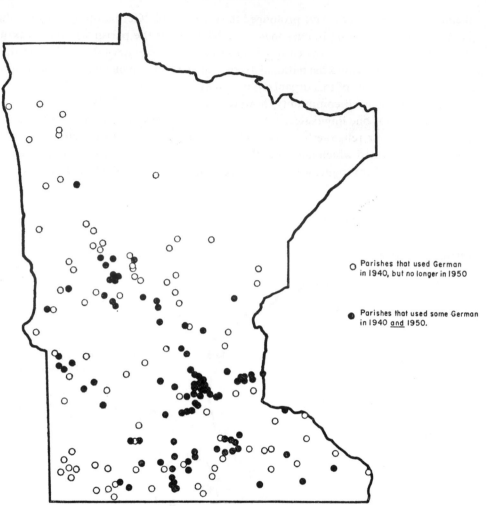

Fig. 4. The use of German in Minnesota parishes of the Missouri Synod.
Source: Adapted from *Statistical Yearbooks of Missouri Synod*, 1940, 1950.

all bilingual parishes in the districts of Michigan, Minnesota, and North Dakota are
plotted for 1940 and 1950. The white circles represent bilingual parishes in which at
least some German was used in 1940, but in which no German was used in 1950. The
black circles designate parishes that maintained the use of some German into 1950.
Thus the distribution of circles provides a picture of the direction of linguistic retreat.
Bilingual parishes, already concentrated in 1940, became even more concentrated by
1950. The linguistic transition can, therefore, be described as a whittling away toward
one or more core areas, that is, an "in-gathering" rather than a "thinning-out"
process. This is especially apparent in the case of Minnesota. The process of concentration makes good sense if we can demonstrate that the areas toward which it

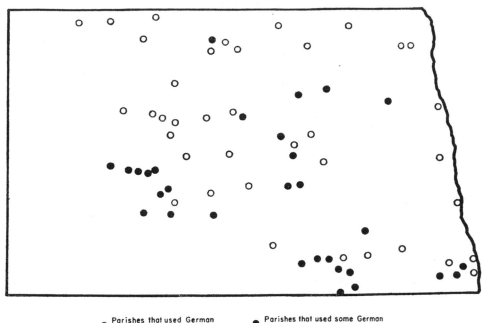

○ Parishes that used German
  in 1940, but no longer in 1950.

● Parishes that used some German
  in 1940 and 1950.

Fig. 5. The use of German in North Dakota parishes of the Missouri Synod.
Source: Adapted from *Statistical Yearbooks of Missouri Synod*, 1940, 1950.

moves display the characteristics of religio-ethnic concentration and continuity posed in our hypothesis. Globally, this can be shown by a mere inspection of the ethnic tables in the Paullin-Wright Atlas. Areas such as the Michigan Bay area, known as "the Thumb", and the region south-west of the Twin Cities in Minnesota are traditionally "German". In areas more sparsely settled by Germans, the language transition would yield a pattern of "thinning-out" rather than "in-gathering", since no one subregion would be strong enough to form a central core.

Einar Haugen, in his study of the Norwegian language in America, has made a similar point (Haugen 1952, pp. 5-6):

The areas where Norwegian has survived the longest in popular speech are not necessarily those areas where the number of persons born in Norway is largest not those which were settled most recently.... Of course, such factors as continued immigration have played an important role, since much of the recent immigration has gone to the same areas as did the earlier, thereby reinforcing the use of the language. But, immigration which is dispersed in the cities or in marginal rural areas is more quickly Anglicized than that which maintains its solid neighborhood core. In the latter, people speak Norwegian simply because everybody else does without reflecting much about it. For them it is not a cultural duty or a program of behavior. If you ask why they do so, it is difficult for them to find an answer.

The core areas are characterized by both early concentrated settlement and continued immigration. If, in addition to what we have observed about the process of concen-

JOHN E. HOFMAN

TABLE 6.15

Size and Age of Average Linguistically Retentive and Non-Retentive Parishes, 1950, 1958

	Missouri Synod						Wisconsin Synod	
	Minnesota 1950		Michigan 1950		Iowa 1950		Wisconsin, West 1958	
	Some G	None	Some G	None	Some G	None	Some G	None
Number of Parishes	99	78[a]	76	63[a]	26	225	89	68[a]
Average Founding Data	1888	1916	1880	1916	1889	1906	1878	1897
Souls per parish	432	250	647	287	448	210	808	589

[a] Random Sample.
Source: Adapted from *Statistical Yearbook of Missouri and Wisconsin Synods.*

tration in Michigan, Minnesota, and North Dakota, we realize that a considerable organizational effort must have been involved in the maintenance of bilingual parishes, it follows that the more retentive parishes should also be the better established and more populous ones. Indeed, Table 6.15 shows this to be the case with respect to a number of parishes picked at random from Yearbooks of the Missouri and Wisconsin Synod. Similar results were obtained when rententive parishes, those using German in 1940 and 1950, were compared with non-rententive parishes, those using German in 1940 but no longer in 1950 (Table 6.16). Thus in Table 6.16 we see that the linguistically

TABLE 6.16

*Linguistically Retentive vs. Non-Retentive Minnesota Parishes
in Missouri Synod, 1940, 1950*

	Institutional Retentiveness	Institutional Non-Retentiveness
	83 Parishes Using German in 1940 *and* in 1950	129 Parishes Using German in 1940, but *not* in 1950.
Souls per Parish, 1940	544	289
Communicants per Parish, 1940	394	196
Ratio of Communicants to Souls	.72	.67
Number of Parochial Schools	44	40
Pupils per Parish	2766/83 = 33.3	1158/129 = 9.0

Source: *Statistical Yearbooks of Missouri Synod*, 1940, 1950.

more retentive parishes were larger, had a greater church-going ratio (a fact that holds for other samples as well), and supported more parochial schools.

The available data do not tell us whether the larger parishes became so as a result of internal growth or of external consolidation, i.e., mergers between parishes. The weight of circumstantial evidence is on the side of organic, internal growth inasmuch as the total number of parishes in the most retentive areas remained rather stable over many years. Still, a certain amount of absorption of the smaller parishes by the larger, especially in rural areas, cannot be ruled out.

A picture has emerged of the linguistically retentive parish in the Missouri Synod as a typically larger, older, and possibly better organized unit than its "non-retentive" counterpart. In our consideration of regional trends, we hypothesized that church-associated retentiveness of the ethnic tongue prevails in areas where the ethnic and/or religious group is relatively concentrated over time. We also hypothesized that other conditions, such as occupational stability and a traditional frame of reference, would reinforce religio-ethnic homogeneity as conditions of linguistic retentiveness.[4] Minnesota was chosen as the locale for testing this hypothesis, inasmuch as it has passed through many of the phases typical of other districts; it has one of the largest memberships in the Missouri Synod; and, being predominantly rural, it does not present some of the special problems of more urbanized districts.

TWELVE MINNESOTA COUNTIES: AN AREA STUDY

Twelve counties, six of them containing the most "retentive" parishes and six of them the least, were selected for a comparison of ethnic and religious concentration (Table 6.17). Church-associated (institutional) linguistic retentiveness served as a bssis for assigning the twelve counties to the two categories. The main criterion of retentiveness was *stability* of bilingualism rather than absolute number of parishes at any one time. Only Carver, Sibley, and McLeod Counties, however, can be classed as really retentive. Blue Earth, Watonwan, and Martin are rather wobbly cases of linguistic retentiveness, and should be regarded as intermediate in position.

Table 6.17 illustrates ethnic and denominational indices, based on census data, for the twelve counties. The table appears to confirm the major hypothesis. The linguistically retentive counties are characterized, generally, by larger concentrations of German-Americans organized in their own national church. Here the retention of the German language has the benefit of relatively greater secular and sacred reinforcement. The picture is particularly clear in the case of the three most retentive counties, Carver, Sibley, and McLeod, especially when these are contrasted with the

---

[4] Today, no occupation serves as a surer basis of family-centered continuity than agriculture. When this rural bias is seen in conjunction with membership in the most conservative of Lutheran denominations, the traditional frame of reference should be obvious. At the same time, any statement of this kind has to be quite tentative until more direct figures on the actual occupational distribution of parishioners from both kinds of parishes can be ascertained.

TABLE 6.17

Denominational and Ethnic Configuration in Selected Counties, Minnesota, 1930

	German Lutherans	Scandinavians	Roman Catholics	Others	German Stock[a]	Scandinavian Stock[a]
	%	%	%	%	%	%
Carver	48	8	32	12	33	7
Sibley	61	9	18	12	34	11
McLeod	45	1	32	22	32	6
Blue Earth	33	12	27	28	23	10
Watonwan	22	49	15	14	19	29
Martin	38	13	13	36	25	14
Most Retentive Counties	26.1	13.0	24.2	26.7	26.4	11.7
Ottertail	28	36	17	19	15	32
Lac Qui Parle	10	63	16	11	24	40
Morrison	8	75	5	12	22	15
Todd	21	9	41	50	19	16
Faribault	13	27	24	36	18	17
Pipestone	22	4	21	75	19	18
Least Retentive Counties	16.2	26.4	32.6	24.8	17.6	23.8

[a] Foreign born and Native of Foreign and Mixed Parentage.
Source: U.S. Census, 1930: Report on Religious Bodies, 1936.

six least retentive counties. In Ottertail, Lac Qui Parle, and Morrison counties, the presence of many Scandinavian-Americans organized in parishes of their own denominations have provided competition and ample opportunity for intermarriage. Warner and Srole (1954, pp. 290-293) have pointed to the affinity between these two ethnic groups. Their coexistence should Anglify both groups at a quicker rate, with English taking the role of common denominator. As Haugen has observed (Haugen 1953, p. 280): "We may also assume that no one learned English and began using it because they wanted to, but only because practical necessity forced them to.... Any facts we can find out about linguistic retentiveness are thus in large measure bound to reflect the degree of social isolation of the group." In Todd and other counties, the presence of many Catholics who are not committed to national churches and probably not as motivated to maintain any ethnic mother tongue would create a situation similarly conducive to more rapid Anglification. Todd, Faribault, and Pipestone counties in addition, comprise large segments of other competing sects and nationalities.

On the whole, the more retentive counties appear to be higher in percentage of church-going. This may be circumstantial evidence of greater conservatism, but it may also be the result of many other variables. It could also be argued that "con-

servatism", if it can be thus identified, is associated with agriculture. The more retentive Missouri Synod parishes typically are more rural than the less retentive ones. The
rural parish, however, is not necessarily located in a predominantly rural county. While
it is true that Carver and Sibley counties are completely rural, the same can be said
for Lac Qui Parle. If occupational pursuit does indeed discriminate between the more
and the less retentive parish, this does not necessarily characterize the county as a
whole in which the parish is located. Thus the degree of rurality of a county does not
help to discriminate between counties of more or less linguistic retentiveness.

Ethnic and denominational homogeneity remain as the only other independent
sociological variables that can be isolated on an extensive, county-wide basis as having
probable bearing on the linguistic retentiveness within the parish.

A SAMPLE PARISH STUDY

A small sample (N=60) of pastors of Minnesota parishes was selected to include all 35
parishes reported by the Missouri Synod to be using some German as late as 1958;
of the other 25 parishes, all but two had been bilingual until at least 1950. On the
basis of previous findings, we expected the retentive parishes to be more homogeneous
in ethnic and occupational makeup, to be somewhat older and larger, and to display
other signs of greater organizational strength. By and large, the earlier findings were
sustained. Again the "ethnic predictor" emerged as most clear-cut of all. The
retentive parish of 1962 was more homogeneous (76.5% German stock) than the non-
retentive (66.4). The extent of interethnic marriages was also smaller for the former,
with intermarriage cited by several pastors as a factor in the Anglification of the parish.
Correspondingly, ingroup marriages were recognized to favor retention of the ethnic
tongue. As one pastor put it: "In the last 25 years the lines of demarcation [between
the ethnic groups] became less and less distinct. Little attention is paid to it now. Yet,
when marriage takes place, most are within one language group."

Most of the differences between the two types of parish were exceedingly slight.
However, the present comparison is an extremely rigorous test of our hypothesis.
Our present subdivision may be said to classify *retentive* parishes as more retentive or
less retentive, rather than as retentive or non-retentive. Still we may ask why the
differences between retentive parishes are not any more clear-cut than they are.

For one thing, these concepts have become relative to a generally high level of
Anglification so that the distinction is just the least bit arbitrary. After all, a parish
which gives one monthly service in German, or fewer, is not really much more retentive
than one in which German has been altogether discontinued. Moreover, by this time,
at a point near the end of the language transition, the forces of religio-ethnic-occupa-
tional homogeneity and organizational strength that originally combined to generate
greater linguistic retentiveness can no longer be clearly operative inasmuch as they
have very little left to operate on. As the curve of the linguistic transition approaches

its asymptote of complete Anglification, the possibilities of orderly fluctuations become increasingly limited, and a rising share of the variance in observable linguistic phenomena may be "error" variance. Stating it differently, "chance" factors become of increasing importance in determining the retentiveness and non-retentiveness of a particular parish. Chance factors, in the context of this study, should be understood to refer to factors other than statistically measurable sociological variables, e.g., the the presence of a German-speaking pastor (twice as many pastors in retentive as in non-retentive parishes were reported as having a very good knowledge of German), the activities of an energetic group of elders, the relative recency of German instruction in Lutheran day schools, subtle differences in attitudes among certain segments of the parish membership, and so on, singly or in any combination.

The approach throughout the study has been to focus on sociolological variables rather than on motivational ones. The composition of a population was held to set the conditions for whatever attitudes underlay institutional retentiveness. Undoubtedly there was a time when this pre-eminence of demographic factors was not so clear-cut, when attitudes of religious conservatism and ethnic identification did play a major role. As Nelson (1960, p. 243) writes:

Moreover, the arguments which were to be repeated in other foreign language groups were articulated there [among German-speaking parishioners]: (1) the use of English must be promoted in order to save the second and succeeding generations for the Lutheran Church; and (2) the use of German must be continued in order to (a) preserve the true faith which was diluted when Anglicized, and (b) to conserve the cultural heritage.[5]

Indeed, it would not have been surprising had the Missouri Synod, known to be one of the most conservative Lutheran bodies, persisted in an ideology of church-associated linguistic retention. Such a development has precedents in the history of religions. The fact is that this did not happen. On the contrary, there are a number of indications that, if anything, the Synod shifted to an ideology of non-retention. Ethnicism, once a pillar of the church, came to be viewed as a deterrent to expansion. As one of the pastors put it: "It became apparent that restricting the church to German would stifle further growth". Haugen (1953, p. 238) makes this point quite clearly:

... eventually the rebellion against the immigrant language reared its head in the church also. Faced with this problem, the church compromised its lesser goal for the sake of its larger one. To stay alive and carry on its spiritual message, the church had to yield and become first bilingual, then increasingly English.

The questionnaire data suggest that the 1962 *home* may actually have been more retentive than the church. This strengthens the impression that the prime mover of retentiveness has been non-institutional and non-ideological during the last few decades. Many statements made by pastors in reply to a variety of questions indicate that the last institutional prop was removed when Lutheran schools cased to teach the German language in the 30's and 40's. The very naturalness of the language transition

[5]   See also Dietz (1949).

is reflected in the type of reason given again and again to account for the remaining persistence of German: "To serve older folks and recent immigrants." The matter-of-factness with which the transition is viewed comes out very clearly in the following: "Originally the majority were of German extraction. For a certain period they endeavored to preserve that language as long as they could, somewhat for sentimental reasons and somewhat because they enjoyed the services made in the language in which they had been brought up. The majority, however, soon prevailed who were interested in helping the people spiritually as much as possible and thought that this could be done best in the language which all understood."

One might even speculate that it is precisely this apolitical, non-ideological, unconscious inertia of old habit that has made the long persistence of German possible. For had there been a strong movement of retentiveness subsequent to the First World War, formidable counter-currents might have generated opposition and smothered the use of German in a hail of politics. (This may hold for other ethnic tongues as well.) As it was, German was rarely actively threatened from the outside because it did not itself constitute a threat. It may be the innocuous naivete of its popular use that, ironically, has kept the language alive so far.

REFERENCES

Auvray, P., P. Poulain, and A. Blaise, *Sacred Languages* (New York, Hawthorn, 1960).

Brady, M. F., "Why American Catholics Conduct Schools", in *The Role of the Independent School in American Democracy*. Paper delivered at a Conference on Education (Milwaukee, Marquette University Press, 1956).

Dietz, P. T., "The Transition from German to English in the Missouri Synod from 1910 to 1947", *The Concordia Historical Institute Quarterly*, XXII (St. Louis, Mo., Concordia Publishing House, Oct. 1949), 97-121.

Fichter, J. H., *Dynamics of a City Church* (Chicago, University of Chicago Press, 1951).

——, "Conceptualizations of the Urban Parish", *Social Forces*, 31 (1952), 31, 43-46.

——, *Parochical School* (Notre Dame, Ind., Univ. of Notre Dame Press, 1958).

Handlin, O., "The Church and the Modern City", *Atlantic Monthly*, 210, 2 (1962), 101-05.

Haugen, E., "The Struggle over Norwegian", in *Norwegian-American Studies*, XVII (Northfield, Minn., Norwegian-American Historical Association, 1952).

——, *The Norwegian Language in America*, Vol. I (Philadelphia, Univ. of Pennsylvania Press, 1953).

Nelson, L., "Speaking of tongues", *American Journal of Sociology*, 54 (1948), 202-210.

Paullin-Wright, *Atlas of the Historical Geography of the United States* (New York, 1932).

Report of Board of Parish Education, *The Lutheran Church-Missouri Synod*, 210 N. Broadway, St. Louis 2, Mo., 1961.

Statistical Yearbooks of the Evangelical Lutheran Synod of Missouri, Ohio, and other States (St. Louis, Mo., Concordia Publishing Co.).

Warner, L., and L. Srole, *The Social System of America* (New Haven, Yale University Press, 1954).

7. ORGANIZATIONAL AND LEADERSHIP INTEREST IN LANGUAGE MAINTENANCE

JOSHUA A. FISHMAN AND VLADIMIR C. NAHIRNY

The United States has often been called "a nation of joiners". Perceptive foreign visitors to our shores have frequently commented on our proclivity for establishing and joining organizations. Social scientists, too, have recently given the socio-psychological dynamics of American organizational activity greatly increased attention.

If there *is* a general American tendency to establish and join organizations, it is one which seems to be equally strong among individuals of fairly recent immigrant-ethnic background, who have not yet become sufficiently de-ethnicized to be accommodated fully and exclusively into the general, non-ethnic "core society". The exigencies of life in a new environment – entailing new customs, a new language, different values, and novel social and economic pressures as well as opportunities – are important factors in leading individuals of similar ethnic, religious, and linguistic backgrounds to come together for solace, for mutual assistance, and for more comfortable interaction.

The ethnic organization has been a doubly novel enterprise for individuals and groups whose roots are in rural or semi-rural ethnic communities, whether those of Europe or of the Hispanic southwest – first, because of their inexperience with formal organizations, and second, because of their inexperience with conscious culture maintenance activity. As a result, the ethnic organization, particularly the ethnic cultural organization, has been patterned either on non-ethnic models adopted from co-territorial Americans who had already shed their ethnicity, or on models brought here by countrymen coming from large cities and accustomed to the consciously created mechanisms growing equally out of ideology and transmuted ethnicity on the one hand, and out of urbanization and secularization on the other. In either case, ethnic organizations represent a partial contradiction, a retreat from authentic ethnicity. The ethnic *organization* has increasingly *replaced* the ethnic *community* in the United States, rather than being either its servant or its reflection.

For this very reason, as well as because the "100% American" de-ethnicized sons and grandsons of many ethnics also require a sense of community, many immigrant-ethnic organizations have continued to function when neither their activities nor their members were primarily ethnic in outlook or behavior. The student of ethnic organizations in the United States is currently faced by a great diversity, running the entire gamut from organizations that serve very recent immigrant groups and are completely oriented toward Old World ideologies and behavior patterns, or toward the problems of immigrant life, to organizations whose very names and activities no longer reflect any immigrant or ethnic interests at all. These organizations vary in size from small local clubs to nationwide organizations-of-organizations. Actually, there is no way of accurately telling how many ethnic organizations there are in the United States today. It has never been part of our national book-keeping to keep records of such matters. On the basis of our own inquiries it seems safe to say that there are at least 15,000, and probably as many as 20,000, functioning formal organizations founded by and for particular groups of ethnics and still largely maintained by them or their descendants. Of this large universe, the ethnic *cultural* organization is only one rather small segment (Dunn 1924, Fishman 1964, Kip 1953, Meyer 1900, Sackett 1914). We shall be better able to appreciate the unique prospects and problems of language-maintenance oriented organizations (ostensibly some 72% of ethnic cultural organizations) if we know something about the general universe of which they are a part. Contrasts between the background characteristics of linguistically retentive and non-retentive organizations, members, and leaders can provide many clues as to the meaning and intensity of language maintenance among the former, as well as clues concerning the meaning and intensity of ethnicity per se in organizations of both types.

If linguistically retentive organizations, referred to as "positives" throughout this discussion, are found to be systematically smaller in membership, composed of relatively more foreign-born members, and more frequently local in organizational scope, it is obvious that such characteristics have definite implications for language maintenance as well as for the direction of adaptive continuity among ethnic cultural organizations in general. If, on the other hand, no systematic differences appear, we might well suspect that the discontinuance of language maintenance concerns in ethnic cultural organizations is related more to ideological, functional, or ethnic specificity than to a general developmental sequence within ethnic cultural organizations. Finally, if language maintenance "positives" are more frequently found to be *younger organizations* composed of relatively *older members*, this would not merely be an interesting isolated finding but one implying that the de-ethnization process produces a break with certain elements of the complete ethnic constellation (e.g., language) much more quickly than it does with others (e.g., more generalized and commemorative cultural interests). This, in turn, implies that marginal ethnicity develops gradually and requires cultural organizations with emphases peculiarly their own. Thus, the background characteristics of ethnic cultural organizations in general, and the existence as well as the direction of systematic differences between linguistically retentive and non-retentive units, can provide orientational clues for subsequent and more central inquiry into organizational activities and ideologies (Blau and Scott 1962, Etzioni 1961, Parsons 1961, Weber 1956).

ORGANIZATIONAL CHARACTERISTICS

Approximately 45% of the responding ethnic cultural organizations claim to be countrywide in scope and a similar percentage to be local. The third organizational pattern – the regional – is definitely a minority pattern, and may well be considered an unstable state; "successful" organizations develop beyond it to nationwide scope, while "unsuccessful" organizations slip back from it to local scope. It is all the more significant, therefore, that as we progress along the continuum of geographic scope from local to countrywide organizations, the percentage of language maintenance "positives" declines regularly: 77%, 73%, 68%. This more frequent "grass roots" status of language maintenance in the United States indicates that it is more "functional" for smaller, face-to-face groups than for larger, more impersonal organizations. The relationship between the two variables – geographic scope and organizational espousal of language maintenance – does not depend on the population of the "places" in which the two types of ethnic cultural organizations are located, since "positives" and "negatives" alike reveal the following distribution:

Population of "Place"	% of Organizations
750,000 or more	36%
500,000 to 749,999	21%
250,000 to 499,999	7%
Under 250,000	36%

While both kinds of ethnic cultural organization follow the distribution of foreign-born and foreign-stock populations in the United States much more closely than they follow that of the general American population,[1] it is apparent that linguistically retentive units are likely to be smaller and, therefore, weaker organizations regardless of the population of the "place" in which they are located. Their more frequent local scope leads us to suspect that language maintenance in the United States is rarely a cause that unites erstwhile countrymen under a common banner, but rather that it appeals to selected individuals only, whether on the basis of ideological or traditional grounds. It seems to be intimately particularistic and exclusive more frequently than it is unifying and expansive. As such, it may represent a behavior pattern or an ideological position which is inimical to membership growth, organizational expansion, and intergenerational organizational continuity.

If it is true that organizational growth depends on compromises with language maintenance, then it may also be true that organizational supremacy leads to compromises with ethnic affiliation. Although all organizations included in this study were selected on the basis of their definite ethnic affiliation, only 76% of responding

---

[1] The population of the United States in 1960 was distributed as follows:

Population of "Place"	% of Population
500,000 or more	16%
250,000 to 500,000	6%
250,000 and under	78%

TABLE 7.1

Ethnic Association and Belief in the Importance of Mother Tongue Maintenance

Belief in Language Maintenance	Ethnic Association: Past and Present			
	Yes – Yes	Yes – No	No – No	Total
Yes	392 (80%) (84%)	41 (49%) (9%)	31 (44%) (7%)	464
No	97 (20%) (54%)	42 (51%) (24%)	39 (56%) (22%)	178
Total	489 (76%)	83 (13%)	70 (11%)	642

units viewed themselves as having an ethnic affiliation (Table 7.1). Another 13% admitted that they did "at one time draw ... [their] membership from and seek to serve individuals from a particular ethnic or nationality background", but claimed they were no longer doing so. The remaining organizations (11%) maintained they never had served nor drawn their membership from individuals of a particular ethnic or nationality background. These disclaimers are important in revealing organizational self-concept and aspiration, particularly in view of the fact that initial evidence (which served as the basis for selection) and subsequent evidence obtained in the course of the study both imply that these disclaimers are less than fully accurate or reliable. A careful study of those organizations that completely denied any association with ethnicity revealed that all of them had definitely had such an association – indeed, that many of them were still functioning with a predominantly ethnic membership, and, not infrequently, on the basis of predominantly ethnic appeals and programs. Clearly, the de-ethnization of organizational self-concepts, the generalization of organizational goals, and finally the denial of ethnicity itself must all be of concern to us for these are matters which necessarily have a decided bearing on language maintenance and on ethnic continuity more generally.

The very fact that these are cultural *organizations* may simplify the process of de-ethnization. Organization implies organizational adaptive capacity, on the one hand, and the predominance of structure over function in human affairs, on the other. Thus, an organization originally founded to serve the cultural needs of German-Americans – and, therefore, "self-evidently" (i) a German-American organization, and (ii) an organization interested in language maintenance – tends to gravitate toward the organizational self-concept of a "cultural organization open to all who are interested in German culture" and, therefore, neither limited to those who command the German language nor to those who are German-American. This generalization of intellectual-cultural-religious functions is a necessary concomitant of de-ethnization, generational turnover, and the predominance of organizational continuity over initially "self-evident" purposes and affiliations. In an early de-ethnicizing stage of this developmental sequence, organizations may still define themselves as having once been associated with particular ethnic groups. Subsequently, these initial ethnic associations come to be considered as "self-evidently" incidental rather than as purposive with respect to the redefined goals of "genuinely cultural" organizations. Indeed, organizational goals and self-concepts can change much more rapidly than the demography of organizational membership. Membership may continue to be very largely foreign born and foreign stock while organizational goals proceed to change along an adaptive sequence toward greater functional generalization and de-ethnization.

Just as an impending or recent break with ethnicity may lead first to rejections of language maintenance and then to disclaimers of ethnicity per se, so greater security with marginal ethnicity may lead to cultural reassertions. The organizations of grandchildren may no longer be ethnic nor consider themselves as such, and yet the long dormant ethnic mother tongue may delight their fancy as a sentimental and a cultural desideratum. This is hardly a "return to ethnicity" (for the ethnicity of the immigrant grandfathers can no longer be recaptured, not only because that is not really what the grandchildren want but also because the ethnicity of the grandfathers was rarely transmissible to begin with), but it does explain the appearance of ostensibly non-ethnic organizations devoted to the ethnic mother tongue. However, while such organizations are clearly more than "never ethnic", their language-maintenance interest may be less than fully functional.

The developmental sequence hypothesized above suggests the possible importance of specific ethnic group contexts within which both "positives" and "negatives" function. We have aimed at theoretical parsimony by ignoring the multiplicity of ethnic groups and by dealing with "positives" and "negatives" directly, as if they were recognizable social and organizational entities; yet it may be that the developmental sequences we have hypothesized in connection with language maintenance and the assertion of ethnic affiliation are not primarily based upon distinctions between "positives" and "negatives" but rather upon distinctions between specific ethnic groups in which "positives" and "negatives" are differentially represented. As long as this possibility remained, it seemed appropriate to reanalyze these relationships for the purpose of determining whether they still obtained when the predominance of language-maintenance interest in the ethnic group context was held constant. Since 72% of the responding ethnic cultural organizations had indicated an espousal of language maintenance, two large sub-clusters of ethnic groups were examined, one in which *72% or more* of the constituent ethnic organizations espoused language maintenance and another in which *less than 72%* did so. We were then able to re-examine the relationship between language-maintenance espousal and assertion of ethnic affiliation. If this relationship had been appreciably strengthened or weakened within either or both of the sub-clusters, then we would have had to conclude that it was initially a reflection primarily of a group effect, i.e., that it was due primarily to certain group-specific ideological, cultural, or even immigrational factors. However, the relationship between ethnic affiliation and language maintenance espousal remained essentially unchanged in both clusters, enabling us to conclude that it transcended group-specific factors and that it could appropriately be analyzed at the level of language maintenance "positives" and "negatives". It appears that regardless of the predominance of language-maintenance espousal in specific ethnic contexts, any "slippage" from organizational ethnic affiliation is likely to lead to a discontinuance of language-maintenance espousal, at least until the third generation becomes predominant. Several strong forces lead toward increased "slippage" from ethnic organizational moorings over time.

Since authentic ("ideal") primordial ethnicity based on the traditions of daily, communal life is rarely and decreasingly possible in the United States, ethnic continuity has been increasingly channeled into the organizational structure amenable to transmuted ethnicity. However, insofar as transmuted ethnicity in the United States cannot long remain ideologically exclusivistic and separatistic, it must tend toward ever greater purposive generalization and de-ethnization. Just as originally ethnic cultural organizations must tend toward becoming "open" cultural organizations, albeit with a particular language-and-area focus, so ethnic religious organizations must tend toward becoming "open" religious organizations, and ethnic mutual welfare organizations toward "open" benefit associations. Such processes begin with the very first generation – i.e., those immigrants who are forced by circumstances to leave authentic or nationalistic ethnicity behind – and are carried on at an increasing

TABLE 7.2

Decade of Founding and Belief in Importance of Mother Tongue Maintenance

Belief in Language Mainte- nance	Decade of Founding								
	N.R.	−1899	1900-09	1910-19	1920-29	1930-39	1940-49	1950−	Total
Yes	5 (1%)	66 (14%)	46 (10%)	48 (10%)	47 (10%)	47 (10%)	76 (16%)	129 (28%)	464
No	*1 (1%)*	*51 (29%)*	*16 (9%)*	*18 (10%)*	*28 (16%)*	*12 (7%)*	*27 (15%)*	*25 (14%)*	*178*
Total	6 (1%)	117 (18%)	62 (10%)	66 (10%)	75 (12%)	59 (9%)	103 (16%)	154 (24%)	642

pace by subsequent generations with their need for a progressively more transmuted and marginal ethnicity. Ethnic organizations that can make such changes are able to grow in membership and in geographic scope. Those that cannot – e.g., those more exclusively oriented toward language and culture maintenance – are destined to remain smaller and weaker if they remain at all. Many ethnic cultural organizations presumably cannot make the adaptations required to insure their continued functioning. The roster of merged and discontinued ethnic organizations testifies that they have more often been lacking in adaptiveness than eager to compromise initial goals for the sake of organizational "success".

On the basis of available information on immigration and repatriation, it appears that roughly 70% of post-1890 immigrants remaining in the United States arrived between 1890 and 1920. One might expect a similar proportion of existing ethnic cultural organizations to have been founded before 1920. Although many ethnic cultural organizations have undoubtedly suffered an early demise, a number of such organizations founded prior to 1890 have been continued by second, third, and subsequent generations. However, the life expectancy of immigrant organizations is considerably briefer than the life expectancy of the immigrants founding them. As shown in Table 7.2, more than 60% of our respondents report their date of founding as post-1920; indeed, about a quarter of them were founded after the conclusion of the Second World War. Moreover, recency of founding is more generally the rule for those organizations espousing language maintenance than it is for those denying its importance. Thus, 65% of "positives" have been founded since 1920 as opposed to 52% of "negatives".

Three distinct factors appear to be involved here. One, language maintenance is more likely to be espoused by organizations of recent immigrants. Two, it is more frequently espoused by organizations of those immigrant groups that have more recently come to the United States. The first factor, is a product of immigrational recency alone, (i.e., there has been less time for the immigrants to become de-ethnicized and for their "positive" organizations to be discontinued), while the latter posits certain ideological-cultural features that are particularly supportive of language maintenance. The third factor, already alluded to, is that an interest in language maintenance does not augur well for the longevity of an ethnic cultural organization.

The relationship between decade of founding and belief in language maintenance is intensified when we examine those ethnic groups in which "positives" are more than usually predominant. Among these, 71% of "positives" have been founded since 1920. As a result, although "positives" undoubtedly have a shorter life expectancy, they should continue to be in a majority among ethnic cultural organizations for many years. The interdependence, nevertheless, of organizational language maintenance and ethnic identification cannot be overstressed. The factors that affect one affect the other. This is clear from the fact that cultural organizations admitting to a current affiliation with a specific ethnic group tend to have been established more recently than

TABLE 7.3

Ethnic Association and Decade of Founding

Ethnic Association (Past-Present)	Decade of Founding								
	N.R.	−1899	1900-09	1910-19	1920-29	1930-39	1940-49	1950−	Total
Yes-Yes	6 (1%)	68 (14%)	48 (10%)	48 (10%)	62 (13%)	43 (9%)	81 (17%)	133 (27%)	489
Yes-No	—	14 (17%)	8 (10%)	11 (13%)	5 (6%)	11 (13%)	17 (21%)	17 (21%)	83
No-No	—	35 (50%)	6 (9%)	7 (10%)	8 (11%)	5 (7%)	5 (7%)	4 (6%)	70
Total	6	117	62	66	75	59	103	154	642

those that no longer make such an admission (Table 7.3). Furthermore, even within the latter category those cultural organizations admitting they at one time were associated with a particular ethnic group have a somewhat more recent average date of establishment than those claiming never to have been associated with a particular ethnic group. The preservation of organizational structure thus seems continually to be purchased at the price of ethnic disaffiliation. If avowed ethnic affiliation decreases over time, and if such affiliation is an important initial predisposer to language maintenance then language maintenance itself may well become further jeopardized in the surviving cultural organizations that were originally ethnic in origin.

MEMBERSHIP CHARACTERISTICS

Among the most obvious membership characteristics of concern to organizations and to students of organizations is membership size (Barber 1954; Terrien 1955). This is particularly true in the present case since we have already seen that espousal of language maintenance may become organizationally dysfunctional to an appreciable degree. Table 7.4 shows that, on the whole, "positives" tend to be smaller in member-

TABLE 7.4

Membership Size and Belief in Importance of Mother Tongue Maintenance

Belief in Language Maintenance	Membership Size						Total
	N.R.	−100	101-500	501-1000	1001-2000	2001+	
Yes	69 (15%)	144 (31%)	118 (25%)	24 (5%)	27 (6%)	82 (17%)	464
No	50 (28%)	35 (20%)	33 (18%)	10 (6%)	6 (3%)	44 (25%)	178
Total	119 (18%)	179 (29%)	151 (23%)	34 (5%)	33 (5%)	126 (20%)	642

ship than "negatives". Thus, 56% of "positive" organizations have a membership of 500 or less whereas only 39% of "negative" organizations are thus limited in the size of their membership. Similarly, while 80% of all organizations with 500 or fewer members are "positives", only 65% of all organizations with 2001 members or more are "positives".

That this negative relationship between membership size and belief in language maintenance is not simply due to most "positives" being local organizations and, therefore, necessarily smaller in terms of membership is borne out by additional data. "Positives" claim fewer members than "negatives" at *each* level of organizational scope. Be they nationwide, regional, or local, organizations which put numerical and financial success, or more generally organizational continuity, ahead of ideological or traditional considerations are inclined to abandon their initial language maintenance interests. Indeed, given the rarity of mother tongue mastery and the marginality of ethnicity among second, third, and subsequent generations, there may be no other approach to organizational success, barring major revitalization movements.

This supposition is strengthened when we consider another aspect of growth trends. Both "positives" and "negatives" make essentially similar claims regarding membership trends over the past decade with respect to foreign-born members. Very few organizations of either type claim an increase in this category of membership (4% and 7% respectively). As for "second-generation" members, the two types of organization once again make very similar claims, although claiming a somewhat larger number of such increases (15% and 13%). However, with respect to membership trends for "third-generation" members, the two types differ quite markedly in their claims. Only 13% of the "positives" claim an increase during the past decade in this category of membership as opposed to 21% of the "negatives". Thus while the two types of organization may be about equally successful (or unsuccessful) in attracting additional first- or second-generation members, when it comes to attracting third- or subsequent-generation members the "negatives" claim increases much more frequently than do the "positives". It is instructive, moreover, to note that foreign-born individuals represent the least important avenue of growth potential for both types of ethnic organization. The second generation still represents a relatively important growth potential for organizations that do believe in language maintenance, but the fact that these organizations are far less successful than "negatives" in finding new members in the third and subsequent generations speaks clearly to the purported "third-generation return" to ethnicity. If there is a "return", it is certainly not to language maintenance.

The membership trends noted above are probably related to organizational age as well as to the period of mass immigration of the associated ethnic groups. Younger ethnic organizations are more likely to be serving ethnic groups that have more recently arrived in large numbers in the United States. Since these are also more likely to be organizations concerned with language maintenance, it is clear why they are not yet as oriented toward third and subsequent generations as are organizations not interested in language maintenance. Nevertheless, "positives" remain less likely to reach a "ripe old age" than "negatives", primarily as a result of their lesser ability to attract members among third and subsequent generations to replace the shrinking universe of foreign-stock members. Only 24% of "negatives" claim that a majority of their members are foreign born. On the other hand, 50% of the "positives" make such a claim. Thus the major current *membership category* of "positives" is no longer a major *membership source*. Whether the newer "positives" (those more recently organized) will succeed in attracting sufficient numbers of American-born members – something the older "positives" have not seemed able to do – remains to be seen. The fact that *only* 50% of current "positives" consist of a majority of foreign-born members may even be viewed as a hopeful rather than a discouraging sign in respect to continued organizational support for future language-maintenance efforts. But, this proportion may also indicate that many "positives" are nearing the "turning point" when language maintenance, and ethnic affiliation more generally, will come into question. Finally, it may imply quite a gap between attitudinal positiveness and its overt implementation.

MOTHER TONGUE USE AND ORGANIZATIONAL ACTIVITY

Apropos of language maintenance it is not enough to know that "positives" differ from "negatives" with respect to certain organizational and membership characteristics. It is even more important to determine whether these two types of ethnic cultural organization differ in the activities they pursue, and how much they differ in frequency of involvement in activities likely to be of major importance for language maintenance. If there are no significant differences, then the distinction between "negatives" and "positives" is only a superficial one, related more to background sentiments and memories than to operative functioning. Some organizational activities are oriented toward older members and others toward younger ones, some are oriented toward a more general public and others toward the "inner membership" or particular subgroups of the membership (officers, committee members, etc.), some are oral activities and some are written, and so on. In view of the possible variations in mother tongue usage that might obtain from one to another, data were collected on six separate areas of organizational activity.

Table 7.5 indicates that "positive" respondents consistently claim much higher rates of mother tongue use than do "negative" respondents. This holds for each one of the six activity areas as well as for the overall average of organizational activity. Whereas 39% of "positives" average between 76% and 100% mother tongue use across all six areas (formal programs, regular meetings, informal gatherings, committee or board meetings, official correspondence, and official minutes), only 16% of "negatives" achieve such a high average. At the lower end of the scale these proportions are reversed. Only 31% of "positives" average less than 25% mother tongue use, whereas 72% of "negatives" show such a low overall average. It is clear, then, that the espousal of language maintenance is usually accompanied by a much higher claim for mother tongue use in organizational activities. Although our data do not permit us to establish the direction of cause and effect, quite a bit of causal circularity is likely. Some clue as to the transitional sequence between use and disuse of the mother tongue in organizational activity is provided by the very use-pattern discernible among the "positives" themselves. Although differences between areas of activity are small, "informal gatherings" and "formal programs" constitute the areas in which mother tongue is *least* frequently used, while "committee meetings" and "regular meetings" constitute the areas in which it is *most* frequently used. This would imply that the core membership and leadership are more likely to use the mother tongue than are either the general membership or the surrounding public to which "positives" bring their programs and services. Beyond the circles of organizational elites and activists

TABLE 7.5

Frequency of Mother Tongue Use in Organizational Activities and Belief in Mother Tongue Maintenance

	LANGUAGE MAINTENANCE BELIEF											
	"POSITIVES"						"NEGATIVES"					
	FREQUENCY OF ETHNIC MOTHER TONGUE USE											
Organizational Activity	NR and None	01 to 25%	26 to 50%	51 to 75%	76 to 100%	Total	NR and None	01 to 25%	26 to 50%	51 to 75%	76 to 100%	Total
Formal Programs	115 (25%)	53 (11%)	99 (21%)	32 (7%)	165 (36%)	464	102 (57%)	25 (14%)	24 (13%)	6 (3%)	21 (12%)	178
Regular Meetings	130 (28%)	40 (9%)	67 (14%)	22 (5%)	205 (44%)	,,	117 (66%)	16 (9%)	12 (7%)	5 (3%)	28 (16%)	,,
Informal Gatherings	116 (25%)	48 (10%)	107 (23%)	36 (8%)	157 (34%)	,,	106 (60%)	20 (11%)	24 (13%)	4 (2%)	24 (13%)	,,
Committee Meetings	140 (30%)	39 (8%)	57 (12%)	23 (5%)	205 (44%)	,,	126 (70%)	13 (7%)	11 (6%)	1 (1%)	27 (15%)	,,
Official Correspondence	131 (28%)	53 (11%)	76 (16%)	27 (6%)	177 (38%)	,,	119 (67%)	15 (8%)	16 (9%)	4 (2%)	24 (13%)	,,
Official Minutes	176 (38%)	21 (5%)	52 (11%)	15 (3%)	200 (43%)	,,	136 (76%)	4 (2%)	7 (4%)	0 (0%)	31 (17%)	,,
Overall Average Use	66 (14%)	80 (17%)	86 (19%)	51 (11%)	181 (39%)		78 (44%)	51 (29%)	15 (8%)	6 (3%)	28 (16%)	

functioning in their official capacities, use of the mother tongue tends to fall off. A language which is no longer appropriate or natural for informal gatherings and interpersonal contacts is evolving from the status of active mother tongue to that of ethnic (or historical) mother tongue.

The nativity of chief officers (and, most probably, the nativity distribution within the membership proper) is an important determinant of the extent to which the mother tongue is employed. Among "positive" organizations with foreign-born chief officers, only 21% report an average rate of mother tongue use lower than 25%, while 49% report an average rate of mother tongue use above 75%. Among "positive" organizations with "native-of-native" chief leaders, the corresponding values are 47% and 28% respectively. The predominance of "positive" organizations in particular ethnic groups is also an important influence. "Negative" organizations embedded in a group context in which over 72% of all organizations are "positives" make more frequent use of their mother tongue than do "positive" organizations embedded in a group context in which fewer than 72% of all organizations are "positives". Thus, while belief in language maintenance is a most important predictor of language use in organizational activity, many other variables – either internal or external to the specific responding organizations – may be even more influential.

Various characteristics of "negatives" led us to hypothesize that their programs would be more "generalized" in the sense of being less anchored in ethnic particularity and ethnic purpose. But generalization may carry over into the *range* of activities rather than being restricted to qualitative content alone. Because "negatives" are older, larger, stronger, and bureaucratically more developed organizations, they should therefore, be better suited for a wider variety of organizational activities. This has frequently been found the case in studies of American organizational patterns and is usually considered an indication that "nothing succeeds like success" in the world of organizational functioning as in most others. Our data on ethnic cultural organizations, however, point consistently to quite a different state of affairs. "Positives" are overrepresented rather than underrepresented in almost all areas of organizational activity (Table 7.6). This is particularly true with respect to "political" activity, defined as "supporting the program of a particular political party or group through meetings, publications, or financial aid". While politics is a rather rare activity for ethnic cultural organizations, of all the organizations admitting to such activity, 87% are "positives". On the other hand, "positives" seem to be somewhat underrepresented among organizations engaging in religious activities. The difference between the frequency of "positive" involvement in these two domains may indicate that the unique wellsprings of language maintenance in America lie closer to communal-political-ideological continuity than to religious continuity. Indeed, ethnic religions may well have attained de-ethnization and bureaucratization more quickly and more "successfully" than other ethnic institutions because they arrive in the United States in a more advanced organizational state relative to other aspects of ethnicity. Moreover, religion tends toward universalistic concerns and toward organizational struc-

TABLE 7.6

Areas of Organizational Activity and Belief in Mother Tongue Maintenance

Organizational Activity	Organizational Belief in Language Maintenance		
	Yes	No	Percent "Yes" of Total
Cultural	367 (79%)	92 (52%)	80
Educational	257 (55%)	74 (42%)	78
Fraternal	125 (27%)	50 (28%)	71
Political	58 (12%)	9 (5%)	87
Social	295 (64%)	79 (44%)	79
Scientific	55 (12%)	15 (8%)	79
Religious	32 (7%)	19 (11%)	63
Other	133 (29%)	54 (30%)	71
Total Organizations	464	178	72

tures which relate individuals to one another across ethnic and linguistic lines. Thus on ideological as well as organizational grounds religious activity is not likely to be consistently supportive of language maintenance over the long run.

The more diversified range of activity on the part of language maintenance "positives" – notwithstanding their more frequent organizational limitations – implies a more active relationship between them and their membership. "Positive" organizations seem to stand closer to an ongoing community, and to be of greater importance in the lives of their members. Whether they are carriers of traditional or of ideological ethnicity, there is about them an air of intensity, of activity, and of personal involvement. They are more inclined to meet all the ethnic needs and interests of their membership, and these ethnic needs and interests tend to be more numerous and varied than is the case with "negatives". The latter have become more specialized as well as more bureaucratic organizations, and their members interact with them peripherally rather than centrally.

Additional evidence consistent with the finding that "positives" engage in more diversified areas of activity is that they more frequently sponsor radio programs and summer camps, as well as junior divisions and schools for children. And, notwithstanding their more limited financial resources, they more frequently sponsor publications. Furthermore, there is ample evidence that in each of these activities "positives" utilize the mother tongue much more frequently than do "negatives". Language maintenance is in itself frequently the major purpose served by many of their activities whereas among "negatives" many more general educational and community-service purposes are advanced. These characteristics are easily corroborated by examination of the publications currently sponsored by both types of ethnic cultural organization.

The ethnic group press has frequently been referred to as "the backbone of language-maintenance efforts" among ethnic groups in the United States. A sizable proportion of this press is organizationally sponsored or subsidized, and were it not for such organizational support both the circulations and the resources available to it would be drastically curtailed. Our data reveal a striking difference between "negatives" and "positives" as to whether organizationally sponsored publications appear in the ethnic mother tongue. Half of all "positives" sponsoring publications do so in the mother tongue only. All in all, 80% of the publishing "positives" utilize their mother tongue in their publications, although some 30% of these sponsor bilingual or tri-lingual publications in which other languages (usually English) are also employed. When we examine the publishing "negatives", we find that only 15% publish exclusively in their mother tongue and only 43% in some combination of mother tongue and other languages. Conversely, whereas 55% of the publishing "negatives" publish in English alone, only 17% of the "positives" do so. From whatever point of view we examine the matter, "positives" not only sponsor publications more frequently than do "negatives" but their publications more frequently utilize the ethnic mother tongue.[2] Much the same tendency can be seen in the schools, camps, radio programs, and junior divisions of "positives" as contrasted with those of "negatives", the "positives" viewing them as means of linguistic and cultural continuity, almost as weapons in a battle for ethnic or ideological survival, rather than as primarily organizational devices for organizational growth and development. Thus it would seem that language maintenance and culture maintenance are simultaneously energizing and focusing principles, leading to a different tempo as well as to different content in the activities of "positives" and "negatives".

To sum up, "positives" and "negatives" show similarities as well as differences in their self-maintenance activities. Whereas the differences are rarely great enough or sharp enough to indicate a secure future for functional bilingualism or even for cultural bilingualism among the "positives", the similarities are sufficiently pervasive to imply that the de-ethnization process is long and slow. Many "negatives" continue to utilize the mother tongue even after they no longer consider language mainte-nance to be an organizational or an ideological imperative. They long continue within a recognizably ethnic (even though marginally ethnic) framework even after they have become language-maintenance "negatives", and still attract members of recognizably ethnic background and pursue activities of recognizably ethnic content after they no longer subscribe to goals that are rationalized in terms of ethnic group maintenance. Their very retreat from "full-blooded" ethnicity and from overt language maintenance may make them more attractive for successive generations of members. Moreover, even first-generation members may be attracted to them, since the ethnicity of many recent immigrants of urban and industrialized backgrounds is sufficiently transmuted and generalized from the very outset to orient them more toward language mainte-nance "negatives" than toward more particularistic "positives". Thus, while "nega-tives" play a passive role at best with respect to language maintenance, their existence,

[2] Following this same pattern, "positives" are less likely than "negatives" to discontinue mother tongue publications and more likely to discontinue English- and other-language publications.

their strength, and even their very passivity make available a mode of ethnic continuity and ethnic identification which not only may be personally and collectively adaptive but may extend the period of language maintenance rather than cut it off quickly and irrevocably.

IDEOLOGICAL APPROACHES TO LANGUAGE MAINTENANCE

We have already noted that many "negatives" make some use of their mother tongue in various organizational activities. We have also noted that there are "positives" that make little, if any, overt organizational use of the mother tongue. Therefore, the very fact that attitude and action are not fully consistent with each other must indicate that language maintenance itself is viewed or defined in diverse ways.

Language maintenance may be vigorous and central whether or not it is ideologically elaborated. Certainly, the traditional ethnic community was a staunch fortress of language maintenance without any ideological-symbolic commitment, indeed even without language consciousness *per se*. At the other extreme, language maintenance in urban industrial and intellectual centers is firmly embedded in an ideological matrix which combines ingredients of national unity, national mission, national creativity, and national distinctiveness and places them on a "moral" level. Although most immigrants to the United States have come from rural rather than urban settings (except in quite recent years) – and might, therefore, have been inclined toward habitual rather than ideological language maintenance – their dependence upon formal means of promoting communal cohesion in the American metropoli in which they were concentrated, and their increasing reliance upon transmuted ethnicity rather than upon a daily ethnic way of life, may also have resulted in a noticeable ideologization of language maintenance on their part. Whether language maintenance among "positives" has frequently attained (or retained) elements of the "fiery sword" associated with nationalist movements, and whether "negatives" reject language maintenance on ideological or purely on functional grounds, are questions of equal concern to us here. Certainly, the absence of ideology among "positives" would seem to be adverse to language maintenance, given the disappearence of traditional ethnicity. On the other hand, the absence of ideology among "negatives" would only indicate that the retreat from language maintenance can become a gradual "fact of life".

Eight content analysis categories were found to adequately cover all the collected free-response statements of language maintenance positions. "Positive" and "negative" statements alike encompassed both ideological and practical responses, and in both types of statement there were ethnic as well as non-ethnic rationales. Although the content categories are referred to by explanatory descriptive titles, each category calls for at least a brief introduction at this point.

Category 1: "Nationalistic or separatistic ideology". Responses that deal with the "glorious history", the "great heroes", the "national mission", the "cultural values", or other ideological, symbolic, nationalistic values.

Category 2: "Ethnic-instrumental self-maintenance". As contrasted with the symbolic emphases of the previous category, responses that speak of preserving the group as a cultural-behavioral entity in the United States.

Category 3: "General cultural and educational values". Humanistic-behavioral rather than ethnic-instrumental or ideological rationales; viz., "it is always good (for a person or for a society) to know another language" in order to be "truly educated and cultured".

Category 4: "American national needs". Like the preceding category, responses that justify language maintenance without explicit reference to ethnic groups or their cultures, with a further generalization of language maintenance by pointing out that the current world situation is such that America must preserve its non-English language resources.

Category 5: Other positive replies.

Category 6: "Unpatriotic (un-American)". Replies indicating that the preservation of a non-English language is rejective of America, Americans, or Americanism.

Category 7: "Unimportant to organizational goals". All responses indicating that language maintenance is unrelated to or even deleterious to the welfare of the organization. These are practical rather than ideological disclaimers.

Category 8: Other negative replies.

Two reply categories account for the lion's share of positive rationales (Table 7.7). The largest – "ethnic-instrumental self-maintenance" – was indicated by 44% of all "positives", the next largest – "general cultural and educational values" – was noted

TABLE 7.7

Belief in Language Maintenance and Reasons For or Against It

Belief in Language Maintenance	Reasons For or Against Language Maintenance[a]									
	1	2	3	4	5	6	7	8	NR	Total
Yes	43	205	138	83	38	—	8	—	102	464
%	9	44	30	18	8	—	2	—	22	
No	—	6	9	2	4	7	52	3	105	178
%	—	3	5	1	2	4	29	2	59	

[a] *Categories*: 1. Nationalistic or separatistic ideology; 2. Ethnic-intrumental self-maintenance; 3. General cultural and educational values; 4. American national needs; 5. Other positive replies; 6. Unpatriotic (un-America); 7. Unimportant to organizational goals; 8. Other negative replies.

by 30%. Significantly enough, only 9% of the "positives" gave replies that dealt with nationalistic or ideological ethnicity, and only 18% advanced American national needs. Thus, the more clearly ideological-symbolic categories (1 and 4) are little utilized, whether they refer to specifically ethnic or to general American content. On the other hand, the concrete behavioral categories (2 and 3) are most frequently espoused – but with differing implications. Those "positives" mentioning "ethnic-instrumental self-maintenance" in the United States are undoubtedly more language-maintenance oriented than those which justify maintenance on the grounds that "it is always good to know more than one language". The latter view clearly represents de-ethnization and a generalization of language maintenance. Such a rationale may help bring about the introduction of the ethnic mother tongue into American schools, colleges, and polite society more generally, but it also foreshadows a lessening of personal and organizational obligation, involvement, and commitment to particularistic language maintenance or group maintenance. As the burden of language maintenance is shifted to society in general and its benefit becomes viewed as educational and cultural enrichment of a general kind, the ethnic embeddedness of language maintenance fades. Just as the mother tongue can shift to become an ethnic mother tongue, so the latter can become "another language" which "it is always good to know".

The absence of symbolically elaborated ideology is also apparent among the "negatives". Only 4% believe that the preservation of a non-English mother tongue stamps individuals or organizations as un-American; thus melting-pot philosophies are practically absent. On the other hand, 29% flatly state that language maintenance is simply unimportant for the furtherance of their organizational goals. Just as "positives" may come to believe that language maintenance is merely "nice" rather than crucial, so "negatives" may feel that language maintenance is merely "unnecessary" rather than ugly. While "positives" utilize the mechanisms of transmuted ethnicity, they do not seem commensurately attracted to its slogans and passions. Schools, publications, organizations, theaters, and other formal means of promoting communal cohesion and language maintenance are utilized mainly because they are recognized group methanisms for goal-directed behavior in an associational society. Transmuted ethnicity has penetrated into the consciousness and the overt behavior of the rank and file of ethnics and their cultural organizations only superficially. As a result, language maintenance at the "high" culture level tends to shade off into ideologically less elaborated and even ideologically inert rationales. Given the interacting participationism of urban American life, de-ideologization superimposed on a narrow and narrowing behavioral base must and does lead to de-ethnization and generalization. In time, non-ethnic considerations come to be primarily advanced on behalf of what once was an ingredient in the "fiery sword" of flaming nationalism. Indeed, nonethnic or extremely generalized ethnic rationales constitute a step on the third generations's road back from the negativistic and rejective rationales which developed out of their parents' discomfort with, on the one hand, the nationalistic and separatistic ideologies of transmuted ethnicity in its most active stage, and, on the other, the shrinking and fractionated world of behavioral ethnicity. Both "positives" and "negatives" appear to have withdrawn from the ideological and behavioral extremes which once made communication between them impossible. As a result of this developmental sequence, there seems to be very little ideological rancor or fervor with respect to language maintenance among ethnic cultural organizations in the United States today.

Ethnic-instrumental self-maintenance, the continued will to survive as a segment of the American population with unique cultural-historical roots and behavioral expressions, thus appears to be the most retentivist rationale currently espoused by any large number of ethnic cultural organizations. Although this rationale receives scant overt or dependable reinforcement either from American core society or from the entire ethnic community as such, it is, nevertheless, still accompanied by more active language maintenance in terms of mother tongue use and of range of organizational activities and avenues than the next most popular rationale, which merely ascribes "general cultural and educational value" to language maintenance. Self-maintenance as a "philosophy" may still have definite energizing value for ethnic cultural organizations without placing them or their members under the shadow of un-American nationalism. It may preserve in them a sense of urgency, of purpose, and of uniqueness far greater than that provided by less retentivist philosophies, at the same time not separating them ideologically from American life.

The ideological calm of mid-century American life has undoubtedly contributed to many of the findings reported above. There is much less concern with immigrant groups and with "foreign" ethnicity than was the case during the first third of this century – perhaps less than at any time since the beginning of mass immigration in the 1880's. As a result, immigrants as well as their children and grandchildren are under less pressure. Their de-ethnization proceeds more from internal dynamics than from external expectations. As the first generation withdraws from active ideological ethnicity and from public behavioral ethnicity into passive, group-maintenance retentivist sentiments, the second generation revolt also becomes de-ideologized. As the second generation itself reaches middle adulthood and acquires security in its Americanism, it provides a meeting ground between the now attenuated and transmuted behavioral ethnicity of the first generation and the generalized, intellectualized, selective ethnicity of the third generation. A long contiuum of marginality appears, obviating the earlier headlong flight from ethnicity. Thus the dearth (if not the death) of ideology in non-ethnic American life has facilitated both the de-ideologization of ethnicity and the organizational and behavioral establishment of marginal ethnicity.

However, concomitant with the above developments, one also notes the curious evolution (perhaps "elevation" is a more appropriate term) of behavioral ethnicity, in both its linguistic and non-linguistic manifestations. From its non-rationalized, non-ideological origins in traditional "low" culture, it has evolved into a "position", a "rationale", which is communicated and defended. Although seriously fractionated in comparison to its originally complete gestalt, it has become verbalized, embedded in consciously formalized and organized structures, and, therefore, more protectable under modern urban conditions. Under all the circumstances currently impinging upon it, functional language maintenance is (and will remain) a rare phenomenon in the United States. Nevertheless, cultural bilingualism still appears to be salvageable and reasonable in conjunction with marginal ethnicity under one or another of the rationales that are currently available to it.

ROLE OF ETHNIC CULTURAL LEADERS

It has frequently been asserted that mass immigration to the United States (roughly 1880-1920) consisted primarily of individuals recruited from the lowest strata of society. To follow the popular cliche, these immigrants were young and energetic, hard-working and ambitious; at the same time, their very costumes, facial features, and calloused hands underscored the fact that their background was one of traditional poverty and ignorance. By and large, the widely accepted stereotype is true; yet, like any other stereotype, it oversimplifies reality (Fishman 1955). It glosses over the fact that these same immigrants were accompanied, as a rule, by individuals of urban background and higher education. The latter included not only educated religious leaders but also a sprinkling of secular intellectuals – writers and journalists, teachers and lawyers, doctors and scholars. Some joined the mass exodus from their homelands out of sheer populist commitment to the insulted, injured, and exploited; others searched for adventure and for careers in this country of expanding opportunity; still others hailed from the growing stratum of declassed intellectuals – teachers without students, journalists without newspapers or readers, and lawyers without clients. Last but not least, there have always been present among educated immigrants a small but significant group of political refugees and exiles whose arrival on these shores has continued since earliest colonial days. The number and proportion of intellectuals have varied from one ethnic group to another and from one wave of immigration to the next; nevertheless, they have been present in every group and in every wave.

At one time or another, most ethnic groups in this country have possessed their own cultural leadership, including not a few highly creative writers and intellectuals. For this reason alone ethnic cultures in the United States must not be equated with venerable but inert traditions consisting of anonymous folk elements such as costumes, songs, and dances. Reliable estimates show that Germans and Norwegians alone have published no less than sixty-five different literary magazines in the United States since the late 1860's. One may justifiably speak of German-, Norwegian-, Jewish-, Polish-, or Ukrainian-American literature, art, and even music. The very existence of these elements of "representative" culture clearly reflects the creative efforts of ethnic cultural leaders and the receptive cultural interests of sizable audiences for whom their creations were most directly intended. Such leaders and such audiences exist to this day, even in the face of ample evidence and expectation that ethnic minorities in the United States cannt long remain culturally creative and dynamic.

Our concern here is primarily with the cultural and organizational leadership of four American ethnic groups: German, Jewish, Polish, and Ukrainian. More specifically, its purpose is a dual one: to determine, first of all, the extent to which ethnic leaders and their children are involved in organized ethnic life, and, secondly, to assess the maintenance of ethnicity among ethnic leaders and their children via the continued use of appropriate ethnic mother tongues in diverse domains of interpersonal life. The close linking of ethnicity and language stems partly from the particular focus of the Language Resources Project. But it is not without its historical justification, especially in that language has both carried and symbolized the basic ideals and values of many modern nationalities. Often the sole determinant of such a collective designation as nationality has been in terms of language and/or language-related criteria.

The universe of the present study consists of those leaders of these four specific ethnic backgrounds considered to be most actively engaged in the maintenance of ethnic communal and cultural life. On the basis of a compiled list of names,[3] 826 data gathering contacts were attempted and 222 (27.0%) were successfully completed during the 1961-62 academic year. The rates of response from these four ethnic groups tend to be inversely related to the proportion of foreign-born leaders among their respondents. Jews and Ukrainians have higher percentages of foreign-born leaders (82% and 92% respectively) and their relative rates of response are lower, while the percentage of foreign-born leaders among Germans and Poles is lower by far (68% and 64%) and their rates of response are appreciably higher. This nativity-linked differential leads us to suspect that first-generation leaders – the very individuals who represent the most intensive type of ethnic leadership – are likely to be underrepresented in each of our responding groups.

In terms of age, education, and recency of arrival in the United States, the Ukrainian communal and cultural leaders constitute a highly dynamic group of ethnic activists. A high proportion are active in ethnic cultural life on a part-time basis only. On weekends, within the context of ethnic "communal" life, they carry the burden of cultural leadership; on weekdays, in the occupational structure of the dominant society, they are frequently unskilled and semi-skilled laborers – dishwashers, elevator operators, etc. Like many other recently arrived educated immigrants, they may best be viewed as declassed ethnic intellectuals. On the other hand, Jewish cultural leaders, although equally of foreign birth, can hardly be considered as declassed with respect to their present occupational standing. Either their occupational position in general American society is congruent with their leadership status in ethnic communal life or, as is more usual, their ethnic leadership is expressed via full-time occupationsl involvement on behalf of their ethnic group. Finally, the Germans and Poles present still a third picture, in that a high proportion of them (about half) are professionals in the occupational system of the dominant society. Many of these leaders are "ethnic" primarily in the sense that the area of their specialty happens to be their ethnic language, literature, art, or history. Such an interest in the ancestral culture (whether among foreign-born or native-born leaders) need not entail personal involvement in ethnic cultural life or, for that matter, active participation in ethnic organizations. Thus the ethnic heritage, including language, may even become solely an object of cognitive orientation, not unlike Greek, Roman, or other national cultures of general intellectual import.

The extent to which English has replaced the ethnic mother tongue, even within

---

[3] Names were derived from discussions, interviews and correspondence with members and observers of the four ethnic groups and via perusal of the ethnic group press and organizational publications.

the context of highly informal and personal relations, is particularly noticeable among native-born communal leaders. Of fifty-two native-born leaders, 44.2 per cent use English exclusively in conversations with their three closest friends, even though in only two cases are all three of these friends non-ethnic Americans. On the whole, native-born leaders tend to maintain friendship ties primarily with individuals of their own ethnic origin. Foreign-born ethnic leaders, besides being ethnically somewhat more homophilous than their native-born counterparts, also display some propensity to maintain friendship ties with foreign-born individuals of other than their own ethnic group. This is especially true among Poles and Ukrainians. The Jewish group, however, stands out as different, in that it is most exclusive in this respect. Its leaders – foreign- and native-born alike – confine their friendship contacts almost completely to other Jews. Seventy-eight per cent of them have exclusively Jewish friends (three closest friends), as compared to sixty per cent among Ukrainians and forty-four and thirty-eight per cent among German and Polish leaders, respectively.

The noticeable dearth of enduring personal relations between Jews and non-Jews (be they other-ethnic or non-ethnic Americans) only confirms what has been known for some time to students of American minority groups. Yet, it is rather difficult to meaningfully interpret this unique insulation of the sphere of privacy and intimacy in the face of ever-declining communal segregation, linguistic difference, and even ritual separation. Bearing in mind the kind of population sampled, such obvious variables as occupational status, age, or even generational composition are scarcely of any value. The nature of Jewish communal existence in the Torah-centered *shtetl* must be carefully distinguished from Jewish communal existence in American urban centers. For the unique feature of American ethnic life lies precisely in the fact that it does not constitute a separate *communal* but a separate *associational* existence. The very proliferation of ethnic voluntary organizations (Jewish and non-Jewish) lends ample testimony to the associational character of ethnic "communal" life in this country. To the extent that this is true, patterns of friendship and interpersonal relations in general cannot but heavily depend upon participation in ethnic organizations.

In view of the foregoing, it might be hypothesized that ethnic homophily would be closely associated with the frequency and intensity of involvement in ethnic organizational life. Our data show, however, that existing variations in organizational membership scarcely approach a significance capable of accounting for the highly exclusive friendship patterns among Jewish leaders. Organizational affiliation among Jewish and Ukrainian communal leaders tends to be strikingly similar. Relatively few of either report being unaffiliated, and, likewise, a considerably high proportion of them (63.0% Jewish and 61.2% Ukrainian) maintain membership in as many as three or more ethnic organizations. German leaders report the least affiliation with organized ethnic life, about one-fourth of them (25.8%) being presently unaffiliated and only 16.0 per cent reporting membership in three or more ethnic organizations. Polish leaders occupy an intermediate position, being less extensively affiliated than Jewish and Ukrainian leaders but appreciably more so than German leaders.

Organizational affiliation does not necessarily entail intense involvement in ethnic organizations. But, if "offices currently held" are taken as a partial measure of involvement, the less extensively affiliated leaders – Germans and Poles – appear to supply the largest number of individuals (47.7% and 47.1% respectively) who are actively involved in ethnic organizational life. The two more extensively affiliated groups – Jews and Ukrainians – currently have fewer organizational activists, only 41.2 per cent of Jewish and 44.7 per cent of Ukrainian communal leaders holding some office in ethnic organizations. These variations in intensity of ethnic organizational involvement, while not appreciable, are nevertheless of some interest. They indicate that the propensity to join many ethnic organizations is not necessarily conducive to intense participation in any of them. Active involvement may accordingly be more typical among those leaders who are affiliated with fewer ethnic organizations. The differences in involvement also suggest that ethnic cultural or communal leaders need not be ethnic organizational leaders.

A different variation obtains when we consider the organizational affiliation of ethnic leaders in the host society. Leaders of the two immigrant groups – Jews and Ukrainians – are least commonly associated with general American (non-ethnic) organizations, 44.9 per cent of Ukrainian and 40.0 per cent of Jewish leaders reporting no membership in American organizations. Similarly, very few Ukrainian (6.1%) and Jewish (18.0%) leaders claim affiliation with as many as three or more organizations. In contrast to the above, membership in American organizations is significantly more extensive among German and Polish leaders. There are fewer non-members among them and also an appreciably larger proportion who are affiliated with three or more ethnic organizations.

Overall the organizational membership of ethnic leaders, in both ethnic and American organizations, reveals a distinct pattern. Except for the German, ethnic leaders continue to remain predominantly ethnic in that they are more extensively involved in ethnic than in American associational life. German-American leaders stand out as different, inasmuch as they are reportedly more involved in the organizational framework of the host society than of the ethnic community.

Another pattern that emerges is that native-born ethnic leaders are both more active and more extensively involved in ethnic organizations. With some few exceptions, these leaders are occupationally integrated in the dominant society as well as culturally de-ethnicized in comparison with foreign born ethnic leaders. This is clearly reflected in the fact that the ethnic mother tongue has become largely dormant among them, even in the sphere of interpersonal relations. At the same time, obviously enough, these are precisely the very native born individuals who are still most intensely interested in organized ethnic life, if not in the ethnicity of their fathers and forefathers. What communal arrangements, then, are available to *native born* and largely de-ethnicized individuals capable of expressing an interest in and attachment to some version and level of ethnicity? We venture to suggest that organizational affiliation remains one such major arrangement available for this purpose. This view is indirectly supported by the fact that one other and equally salient characteristic of native born leaders is their active *participation* in organized *ethnic* life. They are not solely extensive *joiners* of ethnic organizations; they also more frequently assume *positions of leadership* in ethnic organizations. The higher rate of office holding among Poles and Germans appears, then, to be linked to the generational composition of leaders of these two groups.

However, native-born leaders are least frequently members of literary and cultural organizations, that is, of those very organizations that are most directly relevant to the maintenance of ethnic cultures, including ethnic mother tongues. In fact, only 14.5 per cent of native-born ethnic leaders currently belong to ethnic cultural and literary organizations. On the other hand, the highest percentage of native-born leaders (58.2%) report membership in fraternal societies, that is, in those ethnic organizations which now have only the most indirect bearing upon the maintenance of ethnic cultures. Two other types of ethnic organizations with which native-born leaders report frequent association are scholarly (40.0%) and religious (30.9%), i.e., organizations that are also oriented toward the more marginal forms of ethnicity.

It is this shift from personal involvement in ethnic cultures to involvement in ethnically-peripheral organizations that is of crucial significance here. It prompts us to conclude that native-born leaders, far from being ethnic *cultural* leaders, should more properly be considered ethnic *organizational* leaders. Of course, by actively participating in ethnic organizational life native-born leaders may be trying to reassert their attachment to ethnicity. But organizational participation does not necessarily lead to personal and creative involvement in the ancestral culture. In point of fact, native-born leaders are largely de-ethnicized (both linguistically and otherwise) while, at the same time, they remain extensively involved in organized ethnic life.

Differences in the occupational status of ethnic leaders are reflected in their organizational affiliation. The majority of foreign-born leaders who are occupationally integrated in American society maintain only tenuous ties with organized ethnic life. It may even be warranted to contend that some are ethnic leaders simply by virtue of their foreign birth and professional interest in the national culture of their ethnic group. Whatever the specific nature of this interest – be it national history, literature, or even language – its bearing upon ethnic cultural life in this country is likely to be only marginal and indirect at best.

Foreign-born and native-born ethnic leaders are clearly two different generations. Nevertheless, the generations are not necessarily related to each other in the sequential fashion of fathers and sons. Although there exists, on the whole, a substantial correlation between the frequencies of ethnic organizational association of leaders and their children, that of the children lags consistently behind that of their fathers. However, the children's involvement in organized ethnic life is related not only to the involvement of their parents but to their nativity as well. Membership among children of native-born Polish and German leaders is somewhat less common than it is among children of foreign-born Ukrainian or Jewish leaders, even though native-born

Polish and German leaders are themselves more extensively affiliated with ethnic organizations than are foreign-born Ukrainian and Jewish leaders. Organizational membership among the children also appears to be associated with age. The relationship is sufficiently regular to underscore the fact that as children grow older they also tend to outgrow ethnic organizational affiliations. It is particularly striking that after the age of twenty-two the extent of organizational involvement among them shrinks to one or two organizations at best.

MOTHER TONGUE MASTERY AND USE

The above observations on children's involvement in ethnic organizations have decided implications for the continuity of organized ethnic life in this country. First, they suggest that ethnic organizational ties become attenuated with the transition from youth to adulthood and with the integration of adult individuals into the occupational structure of American society. Second, they throw light on the temporary and untransmittible nature of the heightened ethnic organizational involvement of de-ethnicized ethnic group leaders. Indeed, they imply that one can literally outgrow ethnic organizations and ethnic communities alike. Third, they lead us to suspect that ethnic organizational involvement ultimately decreases from one generation to the next and that no return to the fold of organized ethnic life takes place among the members of the third generation. "Organizational ethnicity" may have a special appeal for de-ethnicized second-generation individuals but it is an appeal which it is difficult to pass on – for both structural and psychological reasons – to the third.

What is the bearing of the nature and frequency of organizational affiliation among children of ethnic leaders upon the maintenance of minority ethnic cultures and of ethnic mother tongues in particular? Our data disclose a marked relationship between these two variables (Table 7.8). While it is true that one finds unaffiliated children whose mastery of their ethnic mother tongue is reported as being "very good", and extensively affiliated children whose knowledge of it is reported as being "poor", the relationship between the variables is strongly in the opposite direction. Noteworthy is the fact that very few children reported by their parents as possessing poor mastery of their ethnic mother tongue hold membership in three or more ethnic organizations, but rather are concentrated in the category of the organizationally unaffiliated. Thus, 72.4 percent of the oldest and 75.0 per cent of the youngest children whose mastery of the mother tongue is reported to be poor have no ties with ethnic organizations.

If children of ethnic leaders tend to outgrow ethnic organizational affiliation with increased integration in the educational and occupational structure of American society, it is to be expected that age is another factor associated with knowledge of the ethnic mother tongue. It must be granted that our measure of children's knowledge of their ethnic mother tongue, based as it is on the subjective judgment of their

TABLE 7.8

Average Knowledge of Mother Tongue and Ethnic Organizational Affiliation

Average Knowledge	Organizational Affiliations					
	0		1-2		3 or more	
	N	%	N	%	N	%
	Oldest Children					
Very well	21	35.6	21	35.6	17	28.8
Moderately	29	56.9	11	21.6	11	21.6
Little or None	21	72.4	5	17.2	3	10.3
	Youngest Children					
Very well	8	30.8	9	34.6	9	34.6
Moderately	22	47.3	13	28.3	11	23.9
Little or None	21	75.0	5	17.9	2	7.1

parents, is rather crude and imprecise. Nevertheless, even after allowing for the unavoidable crudity of this measure, the relationship between mother tongue mastery and age remains sufficiently revealing and may be briefly explicated as follows. As children pass through adolescence, the influence of their major age-heterogeneous group – the family of orientation – becomes increasingly circumscribed; at the same time, the influence of age-homogeneous groups – peer groups – tends to be progressively extended. Within this latter and expanding sphere, the English language becomes increasingly dominant, while the ethnic mother tongue remains prevalent within the family and other formally prescribed situations – be they mother tongue classes or ethnic youth organizations. As a result of studying the mother tongue in ethnic schools and continued recourse to it at home and in ethnically sponsored organizations, the child's mastery of it may be appreciably enhanced. But even so, "learning" of the ethnic mother tongue comes face to face with pressures for "unlearning". In fact, the mother tongue not only comes to be less frequently used by children within the family as they approach the end of adolescence, but it increasingly fails to serve them outside the family and similarly delimited institutional settings. Table 7.9, contrasting ethnic mother tongue use among oldest and youngest children, clearly discloses the decreasing frequency with which the mother tongue is used as children move from their *family of orientation* to *peer groups* to their own *family of procreation*. Our data likewise point to the important role that grandparents play in reinforcing use of the ethnic mother tongue among children of the second and third generation alike. It appears that this is precisely the context in which children most frequently continue to avail themselves of the ethnic mother tongue as they grow older. No less suggestive is the extent to which English prevails in conversations among siblings, indicating that even within the family of orientation the ethnic mother tongue is far from being the dominant, let alone the exclusive, medium of communication. So pronounced is this lack of intergenerational continuity in the use of the mother tongue

TABLE 7.9

Frequency of Mother Tongue Use in Conversations by Oldest and Youngest Children

In Conversation with:	Oldest Children						Youngest Children					
	Almost Always		Frequently		Almost Never		Almost Always		Frequently		Almost Never	
	N	%	N	%	N	%	N	%	N	%	N	%
Grandparents	34	55.7	12	19.7	15	24.6	19	39.6	11	22.9	18	37.5
Father	49	39.8	37	30.1	37	30.1	27	31.0	19	21.8	41	47.1
Mother	43	40.6	27	25.5	36	34.0	24	30.8	15	19.2	39	50.0
Brothers and Sisters	16	23.2	18	26.1	35	50.7	13	19.4	14	20.9	40	59.7
Friends	13	14.8	31	35.2	44	50.0	9	12.5	15	20.8	48	66.7
Husband or Wife	5	12.5	4	10.0	31	77.5	4	12.9	1	3.2	26	83.9
Own Child or Children	6	18.7	3	9.3	23	71.9	2	7.1	4	14.2	22	78.6

that ethnic leaders, their children, and their grandchildren literally represent separate linguistic subgroups segregated along generational lines. Whereas the ethnic mother tongue is most likely to be used by children in conversations with grandparents and parents, in conversations among themselves, their peers, and their own children English is almost always employed. Indeed the fact that frequency of mother tongue use with siblings (i.e., within family) and with friends (i.e., outside of family) is quite similar is a further indication that generational differences are more potent than family vs. non-family distinctions.

The above findings on mother tongue use deserve our attention if only because they show that the family, far from being an exclusive sphere of mother tongue dominance, appears to be a meeting ground for two competing languages – the ethnic mother tongue and English. In a sense, the immigrant family plays a dual and scarcely reconcilable role. On the one hand, by transmitting the ethnic mother tongue and ethnic ways to American-born children, it serves as a bulwark of ethnicity. On the other hand, by bringing together siblings whose use of English continues to rise as they grow older, it also becomes an agency of Americanization for immigrant parents and their children alike. Viewed in this light, the immigrant family is revealed as a structure highly vulnerable to competing cultural influences, which in former years and different milieux were frequently expressed in the conflict of generations. These two related processes – the intrusion of English into parental interaction and its dominance among siblings – are of far-reaching significance for the transmission of the ethnic mother tongue from generation to generation. They most certainly touch upon the basic difficulty that immigrant parents face in attempting to transmit ethnic behaviors – and the ethnic mother tongue in particular – to their American-born children and grandchildren.

Directly reflective of intergenerational discontinuity is the appreciably lower frequency of mother tongue use, as well as the less proficient mastery of it, on the part of youngest children. Relatively fewer youngest children avail themselves of the ethnic mother tongue. This is true not only of their conversations with personal friends and brothers and sisters, but also of their conversations with parents and grandparents. Similarly, knowledge of the ethnic mother tongue on the part of youngest children consistently lags behind that of oldest children. This difference in mastery of the ethnic mother tongue is especially pronounced with respect to fluency in speaking. Compared to 48.9 per cent of oldest children, only 31.3 per cent of youngest children are reported by their parents to be able to speak the ethnic mother tongue "very well".

One other piece of evidence relating directly to this is the prevalence of English within the family of procreation of oldest and youngest children alike. Of the seventy-one married children (oldest and youngest), only nine (12.6%) use the ethnic mother tongue "almost always" in conversations with their own spouses, while five (7.0%) do so from time to time and fifty-seven (80.4%) "almost never". Moreover, four of the nine married children who speak their ethnic mother tongue "almost always" with their spouses happen to be immigrants of Ukrainian refugee parents (Table 7.10).

Also of interest are differences in the frequency of mother tongue use among children of these four ethnic groups. The ethnic mother tongue has fallen into almost complete disuse among children of Jewish leaders – oldest and youngest alike. Not a single child of Jewish parentage avails himself of the ethnic mother tongue "almost always" in conversations with his personal friends, brothers and sisters, spouse, or children. Only one out of twenty-two married children of Jewish leaders is reported to use the ethnic mother tongue "frequently" in conversations with his spouse.

As might be expected, children of Ukrainian leaders speak their mother tongue more often than do children of leaders of the other three groups. Half of them, for example, speak the mother tongue "almost always" in conversations with brothers and sisters, as compared to 8.7 per cent for the children of German and 19.4 per cent for the children of Polish leaders. Furthermore, very few (5.0%) Ukrainian oldest and youngest children use English exclusively in conversations with their brothers and sisters. However, the proportion of Ukrainian children who speak the mother tongue "almost always" drops appreciably outside the family in conversations with personal friends. Only 27.3 per cent of the children of Ukrainian leaders use Ukrainian "almost always" in conversations with friends, whereas 36.4 per cent use it "almost never".

Notwithstanding these between-group differences, the overall trend unmistakably points to: (1) an "outgrowing" of ethnic mother tongues within the family of orientation that parallels organizational "outgrowing", and (2) further erosion of ethnic mother tongues within the family of procreation among the offspring of immigrant or second-generation leaders. With few exceptions the third generation virtually ceases to use the ethnic mother tongue in conversation with its own parents, even if both

TABLE 7.10

Frequency of Mother Torgue Use in Conversations by Oldest and Youngest Children of Four Ethnic Backgrounds

In Conversation with:	German						Jewish						Polish						Ukrainian					
	Almost Always N %		Frequently N %		Almost Never N %		Almost Always N %		Frequently N %		Almost Never N %		Almost Always N %		Frequently N %		Almost Never N %		Almost Always N %		Frequently N %		Almost Never N %	
Grandparents	6	26.1	6	26.1	11	47.8	6	20.0	9	30.0	15	50.0	15	57.6	5	19.2	6	23.2	26	96.3	—	—	1	3.7
Father	7	18.4	10	26.4	21	55.2	5	15.0	23	34.3	34	50.7	22	38.3	17	26.7	21	35.0	42	84.0	6	12.0	2	4.0
Mother	5	16.1	4	12.9	22	71.0	5	9.8	19	37.4	27	52.9	16	29.1	14	25.4	25	45.5	41	89.1	5	10.9	—	—
Brothers and Sisters	2	8.7	2	8.7	19	82.6	—	—	7	18.9	30	81.1	7	19.4	5	13.8	24	66.7	20	50.0	18	45.0	2	5.0
Friends	3	10.0	7	23.3	20	66.7	—	—	10	22.7	34	77.3	4	9.8	9	21.9	28	68.3	15	27.3	20	36.4	20	36.4
Husband and Wife	2	11.1	1	5.6	15	83.3	—	—	1	4.5	21	95.5	3	15.0	—	—	17	85.0	4	36.4	3	27.3	4	36.4
Own Child	1	5.6	3	16.7	14	77.8	—	—	1	5.3	18	94.7	3	20.0	—	—	12	80.0	4	50.0	3	37.5	1	12.5

TABLE 7.11

Knowledge of Mother Tongue on the Part of Oldest and Youngest Children and Oldest Grandchildren

	Understanding							Speaking							Writing						
	Very Well N %		Moderately N %		Little or None N %		Total	Very Well N %		Moderately N %		Little or None N %		Total	Very well N %		Moderately N %		Little or None N %		Total
Oldest Children	78	56.5	33	23.9	27	19.6	138	66	48.9	37	27.4	32	23.7	135	38	29.2	43	33.1	49	37.7	130
Youngest Children	43	43.0	32	32.0	25	25.0	100	30	31.3	38	39.6	28	29.2	96	13	14.3	26	28.6	52	57.1	91
Oldest Grandchildren	8	23.5	5	14.7	21	61.8	34	6	19.4	4	12.9	21	67.7	31	1	3.3	4	13.3	25	83.3	30

these parents are of the same ethnic background; at the same time, our data also show that a relatively high percentage are still reported as able to understand and speak their ethnic mother tongue in spite of the fact that they so infrequently employ it (Table 7.11). What do these findings mean and how are we to account for them? Obviously, knowledge of the ethnic mother tongue is not solely a result of extensive inter-personal use between children and their parents but also of formal educational efforts. Many third-generation children of German descent have studied their ethnic mother tongue in American high schools and colleges. Many children of other native-born leaders have received mother tongue instruction in ethnic group schools. In some cases, ethnic organizational affiliation reinforces mastery of the ethnic mother tongue, although this can scarcely be typical in view of the predominant membership by third generation children in those very organizations which are, at best, only marginally concerned with maintenance of the ethnic mother tongue. There remains but one major context in which children of native-born parents actually continue to use their ethnic mother tongue after discontinuing such use more generally, and that is in conversations with their grandparents. In this sense, it may well be appropriate to consider English as the functional *mother tongue* of the third generation, while its ancestral language is neither mother tongue nor ethnic mother tongue but *grandmother tongue*.

To emphasize the gradual character of children's disengagement from ethnic cultural and organizational life (at least insofar as this process is viewed by their parents) we have referred repeatedly to the developmental analogue of "outgrowing". Underlying this usage is the assumption that de-ethnization in the population under study rarely engenders extreme attitudes either of violent dissociation from or nativistic recommitment to ethnicity. An attempt to determine the extent to which this process of "outgrowing" entails changes in children's attitudes toward their ancestral heritage in general and toward their ethnic mother tongue in particular led us to inquire whether children's *knowledge* of their ethnic mother tongue is in any way related to their *attitudes* toward using it in conversations with their parents and other relatives. Our data disclosed that the more proficient their mastery of the ethnic mother tongue the more likely they were to be favorably predisposed toward its use – or vice versa, any causal sequence not being established. In either event, since we saw previously that knowledge of the ethnic mother tongue is positively related to organizational involvement (Table 7.8), we would expect significant differences between the mother tongue attitudes of organizationally affiliated and unaffiliated children. The evidence reported in Table 7.12 confirms this expectation, showing that more extensively affiliated children are much more likely to hold favorable attitudes toward the ethnic mother tongue. Having also found that age is related both to mastery of mother tongue and to organizational affiliation, we would expect too that children's attitudes toward their mother tongue change with age. Comparing the two age categories, 6-22 and 23-over, we find that younger children are indeed more likely to have favorable attitudes toward use of the ethnic mother tongue than are older offspring. Only 64.1 per cent of

TABLE 7.12

Attitudes toward Mother Tongue Use of Oldest and Youngest Children

Attitude	By Organizational Affiliation			
	0 N %	1-2 N %	3 or more N %	Total
Favorable	56 51.8	45 70.3	39 78.0	140
Neutral or Unfavorable	52 48.2	19 29.7	11 22.0	82
Total	108 100.0	64 100.0	50 100.0	222

Attitude	By Age			
	6 to 22 N %	23 and over N %		Total
Favorable	43 79.6	34 64.1		77
Neutral or Unfavorable	11 20.4	19 35.9		30
Total	54	53		107

those in the older age range are rated as favorably disposed toward use of their ethnic mother tongue, as compared with 79.6 per cent of children between six and twenty-two.

All in all, the weight of our evidence suggests what one would expect – that the more involved children are in ethnic life, the better they know and the more frequently they use the mother tongue, and the more likely they are to be interested in and to appreciate their own ancestral heritage. It also suggests that ethnic leaders view the de-ethnization of their children as a process engendering attitudes and behaviors that are neither painful nor violent. Rather, the process they report resembles an accumulation of experiences in life all of which gradually lead both parents and children away from the ancestral heritage. Very few children are reported to hold openly unfavorable attitudes toward their ethnic mother tongue. Very few leaders express great sorrow or shock at the de-ethnization of their children. In commenting on their children's unwillingness to speak the ethnic mother tongue, the most frequent parental remark (37.6%) is that there is simply "no opportunity" for them to use it, since most of their children's friends and the people with whom they come in contact speak only English. Another frequently given reason (23.2%) accounts for children's attitudes in terms of their inadequate knowledge of the mother tongue. Very infrequently is there any indication that some children display attitudes of apparent hostility, that they are ashamed of their ethnic identity, that they seek to divest themselves of lingering "foreign stuff", or that they seek to abandon their ethnic identity by stressing their Americanness. This is a much different picture of parent-child relationships in the arena of ethnicity than that which has come down to us through earlier research and speculation on Americanization. The greater amicableness of modern day de-ethnization within the sphere of the apparently ethnic family may well be a result of greater permissiveness and of the greater de-ethnization that has already come to pass. Indeed not all ethnic leaders are concerned with the preservation of ethnic mother tongues, nor are they all equally interested in the maintenance of ethnic organizations or ethnically related traditions and customs. Thus, eight respondents in our sample were opposed to the preservation of their ethnic mother tongue by their own children and grandchildren; thirteen opposed the retention of ethnically related customs and traditions; and thirteen disapproved of the very existence of separate ethnic institutions and organizations. While the number of such "anti-ethnic" cultural and organizational leaders is quite small, their very presence on the ethnic scene is hardly without significance.

Far greater is the proportion of ethnic leaders who claim to favor ethnic continuity but also claim that the continuity of ethnic cultural and communal life in the United States may be secured without the preservation of ethnic mother tongues. Almost half (47.1%) of native-born and slightly less than a third (29.3%) of foreign-born ethnic leaders share this view. Not a few – 19.6 per cent of the native born and 30.7 per cent of the foreign born – are also of the opinion that the retention of ethnic customs and traditions is unnecessary for the continuity of ethnic life in this country. What most ethnic leaders – native born (84.3%) and foreign born (88.2%) alike – do believe to be extremely important for the continuation of ethnic group identity are knowledge and appreciation of past and present national achievements in art, literature, religion, and other areas of cultural endeavor.

Taken at face value, the above findings may seem to be of little moment. However, they should not be dismissed too lightly, if only because they touch upon the very survival of ethnic groups in the United States. For these beliefs as put forth by ethnic leaders amount to a conviction that knowledge of and attachment to such unique and "particularized" values as language and tradition are less important and less necessary for ethnic continuity and group identity than are knowledge of and attachment to such highly "generalized" ethnic representations as Goethe's *Faust*, Sienkiewicz's *Quo Vadis?* or Beethoven's Ninth Symphony. The least tangible attributes of ethnicity – the ones that are of least significance to the daily life of the ethnic family and the ethnic community – are thus rated by ethnic leaders to be more important for ethnic continuity than the very attributes – language and tradition – which most clearly differentiate one ethnic collectivity from another.

This depreciation of "folk" components of ethnicity, the non-admissability of ideological ethnicity and the simultaneous preference for ethnicity's more dignified "representative" components may but reflect the intellectual perspectives of our respondents. It may also represent an experienced response to the hard facts of life, particularly inasmuch as native-born leaders and their children alike have largely become behaviorally and linguistically de-ethnicized themselves. There is certainly no denying the fact (whatever the reasons, and they are many) that ethnic leaders view the retention of their ethnic mother tongue to be relatively unimportant for ethnic group continuity in the United States.

Nevertheless, this tendency on the part of ethnic leaders, and especially the native born among them, to belittle the importance of language for the future of ethnic life in the United States does not mean that they oppose present language maintenance efforts. Indeed, most ethnic leaders approve its continued use, albeit not always for the same reasons. Foreign-born ethnic leaders tend to justify language maintenance on somewhat different grounds than do native-born leaders, in part because their mother tongue is basic to their own activity and to their own leadership. However, it is valued by them not only for its use; it also represents a value in itself, that is, the mother tongue is cultivated and appreciated intrinsically, for its own sake. Accordingly, those leaders who are more frequently of immigrant origin – Jews and Ukrainians – typically favor the retention of the mother tongue on the ground that it both *expresses* and *symbolizes* the cultural heritage of the group. Exactly half of Ukrainian and 86.8 per cent of Jewish leaders justify the retention of the mother tongue for this reason, as compared with 24.6 per cent among Polish and 30.0 per cent among German leaders. On the other hand, ethnic leaders who are more generationally "mixed" in background – German and Polish – most frequently justify the retention of the mother tongue on the basis of more "practical" considerations. They simply argue that, in general, "knowledge of languages" yields many advantages – whether in scholarly, commercial, diplomatic, or other spheres of life – and that, consequently, the ethnic mother tongue ought to be retained in order to make instrumental bilingualism possible. Thus, 56.7 per cent of all German and 49.2 per cent of all Polish responses in defense of ethnic mother tongue maintenance are couched in terms of such pragmatic considerations.

The above differences in response pattern lead to the conclusion that native-born leaders are likely to be pragmatically oriented toward the retention of the mother tongue and *pari passu* toward ethnicity itself. To the extent that this is true, the ethnic-mother tongue ceases to be of unique or intrinsic value to native-born ethnic leaders. The very reasons advanced in favor of language maintenance, being basically utilitarian, are applicable to languages in general rather than to mother tongues in particular. Indeed, native-born ethnic leaders appear to be interested in ethnic mother tongue maintenance on a non-ethnic basis. Their interest and that of many American leaders concerned with the language resources of the American population seem to be similarly practical and similarly de-ethnicized.

We have discussed a number of findings that have a vital bearing upon the continuity or, rather, discontinuity of ethnic cultural life in the United States. With the passing of the immigrant generation the reservoir of cultural leadership becomes greatly depleted. From this point onward, it would seem, ethnic cultures tend to become increasingly "organized", and, ultimately, cease to be dynamic. The generational turnover in ethnic leadership affects most adversely the ethnic mother tongue, especially its use in interpersonal relations, in ethnic publications, and in ethnic organizations. All the evidence points unequivocally to the progressive disappearance of the ethnic mother tongue from both family and communal life. We know, for example, that the average number of books in the ethnic mother tongue or on ethnic topics published by German and Polish ethnic leaders during the last decade is much smaller than the average number of such books published by Jewish and Ukrainian leaders during this same period, even though the former have published more books during this period than the latter. Similarly, we know that the proportion of ethnic leaders who have contributed literary works (novels, short stories, poetry, articles) to their respective ethnic publications during this period varies directly with the proportion of foreign-born respondents among them.

But while *cultural leadership* becomes seriously depleted with the passing of the immigrant generation, American ethnic groups continue to be successful for an additional period of time in recruiting *organizational leadership* from the native-born generation. This finding is of considerable interest, particularly in that it throws light on the well-known thesis that the assimilation ("structural assimilation") of ethnic groups tends to lag behind their acculturation ("behavioral assimilation") (Gordon 1961). Spiro (1955) accounts for this discrepancy between acculturative and assimilative processes as follows:

... The acculturation of an ethnic group in the United States – its acquisition of the culture of the dominant group – is an exclusive function of the group's desire and capacity for acculturation; but assimilation – the disappearance of the group's identity through non-differential association and exogamy – is a function of both dominant and ethnic group behavior.

The underlying assumption is that assimilation, unlike acculturation, ultimately hinges upon the consent of the dominant society, even though the minority group may desire to be assimilated. Whatever its general explanatory merit, there is hardly warrant for the conclusion that second-generation ethnic activists in our sample are primarily recruited from among those individuals who have been jilted or cast off by American core society. On the contrary, their ethnic organizational involvement is most usually and basically a function of their continued loyalty to ethnicity, even if this loyalty represents little more than loyalty to ethnic organizations, and even though it is patently insufficient for and unrelated to the support of language maintenance.

Finally, the continued role of "organizational ethnicity" in the lives of second-generation leaders, on the one hand, and the declining role of either primordial ethnicity or symbolically elaborated ethnic particularism on the other, prove to be significant keys to parallel developments among the rank-and-file membership. There seems to be no discord between organizational leaders and the organizational membership. The leaders are neither more nor less behaviorally retentive or ideologically oriented than their followers. If there were periods of discord (initially, between older leaders and younger members or, subsequently, between younger leaders and older members) such as those described by Tavuchis (1963), such discord is now but a distant memory among most surviving organizations. Nevertheless, the harmony that typifies the current stage in ethnic leader-follower relations is only superficially similar to that described by Eisenstadt (1951, 1956) in his discussions of early post-immigrational phenomena in Israel. Today's agreement in the United States is marked by a concern for efficient and purposeful organizational functioning. In pursuit of this concern both ethnicity and language maintenance are assigned increasingly marginal roles, ones that do not conflict with organizational continuity and growth, and that permit them to be abstractly valued even though no longer concretely implemented. Among members, leaders, and organizations language maintenance and ethnicity are not cast out or attacked as they become less and less important or realizable. They merely fade away through successive reinterpretations which preserve attitudes of respect toward them while the major foci of organizational concern shift increasingly to organizational continuity and non-ethnic affairs.

REFERENCES

Barber, Bernard, "Participation and mass apathy in associations", in *Studies in Leadership*, Alvin W. Gouldner, ed. (New York, Harper, 1950).

Blau, Peter M., and Scott, W. Richard, *Formal Organizations; A Comparative Approach* (San Francisco, Chandler, 1962).

Dunn, E. J., *Builders of Fraternalism in America* (Chicago, Fraternal Book Concern, 1924).

Eisenstadt, S. N., "The Place of Elites and Primary Groups in the Absorption of New Immigrants in Israel", *American Journal of Sociology*, 7 (1951), 222-231.

——, "The Social Conditions of the Development of Voluntary Associations; A Case Study of Israel", *Scripta Hierosolymitana*, 1956, 104-125.

Etzioni, Amitai, *A Comparative Analysis of Complex Organizations* (New York, Free Press, 1961).

Fishman, J. A., "The process and function of social stereotyping", *Journal of Social Psychology*, 43 (1956), 27-64.

——, "Organizational interest in language maintenance", in Fishman, et al., *Language Loyalty in the United States* (New York, Yeshiva University, 1964), Chapter 5. (Mimeo.)

——, "Childhood indoctrination for minority-group membership", *Daedalus*, Spring, 1961, 329-349.

Gordon, M. M., "Assimilation in America; Theory and Reality", *Daedalus*, Spring, 1961, 263-285.

Kip, Richard de Raismes, *Fraternal Life Insurance in America* (Philadelphia, College Offset Press, 1953).

Meyer, B. H., "Fraternal beneficiary societies in the United States", *American Journal of Sociology*, 6 (1900), 646-661.

Parsons, Talcott, "Suggestions for a sociological approach to the theory of organizations", in *Complex Organizations*, Amitai Etzioni, ed. (New York, Holt, Rinehart, Winston, 1961).

Sackett, Myron W., *Early History of Fraternal Beneficiary Societies* (Meadville, Pa., Tribune, 1914).

Spiro, M. E., "The Acculturation of American Ethnic Groups", *American Anthropologist*, LVII (1955), 1244.

Tavuchis, N., *Pastors and Immigrants: The Role of a Religious Elite in the Absorption of Norwegian Immigrants* (The Hague, Nijhoff, 1963).

Terrien, Frederic W., and Mills, Donald L., "The effect of changing size upon the internal structure of organizations", *Amer. Sociol. Rev.*, 20 (1955), 11-14.

Weber, Max, *Wirtschaft und Gesellschaft* (Tübingen, J. C. B. Mohr, 1956). (See Section 2, pp. 551-558).

8. SOME COMMUNITY DYNAMICS OF LANGUAGE MAINTENANCE

ROBERT G. HAYDEN

The present chapter constitutes an exploratory investigation of the community context of ethnic mother tongue maintenance. It was hoped that an attempt of this kind, based upon intensive interview materials, might complement other relevant data obtained by the Language Resources Project from questionnaires, census materials, and published sources. The investigation involves three languages: *French* in Fall River (Massachusetts), *Spanish* in San Antonio and New York, and *Ukrainian* in Olyphant (Pennsylvania) and Newark (New Jersey). In all, 180 purposive interviews were obtained and provide the data for this study.

ETHNIC COMMUNITIES: GENERAL CHARACTERISTICS

Spanish Communities: A fairly good and extensive literature exists dealing with Puerto Ricans in New York and with Mexican-Americans in San Antonio. Although no attempt will be made here to summarize these informative studies, they will be relied upon briefly in presenting some of the relevant social background characteristics of the two communities.

Spanish-speaking settlements in the San Antonio area date back several centuries. Their contacts with Anglos also have an extensive history going back at least to the early part of the 19th century. Up to the end of that century Mexican-Americans had long constituted a dominant social group in and around San Antonio, both in numbers and in status position. It is only comparatively recently that the situation has been reversed, and that Hispanos have found themselves in subordinate status. Thus, Mexican-Americans in the San Antonio area possess an historical and cultural tradition that can be looked back upon and that can even be resorted to in considering their relationship to dominant Anglo society. Obviously, this situation does not obtain for Puerto Ricans in New York, primarily because most of them arrived there either just before or after World War II, when economic and cultural patterns were already well established.

The above differences suggest that the Hispanos of San Antonio have more stable and stronger roots in their ethnicity. Although it is true that members of both communities make frequent visits to their respective home countries (and that they are visited, in turn, by relatives from their homelands), the very nature of ethnic closures in these two communities is such as to continue the nature of the differences between them.

In New York opportunities for upward social mobility by Spanish speakers are considerably higher than they are in San Antonio. On the other hand, the San Antonio Mexican-American community has evolved over many years into a relatively differentiated structure, allowing some individuals to move upward within its own social hierarchy. In fact, Mexican-Americans in San Antonio can boast of an elite that has at least three distinct origins: (i) those tracing their ancestry to very early settlers and landowners; (ii) professionals, intellectuals, and businessmen who fled their homes at the time of the Mexican Revolution; and (iii) "self-made" men of more recent origin who have risen to professional status, have become successful businessmen, or have been elected to public office by dint of their own efforts and abilities.

Below this upper stratum there exists a sizable category of middle-class individuals who are engaged in semi-professional occupations or in small business ventures. But by far the largest number of Mexican-Americans continues to constitute an exploited and underprivileged group, engaged in low-level service occupations, in agricultural labor, or in other unskilled occupations. The latter live in an area geographically and materially distinct from that inhabited by most of their more fortunate compatriots, Hispano or Anglo.

In contrast, Puerto Ricans in New York have no well-established elite that can point to its "ancient and honorable" past in that city. The status hierarchy among Puerto Ricans in New York City is, therefore, more fluid; it is dependent upon, and structured to a much greater degree in, the pre-existing framework of the dominant society. In short, the Puerto Rican community strikingly resembles many another immigrant community composed of recent immigrants even though Puerto Ricans hold American citizenship.

Ukrainian Communities: Olyphant is a small town near Wilkes-Barre, Pennsylvania. Until recently its main industry has revolved around coal mining. It is settled almost entirely by descendants of various Slavic peoples. The forebears of today's residents arrived in greatest numbers just before and at the turn of the century. They were, almost without exception, of peasant background and were brought to Olyphant for employment in the coal mines. There are virtually no residents of Ukrainian origin who have settled in Olyphant since 1930.

Because of the generally prevailing depressed economic conditions in the coal industry, the population of the town dwindled between 1950 and 1960 from about 10,000 to about 5,000. But even with this decrease of available workers, unemployment continues to be both widespread and constant. As a result, a large proportion of males who are employed work at a great distance from their homes, and are frequently absent from their families. This fact has accentuated the dislocation of traditional family patterns that immigration, Americanization, and unemployment ordinarily have brought to pass.

In Newark, which is also an industrial city, conditions are quite different. Unemployment is not a serious problem in the Ukrainian community. In addition, there exist more diverse opportunities for employment and education in non-ethnic settings. The majority of Ukrainian immigrants arrived in Newark between 1880 and 1910. However, in contrast to Olyphant, Newark also has a sizable contingent of recent Ukrainian refugee immigrants. Unlike their countrymen who preceded them, very few of these new immigrants were peasants in the Ukraine. Many of them possess professional and semi-professional skills. However, this is not always reflected in their present status since many are occupationally declassed.

Our respondents in both Ukrainian communities (like the bulk of the entire Ukrainian population in these two cities) profess to be Catholics of the Byzantine Rite. Parishes in both communities sponsor parochial elementary schools in which Ukrainian is taught, although instruction in all other subjects is entirely in English.

Organized ethnic life in Olyphant currently centers almost completely around the parish church. Consequently, the church and the priest exert great influence on the ethnic activities of Ukrainian-Americans in Olyphant. On the other hand, the Newark community is socially much more differentiated. In addition, the organized Ukrainian life in the community is considerably secularized. Nevertheless, a much higher level of language maintenance obtains for Ukrainians in Newark than in Olyphant.

French Community: Fall River is a town of about 100,000 inhabitants. For many years, like Olyphant, it was basically a one-industry town, depending almost entirely on its textile and shoe factories. But virtually all of these have moved south in search of cheaper labor, creating a serious unemployment problem though not on the dimensions of that in Olyphant. The forebears of Franco-Americans in Fall River came from Canada, the bulk of them arriving in the period between 1880 and 1918. By now most of them have been appreciably assimilated to New England life. A Franco-American Roman Catholic parish continues to function in Fall River, but its role in language maintenance is rapidly diminishing.

The overall social level of the Franco-American community in Fall River is predominantly tied to the skilled trades and to semi-professional or secretarial-clerical occupations. The most successful individuals are concentrated primarily in mercantile pursuits. Whereas Franco-Americans formerly occupied the lowest rung in Fall River's social status hierarchy, that position is now occupied by more recent arrivals, primarily Portuguese-Americans.

Despite the decided inroads of assimilation, there remains a dedicated and tenacious hard core of Franco-Americans who exert every possible means to keep the French language and customs alive. This is done primarily by sponsoring activities in ethnically maintained secular and religious organizations. More informal attempts – such as the establishment of a "French Literary Circle" – have had but limited influence on language maintenance among most Franco-Americans in Fall River.

ATTITUDES AND ACTIVITIES PERTAINING TO ETHNICITY

Our interest in this study is focussed mainly on the most direct indicators of ethnic mother tongue maintenance. However, prior to probes bearing upon such maintenance, a more general question was asked, whether the ethnic group as such should be preserved in the future. The Newark Ukrainians responded most favorably, all of them approving the continued existence of their ethnic group in the United States. Most Ukrainians in Olyphant and most Franco-Americans in Fall River shared these sentiments. Least favorable toward the maintenance of their respective ethnic groups were both Spanish-speaking communities. The proportion of favorable responses from all communities was relatively high. However, these are merely attitudes, and as such are not necessarily related to overt actions. Comparisons of several of the tables that follow reveal large discrepancies between favorable attitudes and supportive actions, with attitudes being generally far more positive than actions.

By and large, many respondents may have expressed merely conventional attitudes concerning the continued existence of their ethnic groups. Only San Antonians represent an exception, inasmuch as they were the only group which responded unfavorably more often than favorably. This higher proportion of unfavorable responses cannot be attributed to "negative activists" or to linguistically assimilated "non-speakers" among San Antonians since these categories were equally represented in the other communities as well. It is more likely that the very term "ethnic group" has quite different overtones for French and Ukrainian respondents, on the one hand, and for Spanish-speaking San Antonians and Puerto Ricans in New York, on the other. The former two groups seem to interpret the term "ethnic group" in terms of a network of ethnically-related organizations and voluntary associations. The Spanish-speaking respondents, on the other hand, react primarily in terms of segregated slum areas in the two cities in which they reside. When respondents who believed that their ethnic groups *should* be maintained were asked to suggest how this might best be accomplished, the answer given most consistently was "through clubs and organizations". Significantly, however, Newark and Olyphant Ukrainians gave this answer most frequently while San Antonio and New York respondents did so least frequently. These organizationally-oriented answers reflect currently existing means rather than any not yet widely available. For both Ukrainian communities rest basically on a network of organizations; in fact, these organizations constitute the main focus of communal integration. Without such an organizational framework, Ukrainian communities would simply cease to exist or at best would be transformed into a myriad of unrelated cliques and informal groupings. In contrast, Spanish speakers, particularly in San Antonio, are far less dependent on formal organization approaches for the maintenance of their ethnicity.

Related to the above observations are data bearing upon the maintenance of three specific component-clusters of ethnicity – observance of ethnic customs and traditions, knowledge and use of the ethnic mother tongue, and knowledge and appreciation of ethnic values and ideals. Here we are not considering attitudes toward the preservation of these components of ethnicity, but beliefs about their necessity in order to secure ethnic group identity and communal continuity. As can be seen from Table 8.1, the

TABLE 8.1

Belief that Certain Components of Enthicity are Necessary
for the Preservation of the Ethnic Group

Component	Degree of Necessity	Spanish		Ukrainian		French
		SA	NY	Oly.	Nwk	FR
Observance of Ethnic	High	56%	72%	90%	89%	67%
customs and traditions	Med.	20	24	10	11	27
	Low	22	3	0	0	6
Ethnic mother tongue	High	57	72	69	86	76
	Med.	20	18	31	14	18
	Low	20	9	0	0	6
Knowledge re cultural	High	61	76	76	86	52
achievements and ideals	Med.	22	24	24	14	33
	Low	15	0	0	0	12
Average rank		5	3	2	1	4

large majority of respondents regard all three components of ethnicity as necessary for the maintenance of ethnic group continuity. Worthy of note are the differences in emphasis given to particular components of ethnicity by the various groups of respondents. Ukrainians of Olyphant and Newark alike most frequently ascribe the greatest significance to ethnic traditions and customs. The Spanish-speaking respondents in both San Antonio and New York most frequently consider the appreciation of ethnic achievements and ideals as necessary for the continuity of ethnic group life. The French speakers of Fall River are relatively less interested in either traditions or ideals. Instead, they emphasize the importance of *language*.

San Antonio respondents assign a lower degree of necessity to all three components of ethnicity than do those in any other community. One suspects that for San Antonians the possible disappearance of their ethnic community is simply not a reality. It is so large, absolutely as well as proportionately, and it is so old, that its existence is simply taken for granted. Moreover, it continues to survive on a daily functional level, as distinct from a periodic organizational level, despite the fact that some of its members disapprove of its very existence. Are we to conclude, then, that San Antonio Spanish speakers (and to a somewhat lesser extent those of New York) remain ethnic by virtue of "fate" rather than by virtue of "faith"? Other data acquired in the study will help in answering this question.

Few uniform answers were obtained when respondents were asked to specify the activities of their parents relative to the maintenance of the mother tongue. What is significant, however, is this: in all but two communities (Newark and New York, both of recent immigrant origin), a relatively high proportion of respondents reported that their parents exerted themselves in one way or another on behalf of their respective ethnic cultures. In Fall River, as in Olyphant, it was frequently reported that parents sponsored ethnic schools, that they insisted upon the observance of ethnic holidays and on the use of the ethnic mother tongue. Encouraging the use and knowledge of the mother tongue as an end in itself (i.e., unrelated to encouragement of other components) was referred to only infrequently. Usually it was mentioned in connection with diverse other efforts. Some such parental activities were reported by almost one-half of all respondents. Except for Fall River, where respondents were markedly less active than their parents had been, most respondents reported they were as active as, or only slightly less so than, their parents. The "holding of the line" appears to exceed what one might expect, and indicates that there may be more interest in intergenerational continuity than is usually suspected.

However, a noticeable intergenerational shift in emphasis apparently occurs.

TABLE 8.2

Belief in and Active Involvement on Behalf of Language Maintenance

Community	Percent believing preservation of EMT is necessary	Percent "actively" engaged in preservation of EMT	Discrepancy
Newark	86%	43%	−43%
New York	72	35	−37
Fall River	76	52	−24
San Antonio	57	43	−14
Olyphant	69	66	− 3

Ukrainian respondents in Newark, for example, tend to pay increased attention to schooling, as compared to their parents, in connection with maintenance of the ethnic mother tongue. The implication appears to be that a continuation of natural home and neighborhood ethnicity has become far less feasible. Ukrainians of Olyphant are even more strongly aware of the role of institutions – and of educational institutions in particular – in the maintenance of language and ethnicity, relying on schooling more than their parents did. This shift is less true of Franco-Americans, and is absent entirely in both Spanish-speaking communities, where neither schools nor organizations seem to have much importance in self-maintenance.

Wide differences obtain between attitudes toward the maintenance of various components of ethnicity and the extent to which respondents are involved in activities designed to preserve these components. These differences with respect to the mother tongue are shown in Table 8.2. What is probably reflected here is that the newest immigrants perceive the greatest intergenerational losses in mother tongue facility between themselves and their children, while in older groups expectation, on the one hand, and motivations and actions on the other have come into closer and presumably more stable alignment. Although there is some discrepancy between attitudes and involvements in all communities – with involvement of course always being the scarcer commodity – it nevertheless remains true that the mother tongue continues to be widely regarded as important for the continuity of ethnic group life, and that a significant proportion of respondents are engaged in activities concerned with its preservation.

The perception of intergenerational losses in mother tongue facility takes on additional meaning when we recall the differing attitudes toward the maintenance of group continuity and identity. Thus the Newark Ukrainians, who were completely in favor of group continuity, presumably view the language loss between themselves and their children as highly regrettable. On the other hand, among Puerto Ricans, who rank next to last in their desire to secure group continuity, this same language loss may well be welcomed, since it may be taken as a sign of successful assimilation to the general community.

Attitudes and activities connected with mother tongue maintenance may well be unrelated to interest in the maintenance of ethnic communities and cultures. This is perhaps particularly true in the case of highly prestigeful or popular languages such as Spanish and French. It is not at all unusual to view facility in Spanish and French as being highly desirable, whether in respect to ethnics or non-ethnics. Accordingly, knowledge and even use of these two languages may be fostered because of their utility and/or prestige in American society. Indeed, the view that bilingualism is desirable, aside from any role that it may have in ethnic life, represents the most frequent response to the question: "Why should your ethnic mother tongue be preserved?" in all but one community. Only three per cent of Ukrainians in Olyphant offer this reply, while thirty to forty-five per cent respond in this manner in each of the remaining communities (Table 8.3).

The Olyphant results can only be partly accounted for in terms of the limited utility

TABLE 8.3

Reasons Why the Ethnic Mother Tongue Should be Preserved
by One's Children and Grandchildren

Reason	SA	NY	Oly.	Nwk.	FR
1. Bilingualism is intrinsically desirable	30%	45%	3%	32%	39%
2. Ethnic identity should be preserved	17	0	35	34	6
3. Helps preserve ethnic beliefs	2	0	21	3	3
4. Both 2 and 3, above	4	0	24	3	0
5. Other reasons	43	38	17	22	49
No response	4	17	0	6	3
	100	100	100	100	100

TABLE 8.4

Family Efforts toward Instruction of Children in the Ethnic Mother Tongue

Activity	SA	NY	Oly.	Nwk.	FR
1. Teach it at home	22%	45%	0%	0%	0%
2. Send children to parochial school	0	0	45	3	0
3. One and two	0	0	24	3	0
4. Have tutors, special schools, classes, Public School courses	6	3	17	26	76
5. Use Mother tongue only, at home	26	17	0	0	0
6. Four and Five	9	0	0	6	15
No response	37	35	14	62	9
	100	100	100	100	100

that Ukrainian has in this country, as contrasted with that of French or Spanish. The response pattern of Ukrainians in Newark clearly suggests that factors of ethnic mother tongue utility and/or prestige cannot fully account for views toward language maintenance. Like Franco-Americans and Hispano-Americans, Newark Ukrainians do tend to recognize the value of bilingualism, even though the utility of their mother tongue in our society is most certainly limited. However, it is not utility as such that prompts Newark Ukrainians to emphasize bilingualism, but rather appreciation of the cultural value of bilingualism coupled with the conviction that their national language is inseparabley related to their national heritage. On the other hand, Olyphant respondents are scarcely appreciative of cultural bilingualism, partly due to their peasant origins and partly as a result of their own relatively low educational achievements. While they are cognizant of the significance of language for the continuity of ethnicity, the specific content of this ethnicity largely coincides with their religion. Bearing in mind the class origins of these respondents, it is likely that ethnicity and ethnic identity still continue to be inextricably interwoven with religion and religious identity in their case, whereas this is not nearly as likely among Newark Ukrainians.

The manner in which ethnic mother tongues are maintained in various ethnic communities acquires additional interest if viewed in the light of the data already discussed. To begin with, let us note that despite a relatively high percentage of negative responses by the two Hispanic communities regarding the preservation of their ethnic groups, and despite their generally low level of involvement in various activities relevant to the maintenance of their ethnic mother tongue, we find that quite a few families in these (as in all other communities) continue to assist their children in learning the ethnic mother tongue.

In what ways, then, do they assist their children? In both Spanish-speaking communities such assistance appears to be centered in the home. In Ukrainian communities marked emphasis is given to parochial schools (Olyphant) or to special language classes (Newark). Reliance on the public schools and on special classes is typical for the French community (Table 8.4). Such between-group differences deserve attention. They strongly suggest that among these respondents and their children, only Spanish is still fully functional in the sense that it continues to be used in daily life. On the other hand, the Ukrainian and French communities increasingly tend to transmit their respective ethnic mother tongues via ethnic and even non-ethnic educational institutions. If this trend continues, it is only to be expected that these two languages will become increasingly non-functional in daily life. First-hand observations in the Ukrainian community at Olyphant confirm this expectation. The children acquire only a halting knowledge of Ukrainian, and this is gained almost entirely in the elementary grades of their parochial school. The ethnic mother tongue has come to be little more than another "subject" in which one receives a grade.

TABLE 8.5

Respondents' Estimates of Family Success in Motivating Children to Learn Mother Tongue

Estimate	SA	NY	Oly.	Nwk.	FR
All families	2%	14%	0%	0%	0%
Most families	26	45	7	66	21
Some families	30	17	31	20	52
Few families	33	17	62	6	27
None	4	0	0	0	0
No response	5	7	0	8	0
	100	100	100	100	100

Table 8.5, showing respondents' estimates of how successful families are in motivating children to learn the ethnic mother tongue, lends additional support to the above expectation. In Olyphant, 93 per cent of the respondents state that only "some" or "few" families are thus successful. Fall River is also marked by little success in motivating its children to learn the ethnic mother tongue. However, in the two Spanish-speaking communities 28 and 59 per cent reply that "all" or "most" attain such success. The Ukrainian community in Newark is apparently most successful, with 66 per cent of its respondents stating that "most" of the families successfully motivate their children to learn the ethnic mother tongue. Such a finding is scarcely unexpected in view of the high proportion of recent refugee immigrants among the parents of Newark respondents.

All in all, one general finding stands out clearly. The active use of the ethnic mother tongue in the home is primarily responsible for enabling children to attain mastery of it. Without this the best of school instruction is likely to fall far short of functional mastery. Consequently, the most successful retentivists are to be found among recent immigrants – Puerto Ricans in New York and Ukrainians in Newark – although the San Antonio case makes clear that recency of immigration is not the only relevant variable. But desire to preserve the ethnic mother tongue, even though expressed as highly favorable attitudes, contributes but little toward language mastery when the language is no longer used in the home.

RELATIVE "PREFERENCE" AND "USE" OF THE MOTHER TONGUE AND ENGLISH

Since active use of the ethnic mother tongue appears to be crucial for maintaining functional mastery of it, inquiries were made concerning both *preference* for and *use* of the mother tongue as compared to English in a variety of situations. Eleven specific situations were examined ranging from conversations with closest relatives to those taking place in public situations, e.g., while shopping or at work. In all five communities the mother tongue was preferred (i.e., it was considered easier and more satisfying) when speaking to parents, although in Fall River and Olyphant the mother tongue was accorded only a slight preference (Table 8.6). A striking and significant

TABLE 8.6

Ethnic Mother Tongue Retentiveness in Eleven Situations For Which Respondents Indicate "Preferences" and "use" In Comparison with English

Respondent prefers/ uses EMT vis-a-vis:		SA		NY		Oly.		Nwk.		FR	
		Rank	%	Rank	%	Rank	%	Rank	%	Rank	%
1. His parents	Prefer.	2	70	1	86	5	45	3	63	4	48
	Use	3	59	1	83	5	41	2	66	4.5	58
2. His spouse	Prefer.	4	30	3	34	5	03	1	71	2	42
	Use	4	19	2	34	5	03	1	69	3	30
3. His children	Prefer.	4	17	3	34	5	03	1	71	2	42
	Use	4	07	3	14	5	03	1	69	2	21
4. His siblings	Prefer.	4	31	2	48	5	10	1	60	3	39
	Use	4	22	2	38	5	07	1	54	3	33
5. His close relatives	Prefer.	3	44	1	83	5	10	2	69	4.4	42
	Use	4	43	1	77	5	14	2	60	3	45
6. His friends	Prefer.	2	55	3.5	24	5	00	1	77	3.5	24
	Use	3.5	19	2	48	5	03	1	71	3.5	18
7. His co-workers	Prefer.	3	19	1	41	5	00	2	31	4	12
	Use	3	17	1.5	17	5	00	1.5	17	4	06
8. His acquaintances	Prefer.	3	11	2	31	5	00	1	34	4	06
	Use	3	07	2	21	5	00	1	29	5	03
9. Sales clerks	Prefer.	4	11	1	34	5	00	2	26	3	21
	Use	4	06	1	17	5	00	3	09	2	15
10. His fellow club members	Prefer.	4	13	2	41	5	03	1	69	3	30
	Use	4.5	04	3	21	4.5	03	1	66	2	27
11. During his religious services	Prefer.	5	22	3	34	4	24	1	89	2	70
	Use	5	09	4	24	3	29	1	86	2	73
Average Pref. and Use Rank		4		2		5		1		3	

TABLE 8.7

The Direction of Differences Between Expressions of "Preference" for the Ethnic Mother Tongue And its "Use"
[Signs denote (use) – (preference)]

Situations in which used	SA	NY	Oly.	Nwk.	FR
1. With parents	−	−	−	+	+
2. With spouse	−	0	0	−	−
3. With children	−	−	0	−	−
4. With siblings	−	−	−	−	−
5. With close relatives	−	−	+	−	+
6. With best friends	−	+	+	−	−
7. At work	−	−	0	−	−
8. With acquaintances	−	−	0	−	−
9. While shopping with sales people	−	−	0	−	−
10. In clubs and organizations	−	−	0	−	−
11. At religious services	−	−	+	−	+
Agreements	0%	9%	55%	0%	0%
Constraint: Percent (−)	100	82	18	91	73
Facilitation: Percent (+)	0	9	27	9	27
	100	100	100	100	100

change in favor of English occurs when respondents report on preference and use in conversations with their spouses. In this situation we find that the ethnic mother tongue is preferred only among Newark Ukrainians. The similarity between parental and spouse contexts among Newark respondents is certainly due to their immigrational recency. On the other hand, a significant language shift occurs between the parental and spouse contexts among the Puerto Ricans of New York, another recent immigrant group. In the other three communities as well English is both preferred and used more often than the ethnic mother tongue among spouses.

In conversation with the third generation (i.e., with their own children) English is once more usually preferred and used in all communities except Newark. In terms of both ethnic mother tongue preference and reported use, Newark Ukrainians rank first more frequently than any other group. In only four out of eleven situations are they replaced in the first rank by Puerto Ricans.

"Close relatives" provide the only context besides parents in which many respondents report that the ethnic mother tongue is usually preferred and employed. Indeed, it would appear that for the great majority of respondents English has displaced the mother tongue in almost all domains of language. On the other hand, since there are reasons to conclude that the members of nearly all communities investigated exist in an environment scarcely favorable to mother tongue maintenance, the extent of linguistic retentiveness may well be judged to be quite considerable under the circumstances. By analyzing the direction of differences between frequencies of preference and frequencies of use, an index of mother tongue constraint and facilitation can be developed for the social environments of the respondents (Table 8.7). In all but one community, Olyphant, the use of the ethnic mother tongue is constrained far more frequently than it is facilitated. Only in Olyphant and Fall River does considerable facilitation appear, particularly in connection with close relatives and religious services. Significantly enough, "preference" and "use" coincide in fifty-five per cent of contact situations in Olyphant, where mother tongue use is lowest.

It is tempting to suggest on the basis of these data that the least retentive communities (Olyphant, Fall River) do not necessarily exhibit these characteristics at the present time because of external pressures, but rather because of internalized preferences for English. Indeed, many respondents in Olyphant and Fall River find themselves using the ethnic mother tongue more frequently than they would like to. On the other hand, the most highly retentive communities (Newark and New York) show high levels of constraint in the use of the mother tongue. These are likely to be *external* rather than *internal* constraints. In other words, the preference for the mother tongue may be so strong as to cause respondents to want to use it on more occasions than is practical or comfortable (e.g., with children, siblings, acquaintances, at work, while shopping, etc.).

In order to explore further the existence of such constraints, respondents were asked to indicate the social situations or contexts in which they did not experience discomfort when using their ethnic mother tongue. As can be noted from Table 8.8, Newark

TABLE 8.8

Lack of Discomfort in Use of the Ethnic Mother Tongue

Respondents	Percent of Situations free of discomfort				
	SA	NY	Oly.	Nwk.	FR
Parents	55	52	76	94	52
Oldest Child	80	86	93	91	76
Rank	4	3	2	1	5

and Olyphant – the most and least retentive communities, respectively – are freest from discomfort, while Fall River, San Antonio, and New York rate highest in discomfort. The absence or presence of discomfort may be traceable to several sources. Where respondents make little use of the ethnic mother tongue, discomfort experiences must be correspondingly low. On the other hand, in Newark, where the ethnic language is most frequently employed, the low discomfort score is probably due to group cohesion and to its insulation from the larger community.

The relative frequency of discomfort among Puerto Ricans in New York is more easily accounted for than that of Franco-Americans in Fall River. Puerto Ricans are socially marginal and are subjected to hostility and discrimination by the larger community. As a result, the use of Spanish, both inside and outside the ethnic community, may be suppressed, at least by more "practical" and "sensitive" individuals. But it seems unlikely that this is the case among Franco-Americans today, although they too were exposed to similar difficulties in former years.

It is interesting to note that there is also a great deal of discomfort about using Spanish in San Antonio, in spite of the fact that one third to one half of the population has been of Hispanic extraction for many, many generations and that the use of Spanish in public and private alike is still extremely common. Nevertheless, excellence in English is emphasized by those Mexican-Americans concerned with fighting discrimination and with rising in the class hierarchy. Thus, the more socially mobile as well as the more socially conscious may refrain from using their ethnic mother tongue to avoid being taken for ignorant "Mexs" or "Canucks", either by Anglos and Yankees or by their "own-ethnics".

If we consider all five communities with respect to the most prevalent type of intergenerational interest in transmitting the ethnic mother tongue to the children, we find

TABLE 8.9

Relatives Designated as "most Interested" in Having Respondents' Children Learn Ethnic Mother Tongue

Relatives	SA	NY	Oly.	Nwk.	FR
Grandparents	50	34	79	11	67
Parents	33	41	3	66	24
Both Parents and Grandparents	13	21	17	20	6
Total Parents	46	62	20	86	30
Parent Rank	3	2	5	1	4

that parent-to-child motivation exists most frequently among Newark respondents (Table 8.9). On the other hand, in Olyphant and in Fall River language transmission is more frequently left to the children's grandparents. (It must be remembered, though, that in the cases of Newark and New York respondents it is less likely that grandparents reside in the United States.) Obviously, parents exert much more direct influence favorable to Spanish among Puerto Ricans than is the case in San Antonio. This, indeed, is what one would expect purely on the basis of recency of immigration. However, the situation is not as simple as it seems. There is evidence that often, despite or because of strong parental interest, children resist the maintenance of the ethnic mother tongue, while *their* children, in turn, may hold a more benign attitude toward it. But by that time such a change of heart seems to be of little value for language maintenance, since the essential ingredient, the language itself, can no longer be adequately transmitted by parents. If the role of parents and grand-parents described here is true, one would expect Puerto Rican children in New York currently to have greater facility in Spanish than Mexican-American children in San Antonio, despite the former's possible aversion to it. However, in the long run the skills involved are more likely to be perpetuated by the bilingual history of the whole community of San Antonio than by the history of New York City which has characteristically absorbed its immigrants into the vortex of the linguistic melting pot. Despite the greater distance between San Antonio children and the traditions of their forebears, the nature of the local ethnic closure is such that knowledge and use of Spanish remains a distinctly functional, although not necessarily prestigeful attribute. Thus, Spanish-speaking children in San Antonio may indicate their disdain for Spanish by cultivating an English accent, but they nevertheless continue to have facility in the language because of its immediate usefulness. This is not to say that Spanish is of no practical value to the Puerto Rican child in New York. Yet, the pressures of the social environment are such that the Puerto Ricans are more likely to rapidly deemphasize the use of Spanish or its transmission to their own children in connection with most domains of language.

CONCLUSIONS

Analyses of interview data have provided several worthwhile vantage points from which to view the present status of language maintenance in five different ethnic communities. If ranked in terms of overall maintenance these five communities fall into two distinct clusters. Two communities – Fall River and Olyphant – clearly and consistently appear to be least retentive. In these communities the ethnic mother tongue is on the verge of complete functional erosion. It has already largely disappeared from the variegated encounters of daily life. It has also ceased to be transmitted via continued use within the domain of intimacy – the family hearth. Nevertheless it lingers on, albeit no longer as a mother tongue, among the children of the respondents.

Ethnic institutions – and parochial schools in particular – have been assigned the burden of language maintenance in these two communities. Even further in the direction of functional de-ethnization is the tendency of Fall River respondents to relegate the responsibility for ethnic mother tongue survival to non-ethnic institutions, namely, the public schools. What many Fall River respondents expect their children to learn is neither their mother tongue nor even their ethnic mother tongue but the language of Voltaire and Flaubert, a language of culture and of practical significance in social advance.

Fall River and Olyphant respondents and their children are no longer *functionally bilingual*, even though many, if not most, possess considerably facility in French or Ukrainian. If they continue to be exposed to their respective ethnic mother tongues, it is not so much through active daily use as through involvement in narrowly delimited and segregated activities such as attendance at schools, church services, or other organizational pursuits.

In striking contrast to the above picture, three other communities – two Spanish and one Ukrainian – still remain largely bilingual and, what is more, functionally bilingual. Two of these most retentive communities do not pose any special inter-

TABLE 8.10

Bases of Ethnic Mother Tongue Maintenance in Five Ethnic Communities

| Community | Informal Familial and Personal Context | | Formal Organizational Context | | |
| | | | Ethnic Community | | Core Society |
	Home	Friendships and Neighborhood	Language Schools	Parochial Schools	Public Schools
Newark	decreasing	decreasing	stable	stable	—
New York	decreasing	decreasing	—	—	minor
San Antonio	stable	stable	—	—	minor
Fall River	—	—	—	decreasing	stable
Olyphant	—	—	—	decreasing	—

petative problems, since whatever success they currently experience in connection with language maintenance can be readily accounted for on the basis of their greater immigrational recency. Indeed, there is no reason to believe that the Ukrainian community of Newark, or the Puerto Rican community of New York, will not ultimately traverse the path of Olyphant and Fall River. On the other hand, the Mexican-American community of San Antonio presents a unique and highly interesting phenomenon for the student of language maintenance in the United States. The evidence at hand strongly suggests that this community has reached an accommodation, however precarious it may be, that is retentive of functional bilingualism. There is little doubt that Spanish in San Antonio is viable not only among the impoverished masses but also among well-educated and successful professionals and businessmen. Indeed, Spanish continues to be used even by those "negative activists" who have attempted or still attempt to eliminate it.

This is not to imply, of course, that the process of linguistic assimilation is entirely absent in San Antonio, although its rate would seem to be far less rapid than that in the other four ethnic communities studied. The crux of the difference lies in the continued viability of Spanish in the family and in the context of intimate relations more generally. The use of both Spanish and English among Mexican-Americans in San Antonio shows many signs of at least partial *contextual stabilization*. The former language continues to be encountered frequently in the sphere of many informal relations while the latter dominates in the formal spheres of work, school, business, and so on.

In the case of the other four ethnic communities the ethnic mother tongue tends to be displaced in the sphere of intimacy by the time the second generation establishes its own families. For the third generation English becomes the dominant language in the parental home. As a result, facility in the ethnic mother tongue for these children tends to depend increasingly on instruction offered by ethnic and non-ethnic schools and organizations. What is accomplished under such circumstances, at best, is scarcely functional but rather cultural bilingualism.

It is suggested, then, that greater *contextual* and *inter-generational stability* under-lies ethnic mother tongue maintenance in San Antonio. Contextual stability provides for the continued use of the mother tongue, while generational stability provides for its transmission from parents to children. As a result, the San Antonio community can still rely upon the home for the maintenance of the mother tongue, whereas Olyphant and Fall River alike have delegated this responsibility to ethnic and non-ethnic agencies outside the family. The different bases of mother tongue maintenance in the five ethnic communities investigated are schematically presented in Table 8.10.

Thus, it would seem that Spanish survives in San Antonio precisely because it con-tinues to be used in the domains most crucial for functional bilingualism. This seem-ingly redundant statement raises a plethora of considerations which require much more intensive study by students of language maintenance.

9. GERMAN-AMERICAN LANGUAGE MAINTENANCE EFFORTS*

HEINZ KLOSS

CONCEPTUAL BACKGROUND: AN ANALYSIS OF FACTORS INFLUENCING LANGUAGE MAINTENANCE OUTCOMES

Factors Favorable to Language Maintenance

Six factors contributing to language maintenance in the United States can currently be isolated on the basis of careful study. One of these is so powerful as to enable those groups endowed with it to resist assimilation on the ground of this one circumstance, no other factor being necessary. This factor (Factor 1) has occurred only among small groups. The five remaining factors have occurred in connection with large groups as well as small, and frequently in a manner that has made them appear interlinked and interpenetrating.

The six factors are:

1. religio-societal insulation;
2. time of immigration: earlier than or simultaneously with the first Anglo-Americans;
3. existence of language islands;
4. affiliation with denominations fostering parochial schools;
5. pre-immigration experience with language maintenance efforts;
6. former use as the *only* official tongue during pre-Anglo-American period.

Factor 1. Religio-societal insulation occurs when the members of some religious group "withdraw from the world" that surrounds them and build up a self-sufficient society of their own, which rejects not only most of the common tenets, but also many tools (such as automobiles, telephones, electric gadgets) of their environment. By shutting themselves off from the dominant cultural trends of their time, they succeed in keeping alive their ancestral tongue. In the United States their point of departure has always been religion rather than nationality or language. They maintain their language in order to more fully exclude worldly influences and, perhaps, because change in itself is considered sinful. Neither language nor nationality is valued for its own sake.

Obviously, groups pursuing this course are doomed to remain small. While they

---

* For a more detailed presentation of this material, including many additional statistical and bibliographic references, the reader is referred to the original report which appeared in Fishman et al. 1964.

usually are prolific, they recurrently lose some of their members, either directly to the "world" at large or to newly-founded splinter groups that try to steer an intermediate course. The latter ultimately find themselves closer to the "world" than to their former co-religionists and, as a result, lose their linguistic separateness as well.

Factors 2, 3, 4, 5, and 6, on the other hand, may be considered most important for language maintenance among normal, non-insulated minority groups. Factors 3 through 6 bear chiefly on the attitudes of the members of such minority groups, while Factor 2 pertains chiefly, although not entirely, to the behavior of the majority group toward the non-dominant groups. While much depends on the language maintenance attitudes of minority groups themselves, the majority group is usually in a position to either facilitate or impede their language maintenance efforts.

Factor 2. This refers to continuity of residence and/or priority of colonization. For a number of reasons, Anglo-Americans have always been much more prone to respect the languages of those groups whose history on American soil harks back as far as that of the "Yankees". Legislation concerning non-English languages has been far more generous toward older minorities. In Hawaii, for example, the little known language of a relatively few Polynesians was more readily accepted than that of the many Japanese who at times formed 40% of the total population. Historical priority has also been of importance in connection with several other non-English languages in the United States, among them French and Spanish. At best, the German element could claim simultaneousness rather than priority.

Factor 3. Another factor favoring the retention of a non-dominant language is the existence of language islands (Sprachinseln), i.e., of circumscribed territories where the minority tongue is the principal tongue used in daily conversation by at least four-fifth of the inhabitants. The larger the island, the greater its ability to resist assimilation. There are two functional categories of language islands:

i. Islands that are large enough, or isolated enough, to retain their language in an effortless way, automatically as it were, without particular language maintenance efforts.

ii. Smaller islands which are in danger of being swallowed up by the surrounding majority tongue unless systematic efforts at language maintenance are adopted.

Thus, linguistic developments in these two types of language island start from different points of departure. The former requires *language assimilation* (or prohibition) *efforts* in order to *bring about* a change in the status quo; the latter requires *language maintenance efforts* in order to *prevent* a change.

The requisite size of a language island or the number of inhabitants required in order to qualify for inclusion in category i, has greatly changed in recent times. Before the time of modern mass communication and transportation media, a much smaller island was sufficient to render deliberate language maintenance efforts unnecessary. At least four language islands in the United States fall into this category: the Spanish-speaking of northern New Mexico and southern Colorado, the French-speaking in southern Louisiana, the German-speaking in eastern and central Pennsylvania, and the German-speaking in southern North Dakota and north-eastern South Dakota. It is apparent that Factors 2 and 3 frequently go together, early settlement being favorable to the formation of large, even huge, language islands in the large and previously unsettled American continent.

The significance (and even the very existence) of these non-English language islands has frequently been overlooked in American literature. They do not seem to fit in well with the conceptual framework of many sociologists and social historians (e.g., with Turner's leitmotiv of the frontier). Here, as elsewhere, "conceptual non-existence" has resulted in ignoring the facts. However, the fact that they were largely overlooked also helped these islands to lead a more secluded and unthreatened existence.

The 1940 census supplies us with a reliable yardstick for measuring the relationship between language islands and language maintenance. If we arrange the native-of-native parentage (third generation) according to the percentage that they represented of their entire mother tongue group, and if, in addition, we mark off by an asterisk those groups which consist of a sizable percentage of "islanders", we arrive at the following picture:

*1.	Spanish	38.6	*6.	Norwegian	12.3
*2.	French	36.7	7.	Polish	7.7
*3.	German	18.7	*8.	Swedish	7.1
*4.	Dutch	17.4	9.	Finnish	6.5
	(without spurious "Dutchmen"		10.	Slovak	6.0
	in Pennsylvania and Ohio)		11.	Portuguese	5.4
*5.	Czech	15.7	*12.	Danish	4.0

Of the twelve most retentive nationalities, eight (among them the first six listed) have language islands. In the case of the highest rating non-island group – the Polish-Americans – Factor 4 (parochial schools) and Factor 5 (previous maintenance experience) come into play.[1]

Factor 4. It is of paramount importance whether a linguistic minority group belongs to a denomination which requires its members to set up its own parochial schools, even though common schooling at public expense is available. Two such religious bodies have been the Roman Catholic Church and the "Old Lutheran" synods named after the states of Missouri and Wisconsin (in German: Missourisynode and Wisconsinsynode). The school policy of a given non-English denomination is more important for the future of the language in question than another aspect of denominational affiliation which is mentioned much more frequently in the pertinent literature, namely, whether the denomination is peculiar to the specific ethnic group or has its theological counterpart among the English-speaking majority populace. That

---

[1] The differences in percentages are, of course, partly due to the fact that the more urbanized groups were also of more recent immigrants status, and, therefore, had had less time in which to produce third generation descendants by 1940 (See Fishman and Hofman, Chapter 2, p. 41).

German-speaking Roman Catholics had their counterpart among English speakers (e.g., among Irish-American Catholics) was a *secondary* factor influencing the extent to which German-American Catholics kept their schools monolingual and the rate of speed with which they later embraced English as their second and even primary medium of instruction. The *primary* factor in language maintenance was that their religion led them to found and retain parochial schools more consistently than did most other German-speaking groups.

Factor 5. Pre-immigration experience with language maintenance efforts is a factor influencing Polish and French-Canadian language maintenance, but has occurred only occasionally among German-Americans (e.g., among the Mennonites from southern Russia). These historical experiences have taught leaders of certain minority groups that *language maintenance cannot be accomplished without "quality maintenance"*. A language which ceases to be a medium of subtle thinking, lofty ideals, diversified occupational interests and skills, which is restricted to the primary grades in parochial schools, and which is capable of serving none but primary group functions – such a language may live on for some generations, but will constantly lose in prestige when contrasted with dynamic American core-culture. As a corollary, it will tend to be less used, qualitative shrinkage being the forerunner of quantitative shrinkage.

Consciously planned language maintenance experiences are to be distinguished from unplanned, effortless pre-immigration language maintenance experiences. The latter situation obtained among most Russian-Germans and also among many Czechs under Habsburg rule. Although it also favors language maintenance, it is a less effectively positive factor than planned maintenance. While it accustomed some immigrants to governments and to host societies using languages other than their own, it did not foster the crucial arts and skills of cultural self-maintenance. It did not provide specific techniques for struggling for language maintenance under circumstances where only directed and coordinated efforts have some chance of success.

Factor 6. This refers to prestige resulting from former monopoly. Non-English-speaking powers preceded the Anglo-Americans in a number of states and established their languages in these areas as the only official languages. Thus, Dutch was the only official language along sections of the middle Atlantic sea coast, Spanish in New Mexico, French in Louisiana. Their official status accorded these languages a specific prestige-value which was subsequently felt and recognized by both non-English and English settlers. The descendants of the original speakers of these languages have clung to them more tenaciously than has been the case with speakers of other immigrant tongues – as testified by the almost miraculous survival of Dutch in parts of New Jersey down into the 20th century.

Ambivalent Factors

There are a number of other factors (7 through 15) which frequently contribute either to the success of language maintenance efforts or to effortless (and sometimes merely temporary) language survival. What distinguishes them from the foregoing factors is their ambivalence. They are apt to work both ways, in some instances *for* and in others *against* language maintenance. Yet, most of them have, at times, been credited by scholars as well as by popular opinion with being favorable to language maintenance. These ambiguous factors are listed here without any claim of exhaustiveness and without regard to their relative importance, which is difficult to ascertain.

Factor 7. High educational level of immigrants.[2]

a. *Favorable effects*: A high educational level enables groups to maintain a lively, intellectual life, a flourishing vernacular press, and, in general, is conducive to self-respect and self-assertiveness. It also encourages the establishment of vernacular schools or of bilingual schools and results in early insight into the necessity of "quality maintenance"; hence the early founding of high schools, seminaries, colleges, etc.

b. *Unfavorable effects*: A high educational level makes for occupational and – as a frequent corollary – geographic mobility, rapid urbanization, and an eagerness to interact with Anglo-Americans and to participate in their economic, social, and political affairs. The unfavorable effects are clearly discernible in the case of Scandinavian immigrants, many of whom arrived with a fair knowledge of English even prior to World War I. As a result, they were more rapidly tempted to neglect the maintenance of their own group life.

Factor 8. Low educational level of immigrants.

a. *Favorable effects*: A low average educational level perpetuates strong group cohesion among the foreign-born generation, a tendency to keep aloof from the mainstream of American life, and to perpetuate institutions and customs that preserve the traditions and values common in their former homelands.

b. *Unfavorable effects*: It is difficult, if not impossible, for immigrants at a low educational level to establish educational institutions of sufficient quality and quantity to shield their children against the overpowering influence of English. The second generation is usually unwilling to accept educational inferiority for itself and rejects that of its parents. As a result of this rejection and the concomitant self-identification with the dominant (i.e., the English-speaking) group, the ethnic mother tongue is also rejected. This adverse effect of low educational attainment on the part of immigrants has been most noticeable in the case of Italian-Americans.

Factor 9. Great numerical strength.

a. *Favorable effects*: Great numerical strength permits the establishment of numerous educational and other institutions, provides a solid financial base for the minority press, permits political influence in state and/or local affairs, and lessens the necessity for intermarriage.

b. *Unfavorable effects*: Great numerical strength inevitably multiplies contacts with the "English" environment, increases the likelihood of factions or wings within the

---

[2] Here, as elsewhere in this conceptual scheme, reference is made to average group standards and not to conditions characterizing selected individuals.

minority groups, makes it difficult for leaders of the group to attain and preserve a general view of the minority's situation, and is conducive to apprehension and animosity on the part of the majority group. Most typical example: the German-Americans.

Factor 10. Smallness of the group.

a. *Favorable effects*: It is much easier for the leaders of an ethnic minority to control or direct a small group, where each minister, organizational officer, and activist is personally known. In large groups, human relations are more impersonal and some subgroups as well as their leaders tend to evade control.

b. *Unfavorable effects*: Where manpower and wherewithal are in short supply, the maintenance of separate cultural institutions (press, schools, organizations, etc.) is extremely difficult. In addition, numerical limitations tend to lead to feelings of hopelessness with respect to the future of language maintenance.

Factor 11. Cultural and/or linguistic similarity to Anglo-Americans.

a. *Favorable effects*: Similarities to Anglo-Americans are conducive to acceptive and sympathetic attitudes on the part of the linguistic majority. As a result, the minority group members maintain positive self-concepts which transfer to language maintenance as well.

b. *Unfavorable effects*: Similarities to Anglo-Americans lead to the erosion of group consciousness and group differences on the part of the second and subsequent generations.

Factor 12. Great cultural and/or linguistic dissimilarity between minority and majority.

a. *Favorable effects*: An awareness of distinctiveness and dissimilarity enhances group consciousness among members of a minority group. Even where dissimilarity leads to animosity, prejudice, discrimination and, in extreme cases, segregation, language maintenance may be strengthened as a result of greater self-reliance in the cultural and economic domains.

b. *Unfavorable effects*: Great initial dissimilarities lead to more eager attempts on the part of the younger generation to become as "American" as possible and not to share the disadvantages of their parents or grandparents. In attempting to overcome great dissimilarities, language differences are rapidly shed.

Factor 13. Suppression of minority tongue(s).

a. *Favorable effects*: The official suppression of a minority tongue by the state (or its unofficial suppression by various social groups) has often strengthened the minority's will to live. As a result, language maintenance becomes a component of resistance to suppression.

b. *Unfavorable effects*: Suppression may bring to pass the partial or even complete collapse of a minority, this latter effect being illustrated by the nadir of German-American language maintenance efforts in the period 1917-23.

Factor 14. Permissive attitude of the majority group.

a. *Favorable effects*: When the majority group freely permits the cultivation of the minority tongue, this naturally encourages the establishment of organizations and institutions to serve the various specific interests of the group, including its linguistic, cultural, and literary heritage. The early history of most western European immigrant groups on American soil illustrates this point.

b. *Unfavorable effects*: The complete lack of any obstacle to cultural development easily produces a lulling effect and results in false feelings of cultural security on the part of minority groups. The more recent history of most western European immigrant groups may serve as an example of this effect.

Factor 15. Socio-cultural characteristics of the minority group in question.

The socio-cultural characteristics of a given minority group constitute one of the most important as well as one of the most elusive factors in language maintenance. Frequently we are at a loss to predict what a given characteristic will signify in a given situation or vis-à-vis a specific challenge. A high degree of ethnic pride and self-reliance may, at first glance, seem definitely favorable to language maintenance. Actually, these characteristics may hasten the process of assimilation since they may lead to the view that group life can be maintained without linguistic continuity.

Summary

The presence or absence of the various factors listed above conditions the rise of language maintenance efforts as well as their prospects of success. They are so variegated that the outcome of their interplay cannot be summed up by a simple formula. Neither Hansen's view that the sons of immigrants flee from ethnicity while the grandsons return to the fold of ethnicity, nor the opposite thesis that the linear disappearance of ethnicity is accomplished within the course of three generations, is sufficiently subtle to be accurate in a given case or to be revealing in the general case. No single formula will prove to be applicable in the case of a very large nationality group such as the German-Americans. No single factor will permit us to explain how early (or how late) in the chain of generations the German language disappeared in the past, or to predict its retention in the future. Among German-Americans, we can find examples of all of the above-mentioned factors. The spirit of ethnicity disappeared among some subgroups within the first American-born generation. In other subgroups it lived on for five, six, and more generations; indeed, in some few instances, it is alive today after a long history of development and shows every sign of living on into the distant future.

STATISTICAL BACKGROUND

The foremost datum in connection with the German-American group is the huge number of speakers of German who, at one time or another, have lived in what today constitutes the United States. A report issued by the American Council of Learned

Societies (1932) estimated that as early as 1790 there were 279,200 Germans on the soil of what is presently the United States. These were distributed by states as follows: Pennsylvania, 141,000; Virginia, 27,900; New York, 25,800; Maryland, 24,400; New Jersey, 15,600; North Carolina, 13,600; Kentucky and Tennessee, 13,000; South Carolina, 7,000 and Georgia, 4,000. The number of immigrants arriving subsequently in the United States from Germany is estimated as follows:

> 1820-1870 (50 years) 1,500,000
> 1870-1917 (47 years) 3,100,000
> 1920-1962 (42 years) 1,300,000

In 1910, when the German-speaking element in the United States was at its peak, we find

> 2,759,000 foreign-born individuals whose mother tongue was German ("German speakers") and
>
> 6,058,300 American-born children of foreign-born "German speakers" or, all in all, a total of
>
> _____
>
> 8,817,300 German-Americans.

Of the 6,058,300 second-generation German-Americans, roughly two-fifths had only one American-born parent. While many members of the second generation either could not or did not habitually speak the language of the forefathers, it may safely be assumed that their number was more than counterbalanced by third or subsequent generation *native Americans of native parentage* whose home tongue was still German. Thus the sum total of persons who spoke German natively in 1910 may well have been in the neighborhood of 9 million. No other non-English language has been spoken by as large a proportion of the residents of the United States at any one time in American history. Similarly, no other non-English group has been represented by more than a handful of persons in all of the 50 states that presently constitute the United States.

Since 1910 a sharp decline has occurred in the number of German speakers in the United States. By 1940 the census disclosed the following figures with respect to German mother tongue:

Foreign born	1,589,000
Native with at least one foreign-born parent	2,436,000
Native of native parentage	925,000
	4,950,000

For our present inquiry, the above figure of 925,000 points to an interesting and important problem. If as late as 1940 there were still nearly one million natives of native parentage for whom German was the language of their early childhood, then the 1940 census must have been preceded by decades, perhaps centuries, of very considerable language maintenance efforts on the part of first- and second-generation German-Americans.

The 1960 census placed the number of foreign-born whose mother tongue was German at 1,278,000. On the other hand, 4,320,100 individuals of foreign stock (i.e., foreign-born and children of foreign-born) named Germany as their country of origin. Since in recent years we can only (at best) expect the children of German immigrants, but *never their grandchildren*, to consider German as their native tongue, the number of American residents whose mother tongue was German was unlikely to have been much above the 4 million mark in 1960. It is also important to realize that a great many "German speakers" came to the United States from countries other than Germany. In the 18th century and until the 1870's, these came mainly from Switzerland, Alsace-Lorraine, and Luxembourg. After 1880 many also came from eastern Europe. In 1910, 1,100,000 persons of "foreign white stock" who claimed German as their mother tongue claimed a country of origin other than Germany. A majority came from Austria-Hungary (374,000), Russia (former boundaries, 245,000), and Switzerland (263,000). No other single country of origin was reported by more than 40,000 claimants of German mother tongue.

It almost goes without saying that in many of the 50 states the German element, while by no means unimportant, was always too weak numerically ever to have had a chance for language survival. This holds true even for some of the isolated German-speaking settlements such as Waldoboro in Maine, the German Coast in Louisiana, Lihue in Hawaii, and Cullman in Alabama. Small settlements like these could never hope to preserve their language permanently. As a matter of fact, the German Coast became Frenchified before succumbing to English. Nevertheless, in at least 24 states the German language at one time or another seemed to have had such a chance either (a) because of its numerical strength, (b) because of the existence of at least one other major non-English language island, or (c) because of both factors. These states and their concentrations are:

(as a result of colonial immigration):
> one major German group in Pennsylvania, and seven minor German groups in New York, New Jersey, Maryland, Virginia, North Carolina, South Carolina, Georgia – each comprising one or several language islands;

(as a result of 19th and 20th century immigration):
> large urban groups in New York, New Jersey, Connecticut, Mississippi, California, Maryland, Kentucky, Louisiana; and numerous urban *and* rural groups, the latter often forming outright language islands, in Texas and in all of the Midwestern States (Ohio, Michigan, Indiana, Illinois, Wisconsin, Missouri, Minnesota, Iowa, North Dakota, South Dakota, Nebraska, Kansas).

It is to these states and periods that we must turn in our search for German language maintenance efforts in the United States.

THE COLONIAL STOCK[3]

Tiny nuclei of German-speaking individuals developed on North American shores in the first half of the 17th century. It is from soon after this period that we hear of their first language maintenance efforts (Lohr 1962, pp. 162-63, 187). In 1655, the Lutherans of New Amsterdam sent a delegate to Holland in order to procure a minister who could preach to them in High German. In 1657 there arrived J. E. Gutwasser, henceforth to serve the High German congregations of New Amsterdam and of Albany (then Beverwyck). It is not improbable that even catechistical instruction (Konfirmandenunterricht) was given in German for a time. However, these earliest German congregations became Dutchified after two or three decades.

In the 18th century there developed a huge German-language island in Pennsylvania and substantial language islands in at least eight other states. For a long time these islands endeavored to preserve their language, their chief weapon being the parochial school. Their efforts continued into the 19th century, as evidenced in a resolution passed in 1815 by the "Special Conference of the Evangelical Lutheran Teachers in Virginia" at Woodstock, Virginia, that ministers either should hire competent German teachers or should themselves teach school in German for at least three months each year. A resolution was also adopted by the Lutheran ministers of Ohio and Western Pennsylvania at their 1816 meeting in New Lancaster, Ohio, that each minister should make the cause of the German school the main topic of at least one sermon a year. Yet, beginning with the 1820's the schools of these diaspora groups became Anglified or were replaced by public schools where only English was taught.

During the first few post-revolutionary decades, most German-language islands manifested great self-assurance as well as considerable pride in being, or so they felt, partners and equals in the republic they had helped to establish. Yet, even at that early date marked differences appeared in the attitudes of the various German groups. In some cases the basis of these differences was clearly sectarian. For instance, the Moravians in Pennsylvania and North Carolina were more progressive than the other denominations in that they more quickly added secondary schools to the elementary ones, establishing the first Moravian academy in 1749. In other instances, the basis of the attitudinal differences seem, at first glance, to have been sectional rather than sectarian. In the Mohawk Valley of upstate New York and in western Maryland the Germans were definitely less concerned about the preservation of their mother tongue than were their co-nationals in Virginia and Ohio, where beginning in the late 18th century thousands of emigrants from eastern Pennsylvania had founded settlements. Yet, upon close scrutiny, we discover the sectarian factor to have been at work here as well. The Lutheran synods in New York and Maryland were more liberal than their sister synods in Virginia and Ohio.[4] While this attitude bore primarily on theo-

---

[3]   The basic reference on pre-1800 immigrants is Emil Meynen 1937.
[4]   For a discussion of the theological views of the 18th and 19th century Lutheran Synods see *Concordia Cyclopedia* 1927.

logical problems it influenced their outlook on the language problem, the New York and Maryland Germans being less conservative in both respects.

Even after the breakdown of the German church schools in the 1820's and the gradual disappearance of High German from sermons, the early outlying settlements were by no means fully Anglified. Their dialects, in most instances varieties of the so-called "Pennsylvania Dutch" dialect, lingered on. Even in the Mohawk Valley and in western Maryland, we know the dialect to have outlived the 19th century in a number of localities. In Virginia and in Ohio (particularly in the neighborhood of Canton) it survives in remote spots even today, primarily but not only among the Amish (Stewart and Smith 1963).

Throughout the 19th century a considerable number of Germans emigrated from eastern Pennsylvania and from the other colonial settlements in the eastern coastal states. Although much of the emigration was scattered, a number of predominantly German settlements was founded. Of these, the dialect is still vigorous today only among the Amish and the Old Order Mennonites. The Mennonite settlements in northern Indiana proved particularly retentive and creative, and even produced a modest body of High German literature. When Eisenhower became president in 1953, reporters were amazed to find that in his family's home town of Abilene, Kansas, there were still a number of elderly people who spoke the dialect. Eisenhower's grandfather had been a German preacher and his father was still fully bilingual.

In Pennsylvania the German language had a much stronger hold than it had in the outposts. A large language island had developed, comprising seven entire counties and large portions of twenty-one others – roughly 15,000 square miles in all. This island may be said to have been large enough that for a long time no special effort was necessary to maintain the German language. It was a "natural thing" for German to live on. In order to bring about a change, special *language-riddance efforts* would have been needed (cf. Factor 3, above).

Regular teaching of German is supposed to have been offered near Philadelphia as early as 1694 by a group of German mystics under Kelpius (Lohr 1962, p. 166). The number of German church schools multiplied rapidly in the following century. By 1750 the Moravians alone had founded 13 schools. In 1775 there were 40 Lutheran and 78 Reformed schools; in 1800, a total of 254 Lutheran and Reformed schools (Livingood 1930; p. 199; Maurer 1932, p. 200). To these must be added the schools founded by Mennonites, German Baptist Brethren (Dunkards), Moravians, River Brethren, and other sects. As a rule these schools were wholly German at that time, although there were early instances of bilingual education, e.g. the Schwenkfelders, who foresaw the indispensability of English and, therefore, stipulated from the outset that their schools should teach both languages (Gerhard 1943). On the other hand, the famous attempt by the London "Society for the Propagation of Christian Knowledge among the Germans in America" to bring about a gradual Anglification by means of bilingual schools (1754-1763) failed miserably even though aided by such prominent Germans as the Reformed leader, Michael Schlatter (Weber 1905).

A major weakness of 18th century German language maintenance effort in Pennsylvania was the tendency to neglect secondary and higher education. The Germans were eager to combat illiteracy. But whereas the Louisiana Creoles were eager to create and maintain academies and colleges, the Germans, with the notable exception of the Moravians, were slow to do so. In some instances, the main impetus to set up bilingual centers of learning (Philadelphia 1780, Lancaster 1787) appears to have come from their Anglo-American neighbors.[5] By and large, the American-born sons and grandsons of German immigrants obtained whatever secondary and higher learning they could at institutions where English was the sole language of instruction. Thus, while German remained for many decades the only language of the elementary school and, of course, of the pulpit and the press, English became the language in which the comparatively few native scholars and intellectuals among German-Americans received their technical training and wrote their books.[6] Thus a rift developed between the bilingual and increasingly English monolingual intelligentsia, and the masses who long remained German monolingual. A special factor in this situation was the persistent aversion of some of the early "plain" sects, chiefly the Mennonites and the Dunkards, toward secondary and higher education. They wanted their children to learn nothing but the most elementary skills. When in the course of the last century they gradually overcame this attitude, English had long since become the only conceivable medium of secondary and college-level teaching. Among the Amish, originally a subgroup of the Mennonites, this distrust of booklearning is very much alive even today.

Nevertheless, the Pennsylvania Germans continued to cultivate their special brand of High German, "Pennsylvania High German", the pronunciation of which followed the 16th-17th century South German pattern, as may be noted from C. Becker's "Allgegenwärtiger Deutscher Sprachlehrer", published in 1818 (Wood 1945). They also developed a considerable body of literature, comprising in the 18th century chiefly poetry, but restricted in the early 19th century chiefly to prose books that were religious in character. The original literature of the Evangelical Association, a revivalist church body founded after 1800 by and for Pennsylvania Germans, was written in High German, mostly, it seems, by American-born authors.[7]

The 1830's, which saw the influx of a new German immigration into the United States, were to be the turning point in the history of High German among the colonial stock in Pennsylvania. The 1834 free school law, while silent about the language of

---

[5] A bilingual academy (founded 1761) and a seminary (founded 1773) collapsed during the Revolution. Cf. the bilingual instruction introduced at the University of Pennsylvania in 1780, at Franklin College (Lancaster) 1787.

[6] In 1819 John H. Livingston informed the German Reformed Church that the German Churches in America were the only ones that had not yet set up training institutions of their own (Livingston 1819, pp. 20-21). When, at long last, the two leading denominations founded such seminaries (the Reformed in Carlisle, 1825, and the Lutherans in Gettysburg, 1826) the predominance of English in college level education was taken for granted.

[7] A collection of such books is to be found in the History Library of Albright College, Reading, Penna.

instruction, was generally understood by the population to mean English-only schools. The Pennsylvania German intelligentsia, due to their lack of secondary and higher training in the German language, had already become somewhat lukewarm toward German language maintenance. When Charles Jared Ingersoll, an Anglo-Saxon lawyer from Philadelphia, moved at the 1837 State Constitutional Convention to adopt an article providing for common schools "in the English and German languages", a number of Pennsylvania German delegates sided with his opponents, and the motion was tabled. This was but one event in an uninterrupted history (still largely unwritten) of "language riddance" efforts beginning in 1834.[8]

Nevertheless, during these very same 1830's, a movement swept through eastern Pennsylvania calling itself the "Deutsche Reform" and clamoring for the admission of German in the courts, public documents, schools, etc. It was partly successful. In 1837 and 1840 laws were enacted providing for German editions of the session laws and in 1843 the position of "German State Printer" was created. The Free School Superintendent's Report for 1836 affirmed: "Care has been taken to correct the impression that a German school cannot be a common school". But very few German districts availed themselves of the opportunity created by the 1834 Free School Law, and so the inevitable came to pass. Neglected in the schools, literary German found a temporary refuge in the Church and in the newspapers, the former refuge being much more significant than the latter. Soon a bifurcation could be noted. In the western half of the German territory, High German was abandoned by Church and press much more quickly than in the eastern counties. Two reasons seem to have been at the root of the "western" attitude. In most of these counties there was a much stronger admixture of English-speaking (largely Scotch-Irish) settlers, and German had never been the only language in common use. In addition, the Lutheran synods prevalent in these sections were more liberal in their theological views and, "consequently" (though there is no necessary causative connection between the two issues), also more liberal in their attitude toward English than was the venerable and conservative "Pennsylvania Ministerium" dominating the eastern counties. Some of the western counties (e.g., Cumberland, Perry) also abandoned the vernacular soon after the discontinuation of High German Church services and the press. But in most of them (e.g., Center, Snyder, Somerset, York), the vernacular has persisted to this day.

Far more complicated were the developments in the eastern region comprising, roughly, the counties Berks, Lehigh and Lebanon, and parts of Bucks, Lancaster, Montgomery, Northampton, and Schuylkill. Here the congregations and synods clung to High German more tenaciously, and a flourishing German press, though sometimes archaic and primitive in its usage, did much to keep interest in the old tongue alive. For decades the Bible and the German-language periodicals of eastern Pennsylvania substituted for the lack of schools. Parents, themselves, taught their

---

[8]   See A. L. Shoemaker, *The Pennsylvania Dutchman*, Jan. 1, 1952: "None of our scholars has as yet undertaken a study of that explosive subject: the efforts, particularly by our educators, to wipe out Pennsylvania Dutch." See also Clyde Stine in R. C. Wood (ed.) 1943, pp. 116-124.

children to read German. Records reveal that the editor of a German-language newspaper used his business trips not only to raise funds, but also to instruct the younger generation in the German language. Other records reveal that public school teachers taught German to their pupils during recess (Wood 1943, p. 140; also Shoemaker in the *Pennsylvania Dutchman*, 1952, 3, p. 2). Obviously, the language still elicited great devotion.

It was here that a last determined attempt to stem the tide of Anglification was undertaken by means of an alliance between Church and press. This attempt at language maintenance was sufficiently broad-based to include the liberal papers and clubs of all (even the most radical) German immigrants in the big cities. Known as the "Verein der Deutschen Presse von Pennsylvanien" (founded in 1862), the alliance succeeded in forcing a law through the state legislature (1863), which made it mandatory to have official notices published in the German newspapers of eight (since 1868, of nine) designated counties. The Press Association promoted the founding of German Sunday schools or weekday schools, supplementary to the public free schools. In a number of instances it caused Anglified German-American Sunday schools to be reconverted into German ones; it effected the creation of bilingual public schools in a few cities (Harris burg, 1866; Lancaster, 1868), and the introduction of German as a branch of study in many others (Scranton, 1870; Williamsport, 1871; Allentown, 1873; Womelsdorf, 1875); it agitated for the founding of German libraries and (private) literary societies; etc. There were also attempts to make the new State Normal School at Kutztown (1867) a center for German instruction and to set up a private bilingual teachers' seminary at Broadheadville (1870). So encouraging were the results that it was decided to transform the Press Association into a nationwide organization. But all quickly came to a standstill with the death of the Presseverein's founder and president, S. K. Brobst, in 1876. Brobst was a Lutheran minister and a gifted journalist whose magazines – among them a youth paper, *Jugendfreund* (1847), the first German periodical of its kind in the United States or, for that matter, anywhere outside Europe – reached a combined circulation of 30,000, a remarkably impressive figure given the time and the circumstances. After his death, the position of High German among the Pennsylvania Germans of colonial descent crumbled irreparably. At the outbreak of World War I, the German press in Pennsylvania had all but disappeared. By the outbreak of World War II, the last traces of High German preaching had followed.

In the meantime, a third prospect had appeared on the scene – the Pennsylvania German dialect called Pennsylvania Dutch by the masses and Pennsylvanish by some (Wood 1952, Kloss 1954).[9] The colonial Germans in Pennsylvania clung to their vernacular much more tenaciously than did later German immigrants. In his autobiography, G. von Bosse tells that when he studied at Mt. Airy Lutheran Seminary (ca. 1890) his co-students of recent German origin conversed in English outside the

---

[9]   Different spellings have been used at various times: Pennsylvaanisch, Pennsylvanish, Pennsylfaanisch, and Pennsylfawnisch. In this essay the form Pennsylvanish is used throughout except in quotations and references.

classroom, but those of colonial stock conversed in the dialect (von Bosse 1920, pp. 15-16). Revivalism among Pennsylvania Germans, in the shape of the Evangelical Association (Albright), the United Brethren in Christ (Otterbein), and the Church of God General Eldership (Winebrenner), long depended upon the dialect for much of its preaching and hymn-singing.

Beginning in the late 1860's, a number of books were published in the dialect, and dialect columns, mostly "just humorous" but frequently "serious in disguise", became common in the newspapers of eastern Pennsylvania. As R. C. Wood has pointed out, the continued contraction of the High German press after 1880 presented a great opportunity for dialect speakers to make Pennsylvanish (instead of English) the successor of High German in the realm of journalism (Wood 1943, pp. 165-57). That this was not altogether out of the question is shown by contemporaneous developments in South Africa where, beginning in the 1870's, literary Dutch was replaced not by English but by a vernacular which today we call Afrikaans (Kloss 1939b). There were also a few educators (such as A. R. Horne) who spoke of the advisability of granting Pennsylvanish and its literature[10] access to the primary grades, but little was done in this direction. The general trend was toward a steady expansion of English in every sphere outside the home. A slow, but quite perceptible, retrogression of the dialect took place, especially in central Pennsylvania and in the cities. During World War I, the general aversion against everything "German" also had some repercussions on Pennsylvania Dutch "even in Pennsylvania".

The decade after World War I was one of apparent apathy; the ultimate extinction of Pennsylvanish seemed inevitable. Yet it was an extremely slow process. In 1937-39 Clyde Stine conducted a survey among public school pupils in the Pennsylvania German sections of seven counties. Among 41,000 children, he found 20,000 who were bilingual. Of these, 33.4% (6,700) declared that they preferred the vernacular to English.[11] Almost two decades later, Buffington and Barba stated, in the appendix to their dialect grammar, that according to investigations in some high schools in the dialect area, 92% of the students spoke "Deitsch" (Buffington and Barba 1954, 132).

A new phase of Pennsylvania German life began around 1930. Suddenly, and almost inexplicably, there appeared a resurgence of interest and vitality. This re-awakening occurred at about the same time that descendants of more recent German stock also began to recover from their post-war shock. Yet apparently, there was no relationship between these two phenomena, nor was the Pennsylvania German revival subsequently stifled by the chilling winds of Nazism. This resurgence has been strikingly likened to the last flickering up of a candle before its flame dies out. Perhaps the life of a linguistic community is governed by emotional responses which make this comparison quite apt. Be that as it may, new plays were written in the dialect and

---

[10]   Histories of the Pennsylvania German dialect literature have been published by H. H. Reichard (1918), H. Kloss (1932), E. F. Robacker (1943).
[11]   Clyde S. Stine, "Bilingualism in the Pennsylvania Schools", *Pa. Sch. J.*, 87 (1939), 339-340.

huge audiences attended their performances. New dialect columns appeared in a number of newspapers; new radio hours were inaugurated over a number of stations. In 1933 and 1934, organizations were founded – the "Fersomlinge" (assemblies) and the "Grundsow" (groundhog) Lodges – with the one and only goal of conducting gatherings entirely in the native tongue.

Since the venerable Pennsylvania-German Society seemed to be neglecting the dialect, a Pennsylvania-German Folklore Society was founded in 1935 which was to pay more attention to the linguistic heritage. In 1935 the Allentown "Morning Call" started a "Pennsylfawnisch [later changed to Pennsylvaanisch] Deitsch Eck" in its Saturday issue which was open to contributors – not all of them writing in the dialect, however – from all over the dialect area. In 1938 a conference of Pennsylvanish writers, meeting in Hershey, Pennsylvania, agreed upon a standardized spelling based on High German with only one major deviation – y for the High German j. In 1946 the Pennsylvania State University introduced a regular course in Pennsylvania-German in its German Department, an event that caused Mario Pei to speak of Pennsylvania-German as a "brand new Germanic language". The two crowning events of the "revival" were the publication in 1955 of a translation into Pennsylvania-German of the Gospel of St. Matthew, and in 1954 of a modern grammar of Pennsylvania-German designed for use by high schools and colleges.

The resurgence of interest in "things Pennsylvania Dutch" led to an enduring rehabilitation of several features of the regional cultural heritage, notably the folk arts. But with respect to the vernacular progress was merely temporary and deceptive, and in the long run all efforts proved futile. The unified spelling was not generally adopted. The appearance of the gospel in Pennsylvanish did not induce congregations to conduct church services in the dialect, except for one each year, which became, and still is, customary with a number of congregations. Few, if any, high schools and colleges made use of the new grammar, although there have been sporadic instances where Pennsylvanish has been taught as an adult education offering. In retrospect, three omissions were of paramount importance in the inability of Pennsylvania-German to "take hold" at that time. Nothing was done to provide elementary education in the dialect, if only temporarily and in a few rural demonstration schools. Few efforts were made to have Pennsylvanish books printed in cheap, uniform, popular editions; the few publications that did appear were mostly enshrined in de luxe editions. And the "Fersomlinge" and "Grundsow" Lodges did little more than stage a few hours of jolly fun-making. They did not have the necessary awareness that what was needed was a measure of dignity at their meetings, which would lend dignity to their tongue. The "Dutchman's" irresistible lust for fun won out over the few devotees who conceived of these organizations as weapons and shields for the preservation of the vernacular.

Among the forces contributing to this fizzling out of what had occasionally been called the Pennsylvania Dutch Revival was the magazine *The Pennsylvania Dutchman* (1949-1957). Edited by a team of able and unusually knowledgeable men of the younger generation, chiefly A. L. Shoemaker, it did its best to promote the antiquarian aspects of Pennsylvania-German lore, digging up a wealth of little known facts in the fields of folklore and history. At the same time, the magazine produced the impression that (a) nothing had been or could be written in Pennsylvanish other than things jocular or trivially nostalgic, and that (b) the Pennsylvania-Germans had nothing whatsoever in common with the descendants of the 19th century German immigrants. Much printer's ink was spilled to emphasize that Pennsylvania-Dutch was the only term permissible, and that the rival term Pennsylvania-German had to be done away with. At the outbreak of the Korean crisis, Shoemaker editorially exhorted the Pennsylvania-Germans henceforth to exclude, totally, the term Pennsylvania-German and to use even "Pennsylvania Dutch" only sparingly so as to strengthen the cohesion of an unhyphenated American nation.

In 1957 a leading Pennsylvania German (who is known to have held a different view in later years) stated in a speech to a Pennsylvania-German organization in Canada that he considered it "stupidly reactionary" to resist the decline of Pennsylvanish. "Even if the dialect, as such, were still the oral vehicle for many millions, it would not serve any utilitarian purpose".[12] These words reveal more than the historian himself may have wished to reveal. By denying any utilitarian value to Pennsylvanish, he implicitly denied its closeness to High German – still one of the great tongues of the world, though no longer among the two or three leading ones. And by mentioning only a utilitarian purpose, he implicitly ruled out another aspect of language so dear to all language loyalists, namely, that language is not a mere tool and, as such, interchangeable with other tools, but that it is also a moulding factor which co-determines patterns of thought and outlooks on life.

It seems clear that not only external forces (e.g. motorized traffic, the radio and television, consolidated schools, etc.) have been involved in bringing about the decline of Pennsylvanish, but also internal forces at the very heart of the speech community's will to live. Among these internal forces must be included the corrosive effect constant merry making exerts from within on a minority and the almost complete lack of feeling toward literary German as part of the Pennsylvania-German heritage. In 1959-60 the FLES-language programs among Pennsylvania Germans, according to an MLA report (Breunig 1961, pp. 29-30), were Spanish in Harrisburg, Emmaus, Lehighton, Lititz, Mifflintown, Hummelstown, Middletown, Millersburg, and Strasburg; French in Shanksville, Somerset, Carlisle, Hanover, Lewisburg, Littletown, and York; Spanish and French in Richboro; Spanish and German in Allentown; French and German in Schwenksville. The Pennsylvania Germans seem to be actively cutting themselves off from their past. Since 1960 the picture has become only somewhat brighter. German became a branch of study in the grade schools of Reading and – together with French and Spanish! – in the Lab School of Millersville Teachers College. Nevertheless, German is still far behind French and Spanish. A leading teacher of German, himself of Pennsylvania German extraction, writes:[13]

---

[12] *Canadian German Folklore* (Pennsylvania Folklore Society of Ontario), 1, 1961, p. 9.
[13] Personal communication.

There is no relationship – UNFORTUNATELY – between the status of Pennsylvania-German and that of German F.L.E.S. in southeastern Pennsylvania. I have always felt that the Pennsylvania German and the Pennsylvania German Folklore Societies should "push" German in the public schools. This they have failed to do for reasons too numerous to detail. Suffice it to say that both organizations are bookish in an old-fashioned way and one step removed from reality!

Most reports agree that the 1950's marked the final turning away of children and adolescents from the old tongue.[14] One of the few remaining optimists, J. J. Stoudt (1951, p. 24), wrote that "it will take another century before this new Germanic language will achieve full maturity...".[15] But R. C. Wood, another lover of the language, was probably more aware of the sad facts of life when he predicted in 1952 that the vernacular would succumb within the next twenty years unless its speakers cease to be illiterate in their mother tongue (Wood 1952). The battle, he felt, could still be won if only one out of every four Pennsylvania Germans who attended Fersomlinge or enjoyed theatrical performances and radio broadcasts in the dialect would make it a point to buy one Pennsylvanish book per year. The first of these two decades has run out without Wood's last best hope having been realized.[16]

THE POST-COLONIAL STOCK: 1830-1914

The Pennsylvania Germans remain a *sectional* group. However, in attempting to understand 19th and 20th century German immigrants,[17] it is of even greater importance to bear in mind their *sectarian* rather than their *sectional* distribution. That the chief loyalty of German Americans was to their adopted country, once they had settled down for good and had given up hopes of returning to Germany, there is no doubt. But even modern man is not entirely nation-oriented. There are minor loyalties, subordinated to his main devotion; sub-loyalties, we may call them. Frequently, such sub-loyalties are sectional in character, i.e., they are directed toward the locality and the state or province wherein one dwells. In the case of the post-1830 German Americans, comparatively little sectional sentiment developed, but divided sub-loyalties of another kind did arise. While probably 95% of the immigrants had come to this country for economic reasons, their mental outlook was shaped by those 5% who were driven by ideological motives, whether political or religious. The members of this minority created the spiritual atmosphere of *Deutschamerika*. Among them we find four main categories:[18] Roman Catholics, Orthodox Lutherans,

[14] See the emphatic statement by Frederic Klees (1950), p. 279.
[15] Also see J. J. Stoudt, *Pennsylvania German Folklore Society*, 20 (1956), 16-20: "Pennsylvanish has managed to thrive ... (and) is still as secure as ever."
[16] The current status of Pennsylvanish among the Amish and the Old Order Mennonites is discussed below, see p. 247.
[17] The main sources for the post-colonial stock are listed in H. A. Pochmann and A. R. Schultz, *Bibliography of German Culture in America* (Madison, University of Wisconsin Press, 1953). All references to periodicals are based on Arndt and Olson (1961).
[18] For further information on this segmentation see the introductory parts of H. Kloss (1937).

other Protestants, and Liberals. The first three groups formed religious congregations. For Liberals, secular clubs (Vereine) and federations of secular clubs (Verbande) were the common rallying centers. Around 1900, the technical term for the members of the first three groups became *Kirchendeutsche* (Church Germans), while the members of the fourth category came to be called *Vereinsdeutsche* (club Germans). Almost the entire rural population – the many language islands, small or medium-sized, that sprung up chiefly in the midwest – belonged to the "Church Germans". Texas was the only state where a significant number of rural Germans belonged to the liberal camp.

On the other hand, urban German Americans were to a large extent club Germans, with the ratio between club and Church Germans varying according to locality. By and large, the percentage of Church Germans was greater in the midwestern cities than in the agglomerations near the Atlantic seacoast; it was probably greatest in St. Louis which became a kind of spiritual capital for both Orthodox Lutherans and Roman Catholics of German extraction.

In the long run, the sub-loyalty of most German Americans went more to their credal group than to their state or region of residence. In analyzing 19th century German-American literature, much more attention has to be given to an author's membership in one of the four main factions, and their many sub-factions, than to his regional location. Whether a writer was a rigid Old Lutheran or a freethinker was more significant than whether he lived in Iowa or in Ohio. Most of all, educational efforts have to be viewed chiefly in terms of their sponsorship by nationwide denominational or liberal groups.

The small groups of men and women who had left Germany because of their devotion to some cause, some ideal, some Weltanschauung, were the ones who shaped the organizational life of German Americans, gathering around themselves the masses who had come without a specific lodestar. There were the Alt-Lutheraner (Old Lutherans) who rejected the union between the Reformed and Lutheran Churches which Prussian and other German governments tried to force upon their subjects. There were the *Dreissiger*, the political refugees of the early 1830's who combined a fervent love for their ancestral language with an enlightened republicanism, and an outspoken religious feeling with a deep distrust of the more orthodox Church groups. There were the famous *Achtundvierziger*, less unbendingly attached to their mother tongue, more radical in their political liberalism (and, therefore, more critical of conditions in the United States), and frequently devoid of Church affiliation or even of religious sentiment. There were the socialists who fled Germany under the Sozialistengesetze. And there were those Roman Catholic priests, monks, and nuns who left Germany during the Kulturkampf between Bismarck and the Catholic Church.

These political or religious refugees were possessed by a missionary spirit. They addressed themselves to their co-nationals in the New World and won them over to their own creeds. The liberals did so chiefly by founding well-managed newspapers, the Protestant leaders by founding congregations, synods, and other federations. The outcome was that after a while the bulk of German Americans were grouped around these small nuclei, even though most of them had entered the country either without a pronounced Weltanschauung or with one that differed from the one that they adopted here. Thus, in 1930 there were in Germany perhaps 80,000 Old Lutherans, whereas in the United States we find in 1926 some 1,800,000 Old Lutherans, nearly all of German descent (1,300,000 members of the Synodical Conference uniting the Missouri and Wisconsin Synods; 500,000 members of the American Lutheran Church uniting the former Buffalo, Iowa, and Ohio Synods). At most, only one-tenth of these individuals were descendants of persons who had been Old Lutherans before their immigration to the United States. Until 1914 the future ministers of Germany's Old Lutherans received their theological training in St. Louis. Old Lutherans had definitely become an American religious grouping.

From the standpoint of language maintenance efforts, the main dividing line was not between Kirchendeutsche and Vereinsdeutsche. It ran between Roman Catholics and Orthodox Lutherans on the one side and other Protestants and the secularized Liberals on the other. Originally, they had all tried to uphold their language – the Church Germans by founding parochial schools, the club Germans by founding independent schools or by having German introduced into the public schools. In the 1860's German became rather widespread as a branch of instruction in public elementary schools serving communities with large German-American populations. As a result, the Liberals as well as most Protestant denominations abandoned their own German schools. Only two major groups resisted this temptation and succeeded in maintaining and even enlarging their own school systems – the Old Lutherans and the Roman Catholics. These two differed, however, in one important respect. Almost from the beginning, the Roman Catholics stressed the bilingual aspect of parochial education, while the Old Lutherans tenaciously tried to preserve the predominance of German over English within their schools. Similar differences prevailed in the realm of secondary schools and colleges. Among German Catholics, English soon became the leading language of instruction. Old Lutherans, on the other hand, created Gymnasiums and colleges where German long remained on an equal footing with English.[19]

---

[19] Two major German-American groups displayed much less sectarian fragmentation. The Texas Germans (with a long history of their own rooted in pre-annexation days and with a stronger admixture of Liberals in rural and small town areas) constituted a more homogeneous group than did the Germans in most midwestern states. They possessed a peculiar consciousness of kind and group loyalty of their own which protected their language from erosion. Similarly, the Russian-Germans (Russlanddeutsche or Russländer) who began settling in the westernmost frontier areas, from North Dakota to Kansas, in the early 1870's also displayed a feeling of belonging together, regardless of creed, seldom found among other Germans. The outward sign of their "togetherness" was their deliberate tendency to settle entire counties almost to the exclusion of other ethnic elements. In South Dakota, for example, the number of Germans from Germany was greater than that of the Germans from Russia; but, while the latter formed a clear majority of the population in at least five counties, the Germans from Central Europe predominated in not a single one. More Central European Germans than Russian-Germans went into urban occupations. They were also less averse to mingling with non-Germans. Rural

Even where the religious group abstained from or gave up systematic language maintenance efforts, other "natural forces" often remained at work for a while to keep the language alive at least in its dialect form. This was possible chiefly in outright language islands. The 19th century immigrants formed numerous language islands, many comprising a number of counties, others a single town (such as Carlstadt, New Jersey) or a single township (Kloss 1939a). The large language islands were, as a rule, far less homogeneous than those of the Pennsylvania Germans for they comprised both Protestants and Roman Catholics and fell into a number of dialect areas. There might be Lutheran Pomeranians in one township, flanked by Roman Catholic Franconians on the one side and by Roman Catholic Rhinelanders on the other. This, of course, made for linguistic instability. When the newer generations no longer knew how to handle literary German – the Hochsprache – there was no single substitute in the form of a vernacular common to the entire language island as there was in Pennsylvania. Swabians and Pomeranians quickly concluded that they had to resort to English as the only linguistic tool they had in common. Thus, not even in rural areas – let alone in cities – could German maintain itself when left to "natural processes" alone. As a result, planned efforts became the only remaining means of effective language maintenance.

Some Factors Underlying Language Maintenance Efforts

What were the factors inducing German Americans to strive, at least temporarily, for the preservation of their mother tongue? First of all, their sheer numerical strength almost compelled them to do so. When millions of monolingual immigrants stream into a country that speaks a language different from their own, the natural thing for them to do is to form a semi-autonomous community of their own, with their own churches, clubs, business establishments, and schools. What is surprising is not that German Americans of the 1830-1880 period tried to perpetuate their language, but rather the lack of similar endeavors among the millions of Italians who entered the United States after 1880. Under comparable (though certainly not identical) circumstances, the latter failed to display a similar zeal. Besides numerical size – a factor which we believe to be basically ambivalent but which *in the beginning* certainly favored the survival of the German language – other factors contributed heavily to the establishment of a network of institutions for language survival. A great many German immigrants lived either in language islands or in monolingual urban sections. They settled in states and territories which were still in a pioneering stage and where newcomers were largely thrown upon their own resources. As a result, they did not look upon themselves as guests in a well-established commonwealth, but as co-founders and partners in a newly-founded enterprise. Also unlike the Italians, they came at a time

---

traditions and separatist gregariousness persisted among the Russländer, as did, therefore, their use of German.

when relatively few other non-English groups had arrived, and these only in small numbers. Consequently, theirs was the only language bidding for large-scale co-existence with English. By 1900 it was obvious that the United States would not grant equal rights to the dozen or more immigrant languages. But in 1850 it did not seem unrealistic to hope that at least some states (e.g., Ohio) might remain officially bilingual in at least some respects (e.g., with regard to public schools and public notices).

Urban Germans frequently were aware of having received better vocational training in Europe than their American countrymen. Others, possessed by an almost missionary eagerness to propagate and spread their particular Weltanschauung, looked upon Americans as spiritually dormant worshippers of the golden calf. They looked upon themselves and upon others of German stock as the leaven that would bring about the spiritual awakening and maturing of the Yankee loaf.

In addition to the natural tendency for adherents of such specifically "German" persuasions as the Old Lutherans to maintain their religious identity, there was a general aversion among German Americans toward modes of worship prevalent among Anglo-Americans. This dislike was shared by members of those denominations whose creed was not limited to Germans alone, e.g., by German Roman Catholics and by German Reformed. The Reverend Anton H. Walburg, an American-born Roman Catholic priest, in 1889 described the Anglo-American as "a boaster, arrogant, pharasaical, worshipper of gold and material quantity, hypocritical, especially in regard to temperance, vain, wedded to this world, bent upon riches" and asked, "Are we going to lead our simple, straight-forward, honest Germans and Irish into this whirlpool of American life?" (Barry 1953, p. 84). In a discourse delivered in 1913, the Reverend F. Mayer of the German Evangelical Synod (a combined Lutheran and Reformed body) heaped blame after scorn upon the "English" Churches which allegedly dealt with secular rather than Biblical topics in their sermons, neglected the religious education of the youth (being unacquainted with the German *Konfirmandenunterricht*), were superficial and noisy in their revival meetings and gospel hymns, etc., etc. (Mayer 1913). He claimed that a far larger percentage of the German-speaking rural population had kept the faith than was the case among rural English speakers. "Language saves faith" was an oft-repeated watchword among German Americans. Thus, to the pious, the German language became a symbol of quiet, honest religiosity as against the Yankee's alleged noisy superficiality. To the German liberal it became the symbol of intellectual and cultural alertness as against the Yankee's alleged intellectual and cultural disinterest.

Many of the German immigrants who entered the United States soon after 1830 fell under the spell of the political refugees who left Germany in the years after the Hambacher Fest (1832) – the so-called *Dreissiger*.[20] These less well-known forerunners of the Forty-Eighters were men and women of high calibre, genuine liberals, but seldom atheists or agnostics, and in the majority devoted to the ideal of keeping the German language alive among their children and grandchildren. They were schooled

[20] On the Dreissiger see Körner (1884), Rattermann (1912), Löher (1885).

in the writings of the German classicists, and many of them were excellent writers themselves. Of the newspapers they founded (all of which were much more intellectual and up-to-date than those of the "Pennsylvania Dutch"), four at once became known far beyond the cities in which they were published: the *Anzeiger des Westens* (1835-1912) in St. Louis, the *Staats-Zeitung* in New York (1834-present), the *Alte und Neue Welt* in Philadelphia (1834-1844),[21] and the Cincinnati *Volksblatt* (1836-1919). While the New York and St. Louis publications were at that time rather lukewarm about the language question, those in Cincinnati and Philadelphia most certainly were not.

Among the *Dreissiger* and their followers, a new type of organization became very popular – the secular club or lodge, of which there had been only a few examples prior to 1830. In 1835 the first German glee club was founded, the "Philadelphia Männer-chor", followed by the Baltimore "Liedertafel" in 1836. In 1840 in New York, the first of many lodges came into being, which in 1848 were to form the important "Order of Sons of Herman", while in 1847 (also in New York) the "Deutsche Orden der Harugari" was founded. These and many other organizations did much to make German a living tongue in urban settings beyond the narrow sphere of hearth and home. They gave it both social function and social standing.

The period 1832-1848 saw the emergence of a new body of German writing. It is the only period in which German-American literature included not only books on poetry, local history, theology, and philosophy, but also some non-narrative prose covering various branches of the sciences and humanities, such as zoology, archaeology, medicine, general history, linguistics, etc. An attempt was made to keep German alive as a medium of intellectual activities appropriate to a highly differentiated modern civilization.

No period in German-American history is more famous than the one lasting from 1848 down to the early 1880's. It witnessed the arrival of the largest number of highly cultured German intellectuals ever to come to the United States prior to the anti-Nazi emigration of the 1930's;[22] the greatest numerical strength of German immigration (215,000 in 1854 and 250,000 in 1882, two peaks never since equaled); a corresponding unfolding of German letters – an influential, well-written press, a varied belletristic literature, numerous books on philosophy and religion; an enormous expansion of the teaching of German, both in public schools and through the founding of parochial and independent schools; and an equally important increase in the political influence of the German element, making itself felt especially in the ranks of the Republican party which monopolized political power after the Civil War. Many observers have been prone to link these facts together in a chain of cause and effect, ascribing e.g., the

[21] The term Deutsch-Amerikaner appears for the first time in *Atle und Neue Welt*, 6/21/1835, 11/28/1835, 12/5/1835.
[22] On the Forty-eighters see Bruncken (1904), Zucker (1950), Wittke (1952), Dobert (1958). Among the peculiarities of this period we find individuals who hoped to found a "New Germany" by concentrating German immigrants within the confines of a given region until their numbers would enable them to join the union as a separate state. Their efforts led to the founding of only a few German settlements in Texas, Missouri and Illinois (Hawgood 1940, p. 93).

upward trend in the number of German schools and courses to the influence of these highly-gifted Forty-eighters. A leading historian, Hawgood (1940), has adduced an additional factor, Know-Nothingism, which he singled out as having deterred German Americans from quick assimilation by frightening them into an almost traumatic withdrawal from the general American scene. He holds that during the period 1850-1917 German Americans were more "German" than "American" and that it was World War I which finally forced them to drop inherited loyalties and to become, at long last, full-fledged Americans.

This unilinear perspective is rather misleading. A much more appropriate judgment was passed by Max Weber[23] who a few years before World War I compared the possible attitudes of German Americans and German Austrians in the case of a hypothetical war between Germany and their respective motherlands. He held that many German Austrians would march against Germany "with utmost reluctance and without dependability" but that "even the most fervent nationality devotees among the German Americans would do so unconditionally, even if without pleasure". Hawgood's opinion is based on the equation "Americanization = Anglification", an equation which is manifestly absurd if applied to the Louisiana Acadians, the New Mexico Hispanos, or the Pennsylvania Germans. It is equally untenable with regard to the 19th century German immigration. For these German-Americans, "Americanism" represented a metalinguistic concept, an inter-ethnic dream to which people might adhere regardless of mother tongue. The Old Lutherans were violently anti-Prussian on theological grounds, the Roman Catholics were not enthusiastic about a Reich bearing a distinctly Protestant stamp and became strongly anti-Bismarck during the *Kulturkampf*; the Forty-eighters at first hated, then resented, and at last put up with conservative Prussia; the Socialists of whom many fled to America during the last decades of the century never made their peace with Berlin; but most of them favored, with more or less intensity, the retention of their native tongue. It is true that many of the post-1871 immigrants were far less critical of German political conditions than were their predecessors, and that their liberalism was less outspoken and more permeated by sentiments of ethnic pride. But they too were seldom in harmony with conditions at home and they certainly never dreamt of reshaping New World political institutions according to Old World traditions. Nor did they ever dream that maintaining the German language might be incompatible with becoming thoroughly American in outlook and sentiment. At German American festivals it became customary to exclaim that in order to be loyal to his bride, a man did not have to forsake his mother ("Germania meine Mutter, Columbia meine Braut").

As for the Kirchendeutsche, Protestants and Catholics alike, it is safe to say that their history would not have been very different had there been neither Forty-Eighters nor Know-Nothings. Their group life would have evolved along much the same line

[23]   Max Weber, *Wirtschaft und Gesellschaft*, 3rd ed. (Tübingen, Mohr, 1947), p. 629. (This work was written in 1911-13, posthumously edited in 1921. German-Americans and German-Austrians, the latter then including the Sudeten Germans, were at that time about equal in number.)

as it eventually did, and the language of their sermons, schools, and conventions would have remained German at any rate. With regard to the Old Lutherans we have the statement of Maurer who pointed out that

for the preservation of the German language in their schools, the Orthodox Lutheran fellow-ship of the Missouri Synod has made greater sacrifices then any other German society or culture group,

but who added that

the German language itself, however, is a non-essential in the technical language of its theology .... The German language was here a principal fighting organ, not for or against this or that nationalism, but against the rationalism of the "natural man". (Maurer 1928)

Thus, the Forty-Eighters rather than being in the vanguard of the struggle for language maintenance, appear to have been the one group which developed in a different direction. From the very beginning they embraced a wing favoring rapid assimila-tion – a tendency later shared by Carl Schurz,[24] who declared that the cultivation of the German language should be left to the individual family – quietly keeping aloof from all pertinent institutional efforts. Their role has been aptly summed up by Ernst Bruncken (1904, p. 41) as follows:

While the activity of the refugee element among the Germans attracted the attention of native Americans, it must by no means be understood that they were the real leaders of the mass of their countrymen. Among those affiliated with the Catholic Church they found, of course, nothing but bitter hostility, and the Catholics were estimated at one-third of the German ele-ment. The large numbers of peasants from northern and eastern Germany, who took up farms or remained in the cities as laborers, were utterly impervious to radical and infidel influences. They were then, as now, the mainstay of Lutheranism. The most fruitful field for radical ideas, both in religion and politics, was found among the skilled workmen of the cities. The well-to-do business element, also, may be said to have felt a mild sympathy with the anti-religious ideas of the Radicals. But political Radicalism was abhorrent to this class, and their attitude toward the Church was that of indifference rather than hostility. Thus, it will be seen that the influence of the Radicals was not altogether proportionate to the noise they made. Still, they were the most conspicuous men among the Germans in all public activities. The Catholics and other church people had a tendency to separate themselves from the rest of their countrymen, and to take part in public affairs only when their own immediate interests were at stake. "Forty-Eighters" were the orators at most German festivities; they dominated many singing societies, social clubs, and other organizations that had nothing in particular to do with religion or politics, but which gave their leading spirits opportunities to become known and influential. Furthermore. they edited most of the German papers.

After 1848 the schism between Church-minded and radical German Americans became definite and permanent. In both wings the extremists gained in number and in in-fluence. Many of the former revolutionaries, who arrived after the 1848 upheaval,

[24] Schurz demonstrated his ambivalence toward language maintenance in a letter to Julius Goebel (1883) in which he wrote that it was an "iron rule" in his family to speak only German, but that his younger children already preferred English when left to themselves and, for his grandchildren, German would be a foreign tongue (Goebel, J., *Deutsch-Amer. Geschichtsblätter*, 29, 1939, p. 108f.). In 1873 Schurz actively opposed the founding of a private German school in Washington.

were not merely opposed to what they considered sectarian narrowness, but to religion in general. Instead of religion, they brought with them and offered to their new homeland a variety of programs for social, educational and political reform. A good many of them were socialists. Any collaboration with German-American church bodies for the sake of maintaining the German language was out of the question for them. Consequently, whenever attempts were made to unite "the" German element, they sought a strictly secular and nominally non-sectarian basis for all such cooperative efforts. However, what they really meant by non-sectarian was non-religious (if not anti-religious), thus tacitly excluding the German-American Church bodies, their synods, federations, and, most of all, their institutions of learning.[25]

The period from 1882 to 1914 was governed by two contradictory tendencies, one of quite visible strength and expansion, and the other of largely invisible weakness and decline. Numerically, all those organizational nuclei which make for language maintenance flourished as never before. The circulation of German daily newspapers rose from 405,000 in 1884 to nearly double that number two decades later. The clubs flourished even more than the newspapers. By 1914 there may have been 10,000 of them. As a result of the language maintenance efforts of the many clubs and organizations, there developed a distinctive German-American cultural atmosphere. Many German books were written and printed during this period, and quite a few by American-born authors, especially in Texas (Metzentim-Raunick, 1939). Yet, with the exception of philosophy and religion, German-American history, and Germanistics, the field of non-narrative prose was largely neglected – a gap which points to the lack of secular German institutions of higher learning.[26]

The German element was, as a matter of fact, not nearly as strong and solid a block as the plethora of publications and clubs might lead one to believe. The Liberals, the Catholics, and the Protestants continued to form separate camps. The Roman Catholics, in particular, succeeded in bringing about an almost complete secession, forming a cultural-linguistic province of their own with their own press, their own teachers' seminary and theological seminaries, their own federation of Catholic clubs (the Centralverein, 1855; since 1956 called Central Union), Priesterverein and a Presseverein (both 1887), and a Lehrerverein (1898). Perhaps nowhere is the existence of cultural subloyalties among German Americans more noticeable than in the emergence of their "autonomous" and segregated Roman Catholic segment.

Far from uniting the entire German element, the National Alliance of secular clubs – the Nationalbund, founded in 1901 – remained restricted to the club Germans, the

---

[25] A new type of club peculiar to the Forty-eighters was the Turnverein. These were centers of cultural as well as of physical activities, many becoming important promoters of free thought and of language maintenance. Adult education by means of Bildungsvereine also flourished among Forty-eighters.

[26] While native-born authors preferring German as their literary medium were quite rare, there were nevertheless hundreds of native-born individuals who preferred German reading-matter and who saw no contradiction between being politically and ideologically American, linguistically German, and culturally German American.

Catholics and all major Protestant church bodies holding themselves apart (Kloss 1937, Child 1939). The Nationalbund long emphasized the struggle against prohibition or, as the German liberals chose to style it, for "personal liberty". "The German vote", as G. S. Viereck put it, "has floated on an ocean of beer", The Nationalbund did little to promote the teaching of German in public schools and next to nothing to found or support non-public German institutions of learning. When, in 1911, the Nationalbund collected money for special purposes, it received:

$1,272.00 for the "preservation of personal liberty"
  490.00 for contacting other national federations
  271.00 for German schools
   62.00 for combating nativism
   10.00 for improvements in school textbooks.

Significantly, English made heavy inroads as a language of worship, particularly after 1900. In 1916 there were 3,768,000 members of Christian congregations with regular German sermons. Of these, a majority already belonged to bilingual congregations,[27] as can be seen from the following figures:

No. of Members of Congregations without any English Services		No. of Members of Congregations with English and German Services	
Protestants	519,000 (71%)	Protestants	1,460,000 (48%)
Catholics	209,000 (29%)	Catholics	1,580,000 (52%)
Total	728,000 (19%)	Total	3,040,000 (81%)

However, many so-called bilingual congregations offered English services only once a month, and that not because German was no longer understood, but because a fraction of the members preferred the national language. Nevertheless, the trend toward English was well under way, particularly among Catholics.

What may well have constituted one of the greatest handicaps of the German Americans was, at that time, generally considered to be a decided asset, namely, the continual reinforcement from new waves of immigrants. Quantitatively, the newcomers meant a strengthening of the ranks. But, at the same time, they prevented the earlier arrivals and their children and grandchildren from consolidating their gains, from assuming a set attitude, from acquiring an outspoken and specifically German-American (i.e., neither European-German nor Anglo-American) outlook of their own. The newcomers both served as a crutch and undermined the self-reliance of the old stock by driving home to them that their language was tainted with Anglicisms, their acquaintance with the latest developments in literary German defective, and their way

[27] According to the religious census of 1916, United States Census Bureau, *Special Reports: Religious Bodies, 1916*, Parts 1-2 (Washington, Government Printing Office, 1919). See also Kloss, "Deutsch als Gottesdienstsprache in den Vereinigten Staaten", in: *Der Auslandsdeutsche*, 14 (1931), pp. 630-634, 689-692, 715-721. The 1916 figures for members of German-Jewish congregations are too incomplete to be of any value.

of life devoid of higher graces. They deflected the oldtimers from a sober appraisal of the language situation and from a realization of how much still had to be done to preserve the German language in the United States; it became easy to conclude that the influx from Germany would always take care of the problem. Finally, the new-comers kept alive among many American-born German Americans a feeling that the German language was somehow bound up with foreigners and with foreignness, something not entirely rooted in New World soil. It is, therefore, no accident that the persistence of the language was greatest in those sections where, since the 1890's, the number of recent immigrants remained comparatively small, such as Texas and certain parts of rural Wisconsin and Minnesota.

Language Maintenance in the Classroom

During the period 1830 to 1848 a memorable breakthrough had been achieved in the field of elementary education.[28] An 1839 Ohio law set forth that: "In any district where the directors keep an English school and do not have the branches taught in German, it shall be lawful for youth in such districts who desire to learn in the German language, to attend a district German school". This provision, only permissive for the state at large, became mandatory for Cincinnati by an 1840 law amending the city charter as follows: "It shall be the duty of the Board of Trustees and Visitors of Common Schools to provide a number of German Schools under some duly qualified teachers for the instruction of such youth as desire to learn the German language or the German and English languages together". After some disagreement as to whether monolingual German schools (with English being merely a branch of study) were desirable, preference was given to the bilingual schools, for which Cincinnati became famous, and which lasted until 1917. Other cities followed suit, for example Dayton in 1844.

This same period also witnessed the beginning of new systems of German parochial schools. The first German Catholic school was founded in Cincinnati in 1836. Equally active were the orthodox Lutherans of the Missouri Synod and other newly founded Lutheran synods. The German Methodists and other denominations of Anglo-Saxon background, which at that time gathered within their fold large groups of German-speaking members, also set up schools. Success in the realm of higher education was less spectacular.[29]

---

[28]   Most pre-1940 American state laws concerning the teaching of foreign languages in elementary schools are quoted (in English) in Kloss (1940 and 1942).

[29]   In Allentown, Penna., in the heart of Pennsylvanish-speaking area, a homeopathic faculty, the first of its kind in the world, functioned from 1835-1842. In 1844 the Texas legislature granted a charter to an abortive Herman's University. More permanent were some of the institutions set up by religious bodies. In 1830 a Lutheran "Deutsches Seminarium" was founded in Canton, Ohio, the nucleus of today's Capitol University at Columbus. Also still active is Concordia Seminary, founded in 1847 by the Missouri Synod (Allenburg, Mo., soon transferred to St. Louis). St. Vincent's College at Latrohe, Penna. (1846), was the forerunner of many similar German-Catholic institutions founded between 1850 and 1900.

A number of independent (i.e., non-sectarian secular) private schools were established in the post-1848 period. Some became model schools where "object lessons" (*Anschauungsunterricht*) and other achievements of modern central European pedagogy were introduced (Dulon, 1866). At the same time, the parochial schools of the Protestants and Catholics alike grew even more rapidly in number and in strength. In addition, many public school systems introduced German into their curricula, especially during the late sixties.

TABLE 9.1

The Study of German in Public and Private Schools 1886 and 1900

Types of Schools	No. of Schools		No. of Students	
1886[a] A. Public Elementary Schools		70		150,000
B. Non-Public Schools				
1) Independent (Secular)	119		15,800	
2) Protestant	1,119		99,300	
3) Roman Catholic	825	2,063	164,800	279,900
		2,133		430,400
1900[b] A. Public Elementary Schools		243		231,700
B. Non-Public Schools				
1) Independent (Secular)	871		18,700	
2) Protestant	2,067		105,800	
3) Roman Catholic	1.046	3,984	193,600	318,100
		4,127		549,800

[a] Based upon K. W. Wollfradt, "Die Statistik des Deutsch-Amerikanischen Schulwesens", *Deutscher Pionier* (Cincinnati), 1886, 18, 50-55.
[b] L. Viereck (1902), states the number of pupils in Lutheran schools to be above 147,100, plus 17,980 in schools of the Evangelicals and "Unierte".

The German, or German-English, public school stemmed from two roots. In some cases it was the outcome of natural, almost instinctive growth, in others the result of conscious efforts. Schools of the first type occurred exclusively during the first decades of this period; practically none existed after 1900. In the midwest, wherever a newly created school district, or number of school districts contained a solidly German population, there was an irresistible temptation to hire a German teacher and to have the school conducted exclusively in German, or in both tongues, no matter what the statutory provision might be. Missouri's Superintendent of Public Instruction complained in his report for 1887-1888 (Handschin 1913, pp. 67-68) as follows:

In a large number of the districts of the State, the German element of the population greatly preponderates and, as a consequence, the schools are mainly taught in the German language and sometimes entirely so. Hence, if an American family lives in such a district, the children must either be deprived of school privileges or else be taught in the German language. In some districts the schools are taught in German a certain number of months and then in

English, while in others German is used part of the day and English the rest. Some of the teachers are scarcely able to speak the English language.

And in his report for 1889 he urged:

The law should specify definitely in what language the instruction of our public schools is to be given. It is a shame and a disgrace to have the English language ruled out of our public schools and German substituted, as is done wholly or in part in many districts in this State .... Representatives and senators admit that German can be put out of a public school by an injunction served upon the (district) board; but why shall a citizen be compelled to resort to the courts to secure that which should be provided by legislative enactment.... This wrong will not much longer be tolerated.

Similar conditions prevailed elsewhere, for instance in Wisconsin and in the Territory of Dakota, where the Russlanddeutsche dominated local boards and dictated local policies in newly-settled areas. The Territorial Board of Education, in its report for 1886-1888 stated (Handschin 1913, p. 68):

Some instances came to the attention of the board where the teacher was not even able to speak the English language and nothing could be done about it, as the foreign element was so strong that they not only controlled the schools, but the election of the county superintendent also.

More important and more enduring were those efforts which aimed not merely at having German taught locally, but simultaneously at creating a legal framework for preventing state authorities from interfering with such teaching. In 1887 a Colorado law permitted the bilingual public school; in 1872 an Oregon law even permitted the monolingual German public school. While only the German language was admitted in a few instances, in most cases the legal provisions were all-inclusive; but nearly always the German Americans were the ones who brought such laws into being and who drew the chief benefit from them. Some of the most pertinent laws of this type were:

Year	State	Referring to which Foreign Tongue?	To be Taught at Whose Direction?
1854	Wisconsin	all	School Board
1857	Illinois	all	—
1861	Iowa	German or other languages	majority of school district's voters
1867	Kansas	German	"freeholders representing 50 pupils"
1867	Minnesota	all	School Board
1869	Indiana	German	parents of 25 pupils
1872	Illinois	all	School Board or voters of district
1877	Minnesota (grade schools only)	all	School Board (if unanimous)
1913	Nebraska (urban schools only)	all	parents of 50 pupils

In a number of localities the local authorities went much further than the lawmakers had envisaged or authorized. In Baltimore (1874) and in Indianapolis (1882) bilingual schools were established comparable to those of Cincinnati. These bilingual public school systems were shining achievements in the fields of language maintenance, bicultural education, and minority rights. They were very modern in their rationales – too modern to outlive the tempests and crises of developing American nationalism.

In the late 1880's three nationwide storms swept the country and seriously weakened German-American life. The first was directed against the teaching of German in public schools. As a result, it was dropped, e.g., by the Louisville (Kentucky) authorities in 1887, by the St. Louis authorities in 1886-1889, and in St. Paul, and other cities at roughly the same time. The second hit the German Catholic school system (Barry 1953). It originated among the leaders of the Irish Catholic clergy and the issue at stake was a complicated one. Exception was taken by English-speaking members of the episcopacy not only to an alleged overemphasis on German in the parochial schools, but also to the founding of a separate federation of German priests (with roughly 900 members) and to the ever-recurring German Catholic demand for full equality of German parishes with English (Irish) parishes. Nationality problems were interwoven with others of a purely ecclesiastic nature, Irish "liberalism" or "Americanism" clashing with German Catholic "conservatism". The third storm was directed chiefly against the Lutheran schools, with the Edwards law in Illinois (1889) and the Bennett law in Wisconsin (1889) prescribing English as the only medium of instruction for most subjects in non-public schools (Hense-Jensen and Bruncken, 1902, pp. 144-69, 278-99).[30]

Little by little the teaching of German in public schools was relegated to the upper grades. It was a far cry, indeed, from the bilingual schools of Baltimore, Cincinnati, and Indianapolis to the Nebraska school law of 1913, which permitted the teaching of German only above grade 4, and only for one period per day. As a corollary to this change, we observe a shift in theoretical argumentation: the cultivation of German in public schools was no longer advocated because it was the mother tongue of the pupils, but because of its cultural value. On behalf of the Nationalbund, Professor M. D. Learned stated in 1901 (*Pedagogische Monatshefte*, 3, no. 3, p. 88):

(1) All American public schools should recognize English as the official language of the school and of general instruction.
(2) No foreign language should be taught in the American public schools simply because the pupils and patrons of the school speak the foreign languages in question. If this principle will not be recognized, we will not only have German schools but Hungarian, Polish, and Italian ones as well.
(3) Only such foreign languages should be introduced as have a general cultural importance or commercial value for Americans....
....
(8) Of all the modern languages, German at present deserves the first place, both for its cultural and commercial values.

[30] Cf. also Whyte in *Wisc. Mag. Hist.*, 10 (1927/28), 363-90.

Impressive advances were made during this period, however, in the field of higher education. Here the Church bodies clearly led the field. Theological seminaries were founded by the Lutherans in St. Louis (1847) and in Dubuque, Iowa (1853), by the Evangelicals in St. Louis (1850), and by the Roman Catholics in St. Francis, Wisconsin (1856) and Columbus, Ohio (1888). Teachers' seminaries were established by the Lutherans in Addison, Illinois (1864), New Ulm, Minnesota (1884) and Seward, Nebraska (1894), and by the Roman Catholics in St.Francis, Wisconsin (1871). It would lead us too far afield to enumerate the many denominational German-American colleges. Besides those set up by the Roman Catholics and the Lutherans, a great many were founded by other Protestant groups. The Orthodox Lutherans duplicated in their colleges the Old-World German Gymnasium, with the additional burden of bilingualism. At Concordia College in Ft. Wayne, Indiana, which may be typical, the classical languages were taught until 1917 through the medium of German, and the use of English was restricted to the sciences and mathematics.

Secular German-American institutions of higher education were rare phenomena. In May 1860 many prominent Germans, among them Carl Schurz, issued an appeal to establish a German teachers' seminary which was to be the nucleus of a liberal (freiheitliche) German university. In 1869 two committees (in Detroit and Milwaukee) that had been organized for the preparation of the Humboldt centenary, launched an appeal to found a university, with a museum as its first stepping-stone. It was hoped that the champions of philosophical materialism would be able to lecture at such a university. The university concept cropped up again as part of the program of a short-lived Deutschamerikanischer Nationalverein founded in 1871 under the impression of Germany's victory over France. The concept was once more conjured up in 1876 by the German Press Association of Pennsylvania, when it tried to transform itself into a national organization. In 1904 Julius Goebel suggested that the Milwaukee Teachers' Seminary might be broadened into an institution of higher learning. In 1906, Professor Detlev Jessen pleaded in the Chicago *Glocke* (1906 vol. 1, no. 8, pp. 281-283) for a "grosse, wissenschaftliche, vorbildliche Akademie", where highly-paid and prominent German scholars would teach. In 1914 (and again in 1924!) Julius Goebel stated that the time had passed when founding a German university was a workable scheme, but that it would still be a timely undertaking to establish a German-American research institute which might serve the twofold purpose of exploring the German-American element, its history, composition, etc., and of acting as a cultural link between Germany and German cultural efforts in the United States.

THE POST-COLONIAL STOCK: 1914 TO PRESENT

World War I led to climax and anti-climax.[31] Its first effect was that German Americans felt, more than ever before, the implications of being members of a world-wide

---

[31]   On the period from 1914-1917 see Child (1939) and Kloss (1937, pp. 276-285).

German linguistic community. German clubs, German meetings, German classes drew larger numbers than ever. The Nationalbund, at long last, subordinated its fight against temperance and prohibition to the worthier fight for political aims – in this case, American neutrality. It was joined by the Irish-Americans and other nationalities, notably many anti-czarist Russian Jews. An interdenominational "Verband Deutscher Geistliche", and a probably more successful Deutscher Akademikerbund were founded; also a National Association of German Newspaper Editors (February, 1916), which for the first time united editors of secular, Catholic, and Protestant papers. But by far the most impressive event was the organization in Chicago of a seven-man "Conference Committee" (Konferenz-Ausschuss) by the German-American National Conference, which brought together leading representatives of the Nationalbund and of the larger religious bodies, including Old Lutherans and Roman Catholics, in May 1916. Here the Nationalbund's pretention to represent the entire German element was implicitly dropped. There is reason to believe that the Chicago conference was a decisive factor in the Republican Party's subsequent nomination of Hughes rather than Roosevelt for the presidency. This represents a degree of political influence never before nor since achieved by a non-English ethnic group in the United States.

This unparalleled political and cultural growth was followed in 1917 and thereafter by an equally unparalleled downfall. Most major secular German associations (including the Nationalbund, Akademikerbund, and Press Association) felt obliged to dissolve. The teaching of German was forbidden in many private as well as public schools. An outburst of fervent anti-German feeling[32] swept over the country, which we might find understandable on the basis of atrocities committed by Germans in World War II, but which in retrospect remain almost inexplicable in the context of those earlier times. Many states prohibited the use of German at meetings, over the telephone, or on the streets. Persons known for pro-German activities (which prior to 1917 had been perfectly legal) were persecuted by mobs or by self-appointed courts of "justice". George Creel writes that in certain states "tarring and feathering became a popular outdoor sport". Many persons were whipped, humiliated, and driven from their jobs. No punishment or reprimand awaited those who at night daubed in yellow the homes of ministers daring to preach in German. Much of this may be characterized as semi-anarchy, wherein events were pretty much beyond control of the regular authorities. However, this phase was followed by one in which anti-German sentiments were broadened into anti-foreign sentiments more generally and were crystallized into legislation which forbade the teaching of languages other than English in all schools, public or non-public, day schools or supplementary, to pupils below grades 8 or 9. The German Lutherans, whom these laws hit more severely than other Church bodies, instituted a number of lawsuits, and finally in 1923, the United States Supreme Court declared the laws to be incompatible with the due process of law clause of the 14th

---

[32]   The key publication concerning the persecution of the German-Americans since 1917 is Wittke (1936), esp. chapter VI, "Furor Americanus".

Amendment.[33] This victory was in the interest of all minority groups on American soil that endeavored to uphold the language of their forefathers.

The dissolution of the earlier leading secular German-American organizations with broad political and cultural objectives necessitated the founding of new ones. At least three deserve to be mentioned. The German-American Citizens League (founded in Chicago, June 6, 1918 and dissolved in 1959) and the Steuben Society (1919) tried, but with small success, to stimulate political activity among the crestfallen German Americans. The Concord Society (1919) tried to stimulate self-pride and "consciousness of kind" by publishing pamphlets illuminating certain phases of German-American history. The Society quietly passed out of existence in the late 1930's. Characteristic of the changed times, the two last-named bodies, Steuben and Concord, had made English their only official language.

In the history of German immigration between World Wars I and II, the events of 1933 mark a deep divide. Prior to that year most German immigrants had come chiefly as a result of economic motives and largely without much intellectual training or interest. As a rule their attitude toward language maintenance efforts was one of complete indifference. In this they were confirmed by the adverse atmosphere surrounding everything German which had been built up during the 20's, to say nothing of the unfortunate legislation in force until 1923. In addition, they had the very understandable feeling of being members of a vanquished nation living in the land of the victor and, therefore, having to move with prudence and caution.

A distinct lessening of interethnic tensions may be noted around 1930 and, consequently, a new wave of self-assurance among the Germans. In 1931 the state federations of German Vereine in the states of Pennsylvania and Illinois organized a new nationwide federation, the feeble second Deutsch-Amerikanischer Nationalbund. Much more important was the "National-Kongress der Amerikaner Deutschen Stammes" held in New York in 1932, whose sponsors realized that it was inadmissible to equate "the Germans" with "Die Vereinsdeutschen" and that, therefore, a convention was needed which explicitly catered to the various Weltanschauung groups. Moreover, they realized that the German element needed more than a superficial summation of organizations and of membership figures in order to become, at best, an influential political pressure group. They thought in qualitative as well as in quantitative terms.[34] However, in spite of two follow-up conventions (Philadelphia, 1933 and Cleveland, 1934), the Congress was doomed to failure in view of the increasing prominence of German-American Nazis, who deepened and augmented the existing cleavages between the German groups. They spent their crude strength in noisy agitation and contributed next to nothing to language or culture maintenance efforts.

[33] Meyer *vs.* Nebraska, 262, US 390.
[34] The Congress recommended the establishment of a central research agency (to be called Pastorius Institute) to serve as an intellectual center for German Americans. See *Erster National-Kongress der Amerikaner Deutschen Stammes; Sitzungsberichte u. Erläuterungen* (N.Y., 1933).

Once more, German Americans were made ashamed of their ancestry and sensitive to criticism from other Americans.

At this same time the political refugees from Nazi Germany – 80 to 90 % of Jewish extraction – began to enter America. Their attitude toward the German language was ambivalent. Among them were a greater proportion of highly cultivated men and women than even the Forty-Eighters had been able to boast, persons accustomed to the best that had been produced in the spheres of art, music, and letters. Scholars and writers abounded among them. Probably never before was so much written (though not always published) in German on American soil on so high a level as in the period 1933-1945. But these very men and women, rejected politically and culturally by their country of origin, finding their right to call themselves Germans abrogated, and having had their works humiliated, were understandably disinclined to do much to uphold the German language. Never before had a wave of German immigrants accepted the equation "Americanization=Anglification" so wholeheartedly and unreservedly.

Yet, even during this period there was an attempt to establish a center of learning where German would be the leading language. The University in Exile, set up in 1934 as a part of the New School for Social Research in New York (and forming today the backbone of its graduate faculty), was conceived by its spiritual fathers, Professors Lederer and Staudinger, as a university wholly German in spirit and language so that it might be transplanted onto the soil of Germany immediately following the hoped-for downfall of Hitler. Actually, however, little of its teaching seems to have been done in German, and that only during its very first years. Also during this period, the denominational institutions of higher learning moved swiftly toward English. In 1914 at the Eden Seminary of the Evangelical Synod, only one professor out of eight had lectured in English; in 1929 there was only one who still lectured in German (Hawgood 1940, p. 300). The orthodox Lutherans were somewhat less hasty. At the Thiensville Seminary of the Wisconsin Synod quite a bit of lecturing was done in German as late as 1937. Also concurrently the German-language press underwent a constant shrinkage – from nearly 300 publications in 1920 to about 200 in 1930 to only 60 in 1950. By 1950 there were only seven dailies left whereas in 1920 there still had been twenty-six.

Radio broadcasting came into play as a new language maintenance factor during this period. However, while it was and still is very instrumental in keeping certain languages alive in the United States, it came too late to slow down the rapid decline of the German language. Had broadcasting come a few decades earlier, it might have become a powerful agent in favor of German. If the Missouri Synod's own radio station – KROW, St. Louis – had been set up before 1917, it would have done at least half its work in German; instead it became an additional channel for the spread of English. Nevertheless, a 1937 study reported that four-fifths of foreign-language broadcasts were in Italian, Polish, Spanish, Yiddish, and German (Brown and Roucek 1945, pp. 384-391), i.e. German at that time was still a major strand in the fabric of non-English transmissions. Since then the situation has deteriorated, with a much lower average of hours per week devoted to German as compared with other major languages.

As always in the case of language survival, the decisive battle is the one that is fought in the elementary schools. In Texas, German Americans in 1933 succeeded in having enacted into law permission for foreign language instruction in public schools above grade 2. In Wisconsin, by joining hands with Poles, German Americans were instrumental in obtaining permission in 1935 for foreign languages to be taught at any school upon the request of at least 50 parents. When, thereupon, the Milwaukee City School Board conducted a survey in order to ascertain the wishes of the parents, 18,236 voted for German, 2,929 for Polish, 2,371 for French, 1,295 for Italian, 924 for Spanish, and 367 for Hebrew. Nevertheless, German was not reintroduced at the grade school level in the state of Wisconsin and was reintroduced in only a few rural localities in Texas. On the other hand, the Iowa state authorities made German compulsory in all grades in the settlement of Amana because they felt that this unique and venerable settlement might become less colorful (and less attractive for tourists) if it were to shed the German language.

As for the parochial schools, the Missouri Synod – after its United States Supreme Court victory in 1923 – and the Wisconsin Synod were the only Church bodies to continue to teach German in day schools to any considerable extent.[35] But we notice a constant and uninterrupted shrinkage, as shown by the following figures for the Missouri Synod:

Year	Number of		Still Bilingual	
	Schools	Students	Schools	Students
1927	1,368	80,300	555	35,000
1931	1,358	81,500	451	28,000
1936	— —	76,800	281	17,800

In 1931, bilingual schools still formed a majority in the district synods of northern Illinois (72:39), southern Illinois (30:23), Wisconsin (74:35), and Minnesota (73:20); however, bilingual schools were a minority in the districts of Indiana and Ohio (28:89), Iowa (20:42), and Nebraska (28:71), that is, in states where anti-German legislation had been particularly harsh. As late as 1930 the Synod published a new manual for the teaching of German in parochial schools, but the preface stated that for a majority of the first-graders German was already a foreign language. It was suggested that German lessons should start in the second half of the first school year. In most bilingual parochial schools the teaching and use of German were now confined to the language lessons themselves, plus – in many but not all instances – the teaching of religion.

[35] I have made use of an unpublished article by Professor Hattstaedt, Milwaukee, and of my own excerpts from the Synod's unpublished statistics for 1936.

There were exceptions. In the Lutheran school in Ixonia, Wisconsin, German writing, spelling, composition, grammar, Church hymns and folksongs were taught as late as 1937. Also at that time the theological seminaries of both the Missouri and Wisconsin Synods still made some use of German in their teaching.

With the decline of day school teaching, German supplementary schools became more important than they had been prior to 1917. The Steuben Society became the leader in this field. A list of these supplementary schools, drawn up by C. G. Orgell in 1937, indicates (not including Wisconsin):

- 35 Sprachschulen (Saturday Schools) set up by religious congregations
- 65 Secular Saturday Schools
- 3 Summer Schools
- 3 Evening Schools
- 17 Religious Sunday Schools.

Of the 65 secular Saturday Schools, 19 were sponsored by the Steuben Society and 6 each by the German-American Federation of Hudson County, New Jersey, and the Federation of German Vereine in Omaha, Nebraska. The Amerikadeutsche Volksbund, the Nazi organization, was responsible for 4 schools. Ten schools were sponsored by special Schulvereine, while roughly 30 had been founded by other Vereine, for example, glee clubs.

Of those German Church bodies which in former decades had given up their parochial schools, some still conducted many of their Sunday Schools in German or in both German and English. In 1937, 242 of the 1,741 Sunday Schools of the American Lutheran Church were still non-English or bilingual (Wartburg-Kalender, 1939, p. 75). It would seem reasonable to estimate that of the 170,000 pupils attending these schools in 1937, approximately 38,000 were German-speaking or bilingual. In all, the following figures give a rough indication of the extent of German teaching to students of grade school age in the late 1930's:

I. *In All-Day Schools*

In day schools of the Missouri Synod	17,800 (A)[36]	
In other parochial schools and in public schools	2,200 (C)	20,000

II. *In Supplementary Schools*

In language schools (usually Saturday schools)	8,000 (B)	
In American Lutheran Church Sunday schools	38,000 (B)	
In Saturday and Sunday schools conducted by the Missouri Synod in congregations without parochial schools	10,000 (B)	
In other Sunday schools	14,000 (C)	70,000
Total		90,000

[36] A = Accurate count; B = Estimate based on reliable information; C = Rough guess.

It should be noted that almost three-fifths of the total number attended Sunday schools which (a) could have among their pupils a considerable number of grownups and (b) are far less effective from the point of view of language maintenance than either parochial schools or language schools.

A bulwark of the German language, in both its dialectal and its literary form, were the settlements founded by the Russian-Germans (Sallet 1931). A considerable number of their congregations had no English church services up to the time of World War II. But these roughly 300,000 Russian-Germans suffered from two great shortcomings. First of all, they had brought with them from Russia a very modest intellectual level which led to their neglecting the problem of secondary and higher education to a degree reminiscent of the late 18th century Pennsylvania Germans. What the Moravians were among the Pennsylvania Germans, the Mennonites were among the Russian-Germans – lone pioneers of secondary and higher education and, therefore, able to train a bilingual elite. Secondly, only a minority of the Protestant Russian-Germans joined the powerful German-American Church bodies such as the Lutherans and the "Unierte". A majority joined various sects of Anglo-Saxon origin (e.g., the Congregationalists) and saw no point in deliberately cultivating the German language. In addition, their sectarian divisiveness made for many small rather than fewer and larger congregations. Thus, German lived on among these people, not because of organized endeavors, but because of the unplanned, almost instinctive efforts of families to hold on to their traditional way of life. Since they had come from a non-German speaking country, they were more accustomed than most other Germans to remaining German in an environment which utilized a language other than their own.

Language Maintenance Efforts since 1941

While World War II did not engender a new violent anti-German outbreak, it naturally did much to accelerate and complete the disappearance of German teaching at the grade-school level. Of the supplementary schools, the Sprachschulen (Saturday schools) ceased to function. The Sunday schools made English their only medium as did the last bilingual parochial schools. A few years after the war, during the 1950's, a limited number of new supplementary Sprachschulen were founded. In 1961 there were twenty-three in all. If we assume the number of pupils per school to average 80, some 2,000 pupils must currently be studying in these schools. Only four were sponsored by religious congregations, and none by the Steuben Society, which today prefers to promote the teaching of German in high schools. Three schools with 550 pupils were maintained by the Deutsch-Amerikanischer Schulverein in New York (established 1873). A private German day school, founded in Washington, D.C., in 1961, following the model of a local French school, has thus far primarily served the capital's aliens.[37] By April 1963 only 5 out of the 61 pupils were children of

---

[37] Among the School's chief supporters were ethnic Germans ("Volksdeutsche") who had originally lived in Southeastern Europe.

American citizens, while 36 held German, 12 dual, and 8 some other citizenship.

Although the post 1950 FLES movement has brought about the teaching of German in a few public elementary schools, there appears to be only one instance where the teaching of German in a public grade school is due to German still being the mother tongue of the pupils – in Amana, Iowa, where German has been reinstated from grade 4 upward. By and large language retention has been left to the inadequate efforts of the family.

The role of the orthodox Lutheran Church bodies after 1945 became almost the reverse of what it had been before 1917. Originally, they had been the staunchest defenders of the language. Now, however, Church policy became a contributing factor to the final doom of the German tongue. Since their seminaries and colleges had given up German, except as a branch of study, they were no longer able to supply ministers, teachers, or editors who were fully at home in both German and English. In many a congregation, after the death of the old bilingual minister, his young successor tried to accelerate the transition to English. Also typical is the case of the Missouri Synod's German church paper in Canada, which had to be discontinued in 1960, not because of a lack of subscribers, but because it was impossible to find a new editor of sufficient linguistic competence.

A statement in reference to Canada by the Kirchliches Aussenamt of the "Evangelische Kirche in Deutschland"[38] seems to be equally applicable to the United States: "The (by now) English-speaking Lutheran Church bodies appear to be definitely averse to the formation of non-English congregations for post-war immigrants, and therefore many originally Lutheran immigrants have joined the Baptists and Methodists because these Church bodies have much more readily responded to their linguistic needs".

Within this general framework, the transition to English has proceeded most rapidly not in the oldest settlements but in the more recent ones. Except for a very few post-1920 congregations, the Lutheran congregations that have stuck to German most tenaciously are those founded by the Old Lutheran "pilgrim fathers". In these Urgemeinden the monthly Church services were preponderantly German as late as 1931.

		Monthly Services	
		German	*English*
Missouri (Saxons)	Altenburg	4	1
	Frohnau	4	1
	Wittenberg	3	1
Michigan (Franconians)	Frankenmuth	5	1
	Frankenlust	4	1
	Frankentrost	4	0
Wisconsin (Pomeranians)	Cedarburg	4	2
	Lebanon	4	1

[38] *Tätigkeitsbericht des K.A. für die Zeit vom 1.1.1961 b.z. 31.12.1962* (Frankfurt, 1963), p. 24.

Obviously, a feeling of "indigenousness" has slowed down the language shift in quite a number of cases. More recently, all German "islands", whether old or new, have been hit by the mass exodus from American farmsteads which began during this period (as a result of large-scale mechanization) and reached its height in the post-1941 period. It has led to a demographic thinning out, especially of German and Scandinavian rural "islands".

While it is not possible to give a complete description of the present state of affairs, it may be useful to look at two cross-sections, one of urban Chicago and one of rural Kansas. In Chicago,[39] an important center of post-1920 German immigration, we find roughly 350,000 German-speaking inhabitants, i.e., one-tenth of the total population. Their chief rallying centers are 115 Vereine, many of them uniting descendents from a single German province or locality. Numerically, the two strongest Vereine are the Deutsch-Amerikanischer National Kongress (4,000 members in three states, founded in 1959 with a view toward uniting Germans on a nationwide scale for political purposes, but until now restricted to Illinois, Wisconsin, and Indiana) and the Schwaben-Verein (1,300 members, founded in 1878; its Cannstatter Volksfest is the biggest and gaudiest annual event for the entire German community). But other clubs with smaller memberships are actually more important. The wealthiest members are to be found in the ranks of the non-political Germania Club (1864, 600 members). It is significant that its current (1962) president does not speak German. In the political area, the Chicago branch of the Steuben Society is quite active. They have few members but, unlike the National Kongress, they are part of a truly nationwide organization and are not without practical experience. Their activities, however, are carried on largely in English. The spiritual heritage of Germany is cultivated by the Columbia, the Literarische Gesellschaft, and, in a more narrowly confined area, the Deutsche Medizinische Gesellschaft (1897). The latter has a membership of about 100 physicians (60% of them graduates of German universities), arranges lectures, often in German, and is in close touch with medical societies in New York and central Europe. Its present president is a refugee of the 1930's. German worship is held regularly at least once a month in 45 churches of Greater Chicago, 36 of them Lutheran, 8 Protestant other than Lutheran, and 1 Roman Catholic.

Of the once influential and varied Chicago German press, there still remain the daily "Abendpost" (founded 1889; circulation 26,000) and the weekly "Eintracht" (founded 1923; circulation 1,100). Chicago is also the home of the monthly "Hausfrau" (founded 1904; circulation 49,000) which caters to a nationwide public. German radio broadcasts are to be heard from WGES (6 hrs. per week), WOPA in Oak Park (3 hrs.), WMRO in Aurora (1 hr.), and a non-commercial program is carried by Station WRHS in Forest Park (1 hr.). Four Sprachschulen, one maintained by Protestant congregations, two by the Donauschwaben (ethnic Germans from southeastern Europe), and one by the German Aid Society, are teaching the ancestral tongue to about 300-400

---

[39]   The Chicago survey is based chiefly on communications from the Chicago Consulate General of the Federal Republic of Germany.

youngsters of German descent. Otherwise, German cultural life is pulsing at a low beat in the Vereine, many of which stress little more than beer, fun, gemütlichkeit, nostalgic folk-songs and the yearly carnival.

In contrast to this urban cross-section is the picture of rural Kansas, as reported by Professor J. N. Carman (1961). In a great many rural settlements, German (largely in the form of one dialect or another) is still very much alive among the adult population. In the Low German town of Hanover, only the old folks still speak German fluently, but in the nearby settlement of Bremen, east of Hanover, everyone above the age of twenty still speaks Low German – a fact which must be ascribed, at least in part, to their affiliation with the Missouri Synod. In a remote settlement of Russlanddeutsche near the Colorado border even the children still know some German, and among these settlers "their nostalgia for things German is great". Among the Mennonites from the Ukraine, who have founded numerous settlements as well as Bethel College, practically all men and women "of age" still speak their Low German dialect as do at least some of the youngsters. Among the many Catholic Volga Germans in Ellis county many of the children still speak the ancestral dialect, which Carman calls Swabian but which is probably Franconian or Hessian. Among the Protestant Volga Germans assimilation has made greater progress, chiefly because of religious disunity, "and while there are among them some ferocious advocates of the German language, very few of these are young".

These few examples seem to indicate, one, that despite the disappearance of practically all organized resistance to assimilation among German Americans, the sheer passive strength of the German language in these cultural islands tends to delay the linguistic transformation and, two, that these islands are potential nuclei for German FLES programs should a sustained effort be made to contact them and draw them into the FLES orbit. Unfortunately, the teaching of German in Kansas (Kreye, *AGR*, 27, 1961, 9-11), although in a *relatively* flourishing state, has at present almost nothing to do with the existence of the German settlements. With the help of Professor Carman's magnificent atlas, *Foreign-Language Units of Kansas* (vol. I, 1962), it might not be too difficult to create a bridge between FLES and the remaining semi-submerged language islands. Other states where a comparison between the present status of German as a mother tongue and the local FLES movement might yield results are the Dakotas, Minnesota, Wisconsin, and Texas. Reliable sources in Texas indicate that in at least a few localities there are still some youngsters who speak German natively.

Remaining Candidates for Survival

Five or six small sectarian groups seem to stand some kind of chance of linguistic survival: the Amish, the Old Order Mennonites, the Hutterites, the Hofer Community, the Amanites, and the Deutsche Gemeinde Gottes. Most members of the first two groups are derived from colonial stock, whereas all members of the last four are derived from the post-colonial. In the case of most of these groups, religio-societal insulation (Factor 1 in our conceptual background) has been the decisive factor in safeguarding their language maintenance potential.

The Old Order Amish[40] or House Amish – who worship in the homes of their members – number roughly 35,000 souls, half of whom (those 18 years old and over) are baptized. The group originated in Europe. At first they were a subgroup of the Mennonites, with whom they are still counted theologically. The sociologist, however, is inclined to consider them a group apart. They have spread to a number of states, but their main centers are in Ohio, Indiana, and Pennsylvania. All are farmers. They make no use of such modern devices as motor vehicles, telephones, the radio, etc. Early in the 19th century, they were strongly reinforced by co-religionists from Europe (more so, proportionately, than all other Pennsylvania German denominations), to the extent that they no longer have any co-religionists in Europe. Their vernacular is Pennsylvania Dutch (Pennsylvanish) and their language of worship is a variant of High German strongly influenced by the dialect. Most of them know High German only passively, i.e., they can understand Scriptural passages read to them in High German. There are a number of ways in which this knowledge of High German is inculcated – by the "bishops" (lay preachers) via Saturday afternoon classes during the winter; by public school teachers during lunch hours; by the parents who have already learned it; and "by doing", i.e. by participation in the long, drawn-out divine service.

Far less famous are the Old Order Mennonites, often but erroneously called "Wislerleute". In 1872, a number of Mennonites in Indiana under Bishop Wisler withdrew from their previous affiliation and formed a little Church body of their own. They did so for a number of reasons, one of which was the language issue. Similar withdrawals took place in other states, but the splinter groups as a whole never considered Wisler their leader nor did they name themselves after him. Today there are about 9,500 Old Order Mennonites of whom four-fifths live in southern Pennsylvania, the remainder in Virginia, Ohio, and Indiana. In Pennsylvania two major subgroups have evolved: the "Fuhreleit" (1926-27), who cling to the horse-and-buggy and use German in their church services, and the "Hanningleit" (1893), who drive automobiles painted entirely black (hence, "Black-bumper Mennonites") and are gradually giving up German.

Both Hutterites and Amanites were originally Christian communists. The Hutterites (Friedmann, 1961)[41] came to South Dakota in 1874 and founded so-called "Brüderhofe", collective settlements where there is no private property. Being conscientious objectors, they were harassed by the authorities during World War I so that most of them emigrated to Canada. Between 1936 and 1950 six Brüderhofe returned to South Dakota, and today there are eighteen colonies in South Dakota and Montana, with a

---

[40] There exists a considerable body of literature on the Amish; see especially E. L. Smith (1958) and W. Schreiber (1962). My figures are taken from an article by Professor E. L. Smith in the *Pennsylvaanisch-Deitsch Eck*, August 22, 1959. Other estimates are much higher.

[41] See also *AGR*, 27 (1961), 8-9.

combined population of 2,000 (as compared to at least 6,000 in Canada). They are 100%
German-speaking to this day – a statement hardly applicable to the Amish or the Old
Order Mennonites.

Between 1855 and 1862 the Amanites founded the seven villages of the Christian
Communist settlement of Amana, Iowa (Shambaugh 1932; Yambura and Bodine 1960).
Today their number is slightly below 2,000. In 1932 they gave up communism and
adopted a position between collectivism and unmitigated individualism which they
have termed "cooperative capitalism". Of the six sectarian groups, they were the only
ones to maintain their language with the open support of public schools. Up to 1917
German was the only language used in the lower grades, while in the higher grades
teaching was bilingual. After 1924, when German instruction was reintroduced in
Iowa, German became a branch of instruction from grade 1 upward. Since World
War II it has been restricted to grades 4-6 and the senior high school. For many years
it seemed that the Amanites would turn out to be the only group of German descent
to succeed in retaining its language without completely separating itself from outside
influences. But in a letter dated November 6, 1962, the Amana Society wrote as
follows:

Church services are still conducted in German, but about a year ago English services were
also introduced for those who are not fully conversant with the German language. The local
high school, however, gives a course in German. The present trend seems to imply that German will be maintained among the older people, but it seems that English will be the predominant language of the future.

The Hofer Community in Sutton, Nebraska, numbers nearly 500 members, more than
300 of whom are fifteen years of age or older, of Russian-German extraction. It was
founded in 1896 by Michael Hofer (1840-1929), a Reformed minister. Children are
taught in the German language on Saturdays and Sundays. While still intact linguistically, the group seems too small to preserve its language without outside (e.g., FLES)
assistance.

There also exists a church body calling itself "Deutsche Gemeinde Gottes" (in
English, "German Church of God") with headquarters in York, Nebraska, where the
Christian Unity Press publishes the *Evangeliums Posaune*. In a letter to the editor
dated January 15, 1963, a reader of the Lincoln, Nebraska, *Weltpost* states: "All of
these congregations conduct all their church services in German; all Sunday school
classes for the older people and some for the younger ones are held in German".
Little else is currently known about this group, except that it is affiliated with the
"Church of God" (headquarters in Anderson, Ind.).

CONCLUSIONS

Among the descendants of the 9 million or so German-speakers who lived on American soil in 1910, at most 50,000 of those under eighteen years of age still speak German
natively. Thus the German language seems doomed to extinction, apart from (1) its
lingering existence in a few 19th century language islands; (2) its continuation among

some self-segregated sectarian splinter groups; (3) its constant but ephemeral rein-forcement by new waves of immigrants who, unlike their forerunners, do little or nothing to transmit the language to their children. This is a development whose epic proportions should not be underestimated. The linguistic assimilation of 9 million German Americans – a group, be it remembered, which in 1916 was sufficiently in-fluential to prevent Theodore Roosevelt's renomination – is the most striking event of its kind in the annals of modern history. No other nationality group of equal numerical strength and living in one country has ever been so wellnigh completely assimilated.

The question arises whether some German Americans, seeing their ethnic mother tongue lost as a vehicle of daily communication, do not feel an inclination to maintain their ancesteral language for which in former years they fought so hard at least as a second language. The answer in general appears to be "no", in spite of some few signs to the contrary, such as the leading position that German still holds among the foreign languages at certain (but not all) denominational colleges and seminaries of Germanic background. What little progress the teaching of German may have made under the FLES program, it has made chiefly in states and localities where the German element has never been dominant, e.g., in Detroit (Breunig 1961). In addition to a general loss of prestige which the language has suffered in the eyes of all Americans, two specific reasons for disinterest may be adduced which hold for the Germanic element only. In the first place, the very fact that in the past their language maintenance efforts were so intense and persistent must now engender a psychological block, a pre-conscious feeling that to struggle for this language obviously is useless and can lead nowhere. This resignation is joined in the second place, by the shock produced by the two World Wars, both of which were accompanied by intensive propaganda against the German language and culture. Whether the Germanic element will ever recover from such a combination of events remains to be seen. At any rate, neither the "block" nor the "shock" dominating German Americans of post-colonial origin should be confused with the deep-rooted indifference of the Pennsylvania Dutch toward High German.

The German-American situation calls for a hard look into the past. Repeatedly, leading German-American and Anglo-American personalities have voiced the opin-ion that while German as a spoken tongue is doomed to die out in the United States, it might remain a secondary tongue for Americans of German descent and their specific institutions of learning. In this way German Americans might serve as cultural links between America and the German-speaking parts of Europe. This idea was first proclaimed by two famous leaders of the German Reformed Church, Philipp Schaff and John W. Nevin. Schaff coined the term "Anglo-Germanismus" for that future segment of American culture that would be English in language but largely conditioned by its German background. He propounded the idea in his *Deutscher Kirchenfreund*,[42] perhaps the best German-language magazine ever published in the

---

[42]   See *Kirchenfreund*, 1848, I, no. 1, p. 18, where Schaff speaks of the "German Churches": "Ihre wissenschaftlichen Anstalten ... wollen zwar von ganzem Herzen amerikanisch sein, aber eben darum nicht rein englisch oder schottisch, sondern anglogermanisch sein."

United States. His friend, Professor John W. Nevin, himself not of German descent, in a lecture delivered at Franklin and Marshall College, called Pennsylvania an "Anglo-German state" and went on: "An institution suited to the character of Pennsylvania ... needs to be English altogether in its general course of studies, and yet of such reigning spirit that both the German language and habit of thought shall feel themselves to be easily at home within its bosom" (*Mercersburg Quart. Rev.*, 5, 1853, 396-418). A similar outlook is found in a book by Harvard Professor Hugo Munsterberg, in which he held that the survival of German depended less on its use among the inarticulate masses ("the beer gardens of Milwaukee or the Cincinnati Gemüsemarkt") than on the extent to which it was cultivated as a cultural tongue (Munsterberg 1909). His fellow professor from Harvard, Kuno Franke, is known to have shared this view. In 1931 Professor A. R. Hohlfeld, one of Wisconsin's best known Germanists, in an address to the Steuben Society, spoke of the necessity to approach the Anglicized Americans of German descent and convince them of the values of German culture and their opportunities as mediators (*Monatshefte*, Madison, Wisc., Jan. 1932). Hohlfeld may or may not have known about Schaff and Nevin and their Anglo-Germanic concept. But there is a thread into the past deserving to be traced very carefully and to be woven into a new pattern of German-American cultural activities. That it can be done is illustrated by the example the Franco-Americans of New England are setting. While gradually giving up French as their primary means of expression, they are studiously making it over into a cherished and well-cultivated second language.

REFERENCES

American Coucil of Learned Societies, *Report of the Committee on Linguistic and National Stocks in the Population of the United States* (Washington, ACLS, 1932). (Also, in *Rep. Am. Hist. Assoc.*, 1931.)

Arndt, K., and Olson, M., *Deutsch-Amerikanische Zeitungen und Zeitschriften* (Heidelberg, Quelle & Mayer, 1961).

Bagster-Collins, E. W., *The History of Modern Language Teaching in The United States* (New York, Columbia Univ. Press, 1910).

Barry, C. S., *The Catholic Church and German-Americans* (Milwaukee, Bruce Publ. Co., 1953).

von Bosse, G., *Ein Kampf um Glaube und Volkstum* (Stuttgart, C. Belser, 1930).

Breunig, Marjorie, *Foreign Languages in the Elementary Schools of the United States, 1959-60* (New York, Mod. Lang. Assoc., 1961).

Brown, F. J., and Roucek, J. S., *One America* (New York, Prentice Hall, 1945).

Bruncken, E., *German Political Refugees in the United States During the Period 1815-1860* (Chicago, 1904). (Reprinted from *Deutsch-Amer. Geschichtsblätter*, 1903/04, 3 and 4.)

Buffington, A. F., and Barba, P. A., *A Pennsylvania German Grammar* (Allentown, Schlechter, 1954).

Carman, J. N., "Germans in Kansas", *American-German Review*, 27 (1961), No. 4, 4-8.

——, *Foreign-Language Units of Kansas; Historical Atlas and Statistics* (Lawrence, Univ. of Kan. Press, 1962).

Child, C. J., *The German-Americans in Politics, 1914-1917* (Madison, Univ. of Wisc. Press, 1939).

Dobert, E. W., *Deutsche Demokraten in Amerika; die 48er und ihre Schriften* (Göttingen, Vandenhoek & Ruprecht, 1958).

Douglas, Paul F., *The Story of German Methodism* (Cincinnati, 1959).

Dulon, R., *Aus Amerika. Über Schule, Deutsche Schule, Amerikanische Schule, Deutschamerikanische Schule* (Leipzig und Heidelberg, C. E. Winter, 1866).

Engerand, G. C., "The so-called Wends of Germany and their colonization in Texas and Australia", *Univ. Tex. Bull.*, 1934, no. 3417.

Fishman, J. A., et al., *Language Loyalty in the United States* (New York, Yeshiva University 1964), three volumes. (Mimeographed Report to the U.S. Office of Education.)

Friedmann, R., *Hutterite Studies* (Groshen, Ind., Mennonite Historical Society, 1961).

Gerhard, E. S., "The history of Schwenkfelder schools", *Schwenkfeldiana*, 1 (1943), No. 3, 5-21.

Handschin, C. H., *The Teaching of Modern Languages in the United States* (Washington, U.S. Govt. Print. Off., 1913).

Hawgood, J. A., *The Tragedy of German-Americans in the United States* (New York and London, Putnam, 1940).

Hense-Jensen, W., and Bruncken, E., *Wisconsin Deutsch-Amerikaner* (Milwaukee, Deutsche Gesellschaft, 1902), vol. II.

Klees, F., *The Pennsylvania Dutch* (New York, Macmillan, 1950).

Kloss, H., *Um die Einigung des Deutschamerikanertumes; Die Geschichte einer unvollendeten Volksgruppe* (Berlin, Volk und Reich Verlag, 1937).

——, "Über die mittelbare Kartographische Erfassung der jüngeren deutschen Volksinseln in den Vereinigten Staaten", *Deutsches Archiv für Landes- und Volksforschung*, 3 (1939a), 453-474.

——, "Afrikaans and Pennsylvanish", *Pennsylvaanisch-Deitsch Eck*, 1939b, March 25.

——, *Volksgruppenrecht in den Vereinigten Staaten von Amerika* (Essen, Essener Verlagsanstalt, I 1940, II 1942).

——, "What's in a name", *Pennsylvaanisch-Deitsch Eck*, 1954, Oct. 2.

——, "Die deutschamerikanische Schule", *Jahrbuch f. Amerikastudien* (Heidelberg), 7 (1962), 141-175.

——, *Das Nationalitätenrecht der Vereinigten Staaten von Amerika* (Wien, Braumüller, 1963).

Körner, G., *Das Deutsche Element in den Vereinigten Staaten von Nordamerika 1838-1848* (New York, Steiger, 1884).

Levi, K. A. E., "Geographical origin of German immigration to Wisconsin", *Coll. Wisc. State Hist. Soc.*, 14 (1898), 341-398.

Livingood, F. G., "Eighteenth century Reformed Church Schools", *Proc. Penn'a-Germ. Soc.*, 38 (1930), 199.

Livingston, J. H., *An Address to the Reformed German Churches in the United States* (New Brunswick, Wm. Myer, 1819).

Löher, F., *Geschichte und Zustände der Deutschen in Amerika* (Cincinnati, Eggers and Wulkop, 1847); 2nd edition: Leipzig, Kohler, 1885.

Lohr, O., *Deutschland und Übersee* (Herrenalb, Erdmann, 1962).

Maurer, C.L., "Early Lutheran Education in Pennsylvania", *Proc. Penn'a-Germ. Soc.*, 40 (1932), 200.

Maurer, H. H., "The Lutheran community and American society; A study in religion as a condition of social accomodation", *Am. J. Soc.*, 34 (1928), 386-389.

Mayer, F., *Die Zukunft der Deutschen Evangelischen Synode von Nord-Amerika* (Michigan City, Michigan District of the German Evangelical Synod, 1913).

Metzentim-Raunick, Selma, "A survey of German literature in Texas", *Southwestern Quarterly*, 33 (1939), 134-159. (Same: "Deutsche Schriften in Texas", *Freie Presse für Texas*, San Antonio, 1935 I; 1936 II).

Meynen, E., *Bibliography of German Settlements in Colonial North America, 1683-1933* (Leipzig, Harrassowitz, 1937).

Muensterberg, H., *Aus Deutsch-Amerika* (Berlin, Mitller & Sohn, 1909).

Ratterman, H. A., "Das Element in den Vereinigten Staaten von Nord-Amerika, 1800-1850", *Gesammelte Ausgewählte Werke*, vol. 16 (Cincinnati, Selbstverlag, 1912).

Sallet, R., "Russlanddeutsche Siedlungen in den Vereinigten Staaten", *Jb. der Dt.-Am. Hist. Ges.*, 3 (1931), 5-126. (Also printed separately, Chicago, 1931.)

Schreiber, Wm., *Our Amish Neighbors* (Chicago, Univ. of Chicago Press, 1962).

Shambaugh, Bertha M., *Amana That Is and Amana That Was* (Iowa City, State Historical Society, 1932).

Smith, E. L., *The Amish People* (New York, Exposition Press, 1958).

Stewart, J., and Smith, E. L., "The survival of German dialects and customs in the Shenandoah

Valley", *Soc. for the Hist. of Germans in Md.* (Baltimore), 31 (1963), 66-70.

Stoudt, J. J., *The Pennsylvania Dutch* (Allentown, Penna., Schlechter, 1951).

Viereck, L., "German instruction in American schools", *Report of the Commissioner of Education for 1900-01* (Washington, U. S. Govt. Print. Office, 1902), pp. 531-708. (German edition: *Zwei Jahrhunderte der Unterricht in den Vereinigten Staaten*, Braunschweig, Vieweg, 1903.)

Weber, S. E., *The Charity School Movement in Colonial Pennsylvania* (Phila., Wm. J. Campbell, 1905).

Wittke, C., *German-Americans and the World War* (Columbus, Ohio, Ohio State Archeol. and Hist. Soc., 1936).

——, *Refugees of Revolution; The German Forty-Eighters in America* (Phila., Univ. of Penn'a Press, 1952).

——, *The German-Language Press in America* (Lexington, Univ. of Kentucky Press, 1957).

——, *William Nast; Patriarch of German Methodism* (Detroit, Wayne State Univ. Press, 1960).

Wollfradt, K. W., "Die Statistik des Deutsch-Amerikanischen Schulwesens", *Deutsches Pionier* (Cincinnati), 18 (1886), 50-55.

Wood, R. C. (ed.), *The Pennsylvania Germans* (Princeton, Princeton Univ. Press, 1943).

——, "Pennsylvania High German", *Germanic Review*, 20 (1945), 299-314.

——, "Pennsilfaanisch", in *Dt. Philologie im Aufriss*, I (Berlin, Erich Schmidt, 1952).

Yambura, B. S., and Bodine, W. D., *A Change and a Parting*; *My story of Amana* (Ames, Iowa, Iowa State Univ. Press, 1960).

Zucker, A. E., *The Forty-Eighters* (New York, Columbia University Press, 1950).

10. FRANCO-AMERICAN EFFORTS ON BEHALF OF THE FRENCH LANGUAGE IN NEW ENGLAND

HERVE-B. LEMAIRE

Over a million people in the United States speak French natively, the largest concentration residing in New England. Franco-Americans, as New Englanders of French-Canadian descent like to be called, pride themselves in having developed a bilingual culture. In general they speak Canadian-French as it was spoken in the Province of Quebec at the turn of the century, with a liberal admixture of Americanisms. Save for some minor problems of a lexical and phonetic nature, the average native of France has little, if any, difficulty in understanding educated Franco-Americans of New England. Franco-Americans readily understand the spoken and written standard language of modern France. There are, as a matter of fact, many places in France where the language customarily spoken by a majority of the population deviates much further from standard French than does the French spoken in New England (Carrière 1949, p. 10).

Compared with most other immigrant languages in the United States, French survives with surprising vigor. This is chiefly due to the determined efforts of the first Franco-Americans, who had the vision to establish a vast network of interlocking religious, educational, cultural, and fraternal organizations at a relatively early date. Today, their 284 parishes are still strong ethnic entities. Their 253 institutions of learning, including seven liberal arts colleges, 51 high schools, and 195 elementary schools, offer one hour or more of French each day in all grades and at all levels. Franco-Americans in New England support several societies whose primary function is to promote ethnic survival. They have an active French-language press and scores of radio stations carrying special French language programs. In some cities, French continues to be spoken in the home, at work, and at play. However, in many other areas Franco-Americans are abandoning the daily use of French, and those who still show a marked interest in the language ordinarily do so as a cultural pursuit. Considered unassimilable a generation ago (Gunther 1947, p. 487), Franco-Americans have in recent years become acculturated to a remarkable degree.

The French-Canadians came to this country, originally, to earn a decent living and to save money with which to return to their beloved farms in Quebec. They lived in New England, in the 19th century, much as they had in French-Canada. Although many now worked in the mills, their real interest lay with their families, their fellow "exiles", and their ethnic organizations. They lived in French-Canadian neighbor-

TABLE 10.1

U.S. Census Data on French Mother Tongue

	Foreign Born	Native of Foreign or Mixed Parentage	Native of Native Parentage
1910	528,842	828,327	X
1920	466,956	823,154	X
1930	523,505	X	X
1940	359,520	533,760	518,780
1960	330,220	X	X

Increases Relative to Earlier Figure

	Foreign Born	Native of Foreign or Mixed Parentage	Native of Native Parentage
1920	−11.7%	− .6%	X
1930	12.1	X	X
1940	−31.3	−35.2	X
1960	−8.15	X	X

hoods, usually by choice, frequently in corporation houses. The ghetto-like French quarters gave them a feeling of security and provided a semblance of the villages they had left behind. In their *petit Canada*, the French-Canadians led a simple life, observing their traditional holidays, singing their folk-songs, dancing their jigs and quadrilles, and relating their marvelous tales. All this they did in French, for at that time they spoke very little, if any, English. The little English they did know, they used only with "outsiders" when absolutely necessary.

French-Canadians, then, fully intended to preserve their ethnicity. Proud of their heritage, they took it upon themselves to perpetuate it. They deemed it essential to preserve their faith and their traditions, and were convinced that loyalty in these two areas depended fully upon the preservation of the French language. Loss of language meant loss of faith, and loss of faith meant loss of eternity (Ducharme 1943, p. 92). For many generations, this was to be the basic tenet of the Franco-American creed, shared by official organizations as well as by the masses.

THE EARLY DAYS: THE CHURCH

Prior to the foundation of their own parishes, Franco-Americans attended territorial churches where they often were merely tolerated. They found no warmth and little meaning in churches where everything but the Latin rite was foreign. They prayed to the same God as their English-speaking Catholic co-religionists, but the sermons and other interpersonal relationships important to their religious practice were less meaningful to them because of the language barrier. They had no schools where their children might pursue their education in French. Their children normally attended public schools where contact with youngsters of other backgrounds fostered much-dreaded assimilation.

In 1850, Franco-Americans opened the doors of their first "national" church in New England, Saint-Joseph in Burlington, Vermont. As the numbers of immigrants grew, more French parishes were established and the search for a French-speaking cleargy began. This search ultimately brought priests from Belgium and France as well as from the Province of Quebec (Walker 1961, p. 11). As in Canada, these churches became the focal point for nearly all phases of community life: social, cultural, and educational, as well as religious. "The mystic bond" that existed between the language and the religion of the Franco-Americans was thus reconfirmed (Ducharme 1943, p. 66). As a rule, the only focus of immigrant activity was in religion; with few exceptions, the only "intellectuals" who had emigrated along with the artisans and farmers were the clergy; the only organization which could maintain the unity of the group was the Church (Niebuhr 1929, p. 223).

However, Franco-Americans encountered serious difficulties in the very organization upon which they relied so completely. The number of French-speaking priests was never sufficient. The American bishops, predominantly Irish, were increasingly reluctant to name French-Canadian pastors. They alluded to the difficulty of convincing the more desirable French-Canadian priests to leave Canada (Rumilly 1958, p. 101). Franco-Americans, who were accustomed to look upon their bishops and their priests as leaders of the people and champions of their ethnic survival, soon found that this was not always to be so in the United States. Irish bishops and priests looked forward to the assimilation of the Franco-Americans (Rumilly 1958, p. 90). America's bishops wanted to destroy the image that Catholicism was a "religion of foreigners" in the United States. Cardinal Gibbons and the bishops strove to "break nationalism within the Church" (Siegfried 1927, p. 50).

Franco-American history abounds with anecdotes and opinions concerning the official policy of the Catholic Church toward the use and maintenance of the French language in this country. For example, one reads of Bishop O'Reilly, of Springfield, Massachusetts, who proclaimed that "the best means for the Franco-Americans to preserve their faith is to preserve their language, to remain attached to their customs, to educate their children in their mother tongue" (Lauvrière 1924, p. 520). On the other hand, a much more typical view was that of the Reverend James E. Cassidy, Chancellor and later Bishop of the diocese of Fall River, Massachusetts, who declared at a ceremony in New Bedford, Massachusetts: "The grandeur of a nation depends upon the assimilation of the diverse races that come to live in that country" (Rumilly 1958, p. 204). Bishop Thomas Hendricken of Providence, considered a proponent of assimilation, found the Franco-Americans very exacting and hard to satisfy. In answer to delegates of a Franco-American parish pleading for French-speaking priests, he replied: "Why do you want French-speaking priests? In ten years everyone will speak English in your parishes" (Rumilly 1958, p. 106). Such replies undoubtedly irritated those who considered themselves to be defenders of the faith.

TABLE 10.2

U.S. Census Data on French Mother Tongue 1910-1960[a]

State	Population	% Foreign Born	% Native of Foreign or Mixed Par.	Foreign Born: % non-English Mother Tongue		Total	Urban	Rural N F	Farm	1940	1930	1920	1910
									(FOREIGN BORN)				
Connecticut	2,535,234	11	28	77	b	227,200	196,873	27,317	3,010	248,960	298,418	289,867	232,777
					c	23,303	18,811	4,288	204	20,400	28,919	18,376	22,118
					d	10	10	16	7	8	10	6	10
Maine	969,265	6	17	50	b	40,472	28,303	10,741	1,428	43,660	52,632	55,373	53,220
					c	21,091	16,683	3,997	411	29,140	37,325	36,071	35,342
					d	52	59	37	29	67	71	65	66
Massachusetts	5,149,317	11	29	61	b	389,116	351,818	34,753	2,545	493,780	598,192	615,332	544,982
					c	59,125	51,647	7,164	314	86,740	121,712	116,364	141,266
					d	15	15	21	12	18	20	19	26
New Hampshire	606,921	7	22	66	b	33,347	25,412	7,257	678	46,480	57,519	62,951	62,237
					c	17,664	14,135	3,244	285	28,720	38,024	38,609	41,060
					d	53	56	45	42	62	66	61	66
Rhode Island	859,488	10	30	70	b	66,272	60,683	5,282	307	92,520	113,367	111,538	105,962
					c	14,542	12,620	1,889	33	25,440	33,954	31,270	36,549
					d	22	21	36	11	27	30	28	34
Vermont	389,881	6	16	61	b	15,688	7,059	6,121	2,508	19,840	27,400	26,295	27,498
					c	9,159	3,678	3,500	1,981	11,820	17,524	14,406	14,902
					d	58	52	57	79	60	64	55	54
Louisiana	3,257,022	.9	3	67	b	25,507	22,077	2,843	587	21,740	31,597	38,965	44,336
					c	1,642	1,450	178	14	1,880	3,263	4,425	5,828
					d	6	7	6	2	9	10	11	13
U.S.A.	179,325,671	5	14	74	b	7,885,151	6,895,466	793,645	196,040	8,603,200	10,886,384	10,704,822	9,981,753
					c	330,220	276,186	45,533	6,562	359,520	523,505	466,956	528,842
					d	4	4	6	3	4	5	4	5

[a] All columns not otherwise designated pertain to 1960.
[b] Number of foreign born claiming non-English mother tongue.
[c] Number of foreign born claiming French mother tongue.
[d] b/a as a percent.

The situation grew progressively more acute. One of the chief causes of dissension was the basic difference in church management in Canada and in the United States. In Canada, French Canadians had elected their *marguilliers* or church wardens who supervised the financial affairs of the parish. They naturally assumed that they would also control the monetary affairs of their churches and their schools in New England. They were, therefore, rudely awakened when American bishops attempted to channel Franco-American parish funds toward other diocesan charities.

In the State of Maine the Corporation Sole system was in effect, whereby the bishop, by state law, was the sole proprietor of any and all church property. This law prevented Franco-Americans from administering the real estate which they had financed. They were informed that the schools and churches they had built did not belong to them but to the bishop. A similar system, the Parish Corporation, existed in the other New England states where the bishop, his vicar general, and the pastor of the parish selected two laymen to act as syndics. Again, the bishop, to whom the vicar general and the pastor were subject, was in control. In practice, the pastor assumed the role of administrator, and the lay members of corporations had neither the rights nor the obligations of the *marguilliers* of the Province of Quebec (Rumilly 1958, pp. 115-116, 238-39).

This development, together with the firm conviction shared by Franco-Americans that the Irish clergy intended to destroy their ethnic values, readily indicates why clashes became inevitable. They all revolved directly or indirectly around the French language. Rumilly, in his *Histoire des Franco-Américains*, lists a large number of conflicts of varying degrees of seriousness. In 1894, in Danielson, Connecticut, Franco-Americans refused to contribute to the construction of a school where French would not be taught. This occurred in a parish where there were 1800 Franco-Americans and only 300 Irish. In 1900, in North Brookfield, Massachusetts, parishioners revolted because they were not given a French-speaking pastor. They sided with their Franco-American curate who was under suspension, until they were given assurances that one of their own nationality would eventually become pastor. In 1909, the famous Corporation Sole case in the State of Maine came about as a result of Church-sponsored attempts at assimilation through the naming of English-language priests to French-speaking parishes. The fact that Franco-Americans lost their case before the Maine civil court, and for all practical purposes in Rome, augmented their anguish. Situations such as these spurred the historian Edmond de Nevers to say: "The Irish clergy in the United States is the most ferocious enemy of the French, German, Polish, and Italian Catholics" (de Nevers 1900, pp. 321-344).

THE SCHOOLS

When the Third Council of Baltimore decreed that Catholics were required to erect parochial schools wherever possible the order was superfluous as far as Franco-

Americans were concerned, since from the time they had built their very first church they had also built schools, staffing them with nuns belonging to religious orders founded in Canada or in France. At first, these schools adopted the French-Canadian curriculum and methods, with most subjects being taught in French. However, as Franco-Americans adjusted to their new environment, they felt a greater need for the English language, although most still considered it to be no more than secondary in importance. They devised an elementary school system consisting of eight or nine years, depending upon the public school organization in the local area. The school year consisted of forty weeks, and the school day lasted, on the average, five and one-half hours. Usually the morning session was devoted to subjects more easily taught in English, while in the afternoon the French language, religion, and the history of Canada were taught in French. While many of these schools were very successful and acquired a high degree of respectability, others were inadequately staffed and lacked proper equipment. The term "French school" was not always meant to be flattering.

In 1904, the Assumptionist Fathers opened a school in Worcester, Massachusetts, which was soon transformed into a liberal arts college, Assumption College, where Franco-Americans might send their children for advanced French training. Many still sent their sons to schools in the Province of Quebec.

By 1912, there were 123 Franco-American parochial schools – a striking testimonial to an ethnic group that would not die (Bachand and Louis 1938, p. 200).

THE SOCIETIES

Parallel to the development of churches and schools was the organization of ethnic societies. Feeling the pressures of other nationality groups and wanting to rub elbows with their own, Franco-Americans sought fraternal gatherings. Societies stood for certain ideals, helped to maintain a nationalistic spirit, and thus filled a real need (Leboeuf 1938, p. 203). Every parish had the customary assortment of religio-social groups such as the *Ligue du St. Nom de Dieu*, the *Dames de Sainte Anne*, and the *Enfants de Marie*. Moreover, Franco-Americans organized into purely social and fraternal societies, where their language and their customs became an integral part of organizational activity. As early as 1859, the first such Franco-American society was founded in Burlington, Vermont, to preserve and propagate the ancestral traditions and the cherished French language.

In 1865, the *Société Saint-Jean-Baptiste de Bienfaisance de New York* invited all existing French-Canadian associations to convene to discuss the major problems confronting the survival of the French group in the Northeastern States (Therriault 1946, pp. 50-51). The constitution of the convention had the following preamble:

The French-Canadian mutual societies in the United States, having been founded for the dual purpose of serving the cause of the French-Canadians in America and of encouraging mutual assistance, cannot hope to accomplish this mission as long as they act separately.

For this reason, they have organized in a common association and have adopted a constitution which will facilitate its operations.

In article 4 of this constitution, it was enacted that all deliberations be in French.

Beginning about 1880 and continuing into the succeeding decades, local Saint-Jean-Baptiste societies sprung up all over New England. In 1889, La Société Jacques Cartier was founded in the State of Rhode Island as a fraternal order. On November 26, 1896, the first mutual insurance society, L'Association Canado-Américaine, was founded in Manchester, New Hampshire. Two main reasons prompted the birth of the ACA. First, there was a strong desire to have a large ethnic society. Many Franco-Americans wished to unite into a single powerful federation all the local Saint-Jean-Baptiste societies which were then maintaining themselves with lacklustre success. Second, they wanted to discourage their brethren from swelling the ranks of neutral or "banned" societies (Lemoine 1921, p. 143). In October 1905, a meeting of members of different mutuals, dignified by the presence of leading Franco-Americans, was held in Springfield, Massachusetts. It was decided to sever relations with the Catholic Order of Foresters and to form a separate *Ordre des Forestiers Franco-Américains*. This new association would be a federative society of mutual aid and would comprise persons of French descent and Catholic affiliation (Guillet 1914, p. 516). *L'Ordre des Forestiers Franco-Américains* amalgamated with *L'Association Canado-Américaine* in 1939.

Franco-American societies were in fairly close contact with their counterparts in French-Canada. Exchanges of visits and of ideas were frequent. In June, 1912, *La Société du Parler Français* in the Province of Quebec organized a French language congress in Quebec city and invited the collaboration of Franco-American groups. Monseigneur Paul-Eugene Roy, Auxiliary-Bishop of Quebec and soul of the Congress, toured the New England states to urge active participation in the convention. Franco-Americans attended the congress in large numbers and were officially represented by their leaders, who described their ethnic situation in New England in optimistic terms. However, one could detect an underlying current of anxiety in their all-too-frequent reminders that the French language would finally win out despite the many attacks made on it in New England.

THE PRESS

With the growth of the Franco-American population and its many ethnic enterprises, a need was felt for a French language press. Franco-Americans have understood well the power of the press and have exploited it to the extent of being accused of a "mania for founding newspapers" (Bracq 1927, p. 335). In less than a century they inaugurated nearly 250 newspapers of every format, from short-lived pamphlets to grand political and national daily tribunes.

The first periodicals published by the Franco-Americans were really French-

Canadian journals on American soil, characterized more by a series of sporadic and temporary efforts than by any lasting quality. However, the increasing struggle for survival, conflicts with Church authorities, and efforts to stave off assimilation were ideal fuel for journalists. In 1898, there were four daily French newspapers, three in Massachusetts – *L'Indépendant* in Fall River, *L'Etoile* in Lowell, and *L'Opinion Publique* in Worcester – and one in Woonsocket, Rhode Island, *La Tribune*. There were also a dozen or so weeklies. In 1911, Alexandre Belisle, president of *L'Opinion Publique*, published a history of the Franco-American press in which he reported seven dailies, almost as many as in the Province of Quebec. In addition to the four mentioned above, there was now *L'Avenir National* in Manchester, New Hampshire and *L'Echo* and the *Journal*, in New Bedford, Massachusetts.

These newspapers defended the two causes considered most vital by Franco-American leaders: French parochial schools and a French-speaking clergy. They tilted not only with the non-Catholic press, but with such Irish publications as the *Catholic Review*, the *Freemail*, the *Catholic Union*, and the *Boston Pilot*, all of which never ceased to advocate assimilation.

THE OFFICIAL ORGANIZATIONS AND THE PEOPLE

The close cooperation which initially existed between the Franco-American masses and their formal organizations weakened with the years, particularly among the newer generations. Having become better adjusted to the American way of life, they developed a self-confidence which lessened their dependence on the ethnic group and its organizations, and to some extent diminished their effective attachment to their ethnic origins.

On the other hand, Franco-American leaders, who had been primarily engrossed in efforts to promote the cultural continuity of their group, gradually evolved a philosophy of "political militancy". Reacting against the spirit of Americanization which swept the country in the early 20th century, they sought to redefine Americanism to mean cultural pluralism, arguing that Franco-Americans were American citizens who retained their French language and their Roman Catholic faith. Imbued with this lofty ideal, but failing to appreciate fully the concerns and aspirations of the common people in their daily struggle with down-to-earth realities, the leadership of the societies slowly drew ever further away from the views and attitudes of the majority of Franco-Americans.

The ethnic involvement of the early Franco-Americans had been almost complete. Their frequent relations with Canada and continued immigration kept the old culture alive. Intermarriages with "outsiders" were rare. Most Franco-Americans adjusted slowly to the idea of permanent settlement in America and long maintained an interest in French-Canadian happenings. However, more and more of them came to realize that their lives were to be spent in the United States where their children were born and educated. French-Canadian farmers, who came to this country ostensibly to earn a little more money and return home, slowly took on new habits and attitudes and, eventually, abandoned forever the idea of repatriation.

Many believe that Franco-Americans would have been quickly assimilated had it not been for the Irish challenge which prompted them to organize. As it was, most first-generation Franco-Americans believed that their language had to be preserved because their faith and hence their salvation depended on it. In fusing the religious and ethnic norms, a powerful emotional force was generated which permeated nearly all facets of Franco-American life and made of this minority group one of the least assimilable of all the ethnic groups in America (Walker 1961, p. 16).

The first Franco-American novel, Honoré Beaugrand's *Jeanne la Fileuse* (1878), is a romanticized report of the French-Canadian migration to the United States. Although Beaugrand's major interest was to refute the unfavorable coverage emigrants received in the Canadian press, we are more interested today in his description of the increasing prosperity of Franco-American mill workers. This prosperity, limited as it might have been, became a cause of assimilation. By Beaugrand's time it had already produced a few individuals who had decided to "go up the hill", that is, to leave the *petit Canada* and settle in a more prosperous section of the city. Separated from their national parishes, they attended the territorial churches and their children soon became assimilated.

Second-generation Franco-Americans became even more absorbed in the American way of life. The young were entranced by the mass media and by the variety of other attractions which abounded in urban centers. Evenings spent in the family circle became less frequent, and when young Franco-Americans met amongst themselves the French language was not always used. The latest American show-tunes soon replaced the old Canadian folksongs (Cadieux 1914, p. 362). They lived in an era and in a milieu where everything hailed American superiority. They did not want to pass for immigrants in the richest country in the world. If they attended parochial schools, a large part of their schooling was in English. All of their education was in English if they attended public schools. They spoke English with their de-ethnicized or other-ethnic playmates. Later they would speak English with their co-workers and with their employers, in fact, with almost everyone in the business world. If they married a non-French girl English would be the only language spoken in the home (Rumilly 1958, p. 176). Most people understood that the sine qua non for success in this country was a practical knowledge of English and of American institutions and methods. Those immigrants who knew English before entering the United States progressed more rapidly than others. Furthermore, among those who spoke no English upon arrival, the quickest to succeed in America were those who were also quickest to understand the importance of mastering the language of the country (Cadieux 1914, p. 255).

THE INTER-WAR YEARS

The turn of the century and, notably, World War I brought about important trans-formations in social attitudes and behaviors in the United States. Patriotism was fired up during the world conflict and, along with a belligerent attitude toward Germany, there arose a sentiment of distrust for almost anything foreign. There was a widely-shared feeling that an American should be English-speaking, follow Anglo-Saxon traditions, and, preferably, be imbued with our Colonial heritage. At about the same time, relative prosperity and comfort reinforced the great equalizing pressures of con-formity. The subsequent evolution of the family, the school, and even the Church resulted in a considerable degree of cultural homogenization. During the 1920's Franco-Americans experienced their greatest struggles against total assimilation in what was perhaps their last concerted effort for ethnic survival.

The Great Depression of the early 1930's was the catalyst which produced a critical reaction among many Franco-Americans against "*la survivance*". The textile workers, especially those who were on relief and at the mercy of government subsidy, slid rapidly into the "melting pot". With the return of relative prosperity, the middle-class urge gripped the nation, touching off a spontaneous and almost irresistible impulse to get ahead, to be accepted, to attain a certain level of economic and social security. Many Franco-Americans, consciously or not, wished to shed the vestiges of the immi-grant and to approach as much as possible the American's self-image, the "national type", the idealized "Anglo-Saxon" model (Herberg 1956, pp. 33-34).

In addition, there was less and less opportunity to draw inspiration from first-generation immigrants, always an important factor in ethnic survival. Migration from Canada had all but ceased in the early part of the century. In September, 1930, President Hoover had sent the following instructions to American consuls in Canada: If consular officials judge that an applicant might become a public burden, even after a considerable period of time, they must refuse him a visa.[1] For a time, as many migrants returned to Canada as entered the United States. Those who were dedicated to pre-serving Franco-American ethnicity in the parishes, in the societies, and in the press found their influence greatly reduced during this critical period.

THE STRUGGLE IN THE CHURCH

Parishes had grown in numbers and had become institutionally stronger, but the dynamism of earlier years was being replaced by a spirit of consolidation. Struggles within the Church continued to reflect a strong insistence on the part of Franco-Americans upon the right to manage their own affairs in their "national" parishes (Theriault 1960, p. 406). While the overwhelming majority of Franco-Americans resented the forced use of parish funds, they nevertheless submitted to the duly

[1] *New York Times*, September 10, 1930.

constituted authority of the representative of Rome. However, only strong outside pressures were capable of bringing to a close the long, bitter struggle of the anti-Irish *Sentinellistes* and their followers. As was expected by most Franco-Americans, the *Sentinellistes* suffered defeat both in the courts and in Rome.

First, a court decision upheld the Bishop's right to tax parishes for diocesan work (October 4, 1927: Superior Court of Rhode Island: Judge Tanner). Then, as Rome clearly could not condone open revolt against ecclesiastical authority, a third appeal of the *Sentinellistes* was turned down, carrying with it the dreaded sentence of excommunication along with the suppression of the rebel newspaper *La Sentinelle*. Many Franco-Americans claim that the Sentinelle "affair" greatly diminished the political influence and the language maintenance interests of Franco-Americans in Rhode Island.

After the crisis of the mid-twenties, there were few controversies over the appointment of priests, or over diocesan permission for school construction in the "French" parishes. Apparently convinced of the merits of a more tactful approach, and aware of the strength of assimilating social forces, Church authorities relaxed their more stringent policies in these respects. Language loyalists, for their part, remained wary of conflicts in which they stood to lose more than they could gain.

The percentage of Franco-American parishes supporting their own parochial elementary schools was high during the inter-war period. However, Franco-American schools were gradually becoming essentially American rather than French-Canadian. Both the State Education Department's rulings and "common sense" required it. The schools would have remained empty had they continued to educate French-Canadians instead of American citizens. Few, if any, Franco-American teachers would now attempt to develop in their pupils a nostalgic affection for Canada, a country which the children barely knew from occasional visits and where they would surely never live. Preaching French-Canadian patriotism could not strengthen their love for the French language. Indeed, it could only injure it. Persons who persisted in exhorting young Franco-Americans to develop such a loyalty spoke a meaningless language to the younger generation. Survival of the French language had to be based on other motives if it were to appeal to the youngsters. However, a new ideological and pedagogic rationale was hard to come by.

LAW AND REALITY

The right to teach French in the private elementary schools of New England has its guarantee in the Fifth and Fourteenth Amendments to the Constitution of the United States. The Fourteenth limits the legislative powers of the States, while the Fifth limits those of the Federal Government. The pertinent section of the Fourteenth Amendment reads as follows: "... nor shall any State deprive any person of life, liberty or property, without due process of law". A similar provision has been incorporated into the constitutions of the six New England States. Furthermore, the Supreme Court has solemnly declared that the freedom of parents to entrust their children to private schools where they receive, in part, instruction in their ethnic mother tongue, contains nothing counter to the common good[2] as long as certain essential information required by the State is not neglected. Thus this latter guarantee is not absolute, but it does exist to a comforting degree.

Ernest D'Amours has amply demonstrated that the following conclusions may be drawn from the texts of the constitutions of the six New England states regarding the teaching of foreign languages in private schools (D'Amours 1938): private schools are tolerated if their curricula include those studies required by the public schools, and if English is the medium of instruction in these studies. Beyond these studies a private school can teach a foreign language if this in no way prejudices the primary instruction required by the State. That even this toleration is not fully guaranteed can be easily demonstrated. In the period between the two World Wars a vast majority of the education officials in the New England States were English-speaking. Many of them were opposed to foreign language institutions at the elementary level or, at the very best, were apathetic toward such institutions. By overloading the required public school curriculum they could easily circumvent the constitutional guarantees upon which Franco-Americans depended for mother tongue instruction. Consequently, although Franco-American schools had the right to teach French, little time was accorded them in which to do so. The attitude of diocesan officials, whose primary concern, no doubt, was to upgrade elementary education in the parochial schools, but who also surely saw the possibility of working toward a more uniform church in New England through less emphasis on ethnic factors, clearly provided no obstacle to this development and probably abetted it.

THE SOCIETIES AND THE PRESS

The societies and the press also found the task of protecting the French-Canadian heritage increasingly arduous during the period 1918-1945. It was frequently observed that Franco-American children born in the United States did not have the same loyalty for the land of their ancestors that had marked their parents and grandparents (Leboeuf 1938, p. 204). The mission of the societies and the press was now felt

---

[2]   The right of parents to send their children to private schools was upheld in the famous case of *Pierce v. Society of Sisters*, 268 U.S. 510, decided in 1925, and involving an Oregon statute requiring all children to attend public schools. The court held that this statute was in violation of the 14th Amendment. In 1922 the same Court had determined in four different cases that the right to speak and teach a foreign language in private schools was also guaranteed by Article 14 of the Bill of Rights. These cases are *Meyer v. Nebraska, Bartels v. Iowa, Bohning v. Ohio, and Pohl v. Ohio*, all reported in 262 U. S. 390. One year after the Pierce case, in 1926, a statute of Hawaii was the occasion for a declaration by the United States Supreme Court that Article 5 of the Constitution guaranteed that the education of children belonged of right to their parents and any unreasonable restriction preventing the free exercise thereof was prohibited. The case is *Farrington v. Tokushige*, 273 U. S. 284.

to be to support the Church, the school, and the family in their efforts to orient the native-born in the "proper" direction. The trouble, however, was in defining and formulating this orientation. Aside from similarly-phrased, well-meaning manifestoes and public proclamations of lofty principles, no clear, broadly-supported plan of operation, capable of galvanizing the masses into a concerted effort to maintain their cultural and linguistic heritage, came forth. The problem of living biculturally in an environment that tended toward de-ethnicized conformity could not be solved by manifestoes.

TABLE 10.3

All Franco-American marriages contracted in Fall River, Mass.,
for the Years 1880, 1912, 1937, and 1961[a]

	1880	1912	1937	1961	Total
Total Number	97	334	432	373	1236
Both Parties Franco-American	83	231	218	77	609
Percentage	86%	70%	50%	20%	49%
Total One Member non-Franco-American	14	103	214	296	627
Percentage	14%	30%	50%	80%	51%
Total Both Parties R.C.	93	303	352	299	1047
Percentage	96%	90%	81%	80%	85%
Total One member non-R.C.	4	31	80	74	189
	4%	10%	19%	20%	15%

[a] From the records of the City Clerk's Office, City Hall, Fall, River, Mass.

"Resistance" leaders warred as well against the rising trend of intermarriage. Although Franco-Americans rarely married non-Catholics, they now freely intermarried with the Irish and other non-French Catholics. In the strong Franco-American community of Woonsocket, Rhode Island, only 7% of the first generation and 8.8% of the second had contracted mixed marriages. In contrast, fully 35% of the third generation entered into such marriages. Mixed marriages seemed to occur most frequently among educated Franco-Americans. Such individuals frequently preserved their mother tongue after marriage but it was rare indeed for their children to be able to speak French. Often they attended the territorial churches of their spouses and avoided the label "Franco-American".

Most Franco-Americans interested in ethnic survival relied heavily on the family as a significant force for language maintenance. However, this institution was seriously weakened by assimilation in city environments. Although an appreciable number of Franco-Americans had located in American rural districts, it was chiefly in the industrial centers that they were concentrated. Census figures show that in 1920, 84.2% of Franco-Americans in New England lived in cities, while the national urban proportion at that time was 76.8%. Massachusetts and Rhode Island boasted the largest percentages of Franco-American city dwellers, 96.4% and 99.6% respectively. It became fairly common practice for most parents to speak to their children in French and to receive answers in English. All in all, the young spent less and less time at home. Even when the depression of 1929 temporarily put a halt to many outside social activities, evenings were spent listening to the radio, a pastime that was to hasten the assimilation process. Undoubtedly many Franco-Americans were able to listen to French programs from Canada, and there were a few French-language broadcasts in New England. On the whole, however, the habit of family-listening to popular American programs opened the portals wide to the English language within the family context.

In spite of this, the Franco-American family was relatively slow to change. Parents did not encourage their children to leave home in order to "succeed in life". Members of the family frequently lived close together even after marriage, and obtaining positions elsewhere was frowned upon because separation would weaken family ties. They lived the byword of General de Castelnau: "Family first! The rest, if the family is strong, united and prosperous, will come of itself".[3] Nevertheless, family traditionalism could not counteract the environment of the large cities. Faced with the apparent indifference or powerlessness of the masses in the face of assimilation, Franco-American leaders hinged their hopes on an "elite", an amorphous group still vitally interested in the French language and in ethnic values.

ADJUSTING TO THE INEVITABLE: THE CURRENT SCENE

America's contribution to the Allied cause in World War II increased its prestige throughout the world, and civic pride reached an all-time high throughout the nation. More than ever Franco-Americans now wanted to be recognized as 100% Americans. Whatever their occupational or social standing, they cared less and less to be identified with an ethnic group. They read the comic strips every day, watched "soap operas" on TV, and consciously as well as subconsciously identified with these and other projections of the American image. An "American" prototype always proved to be dominant, was predictable in appearance and in name, was always a white-collar worker or a professional, was middle-class in outlook and culture, each family with its home in Suburbia (Herberg 1956, pp. 33-35).

Nevertheless, Franco-American organizations still sought to remedy their waning influence over the masses. After sincere but for the most part ineffectual attempts to recapture their original influence an increasing number of leaders accepted the new "elite" concept. The masses were now only superficially affected by the ethnic organizations. For all practical purposes, the youth ignored the very existence of the societies.

Two main arguments were advanced for the introduction of English in the "French" churches – one financial, the other theological.

---

[3] "Famille d'abord! Et le reste, si la famille est forte, unie et prospère, viendra par surcroît." Congrès de Lille, December 5, 1920.

Franco-American parishes had been losing parishioners steadily, with mixed marriages probably being the primary reason. Experience had shown that couples of mixed national origins do not, as a rule, attend a church in which one of them does not understand the sermon. Catholics in this country have the "right of option", that is, the right to transfer from a "national" parish to a territorial church. Parishioners would learn English and join a territorial parish, so that by 1957, for example, there were 19,000 Franco-Americans in the "French" parishes of Fall River and 11,000 in the territorial parishes of that city. It was felt that the former parishioners were irrevocably lost and that unless the Franco-American pastors could miraculously stem the tide, the depletion of their parishes would continue and their financial problems become increasingly more acute.

From the point of view of theology, pastors realized the necessity to teach the Faith to their parishioners in a language they could understand. Therefore they felt an obligation to provide religious instruction in English to those of their flock who under-

TABLE 10.4

Franco-American Parochial and Private Educational Institutions, New England, 1961[a]

	Maine	%[b]	N.H.	%[b]	Vt.	%[b]	Mass.	%[b]	Conn.	%[b]	R.I.	%[b]	Total	%[b]
Parishes	66	(50)	55	(47)	21	(23)	95	(13)	21	(7)	26	(17)	284	(18)
Clergy	123	(37)	104	(26)	27	(12)	265	(8)	44	(4)	68	(11)	631	(10)
Elem. Paroch. Sch.	27	(52)	27	(47)	6	(24)	81	(22)	14	(9)	24	(25)	179	(24)
Nuns teaching	320		333		71		868	(15)	159		274		2,025	
Brothers teaching	27		4				1						32	
Lay teachers	19		10		8		54	(4)	18		21	(11)	130	
Paroch. High Sch.	4	(50)	7	(41)	1	(13)	12	(12)	1	(6)	3	(25)	28	(17)
Nuns teaching	30		72		5		81		5				193	
Brothers teaching	24		2				17						43	
Priests teaching							1						1	
Lay teachers	8		1				4						13	
Private Elem. Sch.	5	(71)	3	(50)			6	(15)			2	(25)	16	(20)
Nuns teaching	49		20				34				14		121	
Brothers teaching	5						9				14		28	
Lay teachers	1						2						3	
Private High Sch.	6	(75)	3	(60)			9	(23)	1	(6)	4	(50)	23	(31)
Nuns teaching	84		23				109		11		6		233	
Brother teaching	5										34	(32)	39	
Priests teaching	13						28						41	
	2		2				22		1				27	
Private colleges	2	(50)	2	(50)			2	(18)	1	(20)			7	(19)
Nuns teaching			39				22		14				75	
Priests teaching	19						18		1				38	
Lay teachers	9						31		5				45	

[a] Data derived from *Official Catholic Directory* but not limited to schools in parishes officially designated as French "national" parishes.

[b] Percent Franco-American of Diocesan total.

stood little or no French. Instead of being the "keeper of the Faith" that it once was, the French language had become an instrument of religious ignorance (Lemaire 1961, p. 45).

French as a subject of formal instruction in parochial schools likewise suffered setbacks. Inasmuch as the teaching of foreign languages received a strong impetus in the United States in World War II, when the Federal Government became concerned with the serious lack of language training in this country, one would think such a change in national outlook would have stimulated Franco-Americans to a renewed interest in maintaining their mother tongue. However, many former Franco-American G.I.'s remembered that they were embarrassed by deficiency in English during the war – rather than by a deficiency in French. Vowing their children would never have to face such embarrassment, they sent them to public schools or insisted on more and better English (rather than French) in the parochial schools. The national need for language proficiency is less personally relevant than second-generation insecurity and mobility strivings.

Many Franco-Americans who belong to "national" parishes send their children to public schools. Moreover, large numbers have left the Franco-American parish and its schools altogether. Too, the character of the "French" schools is itself changing. Not only do they follow State laws pertaining to the curriculum, they are also more closely supervised by diocesan school directors. The sudden growth of the Catholic population in certain areas – as, for example, when military personnel began establishing themselves with their families near the bases where they were stationed in the postwar period – has forced many Franco-American schools to admit large numbers of non-French children who otherwise would have been denied a Catholic education. Interestingly enough, changes such as these have rarely produced pressure from the parents of the "new elements" to eliminate French from the curriculum. As a matter of fact, they generally consider a strong foreign-language program at the elementary level to be a decidely attractive feature. The French program in Franco-American schools frequently finds its strongest supporters in the parent group having no French linguistic or cultural heritage. The attitude of the parents in this respect is clearly reflected in the strong motivation of non-Franco-American pupils who show a laudable, and to the teacher a somewhat embarrassing, rate of increased proficiency when compared with their native-speaking classmates.

The quality of French taught in many of these schools is good. Practically all teachers are Franco-Americans and are fully bilingual. Most received their early training in similar parochial schools and their later training in institutions where French was heard both inside and outside the classroom. However, French cannot be taught today as it was a generation ago. Then, when a child entered school, he often knew no English while he spoke and understood French fluently. Teachers proceeded to teach reading, writing, and grammar much as English is taught in the public schools today. But the toll of assimilation has been heavy, and today most Franco-American children enter school unable to speak French, often even unable to understand it. Some children, gifted for languages, learn French quickly and speak it well, perhaps better than their parents speak it. Altogether too many, however, do poorly and struggle through eight years of French with little to show for their efforts. Others are withdrawn from the parochial school after a few years and are sent to public schools, for it has become the practice among parents to blame a child's poor performance in the parochial school on the "added burden" of a foreign language.

French has become less attractive to an increasing number of Franco-American parochial school pupils with each passing year, primarily because old-fashioned teaching methods have not kept pace with social transition. In many schools modern instructional equipment is lacking and textbooks are hopelessly outdated and unattractive. Many of the texts employed were printed in Canada years ago; their topics hold little interest for young Franco-Americans today. In Franco-American high schools, teachers are similarly unsuccessful in coping with the new situation even though their pupils are a more select group. They usually manage to "salvage" only one small group of students who can follow a traditional French program. The remainder are taught a minimum of French, often in an ineffectual way, always with poor results.

In past generations, French was taught with little or no regard for comparisons with standard French. Many teachers spoke "Canayen", or "joual" (the current term for "jargon" used in the Province of Quebec today) (Bro. Pierre-Jerome 1960, p. 23). This caused their pupils little or no discomfort since, with few exceptions, the French they heard all around them was non-standard. Indeed, any child attempting to speak standard French would have been considered a snob. The situation today is completely the opposite. Children are fully aware of the stigma associated with non-standard speech, and those whose parents still speak French realize that it is a relatively "poor" brand. They are often ashamed of it and rarely want to speak it even when they know it well enough to do so. This, of course, places an added responsibility on the teachers who must, first of all, realize the problem, and then undertake to cope with it. Most Franco-American teachers of French have sufficient command of standard French and are positively oriented toward it, so that the transition to teaching standard French is usually one of goodwill on their part.

A continued sore point with many conservative Franco-Americans is the teaching of religion, or catechism, in the schools. Many still believe that Faith and language are interdependent, and insist that the catechism be taught in French. Though many teachers might like to do this, it is a very difficult and sometimes impossible goal to attain with children who know little, if any, French. As a result, religion is "explained" in English in most Franco-American elementary schools. In some cases, French texts are still used and "parrot-recitation" is resorted to. The same problem exists in the parochial high schools. French texts are used in some schools but explanations have to be given in English almost everywhere. It is generally felt that most students prefer to study religion in English, that they do not know French well enough to grasp the more difficult dogmas when expressed in that language, and that the English texts are more up-to-date, more attractive, and more "American" (Lemaire 1961, p. 44).

From the foregoing, one might be tempted to conclude that French is now a negligible element in Franco-American education. Such is not the case. Pupils with linguistic aptitude learn as much French as their parents did and speak it as well if not as often. Obviously, slower pupils learn little French because they lack the reinforcement of follow-through at home. Nevertheless, Franco-American schools still teach enough French to enable better students to converse fluently and to fare well in local and regional contests sponsored by various societies. Some go on to major in French and are now doing invaluable work as bilingual teachers of French in public or parochial schools at every level of instruction.

Even Assumption College in Worcester, Massachusetts, the once proud hope of the advocates of ethnic survival, has had to bow to the needs of the new generation. It was always evident that its small enrollment was an obstacle to efficient operation. Only very wealthy American colleges continue to operate with an enrollment of under three hundred students. In 1950, after nearly fifty years of operation, Assumption College still had only 182 students. That same year Holy Cross College, also in Worcester, had 125 students of Franco-American nationality. If to this number were added the Franco-Americans attending Boston College, Providence College, St. Anselm's College and St. Michael's College, to name only the better-known Catholic institutions in New England, not to mention the non-Catholic colleges in the area, the proportion attending Assumption was small indeed. The type of program offered was simply not attractive to the majority of Franco-Americans. The Superiors finally decided that it was better to save the college than to sacrifice it to a lost cause. Assumption has now organized a considerably modernized bilingual program and has opened its doors to students of any ethnic origin interested in a liberal arts education (D'Amours 1960-61, p. 13). Sweeping changes in the regulations governing student life have made the campus atmosphere that of a typical American Catholic college.

The Societies, too, have been adjusting to the inevitable. Organizations have a tendency, anyway, to forget their original purpose and to concentrate on development. This has been true of most Franco-American societies. In the process of bureaucratization many of them lost the personal touch which had once been so attractive to their constituents. Most first-generation and many second-generation Franco-Americans continue their membership in the societies but they are far less active members than they were in former years. The average Franco-American of the third generation is little attracted to them, if at all. Anomalous as it may seem to strong partisans of linguistic and cultural continuity, the French language has become a barrier that keeps the young generation away from the societies. As French is the only language tolerated in official deliberations, the "young element" feels that the type of program offered is incompatible with its ideals and unsuited to its needs.

At the close of the Second Congress of the French Language, in Quebec in 1937, a permanent committee was organized, *Le Comité permanent de la Survivance Française en Amérique.* This was a general council of all French-language groups of North

TABLE 10.5

French Broadcasting in the United States

A. Number of Stations

	1956	1960
No. of Stations in New England according to: Broadcasting[b]	31	25
ACNS[c]	43	43
LRP[d]	—	39
No. of Stations in Louisiana according to: Broadcasting	14	12
ACNS	18	17
LRP	—	17
No. of Stations in Rest of U.S.A. according to: Broadcasting	8	10
ACNS	12	23
LRP	—	21
Total No. of Stations according to: Broadcasting	53	47
ACNS	73	83
LRP	—	77

B. Hours/Week of French Language Broadcasting

	1956			1960		
	N[a]	Hrs./Wk.	Av. Hrs.	N	Hrs./Wk.	Av. Hrs.
Hours/Week in New England according to: Broadcasting	31	80.25	2.59	24	49.50	2.06
ACNS	34	83.50	2.46	40	92.75	2.32
LRP	—	—	—	38	105.75	2.78
Hours/Week in Louisiana according to: Broadcasting	14	74.50	5.32	12	111.75	9.31
ACNS	13	70.75	5.44	15	117.25	7.82
LRP	—	—	—	16	124.50	7.78
Hours/Week in Rest of U.S.A. according to: Broadcasting	8	6.00	.75	10	9.50	.95
ACNS	9	6.50	.72	21	15.50	.74
LRP	—	—	—	19	17.75	.93
Total Hours/Week according to: Broadcasting	53	160.75	3.03	46	170.75	3.71
ACNS	56	160.75	2.87	76	225.50	2.97
LRP	—	—	—	73	248.00	3.40

[a] N = number of stations for which information is available on hours/week of French language broadcasting.

[b] *Broadcasting Yearbook - Marketbook Issue*, 1956 and 1960.

[c] *Radio Stations in the United States Broadcasting Foreign Language Programs*, New York, American Council for Nationalities Service, 1956 and 1960.

[d] Language Resources Project.

America with headquarters in the city of Quebec. All French-speaking groups on the continent thus would work together against the forces of assimilation. This committee encountered no more than indifference in many circles in New England. The very word *Survivance* was unpopular with people who had had enough of clashes and conflicts and was reminiscent of the *Sentinelle* "affair". In 1952, at the Third Congress of the French Language, the name of the committee was changed to *Le Conseil de la Vie Française en Amérique*. This council, very influential in the Province of Quebec, includes several Franco-Americans. It maintains close liaison with the major Franco-American groups in New England. On January 29, 1947, in Boston, the *Comité d'Orientation Franco-Américaine* was founded. This committee, specifically Franco-American, "would study the problem of survival; would establish an historic, concrete, and common goal for all Franco-Americans to pursue; would conduct a survey of the resources available for its realization; in order to unite all Franco-Americans in the methodical and unified pursuit of survival". In the first sixteen years of its existence, the *Comité* organized six conventions of the Franco-Americans of New England: 1949, in Worcester, Massachusetts; 1951, in Lewiston, Maine; 1954, in Manchester, New Hampshire; 1957, in Woonsocket, Rhode Island; 1959, in Fall River, Massachusetts; and 1961, in Hartford, Connecticut. In 1957, when it was felt that the period of orientation had been completed, the committee changed its name to *Le Comité de Vie Franco-Américaine*. It has founded several subsidiary groups in an attempt to consolidate organizations dispersed throughout New England. Although all of these groups are autonomous, they receive guidance and support from the *Comité de Vie Franco-Américaine*.

One of these, *L'Alliance Radiophonique Française*, founded in 1950, is a loosely federated organization of some twenty-five Franco-American directors of French-language radio broadcasts in New England. Their programs vary from serious discussions and the enacting of French classics to soap operas and folk music. Unlike periodic publications, radio programs operate with little overhead. Most are broadcast one hour a week, but some areas such as Lewiston, Maine; Manchester, and Nashua, New Hampshire; Woonsocket, Rhode Island; Holyoke and Fall River, Massachusetts have several programs, some daily and others broadcast for two or three hours per week. Even where total ethnic assimilation has taken place, French radio programs attract the attention of those Franco-Americans who have retained an interest in French culture, as well as the attention of Americans of other backgrounds for whom French language, music, and "culture" are matters of interest or pleasure.

Currently, a new type of club for Franco-American men is winning favor in New England. The *Clubs Richelieu*, organized along the same lines as service clubs throughout the United States, appeal especially to professionals and businessmen. That these clubs are popular in spite of the fact that only French may be spoken at the bi-monthly meetings bears proof that there is a "twice-a-month" interest in promoting French culture. Since 1955, ten *Clubs Richelieu* have been founded in New England, totaling about 350 members.

TABLE 10.6

The French Periodic Press in the United States

Columns 2–13 fall under **A. Publications appearing entirely in French**; columns 14–25 fall under **B. Mixed (French and English) publications**. For each group the sub-headings are Dailies, Weeklies etc., Monthlies etc., and Total, each with N, Circ., and Na.

Year and Region	Dailies N	Circ.	Na	Weeklies, etc. N	Circ.	Na	Monthlies, etc. N	Circ.	Na	Total N	Circ.	Na	Dailies N	Circ.	Na	Weeklies, etc. N	Circ.	Na	Monthlies, etc. N	Circ.	Na	Total N	Circ.	Na
1930: [b]New Eng.	5	213	4	16	678	12	1	480	1	22	1371	17							1			1		
Rest of USA	2	109	2	2	38	1	2			6	147	3				5	105	3				5	105	3
Total	7	322	6	18	716	13	3	480	1	28	1518	20				5	105	3	1			6	105	3
1940: New Eng.	5	222	5	13	373	7	1	447	1	19	1042	13				1	20	1	2	12	1	3	32	2
Rest of USA	1	31	1	1	68	1	2	20	1	4	119	3				3	103	2	1	80	1	4	183	3
Total	6	253	6	14	441	8	3	467	2	23	1161	16				4	123	3	3	92	2	7	215	5
1950: New Eng.	2	85	2	11	298	8	2	469	1	15	852	11				2	22	1	1			3	22	1
Rest of USA				2	33	1	3	48	2	5	81	3				1	14	1	2	44	1	3	58	2
Total	2	85	2	13	331	9	5	517	3	20	933	14				3	36	2	3	44	1	6	80	3
1960: New Eng.	1	37	1	7	201	6	2	625	2	10	863	9							1			1		
Rest of USA				1	17	1	2	300	2	3	317	3				1	12	1	1	47	1	2	59	2
Total	1	37	1	8	218	7	4	925	4	13	1180	12				1	12	1	2	47	1	3	59	2
LRP 1960: N. Eng.	1	37	1	7	349	6	3	457	2	11	843	9							1			1		
Rest of USA				1	12	1	3	19	3	4	31	4				1	12	1	1	47	1	2	59	2
Total	1	37	1	8	361	7	5	476	5	15	874	13				1	12	1	2	47	1	3	59	2

[a] N = number of periodic publications for which circulation data are available. Last two digits have been dropped in circulation figures.

[b] data based upon Ayer's *Directory*.

As for the press, the severe financial problems facing all newspapers in America have contributed to the decline of the Franco-American press. The polemical, even factional character of many of these newspapers has been an additional source of their weakness. But above all, the dwindling interest among the younger generation and the strident ethnic appeals of the more aged editors have hastened the disappearance of many Franco-American newspapers during the last two decades (Walker 1961, p. 13). *L'Indépendant* of Fall River, Massachusetts, became a weekly in November, 1962, marking the end of the last French-language daily in the United States. It was published as a weekly only until mid-January, 1963, when it was discontinued entirely. Six other weekly newspapers remain, with English steadily displacing more and more French from their pages.

Literature and the arts attract increasing numbers of Franco-Americans. Poetry and the Franco-American novel have recently appeared in greater quantity and in far better quality than in earlier years. Historians and journalists have become more plentiful. But most Franco-Americans write in English, probably because the English readership is infinitely vaster in this country. The most famous Franco-American author is undoubtedly Will Durant, the historian-philosopher, considered to be one of America's finest "popular scholars". Although Franco-Americans have excelled in many of the arts, notably music, they have yet to make a highly distinctive or visible contribution as a group to the culture of America.

Along with the weakening of their ethnic involvement, Franco-Americans have experienced in the last two decades their greatest social progress. Most of them credit better education and, notably, increased knowledge of English as the chief factors in their social advancement. Many have ascended several steps higher in the professions and in business and many are becoming property owners and moving to the suburbs. While the advantages of higher education are becoming increasingly more evident to them, this does not mean that they have become a scholarly group positively oriented toward scholarship per se; it does mean that they place greater emphasis on their children's education. More and more Franco-American youngsters graduate from high school and go on to college. This is an investment in social mobility if in nothing else.

Franco-Americans show the undeniable effects of urbanization. The city tends to destroy cultural distinctiveness, family primacy, and traditional behavior – among ethnics and non-ethnics alike. Many Franco-Americans have already lost their ethnic identity. In many cities most of them cannot be differentiated from other Americans.

The ethnic situation of Franco-Americans, then, is self-evident. Their ethnic behavioral particularities have become less distinctive. The institutional structure supporting the unity of *La Franco-Américaine* has shown increasing signs of weakness. The evidence points to further assimilation in the future. The process is unlikely to be reversed. It is equally unlikely that it can be appreciably slowed down. On the contrary, it will very probably be more rapid in the next twenty-five years than it has been in the past.

THE FUTURE OF THE FRENCH LANGUAGE IN NEW ENGLAND

The growing awareness in American educational and governmental circles of the dearth of non-English language skills necessary for the maintenance of optimal commercial, diplomatic, and cultural ties with the rest of the world has given new momentum to foreign languages in the United States. The language resources of American immigrant groups are coming to be seen as a huge and valuable treasure which should be recognized as such and protected from the ravages of apathy and antipathy. Undoubtedly, official support (rather than merely non-interference) is a new departure in American life. Its impact on the language situation could well be decisive, both for the minority groups and for the future of American society itself (Fishman 1962, pp. 60-61).

The Federal Government paid special tribute to Franco-Americans by sponsoring the Franco-American Institute at Bowdoin College, in the summers of 1961 and 1962. This language institute, originated and directed by Dr. Gerard J. Brault, a young Franco-American now Associate Professor of Romance Languages at the University of Pennsylvania, was made possible by the terms of the National Defense Education Act, under the auspices of the Department of Health, Education and Welfare. Unlike any other in the country, it admitted only Franco-American teachers of French. These bilingual men and women were trained to teach French "in the New Key", but with particular emphasis on the Franco-American situation. They studied the basic lexical and phonetic difficulties Franco-Americans encounter when transferring to standard French and prepared an experimental French text and tapes for use with Franco-American pupils. A new doctrine was developed, new methods and techniques were tested experimentally. In each of the summers, 1961 and 1962, there were thirty lay teachers, men and women, and ten religious teachers at the Institute. Many of these teachers returned to Franco-American parochial schools, while others are now teaching in public schools were there is a preponderance of Franco-American pupils.

Six motivational factors were agreed upon as being of importance in attracting young Franco-Americans to study French:

(i) Pupils must be assured that the course will be interesting and worthwhile. They will more readily accept a modern approach than the old-fashioned methods against which they will have been prejudiced by their older brothers and sisters.

(ii) They must be made to feel that they already know a good deal of French and that, with a little effort and good will, they can speak as well as any "Parisian".

(iii) They must be led to love the heritage represented by their language. If they are ashamed of their Franco-American background, they will frequently lose interest in the language. They must be taught the highlights of French-Canadian history with appropriate references to France. The many contributions of France to the origin and to the civilization of the United States will give them reason to be justifiably proud.

(iv) Parents must be asked to help out but there must be no attempt to turn back the clock. That French will probably never be used again in daily communication seems almost a certainty. Rather, parents should be asked to encourage their children to learn French well and to learn it correctly, i.e., to learn standard French if they are going to study the language at all.

(v) For the time being, wherever possible, classes should be organized homogeneously in the first year of high school. There is nothing more dispiriting for those Franco-American students who have had eight years of French in a parochial elementary school than to be placed with pupils who have had no French at all, in a French I class in high school. On the other hand, experience has shown that many of these same Franco-American pupils are overconfident and become discouraged by the different standards of the high school course, neglect to study, and frequently fail to derive any benefit from the course. In a homogeneous group, Franco-American pupils can be taught to use what they already know, which is considerable, and to absorb new vocabulary and acquire standard French pronunciation.

(vi) Finally, the appeal of doing something in the *national* interest is perhaps the most important motive. Learning a foreign language has become the ambition of a great number of Americans. It is now patriotic to want to speak French.

Prestige is an instrumental attachment which moves many people to want to learn standard French. Other instrumental attachments related to the study of French, among Franco-Americans as among others, are the possibility of a good position in the diplomatic service, in the import-export trade, in teaching, in careers on the operatic and concert stage, in newspaper and magazine editing, in translating and interpreting, in bilingual stenography, in employment at United Nations headquarters and at other specialized agencies, and in numerous other endeavors. In general, Franco-American teachers of French must adopt certain "Madison Avenue tactics" if they seek to attract the young.

Parochial schools have always been regarded by Franco-American leaders as the backbone of resistance to assimilation. They have always believed that as long as French was taught in their schools its survival would be assured. In spite of strong opposition from within and without the Franco-American fold, the number of Franco-American parochial elementary schools continued to grow. In 1910, there were 114 such schools and in 1960 there were 179, an increase of 57%. These schools reached their peak enrollment in 1930 with a 66.5% increase over that of 1910. What happened after 1930 is difficult to pinpoint, but the symptoms are rather telling. Although the number of schools continued to multiply and the total Franco-American population continued to grow, the enrollment in Franco-American parochial schools decreased – first by 7% in the decade 1930-40, and then by 17% in that of 1940-50. During this period, pressures of all kinds were placed on religious orders of brothers and nuns to "Americanize" their schools, to give their teachers better training in English, to update their methods and their equipment. Most of them complied with this "new look" in parochial school education. Although there is no unquestionable proof that these efforts had any direct impact on enrollment, it remains true that not only did the downward trend come to a halt, but Franco-American parochial elementary school enrollment increased by 10% from 1950 to 1960.

There are still those who decry the changes that have taken place in these schools, particularly the restriction of French instruction to one period per day. However, such critics are few in number and their influence is felt less and less. There are many more who believe that the French language is now taught as well as, if not better than, in previous years. The Franco-American parochial schools of the future will probably continue to offer essentially the same academic program as the public schools of New England. If they progress as they have in the last ten to fifteen years, they will indeed be an invaluable asset to the nation as well as to the ethnic group they serve.

Many Franco-American high schools, both parochial and private, have opened their doors to youngsters of all backgrounds. Being of more recent organizational origin, they have adapted themselves more quickly to the new order. In consequence, their growth has not been hampered and has continued uninterruptedly to the present day. The whole picture of the Franco-American schools is much healthier and brighter than that of the societies, the press, or other formal organizations.

The two largest Franco-American societies, *L'Union Saint-Jean-Baptiste d'Amérique* and the *Association Canado-Américaine*, boast libraries of French, French-Canadian, and Franco-American publications. The Lambert Library at the *Association Canado-Américaine* in Manchester, New Hampshire, is unequalled in its collection of Franco-American documents and correspondence dating from the early immigration period to the present day. The Mallet Library at *L'Union Saint-Jean-Baptiste d'Amérique* in Woonsocket, Rhode Island, is potentially an equally fine research center in Franco-American lore. These societies, together with the other large mutuals, promote education by granting scholarships to needy members. This type of sponsorship can undoubtedly stimulate a greater interest in French, by encouraging those who show an aptitude for and a desire to further their language studies.

The *Société Historique Franco-Américaine* is potentially the best coordinator of the various Franco-American cultural interests. Its purpose is acceptable to all Franco-Americans, as are its methods and activities. It has its limitations, however. There is only one unit for all New England. Meetings are held twice a year, usually in Boston, where a small group of Franco-Americans hears distinguished speakers, prominent in French circles. These meetings are significant for many reasons but there is a noticeable absence of youth. The goals of the *Société Historique* are too important to be taken lightly. No one advocates abolishing the *Société* or changing its present organization. Rather, there are those who would like it to serve as the guiding light for smaller groups throughout New England. Some would like to see it branch out into local chapters, where discussion groups would do the same work on a smaller scale. Many serious Franco-Americans believe the *Société Historique Franco-Américaine* is the most important medium of cultural exchange and creativity still remaining for Franco-Americans.

Finally, there is *Le Comité de Vie Franco-Américaine* and its subsidiaries. It is a very active and influential group but only at the upper echelons. There are two schools of thought within the *Comité*. Some want to keep it as it is, claiming it was never meant to be a "popular club", that it was organized to serve a more lofty purpose, that of developing a philosophy, a code of ethnics, which would orient the Franco-American toward a more meaningful expression of his ethnicity. Others want to avoid such "ivory tower" connotations. They want the *Comité* to work more closely with the people, to be "practical"rather than "philosophical". The *Comité* as a whole is much interested in youth and plans to invite several young and promising Franco-Americans to join its ranks. It is also considering a modification in its forthcoming conventions so as to provide for greater participation on the part of all delegates, with a serious attempt to get to the heart of certain key problems.

As for the press, the small individual Franco-American newspapers are struggling for survival. Figures on the French-language press show that it has declined so radically in the last fifty years that any extrapolation of the trend would indicate that it is bound to disappear entirely in the near future. At the time of this writing, a study is being made by the *Comité de Vie Franco-Américaine* of the advisability of creating a new French-language newspaper which would appeal to cultured Franco-Americans throughout New England.

Generally speaking, one must conclude that the present generation is forsaking the the French language and Franco-American ethnic traditions and self-concepts. However, new hopes are rising, an expanding elite is studying the French language so as to speak it correctly – and this no longer for sentimental or ethnic reasons only, but with more practical motives, such as ambition, social prestige, and cultural eagerness.

French, therefore, will continue to be spoken in New England; and though it will not be used as widely as before, it will be of a more generally acceptable quality. Those who speak it will do so because they want to. While true bilinguals are a rarity in the United States today, many Franco-Americans *are* bilingual and many more will have an opportunity to *become* so. The rising Franco-American generation speaks English as well as any group in the country. Those who choose to preserve or to learn French will develop a new insight into American culture which should bring them much personal satisfaction, and perhaps profit as well. Whereas many predicted that the history of the French language in New England would come to a close in this generation, it seems rather to have taken on a new aspect and to be proceeding in an unexpectedly hopeful direction.

REFERENCES

Bachand, T. R. P. and Louis, O. M., "L'école paroissiale franco-américaine", *La Croisade Franco-Américaine, Deuxième Congrès de la Langue Française, Québec, 1937* (Manchester, L'Avenir National, 1938).

Bracq, J. C., *L'Evolution du Canada Français* (Paris, Plon, 1927).

Brother Pierre-Jerome, Marist, *Les Insolences du Frère Untel* (Montréal, Les Editions de l'Homme, 1960).

Cadieux, L. E., "L'enseignement du français dans les centres canadiens-français de la Nouvelle Angleterre", *Mémoires Premier Congrès de la Langue Française, Québec 1912* (Québec, Imprimerie de l'Action Sociale, 1914).

Carrière, J. M., *Pronunciation of the French Spoken in Brunswick, Maine* (Greensboro, University of North Carolina, American Dialect Society, 1949).

Daignault, E., *Le Vrai Mouvement Sentinelliste* (Montreal, Editions du Zodiaque, Deon Frere, 1935).

D'Amours, E. R., "La situation juridique du français en Nouvelle Angleterre", *La Croisade Franco-Américaine, Deuxième Congrès de la Langue Française, Québec, 1937* (Manchester, L'Avenir National, 1938).

——, "Le Collège de l'Assomption de Worcester", *Le Canado-Américain*, 2 (1960-61), No. 4, 10-17.

Ducharme, J., *The Shadows of the Trees* (New York, Harper, 1943).

Fishman, J. A., "How Have Franco-Americans Fared in Preserving the French Language in the United States?", *Les Conférences de l'Institut Franco-Américain de Bowdoin College* (Brunswick, Maine, 1962).

Guillet, J. H., "La langue française et les associations", *Mémoires, Premier Congrès de la Langue Française, Québec, 1912* (Québec, Imprimerie de l'Action Sociale Ltd., 1914).

Gunther, J., *Inside U.S.A.* (New York, Harper, 1947).

Herberg, W., *Protestant-Catholic-Jew* (Garden City, Doubleday, 1956).

Lauvrière, E., *La Tragédie D'un Peuple* (Paris, Goulet, 1924).

Leboeuf, T., "Nos sociétés nationales", *La Croisade Franco-Américaine, Deuxième Congrès de la Langue Française, Québec, 1937* (Manchester, L'Avenir National, 1938).

Lemaire, H., "Les Franco-Américains de Fall River", *Les Conférences de L'Institut Franco-Américain de Bowdoin College* (Brunswick, Maine, 1961).

Lemoine, A., *L'Evolution de la Race Française en Amérique*, Tome I (Montreal, Librairie Beauchemin, 1921).

de Nevers, E., *L'Ame Américaine – Les Origines – La Vie historique*, Tomes I et II (Paris, Jouvé & Boyer, 1900).

Niebuhr, H. R., *The Social Sources of Denominationalism* (New New York, Holt, 1929).

Rumilly, R., *Histoire des Franco-Américains* (Montréal, L'Union Saint-Jean-Baptiste d'Amérique, 1958).

Siegfried, A., *America Comes of Age*. Tr. by H. S. and Doris Heming. (New York, Harcourt, 1927).

Theriault, G. F., "The Franco-Americans of New England", in *Canadian Dualism*, Mason Wade, ed. (Toronto, University of Toronto Press, 1960), pp. 392-411.

Therriault, Sister Mary Carmel, S. M., *La Littérature française de Nouvelle Angleterre* (Montreal, Fides, 1946).

Walker, D. B., *Politics and Ethnocentrism: The Case of the Franco-Americans* (Brunswick, Maine, Bowdoin College Bureau for Research in Municipal Government, 1961).

11. SPANISH LANGUAGE AND CULTURE IN THE SOUTHWEST

JANE MACNAB CHRISTIAN AND CHESTER C. CHRISTIAN, Jr.

Spanish, like all languages, simultaneously preserves and is carried by a distinctive culture. It serves to set apart the societal group which adheres to it. For nearly four centuries the Spanish-speaking group in the United States has maintained much of its original character, but it has suffered many vicissitudes of fortune during its sojourn in the Southwest. The status and nature of its language reflect these circumstances.

In 1598 the first relatively permanent Spanish settlements were made in what is now New Mexico, more than half a century after Spanish conquistadores had entered, explored, and claimed the Southwest as part of New Spain. These few proud conquerors optimistically envisioned Spanish sway over all the *tierra del norte* with its benighted natives and vast expanses. For approximately three centuries Spanish remained the tongue of conquerors and rulers in the Southwest, and in each of the native tribes at least a few Indians learned this dominant language.

This is, of course, only part of the story. Spanish expansion into the Southwest was coincident with the decline of Spanish national and imperial power; the northern frontier was safeguarded by Spain primarily to resist encroachment from other nations, an enterprise that proved to be an overextension of her military and populating capacities. Politically, economically, and socially, the Southwest never formed an integral part of New Spain. The hazards of rugged desert terrain, tremendous distances, enemies, poverty, and an official indifference to local conditions forced the early conquerors and settlers into a stalemated position. They became the victims of isolation and neglect, so that their culture and language reflected ever more simply and provincially the glories of Spain. New Mexican Spanish, for example, remained much as Cervantes and Coronado had used it in the 16th century, its archaic character persisting in out-of-the-way places even to the present day. By 1823 Spain had been driven out of the New World and the Southwest was governed by the Republic of Mexico, but the United States moved swiftly onto the scene. In an almost bloodless conquest in 1846, General Stephen W. Kearne occupied the area, urging the residents – in their native Spanish – not to resist. When the Treaty of Guadelupe-Hidalgo assigned the Mexican Cession to the United States in 1848, its predominantly Spanish-speaking inhabitants became citizens of a new nation.

English-speaking migrants flooded into the Southwest, inundating the old settlers with a foreign language and culture. However, they did not force the older residents to relinquish most of their time-honored ways, nor did they mix sufficiently with them to make Anglo ways and the English language readily available. Nevertheless, Spanish became the language of the conquered, of second-class citizens. Although it was retained as an important tongue in the Southwest, spoken by millions of people, it persisted more through lack of overpowering interference than through active efforts to maintain its vigor. The strong persistence of the language in this century is also due in part to the proximity of Mexico and to the immigration of millions of people from that country, most of them coming for short periods and usually without the skills or motivation necessary to acquire a new language and culture. Furthermore, cross-cultural contacts have been discouraged – often by both groups – and this lack of mutual acceptance or understanding between the Hispanos and the dominant English-speaking "Anglos" has also served to inhabit acquisition of English among the former.

Compounding this more general isolation was that of many smaller Spanish-speaking communities throughout the region. The Spanish-speaking people of the Southwest never formed a cohesive unit, even before 1846. Towering mountains, deserts, hostile Indian tribes, a government that did not encourage freedom of movement or of trade and could offer less and less protection, the privation of life in a region where only a few scattered spots were favorable for habitation – all these combined to develop a type of Spanish settlement in the Southwest wherein individual communities increasingly folded in upon themselves. There was little opportunity to encourage literacy, formal learning, or appreciation of the niceties of civilization: beautiful and ornate pieces of Spanish silver brought optimistically by the first settlers from Mexico ultimately found their way into the backyards where they held water for poultry and livestock. Folk tales, song, and drama passed on by word of mouth came to comprise the heights of literary creativity in Spanish. Only the vestiges of a once highly literate Spanish culture could survive the rigors of the Southwest; what remained might best be described as a folk society in which, by necessity, the main concern was with elemental needs – the maintenance of life itself – and only a very few relatively wealthy individuals could afford the luxury of literacy or education in the formal sense. Indeed, very few of this class could be persuaded to come to the Southwest unless so ordered by the dictates of civil, military, or clerical duties.

Three separate areas of the Southwest were colonized at different times by the Spanish. All have survived as identifiable entities, and have remained almost totally independent of one another. In New Mexico, the oldest and most firmly established province, nearly all settlement was limited by water scarcity and by raiding Indians to the upper Rio Grande Valley from Socorro, New Mexico to Alamosa, Colorado. The settlement of Texas occurred at about 1700 in slow stages. The northern frontier of Mexico progressed naturally to include some of the lower Rio Grande Valley. French encroachment into Louisiana brought retaliatory Spanish settlement of east-central Texas, and the creation of the *Provincia de Tejas*. This in turn necessitated the settlement of San Antonio to maintain the far-flung east Texas outposts. Meanwhile, the El Paso region had been settled as a result of Spanish retreat from a major Pueblo Indian uprising in New Mexico. However, the Spanish occupation of Texas was forced to contract more often than it could expand, largely because, in addition to factors listed above, the area between New Mexico and San Antonio was rapidly being taken over by the Comanches during the early 1700's. These Indians scourged the Spanish from Texas as far south as Durango, and effectively prevented much Spanish contact between Texas and New Mexico. Arizona never existed as a separate Spanish province, and received only minor attention as a mission field and as the only land route to California.

California, the third area, was always considered attractive, but ocean contact from Mexico was hazardous; a land route was not discovered until about 1700, and the momentum necessary to colonize the region built up only when the British and Russians threatened to take it. By the 1770's, Spain succeeded in creating permanent communities on the coast of Southern California from San Diego to Yerba Buena (San Francisco). Even though an Indian revolt soon closed Spanish land access to California and left the province virtually isolated, it suffered less than the rest of the Spanish Southwest. Its settlers and area had greater political importance, the land was productive, and the Indians not unfriendly.

Almost without exception, the older and more firmly established Spanish communities have persisted as Spanish-speaking centers to the present day. Early Anglo settlements in the Southwest tended strongly to coincide with older Spanish communities for the simple reason that these were usually the best available locations for an agricultural economy in the desert. Then, as railroads and a whole mechanized society moved west, many of these communities became large industrial cities while retaining their Spanish names and often some of their Spanish character. Thus Spanish and Anglo communities have co-existed for generations with only minimal contact between the two peoples.

In this century some of these cities became meccas for so many newer immigrants from Mexico that the new arrivals nearly overwhelmed the older Spanish-speaking communities. This has not been regarded favorably by the older Hispanic residents, since it usually has diminished their standing with the dominant Anglo community.[1]

SPANISH COLONIALISM

Although Spain's basic reasons for exploration and conquest were not unlike those of other empire-building nations, several characteristics set the Spanish apart and made their colonies differ markedly from the others. For one thing, Spain was deeply im-

[1] Originally, there was little communication or co-operation among the three areas of Spanish colonial settlement. Today, little useful or solidly based communication exists either among areas or between older and newer residents. This is true even though the older upper class groups have tended to become self-styled leaders in growing Mexican-American economic and political associations. On occasion this leadership has been shared with citizens one or two generations removed from Mexico.

bued with Moorish culture, since much of the Iberian Peninsula had been under Arabic rule during the eight centuries preceding Columbus's discovery of the New World. Much of Spanish culture was essentially Moorish and Eastern rather than Western. Military ambition and religious fervor, developed while casting the Moors out of Spain, were turned to the conquest of empire.

Feudalism persisted in the Spanish empire even after it had largely died out elsewhere, and a strict hierarchical system prevailed even on the northern frontier of New Spain. At the apex of the colonial pyramid were the so-called *gachupines*, who had emigrated from Spain and often returned there. On the assumption that they combined loyalty to their own interests with loyalty to their monarch, they were appointed to nearly all high positions. The *criollos* were Spanish in ancestry but born in the New World. They enjoyed fewer privileges since their loyalties might lie in the New World rather than indisputably with their king. This discrimination led them eventually to revolt against Spain. After gaining independence they comprised much of the elite in Mexico and among the Spanish-speaking people of the American Southwest. Much farther down on the social scale were the masses of Indians and *mestizos*. With little education and limited legal rights, they were usually exploited for their labor, although they finally came to outnumber all other groups.[2]

The Spanish came to this area, then, with the ideal of exploiting it in order to return wealthy to Spain, instead of focusing primarily on permanent settlement; they came as ambitious individuals within their society, not as divergent groups seeking asylum. Since they brought few Spanish women, they quickly developed the policy of intermixture with conquered natives. This meant that both cultures and populations were blended, and, to a limited extent, the languages influenced each other wherever the two groups were in stable contact. In the American Southwest, however, only a small minority of the Indians fitted into the feudal *encomendero* system, or into missions. Nearly all of them rejected Spanish intrusion, and few tribes were defeated or assimilated. In no case did the Southwestern Indians make much direct impression on the culture of the Spaniards, or upon their language.

AREAS OF SPANISH SETTLEMENT

Distinctive conditions and events shaped the character of each region of Southwestern colonization, and set each somewhat apart from the others. New Mexico lay far from the nearest Spanish outposts, and Oñate's was the only Spanish migration of any size into the area. Several small, neighboring agricultural communities were established there. Contacts between these Spaniards and the Pueblos were mainly superficial, as evidenced by the facts that only a very few Tewa Pueblo words were ever

[2] The Mexican revolution of 1910 brought amelioration of their status, but the continuing absence of an effective middle class, among other things, has made their actual attainment of formal education, assumption of legal powers, and improved economic standards difficult, even in the United States.

incorporated into Spanish, and the Pueblo continued their own culture with scarcely any change. Their relationship was more that of the weak ruler and peacefully inclined but independent-minded subject, who for reasons of habit and mutual defense make little effort to dissolve their union. From their beginnings in Nuevo México the Spanish had included some *mestizos*; many more were added as a result of intermixture with local Indians, very often with captured members of hostile tribes.

Most of Oñate's original settlers came to Nuevo México directly from Nueva Viscaya or Nueva Galicia, but the Castilian dialect has always been fairly uniform in New Mexico. It has tenaciously preserved much of its classic or archaic form.[3]

Schools in the New Mexican area were almost non-existent in Spanish times. Priests and missionaries were educated elsewhere, as were government officials and any other professional people sent there. Upper-class New Mexicans sent their children south to Mexico to be educated if they could afford it, though normally girls did not leave home. The very few libraries in New Mexico were private collections and were considered rather remarkable locally. To brighten an otherwise drab existence there were dramas – both religious and secular – folk-tales, riddles and proverbs, and poetry of many kinds. Octosyllabic verse was very common and used in such varied forms as the *indita* (danced and sung like an Indian chant), the *verso* (often extemporaneous and humorous), the *decima* (popular in the 1800's, on all subjects from love to politics), the *cuando*, the *corrido*, the nostalgic *romance* and the religious *alabado*. Ballads brought by the conquerors remained popular. Fiestas, with song and dance, feasting and gambling, were enthusiastically organized at every opportunity. The people became, in a way, passively fatalistic, but spontaneity was encouraged and never lost. Thus the Spanish-speaking people of New Mexico preserved a largely illiterate, medieval folk culture, but a vital and meaningful one whose forms and concepts still motivate and direct the thought patterns, emotions, and behavior of hundreds of thousands.

In Arizona and California the Spanish were able to do far less than in New Mexico to create a lasting cultural influence. Much of the "Spanish" influence in these areas is due more to two other factors: the nostalgic and romantic Anglo emphasis on the Spanish heritage (plus its box-office appeal), and, more importantly, the relatively recent arrival in these areas of large numbers of people from Mexico. In general, the early Spanish-speaking settlers of California were more influential, better educated, and economically stronger than those who had earlier settled the forbidding land of Nuevo México. The peaceful Indian population provided relative ease in colonization, though there was little acculturation or language mixture in either direction. California's geographic isolation made its population provincial, but also gave it protection from most of the struggles of the outside world.

[3] In New Mexico, southern Colorado, and the El Paso valley, archaic terms in common use are *naiden, traidra, trujo, dijieron, anque, dende, comigo, cuse, (que es de), mesmo, escuro, ivierno, escrebir,* and well over a thousand other. Espinosa (1909, p. 56) counted some fourteen hundred Spanish dialect forms peculiar to New Mexico alone, of which about a thousand are Spanish, seventy-five Nahautl, and only ten of native New Mexican origin.

These Californians could conceivably have emphasized education, literacy, and creativity considerably more than their poorer cousins in Nuevo México, but evidently they did not choose to do so. They were able to develop a more independent spirit, and possessed a slightly higher level of formal education, but did little to encourage literacy among their less fortunate contemporaries. In their isolation the latter developed a simple pastoral economy. Like the New Mexicans, they found pleasure in religious observances, fiestas, parades, speeches, song, dance, and drama. There was not time enough for the development of a characteristic dialect before the Anglo conquest and the discovery of gold inundated the Spanish culture with diverse, sweeping waves of humanity from all parts of the world.

The Spanish colonization of Texas showed still different characteristics. This area was settled a century after New Mexico, but, by 1800, Spanish Texas consisted of only a few settlements around San Antonio. Few voluntary settler could be attracted, so Spain forcibly moved residents of the Canary Islands to San Antonio, and later established penal colonies in Texas, in efforts to strengthen the province. No acculturation of local Indians was feasible, since even their alliance was often doubtful. Official neglect turned the few Spanish residents of Texas away from any strong loyalty to their government, and made it easy for foreigners illegally to win their confidence and trade. Though the Spanish Texans could scarcely be said to have welcomed the Americans with open arms, they never united against them.

As might be surmised, few of the original Texas colonists were literate. It was always difficult to lure well-qualified officials or wealthy settlers to any such outlying, neglected post. Those who came found it difficult, if not impossible, to encourage creativity or organize formal learning. Then too, ravages of the war for independence from Spain destroyed much of Spanish civilization in Texas.

Texas was never so isolated from foreign influences as New Mexico or California. Like California, it was settled too late in the Spanish period of rule to develop a characteristic subculture (as happened in New Mexico), and so, too late to prevent the submergence of Spanish culture and language under American influences. The very numbers of Americans who flooded into east and central Texas overwhelmed the earlier Spanish population and forced it into a subordinate role. This was not nearly so true of New Mexico, and less true of south Texas or the El Paso region, though Anglo-American political supremacy ultimately flowed into these areas too and destroyed many Spanish patterns. It remained for a 20th century migration from Mexico to repopulate Texas with a large proportion of Spanish-speaking people.

THE AMERICAN CONQUEST

The Mexican War of 1846-1848 passed through the Southwest like radiation, causing little commotion at the time; but leaving a different human environment that continued to change almost as a mutation.

The American conquest of the Spanish-speaking people in the Southwest must be understood primarily in psychological terms, all the more so because they had not put up a real struggle. They had never found out for sure just what they *could* do, given a chance. The conquest was confusing, too, because it sometimes seemed not to be one. The Anglos brought in the vague promise, and sometimes the reality, of civil rights unknown to the people before; they sometimes established schools for children who certainly would have remained illiterate; they brought new kinds of employment in their railroads, mines, and industries. It was quite clear from the beginning, however, which group was in control. The American citizenship granted in the Treaty of Guadalupe-Hidalgo was usually of a second-class variety. People with Spanish names were often discouraged or even prevented from voting. Rarely did they hold office, except in New Mexico. Public services were often less than public as far as they were concerned; justice was sometimes unequal for people named Martinez or Apodaca. Their language was often considered disreputable, or, at best, quaint, in the schools.

Economically, too, the conquest was obvious from the beginning. Land that had been used for generations by Spanish-speaking people was suddenly pre-empted by Anglos. Those who spoke Spanish usually found themselves in the poorest jobs at the lowest wages. Social discrimination was closely connected to economic disadvantage. Housing, services and schools were nearly always the poorest available. The Anglos had unexpectedly stumbled onto a source of cheap labor in their frontier march, and they had no intention of giving it up. Unused to such a luxury, they did not quite know how to handle the situation and were often inconsistent, sometimes motivated by political idealism – as when they indignantly abolished peonage during the Civil War – and sometimes ruthlessly exploiting the advantages accruing from having a conquered population at their mercy. Both of these attitudes and their concomitant behavior patterns have persisted to the present day, to confuse legislation, social programs, education, and the Spanish-speaking people in general.

With his heritage of peonage, the Mexican-American continued for generations with little realization of the abstract possibilities open to him under the new system. And, of course, he was not encouraged to learn. Spanish-style revolutions were obviously futile against the United States, and Anglo-type economic-political pressure was completely foreign, incomprehensible, and unacceptable until considerable acculturation had taken place.

Although this general situation prevailed throughout the Southwest after the American conquest, important differences developed among each of the new states or territories. Texas had already started to develop on the pattern of the southeastern United States, with cotton, slavery, white supremacy, and a dim view of other peoples except as a source of cheap labor. In the early days, the outnumbered and unorganized Mexican-Americans of Texas had little choice but tacitly to accept the majority verdict. This view became entrenched in the laws and traditions of the state. Thus, when thousands of Mexican citizens migrated to Texas in the early years of the 20th century, a ready-made pattern of active discrimination awaited them.

In Arizona the situation resembled that in Texas. The scattered and harassed Hispanic inhabitants exchanged one set of tribulations for another, without quite knowing what was happening. They counted for almost nothing in the developing social order. Education languished, and, where few could read English well, Spanish was not taught at all. Mexicans from Sonora continued to disregard the international boundary, but came to stay as they found more work in the mines or on the railroads. In the 20th century they have come in far greater numbers, but they have not been encouraged to participate in local society or politics.

California quickly became a state, and even more quickly became the scene of mass mania in the gold rush days. Hordes of people from all over the world poured into the state, and somewhere in this maelstrom the earlier Spanish-speaking inhabitants lost out, becoming foreigners in their own land. Even though their numbers were swelled by an influx of gold rushers from Sonora and other parts of Mexico, they quickly became a small minority, and were treated as such. Many formerly prominent Spanish-speaking families lost their lands and declined in wealth and prestige. The use of literate Spanish was engulfed by English; Spanish became one of several minority languages spoken in California. With the early 20th century immigration of thousands of agricultural and industrial workers from Mexico, it came to be almost entirely the spoken language of illiterates.

Only in New Mexico did the Hispanic culture and language remain vigorous. Spanish-speaking people had deep roots in this region and a firm, effective and stable way of life in the desert. Sparsely endowed with either water or minerals, this area could support only a small amount of ranching and farming, so for many years the original Spanish-speaking population could compete in numbers with the few incoming Anglos. Demonstrably practical Spanish laws regarding land and water rights were retained. The upper-class Spanish-speaking people of New Mexico continued to take part in the management of the territory. The struggle for supremacy between them and the Anglos resulted in a sort of stalemate, but, withal, a more equitable distribution of power, wealth, and status than developed anywhere else in the Southwest. Anglo and Mexican-American residents of New Mexico have repeatedly joined forces to exert pressure on the Federal Government. Statehood was gained this way. Literacy was not made a requirement for voting when statehood was acquired, so aspirants to public office have always had to seek the Mexican-American vote. Spanish was long used with English in the legislature and the courts; all public documents were printed in both languages.

Southern Colorado was the northern extension of New Mexico under Spain, but their similarity carried over only partially into American times. Colorado's experiences from 1850 on were quite different from New Mexico's: the Pike's Peak gold rush caused Colorado to become a state quickly, and attracted a relatively large Anglo population that early swamped the small, rural Spanish-speaking element. Still, small and isolated Spanish-speaking communities remained almost untouched in southwestern and southern Colorado. In the early 20th century, when developing modern agriculture demanded a larger labor force, immigration from Mexico was encouraged. Segregation and discrimination have been quite evident in the state, and education for Spanish-speaking youth has not been of high quality. In very recent years spokesmen for the group have been slowly instituting some beneficial changes with regard to economic, educational, and social opportunities.

CONTEMPORARY MEXICAN-AMERICANS

In respect to the 20th century several broad, general problems and conditions may be more profitably discussed as they developed in the entire area. Some of the more important of these are immigration and migration, law and justice, politics, the press, education, occupations, health, welfare, housing, organizations, unemployment, segregation and discrimination and social change. Obviously, these and related problems can be only outlined in a paper of this scope, and their complexity grossly simplified. By mid 20th century, the Spanish-speaking population of the Southwest has not only grown far larger than ever before, but it has become far more complex within itself, and it faces conditions and dilemmas never even considered by its predecessors. While attitudes and value patterns have changed little, outer forces have been almost completely transformed.

Immigration and Migration

There has never been a quota system to regulate the immigration of Mexican citizens into the United States. Even so, immigration is not an altogether simple matter, and acquiring United States citizenship is usually not seriously considered by immigrants from Mexico. Many come for periods varying from a few months to several years, but typically they have rejected the idea of giving up citizenship in their native Mexico. In the Southwest a temporary resident on a visa can obtain work, living conditions, etc., as good as or better than those of Mexican-American citizens. Except for a few benefits accruing to citizens – welfare assistance, for example – there is rather little inducement for a change of citizenship.

The lack of a quota system is not only a "good neighbor" device, it also enables Southwestern employers to obtain labor at a fraction of the cost of citizen workers, with very few obligations to furnish safe or healthful working and living conditions. Migratory agricultural workers, both domestic and foreign, and Mexicans who commute daily across the border to work in the United States, are exposed to the brunt of low wages and poor working conditions. However, this is also an increasingly great problem for permanent and stable Mexican residents and Mexican-American citizens in the Southwest who cannot compete with labor from across the border. Employers frequently reject these indigenous workers as less malleable than the hundreds of thousands of *braceros* (who enter this country yearly to work under the provisions of

Public Law 78), or the similar numbers of *mojados* ("wet backs") whose illegal entry makes them prey to illegal practices by employers.

At present, United States consulates in Mexico have a waiting list of over 125,000 Mexican citizens requesting permanent residence visas in the Southwest, and of these at least 5,000 enter the United States each month. It is not possible to make an accurate count of those Mexicans who cross the border illegally, but census figures on Mexican residents in this country are far higher than Immigration Service statistics would indicate. Spanish-named people of all categories in the United States are variously estimated at from six to eight million. Most of these live, or at least have their home base, in the Southwest. Statistics of the 1800's were even less reliable than those of more recent vintage, and the border situation was very fluid then.[4] By 1900 somewhere between 2 and 3 per cent of all Texans were born in Mexico. This compared with approximately 3 per cent of New Mexicans, less than .2 per cent of Coloradoans, 19 per cent of Arizonans, and somewhat over .5 per cent of Californians. Between 1910 and 1920, however, a major revolution almost tore Mexico apart, upsetting populations that had been stable for centuries. At the same time, irrigation projects and new agricultural techniques and crops opened up more of the Southwest to agricultural exploitation and a new labor force was required. An exodus from Mexico to the United States began, large enough to cause serious concern in Mexico, and to inundate the earlier Spanish-speaking population of the Southwest. An estimated 15 per cent of all Mexicans migrated to the United States during the 1920's, in what Santibañez (1930, p. 48) calls "a hemorrhage from the Mexican nation". By 1930, in spite of a very large increase in the total population, the percentages of those born in Mexico had grown significantly in all five Southwestern states.[5]

The whole problem was intensified by the depression of the 1930's, when conditions for this group became so unfavorable that the trend was reversed, people returning to Mexico in greater numbers than those coming to the United States. Then, with the outbreak of the Second World War, the demand for labor suddenly mushroomed in the Southwest, and the immigration of workers from Mexico was cordially encouraged. A great wave of immigrants answered the demand and undertook war work of various kinds. Thus, rural Mexicans became more urbanized. The war proved a catalyst toward acculturation, perhaps because the Spanish-speaking people were, for the first

---

[4]   Remnants of the informal attitude toward border crossing still exist, and partially account for the large wetback population close to the present border.

[5]   According to Reynolds (1933, p. 6), over one-fourth of Arizona's people were new immigrants from Mexico, as were 14 per cent in New Mexico, nearly 12 per cent in Texas, almost 7 per cent in California, and approximately 6 per cent in Colorado. Though neither Texas nor California had previously possessed heavy concentrations of Spanish-speaking people, by 1930 they had become the two states with the most pressing problems regarding this minority. The acuteness of the problem was perhaps aggravated by neither State's having previously made allowances for the needs or interests of their Spanish-speaking people and because neither had any intention of suddenly doing so. The urban centers in the southern parts of both states proved to be good home bases for the large numbers of migratory agricultural workers in this population, making for a permanently unstable situation regarding their position in state or local plans for education, welfare, health, employment, etc.

time, offered economic and social rewards sufficient to lure them toward American patterns of life and language. The international crisis necessitated the use of all available material and human resources, and the Spanish-speaking people found themselves partially accepted as compatriots by the larger society.

In the slump after the war ended, these Spanish-speaking residents found themselves nearly at the bottom of a fiercely competitive labor market. They had neither the skills, education, training, financial credit, nor political power to establish themselves in the peacetime situation. Spanish-speaking veterans returned to second-class citizenship at home. It was no accident that they began to form associations for amelioration of political and economic discrimination. They clearly saw the close correlation between lack of skills in English and familiarity with Anglo culture, and liability to discrimination and other disadvantages.

The postwar rate of "resident visa" immigration from Mexico decreased markedly and has not since been augmented, partly because automation has decreased the market for unskilled labor. Also, all the old factors inhibiting immigration still operate: obvious discrimination, the relative immobility of the Mexican-American population in low-paying occupations, and the difficulties of living with a foreign language and culture while balancing precariously on the lowest rung of the economic scale. This is not to say, however, that the Spanish-speaking population has remained stable during the last several years. On the contrary, due mostly to natural increase, it is the fastest growing population in the Southwest (with the possible exception of the Navajos). Furthermore, it has experienced a great deal of geographic mobility, not so much because this was desired by the people involved as because their work encouraged or necessitated seasonal moving. Between 1950 and 1960 the Spanish-speaking population of Texas increased by 37%, while that of California grew 88%, that of Arizona 51%, that of Colorado 33%, and that of New Mexico 8%. In terms of the entire Southwest, Arizona has 6% of the Spanish-speakers, Colorado 5%, New Mexico 8%, and Texas and California each approximately 41% (Samora 1963, p. 1; Saunders 1949, pp. 6-7). Plainly, it is California and Texas that have had to deal with the major brunt of the acculturation and discrimination problems in recent years, for together they claim the vast majority of the approximately three and one-half million Spanish-speakers in the Southwest. In recent years, California particularly seems to be regarded as their mecca.

More important than the sheer numbers of Spanish speakers in each of these states is their location. Characteristically, their incidence is heaviest near the Mexican border, and gradually diminishes with distance from it. Cities which lie on or near the border have attracted many newer immigrants, but others such as San Antonio, Houston, Los Angeles, San Jose, and Phoenix each claim many thousands. The most favored cities have had from their inception a strong if not primary Hispanic influence. Rural Spanish speakers have either been stable for generations, or are transitory agricultural workers.

Although the Spanish used in the Southwest is essentially that of Mexico, there are regional and class differences. Archaic Spanish is most common in the upper Rio Grande valley and southern Colorado, while an argot or *calo*, comprehensible only to the initiated of the juvenile pachuco gangs, is common to the slums in cities such as El Paso, Albuquerque, Los Angeles, Phoenix, and San Jose. Very little variation in this gang speech has developed from city to city – a rather surprising uniformity which, with other factors, seems to indicate considerable communication among members of this group. Simple, rural Mexican Spanish, with slight lexical variants corresponding to different sections of Mexico, has been characteristic of *campesinos* who arrived in the Southwest within the last generation or so. This is typical of the lower Rio Grande valley, for example. The majority of Spanish-speaking immigrants to the Southwest have since the turn of the century come from the Mexican states of the central Mexican plateau.

Since the 1840's many English words and Anglicized Spanish expressions have been adopted by Spanish speakers throughout the Southwest. Among more acculturated Spanish speakers, a mixture of oral Spanish and English has developed, involving both lexical and grammatical interference. A few old upper-class families have consistently spoken and encouraged grammatically correct and precise Spanish, but both their numbers and their influence have been dwindling in recent years.

The seasonal migration of hundreds of thousands of Spanish-speaking agricultural workers into northern states must also be briefly considered. These people exemplify to an extreme degree the problems faced by all Spanish-speakers of the Southwest. Some migratory workers have home bases in Arizona, Colorado, and New Mexico, but the really large concentrations of migratory Spanish-speaking workers have always come from south Texas (which now has 127,000 – more than any other state) and southern California (with upwards of 100,000) (Texas Educ. Agcy. 1962, p. 2). These people have been forced by necessity – chronic unemployment – to leave home in family or larger groups in the spring of each year in order to follow whatever crops may be harvested. They usually do not return home until fall. Generally the least acculturated and the least educated of all the Spanish speakers in the Southwest, they have been imprisoned in this position generation after generation by the circumstances of their work. They have developed what might be called a migratory subculture.

In Texas one-third of these migrants have had no formal education whatsoever, while only 5 per cent have gone beyond elementary school; almost all are functionally illiterate – that is, they have attended less than five years of school (Texas Educ. Agcy. 1962, pp. 3-12).[6] Averaging 125 working days in 1960, a worker would have earned $911, but income has been even lower recently because of automation in harvesting (Texas Educ. Agcy 1962, pp. 20-28). For example, until 1958 only about 6 percent of south Texas cotton was machine picked; in 1962 over three-fourths was harvested in this way. The situation of the migrant Spanish-speaking worker is now such that it

[6] Texas and California are second only to New York state in the numbers of functional illiterates, and this is quite obviously due to the plight of the migratory worker.

requires some form of economic rehabilitation if he is not to be a charge to the community. He must be retrained, preferably for skilled labor at higher wages. Some such efforts are currently being made in California (at Santa Clara and San Jose) and in Texas (at the San Antonio Project), via pilot projects witch are yet as drops in an ocean of need.

Law, Politics and Justice

Even though the American frontier, superimposed upon the Spanish frontier in the Southwest, at times created a thoroughly lawless situation, Spanish names were infrequent among the outlaws, or in connection with serious crimes. Nevertheless, as law and order caught up with this frontier, Mexican-Americans began to find themselves in a disadvantageous position, if not under the law itself then under legal interpretations in the courts. As Samora (1962, pp. 2-3) says,

People of low socio-economic status without "purse, power and pull" are disadvantaged before the law. The Spanish-speaking fall into this category, but for them there must be added the dimension of ethnicity. There is some evidence to suggest that they suffer from police brutality, differential arrest and conviction patterns, and exclusion from jury duty. The pattern, however, is quite variable throughout the United States.

The voting pattern and general political participation varies widely. In a few areas there is complete control of town and county; in other areas there is hardly any participation. The exercise of the right to vote, however, whether high or low, does not seem to change appreciably the general socio-cultural situation of the Spanish-speaking nor the opportunities open to them. In some areas there is evidence of barriers to the right to vote.

The Southwestern pattern of legal discrimination, though widespread, has not been altogether consistent. We find that in New Mexico, for example, the Spanish-speaking leaders managed to gain considerable concessions. Though Arizona has always had segregated schools and literacy requirements for voting, California has not since 1931. In Texas, there has been no literacy requirement for voting, but school segregation has been widespread. In recent years school segregation has been rather successfully attacked in several court cases. The Delgado case of 1948 was particularly important. Segregation practices were ruled arbitrary and discriminatory, and in violation of constitutional rights under the Fourteenth Amendment.[7] Even so, they still continued in various places, since this decision did not cover them all. In *Hernández v. Driscoll* (U.S. 1957), the court ruled that arbitrary retention of Spanish-speaking children for four years in the first two grades of school constituted unreasonable discrimination.[8]

Since most discriminatory practices never reach the stage of legal contest, they are difficult to delineate with anything approaching full accuracy. Typical is the case of

---

[7]   Interview with Chester Allison, attorney for the Texas Education Agency, Austin, Texas, July 21, 1963; *Minerva Delgado et al. v. Bastrop, Independent School District et al.*, 388 U.S., (1948).
[8]   *Herminio Hernandez et al. v. Driscoll Consolidated Independent School District et al.*, 1384 U.S., (1957).

Anglos working officially with Spanish-speaking people: few of them have ever spoken Spanish and fewer still have been required to do so. Public school, health, law enforcement, and welfare personnel have always needed fluency in Spanish to perform their duties properly, but this has not been asked of them, and very few Anglos in such positions have achieved a workable level of communication in Spanish.

Organizational Efforts

The individuals among Spanish-speaking leaders who are most influential in representing their people to Anglo authorities have almost invariably been those most completely Anglified. Organizations developed by such "leaders" are directed almost entirely toward impressing their people with the importance of conforming to the Anglo mold. Their first and most universal goal is to promote effective fluency in English. That this is done at the expense of Spanish is either ignored or often itself considered as a positive goal. One example of this is the work of the League of United Latin American Citizens (LULAC), which started a campaign to teach children going into elementary school 400 basic English words. The project has since been taken up by state education authorities in Texas. Although LULAC is quite active in Texas, it is not quite so powerful in New Mexico and Colorado and only moderately active in Arizona and California. The LULAC is also a political organization, controlling many votes and sponsoring candidates for public office. Many of the LULAC's public activities seem designed as much for their public relations value with Anglos as for the sake of maintaining traditional Hispanic cultural patterns.

In California, the Community Service Organizations (CSO) seem to be the most effective and influential leadership group. They, like the LULAC, assist Hispanos with legal, health, real estate, education, employment, and welfare problems – enrolling those whom they help into the organization. In some farming areas of California, Anglo farmers have apparently "discouraged" formation of local Hispano organizations through fear that Spanish-speaking farm laborers will be "helped too much" for the good of the farmers.

An organization which incorporates all others in that state, and which seems to be doing much in its own right, is the Colorado Federation of Latin-American Organizations. It deals largely with discrimination in voting and employment, although some attempt is also made to preserve elements of Hispanic culture, possibly because Colorado is an old Hispanic area of settlement. Another strong political organization is the Political Action for Spanish-Speaking Organizations, known in some areas as the Mexican-American Political Association (PASSO or MAPA).[9]

---

[9] PASSO has recently suffered from internal dissension due to its inactivity in connection with an incident in Crystal City, Texas, where the governor of Texas sent in rangers on election day, presumably to discourage the Spanish speakers from voting. Some of the Spanish speakers have come to believe that the national administration of PASSO is pro-Anglo and, as a result, the Texas affiliates indignant about the Crystal City incident, have declared their independence from the national office.

A number of organizations are especially dedicated to furthering the education of the Spanish speakers. Among these are Careers for Youth of Phoenix, and the Vesta Club of Phoenix; the latter, which is formed of both Spanish-speaking and Anglo college graduates, helps "underprivileged" Spanish-speaking students. Its slogan is "Progress Through Education", and it discourages use of the Spanish language. Another such organization is the Latin-American Educational Foundation of Denver which grants scholarship aid to young people. Although few such organizations actually provide financial aid to students, most do encourage students to go as far as possible in school.

We have been unable to locate practically any organizations in the Southwest dedicated solely to the preservation and development of the Spanish language or Hispanic culture, though some make a modest contribution in this direction. The Alianza Hispano-Americana in Phoenix (basically a fraternal organization) holds meetings in Spanish and encourages its use. A few other organizations publish Spanish language newsletters or present Spanish plays and cultural programs.[10] Even so, such efforts do not constitute a full-blown and conscientious program of language maintenance. A great many clubs of Spanish speakers in the Southwest simply provide an opportunity for social conviviality. In such clubs, Spanish is much used (as in the family), but there is little effort to promote or defend it. Many local "pan-American" organizations, such as the Pan American Round Table, are also chiefly social, though in El Paso a joint program with Texas Western College has recently been developed to promote interest in and knowledge of Mexican culture. The Good Neighbor Commission of Texas also attempts to promote Mexican culture and the Spanish language.

In contrast to these local, small, or uncoordinated organizations stands the Catholic Church. Their close and intense identification with Catholicism has produced among Spanish speakers attitudes which often have proved embarrassing to the Church as a whole. Spanish speakers have a strong feeling that in some essential way the Church "belongs" to them, so that they can berate it, vilify it, and attack it at will. It is relatively common for the individual to be deeply religious but strongly anti-clerical. This may be one reason why the Church has made little effort to preserve Hispanic attitudes and the Spanish language in the Southwest. It still is very much conscious of its mission among these people, but, like other organizations, has attempted to "help" them by contributing to their Anglification.

It has also been charged that the American G.I. Forum was established to offset the independent Texas affiliates of PASSO.

[10] One popular organization in Los Angeles, the Teatro de Cámara, is seemingly composed entirely of South Americans and presents in Spanish. Paco Sanchez wrote and directed a Spanish play (*Madrecita del Alma*) which was presented to a full house in the Tabor theater in Denver on May 14, 1963. The University of Denver produced five plays in Spanish in 1962. The University of California at Berkeley maintains an annual series of lectures on "Aspectos de la Cultura Hispánica", but, as with other University cultural programs in the Southwest, there seems to be very little contact with an audience beyond students and professors.

The National Catholic Council for the Spanish Speaking (NCCSS) is the central Catholic organization dealing with problems of Spanish-speakers throughout the United States. The problems of those in the Southwest are handled by the Bishop's Committee for the Spanish Speaking, located in San Antonio.[11] A church pilot project to deal with these problems has also been set up in San Antonio. Its activities include a job-placement office, counseling on personal problems, academic and vocational rehabilitation classes, and an organization to develop community support. Its overall purpose is revealed by this statement (Wagner 1963):

The work of acculturation will not be accomplished by the minority alone. The majority too must be awakened to the responsibility to analyze its own position and make it possible for the new immigrant to assimilate himself into the American way of life.... I think it is clear that eventually the immigrant culture will give way to a form of life which is predominantly American but ... this occurs most regularly and most harmoniously when the culture of the immigrant is respected.

Despite the avowed Catholic program of acculturation, English is rarely heard in many Southwestern parishes. However, if a Spanish-speaking priest is assigned, it is usually because few or none of the parishioners can understand English. A negligible number of priests are recruited from among U.S. Spanish speakers and Mexico cannot supply its own needs; so, for practical reasons, Southwestern Catholic priests vary widely in national background. These factors make it impossible to develop an effectively unified Church policy regarding use of the Spanish language.

There is an increasing trend in all associations to acknowledgement that power on the state or national scene requires an organized, American-oriented, English-fluent membership. This view is probably quite valid in view of the facts of segregation and discrimination still prevalent in most parts of the Southwest. But it often sacrifices Spanish to English, tends to negate many positive values in Mexican culture, and overlooks the possibility that Spanish and its culture could be maintained without hampering economic, civil rights, and status gains. Hopefully, some may come to reconsider the factors involved in cross-cultural relations of Anglo and Mexican Americans in the Southwest.

Press and Radio

Those Southwesterners limited to speaking Spanish have found little access to general information, whether in connection with social services, employment, or more general news. Recently, most urban centers have acquired Spanish radio stations or Spanish programs on predominantly English-speaking stations, but in the many years preceding this development Spanish newspapers tried to fill the need. Even though many Spanish speakers could not read their own language, the number of these

---

[11] This organization, founded in 1945, has accumulated an immense amount of data, covering almost every aspect of Spanish speakers' lives. Most of this has been done under the very able direction of Rev. John A. Wagner, Executive Secretary.

periodicals was fairly large. In the early 1900's, for example, New Mexico and southern Colorado alone possessed at least a dozen of them. Several early English-language newspapers in the Southwest either published Spanish editions or devoted some pages to news in Spanish. However, in recent years, most of the exclusively Spanish newspapers have found a sharply decreasing market. *La Opinión* of Los Angeles, established in 1926, is one of the few remaining Spanish-language newspapers of large circulation. It is competently, and at times expertly, written, but consists of only a few small pages. El Paso has three Spanish newspapers – *El Continental*, *El Fronterizo*, and *El Mexicano* – with a combined circulation of about eight thousand. Brownsville and vicinity has four Spanish-language newspapers – *El Bravo*, *El Noticiero*, *El Regional*, and *El Mañana*. Corpus Christi, Phoenix, Tucson, and other Southwestern cities have small weekly newspapers in Spanish; such newspapers appear and disappear fairly frequently. LaFarge's statement concerning the discontinuation of *El Neuvo Mexicano* in Santa Fe (1958), after nearly a century of operation, is generally applicable (LaFarge 1959):

Although Spanish of all sorts was still the daily speech of several hundred thousand New Mexicans, only a small minority of these could read the language with any ease. Those who could were among the best educated and naturally preferred the much fuller coverage of the various English-language dailies. The fact of the matter is that at the present time New Mexico's school system does not give the masses of Spanish-Americans a complete command of English, yet at the same time it is allowing the common Spanish to degenerate into an illiterate patois which is daily more inadequate for communication with the Spanish-speaking world.

The one and only force which is now promoting Spanish, and is felt throughout the Southwest, is the Spanish-language radio. Serving virtually all Spanish-speaking people in the United States are more than 300 stations broadcasting in Spanish at some time or other during the week; approximately two-thirds of these are in the Southwest. Several broadcast entirely in Spanish. Another dozen or more border stations inside Mexico are directed mostly toward U.S. rather than Mexican listeners.

Spanish radio stations in the Southwest are commercially successful because a large proportion of Spanish speakers prefer to listen to Latin American music and drama (mostly soap opera) in Spanish, as well as to other program materials – such as poetry – not found in English-language broadcasts.[12] A sign of their commercial suc-

[12] Data obtained from a questionnaire distributed to the 15 major Spanish-language stations in the Southwest (to which 13 responded) indicate that 9 of these stations broadcast Spanish poetry regularly, and one more will begin doing so soon. The average time devoted to poetry is 4 hours per week, with a total for all responding stations of 36 hours. There seems no doubt that poetry is an integral part of Hispanic culture while it is a mere vestige in Anglo culture. This is explicable only in terms of the total values of the two cultures. There are approximately 50 hours per week (9 stations, $5\frac{1}{2}$ hours per station) of other "cultural" materials, such as panel discussions, literary readings, etc. In addition, news and editorials average about one hour per station per day. Only two stations currently present plays from classical or modern Spanish literature, but one other is planning to do so. Ten of the 13 responding stations list outside activities on the part of their employees in the promotion of Spanish language and culture. These 13 stations report receiving an average of 2,540 letters per week

cess may be seen in the fact that Spanish broadcasting alone accounted for two-thirds of all foreign language broadcasting in the U.S.A. in 1956 and 1960. Program managers of Spanish stations and Spanish programs would like to see greater interest in and use of the Spanish language because this would increase their potential market. *They comprise the largest single group of leaders of the Spanish speaking who are directly interested in the language and the culture, on the one hand, and in close touch with the Anglo world, on the other.* They try to recognize both the masses who cling to their traditions but who do not know how to safeguard or transmit them, and the assimilated who are either hostile to parental traditions or share them only to a very minor degree. However, unlike "middle men" of other ethnic minorities in the United States, Spanish radio program managers are not organized for the specific purpose of bi-culturism nor have they formulated rationales on behalf of it.

There are several reasons for the success of Spanish-language radio. Basically, it does not require literacy. It is a far more personal means of communication than the newspaper, and, as such, fits better into Hispanic culture. It is, perhaps, comparable to the all-pervading Church, where so much consists of listening and receiving, and which takes a personal interest in its listeners.[13]

Education

Until late in the 19th century there were very few schools of any kind in the Southwest, and fewer still in which special attention was given to the problems of Spanish-speakers. But in 1888 the *New Mexican* of Santa Fe presented an interesting argument:

When the *New Mexican* says that the teaching of English in our public schools should be made compulsory by legislative enactment it does not mean that the Spanish language should be excluded. It would be better, perhaps, owing to the peculiar composition of our population to have the teaching of both English and Spanish made compulsory.[14]

Although a few creative educators have at different times, espoused essentially the same argument in various parts of the Southwest, there has long been almost no serious popular consideration of actually creating a bilingual population in this area where two languages are so prevalent. When viewed objectively, this situation seems rather odd, especially considering the clear, practical advantages of bilingualism. The main key to the educational situation may be found in ethnocentrism. Since Spanish

---

written in Spanish, but only 250 written in English. This indicates that a substantial proportion of the population which is literate in Spanish also listens to the Spanish-language radio. It also implies the rarity of English literacy among the listeners.

[13] Increasingly, television stations are broadcasting a few hours per week in Spanish in large Southwestern cities. There is at least one full-time station in Los Angeles. Also, a number of stations on the Mexican side of the border are popular with U.S. viewers.

[14] (LaFarge 1954, p. 134). In general, the situation long remained "different" in New Mexico, where Spanish and bilingual public schools were dominant until the turn of the century. For a full account see Kloss (1940, pp. 311-425).

is the language of a "conquered" and largely "lower" socio-economic group, it has been almost suppressed in many schools throughout the Southwest. In some schools, children are still punished for speaking their native Spanish on the schoolgrounds. In very few has Spanish been taught well enough to give either Spanish-speaking or Anglo children a reading knowledge of it. Certainly, Anglo children have almost never learned to use Spanish effectively.

All Southwestern states have provided for the teaching of Spanish in the public schools.[15] In 1963, the California legislature made proficiency in Spanish a requirement for prospective teachers of Spanish-speaking children. This, of course, has not yet been thoroughly tested in practice. Most legal provisions in the realm of education tend to be either forced compromises or stop-gaps which fail to recognize or deal in a creative fashion with the basic issues of acculturation, culture conflict, and cultural continuity.

School segregation of Spanish-speaking children has been typically rationalized or excused on the basis that these youngsters knew little or no English on entering school and, therefore, could not compete on an equal basis for the first year or so with Anglo children, when the medium of instruction (as required by law in all the Southwestern states) was English. This pedagogical argument has been so abused that some educators now go to the opposite extreme and advocate combining children at any and all levels of proficiency in English in the same classroom, on the grounds that they will somehow manage to pick up English. This view, too, probably needs some modification in order to give each child an adequate education for the modern Southwest. As George Works (1925, p. 213) wrote:

On pedagogical grounds a very good argument can be made for segregation in the early grades.... This advice is offered with some reluctance, as there is danger that it will be misunderstood by some. By others it may be seized upon as a means of justifying the practices now obtaining in some communities. In some instances segregation has used for the purpose of giving the Mexican children a shorter school year, inferior buildings and equipment, and poorly-paid teachers.

Whatever the theoretical arguments, several problems have existed for generations to limit the educational opportunities and achievements of the Spanish-speaking people of the Southwest. School segregation has continued and will continue so long as many children reach school age without knowing English at all, and so long as housing segregation exists in the Southwest. This has almost inevitably been associated with the continuation of inferior facilities and teaching practices. The schools have consistently failed to give practical training in skills that could raise the socio-economic level of the Spanish speakers. They have generally failed to teach the children good,

---

[15]   Article 2911 of Revised Civil Statutes of Texas, for example, sets up many Spanish courses which, by 1941, included courses from the second grade on. However, this article is followed only in such school districts as desire it. In 1959 the Texas legislature set up a pre-school summer language program to teach some English to children speaking only Spanish, so that they could progress normally through the grades. By no means all communities have taken advantage of this program.

literate English that would have the same effect. And it was only after the states changed the basis of their educational allotments to local communities from a per capita to an average daily attendance basis that school officials made a real effort to improve attendance among the Spanish-speaking.[16]

Plainly, the Spanish language in the Southwest has developed unfortunate associations with low socio-economic status, lack of sanitation, widespread illiteracy, and ignorance. The educational system, until very recently, overwhelmingly discouraged its use, while at the same time it failed to provide an adequate grounding in English, forcing the Spanish-speaking people to remain in a ghetto-like corner of Southwestern society and economy. Low attendance and high dropout rates always complicated the picture, as the Spanish speakers could see very little use in continuing a meaningless struggle with education authorities. This situation has unnecessarily deprived both Anglo- and Spanish-speaking groups of the benefits of bilingualism and equalitarian familiarity with another way of life.

Futhermore, cultural factors within the Spanish-speaking community have dimmed the attractions of education. Most Spanish speakers are of a relatively recent peasant background in which literacy was beyond the realm of need or possibility. Children had to contribute to family income by working in the fields; there was no time for the luxury of schooling. But now most of these people have entered an urban, industrial economy, in which education is a definite asset to social and economic mobility. They have had to compete for jobs in a situation where the best ones went to the best educated. With rapidly increasing automation in agriculture, even rural life has begun to follow this trend. Now, the orientation of the Spanish speakers toward education is slowly undergoing a change shaped by an inexorably shifting economy.

SOCIOCULTURAL ANALYSIS

The present identification of Hispanic culture in the Southwestern United States with poverty, illiteracy, and rurality is ironic in view of the fact that at the time it entered the Southwest, it was at the height of its Golden Age, producing some of the greatest literature and art the world has known. At that time the Southwest was uncivilized and the Anglo-American did not yet exist. This Hispanic culture has remained in the Southwest for nearly four centuries, even though its literary and artistic glories have become only dormant seeds carried by the Spanish speakers of the Southwest.

What was and is the nature of this Hispanic-American culture? How did a language and culture of such high status come to such a low pass? How have Anglo-Americans reacted to this language, its speakers, and their values and behavior patterns? How

---

[16] As late as 1950, the educational level of Spanish-speaking people in four of the Southwestern states hovered around the completion of six to seven grades, though in Texas the median was only 3.6 years. This was very much lower than levels in the same states for Anglos and lower even than the medians for "non-whites" except in Arizona (Samora 1963, Table No. 2). In most states "non-whites" means mostly Negroes and Asians, but in Arizona it refers to a large illiterate Indian population.

have Spanish speakers reacted to Anglo-American culture, to the English language, and to a century of Anglo-American domination? What do all these factors and issues portend for the future of the Spanish language in the Southwest? These questions and others will be examined briefly in the pages that follow.

Theoretical Orientation: *Language and Culture*

It is impossible to understand the history, the contemporary problems, or the future probabilities and possibilities of Spanish speakers in the Southwest without understanding, at least in a general way, the culture in which they have their roots. In addition, such understanding requires some knowledge of differences between Hispanic culture and Anglo culture. The nature of Hispanic culture seems to be *embedded in the language* of Spanish speakers in the Southwest. Furthermore, their culture and the language both seem to be *based upon and derived* from the reality in which they live; at the same time both language and culture seem to *create and mold* that reality.[17]

Language and culture *together* form the basic orientation toward reality of any given person or group of persons. The process of forming this orientation is circular, and may be described as follows: reality creates both language and culture; language creates culture and is created by culture; and language and culture create reality.

LANGUAGE

REALITY CREATES   CREATES   CREATES REALITY

CULTURE

The terms are defined as follows:

(1) REALITY is the total structure of that which is perceived and regarded as objectively valid by any definable social group;

(2) LANGUAGE is a system of symbols with a coherent set of rules of reference and transformation rules by means of which a social group finds it possible to communicate;

(3) CULTURE is a system of meanings, methods, and values which develops from the common frame of reference of a social group, and which remains relatively constant while the composition of the group changes.

Empirically, neither the language, the reality structure, nor the culture exist in a total or pure form. Specific classifications of either may overlap or interpenetrate.

---

[17]   To deal adequately with these interrelations would require a complex and elaborate theory such as is found at present in no social or linguistic science. Within the limits of the present discussion, the best that can be done is to provide an outline which integrates some aspects of what is known, realizing that strict scientific verification or contradiction of most of the statements to be made is impossible at the present time. Rather, a set of relations among language, culture, and the reality perceptions of those members of a culture who speak a given language is stated as an axiomatic position. Thereafter, several hypotheses are derived from this position and related directly to the status of Spanish language and culture in the Southwest.

Though they are in a continuous process of modification, they are founded on certain basic premises which are modified only slowly and minutely, and *which can possibly change only within certain limitations.*

Before proceeding with an analysis of Hispanic culture and the Spanish language as such, the most important conscious assumptions underlying the approach used will be stated.

a. The limits of a culture are at least in part circumscribed by the limits of a language. It is impossible to maintain the use of a language without at the same time maintaining the rudiments of the basic orientation toward reality that the language represents. New World variations of the Hispanic theme have not developed far enough away from the Hispanic system to be considered anything but a part of Hispanic culture. Though our state of knowledge is not advanced enough to develop rigorously the implications of relations between grammatical structure and human behavior, still something like the analysis of "cultural themes" proposed by Nostrand seems to be amenable to research (Nostrand 1963, p. 3). Hispanic literature of the great tradition seems to have grown from and to have molded traditions of Hispanic culture to a surprising extent. As a result, great Hispanic literature remains an important source of the cultural themes of Hispanos, in the Southwest and elsewhere.

Of utmost importance in the analysis of a culture are the unquestioned assumptions about reality, which are a part of the structure and meaning of the language. Each language seems to create an implicit frame of reference with regard to key beliefs regarding the nature of reality, and the educational process reinforces this pattern rather than allowing the student to go beyond or outside it. The mastery of other languages seems to be the only effective way of widening these boundaries.

One implication of the existence of unquestioned assumptions is that each language is only partially translatable, and that the greater the difference in structure from another language, the more nearly it is untranslatable into that language. Einar Haugen (1956, p. 70) discusses this, citing an example:

The French-born American writer, Julian Green ... tells of his attempt to translate one of his own books from French to English; it failed, and he had to sit down and write an entirely new book: "It was as if, writing in English, I had become another person."

This observation has many implications for maintenance of Spanish in the Southwest. It would explain the almost total inaccessibility of the mind of the 'chicano' to that of the 'gringo' or 'gabacho'. It would suggest that acceptance of English by the Mexican-American implies a direct and immediate submission to a foreign culture and frame of reference, as well as to a foreign language. Those who do submit are called *pochos*, bleached or faded.

The study of the "themes" of a culture is also relevant to the representation of its reality structure. The existence of themes of Hispanic culture in the orientation of the Spanish-speaking people of the Southwest may well be a major factor in the preservation of the Spanish language there; there may be a greater resistance to a change of themes than to a change of language because the themes represent more clearly the reality structure of the culture. And it may be that the themes are inextricably interwoven with the vocabulary, linguistic patterns, intonation patterns, etc., of the language itself. They could explain many of the persistent social patterns which lead to clear socio-economic disadvantage, and could partly explain why there is no concerted effort by the mass of Spanish-speaking people to attain socio-economic advantage, and why their "liaison leaders" have generally insisted on the whole-hearted acceptance of English as a first step in their "rehabilitation".

b. The greater the extent and depth of mastery of a language, the more extensive the system of cultural meanings and values that is internalized and the more firmly established is the reality structure given by the language. Language and culture are both the prisons and the liberators of the human soul. The more intimate and extensive contact there is with a given language and culture, the more freedom the individaul has within its framework, because he can respond to far greater subtleties in the adaptation of the culture to personal need. The more languages and cultures to which he becomes able to respond *in terms of their greatest subtleties*, the more complete, authentic, and adaptable an individual he can be, and the more likely he is to contribute something of lasting value to his original culture as well as to universal culture. It is this which makes immeasurable the potential contribution of the Spanish-speaking people of the Southwest. But it is of little personal or social value for the individual to be incarcerated in two prisons, as has happened to the mass of the Spanish speakers of the Southwest. Few indeed are aware of the existence of the liberating forms of either language or culture.

c. Once literary and artistic values have been developed in a language and culture, those who use the language may become psychologically and socially *prepared* to respond to and develop these values. Rarely can this be done with a language and culture learned later in life. Furthermore, failure to attain sensitivity and creative ability in one's native language almost inevitably implies corresponding failure in a second learned language. If Spanish-speaking students in Southwestern schools were taught to read, write, and think in Spanish from the earliest elementary grades, a far greater number of them would become more creative and contribute much more than they otherwise will to society – while at the same time becoming better able to cope with the Anglo world. As it is, their limitations in each language and culture block any higher abilities in the other.

The United States is in a position to produce a significant proportion of the total number of educated Spanish-speaking people in this hemisphere. El Paso, for example, graduates approximately fifteen times as many Spanish-speaking high school students as does Ciudad Juárez, her sister-city of somewhat greater population. If a significant number of such students had a profound and well-developed relationship to Spanish language and culture, we as well would be enriched and more at home with each other and with hemispheric neighbors to the south.

Hispanic Culture: Hypotheses and Observations

Differences in the cultural definitions of the individual's relation to societal authority may have created the greatest source of misunderstanding and conflict between the Spanish speakers and the Anglos of the Southwest. *Hispanic culture is based on extreme individual autonomy within the absolute boundaries created by society.* The regulations and restrictions of religion, government, and other forms of authority are not internalized to form a "conscience" which might restrict inconsequential acts and thoughts.[18] Spanish-speaking persons in the Southwest are accused by Anglos of being rebellious; the latter do not realize that Spanish speakers assume a world in which authorities show little interest in the lives of the people.[19]

In Hispanic culture we hypothesize that control over the individual's life is to a great extent tangible, external, and absolute. There is much empirical evidence for this.[20] It is a form of social control that exists in full force in many Southwestern comunities, and creates numerous problems even in areas where it is not obvious. When the limits of behavior are absolute, they are usually well defined and commonly accepted as prescribed forms; when they are relative, one must become an "expert" in the culture to know what they are. When they are relative *and* in a constant process of change, constant application is necessary to learn how to act. The Spanish-speaking person of the Southwest is not culturally prepared for this learning process. He usually assumes the barriers he finds to be absolute, and his behavior is thereby more restricted than that of the Anglo.

The second most important facet of Hispanic culture is its orientation toward persons rather than toward ideas or abstractions.[21] Among the Spanish speakers of the Southwest, this is reinforced by family structure, socio-economic status, and limited

---

[18] A story is told of a group of Spanish intellectuals who convened to form a constitution perfectly suited to the Spanish temperament. After long deliberations, they simply wrote: *Cada individuo tiene el deber de hacer lo que le da la real gana* (The duty of each person is to do as his heart truly desires). However, a second article was also deemed necessary, namely: *No se exigirá a ningun individuo que obedezca al primer articulo* (It will not be demanded of any person that he obey the first article).

[19] There is also an exaggerated form of individualism called *hombría* or *machismo* which often goes so far as to disregard the absolute limits of behavior. Sabino Ulibarri (1961, p. 320) has stated that the one word which best characterizes Spanish life is "anarchism": "Si hay una sola palabra que se acerque a definir la vida social y pública española, esa palabra tendría que ser: ANARQUISMO." In Spanish, the connotations of this word are different from those of its English cognate: there is more emphasis on freedom and less on disorganization.

[20] The sign *Alto* on a street usually signifies "Stop" only to North Americans travelling in Mexico. If the government really wants a driver to stop, there will be *topos* – one or more obstructions which it is necessary to drive over; to slow down the driver, there will be *corrugaciones*. The tendency to exercise one's freedom to steal is corrected by iron bars which are pulled down in front of the glass windows when a store is closed. The virtuous woman is one with *pierna quebrada, y en casa*.

[21] Nostrand (1961, pp. 465-72) points out that Hispanic culture is at its best in revealing the "complex wholeness of personalities", as in the *Cid*, the *Celestina*, and the *Quijote*. Ulibarri (1951, p. 320). states that the structure and vocabulary of the language itself is subjective, and that it functions impulsively and emotionally. He demonstrates this in the use of the subjunctive, the reflexive, the diminutive, and other forms. This is in contrast to English, which is objective, precise, explicit – depersonalized.

educational attainment. In Spanish, the person exists, functions, and is recognized as a complete whole by others (whereas in English he is perceived in terms of his discrete roles). This is undoubtedly fostered by the rigidity of the Hispanic social system; in Hispanic culture the person begins to know who he is and will remain within the socio-economic frameworks almost as soon as he becomes aware of his own existence. There is more *serenidad* and emphasis on beauty (and fatalism) because people are not generally engaged in a race with their neighbors to climb the social ladder, because the poor need these as compensation for their sufferings, and because the rich can afford them. People work to live and do not kill themselves working, because it is felt that no amount of work would change what they are personally or socially.

A hypothesis closely related to the foregoing is given as a theme by Nostrand (1961, pp. 465-72): Human nature is mistrusted by everyone "from orthodox Christians to scientific positivists". In relation to the first hypothesis, this could result from failure to internalize the formal norms of one's society, so that one expects all to do "lo que le da la real gana" when they are not forcefully restrained. In relation to the second hypothesis, orientation toward persons in terms of their total being, rather than in terms of their roles, may create an awareness of the "dark side" of human nature – an insight into subconscious psychological factors which other cultures keep better concealed. It is not hypothesized that these three themes of Hispanic culture are exhaustive, but most characteristics of Hispanic culture may be subsumed under one of these three headings.

These themes go far to explain the frequency of Hispano-Anglo culture conflict in the Southwest. The Spanish-speaking have always been a thorn in the side of educators. Most Anglo teachers have known little of the Spanish language and less of the rich Hispanic culture; they have assumed that both are weeds to be uprooted so that English and "our way of life" can flourish. The fact that they have not been able to change basically the cultural orientation of the Spanish speakers is indicated by one of the many reports on this group in the public schools (de Leon 1959):

Efforts to identify him [The Spanish speaker] with the representative culture have been attempted in various degrees, depending on the social level of the person and the community in which he resides. Yet, in spite of it all, he still remains a foreigner, a stranger, and for all intents and purposes "a Mexican" with the complete common stereotyped connotations brought on by some one hundred years of cultural conflict.

There are promising indications of change in this conflict. Theodore Andersson (1957, pp. 32-35) has suggested a basic reorientation in the educational system beginning with the elementary school, which would develop pride rather than shame on the part of the Spanish speakers in their cultural heritage. Andersson's program would enable most Spanish speakers to participate more fully and meaningfully in both Hispanic and Anglo cultures than have their Mexican or Southwestern forefathers.

Until recently a sharp increase in English literacy has often worked to the disadvantage of the U.S.-born, Spanish-speaking intellectual. For while lack of precision and poetization of experience seem charming in either native or foreign intellectuals, they are intolerable in our native "run of the mill" sons. The intelligent Spanish-speaking student soon sees this and may discard his language and culture, becoming so 'pocho' that the 'gabachos' look colorful in comparison. His other alternative – the one taken by most of those who could potentially contribute most to the enrichment of U.S. culture – is simply to drop out of school and find himself a job where his alienation from Anglo values will not be noticed.

Julian Samora, who has made a monumental statistical study of Spanish speakers in the Southwest, has stated that (Samora 1963, p. 8):

The American school system ... functions best when conforming middle-class administrators and teachers professing middle-class values address themselves to middle-class students who possess the same value orientation or are in the process of acquiring it.

This situation may change more than it recently has, but it will require a veritable revolution in primary, secondary, and higher education to develop a highly literate Hispanic subculture in the United States, carried forward in great part by those who can best internalize this subculture and thereby contribute to the enrichment of all U.S. culture. If they are allowed and encouraged to do so, they might contribute significantly to making our culture more flexible and adaptable in dealing with both domestic and international problems.

Hispanic Social Structure

The most characteristic features of Hispanic social structure are: strict division of social roles, the importance of the family (which includes both primary and secondary family groups), and religious affiliation with the Roman Catholic Church. These features most strongly differentiate Hispanic from Anglo society, and make adjustment difficult for the Spanish-speaking people of the United States. They also seem to be the most enduring facts of Hispanic social structure, extending back into the Moorish occupation and forward into the Anglo occupation, providing sources of internal strength and internal dissension, and the plots of thousands of novels, short stories, and motion pictures.

Separation of the sexes traditionally begins with the first year of school and extends throughout the life of the individual. This is one area where United States customs and economic facts of life have had a great influence on Spanish speakers, but resistance is still strong. The female is prepared only for family life. Since she rarely uses effective methods of birth control, it is expected that she will bear children regularly, leaving her no time for work outside the home even were it otherwise permissible. She is considered ineligible if she does not marry at least by her early twenties, so has no time to establish a career. She is not expected to "use" the education she receives from the public school, but she is expected to learn to help take care of a family from an early age, and males are expected to offer little if any assistance. Even the most brilliant of Spanish-speaking females, therefore, do not take intellectual activity seriously. Females are more closely tied to their culture than are males, and the culture itself requires greater submission on their part.

The male in Hispanic culture is an explorer and conqueror – of ideas, of lands, and of women. He functions as a unit which defies categorization. He is both a Cortés and a Quijote. And when he cannot be either, he is a *pachuco*. He is first of all a man, and only secondarily a storekeeper, a mechanic, or even a lawyer or physician; the role is not promoted at the expense of the man. This leaves him at a distinct disadvantage in economic competition with the Anglo, but he will get his satisfactions from being ruler in his own family, and master of his own personal destiny. Whether this leads to personal grandeur or petty dictatorship, the male in Hispanic society receives personal gratifications rarely available to the male in Anglo society, and stable expectations develop solidarity within the family.

Complications arise from contact with Anglo society, which is founded on entirely different patterns. The boy is first confused when he enters elementary school and finds that his behavior is not strictly controlled, as it is at home. During his most formative years, he was allowed a great deal of freedom within rigid limits. In school he finds only a persistent, nagging pressure to stay in line. Unconsciously he realizes that "something is wrong", either with him or with the "Americans". If he finds no support from his "compadres", it will probably be the former; if he does, the latter. In the first case, he will probably go along with the game until he is completely defeated or finds a way out; in the second, he may join a more or less rebellious gang.

As C. Wright Mills has pointed out in *White Collar*, the lower echelons of better-educated males in U.S. society are expected to maintain a "salable" personality in their areas of employment and in relations with the public. Such a personality is considered in Hispanic culture as weak and effeminate – directly opposed to the *hombría* or *machismo* of the Spanish-speaking male.[22] It is not that the Spanish-speaking male is overly aggressive. It is that he attains a type of personal integrity which he considers to be inviolate; this is found from the university professor in Spain to the inhabitant of a South El Paso bar. This demand for integrity is not inconsistent with Hispanic traditions of courtesy and formality. The Spanish-speaking male (or female) is capable of engaging in the most hypocritical conversation imaginable – but almost invariably both parties fully realize that neither is telling the truth, or is expected to tell it. The "honesty" generally sought by U.S. employers is attained by a process to which relatively few Spanish-speaking males will submit – by the molding of the personality to fit the job.

Spanish-speaking males in the Southwest who do continue through a university

[22] There is direct evidence of this in the use of the term *bolillo* by the Spanish speakers in referring to to the Anglo male. (It otherwise refers to the bobbin used in making lace, to starched lace cuffs, or to white thread.)

strongly prefer medicine and law as professions. These are traditional educational goals of Hispanic education, and they require a molding of personality which is suited to Hispanic temperament. The Hispanic lawyer or physician is traditionally a man of broad culture, often an artist, poet, or writer, sometimes a social reformer, a part-time teacher, or a politician. These goals of the Spanish-speaking male in the South-west are much the same as they would be if he were living in Spain or in a Latin-American country. Considering the small proportion of Spanish speakers who would be middle or upper class members if they lived in such a country, it is perhaps not surprising that a relatively small number are members of professions in the South-west. Middle-class white-collar work requiring only high school graduation or a B.A. degree is not easily reconciled with their roles as males of Hispanic background.

An experiment conducted by "Careers for Youth", a Phoenix organization designed to acquaint "culturally deprived" Negro, Anglo, and Mexican-American children with middle-class American life, has demonstrated the lack of inherent appeal of the middle-class Anglo world to the Spanish-speaking student. The organization hoped that through field trips, friendly interest, and discussions, these children would be motivated to attain middle class status. The first to drop out have been the Spanish speakers.

The present discussion has shown how this may be an expected outcome of the irrelevance of U.S. school organization and job expectancy to the fulfillment of the role of both the male and the female in Hispanic society. Many Spanish-speaking individuals play the Hispanic sex role whether or not it is appropriate to the external social structure in which they live. They do this because the Hispanic social structure is "there" – partly in the family, partly in objectified language and culture, partly in the church, and partly in the attitudes and words of one's friends.

The Hispanic division of social role on the basis of age is not unusual in terms of the social structure of other European countries, but is unusual in terms of the social structure of the United States as a whole. In Hispanic culture, children are subject to the authority of their parents until they establish a family of their own. Other than that, increase in age generally signifies increase in authority. The wife is subject to the authority of the husband partly because she is female and partly because she is usually much younger than he. It is not at all uncommon for her to be "young enough to be his daughter". Not only does this allow the male to dominate her more effectively, but it puts him in a position of much greater relative prestige with regard to the rest of the family, and has important results in the socialization of the children. The age differential between husband and wife is to a great extent necessary because of other factors of Hispanic social structure: since the family is expected to be large, the wife should begin bearing children when she is young, whereas the husband should be "well established" before he is married.

Family history is still the most effective gauge of status in nearly all the Spanish-speaking world, and the individual's position in society is that of his family. The family is a self-sufficient unit and a mutual aid organization, incorporating many responsibilities and privileges, social and economic. It is often huge by U.S. standards, and composed of three generations, siblings of the parents, etc. Nearly as important is the *compadrazgo*.[23] If one individual should earn more than the family were accustomed to having, there would be little evidence of it once it was distributed among the many family members. Since the wife must not (and frequently has no time to) work, conventional U.S. methods do not enable the Spanish-speaking family to better its economic situation. Therefore, the individual in Hispanic culture can do little but accept the status of his family as permanent and learn to reap the benefits of living at that particular social level. This is one of the most essential elements in the maintenance of Hispanic culture and social life. If pressures toward constant change of socio-economic status became as dominant over other values as they are in U.S. society in general, individual character structure, social structure, and Hispanic culture at large would have to change. Under such circumstances it is very unlikely that the language itself would survive.

Such a large social unit as the Hispanic family requires someone with authority to manage it; this authority is delegated to the father. Noramally he cannot be intimate with or help each child educationally and professionally. Howevei, this distance and authority perhaps focuses the child's attention more on his father as a clear model. The companionate family system of the United States would be ridiculously impractical for Hispanic families. If Spanish-speaking children seeing it to their advantage, attempt to adopt Anglo attitudes and threaten the authority of the father, he may find it preferable that they leave school (the benefits of which he questions) and go to work to help support the rest of the family. The employment available to those without a high school education is likely to reaffirm the structure of authority found in the family, rather than that espoused by the public school.

Religion pervades Hispanic society in a manner that can hardly be understood by those outside it, incorporating all that is perceived of life. It dominates the life of suffering through asceticism – and the life lived with gusto through sensuality. Spanish speakers almost invariably name their children for a saint, and celebrate the saint's day rather than the child's birthday. A child may be named Jesús, José, or María – or perhaps all three. And if the child later becomes an atheist, he still proudly retains his name. In a discussion of Hispanic attitudes toward religion, Tere Ríos (1962, p. 5) says,

Jorge marches his wife and children off without fail; he has them all baptized, sees that they are instructed as well as he (which isn't often well); but for himself: What is church to Him? Church is for women and children and priests. But he's a Catholic – he'll tell you so. And get shot for it – or whatever else is required to be a Catholic – except go to church.

On numerous occasions don Quijote equates the Church with weakness and effeminacy,

---

[23] Those nearest the immediate family are the *padrino* and the *madrina* – the godparents – who are expected to care for their godchildren in the event of death of the parents or any other serious emergency. Practically speaking, this often means that the family includes godchildren from other families.

as do Latin American novelists to the present day. Monuments throughout Mexico represent the great father image, Benito Juárez. And icons everywhere represent the great mother image, La Virgen de Guadalupe. The latter offers solace in illness and misfortune, and heals one's body; the former offers strength and protection – and his basic ideas are incorporated into the Mexican constitution, telling everyone, including the Church, what may and may not be done.

There is much external evidence that religion is an integral part of Hispanic culture: customs of naming, number of religious holidays, using of names of deities in ordinary conversation, prevalence of highly personal stories about the saints, and the fact that churches dominate almost every populated landscape. The less visible role is more difficult to discover, but there is much evidence that the structure and functionaing of the entire society is dependent upon it – and that its role is that of the Spanish-speaking mother who, so long as the children behave, is loving, understanding, and forgiving.

Contact with the English Language and Anglo Culture

It has not been the purpose of the preceding to imply a complete discontinuity or dissimilarity between Hispanic culture or social structure, on the one hand, and Anglo culture or social structure on the other. Actually, the differences between the two are more appropriately understood as differences in the degree of dominance and inter-relatedness of certain themes and institutions. However, since an adequate presentation along such lines is beyond the scope of this essay, it may be permissible to indicate that dominant themes and institutions of Hispanic and Anglo life are quite consistently weighted toward opposite ends of inter-related continua. From the point of view of U.S. attitudes and values in general, Hispanic behavior is irrational. To obtain a better perspective on this situation, we may glance at Anglo social structure and culture from the Hispanic point of view.

Just as "anarchism" is the chief virtue and chief vice of Hispanic society, "order" is the chief virtue and chief vice of Anglo society. And just as "anarchism" can be associated with individuality, vitality, passion, integrity, and freedom – or chaos, inefficiency, crime, violence, and injustice, so can "order" be associated with progress, efficiency, cleanliness, stability, and justice – or innocuousness, sterility, antisepses, rigidity, and timidity. Each society tends to judge the other on the basis of the negative elements of its chief characteristic, of course, and its own by the positive elements. The names in Spanish for Anglos reveal some of these negative associations.[24] More-

[24] The most popular name for Anglos in general throughout the Southwest is *gabachos*. It has come to have connotations of impotence – sometimes even of effeminacy. *Gringo* is of course a much used term, always used disparagingly but sometimes tempered with an attitude of humor. *Yanquis* has connotations of lack of humanity, and economic imperialism. No neutral or flattering terms (except "Anglos") are commonly used. For that matter, neither are there any in English for the Mexican. Even "Mexican" is so often used disparagingly that many who proudly refer to themselves as *mexicanos* in Spanish are insulted if an Anglo calls them Mexican. The only "polite" names are the ones which do not refer specifically to the Mexican, or which even deny his Mexican heritage: Spanish-

over, these negative reactions remain strong and persistent because contact with Anglos is limited almost entirely to lower-middle-class Anglos (the policeman, the teacher, the social worker, etc.) whose attitudes are more unpalatable to Hispanic tastes than those of either higher or lower socio-economic groups in the United States. Graciela Gil-Olivárez states that the greatest critics of "Mexicans" in the Southwest are Mexican-Americans who have become members of the U.S. middle class, and that the few educated Spanish-speaking persons who attempt to maintain their original language and culture are a minority within a minority. These isolated, educated Spanish-speaking Americans are not active members of the Anglo cummunity.[25]

In the Southwestern United States, the problem is seen as a relatively simple one by many Spanish-speaking leaders and sympathetic Anglos: the Spanish speakers suffer from their location at the bottom of the socio-economic scale; education is most likely to put them higher on the scale – into the highly vaunted U.S. middle class; therefore education is *the* solution to the problems of the Spanish-speaking people in the United States. However, this solution is far from being achieved at present. Los Angeles has become the haven for the Spanish speakers in the Southwest; yet in the University of California at Los Angeles Spanish-speakers are numerically the smallest group.[26] Julian Samora reports that dropouts among Spanish-speaking students show a higher rate than among any other social group, especially in the ninth and tenth grades. It may be precisely when he is in high school, at an age when he is encouraged to consider what he is "going to be", that the Spanish-speaking boy decides that he does not want to be "an American man".

Most schools, though fairly eager to keep the Spanish-speaking student in school, have failed to develop effective methods of doing so. A University of New Mexico study concluded:

An analysis of the results indicated that the educational programs had failed to make allowances for the cultural barriers and the language barriers of the majority of the students in that district. We were gearing our educational program to people who were from an entirely different world.[27]

Too often even the Spanish-speaking teacher or school administrator has not fully realized the nature of the problem.

The Hispanic world has developed its own approach to urban life.[28] Many of the

---

speaking, Latin-American, or Spanish-American. Some Mexican-Americans do refer to themselves in Spanish as *latinoamericanos* or *hispanoamericanos*, but most are perfectly content with *mexicanos*, *Chicanos* or *la raza* when they are talking among themselves; if they want to be disparaging, they use the word *pochos* – a term which represents a good part of the spectrum of negative reactions to Anglo society.

[25]   Personal interview with Graciela Gil-Olivárez, July 1963.
[26]   Personal interview with Dr. S. L. Robe, Chairman of Department of Spanish and Portuguese, UCLA, July 1963.
[27]   Ray Leger, *Special Program for the Bi-lingual Child*, Address to the Mexican-American Seminar, January 1963.
[28]   At this point it may seem that we are dealing with two other distinctions: that between rural and

problems brought on by city life are the same for all people – but the interpretations are not the same in various cultures. Hispanic society, like Anglo society, accepts the city's gift of freedom of action, but, unlike Anglo society, it does not accept the depersonalization of city life as a reality to which one simply adjusts – nor the economic scale as the quantifier of human success. Conflict between Hispanic culture and urban life usually ends in the submission of many demands of urban life to those of Hispanic culture. It is true that circumstances have decreed that most Spanish-speaking immigrants to the United States be rural and of the lower socio-economic classes. But the culture of the Spanish speakers who have immigrated to the Southwest is only incidentally connected with rural life and with rural poverty; it would not find great difficulty in making the transition to values prevalent in a city of Spanish speakers. Its great difficulty is in making the transition to Anglo culture.

Life in the Spanish-speaking family and neighborhood is so complete in itself that the child usually makes little contact with Anglo society until he enters elementary school. His emotional satisfactions so far have come from playing with other children, not with toys. The disposition to value human relationships over material welfare is ingrained early and effortlessly. That, as a school child, he does not readily reject his old values and embrace Anglification is a source of never-ending amazement to school officials. Few educators realize that the Spanish-speaking child has never accepted the transcendent value of material goods and socio-economic success, and furthermore, that he has received most of his personal gratifications from a world in which these are virtually unknown.

The elementary school child does not, of course, realize that he is rebelling against Anglo culture as a member of Hispanic culture. However, his identification is with the people who satisfy his needs. He does not realize that his identifications make him a part of a culture which does not traditionally plan for the future but accepts life's situation as it exists at a given moment. He does not realize that his culture emphasizes being, not doing. He simply knows that he becomes increasingly uncomfortable – "not at home" – as he progresses in school. As Carl Rosenquist (1961) has put it,

It is ... difficult if not impossible for a boy in school to disregard completely the values of the dominant culture in which he is immersed. Constantly reminded of his lack of interest in the standard objectives and discriminated against because of the level of his achievement, he is likely to react negatively, that is, he comes to deny the validity of the standard objectives and to embrace values that are diametrically opposed.

Many such children seem to reject both cultures. They often belong to clubs or gangs which use a language, an argot, understood neither by Anglos nor by their own parents.

---

urban life on the one hand, and that between lower-class and middle-class life on the other. To a certain extent this is true. Anglos of lower socioeconomic status may have as much in common with Spanish-speaking persons of similar status as they have with middle-class Anglo society; rural Anglos may have as much in common with rural Spanish-speaking persons as they have with Anglos of a large city. It is indeed practicable to develop a sociology and a psychology of urban life, of rural life, of poverty, and of the middle class in general; research based on this may and should cross the lines of language. But these differences are only incidentally the subject of this paper.

While many of the Spanish speakers in the Southwest also see this superficially as a rejection of both cultures, it seems rather to be an *exaggeration and distortion of the traditional Hispanic male role in society*. As such, it contains elements of the long and rich tradition of the *pícaro* in Latin American and Spanish literature.

There seem to be no adult gangs or groups comparable to the *pachucos*. Barker (1958) found it to be a characteristic of Mexican-American youths to organize into such groups, or to adopt the *pachuco* vocabulary and attitudes individually. Those who did not were considered not to "belong". He found one characteristic of their attitude to be disdain of advancing on the socio-economic scale, planning for the future, or obeying the laws either of the land or of their parents. Their greatest value was placed on present experience – the excitement of sex, drugs (there are at least 18 *pachuco* words for "marijuana"), and defiance of authority. These are simply the exaggeration and distortion of Hispanic values which are found throughout the society and throughout the literature. This exaggeration generally disappears, except for occasional scenes in the bar or *cantina*, once the *pachuco* is married and begins having children, but his basic Hispanic attitudes and values rarely disappear.

Many of the *pachucos* spend some time in high school, and some of them graduate. According to Samora's data for the five Southwestern states, one-fourth to about one-half as many of the Spanish speakers as of Anglos graduate from high school. About the same proportion to twice as many non-whites have graduated from high school (Samora 1963). Of a Spanish-speaking population of approximately three-and-a-half million, there were only 14,000 in college in 1961. The few Spanish-speaking leaders in the United States came almost entirely from this minute, relatively well-educated group. They may be highly disinclined toward continued contact with their illiterate *compadres*. Most of them have sacrificed and worked hard to overcome the "disadvantage" of their origin, of the prejudice against them, and of their own most natural impulses and desires. They may even have side-stepped some of their normal familial and religious obligations to attain their status, and, as a result, have become further alienated through a feeling of guilt. There is much evidence that they have had to break the most essential of bonds to Hispanic society, culture, and language, to attain a desirable position in Anglo society.

One of the predominant characteristics of the Spanish speakers in the Southwest is that their largely non-literate culture reaches them in Spanish, but literate elaborations of culture – particularly high culture – come to them almost entirely through English. This creates a dual environment. One culture provides basic personal and social satisfactions not duplicated in the English-speaking environment. The other culture represents intellectual attainment as well as socio-economic progress which is not available in the Spanish-speaking environment. Spanish represents a world of virtually effortless pleasures and gratifications – a world which may be symbolized by the radio, which permeates the atmosphere and is available at a moment's notice. English represents the dull and demanding world of work – a world which may be symbolized by the clock, which impersonally and relentlessly assigns the task to be done.

It is not surprising that under these circumstances the Spanish-speaking person prefers to live in the first world and contribute as little energy as possible to the second. When he has discharged his obligations to the second, he does not want to put forth more time and effort of the same type into the first. He does not want to read a novel in Spanish, for example, because that is the sort of thing he has been taught to do in the Anglo school. Literature, theater, organized cultural activity is a part of "that world". He prefers to relax in the security of his native world – the world of the language he first learned.

It has been observed that the failure of American educators to take cognizance of the validity of other cultures, except in the abstract, stems from the innocence of the Anglo-American which makes him "wait, as for a natural thing, for all the world to adjust itself to middle class North American culture". It is the innocence of confidence and success, but it has contributed to a lack of understanding, not only with Spanish speakers in the United States but with those of the entire hemisphere.

FUTURE PROBABILITIES AND POSSIBILITIES

There are three possibilities with regard to the future of the Spanish language and Hispanic culture in the Southwestern United States: (1) continued coexistence with the English language and Anglo culture, with each largely satisfying its own needs and demands, and with a minimum of contact between them; (2) assimilation of the Spanish-speaking people into the Anglo culture, first by the exercise of equal educational and employment rights, and later by their acceptance of the small family, the wife's employment, and psychological guidance by the psychiatrist rather than the priest; and (3) synthesis of the two cultures, such that many persons are able to achieve the personal integration and self-direction of Hispanic culture along with the orderliness and efficiency of Anglo culture. None of these three possibilities can exist exclusively of the other two, but the relative balance achieved among them will play an important part in the future of Spanish in the Southwest as well as in the future of the United States as a whole.

For a long time to come there will be two distinct linguistic and cultural groups in the Southwest. Assuring this is the gross difference in standards of living as between the United States and Mexico, with the lowest socio-economic groups in the United States earning from five to thirty or more times what they would earn in Mexico. Mexicans will find some way to get here, and some way to work, legally or illegally, for wages low enough to compete with domestic labor. The experience of hunger is disagreeable enough to assure this. They will live in areas and in dwellings in which Anglos refuse to live, and will create large populations in these areas by following the dictates of their culture and their religion. They will necessarily communicate among themselves in Spanish, and radio broadcasters will tell them in Spanish where to buy their food and clothing. Even should they consider it important, they will find it economically impossible to stay as clean and as neat as the Anglos, and this will provide a source of discrimination and negative stereotypes even should other sources disappear. Many will migrate too often for their children to get the full benefit of the schooling offered them. And when they finally step outside this process and into something like middle-class life, there will be other Mexicans waiting to take their places.

This is not intended to be a depressing picture. It *is* depressing only from the point of view of the American middle class. The *bracero* who comes to the United States does so because he is desperate enough to pay the bribes it takes to get him here, to leave his family, and to risk the horrors of *bracero* life on some ranches about which he has heard. He does not come looking for a $2 per hour minimum wage (about the income of a professional person in Mexico), and he realizes that employers are not looking for him in order to pay him such a wage. Even should he obtain $2 per hour, he will not use it to live a middle-class Anglo type of life; with part of it he will pay even higher *mordidas* to Mexican officials in order to enable relatives and friends to come here, and for the rest there will always be needy relatives here or back home. This is not to say that the Spanish speakers are averse to accepting more money or greater physical comforts than they now have, but that they – like the Navajos in New Mexico and Arizona and the cedar choppers in Central Texas – do not want to accept these for their children at the expense of losing them to a foreign world and a foreign way of life. And, consciously or unconsciously, they realize that this is what "progress" entails.

The children, however, may decide to be lost. As they grow up and must choose a way of life, they are in a position similar to that described by Murphy (1958):

Each [career] could be looked at objectively in terms of earnings, prestige, place in society. But at a deeper level each could be looked at in terms of the *kind of self*, the kind of picture of of one's individuality that one has drawn. Each of the two alternatives, "sweet and good," is now available, but once the choice has been made the other will forever become unrealizable. The student knows he is deciding between two ways of life and deciding *between two selves*. The decision is often postponed because of its formidable and threatening character. When once it is made, however, one soon notices a consolidation and crystallization of the values which band together as expressive of the choice made.

Once a choice is made, the individual frequently mobilizes all his defenses against the choice denied – which partially explains both the exaggerations of the *pachuco* and those of the *pocho*.

Almost by definition, the more complete the Anglification of Spanish speakers, the more complete the loss of their original language and culture. Most of them who become assimilated think of this as the loss of an antiquated culture of poverty and suffering; they have never heard of the Golden Age of Spain, and would not have recognized it as a part of their heritage if they had. Once the Spanish-speaking individual becomes a part of the U.S. middle class, he frequently works through his organizations not only to make it *possible* for other ("less enlightened") Spanish speakers to join him, but actively to discourage such attitudes or actions as would tend to preserve Hispanic values. This seems to him necessary for the effective incorporation of the Spanish speaker into the world of Anglo values – and indeed, at the present time, it may be essential. Spanish speakers may keep only the external forms, even of their religion, if they are to become effective U.S. citizens, living according to the mores of the middle class.

For many, the gospel of assimilation is hard to resist. It is founded on the doctrine that middle-class American society provides the best of all possible worlds. Indeed, the miracles of plumbing, transportation, and television are compelling, objective evidence of this. U.S. citizens cynically observe the alacrity with which other peoples accept these miracles even when they do not accept the gospel. It seems obvious to some that the gospel is to become universal, all others dwindling to nothingness before it: the sooner everyone accepts it, the simpler it will be for all. And those who live within our borders – poverty-stricken, uneducated, and unambitious – need only to become a part of the American public school system for twelve years in order to achieve salvation.

Admittedly, no other view of the strengths of our culture is so attractive. To take another view implies that we are not so near the limits of human potentialities. But if one is willing to assume that other values are tenable, it may become evident that some positive values are in the process of being lost, and that life may become less satisfying as a result. Some of these values may be precisely those which are best preserved in Hispanic culture: values associated with the poetization of life, with the personalization of human relationships, with the full perception of the present, with the completeness and adequacy of the individual, with unquantifiable human experience, with a greater range of inner freedoms, and with a serenity which accepts what is, to make the most of it, rather than restlessly and continuously searching for something different. If these values are worth preserving, we can best preserve them in those persons for whom they are native – persons from a background which for centuries has been a matrix for these values. One way to do this is by giving them contact in our schools, from the very first, with the ancient roots of Hispanic culture, and with the beautiful elaborations of it which are now in formation, as well as with those which have become the heritage of the centuries. It cannot be achieved by the patronizing introduction of sombreros and serapes into the classroom.

Some proposals for the inforporation of this heritage into the larger culture of the United States were presented at a conference in Los Angeles on November 14, 1963, directed by members of the President's Committee for Equal Economic Opportunity. At this conference the need for preserving Hispanic culture in the Southwest was recognized. It was pointed out that such efforts will not only help the Spanish-speaking population to establish a suitable role in U.S. society, but will enable the United States to work more effectively with Latin American nations. With this end in view, officials of the Federal Government pledged themselves to promote the education of Spanish speakers in Spanish as well as in English, by teachers who know and respect the Spanish language and culture, by guidance counselors who are able to advise both students and parents in Spanish and in terms of their own culture, by the development of vocational opportunities for the Spanish speakers which will utilize their particular cultural biases as well as their skills, and by the preparation and utilization of Spanish-speaking persons for overseas assignments in Latin America, both in business and in government. There seems to be only one important element which was not mentioned in the recommendations: the education of the Spanish speakers in terms of the greatest literary and artistic traditions of Hispanic culture. It is the presence or lack of such and education which usually separates the American diplomat who speaks Spanish from the Spanish-speaking Latin American. Its acquisition provides the intelligent Spanish-speaking person with the foundations of transcendent values in his culture. The best that we can do is to offer it to him, and allow him to live with it once he acquires it. The Spanish-speaking people of the Southwest may then become a part of the culture of the United States in such a way that they can make a contribution which no other group on earth can make to us – a contribution which may enlarge and strengthen our own potentialities.

REFERENCES

Andersson, T., "Foreign Languages and Intercultural Understanding", *National Elementary Principal*, 36 (1957), No. 5, 32-35.
Barker, G. C., *Pachuco, An American-Spanish Argot and Its Social Functions in Tucson, Arizona* (Tucson, University of Arizona Press, 1958).
de Leon, M., "Wanted: A New Educational Philosophy for the Mexican-American", Unpublished MS (abridged synopsis in the *Journal of Secondary Education*, 34, 1959, 398-402).
Espinosa, A. M., "Studies in New Mexican Spanish Phonology and Morphology", *Bulletin, Language Series*, No. 2 (Albuquerque, University of New Mexico Press, December, 1909).
Haugen, E., *Bilingualism in the Americas* (University, Ala., American Dialect Society, 1956).
Kloss, H., *Das Volksgruppenrecht in den Vereinigten Staaten von Amerika*, Vol. I (Essen, Essener Verlagsanstalt, 1940).
LaFarge, O., *Santa Fe, The Autobiography of a Southwestern Town* (Norman, University of Oklahoma Press, 1959).
Murphy, G., *Human Potentialities* (New York, Basic Books, 1958).
Nostrand, H., "Literature, Area Study, and Hispanic Culture", *Hispania*, XLIV, No. 3 (September 1961).
——, "Digest of Handbook on the Describing and Teaching of Literate Cultures". Unpublished MS, Univ. of Washington, 1963.
Reynolds, Annie, "The Education of Spanish-Speaking Children in Five Southwestern States", *U.S. Office of Education Bulletin*, 1933, No. 11 (Washinton, Government Printing Office, 1933).
Ríos, T., *Understanding the Latin American* (St. Louis, The Queen's Work, 1962).
Rosenquist, C., "An Intercultural Study of Juvenile Delinquency", Address presented at the Conference on Social and Economic Change in Contemporary Mexico, Monterrey, Nuevo Léon, August, 1961. (Mimeographed.)
Samora, J. "Recommendation", from an unpublished report for the United States Commission on Civil Rights on the Spanish-speaking people in the United States, 1962.
——, "The Education of the Spanish-speaking in the Southwest – an Analysis of the 1960 Census Materials", published in mimeograph by the Mexican-American Seminar, Phoenix, Arizona, January, 1963.

Santibanez, E., *Ensayo Acerca de la Inmigración Mexicana en los Estados Unidos* (San Antonio, Clegg Co., 1930).

Saunders, L., "Address Delivered at the National Convention of the League of United Latin American Citizens", San Antonio, Study of Spanish-speaking People, June 11, 1949.

Texas Education Agency, *Report on the Educational Needs of Migrant Workers* (Austin, Texas Education Agency, 1962).

Ulibarri, S., "La Lengua: Crisol de la Cultura", *Hispania*, XLIV, No. 2 (May, 1951).

Wagner, J. A., *San Antonio Project*, Published in mimeograph by the Bishops' Committee, 551 San Pedro Avenue, San Antonio 12, 1963.

Works, G. A., *Texas Educational Survey Report*, VIII (Austin, Texas Educational Survey Commission, 1925).

12. UKRAINIAN LANGUAGE MAINTENANCE EFFORTS IN THE UNITED STATES

VLADIMIR C. NAHIRNY AND JOSHUA A. FISHMAN

For centuries the Ukrainian nationality has been a stepchild of Europe; its very presence on this shrinking globe has been consistently overlooked or ignored. Not a few of its past rulers exerted themselves to seal off its fate by officially decreeing that there never had been nor would there ever be a Ukrainian language or nationality.[1] Politically and culturally oppressed, economically impoverished, Ukrainians were reminded incessantly in the past that their only opportunity in life lay in becoming either Russians or Poles or even Magyars. At times, they were the object of oppressive assimilationist policies in comparison with which those exerted against Poles, Slovaks, or even Finns may be viewed as humane and liberal. For the Ukrainians were denied not only the right of self-rule, but also the use of their native tongue.

In modern times the Ukrainians have been a battleground for Russian and Polish imperial conflicts. Over one hundred years ago, Havlicek, the disenchanted Czech proponent of Pan-Slavic brotherhood, referred to the plight of Ukrainians in these unequivocal terms (Kohn 1955, pp. 157-58):

At the beginning I sided with the Poles against the Russians. As soon as I recognized the true state of affairs in Poland, as soon as the veil which poetically hid from me the prosaic misery and corruption of the nation (that is, the Polish nobility) dropped from my eyes, my affection changed to dislike, and for a psychologically understandable reason the Russians appeared to me to be better than the Poles. This, however, did not last long. I soon recognized that Peter is like Paul. Russia like Poland. My Slav sympathy disappeared, and I learned to regard the Russians and the Poles, in spite of the affinity of language, origin, and customs, as nations alien to us Czechs ... We must mot look on the Russian-Polish relations with as blind an eye as does the greater part of Europe; we should not think of an innocent lamb and a wolf, but know that the wolf meets wolf, and we shall say later that the lamb among them is the Ukrainian.... The Ukraine is the apple of discord which fate threw between these two nations.

The Poles and Russians buried the national spirit of the Ukraine and began to divided the great body, and, as generally happens in such cases, they began to fight and have not yet ceased. Both the Russians and the Poles regard the Ukrainian language as a dialect of their own language.... Thus we have seen three great Eastern Slav nations, each one of which hates the other two, and also has a just reason for it. Nobody can speak reasonably of brotherhood there.

---

[1] A special decree to that effect was issued in 1863 by Count Valuev, Minister of Interior.

With the partition of Poland in the last quarter of the 18th century, the Ukrainians fell under the political control of two multi-national empires – Austro-Hungary and Russia. Culturally, in turn, they were subjected to at least assimilationist pressures of various durations and intensities – the Russian pressure from the East and the Polish and Hungarian pressures from the West and Southwest. The bulk of the Ukrainian population, however, found itself governed by Russia. Out of a total of 26,700,000 Ukrainians at the end of the 19th century, about 85 per cent lived under Russian rule (Kubiiovych 1949, pp. 133-38). It was in Russia that the Ukrainian culture and language fared worst, due to the relentless pressure of Russification. One decree after another was issued in the course of the 19th century prohibiting the printing of both popular and scholarly works in Ukrainian, or the presentation of theatrical performances, the holding of lectures, the publishing of music, or even the singing of songs in the Ukrainian language. As late as 1887 one of the Russian censors opposed the publication of a Ukrainian grammar on the ground that it would be hardly advisable to print a grammar dealing with a language doomed to extinction.[2]

Not until 1905, under the spell of liberalization which followed in the wake of the First Russian Revolution, did the Imperial Academy of Sciences at St. Petersburg officially confirm the mere existence of a Ukrainian language. With this granting of the long denied right, hitherto suppressed modes of linguistic and cultural expression flared into new life. Literary and even scientific publications began to appear in Ukrainian; the Ukrainian press emerged no less quickly. Despite the fact that martial law was soon proclaimed, some thirty-four different newspapers began publication by the end of 1905. With the onslaught of reaction in 1907, however, the Ukrainian cultural revival in the Russian Empire was harshly curtailed.

On the other hand, the development of Ukrainian national culture in the Austro-Hungarian Empire fared far better during the second half of the 19th century. In pursuing its well-established policy of keeping the Empire intact by playing off one nationality against another, the government granted the Ukrainians certain liberties as a means of securing their political loyalty. This was especially true after 1848, when the clamor of different nationalities for cultural autonomy, if not political independence, threatened the very integrity of the Austro-Hungarian Empire. These

---

[2] The harm inflicted upon the literary language and upon Ukrainian culture in general by this oppressive policy can be seen from the fact that no more than 25 books were published in Ukrainian during the "apogee of autocracy" between 1845 and 1856.

1845	1	1851	2
1846	0	1852	3
1847	0	1853	0
1848	3	1854	3
1849	2	1855	4
1850	1	1856	6

Total 25

Source: D. Antonovych (ed.), *Ukrainska Kultura* (Regensburg, Ukrainskyi Tekhnichno-Hospodarskyi Instytut, 1947), p. 37. See also S. Iefremov, *V Tismykh Riamkakh: Ukrainska Knyha v 1798-1916* (Kiev, 1926), pp. 4-7.

concessions, insignificant though they were in comparison to those granted to Poles, made Galicia a haven for refugee intellectuals from the Russian Ukraine. As a result, that part of the Ukrainian ethnographic territory which was under Austro-Hungarian control quickly became a center of Ukrainian cultural activity and irredentist agitation, and later came to be known as the cultural "Piedmont" of the Ukraine.

The impact of this cultural renaissance upon the mass of Ukrainians in Austro-Hungary deserves to be carefully assessed, since it was this very region that long supplied the overwhelming majority of Ukrainian immigrants to the United States.

UKRAINIANS IN GALICIA

In the latter part of the 19th century Ukrainians were not the sole imhabitants of Galicia; Poles and Jews, for example, comprised roughly 35 per cent of the total population. On the whole, the ethnic composition of that region coincided with its class and occupational distribution. The Jewish group alone numbered 811,371 in 1900, representing 11 per cent of the population in Galicia (Mahler 1952, p. 257). According to the official census of that year, the largest occupational category (about 30 per cent) of all gainfully employed Jews consisted of "merchants, dealers, shop-keepers and brokers" (Mahler 1952; Bujak 1919, p. 17). About 88 per cent of Galician trade at that time was preempted by the Jewish ethnic group. Another, similarly exclusive Jewish occupation in Galicia was tavern- and innkeeping. Over 70,000 Jews in Galicia made their living by selling alcoholic beverages, and they constituted about 80 per cent of all those involved in this occupational pursuit (Mahler 1952, p. 258). With the exception of a tiny stratum of secular intelligentsia (literati, journalists, school teachers) and the Catholic clergy, the bulk of the Ukrainian population (about 94 per cent in 1900) belonged to the mass of illiterate peasantry, steeped in poverty and alcoholism. Under the feudal conditions that prevailed in Galicia at that time, almost half of all cultivated land was in the hands of about 4,000 Polish or Polonized landowners. At the same time, almost 80 per cent of all peasant families had holdings of less than 12.5 acres and about 43 per cent of them less than six acres.

A peculiar social structure thus evolved in Galicia: at its bottom one found a mass of peasantry, representing at once a social class and an ethnic collectivity; at its top a scattered stratum of economically and politically privileged landowners and officials of Polish nationality or cultural orientation. The Jewish ethnic group occupied a precarious position between these two bifurcated extremes of the semi-feudal edifice, fighting both for legal emancipation and to ward off the ever-present danger of economic impoverishment, if not transformation into an *am-haaretz* ("people of the soil", rustics).

Ethnic and class differentiations were reinforced by political power and administrative control, for the administrative and political hierarchies in Galicia were virtually monopolized by Polish and Polonized landowners. Two thousand large landowners were able to elect more representatives to the Diet than could several million peasants. Some, indeed, were elected by as few as twenty voters, while a deputy of the peasantry usually represented no less than 100,000 peasants. Given this configuration of political power and privilege, the Polish ethnic group was able to control and manipulate to its own advantage practically all public educational and cultural institutions.

It is fairly evident, then, that the societal structure was characterized by "superimposed" segmentation; i.e., membership in one social group or category implied, as a rule, membership in another. Most Ukrainians belonged to the socially and politically subordinate class of rustics of Greek Catholic religion; most Jews, to the occupational stratum of petty tradesmen and merchants; and, finally, most Poles to the politically superordinate and socially privileged group of landowners, officials, and administrators of the Roman Catholic religion. Class, ethnicity, religion, economic privilege, and political power were thus largely superimposed. Although this traditional configuration of class and ethnicity had become considerably modified by the first decade of this century, the Ukrainians, the Poles, and the Jews long remained cast in the stereotyped images of "illiterate *khlop*" (peasant), "cultured *pan*" (gentleman), and "petty peddler", respectively. The very persistence of these stereotypes, as the literature of that period testifies, is highly suggestive and cannot be lightly dismissed as an unfortunate survival of traditional attitudes. For these same attitudes were part of the dominant value orientations that effectively influenced individual behavior and ideals. Phrased in concrete terms, a young Ukrainian aspiring to the status position of refined *pan* and urbanite not only sought to acquire a higher education (attending non-Ukrainian schools, of course) but also to discard other cultural attributes related to his Ukrainian ethnicity – foremost among them the Ukrainian language. Vertical social mobility was thus tantamount in extreme cases to ethnic estrangement. No wonder, then, that assimilation took a sizable toll among educated Ukrainians in the course of the 18th and 19th centuries.

The basic character of Galician society at the end of the 19th century may be described as follows: an ethnically-confounded, stratified society based on the axis of dominant city and subordinate countryside. Since Ukrainians belonged overwhelmingly to the peasant class, and thus represented the rural dimension of this society, they constituted only part-society and part-culture. Whatever name one applies to such a peasant part-culture – be it folk-ethnic culture, lay culture, low culture, or little tradition – it is clear that it was shared by the unreflective many and that its continuity depended basically upon direct transmission from generation to generation by spoken word and personal example. This is all the more true in view of the fact that about 75 per cent of the Ukrainian population in Galicia was illiterate as late as the last decade of the 19th century. Implicit in this characterization is the conclusion that the Ukrainian ethnic group was long unable to evolve a national culture composed of both rural (little tradition) and urban (great tradition) dimensions. For the latter dimension of culture requires for its development a special group of individuals directly engaged in cultivating such national values as language, art, literature, and even history.

The autocratic regime of 19th-century Russia greatly impeded the formation of such a nationally-oriented cultural elite among Ukrainians. From Bogdanovich to Potapenko, from Gogol to Korelenko, a long line of educated individuals of Ukrainian ethnic background channeled their creative energies into Russian cultural life, enriching it with some of their finest products. Such ethnically estranged individuals frequently shared the attitudes of urban (Polish, Russian) society and looked down upon the culture and language of their fathers and forefathers. Even if some of them were of the populist persuasion and half-heartedly glorified the "pastoral harmony" of the countryside, they tended to view this same culture as an integral part of the peasant way of life and, as such, unbecoming for a man of refinement and education. This attitude was held not only by the many intellectuals who severed all ties with their Ukrainian heritage, but also by the few who retained considerable interest in it. This latter group of educated Ukrainians enjoyed dancing Ukrainian folk dances and singing melodious folk songs; they gladly availed themselves of the local Ukrainian dialect in addressing village maidens and household servants. But the language of high culture and refined conversation, at times even within the family circle, was predominantly either Russian or Polish. In every real sense, the stratum of educated Ukrainians has been bilingual and bicultural since the beginning of the 19th century. Its members belonged to the subordinate Ukrainian subculture only by virtue of their ancestral ethnic origins and identified themselves with the superordinate Polish or Russian subcultures by virtue of their achieved educational status. Within the family circle, on informal festive occasions, and in church services, they conversed, prayed and confessed in Ukrainian; within the public sphere of life they turned either to Polish or to Russian. Ethnic and familial bonds sustained their loyalty to the Ukrainian spoken tongue; functional requirements and considerations of status made them master either the Polish or Russian literary language.

Toward the end of the 19th century Ukrainian intellectuals in Galicia did undertake to develop a national culture, but their influence upon the illiterate multitudes was most certainly limited. It is hardly an exaggeration to state that this elite remained largely isolated from the very people on whose behalf it labored. For only well-developed and appropriately numerous and diversified educational institutions could have successfully mediated between the reflective few and the unreflective many. Inasmuch as most educational institutions in Galicia at that time were controlled by Poles and, indeed, served as agencies of Polonization among Ukrainians, the popular press remained the only important medium of contact with and influence upon the peasant masses. Yet the press neither was nor could it have been a truly effective instrument for reaching them.

There was, however, in each village one institution and one individual at once intimately acquainted with the peasant way of life and in touch with "high culture" – the Church and its representative, the priest. The priest alone possessed sufficient education and was close enough to the village people to be able to mediate between the outside world and the local way of life. He alone was capable of articulating their grievances and broadening their horizons. If such a priest was neither Polonized nor Russified, he was then able not only to preach and spread the Word of God, but also to strengthen that type of ethnic solidarity that transcended kinship ties and local village attachments. And it must be granted that the Ukrainian clergy in Galicia performed this latter role with considerable success since the end of the last century.

All other contacts that the Ukrainian peasants might have had with the outside and upper world – such as those with local officials and legal authorities, with Jewish tradesmen and tavern-keepers – were too intermittent and too impersonal to have any lasting effect upon their traditional outlook and way of life. From this outside world they learned at best a few Yiddish phrases which they half-jokingly used on recurrent visits to a market town. In some rare instances they also mastered conversational Polish in order to be able to greet arriving and departing "absentee" landowners or persons of authority. At best, these businesslike contacts with the outside world reminded the Ukrainian peasants that their own villages hardly represented the whole of society and culture, that there were above and beyond them people possessing different traditions, religions, and languages. Such situational perceptions of cultural differences helped them to determine, albeit negatively, their own ethnic identity. And while most of them were also aware of the fact that there were Tsars and Kaisers on the thrones and even Popes in Rome, such kinds of knowledge played only an insignificant role in their daily round of activities.

UKRAINIAN IMMIGRATION TO THE UNITED STATES

The history of Ukrainian immigration to the United States may be conveniently subdivided into three distinct periods. The first phase of mass immigration extended from about 1870 to the First World War. Lack of official records for the first three decades of this period (1870-1899) makes it impossible to assess the number of Ukrainian immigrants to the United States. As might be expected, the available unofficial estimates differ rather considerably, ranging from 200,000 to 300,000 (Bachynskyi 1914, pp. 86-114). We do know, however, that before 1880 Ukrainian immigration was sporadic; after that date it increased consistently and reached its highest peak in 1914, with a total of 42,413 individuals in that year alone. The figures in Table 12.1 disclose a steadily increasing flow of Ukrainian immigrants during the years 1899-1914.

TABLE 12.1

Number of Ukrainian Immigrants to the United States 1899-1914

| 1899-1900 | 4,232 | 1903-1904 | 19,437 | 1907-1908 | 36,442 | 1911-1912 | 39,689 |
| 1901-1902 | 12,821 | 1905-1906 | 30,730 | 1909-1910 | 43,715 | 1913-1914 | 66,669 |

Source: Vasyl Halych, "Rozmishchennia Ukrainskoi Imigracii v Zluehenykh Derzhavah", in *Propamiatna Knyha*, L. Myshuha (ed.) (Jersey City, Ukrainskyi Narodnyi Soiuz, 1936), pp. 451-457.

The First World War brought about a sharp decline in the number of Ukrainians admitted to the United States. Although this trend was somewhat reversed in the early 1920's, the promulgation of the Immigration Act of 1924 virtually put an end to the mass influx. During the period 1914 to 1933 no more than 25,000 Ukrainians came to this country. For the five-year period 1931 to 1936, official statistics record a total of 587 Ukrainian immigrants, an average of 96 individuals per year (Halich 1937, p. 12). The second phase of Ukrainian immigration, which coincided with the period between the two World Wars is, therefore marked by a sharp decline in arrivals. World War II refugees represent the third and most recent wave. Ukrainian authors estimate that about 80,000 of these refugees settled in the United States during the decade following the Second World War. This estimate is probably somewhat conservative; a slightly higher figure of 85,000 would seem to be more accurate (Mudryi 1954, p. 131).

There can be no doubt that economic conditions prevalent in Galicia around the turn of the last century prompted the Ukrainians to depart *en masse* from their native land. The constantly increasing rural population and the attendant division and subdivision of the available land brought about a general impoverishment of the peasant class. As one of the early American students of Slavic immigration observed (Balch 1910, p. 138):

Of all agricultural properties in the country, nearly 80 per cent are "small" (that is, under twelve and a half acres), and nearly half consist of less than five acres. That this excessive subdivision is the main cause of emigration from Galicia is undisputed. When a man has so little that it can no longer support him, much less provide for his children, he probably gets into debt, and, at any rate, is in imperative need for money.

In the absence of industry and outside work, disinherited peasants were forced to work on landowners' estates for extremely low wages, ten to thirty cents per day in 1900. Emigration remained the only avenue of escape from the feudal conditions and economic hardships prevailing in the countryside. The class and occupational distribution of Ukrainian immigrants arriving in the United States during the first decade of this century (1899-1910) lends ample support to this interpretation (Table 12.2).

The servants of God from among the educated few, and the servants of Man from among the many illiterate grandsons or even sons of former serfs, were the two most significant groups of Ukrainian immigrants. *Khlopy* (peasants) and *popy* (priests) literally represented the Ukrainian ethnic group on the move. The former had left their villages out of sheer desire to survive, to secure for themselves and their children a means of livelihood; the latter followed their disinherited and hungry brethren in order to save souls. These two immigrant subgroups laid the shaky foundations of Ukrainian social and cultural life in the United States. The arrival of political refugees and several distinguished intellectuals in the early 1920's (including the scholars Kistiakovsky, Timoshenko, and Granovsky; the artist Archipenko; and the inventor Sikorsky) hardly affected the organized communal life of Ukrainian immigrants. At best, their personal achievements might have contributed to the awakening of a feeling

TABLE 12.2

Occupational Composition of Ukrainian Immigrants, 1899-1910

Type of Occupation		Number	Percent
Clergy	47	106	.08
Doctors	7		
Writers	24		
Teachers	24		
Others	4		
Tradesmen		48	.03
Skilled and Semi-Skilled workers		2,602	2.03
Farm Laborers, Servants		125,704	97.86
Total		128,460	

Source: "Distribution of Immigrants", *Senate Documents*,
61st Cong., 3rd Session, pp. 153-155.

of ethnic self-respect, heretofore so utterly lacking among many immigrants and their American-born children.

The most recent wave of refugee immigrants, however, brought about far-reaching changes in almost all large Ukrainian communities in the United States. The refugee immigrants not only reinforced the steadily weakening organized ethnic life but also provided it with new and more competent leadership. Moreover, they founded many new organizations – from scholarly societies to Ukrainian language schools. This came about not only because of their sheer numerical strength, but also because they included, for the first time in Ukrainian-American history, a very considerable number of individuals with urban backgrounds and with higher education (about ten per cent with college education). Available information on the class and occupational distribution of the post-World War II Ukrainian refugee population (Table 12.3), incomplete though it is, strikingly contrasts with that on Ukrainian immigrants arriving in

TABLE 12.3

*Occupational Composition of Adult Ukrainian Refugees
in Three Occupational Zones of Germany, 1948*

Type of Occupation	Number	Percent
Professionals	6,130	13.76
Merchants, Bankers	1,098	2.46
Skilled Workers	11,319	25.41
Unskilled and Semi-Skilled Workers	7,038	15.80
Farmers	18,957	42.56
Total	44,542	

Source: Mudryi (1954), pp. 119-120.

the United States prior to World War I. From among all the Ukrainian refugees leaving their homeland after the Second World War, a disproportionately large number of intellectuals, professionals, and skilled workers settled in the United States – among them about twelve hundred physicians and a thousand engineers.

The impact of these bearers of high culture on Ukrainian language maintenance deserves additional attention. However, before proceeding with an analysis of immigrational influence on language maintenance, let us return once more to the Ukrainian village society in which many Ukrainians still have notable roots.

PRIMORDIAL COLLECTIVITY: PEASANT SOCIETY AND CULTURE

Like other immigrants of peasant origin – Southern Italians, Lithuanians, Slovaks, Poles – the Ukrainians had direct and intimate familiarity with two natural groups, the family and the village. The village consisted primarily of a series of interrelated families, and was only derivatively an administrative and functional unit. In other words, the basic context of the peasant's way of life was the village-embedded kinship group. It encompassed the individual's whole life, from birth to death; it transmitted ancient customs and folkways from generation to generation; and, finally, it provided its young members with all the skills and knowledge required for perpetuating the traditional mode of life. Although politically and socially subordinate, it was culturally a self-sustained entity. We shall call such a territorially-related natural grouping of people, bound together by familistic and personal ties, a "primordial collectivity".

It bears emphasizing that this type of human community hardly provided a fertile soil for the growth of voluntary associations and special interest organizations. For the same reason it hardly recognized specifically defined and segmented loyalties. In contrast to more differentiated societies, in which ties of friendship originate in such specialized institutions as schools or youth movements, the entire village neighborhood constituted the sole reservoire from which friendship choices and personal contacts were available. The dominant pattern of village endogamy and the equally significant dearth of enduring inter-village contacts indicate beyond doubt that a village community was almost completely circumscribed.

Age-peer group and occupational organizations played a relatively insignificant role within the village environment. Some recent studies bearing upon this and related problems convincingly show that "joiners" tend to emerge under social conditions characterized by a growing independence from familial ties (see, e.g., Katz and Zloczower 1961, p. 324). Eisenstadt suggests that the relevance of age-peer groups varies with the difference between the roles and orientations an adolescent or youth has learned within the family and those he is supposed to take over as an adult member of society. Since there was no clear-cut separation of familial and non-familial spheres of life in the Ukrainian village, the patterns of behavior and attitudes expected of adult village members were acquired within the framework of the family. The transition from youth to adulthood thus entailed no major readjustment; it presupposed simply that children follow in the footsteps of their parents.

The centrality of kinship in the integration of the village community is of particular importance to an understanding of Ukrainian life before and since coming to America. It is this structural principle, and not so much the patriarchial type of family or inherent peasant traditionalism, that accounts for the generational continuity (absence of parent-child conflict) and cultural stability of the peasant community. While it is undeniably true that Ukrainian, Polish, or even Italian peasant families give the impression of absolute patriarchal authority, close examination of this alleged patriarchalism reveals a series of striking exceptions. Some authors consider these exceptions as "matriarchal survivals" and, indeed, argue that the father's absolute dominance superseded an ancient form of matriarchal society (Schermerhorn 1949, p. 240). But, whatever type of family might have been prevalent, the authority of father and/or mother was basically a function of the all-pervasive influence of familial relations within a village community. As long as these conditions obtained, the proverbial peasant conservatism as well as the traditional outlook on life also remained intact.

One important peasant institution did stem from outside the village community – the Church. The Ukrainians, like many other people – Italians, Poles, Lithuanians – became Christians by decree rather than out of personal conviction. This meant that Christian beliefs, symbols, and observances were superimposed upon indigenous pagan values and traditions. The diffusion of Christian beliefs and ritual practices by no means eliminated the old beliefs and practices; to the contrary, the peasants continued to hold on to ancient "superstitions" even as the Church fought against them. More often than not, the peasants succeeded admirably in reinterpreting imposed beliefs and symbols in terms of indigenous notions as well as in endowing old customs and observances with new meanings. One cannot fail to recognize that ancient folk customs and festivities were carried bodily into Christian observances, not infrequently without modification. Very often the Christian saints became a new version of the old deities and spirits. Many also acquired qualities derived from the immediate village environment. In the village of Olympus, for example, St. George and St. Martin protected birds and geese; St. Anthony helped to find lost articles and marriage partners; St. Lawrence cured burns; St. Agatha and St. Apolonnia protected from fire and cured toothaches; St. Anne and St. Elias protected from thunder and thunderstorms; St. Andrew helped maids to see their future husbands in dreams; St. Peter saved people from madness; and St. Thomas protected the pigs.

The end result of this process was a close blending and reconciliation of old ethnic and new religious elements on both the symbolic and behavioral levels. There is thus some truth in Foerster's comment (1919, p. 97) that about 50 per cent of the religion of Italian peasants was festivity and the other 50 per cent superstition. For the peasants became responsive to Christian religious beliefs and symbols only after these had become "parochialized" and rendered relevant within the context of the traditional way of life. This process of parochialization affected all aspects of religion. Religious norms and values were translated into specific precepts of interpersonal behavior. Saints and deities were endowed with those attributes and functions which stemmed from the peasant's day-to-day existence. Even central religious symbols were mediated to the village peasants by means of visible images and observable ritual acts. In this way religious beliefs and values were concretized and thus articulated in communal life. They were made to correspond with the character of personal relations dominant in the village; consequently, they came to influence individual behavior in concrete social situations.

This far-reaching syncretism of religious and ethnic values and traditions on the level of village culture led to both the "sanctification" of ethnicity and the "ethniza-tion" of religion. The characteristic response of the Polish peasants to D'Etchevoyen's inquiry strikingly illustrates our point: "La plupart des paysans auxquels on demande s'ils sont orthodoxes ou catholiques répondent: Non, je suis de religion polonaise..." (Grentrup 1932, pp. 260-61). Accordingly, there was no clear-cut distinction between sacred and profane, between religious and non-religious spheres of life on the level of the village community. The *religious institution* itself was not so much a separate religious organization constituted on an officially prescribed set of beliefs and practices as it was the way of life embedded in many a sphere of common-place peasant activities and daily preoccupations.

The social world of the peasant's "daily reach" possessed an aura of immediacy and intimacy; it was charged with affectivity to such an extent that even purely instrumen-tal activity – such as land cultivation – was steeped in sentiment and suffused with "religious feeling". The peasants' orientation to cultural values – whether customs, language, or other cultural symbols – was also immanent and particularized. For example, in comparison to trained linguists, who distinguished at best several regional dialects, the peasants were much more "sensitive", being able to perceive many additional unique and differentiating features in their regional or even in their local speech. And, it was precisely this "parochial" tongue, rather than the "language used by the thirty million Ukrainians", that the peasants were intensely attached to. They were not attached to their tongue because it was Ukrainian, but because it was their own; they were not committed to the language of "the Ukrainian people", but attached to the speech of their kin and dear ones. The tongue was deeply embedded in interpersonal relations and, therefore, highly expressive of personal feelings and emotions. But while the village community cohered on "natural" bonds of kinship and personal ties – that is, on attachments characterized by diffuse, affective, and particularistic relationships – the impersonal world by contrast consisted of outsiders and strangers, whether officials, policemen, or tradesmen. Thus one may say that this was a culture composed of particulars rather than universals, of personal qualities rather than impersonal categories.

The very character of their ethnic symbols, as well as the mode of orientation toward them, left the 19th-century village peasants and the early Ukrainian immigrants in the United States unconscious of belonging to a Ukrainian nationality. So much was this the case that most of them were unaware of the very existence of the terms "Ukrainian" or "Ukraine". They were aware of their local traditional pasts, but unaware of a national historical past. Altogether they possessed many different pasts, but no singular "corporate" past – only *particular historical* continuities. Inasmuch as the peasants' ethnic identity expressed itself through the particular and concrete rather than through the general and abstract, their ethnic consciousness grew out of communal and ancestral values rather than out of values "shared" by the Ukrainian nationality as a whole. Like poets, the peasants appreciated and responded to the particular with no reference to the universal; unlike poets, however, they were scarcely cognizant of the fact that this same particular might encompass, in some way, the universal.

An ethnic group becomes a nationality when it has an image of its collective past and when its members are aware of and responsive to that image. Such a development most certainly presupposes a specialized group of persons exclusively concerned with creating and propagating general symbols and values, at once expressing and expressive of this collective past. We know next to nothing about the conditions under which these plural and parochial values become transformed into or replaced by a singular set of national ones. Clearly enough, there is no *a priori* reason to assert that any ethnic group's awareness of its "common fate" must necessarily swallow up its particular and parochial awareness. There are, however, strong indications that the transition from ethnic group to nationality entails the weakening of local ties and primordial attachments. At the time of the French Revolution the idea of *la patrie* symbolized one single nation and also stood in opposition to the alleged diversity of the *ancien-régime*. The Jacobin nationalists vociferously attacked all local customs and traditions, presumably on the assumption that the individual's commitment to central national values could not but be weak as long as parochial attachments remain strong.

The scope of the present essay precludes our exploring this problem more extensively. What requires emphasis at this point is the distinction between primordial and ideological collectivities. These collectivities – the ethnic and the national – entail different types of symbols as well as different kinds of orientations toward them. Members of a primordial collectivity conceive of their ethnic identity in terms of concrete and particular symbols, that is, in terms of those symbols which are meaningful in communal life. Members of an ideological collectivity attach themselves to some set of general and abstract symbols, that is, to symbols which transcend local attachments and loyalties and pertain equally to all the members of a national collectivity. While the primordial collectivity or ethnic group coheres on tradition spontaneously growing out of communal living, the ideological collectivity or nationality presupposes consciously evolved ideology or, at least, ideologically transmuted tradition.

UKRAINIAN IMMIGRANTS IN THE UNITED STATES:
FROM COMMUNAL TO ASSOCIATIONAL SOCIETY

It should be evident from the foregoing that Ukrainian immigrants arriving in the United States before World War I were recruited almost exclusively from the impoverished peasant class, economically disinherited and torn loose from the fabric of village life. Not unexpectedly, most of them had hardly any schooling. About 55 per cent were illiterate at the time of their arrival in this country (Davis 1922, p. 69). Swarming into the unskilled labor force, these "people of naught" were nevertheless capable of providing for themselves and their children a minimum of economic security. But their new occupations as industrial or mining laborers were far from being an integral part of a way of life – as was farming in the village. The whole major segment of life given over to earning a living was transferred from the jurisdiction of the family and the primordial collectivity. The dissociation of "work" from "traditional ways" made it impossible for peasant immigrants to reestablish in this country the same type of community they had left behind. Detached from the territorial moorings of a village community, the peasant's way of life suffered an irretrievable blow. To exist at all, it had to be *consciously reinstituted* as well as *readjusted* to the conditions of urban life. It is no wonder, then, that the peasant immigrant most successfully transplanted his religion – that aspect of his old way of life which had been *institutionally* sustained in the old country. One of the most perceptive students of American immigrant life has attempted to account for it thus (Handlin 1951, p. 117):

The more thorough the separation from the other aspects of the old life, the greater was the hold of the religion that alone survived the transfer. Struggling against heavy odds to save something of the old ways, the immigrants directed into their faith the whole weight of their longing to be connected with the past.

In this process of transoceanic transfer, the religious institution was separated from the primordial collectivity – the village – and reestablished under new urban conditions as an independent religious organization. It became, in fact, the focal point of the immigrants' communal life as well as the mainstay of their ethnicity – one striking indication that only a well-developed network of organizations is capable of reclaiming the culture of uprooted immigrants. Religious and ethnic values and symbols alike were affected by this sudden separation from the natural community, and some of these symbols were incapable of "adjusting" themselves to new urban conditions. Since dentists, for example, cured toothaches in this country, St. Apollonia could not but lose her clients; since geese and pigs were out of sight in urban centers or even in mining towns, their protectors, St. Martin and St. Thomas, could not but be doomed to chronic unemployment. Not only such cases of peasant superstition but also many other ethnic-religious customs and traditions became irrelevant in the new environment. Removed from the context of village life, they became, as it were, suspended in the air and divested of meaningful function. For what solace could immigrant miners, and even more their American-born children, derive from such a New Year's greeting as "May God bless you with a good crop of rye, wheat, and everything good".

Upon settling in this country, the peasant immigrants needed a kind of communal life which would take them away from daily chores in the factories and mines. The ethnic Church and affiliated organizations provided for this need. Margaret Bynigton (1910, p. 159), for example, described how she had watched for two months "the groups of men that gathered outside the gate after service on a Sunday morning. Some came from neighboring towns and looked forward to this weekly chance for a friendly smoke or chat". Thus, within the context of "week-end" life, the immigrants re-affirmed their ties with people of their own kind – here they mixed freely with old friends and made new acquaintances, here they expressed unashamedly their intense attachment to "strange" customs and traditions. On such festive occasions, indeed, these illiterate "Hunkies" regained in some measure feeling of human dignity and self-confidence.

It has been only too often emphasized that the Church was the "most powerful social institution" among Slavic immigrants. Although this observation is undeniably true, the source and nature of this power or influence in the Old Country and in the United States must be clearly distinguished. The power of religion in the village stemmed from its pervasive and diffuse influence; that is to say, religion constituted an integral part of the peasants' everyday life. What was then "powerful" was the tradition of communal life rather than the religious organization *per se*. Once transplanted to the highly differentiated and urban milieu, religion never regained its intimate touch with life. And yet, the organizational power of the Church, as well as the authority of the priest, was considerably enhanced despite the weakening sway of religion over its immigrant flock. The author of *Quo Vadis* was dismayed to find, upon his visit to America, that his countrymen, the Polish immigrants, were completely "in the hands of priests" (Nobilis 1945, p. 35). It is worthwhile to examine more closely the Ukrainian parish in the United States since it was upon this foundation that language maintenance partly came to depend.

PARISH COMMUNITIES: PAST AND PRESENT DEVELOPMENT

The first Ukrainian churches (Greek Catholic and Eastern Orthodox alike) were organized in the mining towns of Pennsylvania. The evidence available to us indicates that this same state accounted for almost all Ukrainian parishes established prior to 1900. As late as 1915, about 60 per cent of Ukrainian parishes were concentrated in Pennsylvania and another 20 per cent in the neighboring states of New York and New Jersey. By 1960, however, only 34 per cent (65 out of 187) of Ukrainian Catholic and 23 percent (30 out of 130) of Ukrainian Orthodox parishes were located in the state of Pennsylvania. However, three eastern states – Pennsylvania, New York, and New Jersey – still accounted for over one-half (58.4 per cent) of all Ukrainian parishes in the United States in 1961 (Table 12.4).

TABLE 12.4

State and Regional Distribution of Ukrainian Catholic and Orthodox Parishes, 1960

State and Region	Number	Percent
Pennsylvania	95	30.0
New York	59	18.6
New Jersey	31	9.8
New England	34	10.7
Midwest	57	18.0
Other	41	12.9
Total	317	100.0

Sources: *The Catholic Directory: Byzantine Rite Archeparchy Parishes of Philadelphia, U.S.A.* (Philadelphia, 1960). *Parishes and Clergy of the Orthodox and Other Eastern Churches in North and South America* (Buffalo, The Joint Commission on Cooperation with the Eastern Churches, 1960-1961).

As late as 1961 the state of Pennsylvania contained the largest number of Ukrainian parishes in this country; this same state had the lowest increment of new parishes for the decade 1950-1959. The very fact that all six new parishes established in Pennsylvania between 1950 and 1959 (Table 12.5) were required by the arrival of new immi-

TABLE 12.5

State and Regional Distribution of New Parishes Established by Ukrainian Catholic and Orthodox Churches, 1950-1959

State and Region	Ukrainian Catholic Parishes			Ukrainian Orthodox Parishes		
	Number		Percent Increase	Number		Percent Increase
	1950	1959		1950	1959	
Pennsylvania	59	65	11.7	22	25	13.6
New York	26	35	34.6	9	13	44.4
New Jersey	13	17	37.6	5	9	80.0
New England	14	19	35.7	6	9	50.0
Midwest	16	27	68.7	13	21	61.5
Other	15	24	60.0	3	11	266.0

Sources: *The Catholic Directory: Byzantine Rite ...* (1960). *Ukrainskyi Pravoslavnyi Kalendar* (Bound Brook, Ukrainian Orthodox Church of U.S.A., 1961).

grants strongly suggests that the oldest center of Ukrainian religious institutions has reached the point of stagnation. It may well be that many of the old parishes in this state are now passing through a critical period of decline in membership and of organizational disintegration.

The unprecedented upsurge in the number of new parishes in "other" states reveals a growing tendency toward dispersion; furthermore, this tendency has been considerably intensified by the influx of postwar refugees since 1950. With some few exceptions, the postwar refugee immigrants have not been integrated into the existing fabric of ethnic life on the level of the parish community; they have either established their own parishes or rescued the old ones from imminent oblivion. At best, they have numerically strengthened the Church and helped to expand it organizationally by establishing new parish communities.

RELIGIOUS CONFLICT: TRADITIONAL VARIETY VERSUS ORGANIZATIONAL UNIFORMITY

The history of the Roman Catholic Church in the United States is not one of continuous growth and expansion; in fact, its annals are replete with prolonged conflicts and even wholesale desertions. Unfortunately, Catholic historians have largely been insensitive to the human drama hidden behind the facade of organizational achievement. They have been predominantly interested in the growth of religious organizations and edifices, in "hierarchical development", and in the lives and deeds of venerable bishops. Enough is known, however, to indicate that the conflict has been rather extensive and sufficiently deep to adversely affect many an ethnic parish. The traditional explanation of the problem has been couched in terms of "recrudescent trusteeism", that is, in terms of revolt against the decree that Church property be incorporated under the control of bishops and that lay trustees be divested of any power which would interfere with the jurisdiction of the Church. It would seem more appropriate, however, to view "trusteeism" as but one manifestation of the conflict. Stated more generally, it was the conflict between tradition and organization, between traditional authority and organizational power vested in the hierarchy, between diversity of tradition and uniformity of ideology, between ethnicity and religion. This latter aspect of the conflict reflected the slow but steady progress of secularization.

The mass exodus of Italians, Poles, Slovaks, Ukrainians, and Lithuanians to this country coincided with a movement among the members of the American Irish-Catholic hierarchy known as "Americanism". Not unlike many other *isms*, "Americanism" eludes exact definition. One may safely state, however, that it refers not only to a collection of disparate ideas, but also to a particular frame of mind and attitude among its proponents. By way of illustration we shall quote in extenso a few extracts from Monsignor O'Connel's letter to Bishop Ireland, since it makes, according to one Catholic historian, "a very important contribution to a definition of Americanism as conceived by the Americanists" (McAvoy 1957, p. 206).

And now only one word more: all doubts and hesitation to the wind and on with the banner of Americanism which is the banner of God and humanity. Now realize all the dreams you ever dreamed, and force upon the Curia by the great triumph of Americanism that recognition of English speaking peoples that you know is needed....

No more patching of new pieces and old garments; it serves neither one nor the other. And the foundation of religion need be laid anew "in spirit and in truth". Begin there anew with the Gospel and with such accessories and canon law as the Gospel requires without making paramount the interests of comfortable-living personages or communities....

Again it seems to me that above all nations, moving them on along the path of civilization to better, higher, happier modes of existence, it is the constant action of a tender divine Providence, and that the convergent action of all great powers is towards that common and destined end; to more brotherhood, to more kindness, to more mutual respect for every man, to more practical and living recognition of the rule of God.... Now God passes the banner to the hands of America, to bear it: – in the cause of humanity, and it is your office to make its destiny known to America and become its grand chaplain. Over all America there is certainly a duty higher than the interest of the individual states – even of the national government. The duty to humanity is certainly a real duty, and America cannot certainly with honor, or fortune, evade its great share in it. Go to America and say, thus saith the Lord! Then you will live in history as God's Apostle in modern times to Church and to Society. Hence I am a partisan of the Anglo-American alliance, together they are invincible and they will impose a new civilization. Now is your opportunity – and at the end of the war as the Vatican always goes after a strong man you will likewise become her intermediary....

I write this letter after much thought and much hesitation fearing sometimes you would suspect my modesty or again my common sense. And I assure you, however rapidly I may have written I have long pondered these thoughts and if you have had the patience to plow through them I shall be greatly flattered and rewarded if you say you agree with them. I believe you will say they are right and that our destiny was not thrown together for nothing. War is often God's way of moving things onward. The whole realm of life of every kind lay under the operation of one law: struggle. In that way all the plans of nature are worked out and the name for struggle between nations is sometimes "war".....

The whole history of Providence is the history of war; survival of the fittest. There is no room in this little world for anything else and bad as the world is today how much worse it certainly would be if by war and struggle the worse elements had not to go to the wall. (McAvoy 1957, pp. 207-09)

Taken as whole, these passages contain several related themes worthy of further exploration. One of them is the very conception of religion purified of tradition and "old garments" and instituted anew on the basis of the Gospel and organizationally enacted uniform rule of law. As might be expected, an inseparable part of this ideal was an almost obsessive insistence upon uniformity and complete disregard, if not hatred, of cultural differences and ethnic traditions represented by newly-arriving immigrant groups. Translated into a call for action, it led to such blatantly non-sequitur slogans as the one coined by Biship Tierney of Hartford: "One God, one faith, one language and one Church jurisdiction in America."[3]

No less evident is the attempt to reinforce the ideal of Americanism by simply equating it with the "banner of God and humanity". It followed ineluctably from this dubious reasoning that the imposition of Anglo-American civilization was necessary in order that the cause of God and humanity might finally triumph. Only then would the era of "brotherhood", "kindness" and "respect for every man" arrive, even though, as this servant of God informs us, it would be preceded by vulgar Darwinism,

---

[3]   "History of the St. Stanislaus P. N. C. Parish of Scranton, Pennsylvania", *Album Szescdziesiatej Rocznicy Polskisgo Narodenego Katelickiego Kosciola: 1897-1957* (Scranton, 1957), p. 12.

with its struggle, domination, and elimination of "lesser breeds" and "inferior" cultures.

One cannot escape the conclusion that the ideal of "Americanism" was basically the product of people unrestrained by and inimical to ethnic tradition; that it resulted from that type of human orientation which is profoundly intolerant of the historical past and ever ready to be carried away by the expectation of the ideal future. Almost in the manner of sectarian zealots, the "Americanists" were inspired by the Gospel divested of all historical contingencies. Unlike sectarians, however, they realized only too well that uprooted immigrant humanity might not readily see the light of truth and that, consequently, the unity of faith should be guarded also by organizational discipline and control. On a secular plane, in turn, the "Americanists" were akin in many ways to the Jacobin nationalists. For, like Jacobin nationalists, they conceived of human society as integrated exclusively on the basis of a uniform set of values and symbols, and equally despised cultural diversity and plural loyalties. Finally, not unlike the Jacobin nationalists, they carried the banner of nationalism under the aegis of humanity, the major difference being that the Jacobin concept of humanity was emptied of all religious associations.

Ample evidence suggests that this type of Jacobin nationalism infected many a member of the Irish-Catholic hierarchy; in fact, the policy of some bishops with regard to immigrant groups was clearly tainted by it. It is known that some of the "Americanizers" from among the prelates vehemently opposed the establishment of ethnic parishes, very often by resorting to highly questionable methods. Cardinal McCloskey, now referred to by Catholic historians as "this gentle prelate of New York", went so far as to inform the Poles that what they needed was not their own church but a "pig shanty" (Kruszka XII, p. 176). That difficulties of a similar kind occurred in many a community may be gleaned from the few following illustrations:

South River, New Jersey –

After many of us had settled here, it was decided to extablish the Polish Church in 1896. But we were disappointed because the Bishop of Trent refused to grant us permission. He threatened to anathematize us. He ordered us to help financially the Irish parish which was in debt at that time. But this church is not ever in our neighborhood. (Kruszka XII, p. 93)

Adams, Massachusetts –

The Polish settlement here consists of about 1,250 souls. Following many attempts, petitions, and difficulties, the Bishop gave his permission to buy land for the construction of the Church. But this is of no use as long as the Bishop refuses to provide us with a priest in order that he may organize the parish. One more delegation had been sent to the Bishop and four days thereafter the priest arrived. (Kruszka XIII, pp. 127-28)

Easthampton, Massachusetts –

Poles have been residing here for some time. The parish was organized, but, despite many appeals made to the Bishop, we failed to get our priest. The Irish priest opposes the establishment of the Polish parish because the Poles have been hitherto of considerable financial help to him. (Kruszka XIII, p. 129)

Canonsburg, Pannsylvania –

St. Patrick's parish was founded here some time ago. The Irish priest is in charge of it even though the majority of parishioners are Poles. With the rise of "independent spirit," however, St. Patrick's parish accepted the Polish priest. (Kruszka XII, p. 155)

The attitude of the Catholic hierarchy toward the establishment of Ukrainian Catholic parishes was at times even more intolerant and unreserved than the attitudes illustrated above. Some of the prelates became alarmed upon learning that these new Catholics observed different rites, had their own liturgical language and even their own religious calendar. A further complicating factor was the fact that many Ukrainian clergymen were married. The Bishop of Philadelphia greeted the arrival of the first Ukrainian priest by excommunicating him. Another prelate, Archbishop Ireland of Minneapolis, simply could not believe that these people were Catholics. His opposition to the establishment of a Ukrainian parish as well as his refusal to accept the Ukrainian priest into the diocese sparked the conflict that led ultimately to the movement "Away from Rome". The revolt of Ukrainian priests and parishioners alike spread quickly from one community to another and decimated almost all Ukrainian Catholic parishes in the course of two decades. The movement was at least partly contained with the establishment, in 1907, of a Greek Catholic Diocese headed by a separate Bishop of Ukrainian nationality.

Much more serious than the interference of Irish bishops in organizational matters was their attempt to cast ethnic churches into one mold by eliminating (with the help of official decrees) the diverse religious traditions and practices of ethnic groups. There can hardly be any doubt that decisions of this kind were very often arbitrary and represented an abuse of authority. As one Lithuanian clergyman observed: "The Bishop may tolerate some traditions and abolish others completely. For instance, the exposition of the Blessed Sacrament ... before Easter in the Lithuanian churches in the Philadelphia Archdiocese disappeared four years ago because of the ruling from the chancery" (Sirvaitis 1945, p. 630). At least in one community, during the heyday of Americanism, youngsters were employed as the "guardians of uniformity". Whether actively sponsored or merely tacitly approved, these young *druzhinniki* molested the Lithuanian settlement in Aurora, Illinois, during Lent when it was customary for Lithuanians to congregate in each other's homes and sing Christ's Passion Hymns:

They do not have a Lithuanian priest. The American youngsters do not like their singing, so they come to the house in which the singing is taking place and make much noise. (Sirvaitis 1945, p. 512)

It seems clear that ideological aspects of religion were of no significance in the revolt of Ukrainian immigrants against the Catholic Church; that is to say, neither ideological conversion nor the attendant change of ideological allegiance was involved here. If many peasant immigrants refused to obey the Church, it was because their loyalty to tradition was stronger than their loyalty to the authority of religious organization. If some of them dared to desert the Church, it was due to the fact that their attachment to ancestral values was more intense than their attachment to the impersonal organization. They left no room for doubt that they cherished what was their own and what was familiar rather than what was foreign and strange; that what they stood for, in short, was the heritage of their fathers and forefathers.

To the extent that the ethnic culture had to be consciously defended in this country, it is not surprising that it acquired with time an apologetic character and was turned into "a cause" worthy of fighting for. Heightened *national sensitivity* was but one important by-product of this development. In fact, many a Ukrainian immigrant first became keenly conscious of his *national identity* in the United States.

FIRST SECULAR ORGANIZATIONS: MUTUAL AID SOCIETIES

Indicative of the radical difference between the village community and the type of communal life that immigrant groups established upon settling in this country was the proliferation of benevolent associations, the so-called "mutual aid societies". The very attempt to promote communal cohesion by formal means and to organizationally sustain the sentiment of communal solidarity represented an unprecedented development. It amounted, in effect, to the use of formal associational devices for the sake of strengthening communal loyalties and even personal ties. These benevolent societies were not functionally specific organizations – *collegia funeralia* – whose sole purpose was to make provisions for an adequate funeral. For many an immigrant "joiner" they served as a substitute for the communal life of the village. Not unlike the *collegia tenorum* in ancient Rome, they became "homes for the homeless, a little fatherland or *patria* for those without a country" (Dill 1911, p. 271). This was especially true of those small settlements incapable of maintaining their own ethnic churches. With the estrangement of many an immigrant from the Catholic Church, the communal role of local societies was greatly enhanced. Very often they provided the only organized framework for ethnic life.

On the local level, then, these insurance associations possessed all the attributes of nonpurposive personal groups, in spite of the fact that they were founded under the pretext of formally stated objectives. True enough, the peasant immigrants adhered faithfully to all the formal rules and procedures expected of them at regular meetings and gatherings. So much so, that within time these procedures acquired such a ritualistic quality that participants indulged in them unduly even at the expense of efficiency. What counted ultimately, however, was sheer sociability and delight derived from being able to elicit human sympathy and understanding. The few yellow pages of still extant records reveal, more often than not, the predicament of uprooted humanity and scarcely enlighten us at all on organizational matters – be they "things done" or "problems solved". They refer, as a rule, to the injustices and tragedies that befell many an immigrant in the mines and factories.[4] They abound in all kinds of personal

[4] Out of 1,461 members of one Ukrainian insurance society who died between 1897-1914, 229

grievances and difficulties; at times, they are so intimately personal that creative writers could best profit from them.

Organizational expansion coupled with more efficient administrative management soon made some of these mutual aid societies financially strong enough to be able to carry on an array of activities related to the maintenance of ethnic life in this country. They established Ukrainian newspapers and periodicals; they financed the publication of literary works, popular books, and pamphlets – from cookbooks to short histories of the United States and the Ukraine. They helped to organize local centers of communal life – libraries and reading rooms – and even sponsored public lectures and adult classes for the benefit of many illiterate immigrants. Above all, they were instrumental in awakening and strengthening among former peasants a kind of group solidarity that went beyond communal attachments to kinsmen and village neighbors.

Ukrainians in the United States currently support four major mutual aid societies: *Ukrainian National Association, Ukrainian Workingmen's Association, Providence Association of Ukrainian Catholics,* and *National Aid Association.* By the end of 1961, these four organizations had a total of 126,445 members and their combined assets reached $37,220,945. However, the oldest center of Ukrainian organizational life – the ninety-odd communities in the State of Pennsylvania – apparently has reached the point of stagnation. There are good reasons for supposing that not a few Ukrainian organizations in this state – religious and secular alike – have been afflicted with decline in membership and organizational disintegration. Membership in the Ukrainian Workingmen's Association alone decreased in this region by 12.3 per cent between 1953 and 1961. And while it is true that chronic unemployment in the mining towns of Pennsylvania is partly responsible for this development, it is equally true that many Ukrainian-Americans sever their last ties with organized ethnic life upon resettlement in newer regions and urban centers. This is particularly noticeable among members of the second and third generations. When they leave their home neighborhood and home town for "greener pastures" they usually leave their Ukrainian ties behind them

Another consequence of the increasing urban settlement of refugee immigrants has been a growing concentration of Ukrainian institutions and organized activities in large urban centers. Indicative of this tendency toward urban contraction is the change in the relative weight of urban membership in the Ukrainian Workingmen's Association during the last two decades. Those organizations (which are located in the peripheral communities outside of Chicago, Detroit, Cleveland, Boston, and other urban centers) have displayed for the past decade or more all the symptoms of slow but steady dissolution. The very fact that this trend is not confined solely to the depressed areas of Pennsylvania makes inadequate any explanation couched primarily in economic terms. Whatever the underlying causes may be, it is evident that the stability of the relatively strongest and most permanent ethnic organizations – the mutual aid societies – is steadily being undermined.

(15.7 per cent) were killed in the mines. See R. Slobodian, "U. N. Soiuz u Movi Chysel", *Propamiatna Knyha* (Jersey City, Ukrainskyi Narodnyi Soiuz, 1936), p. 246.

THE PROBLEM OF ETHNIC CONTINUITY

The American way of life, if viewed within the context of our approach, may be said to constitute a set of "national" ideals to be aspired to rather than of "ethnic" traditions to be lived by. For the uniqueness of American society lies precisely in the fact that is became a nationality (ideological collectivity) without ever having had an ethnic base, that it devised its own national ideology without the benefit of an ethnic heritage of its own. Unlike Polish, French, English, or other nationalities which developed out of their respective ethnic substrata, American nationality was established by its founding fathers. Its national unity and solidarity was supposed to rest on consciously evolved ideology and hardly on commonly shared ethnic heritage. By its very nature, therefore, it could not but be suspicious of imported traditions and, indeed, has long preferred uniform but rapidly changing fads and fashions to diverse and supposedly "stagnant" traditions. Projected into the future, the ideal of American nationality and national unity precludes ethnic diversity; moreover, it expects that immigrants will be stripped of their native cultures and traditional attachments as soon as possible. As one immigrant author observed some forty years ago (Panuncio 1926, p. 194):

Forget your native land, forget your mother tongue, do away in a day with your inherited customs, put from you as a cloak all that inheritance and early environment made you and become in a day an American par excellence. This was precisely the talk I used to hear when I first came to this country. There was then as now, I regret to say, a spirit of compulsion in the air.

Convincing evidence may be brought to show that extreme proponents of Americanism have adhered to the view that individual or group attachments to ethnic values and traditions – be they ethnic mother tongues or communal customs – somehow undermine the ideologically conceived unity of American nationality. To cite John Quincy Adams: "They must cast off the European skin, never to resume it. They must look forward to their posterity rather than backward to their ancestors; they must be sure that whatever their own feelings may be, those of their children will cling to the prejudices of this country" (Gordon 1961, p. 268). Yet, this "forward-looking" orientation of many an Americanist was itself not free of ethnic "prejudices"; furthermore, most, if not all, of these "prejudices" (if we are to equate them with ethnic traditions) were of English ethnic origin.

These two factors together – American ideological nationalism and English ethnic dominance – have militated against ethnic pluralism and even against the spontaneous blending (melting pot) of diverse and equally valuable ethnic strains. Viewed in this light, the theories of ethnic pluralism and of the ethnic melting pot are scarcely reflective of the dominant historical process; at best, they offer alternative ideas of what might have or should have taken place.

A full explanation of the manner in which English ethnic culture was appropriated by and made standard in American society would necessitate viewing the process as part of a much broader historical development. Suffice it to state here that many prevalent views – such as the contention that English ethnic culture was superior to all others or more consonant with the American way of life – can only in part account for what has happened. Much more relevant is the fact that the dominance of English ethnic culture was closely tied to the dominant socio-economic and political status of the English group. In other words, English ethnic culture has enjoyed the support of basic social institutions and of the social structure as a whole. More recent attempts to transform St. Patrick's Day into a general American Catholic holiday illustrate strikingly how a dominant ethnic group may buttress its traditions via institutional support. While St. Patrick's observances will soon acquire (if they have not already) an all-American (Catholic) significance, all other ethnic saints and religious festivities will be slowly relegated to the domain of immigrant history.

It is suggested here that the institutional and social dominance of the English themselves and of other English-speaking ethnic groups is basic to an understanding of the process of Americanization. At the same time, it must be emphasized that the nature of this dominance is not to be equated with the colonial model – whether dominance through annexation (Austria, German, Russia) or through overseas conquest (Great Britain, Portugal, Spain, France). With the exception of the indigenous Spanish-speaking group in the Southwest, the American pattern of dominance involves subordination of immigrant ethnic groups by an indigenous core society. The colonial pattern of dominance involves subordination of an indigenous ethnic population by an immigrant group. As a rule, the colonial pattern of dominance left intact the cultural heritage and indigenous communal institutions of subordinated ethnic groups, even after prolonged assimilationist pressures. Although reduced to the status of "little tradition", the Ukrainian ethnic culture was never seriously threatened by either Russian or Polish dominance. The Ukrainian language, for example, retained its sway over the peasant masses, notwithstanding the fact that Russian or Polish was employed as the language of instruction in rural elementary schools. Moreover, since the second half of the 19th century, the Ukrainian ethnic group was slowly transforming into a socially and culturally differentiated society, with its own standard literary language and a growing stratum of cultural and even political elite.

The American pattern of dominance and the incoordinate nature of most immigration into the United States precluded the establishment of territorially related and socially differentiated communities capable of securing for themselves generational continuity and institutional stability. The so-called "Little Polands" and "Little Italys" served as temporary devices for accommodating the arriving immigrants to a new social setting. They were expected to and, indeed, did provide a human reservoir for the dominant American society. Given this distinction, it is also necessary to emphasize that the settlement of Ukrainian immigrants in this country (as is true of many other immigrant groups as well) amounted to the transition from a kinship-integrated, relatively undifferentiated and stable type of *communal society* to an occupation-integrated, functionally differentiated and highly mobile type of *associational society*. The major consequence of this transition from communal to associational society was that newly established ethnic communities had to be constituted on a network of voluntary associations and organizations. This consideration suggests at once that the vitality of ethnic organizations and associations – membership growth, organizational strength – represents one of the most meaningful criteria for gauging the generational continuity of ethnic groups in the United States.

ORGANIZATIONAL AND GENERATIONAL CONTINUITY

At present, the Ukrainian Churches and mutual aid societies represent the two numerically strongest foci of organized Ukrainian-American activity. It can be reliably estimated that the total membership of the two largest Ukrainian denominations – Catholic and Orthodox – reached 450,000 parishioners in 1960. This number shows beyond doubt that the overwhelming majority of Ukrainian-American parishioners are by now American born.[5] According to available information on nineteen Ukrainian Catholic parishes located in the states of Pennsylvania and New York, only 31.8 per cent of their parishioners in 1960 were foreign born. The percentage of foreign-born parishioners is likely to be even lower in the mining towns of Pennsylvania as well as in other peripheral settlements.

A look at the generational composition of the largest Ukrainian mutual aid society – the Ukrainian National Association – discloses a drastically different picture. In contrast to the Church, the majority of its members, 65 per cent in 1960, was foreign born.[6] In the junior division alone, one-half of its membership consisted of foreign-born individuals. Between 1950 and 1960 the number of foreign-born members in the Ukrainian National Association increased by 5 per cent (in the junior division by 10 per cent). For the past decade, indeed, the numerical expansion of this organization has depended almost exclusively upon newly arrived refugee immigrants and their children. Membership growth in the largest religious denomination – the Ukrainian Catholic Church – has likewise depended upon postwar refugee immigrants. Between 1950 and 1955, the number of its members increased by 6.4 per cent; however, between 1955 and 1960, it decreased by 2.7 per cent.

Although both the Church and the insurance societies continue to maintain their organizational sway over a considerable portion of the American-born generations, it must be stressed that the numerical growth of these two ethnic organizations since World War II has to be accounted for by the arrival of refugee immigrants. Once this human reservoir is exhausted, as the precarious change in the membership of the Ukrainian Catholic Church suggests, a trend toward relative "normalcy" appears; that is, a trend toward stability or even decline in membership. And while it is difficult to determine the exact points of transition from growth to stability and/or decline,

[5] 1960 data supplies by the U.S. Census list only 106,974 foreign-born claimants of Ukrainian mother tongue.
[6] Language Resources Project, Organizational Questionnaire.

some few general observations are in order. In the first place, it may be safely asserted that in the past the numerical growth of all Ukrainian ethnic organizations has hinged upon foreign-born members and their children. This is particularly true of the two typically "non-voluntary" organizations – the Church and the mutual aid societies. As a rule, American-born individuals become members of these organizations without their own consent; they are simply enrolled by their immigrant parents. As soon as immigrant mothers pass beyond the childbearing age, the proportion of junior members begins to drop. Another wave of immigrants is then necessary in order that its offspring may again rejuvenate these organizations.

While children of foreign-born parentage initially become members of the Church and of mutual aid societies without their own consent, their continued association with these organizations acquires, with time, a voluntary character. Two alternative hypotheses may explain the relative success of religious and mutual benefit organizations in retaining their hold over a considerable segment of the American-born (second, third and even fourth) generations. On the one hand, it may be suggested that the very decision of these individuals to remain members in such ethnic organizations cannot but reflect some kind of attachment to the culture of their fathers and forefathers. According to this view, the continuing sense of loyalty to ethnicity would be considered one of the important determinants of membership in ethnic organizations. On the other hand, it is equally plausible to argue that by the time individuals of the second and, even more so, of the third and fourth generations become dominant in such organizations, the very ethnicity of the organizations has been largely eroded. What survive then are hardly ethnic but religious and economic organizations. Membership in such formerly ethnic organizations would represent, consequently, little more than loyalty to religious institutions and to purely instrumental involvement in economic (insurance) organizations. These two general hypotheses are not, of course, mutually exclusive, but there are many indications that the overall trend is more consonant with the second hypothesis. One indication is precisely the fact that only these two organizations – the Church and the mutual benefit societies – include members recruited from the third and fourth generations. All other Ukrainian institutions and organizations – professional, scholarly, or literary societies, Ukrainian language schools, and youth associations – consist almost exclusively of immigrant members and their offspring. Yet, these are the very organizations which are most directly concerned with the maintenance of the ethnic culture, including the language.

The foregoing considerations underscore once again the central place of religion in maintaining the organized base for ethnic affiliations. But this should not be construed to mean that religious belonging and identity simply serve the members of American-born generations as convenient substitutes for ethnic belonging and identity. With the exception of the Jewish religion, which traditionally constitutes a national ideology, something patently different usually occurs. While it is true that all immigrant religious organizations depend initially on their respective ethnic groups, it is no less true that with the passage of time in the "new country" they discard almost completely the lingering vestiges of ethnicity. Mergers of the Lutheran Churches in the United States strikingly illustrate the way in which ethnically related religious organizations divest themselves of ethnic affiliations. The crux of this development may be briefly formulated thus: the strongest and most enduring ethnic organization – the Church – is least concerned in the long run with the preservation of the ethnic heritage of its founders. The manner in which this development comes about will be explored in the following analysis of ethnic identification.

ETHNIC IDENTIFICATION

It is the basic thesis of this essay that the erosion of ethnicity and ethnic identity takes place in the course of three generations; it involves, in other words, the immigrant fathers, their sons, and their grandsons. In contrast to the widely prevalent notion that there ensues some kind of return to the fold of ethnicity "whenever any immigrant group reaches the third generation stage in its development" (Hansen 1952, p. 496), the view advanced here assumes that the ethnic heritage, including the language, usually ceases to play any vital role in the life of the third generation. Hansen's argument to the effect that "Anyone who has the courage to codify the laws of history must include what can be designated as the principle of the third generation interest" (p. 495) stems largely from his misreading of the basic process involved. Hansen came upon the idea of the "returning grandsons" against the background of the "fleeing sons". To cite him again: "The theory is derived from the almost universal phenomenon that what the son wishes to forget the grandson wishes to remember. This tendency might be illustrated by a hundred examples". The resurgent interest of the grandsons in ethnicity is thus relative to the determinaton of the sons to forget it. Viewed in this light, the revival of the "third generation interest" may be actually no more than a somewhat appreciative, or merely indifferent, orientation of the grandsons in comparison to that of the sons. The very violence with which some of the sons dissociated themselves from their ethnic heritage expressed the extent to which it had taken hold of them. The very attempt of some of these sons to cut loose all the ties that bound them to the ethnic community reflected their manifold involvement in it. Instances of highly negative response testify to the impact of ethnicity upon the attitudes and actions of the sons. The grandsons, in turn, find it possible to become interested in their ethnic heritage precisely because they have been left largely untouched by it. They need not *forget* the ethnic ways since these have scarcely been known to them. They need not *unlearn* the language of their immigrant grandfathers since they have never mastered it. They need not emphasize their Americanism by dissociating from ethnicity because their Americanism is unstrained and their ethnicity attenuated. The sons, still deeply involved in ethnicity, tend to depreciate it for the strength of its claims is a hindrance to them; the grandsons, only slightly affected by ethnicity, tend to appreciate it for the weakness of its claims upon them removes all hindrance. If it be granted, then, that this is the case, Hansen's principle of the "third generation interest" may forestall not only the *end* of ethnicity but its *vital role* in the lives of grandsons as well.

The foregoing comments raise a series of issues that need urgent reappraisal. One is the murky concept of ethnic identification. To suggest, for example, that the grandsons are more appreciative of or less inimical to ethnicity than the sons, is to imply that the concept of ethnic identification lends itself to analysis along a unidimensional attitudinal continuum. Once this dubious assumption is made, of course, the next logical step is to construct a scale capable of measuring the positiveness or the intensity of identification with ethnicity. In fact, this is one of the standard procedures employed by students of ethnic groups in the United States. A careful perusal of the diverse and ad hoc selections of criteria for gauging ethnic identification makes painfully evident the simplistic character of this procedure.[7] It ignores the central fact that the fathers, sons, and grandsons may differ among themselves not only in the *degree* but also in the *mode* of their identification with ethnicity.

It has long been recognized that the generational conflict between immigrant fathers and their sons represents the first major blow to the continuity of ethnic cultures and groups in this country. On the one hand, it has been observed that immigrant fathers desperately tried to instill in their sons their own love for and appreciation of the ethnic heritage; on the other hand, the sons of these immigrant fathers were determined to forget everything – the mother tongue that left (or was rumored to leave) so many traces in their English speech, the "strange" customs that they were forced to practice at home and in church, and so forth. In many an extreme case, to cite Hansen, "Nothing was more Yankee than a Yankeeized person of foreign descent" (p. 494). How general this revolt might have been is only of minor concern here; what deserves careful scrutiny is the limited extent to which the immigrant fathers could ever have led any of their sons to appreciate or to identify with ethnicity in the same manner as they themselves did. For the immigrant fathers, as has been pointed out, ethnicity was literally an integral part of their way of life. Being an outgrowth of past personal experience in the village community, the ethnic identity of the immigrant fathers represented something deeply subjective and yet tangible; that is, it was hardly externalized and expressed in general symbolic terms. For this reason alone the immigrant fathers, unlike the sons, could neither rebel against nor consciously commit themselves to ethnicity. Related intimately to the way of life in the village, ethnicity was simply experienced in the daily round of activities. It was this particular way of life that expressed an individual's ethnic identity, rather than his ethnicity regulating his way of life.

The point made here needs to be carefully considered if only because *ethnic identification* has been commonly defined as "a person's use of racial, national or religious

---

[7]   See Ludwig Geismar, "A Scale for the Measurement of Ethnic Identification", *Jewish Social Studies*, 16 (1954), 33-60; Bernard Lazarowitz, "Some Factors in Jewish Identification", *Jewish Social Studies*, 15 (1953), 3-24.

terms to identify himself, and thereby, to relate himself to others" (Glaser 1958, p. 31). These ethnic terms or categories supposedly provide a universalistic framework for ordering social relationships. *Ethnic orientation*, in turn, has been defined as "those features of a person's feelings and action towards others which are a function of the ethnic category by which he identifies himself" (Glaser 1958). To appreciate the difficulty posed by such definitions of ethnic identification and orientation, it suffices to recall that many peasant immigrants – whether of Finnish, Slovak, Italian, Ukrainian, Norwegian, or even of Polish or German origin – were hardly conscious of the existence of comprehensive categories by means of which they would relate themselves to others. Many a Ukrainian peasant, for example, continued until well into this century to inform census officials who appeared in his village that he was of "indigenous" ethnic background. This response was given for the simple reason that he was utterly innocent of the very existence of the terms "Ukraine" or "Ukrainian". The following statement of one of the foremost students of rural life in Poland shows how utterly confused Polish peasants must have been with regard to their national identity (Bujak 1903, p. 131):

There are still many people in the village of *Zmiaca* as well as in the neighboring villages who identify their nationality by saying that they are either Catholics ... or peasants or, finally, that they are *Kaiser's* people (cysarskimi). If one endeavors to convince them that they are Poles they become disturbed and avoid discussing it altogether.

But what is salient in this context is not so much whether peasant immigrants identified themselves with appropriate ethnic categories (some of them undoubtedly did) as the extent to which any of their attitudes and actions were a *function* of such categories. It may be pointed out, of course, that the establishment of so many ethnic organizations and churches by these peasant immigrants is directly expressive of their ethnic consciousness and solidarity. Yet, it is known that the first ethnic organizations and churches of not a few ethnic groups were set up along local and village lines rather than along ethnic lines as such. The very pattern of settlement in this country proceeded along similar lines. Some 300 present-day Ukrainian organizations in the United States and Canada are still based on such parochial loyalties and attachments. Norwegian-American *bygdelags* provide another illustration of this same phenomenon. One author (Hodnefield 1954, p. 171) estimates that there were fifty such *lags* in 1929, and that each year some 75,000 Norwegian-Americans came under the direct influence of these societies. The foremost objective of the *bygdelags* can be glimpsed from the following quotation (Hodnefield, p. 165):

Immigrants from Norway who during their youth shared a common acquaintance with families and places find at the conventions a ready opportunity to meet neighbors again, refresh half-forgotten memories, and be cheered by the homelike coziness that association with friends of one's youth usually gives. This pre-eminently is the attracting and assembling force connected with gatherings of those from the same home community.

The point made here lends additional support to our previous observation that the first immigrant organizations partook of the nature of communal reunions; indeed, they provided the immigrants with an *ersatz* frame-work within which they could and did recreate their common past experience – from speaking and hearing their dialect to singing and dancing local folk songs and dances. It was not some affectively-charged response to national symbols that made the immigrants band together, but a highly particularized response to many facets of their former way of life. Only those who had personally experienced this way of life in the past – embedded as it was in the local scenery with its fjords, orchards, or white peasant huts, and replete with local festivities and holidays – could draw delight from and genuinely appreciate its recreation in the United States. Sheer human sentiment was involved in the establishment of many immigrant organizations, and their primary function in this country was to foster the friendly ties among former neighbors and, thereby, to keep alive the local customs and precious personal memories of their ancestral homes. Clearly enough, the immigrant fathers and mothers did not respond to a collective and generalized past of their respective ethnic groups; they did not endow with affective and emotional aura all Norwegian fjords, Lithuanian forests, or Ukrainian orchards. Like the ancient hero and wanderer, Odysseus, the immigrants knew only too well that a chimney and the smoke rising from it were not exclusive attributes of their ancestral homes alone; yet, the one and only smoke that they could neither easily forget nor readily find a substitute for was precisely that which had once come from their own childhood homes.

Personal experience and memory underlay this mode of identification with and attachment to ethnicity and ethnic tradition. To dismiss this as a lachrymose hearkening to the past and as nothing but another instance of *Schwaermerei* is to simply disregard the significance of concrete experiences for personal identity and continuity. A cursory look at some Ukrainian-American and Ukrainian-Canadian folk songs, sayings, and folk poems reveals the poignant search of their immigrant authors for such a link with the past. It is worthy of note that those who could read and write frequently turned into amateur poets; that is to say, they resorted to that very medium which enabled them to recreate the past in terms of concrete images. Most of these poems contain hardly any reference to the beloved Ukraine, its culture, people, or to any other such general categories. Instead, they abound in highly singular and unique imagery, as the following verse aptly illustrates:

> O, my Ukrainain song,
>   You sweeten my days,
> For I learned you
>   From my dear mother.
> ....
> My mother rests in the grave
>   Of her native land,
> But her songs still re-echo
>   From my own lips.   (Rudnytskyi 1958, p. 424)

It is certainly appropriate to suggest (as many have done) that the immigrant fathers could scarcely transmit to their sons this kind of orientation and attachment to ethnicity, even when they genuinely tried to train their sons in the *mores maiorum* of their ancestors. By listening to the stories told by parents or by studying ethnically oriented geography and history, the sons were able, at best, to conceive of the old country as possessing some *generalized attributes* – be they Norwegian fjords and folk costumes or Ukrainian orchards and folk dances. But what bearing could such knowledge of the ethnic past have on that special relationship which links the family or individual from generation to generation? Too radical a break in the continuity of generations had made the personal and concrete experiences of the fathers inaccessible to the sons. For the fathers the "old ways" survived as *realities*, meaningfully linking them to the ancestral past as well as to the community of their immigrant contemporaries. For the sons they stood at best for *ideals* to be appreciated and cherished.

Whereas the immigrant fathers continued to accept ethnicity as a way of life and, to that extent, as a living tradition, the sons tended to view it as the "dead hand of the past" which they were taught to hold dear and to respect in their childhood years. Influenced, no doubt, by the dominant society, the sons turned before long to a wholesale purging of that past which they came to consider as reflecting ethnic "superstitions" and "strange" survivals. These alleged superstitions were often equated with the very customs and traditions which were unique and strikingly different from those found in the dominant society. Many ethnic practices (e.g., Ukrainian wedding customs) were cast off in this way and, with time, replaced by supposedly less superstitious practices of the dominant society. One uniquely differentiating quality of any ethnic group – the mother tongue – suffered the most serious blow at the hands of the sons. For it was largely upon their insistence that English was introduced into church services (sermons) and ethnic publications. Ukrainian ethnic parishes were thus made bilingual. In extreme cases, they were even transformed into two socially segregated congregations – one of them ethnic, comprising the immigrant fathers and mothers, the other American, comprising their sons and daughters. Similar patterns of segregation along generational lines also affected local lodges of fraternal insurance societies.

These few illustrations indicate the important difference in ethnic orientation between fathers and sons. While the sons treated ethnicity as something to be manipulated or even dispensed with at will, the fathers still lived by it and, in the process of doing so, spontaneously changed and modified it. In the case of the fathers, ethnicity retained the basic mark of a genuine tradition. In the case of the sons, it ceased being a meaningful pattern of daily existence.

It is impossible to assess how many and what elements of ethnicity were considered by the sons as worthy of retention. The mother tongue was hardly one of them, since there is considerable evidence that many members of the second generation vehemently disapproved of its being taught to their children in parochial schools. Differences in this respect may have existed from one ethnic group to another and certainly from one second-generation individual to another. There is no doubt, however, that the attitude of not a few sons bordered on outright nihilism; that is, they tended to dismiss their respective ethnic cultures *in toto*, either by equating them with ignorance and super-stition, or by equating them with poverty and backwardness. This somewhat crude attack on the ancestral tradition and on the purportedly degrading enslavement of their parents to it, although done in the name of reason, closely resembled the breathless fervor of a conversion experience.[8] To appreciate the tragic predicament in which some of the sons found themselves, suffice it to point out that the more intensely they hated their ethnic heritage the more conscious they were of their ethnic identity. The more ashamed they were of this past, and even of their parents, the more they were aware of their ethnic background. For it should be kept in mind that the sons were bent on suppressing ethnicity. If they insisted, for example, that English be introduced in the church services and sermons, it was not only or even primarily because they were unable to understand the mother tongue, but because they sought to eliminate it from public use. Even today one may encounter second-generation individuals who relish in protesting that they remember but a few phrases of their mother tongue. Yet, it is not surprising to find that these "few phrases" miraculously expand into relatively fluent command of the conversational language when an appropriate occasion arises.

What was the nature of the sons' ethnic identification if, at the same time, they negated its very base – the ethnic heritage? In what ways did the sons relate them-selves to their fathers if they disparaged or dispised the ethnic attributes possessed by them? How did the sons identify themselves with their respective ethnic groups if they were bent on eliminating the very ties that bound them to these groups? The questions posed here raise a series of fascinating problems related to individual and group identi-fication. A relatively simple yet only partially correct answer would be to suggest that the sons severed all the ties (personal and organizational) binding them to their re-spective ethnic groups. There is no doubt that some second-generation individuals did precisely that. At the same time, it is equally evident that even those sons who were most intent on eliminating or suppressing the ethnic heritage frequently continued to participate to some extent in ethnic communal and organizational life.[9]

It is suggested here that one of the clues to the understanding of the sons' ethnic identity is their search for a "usable" past. This search, of course, should not be construed to mean a dispassionate attempt to select and preserve seemingly valuable strains of the ethnic heritage. In fact, the "usable" past consisted not so much of specific elements of the ethnic heritage that the sons were determined to retain and live by, as of an ethnically related ideal they could identify with. To that extent, the "usable" past was also "transmuted" past; it may more appropriately be called an ideology. Drawing mainly upon Jewish-American sources, the few illustrations that follow should makes explicit the distinction between tradition and ideology.

[8]   This type of revolt was especially noticeable among second-generation individuals of Jewish ethnic background. See Jessie Bernard, "Biculturality: A Study in Social Schizophrenia", in I. Graeber and S. H. Briff (eds.), *Jews in a Gentile World* (New York, Macmillan, 1942), pp. 264-293.
[9]   Viewed in this light, any assessment of the sons' positive or negative identification with ethnicity in terms of organizational affiliation alone is highly dubious.

In the two symposia dealing with American-Jewish intellectuals, published in *Contemporary Jewish Record*[10] and *Commentary*[11] one central and recurrent theme is readily discernible. The editor of *Commentary* briefly summarized it as follows (p. 310):

Believing ... that the essence of Judaism is the struggle for universal justice and human brotherhood, these young intellectuals assert over and over again that anyone who fights for this ideal is to that degree more Jewish than a man who merely observes the rituals or identifies himself with the Jewish community.

Some of the participants in this second symposium went so far as to claim that the more thoroughly one divests himself of the ancestral tradition the more he re-affirms the "essence of Judaism", i.e., the more qualified he becomes to play the role of spokesman for "rational social change" or for a "rationally organized democratic world society, unfettered by parochial traditions and superstitions". Even more, the very estrangement from the ancestral tradition or tradition in general was proclaimed to be a positive value since it helped to foster:

... a critical sense out of a role of detachment; it is, if you will, the assumption of the role of prophet ... the one of whom the Hebrew essayist Akhad Ha-am has written: '... he is a man of truth! He sees life as it is with a view unwarped by subjective feelings; and he tells you what he sees just as he sees it, unaffected by irrelevant considerations. (Bell 1946, p. 19)

It is only too obvious that this kind of Judaism, so eagerly embraced by the sons, was not received from the natural fathers and forefathers through a process of transmission from generation to generation. It may be traced to the most diverse sources – to Marx and Trotsky, to Hess and Herzl, or even to Mannheim and Buber – but hardly to the Torah-centered *shtetl* of their fathers and mothers. In fact, any of the above-named "ancestors" could equally have linked the sons to their respective versions of Judaism. In the 1930's, for example, Marx and Trotsky helped many a deracinated son along the road of reaffirmation of Judaism, since they supposedly symbolized the struggle for "universal justice and human brotherhood". Many other and widely different versions of Judaism were also entertained by the sons. Those who were more intellectually oriented tried to convince themselves and others that "... Judaism remained the only culture beside the Greek which believed in learning for its own sake and which honored the sage more than it did the plutocrat. This too was effective, for 'bourgeois standards' constituted another of our violent hatreds" (Podhoretz 1955, p. 453).

It would be highly unrewarding to inquire whether any of these versions of Judaism are true. What is certain is the fact that they are related to historical Judaism only in a tenuous way. Little historical insight is necessary in order to recognize that the French, Italians, Poles, in fact, almost all ethnic groups have unearthed in their collective pasts

---

[10] "Under Forty: A Symposium on American Literature and the Younger Generation of American Jews", *Contemporary Jewish Record*, 7 (1944), 3-36.
[11] "Jewishness and the Youger Intellectuals: A Symposium", *Commentary*, 31 (1961), 306-359.

analogous ideas and ideals. The Poles, for example, are proudly conscious of the daring exploits of their forefathers on behalf of freedom and justice; and have long been stereotyped as perennial freedom fighters. Similar attempts have repeatedly been made by American ethnic groups to provide themselves with a bilateral line of descent by tracing their origins to the American colonial past. Many of these groups have successfully discovered their respective ancestors among the contemporaries of John Smith, George Washington, and Abraham Lincoln. Recurrent rallies and pageants serve as constant reminders of these distinguished ancestors. Poles annually recall the words of Lincoln, who is supposed to have addressed Polish soldiers of the Army of the Potomac as follows:[12]

My friends, it has been a privilege to meet and greet everyone of you.... In the veins of every Pole flows the blood of your heroic ancestors – your soldierly qualities are therefore inherent. ... The United States has a deep feeling and sympathy for Poland and the hospitality of our shores shall always be open to her sons.... We shall not fail to reward those who aided us in conquering a foe who espouses slavery and would destroy our republic....

Students of American ethnic groups disagree among themselves as to whether the creators of this kind of ethnic past are recruited from among the educated immigrant fathers, their sons, or grandsons. Some suggest that the sons could hardly be history-minded since they were much too touchy about their foreign background (Appel 1961, p. 3). On the other hand, the grandsons, much more secure in their Americanness, have displayed an increasing interest and pride in their ethnic origins. But what is significant in this context is not at all the generational composition of the authors, but rather the "elective affinity" between this highly selected and transmuted past and the touchy attitude of the immigrant sons and daughters toward their ancestral background. It may well be that the uneasy and, at times, derogatory attitude of the sons toward the actual heritage of their "close" ancestors made them prone to fall back on the heritage of more "distant" ancestors – from Plato to Buber, from Columbus to Kosciusko. Similarly, the sons' hyphenated status might have predisposed them to define their ethnic ancestry in terms of the bilateral rule of descent. Considerations of this kind strongly suggest that the immigrant sons sought to disavow those aspects of ethnicity which had been directly transmitted to them by their parents. And the more determined they were to dismiss the way of life (tradition) of their natural fathers, the more inclined they were to embrace the intangible ideals and values attributable to the distant past of their respective ethnic groups. The more inclined they were to equate the heritage of their fathers with ignorance and superstition, the more readily they identified themselves with those ethnically related symbols and ideals which transcended the heritage of their fathers. This latter mode of identification with ethnicity required neither attachment to nor involvement in the parental heritage. No wonder, then, that the ethnic identification of the sons strikingly reminds one of another kind of identification, namely, that with the "proletarian class". It is a well known fact that

[12]   "Polish Rally to Recall Civil War", *The Christian Science Monitor*, February 1, 1963, 4.

one may intensely identify with the "proletarian class", and also disavow particular proletarians of this same class. Moreover, one may also deride the interests and values of individual proletarians or even dismiss them individually as typical representatives of the *Lumpenproletariat*, and, at the same time, attribute to or derive from the "proletarian class" (as a collectivity) lofty and noble values and ideals. In the same vein, one may symbolically commit himself to the "Ukrainian people" or, for that matter, glorify them, as many a populist has done with respect to the peasantry, and equally brand individual peasants as "superstitious", "narrowminded", and "ignorant". In all these instances the mode of identification is ideological, since the symbols expressing it transcend particular human beings and their personal attributes. In this sense, the ethnic identification of the sons was characteristically ambivalent, for it allowed them to love, and even pride themselves on their association with, the Jewish, Polish, or Ukrainian people in the *abstract* and, at the same time, also to despise and be ashamed of these people in the concrete.

It should be evident why the ethnic heritage, including the language, was well-nigh inaccessible to the grandsons. The influence of the immigrant grandfathers could not have been sufficiently enduring, since the very structure of the American family precluded it. The grandsons literally became outsiders to their ancestral heritage, even though many still attended churches and schools established by their immigrant grandfathers. The ancestral language became another foreign language which they primarily studied in school as one of the required subjects. There was no doubt about their ethnic identity – they were Americans of Ukrainian ancestry. Neither was there any trace of ambivalence in the ethnic identity of the grandsons for, unlike the sons, they never experienced the full brunt of a marginal status. Like many another fact of ancestral history, the grandsons neither sought to deny nor rushed to embrace it. Increasingly it came to approximate an object of cognition, in the sense that the grandsons had to *study* in order to know about their ethnic heritage and to *appreciate* it. But such knowledge and appreciation of the ancestral past had little or no effect on their daily lives – from the selection of spouses to personal and organizational associations. Studies of marriage patterns, for example, would most likely show that the grandsons far surpass the sons in their tendency toward out-marriage. The genera-

TABLE 12.6

Generational Differences in Orientation Toward Ethnicity

Generations	First Generation (Grandfathers)	Second Generation (Sons)	Third Generation (Grandsons)
Type of Identification:	Primordial	Symbolic	Functional
Mode of Orientation	Personal Affective	Symbolic- Affective	Cognitive- Appreciative
Object of Orientation	Tradition (Ancestral Past)	Ideology (Transmuted Past)	History (Historical Past)

tional differences in the orientation toward ethnicity are schematically presented in Table 12.6.

CULTURE MAINTENANCE

It has been observed on several occasions that the very fact of resettlement brought about a far-reaching dislocation in the traditional way of life of Ukrainian peasant immigrants. It required not only that the immigrants be accommodated occupationally but, more importantly, that their communal and cultural life be restructured on the basis of patterns consonant with the urban setting. The "little worlds" that the peasant immigrants founded in this country resembled but little the natural grouping of people – the village community – they had left behind. Rather they were constituted on the basis of voluntary associations and organizations, in which ethnicity became increasingly fragmented as the children of these immigrants grew up. Both ethnic communal life and the ethnic heritage came largely to depend upon and be sustained by such purposively devised organizational bonds. Only through participation in ethnic organizational life could the immigrants, and even more so their native-born children, reassert their ethnic solidarity as well as express their attachment to ethnic values and traditions. However, this very development only confirms the view that the ethnic heritage had largely ceased to be a way of life – a set of integrated values, attitudes, and behavior patterns appropriate for life in the village community and transmitted almost unconsciously to succeeding generations. It came to approximate the more formally transmitted heritage that one acquires via participation in organized national life.

This organizationally enveloped ethnic communal and cultural edifice crumbled further with the passing of the immigrant generation. The breakdown in its continuity is manifest in many spheres – it is reflected in the cultural estrangement of children from parents, in the disappearance of cultural institutions, and, finally, in the fading away of the mother tongue and of the ethnic heritage in general from immigrant churches, schools, and other organizations.

The patently temporary nature of the institutional system improvised by ethnic groups in the United States precludes any accommodation conducive to *functional biculturism* and *bilingualism*. In fact, it renders unnecessary, if not useless, the retention of the ethnic heritage and particularly of the mother tongue by the sons and grandsons of the immigrants. Reflective of this fact is the gradual "unlearning" of the mother tongue on the part of second-generation individuals. There are good reasons for concluding that children of immigrants possess better mastery of their ethnic mother tongue in their childhood than in their adolescence or adulthood. They virtually "outgrow" the institutional framework created by the immigrant parents and, as a result, find it less and less necessary to employ the mother tongue in most contexts of daily life. This is only too evident if one considers the limited influences of the immigrant family and its utter dependence upon the occupational and educational institutions of the dominant society. Indeed, with the transition from youth to adulthood, there remains but one social context in which the sons and daughters most frequently resort to the mother tongue – during recurrent visits with their immigrant parents and grandparents. Once relegated to the sphere of the parental family, the mother tongue becomes practically dormant among adult members of the second generation.

To the extent, of course, that adult individuals of the second generation remained involved in ethnic organizational life they continued to be exposed to the organizationally sustained heritage of their immigrant parents. But such exposure to ethnicity clearly limits its influence upon the native-born generation to narrowly circumscribed and increasingly insulated segments of life. The so-called "religious revival" in America should help to explicate the problem. Whatever the nature of this revival may be, the consensus seems to be that religious acitivity and involvement in religious organizations increase with increasing Americanization. It is evident that religiosity of this kind is gauged in terms of conformity to organizationally sactioned expectations – be they the frequency of attending church services, making of confessions, or whatever. If assessed on the basis of such criteria, it is only to be expected that native-born sons and grandsons would far surpass in "religiosity" their immigrant parents, since it is well known that immigrants of rural background are notoriously loath to express their "religiosity" through extensive participation in churches and church-related organizations. This fact alone hardly enlightens us on the extent to which the peasants may or may not have been "religious"; at best, it suggests that there are different ways of being "religious". Or, to put the matter more pointedly, the peasants' way of being "religious" did not need to express itself through conformity to such formally prescribed acts as attendance at church services. Rather, it expressed itself in life and, indeed, was inseparably bound to the whole scheme of daily living dominant in the village community. Even if one assented to Pascal's laconic maxim: "Bow thy knee and be religious",[13] it would still remain true that the peasants did their kneeling more frequently and on many more occasions than their organizationally active and conforming American-born sons and grandsons.

Any facile attempt to relate "religious interest" or even "religiosity" to Americanization utterly disregards the nature of religious expression under two widely divergent conditions – in the village community and in the urban milieu. The more active participation in religious organizations on the part of native-born generations may well be symptomatic of the far-reaching change in the nature of "religious expression" in this highly secularized and institutionally segmented society. Interestingly enough, it may even be indicative of the attenuating influence of religion upon American life in general.

The foregoing consideration underscores once again the *organizational context* within which both religious and ethnic values are sustained in this society. The Church was the first ethnic organization that peasant immigrants successfully established upon

---

[13] Quoted in Joachim Wach, *The Comparative Study of Religions* (New York, Columbia University Press, 1961), p. 101.

arrival in this country. From the very beginning, however, it was painfully evident that what they established was a *specifically religious organization*, even though the peasant immigrants tried desperately to salvage not only their ancestral faith but also their ancestral lifeways intimately related to this faith – so much so that some did not hesitate to desert the *religious organization* for the sake of remaining loyal to *religious tradition*. But the most serious blow to ethnicity and tradition came not so much from official Catholic pressure toward uniformity as from within the ethnic community itself – from the very sons and daughters of these peasant immigrants. The complex nature of the sons' hostile attitudes toward ethnicity has been extensively explored in this essay. Here it suffices to recall that some of the sons disparaged it in a wholesale fashion – from the strange "superstitions" to which their fathers were so intensely attached to the peasant dialects spoken by them. In brief, what the sons so eagerly scoffed at was the very and only heritage that their parents knew. The more sophisticated aspects of national culture – national literature, literary language, art, history – were largely unknown and inaccessible to the peasant immigrants. There was thus little in the parental heritage that would make the sons proud, albeit there was much in it that could be appreciated and cherished.

A somewhat different set of considerations is involved in the analysis of culture maintenance among the most recent refugee immigrants. Their higher educational status and urban background, even their intense national consciousness, all these and other characteristics differentiate the refugees from all other Ukrainian immigrants who arrived on these shores prior to or soon after World War I. One striking indication of these differences is the disproportionately large number of ethnic organizations – youth and cultural associations, professional and scholarly societies, educational institutions, and social clubs – that have been established by the newer immigrants during the last decade or so. The thoroughly secular character of most of these organizations is equally reflective of the same differences. The ethnic Church remains, of course, an important focus of ethnic communal life, but its role in the maintenance of ethnicity and of the mother tongue in particular appears to be less potent among the newer immigrants than ever before. The influence of the Church upon ethnic cultural life as a whole has been circumscribed with the arrival of the refugee immigrants. In fact, the secular sector of organized ethnic life presently carries the main brunt of culture maintenance. The two largest youth organizations as well as the mother tongue schools are currently maintained under secular auspices.

In this sense the refugee immigrants have enhanced the process of secularization of ethnic cultural life, and in so doing they have also caused the ethnic Church to increasingly approximate any other religious organization in an urban environment. What, then, is the content of this ethnicity that the refugee immigrants attempt to preserve? First of all, it represents a highly secularized version of ethnicity; second, it contains but few elements of folk culture (traditional ethnicity), i.e., the customs and practices that went to make up the peasants' lifeways. In general, the refugee immigrants know little and care less about traditional ethnicity, partly because it has been associated intimately with the peasant class. Rather, they are determined to maintain and also to transmit to succeeding generations a knowledge and appreciation of *national values and ideals* drawn from history, literature, and the like. Ethnicity of this kind is thus largely *symbolic*, and need not be manifested in overt behavior. It is calculated to sustain national sentiment (national consciousness) rather than ethnic behavioral patterns among American-born generations.[14]

At the present time, knowledge of the ethnic tongue still ranks high in the hierarchy of national values the refugee immigrants deem germane for the continuity of national self-consciousness. But more and more frequently voices are heard which bluntly state that national sentiments may be transmitted to succeeding generations via English or, for that matter, via any other languague. The Jewish group in the United States is often mentioned as a model worthy of general emulation.[15] However that may be, most refugee immigrants still continue to make a concerted effort on behalf of mother tongue maintenance.

It has been emphasized on several occasions that the temporary character of ethnic institutional systems militates against *functional bilingualism*. No definite social arrangements, however, are requisite for the maintenance of *cultural bilingualism*, since the latter can constitute a style of life to which individuals or even groups aspire and conform. Unfortunately, the popular version of Americanism has for long embraced the immage of the "adjusted" American who knows only one language – English. Without doubt this ideology of cultural provincialism adversely affects many an immigrant son and daughter; indeed, it prompts them to view their mother tongue as another "ancestral burden" which should be lifted from their shoulders as soon as possible. Some of its consequences are now becoming painfully evident, as the following comment on translated scholarly works suggests (Hughes 1955, p. 7):

Their contribution is made the greater by the fact that those Americans whose mother

---

[14]   The refugee immigrants and their offspring alike provide an enviable "human material" for Americanization. There is but little in their "designs for living" which would strikingly differentiate them from American urban populations. It appears that the Americanization of recent refugee immigrants proceeds at a relatively fast pace, even when their Ukrainian self-consciousness remains intact. Some fifty years ago the Polish-American Nestor, Father Kruszka, while discussing the Americanization of Polish immigrants, made this suggestive observation:

"... Polish political refugees were the most outspoken Polish patriots. Yet, they failed to save not only their children but also themselves before Americanization.... Had the Polish immigration exclusively consisted of political refugees, we would scarcely have Polish communities in the United States today.... What remained in the end was Polish peasant immigrant..." (Kruszka, 1905-08, XIII, p. 173).

[15]   There is evidence to show that acculturation has failed to erode Jewish self-consciousness. Some authors even suggest that despite (or because of) acculturation the latter has increased. Within the context of this approach, there can be little doubt that Jewish *traditional ethnicity* has been largely eroded, but what lingers on is Jewish *symbolic ethnicity*. This is due mainly to the fact that the Jewish ethnic group is the only group in the United States which has successfully institutionalized its symbolic ethnicity. And it has done so only because Jewish religion itself constitutes symbolic ethnicity – national history and ideology. (On Jewish self-consciousness, see Erich Rosenthal, "Acculturation Without Assimilation? The Jewish Community of Chicago, Illinois", *American Journal of Sociology*, 66, 1960, 275-288).

tongue is English (including those among them whose mother's tongue was not English) are extremely loath to learn other languages. Translations from other languages are also relatively few and are slow in appearing. If we should now stop the stream of immigrants of some measure of higher learning acquired in other languages, our linguistic isolation may become even more embarrassing than it is now.

The effect of linguistic isolation is also felt in many other spheres of American cultural life. Is it not ironic that the representatives of America and Americanism abroad (e.g., many of the guides accompanying American cultural and scientific exhibits) have to be recruited from among the children of the most recent immigrants?

There is no necessity to reiterate that even at present American ethnic groups represent a "natural reservoir" of bilingual individuals. The number of such individuals would most likely increase in the future, provided a determined attempt were made to eradicate prejudices deeply rooted in popular Americanism. The ethnic groups, in turn, still have at their disposal educational institutions capable of offering effective instruction in the mother tongue. The Ukrainian ethnic group presently supports one of the numerically strongest networks of secular (Weekend) language schools located in large metropolitan cities. In the 1962-63 school year some 6,500 children between the ages 6 and 14 were enrolled in these schools. The overwhelming majority of students attending the schools are recruited from among the children of postwar refugee immigrants. Children of American-born parents more usually study the Ukrainian language in parochial All Day and Afternoon schools. In some of the Church-related schools, however, Ukrainian is no longer taught, largely on the insistence of American-born parents. This is particularly true in the Afternoon schools, since they are slowly being transformed into religious classes in which English is used as the language of instruction.

On the other hand, many children of postwar immigrants study Ukrainian in both parochial All Day elementary schools and secular Weekend language schools. Moreover, two youth organizations (Ukrainian Scouting Association and Association of Ukrainian Youth, with a total of 5,830 members) are maintained for these same children and reinforce the use of Ukrainian in more informal peer-group contexts. There is some evidence that those children who attend Ukrainian language schools and belong to youth organizations not only know Ukrainian but are also actively bilingual, in that they tend to converse in Ukrainian outside of familial and organizational contexts. It remains to be seen, of course, whether many of these children will remain actively bilingual during their young adult years and thereafter. But the very fact that they do resort to their mother tongue in the company of peers represents a unique accomplishment for a relatively small and highly urbanized ethnic group. If their bilingualism should meet with a more positive reaction in general American circles, it need not necessarily be "unlearned" as these children grow into mature adults. A mature America will preserve and foster bilingualism in a mature second generation.

REFERENCES

Appel, J. J., "Hansen's Third Generation 'Law' and the Origins of the American-Jewish Historical Society", *Jewish Social Studies*, 23 (1961), 3-20.

Bachynskyi, L., *Ukrainska Immigraciia v Ziedynenykh Derzhavakh Ameryky* (Lviv, Naukove Tovarystvo Imeny Shevchenka, 1914), pp. 86-114.

Balch, Emily, *Our Slavic Fellow Citizens* (New York, Charities Publication Committee, 1910).

Bell, D., "A Parable of Alienation", *The Jewish Frontier*, 13 (November 1946), 12-19.

Bujak, F., *Zmiaca-Wies Powiatu Limanowskiego: Stosunki Gospodorcze i Spoleczne* (Krakow, G. Gebethner, 1903).

——, *The Jewish Question in Poland* (Paris, Imprimerie Leve, 1919).

Bynigton, Margaret, *Homestead: The Household of Milltown* (New York, Charities Publication Committee, 1910).

Davis, J., *The Russians and Ruthenians in America* (New York, George H. Doran Co., 1922).

Dill, S., *Roman Society from Nero to Marc Aurel* (London, Macmillan, 1911).

Foerster, R. F., *The Italian Emigration of Our Times* (Cambridge, Mass., Harvard University Press, 1919).

Glaser, D., "Dynamics of Ethnic Identification", *American Sociological Review*, 23 (1958), 31-40.

Gordon, M. M., "Assimilation in America: Theory and Reality", *Daedalus*, 1961, No. 2, 263-285.

Grentrup, T., S. V. D., *Religion und Muttersprache* (Münster, Aschendorffsche Verlagsbuchhandlung, 1932).

Halich, W., *Ukrainians in the United States* (Chicago, University of Chicago Press, 1937).

Handlin, O., *The Uprooted* (Boston, Little, Brown 1951).

Hansen, M. L., "The Third Generation in America", *Commentary*, 14 (1952), 492-500.

Hodnefield, J., "Norwegian-American *Bygdelags* and their Publications", *Norwegian-American Studies and Records*, 18 (1954), 163-174.

Hughes, E. C., "Forword" in George Simmel, *Conflict*, trans. by Kurt H. Wolff and Reinhard Bendix (Glencoe, Ill., The Free Press, 1955).

Katz, E., and A. Zloczower, "Ethnic Continuity in an Israeli Town", *Human Relations*, 14 (1961), 293-327.

Kohn, H., *Nationalism: Its Meaning and History* (Princeton, D. Van Nostrand Co., 1955).

Kruszka, W., *Historya Polska v Ameryce* (Milwaukee, Spolka Wydawnicza Kuryera, 1905-08), XII, XIII.

Kubiiovych, V., (ed.), *Entsyklopediia Ukrainoznavstva* (Munich-New York, Shevchenko Scientific Society, 1949).

Mahler, R., "The Economic Background of Jewish Emigration from Galicia to the United States", *YIVO Annual of Jewish Social Science*, 7 (1952), 255-267.

McAvoy, T. T., *The Great Crisis in American Catholic History: 1895-1900* (Chicago, Henry Regney Company, 1957).

Mudryi, V., "Nova Ukrainska Emigraciia", in *Ukrainci u Vilnomu Sviti: Iuvileina Knyha Ukrainskoho Narodnoho Soiuzu*, L. Myshuha (ed.), (Jersey City, Ukrainskyi Narodnyi Soiuz, 1954).

Nobilis, Sister M., S.S.N.D., "Sienkiewicz and the Poles in America", *Polish American Studies*, 2 (1945), 34-37.

Panuncio, C. M., *The Soul of an Immigrant* (New York, Macmillan, 1926).

Podhoretz, N., "Jewish Culture and the Intellectuals", *Commentary*, 19 (1955), 451-457.

Rudnytskyi, I., *Materialy do Ukrainsko-Kanadiiskoi Folklorystyky i Diialektolohii* (Winnipeg, Ukrainska Vilna Akademiia Nauk, 1958), V.

Schermerhorn, R. A., *These Our People: Minorities in American Culture* (Boston, D. C. Heath and Co., 1949).

Sirvaitis, C. P., Reverend, *Religious Folkways in Lithuania and Their Conservation among the Lithuanian Immigrants in the United States*. Ph. D. Dissertation: The Catholic University of America, 1945.

13. THE PROCESS AND PROBLEMS OF LANGUAGE-MAINTENANCE: AN INTEGRATIVE REVIEW

NATHAN GLAZER

More than forty years ago, Robert E. Park published *The Immigrant Press and its Control*.[1] No other study has described as well the incredible variety of immigrant experience in America and the way in which it found expression in print. The title clearly indicated that Park had a practical as well as a scholarly objective in undertaking this study. He was answering the question: is the immigrant press a menace? Were subversive and un-American sentiments lurking behind the strange alphabets and ideographs? Was not the immigrant press – not only the German newspapers, but also those of other Central and East European groups – influenced by German money in World War I? Had not immigrant newspapers supported the countries that became our enemies? And were they not maintaining distinct and separate loyalties, and preventing the immigrants from becoming good citizens?

It was part of Park's uniqueness as a sociologist of American ethnic groups – perhaps it came from his journalistic background – that he was able to consider soberly the idea that there was some truth in these accusations and that control of the foreign press was an issue that at least deserved discussion. He was no Pollyanna; he knew perfectly well what subsidies and judiciously placed advertisements could do to influence impoverished editors and publishers struggling to keep a newspaper alive. His conclusions therefore came with all the more force and effectiveness. He opposed any formal controls and favored the natural control that was exercised by a real interest in and knowledge of the foreign communities and their newspapers. "If immigrant editors and readers know that their newspaper is read outside its own language group, that America is interested in what it says and takes account of its opinions – that very fact establishes a measure of control".

But his larger conclusion was that the very nature of immigrant hopes and objectives in this country made this issue a temporary one, and one which would find a solution without the need for any formal governmental intervention: "In America, the immigrant wants to preserve, as far as possible, his heritage from the old country. These are represented pre-eminently by his language and his religion. At the same time, he wants to participate in the common life and find a place in the American community. In these two motives, we have at once the problem of the foreign-language press and its solution."

[1] New York and London, Harper and Brothers, 1922.

Forty years later, and after the appearance of many other books dealing with American ethnic groups, we again have witnessed a heightening of interest in the peculiar cultural treasures which the vast numbers of immigrants brought to this country. Once again, there is both official and scholarly interest in the topic. But immigrant tenacity in holding on to specific cultural characteristics is no longer seen as the problem; rather, the new problem is, as Park's conclusions suggested they would be, the rapidity with which values and resources are abandoned. In particular, our new international position leads us to consider with concern the rapid attenuation of facility in languages, a facility which almost all human beings seem to acquire almost effortlessly early in life, and to which most can add only with great difficulty when they are grown. This country, which can find within its borders native speakers of the most outlandish and exotic languages – and very often sizeable numbers of them – seems to be one of the most linguistically limited of the great nations in its international contacts. Tens of millions of people in this country were raised speaking languages other than English yet these Americans are, it seems, tongue-tied abroad and unable to make use of the huge literature published in other languages – including, commonly, the ones they or their parents used in their childhood.

The nature of official interest has consequently changed. We are no longer interested in the control of a rich, unrestrained and possibly menacing natural growth; we are now more interested in the factors that have led to the rapid decline of language facility and of all the institutions that expressed and to some degree supported it. We have also become interested in the question of whether these institutions might be strengthened for the benefit of the country. And once again, as in Park's book forty years ago, we are confronted with the incredible variety and complexity of immigrant experience in this country.

The major intellectual problem with which we are faced is perfectly clear: how can we explain why, in the country which was most open to immigration, and most undisturbed when it came to the maintenance of immigrant cultures, there was also the most rapid flight from and abandonment of most key aspects of immigrant cultures on the part of the children and grandchildren of immigrants as well as on the part of immigrants themselves?

On the one hand, in contrast to some other countries with sizeable minorities or heavy immigration, immigrants to the United States were allowed a remarkable degree of cultural freedom. There were no established religions, there was rarely any great restraint on private schooling, there was usually no control of publications, and cultural and social organizations of the greatest variety could do what they wished. Indeed, even the public institutions could sometimes be used for language maintenance, as in the case of the many public schools that were conducted wholly or partly in German, and as in the case of the successful effort to introduce the languages of major ethnic groups into public high schools in New York and elsewhere.

It is, of course, only by contrast with *some* other countries that the United States may be considered liberal in its attitudes toward the cultures of incoming ethnic groups,

If we apply more absolute standard of freedom our record is not nearly as good. In many parts of the country native Americans of Anglo-American background resisted public support for other languages. It took a good deal of political muscle by Italians and Jews to introduce their languages into the New York City high schools. And during the first World War and after, there was an hysterical attack on German by public bodies and public opinion, and to a lesser degree on other foreign languages. But apart from any public actions, there is the character of American culture itself, and in particular the strong pressures – remarked upon by Toqueville and other European travellers – toward conformity. Even without any formal legal requirements, these could be devastatingly effective in hastening the abandonment of foreign dress, habits, language, and accent. Just why America produced *without* laws that which other countries, desiring a culturally unified population, were not able to produce *with* laws – is not an easy question.

Elsewhere in this volume, Joshua A. Fishman suggests one important point which explains the enormous assimilative power of American civilization: assimilation in America was not to another folk, another ethnic group, but to a rather abstract concept involving freedom for all and loyalty to democratic ideals. In America one assimilated not to another *people* – which inevitably means abandoning or betraying one's "own" people – but to an ideology marked by an easily attained formal citizenship. Thus, Fishman suggests, even the very first Puritan settlers emphasized ideology rather than ethnicity. The ideology, in time, underwent many changes, and today's "Americanism" is a very different affair from the Enlightenment philosophy of the founding fathers. But all the ideologies held in common a refusal to accept the typical European nationalism which ascribed special virtues, many unanalysed, to a natural phenomenon, the ethnically based nation, which had as one of its natural features a special language. Thus, even the recurrent waves of exclusivism in this country, which were vicious and bigoted in their attitudes towards those they wished to *exclude* (Catholics, Jews, Orientals, Communists), were remarkably *inclusive* in their interpretations of those they considered true Americans. At worst, the true Americans were white Protestant Christians. But this includes Englishmen, Scots, Welshmen, Netherlanders, Germans, Danes, Norwegians, Swedes and members of other ethnic-nationality groups as well.

The significance of this is that American nationalism rarely attacked foreign cultures directly, except in the special case of Germans during and after the First World War. It attacked "ideas" and "conditions": authoritarianism, poverty, ignorance and inefficiency. Since most immigrants were without a sharply developed opposing ideology, it was easy to accept Americanism. And since their specific cultural and linguistic attributes were not under attack directly, they developed little loyalty in defending them. Culture and language became an *embarrassment* and an *obstacle* in the way of becoming true Americanc, rather than something of value to be cherished.

Thus, when compared with many other countries, the United States has put relatively few restrictions on the public and private use of foreign languages. And yet, as so many language loyalists sadly noted, their languages shrivelled in the air of freedom, while they had apparently flourished under adversity in Europe. Obviously, there was more than freedom in the United States. There were other aspects to American society and culture which reduced all languages to the same sad state. Whether it was one of the great international tongues with a vast literature, such as German, Spanish or French; or a language of peasants with a scanty literature or press, such as Ukrainian; or an exotic and proud language not widely known, such as Hungarian;[2] or a language, such as Yiddish,[3] that incorporated in itself a major national and cultural movement – all, it seems, regardless of their position, their history, their strength, the character of the groups that brought them to this country and maintained them through one or two or three generations, have come to a similar condition. The newspapers die out; the schools, full-time and part-time, close; the organizations, religious or secular, shift to English; and the maintenance of the ethnic mother tongue becomes the desperate struggle of a small group committed to it, who will have to find their most effective future support less among the descendants of the immigrants who brought the language to this country than in governmental and educational institutions that might find some practical or scholarly value in training and maintaining a corps of experts who know and can use it.

And yet the diversity among the groups that carried foreign languages to this country, and the circumstances they encountered, was so great, that it is hard to see what common factors could have affected them all. We can document – from the studies reported by Fishman and his colleagues – a number of major types of diversity which logically should have played some role in affecting the use and history of immigrant group languages in this country. Without attempting to order them in degree of significance, we can distinguish at least five factors of major importance.

There was, first of all, the time of arrival in this country of the bulk of the immigrant group. In the first half of the nineteenth century, when many German immigrants arrived, the United States was, in fact, culturally underdeveloped. Colleges and universities were few and inferior to those in Europe; the public school system was just beginning; sectionalism was strong and the Federal government weak. Under these circumstances, it was no special sign of cultural nationalism for German immigrants to feel a strong obligation to maintain what they conceived of as a higher culture. Indeed, the German language gave access to as much or more of science and literature than did English.

The situation after the second half of the nineteenth century was quite different. With the passage of time, American institutions became stronger; their assimilating power much greater. Since the early 1930's, immigrants to this country have been

[2]   Fishman, Joshua A., "Efforts to maintain the Hungarian Language in America", in Fishman, J. A. et al., *Language loyalty in America* (New York, Yeshiva University, 1964), Chapter 17. (Mimeographed report to the Language Research Section, USOE.) *American Studies in Uralic Linguistics*, II (in press).
[3]   Fishman, Joshua A., "Yiddish in America: A Socio-Linguistic Analysis", in Fishman, J. A. et al., *op. cit.*, Chapter 18. *International Journal of American Linguistics*, 31 (1965), no. 2, part II.

distinguished from their same-homeland predecessors by more education, more frequent professional backgrounds, and more experienced intellectual and cultural leadership. Nevertheless, they have come to an America of enormous cultural strength and significance, with powerful educational and political institutions and with tremendous economic opportunities, and this has inevitably inhibited the development of separate social and cultural organizations and of direct language-maintenance institutions (settlements, schools, newspapers, theatres) among these new immigrants, even though they are far more competent to build such institutions than were their predecessors.

In his essay on German in the United States, Heinz Kloss points to an important factor related to the time of arrival of the first large bodies of non-English language users: some of their languages had official status *before* the establishment of the political authority of England or the United States. In particular, one must note the position of Spanish in New Mexico, and of French in Louisiana. One can hardly overestimate the importance of some official status in maintaining a language. It gives it social status among its native users, and serves in part as a barrier against self-deprecation and embarrassment. A little of state support, in the form of official printing presses, court proceedings, and school use, can, at times, do much more to establish a language than can a vast amount of energetic activity by language loyalists. However, we may add to the significance of *official* status in maintaining these early established languages the *social* status derivable from the fact that the first settlers, the makers of history in the area, the givers of names to natural features and towns, spoke these languages. Thus, the colonial tongues, French, Spanish, and German, have been stronger than the more recently introduced languages of the period of mass immigration.

But this factor, of course, is closely linked to a second factor which Heinz Kloss also emphasizes: the area and pattern of settlement. Thus, the mother tongue was maintained longer in the German language islands of Texas or the Great Plains than in mixed areas of settlement, urban or rural. Language maintenance was more successful in smaller industrial and mining towns with large relative concentrations of a particular immigrant group cut off from cosmopolitan influences than in the mixed areas of the great cities where larger numbers of immigrants of diversified backgrounds resided side by side. Ethnic mother tongues were maintained longer where immigrant groups were, in effect, almost geographic extensions of homelands near at hand than where immigrants were cut off from their homelands by oceans. Thus, the French-Canadians in New England, the Puerto Ricans in New York, the Cubans in Florida, the Mexicans in the Southwest, are all better able to maintain their languages owing to the relative ease of contact with Canada, Peurto Rico, Cuba, and Mexico, as well as the relative concentration of their settlements.

But in comparison with these factors of time and pattern of settlement, the social and cultural factors – more elusive and complex – are at least of equal significance. Hasidic Jews created – at least for a time – a community in the heart of Brooklyn as completely cut off from the influence of the city as the German sectarian groups in their colonies in the sparsely populated Dakotas. Immigrant groups arrived in this country with quite different social structures. The Germans represented almost a whole nation – intellectuals, professionals, priests, artisans, farmers, workers. Other groups, such as the Ukrainians, represented a much less extended social range, limited primarily to peasants and workers and a handful of priests. What was the significance of the presence of a substantial intellectual or professional class, or of a large middle class, among immigrants? It would seem that they strengthened the institutions that supported language use directly, such as schools and cultural societies and publications. And yet, a peasant group without intellectuals, such as the Ukrainians, freed from the presence of a Russified or Polonized upper and middle class, could find within itself cultural resources that would not have flourished in the homeland and that offered strong support for language maintenance. Perhaps more important than the simple *presence* of intellectual and middle-class groups among the immigrants was their *relationship* to the less educated masses. In the case of Ukrainians, Russians, Hungarians, Croatians, political history led to a pattern in which one had an earlier working-class migration, followed by later migrations of better educated professional and middle-class groups. In all these cases, the later middle-class immigrants felt superior to the earlier immigrants of the peasant class. They did little or nothing to strengthen the institutions these had created. But if the entire group, those of middle-class and of peasant origin, had been bound together by a national struggle, if a sense of common nationality had been strengthened in them, then undoubtedly the educated middle-class elements were a resource for language maintenance. The Germans in the middle of the nineteenth century, and the Eastern European Jews in the early twentieth century, are examples of such groups.

Of all the groups reported on in this volume, it is the Spanish-speaking of the Southwest, who seem to have been most completely without middle class, intellectual and professional groups. Paradoxically, while less "high cultural" activity is reported for them than for any other group, at the same time they reveal less attrition in the use of their mother tongue than does any other group! Of course, one cannot take the position that the development of any serious cultural interest in a minority language is a sign that it is losing its hold as a medium of daily life. The explanation of the paradox of continued mass use without high cultural development is obviously to be found in the special circumstances of both the early Spanish-speaking population and later immigrants. The early Spanish-speaking groups, largely Indian in origin, developed a folk culture in which there was almost no written communication. Later Mexican immigrants also came from an illiterate environment. In this country, as Chester and Jane Christian have pointed out, both groups adopted patterns of communication and entertainment by means that either preceded or succeeded the age of print – fiestas, markets and family life from the period *before*; radio and television from the period *after*. Certain political services for this group were more often carried out by Mexican consular representatives than by their own leaders. Thus, they may be seen as a lower class extension of a society which, however small its middle, intellectual and professional classes, does have them – back in Mexico.

But this link with Mexico is being broken as the immigrants become city dwellers and American citizens. Mexican-Americans seem to be at a point which French Canadians in New England reached one hundred years ago. If the folk use of the language is still strong, this is primarily the effect of social isolation which is bound to break down as the commitment to American citizenship increases. And yet it would be hazardous to predict that Spanish in the Southwest will go through the same evolution as French in New England. On the one hand, its present complement of high cultural institutions is nowhere near what French had and has. On the other hand, its evolution will take place in an America that may be far more supportive of facility in a language as important to this nation as Spanish. One suspects that just as Spanish in New York is developing an official position that no other immigrant language ever attained, so Spanish in the Southwest has a history marked out for it that will be rather different from the histories of languages spoken by other peasant immigrant groups. Once again – Spanish *is* the official language of one part of the American polity (and Puerto Rico may yet become a state), and this too will certainly make a difference.

As Heinz Kloss has pointed out, these elements of social structure of immigrant groups, have ambiguous effects on language maintenance. We must analyse complex interrelationships of time, place, and social structure for each group. Religion has an equally complex relationship to language-maintenance. One of the most interesting generalizations one can draw from this series of studies on the experiences of many different ethnic groups in the United States is that the Catholic Church became indifferent or opposed to the language maintenance efforts of immigrant groups within its fold. Thus, among the Germans, it was the Lutheran churches rather than the Catholic that were most concerned with maintaining German schools. The French had to fight consistently against the Irish-American hierarchy in order to maintain their French-language schools and French-language parishes. The Ukrainians encountered the same difficulties. Nor was the Roman Catholic hierarchy much friendlier to Italian, Hungarian, Polish, or any other language-maintenance efforts. But if the Roman Catholic hierarchy in America generally played a grudging and unwilling role in helping foreign languages, the situation was, of course, quite different where the group were able to maintain their own distinct parishes, with priests stemming from the language groups itself. The French Canadians were most successful in doing so, and some of their parishes became strong supporters of language-maintenance efforts.

Among the Spanish-speaking of the Southwest, the church is deeply concerned with the social and economic problems of Mexican Americans and accepts the fact that they are Spanish-speaking. However, once again, there is no evidence that it places any great value on this fact. It defends the rights of the Spanish-speaking, and in the present situation this means acknowledgment of the fact that teachers and social workers and policemen and government employees who do not know Spanish cannot do as good a job as those who can. Thus, we find a purely instrumental accommodation to Spanish, rather than – as in the truly nationally oriented churches – a fight for the language itself.

In many ethnic groups there were also non-Catholic, nationally oriented churches, and these were among the most powerful forces in strengthening language loyalty. This was the case among the German Lutherans, the Hungarian Calvinists and among the various Eastern Churches separated in varying degrees from Roman Catholicism. Was the indifference or antagonism of American Catholicism to foreign languages affected by the overwhelming domination of the American hierarchy by the Irish, who spoke English and had become ardent 100 per cent American patriots by the time mass Eastern and Central European immigration had begun? Was "Americanism" in the church related to the strong American nationalism that the Irish developed in the United States?

Religion, we may conclude, played a role in maintaining language skill when it was a *national* religion, closely linked to and identified with the historical trials of a single nation. If it was truly "catholic" then religion could not long serve as a vehicle by which particular national languages, cultures, or customs were maintained. And indeed, with the passage of time, as the religious denominations which stemmed from European national churches came ever closer together on the basis of theological ties – as the lines between German, Swedish, Norwegian, Danish and other Lutherans blurred (and as the same thing happened to Calvinists) – even these national religions no longer played major roles in maintaining language competence. They became American religions, with the same assimilating effects as other American institutions.

We have spoken of the time of immigration, the spatial pattern of settlement, the social structure of the immigrant group (and in particular of the role of professional, intellectual, and middle-class elements within it) and of the role of religion. To these four factors we will add one more: the degree of ideological mobilization in the group. We may ask, is the emigration to be explained solely by economic factors, or are religious and political factors also important? It seems reasonable that if people emigrate because of oppression, because they are not allowed national freedom, cultural freedom, religious freedom, they will cling more strongly to the national language than if they emigrate only to improve their economic situation. If the language has become an instrument in the national struggle – as in the case of Polish – there is even stronger reason to set up communities, schools, newspapers, organizations. We are all familiar with political refugees – whether from Bourbon Italy or Castro Cuba – who expected to return to their homelands and who maintained a vigorous associational life and a lively press in their native languages. And yet, it is also true that, on a lower social level, those who emigrate to make money, and who expect to return to their homes, will also – with less sophisticated instruments perhaps – maintain language facility and move over to English slowly. Their within-group ties and everyday ethnicity may be strong enough to make up for the absence of conscious nationalism.

And yet, having listed all these factors, can one honestly say that they made a great difference in the outcome? Regardless of this wide range of differences in the circumstances of ethnic groups in America, language is always so intimate and valued a part of life that the immigrants clung to it – whether they were religious or freethinkers, in an international or a national church, concentrated in town or country-side or spread thinly over many states, and regardless of whether they had an appropriate complement of intellectuals and journalists and teachers. Indeed, as Fishman points out in several chapters, one of the most striking facts about immigrant languages in America was the way in which groups without intellectuals and ignorant of the approved form of their language were able to develop newspapers, organizations and schools to maintain this valued part of their heritage.

The basic counter-maintenance factor, therefore, may very well have been American civilization. Probably mass, free education played the largest role – it taught almost all the children English, and it insidiously undermined the native language by implying (if not advocating) the superiority of English to any language their parents spoke. But an important role in undermining the foreign languages was also taken by American mass culture. This was gradually shaped under democracy so as to appeal, for the greater profit of its producers, to the largest numbers. American mass culture learned to create products which have, it appears, as great an appeal to the most diverse peoples of the world as to Americans. It has made English – along with its political and commercial importance – the language that the world's youth feels it must acquire first in order to become stylish and modern. If it has this effect in Japan, how much more effective is it in America? American mass culture was created to appeal to people of the most diverse backgrounds. Tested successfully among immigrants here, it now goes abroad to create new emigrants-in-spirit from their own country and from their own cultures.

Along then with the school, we must place mass culture. Consider the impact of television in teaching English – and much more than English – to the immigrants who have come to the United States since World War II. And before television, there were movies, comic strips, popular newspapers, gadgets and innovations doing the same.

The openness of American politics must also be considered. It has made it relatively easy for immigrants to participate in political processes. By offering the rewards of office to a few, it makes the natural leaders of the immigrants the most effective propagandists for Americanization. Thus, instead of defending the group culture and language – as minority leaders do in other countries – the leaders of immigrants join other Americans in urging the immigrant to put away his foreign ways, learn English, and become a citizen. Only then can he vote his leaders into office, and benefit most from the American social and economic system. Aspiring political leaders also appealed to ethnic groups as groups – they sought Polish, German, or Jewish votes by stressing some group demand, or by emphasizing their own identification with these groups. But they could not get the support they sought while the members of these groups remained unchanged. They encouraged a symbolic Polishness, Germanness, Jewishness – loyalty to a vague and contentless symbol, rather than a concrete cultural reality. The latter would threaten them, by preventing their people from entering into general political and communal life; the former mobilized a voting bloc for them. Once this mobilization had taken place, once the specific cultural content of the group had been reduced to almost nothing, then the candidate could propose various symbolic balms to the group ego, such as teaching the ethnic language in public schools.

Finally, the economy also played a major role in undercutting immigrant languages and cultures. Workers were very often concentrated in industries dominated by a single or only a very few ethnic groups. Garment workers in New York, farmers in Minnesota and coal miners in Pennsylvania could manage well enough with Yiddish of Swedish or Lithuanian. But few immigrants and their children wanted to remain workers in a land of expanding opportunities. Many opened small businesses; those who succeeded in educating themselves entered white collar work and became professionals. These could not be effective economically or accepted socially without English.

And so, through education, mass culture, politics, the economy, the immigrant was assimilated. So powerful were these forces, that as Fishman and Nahirny both point out, we find not only the loss of language competence from one generation to another; we find the loss of competence within a single generation. The children of immigrants, fluent in childhood, lose their knowledge as they grow up. This happens even to the immigrants themselves. It is a result of the fact that the most effective and important institutions to which they have access as Americans are conducted in English.

What we must conclude is that many *natural* supports for language use are cut off in America. The family still exists. Insofar as language facility is communicated, it tends to be as a result of language use within the family in the earliest years of childhood. As soon as school begins, another language, of greater status and value, begins to compete. Even before school, television is in the home and with it, the language of television. Associations may support the old language – but the driving force of associations is self-perpetuation, and many an organization which began in a foreign language, and as a supporter of foreign language use, continues its life in English.

But if the natural supports of language are cut down by the homogenizing aspects of American civilization, at the same time it must be pointed out there is no direct hostility to language use and language maintenance. Indeed, the mass media, which we have spoken of as one of the chief creators of a homogeneous culture, are not averse to adapting themselves to a foreign language, if its use is widespread, and if its bearers show little tendency to switch to English – as happens among the Spanish speaking of the Southwest and New York. It is the peculiar nature of American culture and civilization – discussed by many of the chapters in this volume – that seems to undermine differences, in its creation of a common modern, changing, mobile, urbanized, society. Just as the "socialist culture" of Soviet Russia can be spread in many languages, so can the "mass culture" that is one of the distinctive products of American civilization.

If the natural supports of language use remain strong, then American institutions accommodate themselves to the situation. But this seems to be the situation – and it may remain so only temporarily – only in the case of Spanish. For the rest, we can no longer depend on the natural supports, in a distinctive culture, of language use. The people of this country are for the most part too mobile, geographically and socially, to maintain distinctive cultures, whether immigrant or regional. Thus, just as hitherto many other "natural" functions (for example, the maintenance of the aged and of dependent children by their families) became state functions, or at any rate, formally organized functions, so too the natural process of language transmission, if it is to be strengthened and maintained, will very likely need formal and state support. More and more of the things that were done unthinkingly, by groups and nations, in the past, will have to be done in a formally organized way, on the basis of common group decisions – in effect, political decisions – if they are to be done in the future.

Under these new circumstances, the chief supports of foreign language facility – if there are to be any – will have to be found in those relatively efficient organized segments of American life. The schools, first of all; in a more limited way, the mass media and specialized voluntary organizations; and above all, public funds, which become more and more necessary for any large social objective. This is a country in which every natural – or traditional – social form is rapidly undermined by new forms of rational organization. The only hope for the maintenance of the valuable resource of foreign language facility still available to us is for language loyalists and others interested in language maintenance to learn the techniques of using rational organization and public commitment in support of their goals.

14. PLANNED REINFORCEMENT OF LANGUAGE MAINTENANCE IN THE UNITED STATES: SUGGESTIONS FOR THE CONSERVATION OF A NEGLECTED NATIONAL RESOURCE

JOSHUA A. FISHMAN

After many generations of neglect and apathy, American speakers of non-English languages have, of late, become objects of more positive attention than has commonly been their lot in most American communities. They have not been proclaimed national heroes, nor have they been the recipients of public or private largesse. In the eyes of the general public, they continue to be objects of curiosity in that their atypicality is obvious even if it is no longer shameful. Nevertheless, the attitude toward them *has* changed. They are now more frequently viewed as commanding a rare commodity, a skill which has "suddenly" become a valuable asset for the country. As a result, there have been a number of recent efforts to study the distribution of this commodity and to consider ways of safeguarding it. The Language Resources Project itself may be viewed as one such effort; there could be many more if it were fully and finally decided to pursue a consistent and effective policy of language maintenance, reinforcement, and development. Our purpose here is to indicate some possible ingredients of such a policy.

I approach this task with some ambivalence. At a professional level, most social scientists feel more comfortable with diagnosis (study design, instrument construction, data collection, data analysis, data interpretation) than with therapy (recommendations for action, planning action, involvement with action-oriented branches of government or segments of the community).[1] Our self-concepts and our professional standing as scientists and scholars are reinforced and advanced by activities removed from the work-a-day world of political pressures, social tactics, and applied activities. Since our scientific status is often relatively recent and insecure within the academic community itself, we are frequently tempted to pursue security and respectability by increasing our isolation from the complexities and the frustrations of social arenas in which our findings and theories might be put to overly demanding, time-consuming, and frustrating tests. Although it is frequently admitted that applied settings *can* provide powerful stimulation for theoretical developments, the leap from the role of scholar to that of consultant or activist is still rarely attempted among behavioral

---

[1] An interesting exception to this tendency, and one of particular relevance to our topic, is the "Appeal of a Meeting of Professors in Scandinavian Countries on Behalf of Ethnic Groups and of Languages in Danger of Becoming Extinct" published in *Revue de Psychologie des Peuples*, 17 (1962), 350-356.

scientists, and even more rarely pursued to the point of both conceptual and pragmatic "success".[2]

As a research venture the Language Resources Project was guided by an intellectual preoccupation with language maintenance under the impact of social change in the United States. No particular attitudinal position with respect to the language maintenance efforts of American ethnic groups was necessary in order to plan, conduct, or interpret the score of interrelated studies which constituted the Project. Given necessary levels of previous training and concurrent ability, and given an interest in the topic as an area of professional promise, it was rarely necessary either to significantly depend upon or to discount personal sympathies or biases in order to proceed with the Project. This might not have been the case had we made greater use of intensive interviewing, clinical testing, or participant observation techniques. As it was, the structured and quantitative research designs that we initially imposed on ourselves usually limited the impact of values and biases toward language maintenance on the part of the Project staff. Although such biases as did exist (and they were by no means unidirectional) are, at times, apparent upon a careful reading of the reports contributed by various Project staff members, it is rarely necessary to share these biases in order to accept the data presented.

However, when one approaches the realm of recommendations and of social engineering more generally, it is impossible to disclaim the guiding role of values and biases. Recommendations with respect to social policy require a social philosophy. A social philosophy can be adopted in a role-playing sense, i.e., as a purely temporary, expedient exercise. A social philosophy can be a deeply experienced commitment derived from basic value positions pertaining to the nature of man and the meaning of life. In either case, social philosophy results in recommendations that *may* be derived from data but aim at goals which exist above and beyond the reaches of data. In part, the recommendations advanced here are derived from the point of view that language maintenance in the United States is desirable, in that the non-English language resources of American minority groups have already helped meet our urgent national need for

---

[2] The governmental agency which supported the Language Resources Project for three years requested, entirely on its own initiative, that a section devoted to suggestions for planned reinforcement of non-English language resources in the United States be included in the Project's final report. It was never quite clear to me how certain or how extensive such future reinforcement might be. Thus I struggled with the suspicion that the Project itself, which was not supposed to help concretely in language maintenance efforts, was indirectly doing so, while at the same time I suspected that my direct recommendations for future assistance to language maintenance might actually remain a strange and pious document and little more. To complicate the role-problem even further, I was aware of the fact that the Language Resources Project was being viewed as a harbinger of governmental-blessings-yet-to-come by language loyalists throughout the nation. As the director of the Project I was considered, at times, to be an actual or potential savior. In seeking cooperation or information from innumerable individuals, organizations, and groups unaccustomed to social research, I frequently felt that some reference to the possibility of governmental assistance in the future would open many doors for the Project. Nevertheless, I was not at all sure whether there really would be any such assistance, and if there was, for what purposes. As a result, I requested cooperation or information primarily on a research basis.

speakers of various non-English languages, and that these resources can be reinforced and developed so as to do so to a very much greater extent in the future. The recommendations are also derived from an awareness that while competence in two languages can be a decided asset to those who have this command (indeed, most language learning in schools is based on just such an assumption), the bilingualism of hundreds of thousands of Americans is a liability in their lives, and this for no reason inherent in the nature of bilingualism per se. It is our treatment of bilinguals and of bilingualism that brings this sad state of affairs into being and, therefore, it is this treatment that must be altered. Finally, in the realm of sheer practicality, it is obvious that our national resources of native non-English language competence are allowed – even encouraged – to languish and disappear at the very time that unprecedented efforts and sums are being spent to improve and increase the teaching of "foreign" languages in the nation's schools and colleges. The recommendations aim to eliminate this wasteful ambivalence.

At an even more basic (and less instrumental) level, language maintenance support is advocated on the ground that our national genius and our national promise depend upon a more conscious and a better implemented commitment to a culturally pluralistic society. Such support is crucial because neither a fondness for cultural quaintness nor a romantic interest in cultural diversity can materially benefit language maintenance or materially alter its prospects. Only a mobilization of sensitivity, concern, intellect, and means can accomplish this goal. Only an unembarrassed acceptance of the merits of linguistic and cultural variations from the English-speaking norm of American core society can bring such mobilizations into being. Just as Dobzhansky has vigorously maintained thet the merit of a society is significantly dependent on the maintenance of the most varied pool of genes (Dobzhansky 1956), so must there be substantial conviction that the merit of a society – of our American society – is significantly dependent on the appropriate maintenance of the most varied pool of languages and cultures. In present day America such a conviction cannot be derived from nor maintained by a tradition of permissiveness or a spirit of toleration alone. Rather, such a conviction requires that honestly pursued cross-cultural understanding, democratically pursued internal unity, deeply experienced traditional practices, deeply valued cultural creativity, deep sensitivity to the nature of human tragedy and human hope – that all of these be viewed as more than romantic luxuries; indeed, that they be viewed as desiderata that carry with them imperatives for rational action.

The recommendations that follow are offered in the hope they will be implemented and that language maintenance will be strengthened as a result of such implementation. However, these recommendations are not necessarily derived from data reported by the Language Resources Project. Many could have been advanced (and probably would have been) without the data obtained from three years of concerted effort. Others, usually those oriented toward detailed alternatives or priorities, have been influenced by the data to some extent. Nevertheless, all of the recommendations should be evaluated not so much on the basis of accuracy of data as on the basis of extrapolations beyond data into the realm of desirability. Certainly this is not an unusual situation – either in the realm of national planning as a whole or in the realm of language planning more specifically. Students of the sociology of language have been called upon many times to depart from exclusive attention to their basic disciplines and to enter the realm of desirability and possibility. Not only have such students helped create, select, standardize, and develop national (and international) languages but they have also accumulated considerable experience in the realm of planned language protection, maintenance, and reinforcement. Whenever this is to be done, more than technical linguistics and technical sociology are called for. Recommendations leading to language reinforcement imply a willingness to espouse certain values, and to assit certain groups in an informed pursuit of "the art of the possible". Language reinforcement, like all language planning, whether in developing or in developed contexts, deals with much more than language per se; it deals with goals and values, both those of the planners and those of the populace.

Many American intellectuals reveal particular ambivalence or hostility in connection with discussions – whether at a theoretical or applied level – concerning ethnic or ethno-religious participation in the United States. Many are themselves of second and third generation background. More than most Americans they are likely to have been "liberated" (intellectually and overtly, if not emotionally) from the claims and constraints of many primordial ties and biases. As a result, they are less inclined than most to take kindly to serious consideration of the *values* of ethno-religious participation, not to mention consideration of ways and means of reinforcing such participation. To the extent that they acknowledge pervasive value commitments beyond those directly related to their own academic specialties, these commitments usually take the form of assisting various population groups to gain liberation from constraints that impede their full participation in higher levels of socio-cultural life. However, the particular ethnocentric and egocentric ingredients of this value commitment usually remain unexamined. Such commitments may well assume the complete relevance of the intellectual's own experiences and convictions as a goal for all mankind. The very completeness of their own divestment from ethnicity and religion may prompt all-or-none distinctions between primordiality and modernity, between particularism and cosmopolitanism, to the end that reality is severely misconstrued. For most of mankind these guiding forces are in constant and complementary interaction, and are in a world-wide process of mutual accommodation, each providing benefits and exacting tolls unknown to the other. The problem of ethnically-based language maintenance in the United States (and in various other developed or developing nations) is precisely the problem of readjusting an imbalance between these forces so as to permit all men to more freely and more maturely benefit from each, rather than from only one or the other.

The problems of language maintenance in the United States are here considered at the very time that our country is convulsed, as never before, by the need to liberate millions of its citizens from primordial restrictions of a particularly debilitating and shameful kind. This co-occurrence heaps additional difficulty upon any attempt to distinguish between primordial attachments and to strengthen some while weakening others. Since native linguistic competence cannot be preserved without preserving some form of para-linguistic difference, a discussion of language maintenance at this time runs the risk of eliciting charges of parochialism and ghettoization or worse. Actually, two different kinds of ghettos must be overcome. One is the ghetto of ethnic superiority which rejects change and egalitarian participation in modern culture and in society at large. This type of ghetto is far weaker in the United States than it has ever been, and is becoming increasingly enfeebled. The other ghetto is that which considers everything ethnic to be foreign or worthless. This type of ghetto, regrettably, is still all too evident around us. The co-existence of these two kinds of parochialism implies that there is no easy route to language maintenance in the United States. Such maintenance is faced by the task of consciously preserving certain carefully selected cultural *differences* at the same time that we strain to attain other carefully selected cultural *similarities* or equalities. Language maintenance must pursue both unity and diversity, both proximity and distance. However, in this respect it is merely a reflection at the national-cultural level of a problem that every mature individual must solve within himself even when ethnic considerations are entirely absent.

The recommendations herewith presented derive from the author's values and biases concerning not only the general worthwhileness of safeguarding linguistic and cultural diversity in American life, but also from his biases concerning the spheres in which such diversity is desirable and the intensiveness with which language maintenance is to be pursued. Far different recommendations would flow from a model of American society which aimed at securing cultural autonomy within an officially protected multi-language and multi-culture political framework. Far different ones would be offered on the basis of a desire to maintain major population groups on a fully intact, separate, monolingual, non-English speaking basis. No such *verzuiling* is desired (Moberg 1961); nor is it a sine qua non for the successful pursuit of language maintenance. Every nation, new or old, that engages in language maintenance efforts must define the domains (if any) in which cultural and linguistic unity must receive precedence over cultural and linguistic diversity. Every nation, developing or developed, that pursues planned reinforcement of language maintenance must decide on the appropriateness of extensive vs. intensive efforts toward that goal.

The present recommendations neither envision nor seek the disestablishment of English as the common language of American unity and as the basic language of American culture, government, and education for all Americans. Rather, they have in mind the planned reinforcement of non-English languages and their underlying non-core cultures for those who desire them, for those who are willing and able to expend considerable efforts and sums of their own to maintain institutions and organizations of their own on behalf of their languages and cultures, and for those who are willing to do so within a framework of mutual interaction with American core society and its democratically maintained and developed institutions and processes. Thus, not only is cultural pluralism rather than cultural separatism espoused, but cultural bilingualism rather than merely functional bilingualism is emphasized. Non-English languages and non-core cultures are considered to be maintainable and reinforceable primarily within the spheres of American-ethnic family life, of the self-defined American-ethnic community, the self-defined American ethnic school and cultural organization, under the direction of the self-defined American-ethnic teacher, writer, artist, and cultural or communal leader. Both language maintenance and ethnicity have become and must remain entirely voluntaristic behaviors in the United States. Their ideological mainsprings must derive largely from an interpretation of Americanism, American culture, and American national well being. However, such behaviors and interpretations are particularly dependent on an encouraging and facilitating environment. It is to recommendations for maintaining such an environment that we now turn.

ESTABLISHING A CLIMATE FOR LANGUAGE MAINTENANCE

For the foreseeable future there will continue to be non-English-speaking groups in the United States, regardless of either official or unofficial encouragement or discouragement. However, accidents of history and geography are insufficient to assure either the numerical adequacy of proficient speakers of standard and regional variants of most languages, or the required psychological predisposition.

Fundamentally, language maintenance efforts are justifiable and desirable because: either they serve the *national* interest (both in utilitarian and in an idealistic sense), and/or they promote various *group* interests that need not be in conflict with the national interest, and/or they contribute powerfully to the enrichment of *individual* functioning. The cultural and political unity of the United States seems to be sufficiently assured so that there need be no fear of "Balkanization" as a result of non-English language maintenance and "non-core" ethnic cultural diversity within subgroups of the American population. There is no longer any reasonable basis upon which to fear an entrenchment on our shores of the political and social cleavages which cultural and linguistic diversity have forced upon Belgium or Canada in the West, or upon India and Ceylon in the East. A common pattern of commitment to and participation in American political processes and social values has developed and become fully and naturally established among almost all subgroups within American society. Common patterns of food preference, of entertainment, of occupational aspiration, of dress, of education, and of language have become widely and deeply ingrained. However, the process of strengthening these unities and communalities has proceeded so far and so rapidly as to endanger the cultural and linguistic diversity that many subgroups desire and that our national welfare may well require. Our political and cultural foundations are weakened when large population groupings do not feel encouraged to express, to safeguard, and to develop behavioral patterns that are traditionally meaningful to them. Our national creativity and personal purposefulness are rendered more shallow when constructive channels of self-expression are blocked and when alienation from ethnic-cultural roots becomes the necessary price of self-respect and social advancement, regardless of the merits of the cultural components of these roots. For those groups and individuals that desire it there must be openly sanctioned and publicly encouraged avenues of linguistic and cultural distinctiveness which will provide both a general atmosphere and specific facilitation for diversity within the general framework of American unity.

All Americans, and speakers of non-English languages in particular, are aware of the value our society and its institutions place upon cultural and linguistic unity. The desirability of such unity is explicitly or implicitly conveyed by citizenship requirements, by voting requirements, by the common public school, by the many agencies whose task it is to "naturalize" and Americanize immigrants and our indigenous or semi-indigenous ethnic populations, by national holidays, and even by the very openness of American economic and political life which normally requires little else of ethnics than that they join with de-ethnicized Americans in advancing themselves by advancing the common good. There is a "message" which immigrants, other ethnics, and their children quickly get – that ethnicity is foreignness, that both have no value, that they are things to forget, to give up. The frequent and enduring contrast between war, disharmony, and poverty abroad, and relative peace, acceptance, and prosperity here clearly shouts this message. Governmental and private agency conferences on Americanization and on cultural enrichment for disadvantaged ethnic populations reinforce it. Social prejudice and economic competition bring the message home in hundreds of ways, both subtle and obvious, even though both are usually less intense than in most other countries. Given a general climate which constantly reinforces unity – often by assuming it to be so obviously and universally desirable that no public discussion of it is deemed necessary – it is essential that diversity, too, receive constant support at underlying philosophical and operational levels.

Positive statements by leading American personages concerning the merits of cultural diversity and its benefits to American society have been relatively few and have hardly reached the "general public". Sentiments to this effect are directed toward minority group audiences from time to time, but are largely superfluous. A statement by the Governor or the President directed toward Spanish-Americans or Italo-Americans on Columbus Day normally reaches only those who are already aware of their ethnic heritages. It is usually recognized for what it usually is – a politically self-serving appeal or ritual time-filler of little general or genuine significance. Such statements imply a relegation of ethnicity to a "one-day-a-year" affair commemorating the long ago and the far away. They rarely seek to foster a more accepting view of ethnicity among non-ethnics. What is needed, therefore, rather than statements such as these, are statements that will reach the general public with the message that cultural differences – here and now, on an everyday as well as on a "high culture" and festive level – are meaningful, desirable, and worth strengthening. They should be made before non-ethnic audiences assembled to consider non-ethnic problems if they are to have their greatest impact and if they are to be disseminated widely through non-ethnic mass media.[3] If a "special day" for such statements seems desirable, it might be far better to release them on the Fourth of July than to reserve them for Polish-American Day, or German-American Day, or other such isolated "heritage" days.

But statements alone are too intermittent, too fleeting, and too unreliable to bring about a major change of climate. Those of the kind that would do the most good are rare, because few leading figures in American life are concerned with the role of ethnicity and diversity. Few have thought deeply about it and, under ordinary circumstances, few can be expected to do so in the future. Many consider ethnicity to be a far more ephemeral phenomenon than it really is. It is taken to be an issue that belongs to the 19th century, that will die of its own accord, that is petty and sectarian, and therefore one that does not deserve serious attention. This view is mistaken on psychological grounds alone. Although fragments of ethnicity's "little tradition", such as foods and dances, embarrass many second- and third-generation Americans when subjected to outside scrutiny, these same individuals frequently experience a private void which a fuller but selectively synthesized ethnicity might fill. While they have lost contact with the deeper and more meaningful ethnicity, they object to being publicly characterized in terms of the quaint but isolated fragments that they have maintained. Certainly, neither their own foods and dances nor the silent-treatment on the part of "American" peers and leaders will enable them to find personal satisfaction, on the one hand, or to reinforce language maintenance, on the other. In order to accomplish either of these goals *cultural and linguistic diversity must become a serious topic of public interest.* A federal "Commission on Biculturism (or Bilingualism) in American Life" might help bring this to pass. Such a Commission composed of ethnic and non-ethnic leaders, social scientists, educators, and distinguished "cultural figures" would be in a position to focus interest on the meaningfulness, legitimacy, and potential creativity of cultural and linguistic diversity within American unity. Such a Commission – and the recurring national conferences and reports that

---

[3] *The New York Times* reported on May 2, 1963, that Dr. Calvin E. Gross, Superintendent of Schools, made the following statement to "850 teachers and supervisors attending the [New York City School] system's annual curriculum conference. Many in the audience appeared shocked.... Dr. Gross ... urged that Puerto Rican children and other new arrivals to the city be enabled to develop biculturally and bilingustically. Dr. Gross said that instead of trying to remake Puerto Rican children and telling them to forget their language, these children schould be told: 'You are Puerto Rican and you have something to be proud of. Keep your culture – we'll help you develop it – but we also give you something else.' He deplored the 'melting pot' approach in which new arrivals are 'made over in our image.'" Although limited to a specialized audience this statement may be expected to have had greater impact in view of its presentation *in the context of general American educational goals* than a similar statement presented in the context of education for children of foreign backgrounds. Thus, the San Jose (California) *Mercury News* of July 14, 1963, reports a state-wide conference of educators on "Teaching English as a Second Language" under the headline "Schools Fear Enrollment Hike as a Result of Bracero Cutback". At this conference, Helen Hefferman, Chief of the Bureau of Elementary Education of the California State Department of Education, declared that "children of Mexican descent are to be encouraged to retain their first language and become more skillfull in its use [as they learn English]".

it might sponsor – could raise language maintenance to the level of an avowed national concern.[4]

All in all, cultural and linguistic diversity must be publicly recognized, publicly discussed, and publicly supported if languae maintenance is to be quickly, fully, and effectively reinforced. Appeals on behalf of such diversity can be supported by reference to American values, traditions, and history. As a possibly vital and creative force in American life, cultural diversity has all too long been ignored or given only apologetic and embarrassed glances. If language maintenance is to be seriously pursued in the future, public rehabilitation of this topic will be necessary. Bilingualism does not exist in a vacuum; it exists in the context of ethnic, religious, and cultural differences. It cannot be supported on a national scale without supporting biculturism. Biculturism requires awareness of one's heritage, identification with it (at least on a selective basis), and freedom to express this identification in a natural and uninhibited manner. It can only be enriching for our country to discover that the languages which have recently been brought to our attention are inextricably related to diverse behavioral patterns and behavioral products which can be every bit as acceptable and as valuable as the languages themselves. The languages can only function in conjunction with meaningful patrimonies. Intimately meaningful patrimonies can only enrich America and the lives of its citizens.

How can such awareness be made tangible and real for ethnics and non-ethnics alike? One approach having general, climate-building value might be to establish ethnic "Williamsburgs" at appropriate points throughout the United States. Several cities and states could profitably establish "nationality committees" whose purpose would be to preserve ethnic neighborhoods and settlements that might otherwise be scheduled for demolition, abandonment, or oblivion. Much as Williamsburg, Virginia, manifests our continued esteem for the best of colonial architecture, dress, and life style, much as Den Fynske Landsby manifests current reverence for the Danish peasant community of bygone days – so publicly supported museums, libraries, streets, neighborhoods, and settlements dedicated to preserving and honoring the cultural diversity of American life would lend dignity and status to the much maligned immigrant roots of American biculturism.[5] Of course, biculturism must not remain rigidly fixed and rooted in the past. It must not be preservative and nothing more.

---

[4] Other countries too have long traditions of royal or national commissions for focusing attention on and seeking solutions to important social issues. The new Canadian "Commission on Biculturism" (with representatives of the English, French, and "New" Canadians) might serve as a particularly appropriate example, although fortunately the U.S.A. does not have the vexing problems which have led to the establishment of that body.

[5] The entertainability of this recommendation, as well as the greater respectability of American Indian as contrasted with immigrant ethnicity, is indicated by the Department of the Interior's endorsement of the "restoration of Indian culture on the Seneca Reservation in western New York State. It left up to Congress a decision on whether an effort should be made to construct something like the restoration of colonial Virginia at Williamsburg" (*New York Times*, August, 13 1963, p. 33). Amana, Iowa and Solvang, California perform this function for the German and Danish cultures respectively, but are much too isolated and too modest for purposes of major impact.

But it must have tangible – and, if need be, idealized – public access to its earliest American roots. The immigrant past must be as worth preserving as the colonial past, the "old south", and the frontier ghost-town. Each of these provides a point of departure, a point of reference, and a point of pride. Our Chinatowns, our Little Italys, our Little Warsaws could be turned into bastions of support and respect for cultural-linguistic diversity, if they were intelligently and sympathetically redeveloped with this goal in mind. Every national value needs a shrine to embody it. If cultural and linguistic diversities are to become genuine national values – discussed as such by our statesmen, treated as such by scholars, policy makers, and community leaders – then they too must have their palpable shrines, that can be visited by ordinary American citizens of all ages and all backgrounds. It would represent, in short, another effort to make cultural and linguistic diversity "normal", by treating it openly, making it visible, and declaring it valuable.

SPECIFIC SUPPORT FOR LANGUAGE MAINTENANCE

In addition to rehabilitating the mainsprings of language maintenance so that it may have a favorable climate within which to function, language maintenance itself must be reinforced so that it can more successfully aid in attaining the goal of cultural bilingualism. Here too many old taboos must be discarded if language maintenance is to be seriously pursued.

One such taboo is that Americans of immigrant origin must give up their contacts with the countries from which they emigrated. Such contacts have far too frequently and automatically been viewed as indicative of un-American sentiments. Thus, overly long residence in the foreign country of one's birth or overly frequent visits to that country can jeopardize an immigrant's naturalization or lead to the loss of his passport.[6] The implication behind such policies is that America cannot fully trust its naturalized citizens; that it views their relationships with their ethnic motherlands as a species of bigamy; that the motherlands represent a fatal fascination from which the United States must be protected. Even greater opprobrium is attached to motherlands which seek to maintain active contacts with former inhabitants who are now citizens of the United States. Currently, most countries seeking to sponsor clubs, courses, publications, and other means of active and continued contact with their former citizens would be considered as engaging in suspicious activities, the more so the further these countries are from Anglo-Saxon Europe. Such attitudes tend to defeat language maintenance and are rooted in a bygone age. Naturalized citizens residing abroad are our most effective ambassadors. To the extent that their trips abroad renew and update their own language facility, and to the extent that ethnic mother tongues become more attractive or more functional for their children or grandchildren, further gains are effected for language maintenance. These latter

---

[6]   A U.S. Supreme Court decision, rendered May 18, 1964, declared this practice to be unconstitutional.

consequences are much more likely to come to reality than are any of the traitorous suspicions which impart such an unsavory air to our current policies.

"Old Country" contacts with naturalized American citizens and their children should be fostered under favorable international circumstances.[7] Italian governmental efforts to keep Italian language, literature, and customs alive among Italo-Americans may be thought of as a form of reverse lend-lease and may very well be a form of debt-repayment. Such efforts help to keep Italian alive and closer to its standardized form among Italo-Americans. They help overcome the constant Anglification and petrification that obtains when a language of immigrants does not have all of the normal avenues for use, growth, and change. Among second and third generations it helps dispel the lingering association of ethnic mother tongues with poverty, insecurity, immigrant status, mixed speech, and cultural mummification. That this is not an unheard of approach to language maintenance may be seen from recent acts of the government of the Province of Quebec.[8] Surely there is sufficient ingenuity in American governmental circles to enable us to initiate, control, and (if need be) discontinue activities of this kind as international conditions dictate. For the sake of language maintenance it would seem to be worth our while to institute agreements concerning such activities, at least with a few "safe" countries, at the earliest opportunity.

There can be no doubt that the major force weakening language maintenance in the United States today is the restriction of immigration. Not only are the numbers of immigrants admitted far smaller than half a century ago, but the lion's share of the available quota is awarded to immigrants most likely to assimilate and least likely to perpetuate their non-English mother tongues. It is worth speculating what would occur if larger numbers of Eastern and Southern European immigrants, as well as larger numbers of Near Eastern, Far Eastern, and African immigrants, could enter the United States, primarily on the basis of sponsors willing to guarantee that such immigrants would not become public charges. All available evidence indicates that newer immigrants from parts of the globe not favored by current United States immigration policy differ quite markedly from immigrants of half a century ago. They are far less likely to be rural dwellers, far more likely to have received formal education, and far more likely to come with specialized skills suitable for modern technological employment. These characteristics have various implications for language maintenance. Some imply a more rapid assimilability, and some a greater language maintenance potential. Probably both of these directions would be pursued by different clusters of

[7] Note, e.g., *Bill 18, Loi instituant le ministère des affaires culturelles, sanctionnée le 24 mars 1961*, Assemblee Legislative de Quebec. This bill establishes not only "l'Office de la Langue Française" but also "le Département du Canada Français d'outre-Frontières."

[8] *LeDevoir* of Montreal reported on May 9, 1963, that M. Georges-Emile Lapalme "le ministre des affaires culturelles a lancé un appel à la France la suppliant d'apporter une aide concrète à l'essor de la culture française en Amérique du Nord". The week before the Minister was present at the first such act of financial assistance provided by France and announced that additional assistance was expected in the future. He stressed that it was the presence of the government in these matters rather than funds advanced that French-speaking minorities are in need of throughout the continent.

immigrants. A large proportion of newer immigrants of currently "unfavored origins" would become assimilated much more rapidly than did their pre-World War I predecessors. Nevertheless, a small proportion of them would certainly be inclined to oppose cultural and linguistic assimilation and would be more likely to do so successfully – at least for an initial generational period – than was the case for the average immigrant of half a century ago. Their formal training in their respective mother tongues, their greater historical, cultural, and linguistic sophistication, and their greater awareness of language needs in American affairs and of the value of language skills in personal professional advancement would certainly lead toward successful maintenance. Indeed, there is every possibility that both directions (acculturation and non-acculturation) might be integrated and pursued simultaneously by modern immigrants in a manner quite beyond the ken of older immigrants arriving half a century or more ago.

Newer immigrants are far more inclined toward and capable of adopting a pattern somewhat similar to that devised by third-generation Americans of older immigrant stock, namely, a pattern of selective maintenance within the context of pervasive Americanization. They adopt general American speech, dress, food, recreational, educational, residential, and occupational patterns much more rapidly than did pre-World War I immigrants. On the other hand, if properly motivated, they can and do combine these general American patterns with selective culture maintenance patterns which safeguard many linguistic, religious, and representational elements derived from their countries of origin. Thus a consciously balanced cultural pluralism is much more attainable for immigrants today than it was for their forebears. Both the American and the Old World patterns and ingredients that are most meaningful to them may be characterized as urban, "high culture", and selective.

American immigration policy is in many ways still governed by a pre-World War I mentality. Not only is it uninfluenced by considerations of current national needs, it is also curiously innocent of any awareness of the extent to which the entire world has been "Americanized" in the last fifty years. Most immigrants reaching our shores today are much more like Americans than has been the case during the last 100 years or more. While this fact should lay the ghost of separatism and irredentism (which still influences American immigration policy), it should as well facilitate non-conflicted, non-derogatory and non-exclusionary language and culture maintenance. In addition, the advance of automated industry requires an infusion of technical skills and high-level talents which bypass direct competition with unskilled and semi-skilled American labor – another classical source of opposition to immigration. After a hiatus of more than a century, it can once more be said that we are in a period when larger and more diversified immigration can simultaneously contribute to national needs, self-maintenance processes, and harmonious cultural pluralism. It is high time our immigration policy were revised with these considerations in mind.

Even under our current anachronistic policy, priorities might be introduced that would tend to strengthen the language maintenance potentials within the American population. Once language maintenance efforts are recognized as being in the public interest, it becomes simple to recognize that certain types of immigrants are more likely to contribute to language maintenance than others. Once the language loyalist is cleared of the suspicion of being an "enemy of the people" it is but a logical next step to realize that teachers, writers, artists, musicians, religious functionaries, organizational leaders, and other intellectuals are more likely to contribute consciously to the perpetuation of the language resources of the United States than are other categories of immigrants. Actually, such individuals are in terribly short supply among most American ethnic groups, primarily because relatively few sought to come to the United States during the pre-World War I immigration peak. Once language maintenance becomes a national desideratum, it would seem to be possible to select prospective immigrants so as to maximize the likelihood of contributing to this goal.[9]

As for assistance to those segments of American ethnic groups that are already engaged in language maintenance efforts, there are a host of steps that might be taken to strengthen these efforts directly. Certainly dependence on immigration alone is neither practical nor wise. Immigrants and non-immigrants alike require an environment that is supportive of language maintenance in the same way that other matters in the national interest are supported. In an era of unprecedented governmental assistance to American colleges and universities for the establishment and maintenance of language and area study centers (under the National Defense Education Act), it would seem only logical to offer assistance to the institutions of American ethnic groups whose activities are clearly related to language maintenance. In addition to supporting instruction in Chinese, Hungarian, Russian, and dozens of other "neglected" languages now taught to Americans for whom these languages are truly "foreign", it would seem also to be highly desirable to support instructional and other languages maintenance efforts directed at those Americans for whom these languages are still not entirely "foreign". Government aid to ethnic group schools engaged in formal mother tongue instruction would involve only relatively minor innovations and reformulations in current policies. Any financial relief would encourage them to continue what often has seemed a most difficult task, and to im-

---

[9] After the initial formulation of this chapter (Spring 1963) President John F. Kennedy submitted a draft bill to Congress calling for increased immigration without regard to country of origin and giving "first priority to persons of useful skills and attainments ... with the greatest ability to add to the national welfare ... [such as] engineers, doctors, teachers and scientists" (*New York Times*, July 23, 1963, pp. 1, 12-13). In response to a copy of the first draft of this chapter Myer Feldman, Deputy Special Counsel to the President, indicated that "Language has always been a major force for cohesion between nations, a valuable resource at all times, and a useful aid to those seeking to improve their own skills in the articulation of ideas. Your discussion of the immigration legislation is consistent with the basis for the legislation submitted by the President" (letter, July 29, 1963). Political commentators quickly observed that "congressional approval of these [proposed] changes, most of them controversial, is not believed likely this year and promises to be difficult at any time in the House of Representatives" (New York Times, *op. cit.*). Immigration and population experts have long been calling for similar revisions in American immigration policy. E.g., Frank Lorimer, "Issues in Population Policy", in *The Population Dilemma*, Philip M. Hauser, ed. (Englewood Cliffs, N.J., Prentice-Hall, 1963).

prove and intensify their current efforts. In some cases the question of public support for religiously sponsored institutions would doubtless arise (Fishman 1959). But this can easily become a false issue. There are many effective schools to which the religious issue is not applicable at all. At any rate, support for language instruction can be kept quite separate from support for religious instruction. Certainly there is legal precedent for such a distinction and, given sufficient conviction that language maintenance is in the national interest, additional precedents can be established and maintained. Finally, the constitutional restrictions bearing upon the separation of Church and state need not hinder the great private foundations that have done so much to support and replenish the cultural and educational resources of American society. As yet, none has supported the language maintenance efforts of American ethnic groups – whether in the educational, literary, dramatic, musical, or scholarly spheres – and a change in this respect would simultaneously signify the rehabilitation of language maintenance and the social maturation of American foundations.

Untouched by religious complications are several colleges and universities[10] as well as hundreds of periodicals, radio broadcasts, and cultural or scholarly institutions of American ethnic groups. Whether by tax exemption, by direct support, or even by indirect facilitation and encouragement, means could be found for giving recognition and assistance to these vehicles of language maintenance. Not only has there been no studied attempt to do this but negative and exploitative steps have often been taken (or implied), of which language loyalists are painfully aware.[11] They frequently have long memories of hostile governmental attitudes dating back to their home countries. Under the best of circumstances they would tend to be suspicious of governmental "impartiality" since their own is not an impartial posture. Having concluded that language maintenance is in the public good, they frequently interpret governmental disinterest or neglect as thinly veiled opposition and, what is worse, disdain. Why should their work be considered "beneath the dignity" of attention by government,

[10]   Given sufficient support and recognition many ethnically founded and maintained institutions of higher education could train language maintenance leaders in specific "unusual" languages. Among these are: Alliance College (Cambridge Springs, Penn.), St. Mary's College (Orchard Lake, Mich.) and Villa Maria College (Buffalo, New York), in Polish; Suomi College (Hancock, Mich.), in Finnish; Marianapolis College (Thompson, Conn.), in Lithuanian; St. Basil's College (Stamford, Conn.), in Ukrainian; St. Procopius College (Lisle, Ill.), in Czech; Luther College (Decorah, Iowa), in Norwegian; Yeshiva University (New York, N.Y.) and Brandeis University (Waltham, Mass.), in Hebrew and Yiddish. Higher education itself could contribute significantly to language maintenance by the establishment of many more chairs for ethnically infused languages and their cultures, particularly where these enjoy considerable local support. Social research on language maintenance might contribute to this goal by telling the story of the introduction of ethnically based languages into a number of "general" American high schools and colleges much more exhaustively than we have attempted to do in these pages.

[11]   One example is FCC ruling 58-734-61564 referred to on p. 89, above. My attention was directed to this entire episode by language loyalists who had concluded that the decision of the Commission that a number of factors must be considered "in determining the suitability of foreign language programming" was evidence of "intercover" federal policy to discontinue such programming whenever possible.

by foundations, and by the public at large? Why does an unofficial conspiracy of silence and an implication of lunacy surround their efforts? Are they not working on behalf of an intellectually, culturally, and politically valuable goal? Why then have they been ignored and ruled out from Sputnik-inspired largesse available to others? If we, as well, grant that language maintenance is a desideratum, then there can be no argument that it is in grave need of assistance and that it has received neither the support nor the attention best calculated to foster its creative contribution to American life. Given the current status of language maintenance in most ethnic groups in our midst, nothing would seem better calculated to strengthen it than the preparation of cadres of young and rigorously educated bilingual-bicultural cultural leaders. Ethnic group schools are in the best position to accomplish this – but are frequently unable to do so without assistance.[12]

A final area of language maintenance support is to be found in facilities that are or could be entirely under public auspices. Chief among these are the public schools. While our schools are certainly more language conscious than they have been in previous years, they are not nearly as inventive or as concerned as they might be and their official consciousness of language maintenance is practically nil. FLES programs are woefully limited in terms of their numbers and the languages involved, and distressingly ineffective in terms of teacher competence and pupil learning. Foreign language programs at the high school level are only slightly less remiss in each of these respects. Pitifully little is being done today to effectively and widely introduce such major world languages as Russian, Chinese, or Arabic into American public education at any level. The few exceptional schools in which these languages are taught to a few exceptional children received deserved publicity, but their impact on the total picture is meager. The fearful bureaucratic complexity of American educational enterprises is such that all the institutional characteristics tend to discourage rather than encourage either greater variation or wider coverage in language instruction. Thus, it is initially difficult to introduce additional languages because teachers are not available to teach them. It is difficult to locate suitable teachers because training programs are not available to train them. In most states even a completely bilingual individual with university training in both languages is not considered "trained" and eligible for certification as a public school teacher until he has taken a number of college courses in the field of "professional education". Furthermore, it is difficult to hire trained teachers because salaries are so low as to be noncompetitive with other sources of income available to such individuals. And it is diffi-

---

[12] An alternative to the support of ethnic group schools – particularly where such support is rendered difficult as a result of Church-state problems – is the establishment of non-ethnic schools conducted entirely in critical non-English languages. A few private schools of this kind already exist, but these are primarily in French, limited to the "early childhood education" level, non-ethnic (or anti-ethnic) in pupil-teacher composition, and expensive. The possibility of such schools at the college level is demonstrated by the University of the Pacific's "Spanish College", in which "all subjects (except English) are taught in Spanish as a novel step toward better Latin American relations and as a recognition of California's Spanish heritage" (*Palo Alto Times*, Sept. 19, 1963, p. 8).

cult also to recruit teachers willing to accept appointments at current salaries because too few children in any one school would elect to study, say, Russian, to provide a teacher with a full program. Difficulty is thus pyramided upon difficulty and the entire structure moves ahead at a snail's pace. The final irony is that methods and materials of instruction are all geared to teaching monolinguals, with the result that foreign language teachers are least successful when they work with students who possess competence in a second language based upon their out-of-school experiences (Brault 1964).

A number of innovations that might prove to be of some value have either not been tried at all or have been tried on too limited a scale. There have been a few NDEA-sponsored Language Institutes for the express purpose of preparing educators who are themselves of a particular ethnic background so that they might teach the standard version of their own ethnic mother tongue to pupils who are also of this background.[13] These institutes serve several purposes simultaneously: (i) they remove common ethnicity between teachers and pupils from the realm of taboo and place it in the realm of an explicitly acknowledged and functionally activated factor in language learning;[14] (ii) they recognize the particular language learning assets and problems of children with an ethnic mother tongue and they prepare teachers to cope with these constructively; (iii) they prepare special teaching and learning materials oriented toward raising the levels of mastery of, and overcoming the deviations from, standard speech among teachers and pupils; (iv) they explicitly involve the government, the teacher, and the pupil in a joint language maintenance venture. Certainly, such institutes should be increased in size, in number, and in the variety of languages covered. The preparation of teachers and of teaching-learning materials via such institutes will begin to ameliorate the problem of where to recruit appropriate personnel for public school languages programs, that might in the future be related to the ethnic composition of large proportions of the student bodies in many urban centers. However, this approach alone is far too limited to result in any early language maintenance gains. Additional approaches are required and only quite normal degrees of ingenuity and good will are needed to uncover them.

The MLA Foreign Language Proficiency Tests (available only for French, German,

[13]   The major undertaking of this kind is the Franco-American Institute at Bowdoin College (Brunswick, Maine) conducted by Professor Gerard J. Brault of the University of Pennsylvania, during the the summers of 1961, 1962 and 1963. In several instances, other NDEA Language Institutes not explicitly intended for teachers of particular ethnic backgrounds have, nevertheless, been largely composed of such teachers.

[14]   Since teachers of religiously-affiliated ethnic group ("private") schools have been admitted to these institutes on the usual tuition-free basis (although without the weekly stipend normally offered to students at NDEA institutes), one more precedent has been established for language maintenance aid to ethnic groups schools under religious sponsorship. As a result, it might be possible to organize such institutes for teachers employed by ethnic group schools and to offer instruction in Polish, Hungarian, Ukrainian, Greek, Yiddish, and other languages rarely available in public school settings but still amply represented in the American population.

Italian, Russian, and Spanish) already utilized by the State Education Departments of New York, Pennsylvania, Delaware, and West Virginia represent a potentially important facilitative device (Starr 1962). Individuals who have reached necessary levels of language proficiency by informal means (home, neighborhood, travel) – rather than by the "normal" route of accumulating college credits – can attest to their proficiency throught these examinations and obtain state-approved teaching licenses or certificates. This approach to the certification of foreign language teachers should be far more widely adopted.[15] If properly encouraged, it has the potential of providing many localities with teachers of uncommon languages. Such languages almost always have an ethnic base and their availability under public auspices greatly encourages language maintenance. Pupils studying these languages in the public schools would most frequently be of the "appropriate" ethnic background. Even if this were not the case, language maintenance would benefit if only from publicizing that an ethnic mother tongue had "broken through" the silence barrier and had received "public recognition".[16]

Another significant means of public school recognition might well be the granting of formal credit to pupils for language skills acquired outside of school auspices. Thousands of public school pupils, at the elementary as well as the secondary level of instruction, attend one or another type of ethnic group school during after-school hours. Our evidence indicates that mother tongue instruction in these schools is at least as effective as – if not more so than – foreign language instruction under public school auspices. The combination of student background factors, teacher dedication, and appreciable exposure over a number of years results in language skills that are by no means too rudimentary to deserve recognition and encouragement by public schools authorities. Recognition might take one or another of several forms: certificates of merit, advanced placement in public high school language courses, credit toward graduation, etc. In each case, an appropriate yet simple evaluation or review mechanism would need to be instituted. It is difficult to exaggerate the stimulus to mother tongue instruction in ethnic group schools that would result from any form of recognition by the public schools. Again and again teachers, principals, and activists affiliated with ethnic group schools offering mother tongue instruction mention the "double insult" of having their mother tongue "excluded" from the public school program while at the same time the public school refuses to recognize that their children are diligently studying another language and culture at their own expense and on their own time. "If our children were merely collecting stamps or building models,

---

[15] For a report of early successes with the proficiency examination approach in the foreign languages area see "Modern Foreign Language Proficiency Tests for Teacher Certification; Report of Results in 1963 Administrations". Albany, New York State Education Department, 1964.

[16] A first step in the direction of such "recognition" has, on several occasions, been the organization of after-school language clubs for students interested in various languages that are still "uncommon" to the public school curriculum. When a sufficient number of pupils have joined such a club the transition to a regularly scheduled course during the normal school day can be made more easily.

they would get some encouragement from school authorities; for studying Greek they get no recognition at all!"[17]

However, much more than "recognition" or other indirect motivators may be possible in those localities where truly substantial numbers of students enter the first grade with a home-and-neighborhood tongue other than English. Under these circumstances it would be highly desirable for a few public schools to experiment with programs that provide a major part of their instruction in non-English mother tongues, until students have acquired, at the very least, adequate literacy in these languages. In such cases the mother tongue might well remain both a medium and a subject of instruction throughout the elementary school years, with the gradual and appropriate introduction of English beginning on a small scale in the first grade and increasing in each successive year of study.[18] An experimental return to the bilingual public school that functioned in several American cities during the late 19th and the early 20th century would appear to be particularly justified in the case of Mexican-American population concentrations in the Southwest. Such attempts should be labeled frankly as experimantal and as intensive language maintenance efforts so as to avoid any implications of social or cultural segregation. Where such attempts are not feasible it might still be possible to group bilingual children separately for early, intensive and specially devised instruction in their mother tongue, under the guidance of teachers who are themselves fully literate and educated in it. There is recent evidence that even the high school level is not too late for effective and lasting reinforcement of language skills and attitudes among bilingual youngsters (Nance 1963).[19]

There are still other possible approaches to bolstering foreign language programs in our public schools in such a way as to directly or indirectly foster language maintenance. Approximately a thousand exchange teachers from abroad are annually appointed to public elementary and secondary schools throughout the United States. Ordinarily, a condition of such appointments is that exchange teachers possess sufficient mastery of English to teach in that language throughout the school day. Rarely has it occurred to American school authorities that these same foreign teachers

---

[17] *The New York Post*, May 13, 1962, p. 22, reports a precedent of possible importance in this connection: "School districts in the state are giving credits to students for outside-of-school religious instruction with the approval of the State Education Department.... High school students have been granted a fourth of a unit toward their Regents credits for each year of religious instruction.... Such credits fall into the same category as dancing or music instruction given outside the school". Language instruction may also be credited in this fashion. Similar opportunities exist in a few other states but are seldom known or utilized. Certainly, institutions of higher education should pose no difficulty in recognizing language proficiency – however attained – for purposes of admission and placement.
[18] For several alternative suggestions concerning such programs see the section on "Basic Plans for Bilingual [Public] Schools", in Bruce A. Gaarder's "Teaching the Bilingual Child: Research, Development and Policy", *Proceedings of the Conference on Teaching the Bilingual Child* (Austin, Texas State Education Agency, 1964).
[19] For a review of recent public school efforts to conduct special Spanish programs for children of Mexican-American origin, see the *Texas Foreign Language Association Bulletin*, 5 (1963), number 3. Also note the *experimental* bilingual public School as well as the *system-wide* bilingual language arts program in Dade County, Florida, briefly described in *Modern Language Journal*, 48 (1964), 239.

might well be utilized to teach their own mother tongues – either during the regular school day or in after-school classes.[20] Indeed, rarely has it occurred to spokesmen and functionaries of foreign language instruction in American school to utilize even the best local representatives of the few languages taught in our schools. Utilization of native speakers would have more than mere pedagogic value; it would also imply the respectability of ethnicity, the mentionability of language maintenance, the "Americanness", as it were, of speaking and safeguarding languages other than English. Indeed, native speakers could well serve as "cultural representatives" beyond the confines of the school's few language courses. They could and should serve as consultants and participants in various courses dealing with the several cultures that have contributed to ours, and in which the range of creative human diversity is educatively illustrated. Such an enterprise could seek a genuinely comparative approach to the understanding of human institutions and the variability of cultures, showing they need not be "foreign" however much they are "different". This is much more than the antiseptic study of immigrant roots and the songs, dances, and games that pertain to them. It is an acknowledgment that the roots of American life are still capable of legitimate fruits of a "high tradition" to this very day.

All in all, the public school's approach to non-English languages and to non-core cultures in the United States has been that of all official levels of American life, namely, that ethnicity in America and its cultural and linguistic components deserve neither disciplined nor dignified recognition. Thus it would seem that as long as these languages and cultures are truly "foreign" our schools are comfortable with them. But as soon as they are found in our own backyards, the schools deny them. However, by denying them we not only deny a part of ourselves (a dangerous act in any democracy) but we limit the extent to which public school instruction in languages and cultures is live, real, and meaningful. Ethnicity is still so uncomfortable and guilt-laden an area for the essentially middle-class public school teacher, principal, superintendent, and curriculum expert that it is less objectionable to cut pupils off from deep understanding and appreciation than to give ethnically-based linguistic and cultural materials their due recognition.

While the public school can certainly become a much more valuable vehicle of language maintenance, and of language instruction, than it currently is, it does have other and more central goals to pursue. The curricular demands placed upon it and the administrative and social pressures to which it is exposed effectively preclude it from becoming primarily or even significantly concerned with language maintenance. Indeed, there is no public institution in American life whose avowed primary purpose is language maintenance. No other national resource is so unprotected and "unassigned".

---

[20] During the 1962-63 school year, a group of exchange teachers from Puerto Rico appointed to teach in New York City Schools set up after school classes in Spanish in a number of schools with substantial Puerto Rican enrollments. This activity was part of a larger program known as "Operation Understanding" which also sent exchange teachers from New York to Puerto Rico, so that they could become more familiar with the home language and culture of Puerto Rican students in New York schools.

A Language Maintenance section in the Department of Health, Education, and Welfare is urgently needed so that language maintenance becomes someone's full-time responsibility and concern.[21] A network of language camps for selected children and youth could be sponsored for language maintenance purposes – not unlike the 4-H clubs that are sponsored to encourage farm children to become proud and skilled farmers. Guide books and text books could be prepared for parents and teachers.[22] Consultation services could be made available to schools and to cultural institutions. Necessary demonstration projects and research efforts could be assisted or conducted.[23] Financial aid could be channeled. The coordination of FLES programs with the remaining non-English language islands could be attempted. Above all, the veil of embarrassed silence could be pierced and removed. This latter goal must come before all else and must be continually pursued together with all else. Its importance goes beyond language maintenance per se. Intelligent, creative, unembarrassed, unharassed, evolving ethnicity will certainly contribute to language maintenance but it will also contribute to the enrichment of millions of lives and to the authenticity of American civilization.

CONCLUSIONS

It is odd indeed that a nation which prides itself on "know how", resourcefulness, and ingenuity should be so helpless with respect to deepening and strengthening its own

[21] What is proposed here is similar to the special recognition given to "educational media" by the separate establishment of Title VII under the National Defense Education Act of 1958. Educational media research and development might have been included under another title, e.g., with the Co-operative Research Program. However, as a result of their separate legal and budgetary status much more attention has been directed toward them than would otherwise have been the case. Although no separate Title for language maintenance is being advocated here, a separate section with its own staff, budget, and program *is* recommended. Unfortunately, language maintenance does not have nearly as strong a lobby as that which the educational-media-industries (including gadgetry, electronics, radio, and T.V.) were able to marshal on behalf of Title VII.

[22] While our increased sensitivities and needs have prompted the preparation (under NDEA Title VI auspices) of dictionaries, texts, grammars, and records in many exotic languages during the last few years, an anthology of non-English *American* literature for elementary or secondary school use still does not exist. There is also a great dearth of teaching materials and pedagogic tools for teachers working with children of particular ethnic backgrounds. The recent appearance of Gerard J. Brault's "Cours de Langue Française Destine aux Jeunes Franco-Americains" (Phila., Univ. of Pennsylvania, 1963) may serve as a model of what is needed in scores of other languages as well, stressing as it does both language maintenance and greater fidelity to standard French and to the "high tradition" of French culture.

[23] Although further studies are indeed needed, it must be more fully understood that what is sought is more than an analysis of the current situation; it is a search for ways of transcending the present in the future. In view of the greater possibility of cultural bilingualism as compared to daily functional bilingualism, it would seem particularly desirable to initiate studies of ethnic group schools engaged in language maintenance efforts. Since the school is a meeting ground for several generations, since it represents an extended and conscious enculturating effort, and since it deals with both ethnically and ideologically elaborated language maintenance, it would seem to be an important and potentially fruitful arena for immediate inquiry.

inner life. We laugh at the taboos of "backward" peoples and pride ourselves on our own rational procedurees. Yet, in the entire area of ethnicity and language maintenance we are constrained by a taboo in some ways stronger than those which govern our sexual or racial mores. Sex problems and race issues are discussed in the press, debated in Congress, studied in schools and accorded consideration by foundations. In the area of ethnicity, however, wise men react as children – with denial, with rejection, with repression. If language loyalty and ethnicity had truly ceased to function in major segments of American intellectual and cultural life, if they really evoked no pained or puzzled feelings of responsibilities unmet and sensitivities undeveloped, these topics would receive far more open, more dispassionate, and more imaginative consideration.

Nevertheless, on the basis of data obtained by the Language Resources Project and on the basis of impressions gained in the pursuit and analysis of these data, it seems there are still good prospects of maintaining or attaining cultural bilingualism among many different, carefully selected ethnic subgroups in the United States. These groups can be so selected – over and above their self-selection – and so instructed that the advantage of having an ethnic mother tongue would be considerable in developing and maintaining bilingual facility. In many ways human talents are like other resources; they must be discovered and preserved if they are to be available. However, in other ways, human talents are quite unique; they can be prompted, augmented, and created by appropriate recognition, training, and reward. Within every language group studied there are subgroups consciously ready, willing, and able to benefit from a more favorable "language policy" in the United States. The adoption of such a policy would itself create additional subgroups of similar capacity, above and beyond those currently discernible.

In her fascinating volume *New Lives for Old*, Margaret Mead (1956) points out that Western interest in preserving the "quaint" customs and cultures of primitive peoples has often been no more than a thinly disguised means of excluding these peoples from independent regulation of their own affairs and from reaping the fruits of their own personal and natural resources. Certainly, every people must have the right to reject its past, to break sharply with its heritage, and to adopt a new way of life. However, just as "guided traditionalism" may be a subterfuge for exploitation and the prolongation of backwardness, so "guided acculturation" may be a subterfuge serving exactly the same ulterior purposes. Either approach can be used for the self-aggrandizement of the "powers that be". Neither approach is calculated to develop freedom of choice or creative cultural evolution.

Language maintenance in America does not require, nor would it benefit from, the forced ghettoization of linguistic groups. But neither will it benefit from the nonproductive sentimentality of ethnicity for one day a year, from the instrumentalism of "anti-communist letters to the homeland" to influence elections, or from the pollyanna-like pageantry in which little children sing and dance bedecked in partly mythical and wholly archaic folk costumes. Language maintenance will benefit only from explicit and substantial public recognition of its value and its legitimacy, and from public support for those willing and able to engage in it. The same must be said for ethnicity, with the additional emphasis that without greater recognition accorded to meaningful, evolving ethnicity, there can be no enduring language maintenance in the United States. Ethnicity in America is not an all-or-none affair. Nor is it a logical affair. It is not at all understandable or describable in Old World terms alone. For some it is composed of half-forgotten memories, unexplored longings, and intermittent preferences; for others, it is active, structured, elaborated and constant. For some it is exclusionary and isolating; for others it is an avenue toward more secure and more authentic participation in general American affairs. For some it is hidden and has negative or conflicted overtones; for others it is open, positive, and stimulating. For some it is archaic, unchanging and unalterable; for others it is evolving and creative. For some it is a badge of shame to ignore, forget, and eradicate; for others it is a source of pride, a focus of initial loyalties and integrations from which broader loyalties and wider integrations can proceed. For some its is interpenetrated by religion and formal organization; for others it is entirely secular and associational. Not all modes of ethnicity contribute to language maintenance, but many do. All in all, the variations and variabilities of ethnicity in America today are largely unknown. This ignorance represents a stumbling block to the American sociologist or applied linguist, whose approaches to ethnicity are usually far too simple and far too condescending. It represents a major gap in our ability to understand or facilitate language maintenance. But above all else, the absence of such knowledge represents an area of self-ignorance for all Americans – philosophers, scientists, and laymen alike. It is certainly high time that we began to know ourselves, accept ourselves, and shape ourselves in this area just as realistically and as determinedly as we have tried to do in many other areas in recent years.

The point about the melting pot is that is did not happen.... The fact is that in every generation, throughout the history of the American republic, the merging of the varying streams of population differentiated from one another by origin, religion, outlook has seemed to lie just ahead – a generation, perhaps, in the future. This continual deferral of the final smelting of the different ingredients .... suggests that we must search for some systematic and general cause for this American pattern of subnationalities ... which structures people, whether those coming in afresh or the descendants of those who have been here for generations, into groups of different status and character. (Glazer and Moynihan 1963)

The conclusions quoted above require only minor extension from the point of view of this presentation, namely, that precisely because they are true, after two centuries of pretense to the contrary, it is time that the diversity of American linguistic and cultural existence be recognized and channeled more conscientiously into a creative force, rather than be left at worst as something shameful and to be denied, or at best something mysterious to be patronized. If we can rethink in this light our unwritten language policy and our unproclaimed ethnic philosophy, the recommendations presented here on behalf of language maintenance – or others of far greater practical and positive application – may yet be implemented.

REFERENCES

Brault, G. J., "Some Misconceptions about Teaching American Ethnic Children Their Mother Tongue", *Modern Language Journal*, 48 (1964), 67-71.

Dobzhansky, T., *The Biological Basis of Human Freedom* (New York, Columbia University Press, 1956).

Fishman, J. A., "Publicly Subsidized Pluralism: The European and the American Contexts"; also "The American Dilemmas of Publicly Subsidized Pluralism", *School and Society*, 87 (1959), 246-248 and 264-267.

Glazer, N., and Moynhan, D. P., *Beyond the Melting Pot* (Cambridge, M.I.T. and Harvard University Press, 1963).

Mead, Margaret, *New Lives for Old* (New York, Morrow, 1956).

Moberg, D. O., "Social Differentiation in the Netherlands", *Social Forces*, 39 (1961), 333-337.

Nance, Mrs. Afton D., *Spanish for Spanish-Speaking Pupils* (Sacramento, State of California Department of Education, 1963) (Mimeographed.)

Starr, W. H., "MLA Foreign Language Proficiency Tests for Teachers and Advanced Students", *PMLA*, 77 (1962), no. 4, part 2, 1-12.

15. LANGUAGE MAINTENANCE IN A SUPRA-ETHNIC AGE: SUMMARY AND CONCLUSIONS

THE CURRENT STATUS OF NON-ENGLISH LANGUAGE RESOURCES IN THE UNITED STATES

In 1960 the non-English language resources of the United States were undoubtedly smaller than they had been a decade or two previously. Nevertheless, they were still huge, both in absolute terms and relative to their 20th century high-water marks in the 1920's and 1930's.

Approximately 19 million individuals (11 per cent of the entire American population) possessed a non-English mother tongue in 1960. These mother tongues represent a very high proportion of those that have evolved to the point of becoming standard literary languages as well as many that have not yet reached this stage of development. Relative to 1940, the quantitative position of the colonial languages – Spanish, French, and German – has remained superior to that of all but the most recently reinforced immigrant languages. However, even in the case of most of the immigrant languages that did not benefit from post-war immigration and that suffered most from internal attrition and external apathy, some subgroups still retain sufficient cultural-linguistic intactness to maintain functional bilingualism and to provide good prospects of marked gain (in either functional or cultural bilingualism) with well designed and vigorous reinforcement efforts.

The non-English press boasted over 500 periodic publications in 1960 and continued to have a circulation of approximately five and one-half millions, as well as a "pass-along" readership estimated to be equally large. Although non-English dailies and weeklies have regularly lost circulation since 1930, monthlies have experienced circulation gains in recent decades. Non-English broadcasting also seemed to be in a far better state of health in 1960 than was usually expected to be the case – with over 1600 "stations" broadcasting more than 6,000 hours of non-English language programs every week in the continental United States. However, this picture largely reflects the continued strength of Spanish broadcasting, which alone accounts for two-thirds of all non-English broadcasting in the United States. Both the non-English press and non-English broadcasting (with the exception of Spanish broadcasting) are largely dependent upon and oriented toward a first-generation clientele. The latter, in turn, represent slightly less than half the claimants of almost all non-English mother tongues in the United States. Thus, although immigrant status itself is not predictive of either language maintenance or language loyalty, both of these phenomena are heavily dependent upon immigrant status – with the colonial languages marking the only noteworthy exceptions to this generalization.

In 1960 there were at least 1800 (and probably a good many more) ethnic "cultural" organizations in the United States. Many, including the largest among them, serve first-, second-, and third-generation members. Nearly three-quarters of all ethnic cultural organizations favor maintenance of their non-English ethnic mother tongue. However, the very fact that ethnic organizations have been more successful than either the non-English press or non-English broadcasting in attracting second and third generation interest has also led most of them to exceedingly marginal and passive approaches to ethnicity and to language maintenance. The organizations represent bulwarks of structural more than of behavioral-functional pluralism.

The *most* active language maintenance institution in the majority of ethnic communities in the United States is the ethnic group school. Over 2,000 such schools currently function in the United States, of which more than half offer mother tongue instruction even when there are many "non-ethnics" and "other-ethnics" among their pupils. On the whole, they succeed in reinforcing or developing moderate comprehension, reading, and speaking facility in their pupils. They are far less successful in implanting retentivist language attitudes which might serve to maintain language facility after their students' programs of study have been completed, approximately at the age of fourteen. Although the languages learned by pupils in ethnic group schools are "ethnic mother tongues", rather than true mother tongues, the levels of facility attained usually are sufficient to provide a foundation for cultural bilingualism. This foundation, however, is rarely reinforced after the completion of study in the ethnic group school.

Mother tongue teachers in ethnic group schools rarely view themselves as powerful factors in determining language maintenance outcomes. They feel that their pupils do not accomplish much with respect to the more active domains of language maintenance. They typically report that their pupils become increasingly less interested in mother tongue instruction as they advance through the grades and attribute this (and other instructional difficulties) to parental apathy or opposition to the mother tongue. They tend to view the mother tongues they teach as not being among the most prestigeful in the United States (an honor reserved for French and Spanish almost exclusively). However, the determinants of language prestige (unlike the determinants of instructional difficulties) are attributed to "American" rather than to ethnic factors. When group maintenance is seen as being in conflict with language maintenance, the former is frequently preferred, except in the case of mother tongue teachers associated with very recent immigrant groups, most of whom reject the possibility of any such conflict.

The relationship between ethnicity, language, and religion remains strong, although the latter tends to withdraw from the tripartite association. Religion is organizationally "successful" in the United States, and therefore its less successful companions, ethnicity and language, lean upon it heavily for support. But the more "successful" religion becomes, the more de-ethnicized it becomes, the more amenable to mergers with other de-ethnicized churches, and the more disinterested in language maintenance. Language maintenance in historically ethnic churches is continued on a habitual (rather than an ideological-purposive) basis, on ethnic (rather than on religious) grounds, and in conjunction with adult (rather than youth) activities. The triple melting pot – leading toward de-ethnicized Catholicism, Protestantism, and Judaism – and the mere passage of time represent the two most prevalent religious solutions to the "embarrassment" of language maintenance. Traditional *ritual protection* of non-English vernaculars (such as exists in the Greek Catholic and Eastern Orthodox Churches) functions more as a significant delaying factor than as a crucial outcome factor in this connection.

Ethnic cultural-organizational leaders and rank-and-file ethnics display essentially similar patterns with respect to language maintenance efforts and processes. In both instances, immigrants are more retentive – within the family and outside it – than are second-generation individuals. Older children are more linguistically retentive than younger children, first children more so than last children, children more so than grandchildren, organizationally affiliated children more so than unaffiliated children. Whereas first-generation leaders consist of both cultural and organizational activists, second-generation leaders are almost exclusively organizational activists. Although they favor language maintenance, they do so with essentially non-ethnic rationales and their support for language maintenance is attitudinal rather than overt. Philosophies or rationales of bi-culturism and bi-lingualism are weak or non-existent.

There are two large worlds of non-English languages in the United States. One is the officially recognized and supported world of "foreign language" instruction in non-ethnic high schools and colleges. The other is the largely unrecognized and unsupported world of ethnic language maintenance efforts. These two worlds meet in the persons of foreign language teachers, over half of whom are of an immediate ethnic background appropriate to one of the languages they teach. Teachers of ethnically more infused, less prestigeful languages, (e.g., German and Italian, as contrasted with French and Spanish) – particularly those at the college and university level – are most likely to have been ethnically exposed and to be in favor of language maintenance efforts. However, these same teachers are also under the greatest strain toward professionalization and are, therefore, least inclined to utilize the resources of minority cultural-linguistic groups (native speakers, publications, broadcasts, choral-dramatic presentations) for instructional purposes (Fishman and Hayden 1964).

Detailed integrative case studies of six separate cultural-linguistic groups provide much independent support for the above generalizations. In general, language maintenance and language shift have proceeded along quite similar lines in the three high prestige colonial languages (French, Spanish, German) and the three low prestige immigrant languages (Yiddish, Hungarian, Ukrainian). Although differing widely with respect to period of settlement, numerical size, balance between low-culture and high-culture language retentivism, religious protection of the vernacular, and social mobility of their speakers, the drift has been consistently toward Anglification and has become accelerated in recent years. Differences between the six language groups seem to be great only in connection with the *rate of change* toward Anglification.

Among the Spanish and Ukrainian speakers sizable contingents of young and youthful bilinguals are still available. In the Ukrainian case this is primarily due to recent large immigration. In the Spanish case it is due to the absence of economic mobility. Symbolically elaborated ethnicity, language loyalty, and religious protection of the vernacular are absent in the Spanish case and present in the Ukrainian. All in all, certain pervasive characteristics of American nationalism (mobility on a non-ethnic, ideological, mass-culture base) and of most immigrant heritages (non-ideological ethnicity, cultural and economic "backwardness") seem to have been much more effective in jointly producing essentially similar outcomes than have the various uniquenesses of ethnic heritages or of immigrational-settlement patterns in safeguarding cultural and linguistic differences.

The modal characteristics of language maintenance efforts among southern and eastern European immigrants arriving during the period of mass immigration are roughly summarizable as follows:

a. Language is rarely a consciously identified or valued component of daily, traditional, ethnicity. Ethnicity itself is minimally ideologized or organized in terms of conscious nationalistic or symbolic considerations.

b. Rapid immersion in the American metropolis and acceptance of American national values results in the fragmentation of traditional ways. Those fragments of ethnicity that are retained in a disjointed and altered fashion are usually insufficient for the maintenance of functional bilingualism beyond the first generation.

c. Ethnicity and language maintenance become increasingly and overly dependent on that major organizational institution previously available in the "old country" setting and most successfully transplanted to the United States: the Church. However, the Church has increasingly withdrawn from ethnicity and from language maintenance in order to pursue its own organizational goals.

d. Attempts to utilize the formal organizational mechanisms of high culture and of industrialized metropolitan and modern national life on behalf of language and culture maintenance proceed without benefit of a popular ideological base that might either compete with or be joined to American nationalism.

e. As a result, neither traditional intactness nor ideological mobilization is available to the second generation. "Revolts" are common when maximal claims are advanced by the first generation and become uncommon when such claims are no longer pressed.

f. Those of the second generation "outgrow" the fragmented ethnicity of the first but frequently retain an attachment to more marginal expressions of ethnicity via the Church, other organizations, and familial remnants of traditional ethnicity. While these have been insufficient for functional language maintenance, they have often preserved a positive attitude toward the ethnic language and culture. This positiveness becomes more evident as the second generation advances through adulthood.

g. The third generation approaches ethnicity with even greater selectivity, frequently viewing the ethnic mother tongue as a cultural or instrumental desideratum and viewing ethnicity as an area of appreciation or a field of study. De-ethnicized language maintenance elicits interest in the third generation although facility is rare.

Of all the foregoing, what can be considered new or striking in the light of previous studies or common knowledge? Certainly the availability of systematic empirical data – rather than anecdotal impressions – is new for many of the domains under discussion. The vastness of language maintenance efforts, even after generations of attrition, is certainly striking, but so is the fact that these efforts are so largely habitual and unfocused even within the very operation of organizations, schools, churches, and the mass media. The conscious, ideologically based and rationally directed efforts of language loyalists normally reach and influence only a small fraction of even the first generation of speakers of non-English languages. The uniformly changed role of religion with respect to language maintenance – from initially wholehearted support to implacable opposition or unmovable apathy – is also striking and hitherto largely unappreciated. Similarly notable is the fact that opposition to language maintenance in the second and third generations of immigrant stock is now most commonly on a low key and unideologized. The days of bitter language disputes seem to be over, even between the age groups formerly involved in such disputes. The continuation of favorable language maintenance sentiments much beyond the time of functional language maintenance is also striking, particularly in that it goes hand in hand with a continued acceptance of ethnicity and even a search for ethnicity of an appropriately selective and marginal nature. While language maintenance becomes a progressively weaker and smaller component of such ethnicity, organizational (including religious) involvement, cultural interests, and modified-disjointed festive acts become relatively more prominent and are maintained much longer. Thus it is that the most striking fact of all comes into focus – that a vast amount of marginal ethnicity can exist side by side with the gradual disappearance of language maintenance, with the two phenomena inter-acting and contributing to each other.

In summary, language maintenance in the United States is currently strongest among those immigrants who have maintained greatest psychological, social, and cultural distance from the institutions, processes, and values of American core society. Ideological protection of non-English mother tongues without concomitant withdrawal from interaction with American society (i.e., the pattern adopted by urban religionists and by secular-cultural nationalists in the United States) has been a somewhat less effective bulwark of language maintenance than has ethnic-religious separatism based upon intact rural "little traditions". Where neither ideological nor ethnoreligious protection has obtained language shift has proceeded in proportion to mobility within the larger sphere of American society, as reflected by indices of education, occupation, or income. Either type of protection has been exceedingly rare. As a result, between-group differences in language maintenance have come to reflect im-migrational recency, settlement concentration, numerical size, and social mobility much more than differences in post-immigrational maintenance efforts. Within-group differences in language maintenance have also come to depend primarily on the same set of factors, together with rurality, and to a smaller but nevertheless noticeable degree upon conscious maintenance efforts.

Our current information concerning behaviors directed toward ethnic mother tongues on the part of their erstwhile and sometime speakers must be viewed in the perspective of the transitions that these tongues have most commonly experienced in the United States. From their original status as vernaculars of entire religio-ethnic communities they are now the vernaculars only of very recent or otherwise atypical sub-populations. Instead of their earlier use in all the domains of life related to the particular socio-cultural patterns of their speakers, they are now predominantly employed in fewer and particularly in symbolic or restricted domains. Nevertheless, concomitant with accelerated de-ethnization and social mobility, and concomitant with their relegation to fewer and narrower domains, non-English mother tongues have frequently experienced increases in general esteem during the past 15-20 years. They are more frequently viewed positively and nostalgically by older first- and second-generation individuals who had characterized them as ugly, corrupted, and grammarless in pre-World War II days. The third generations view them (almost always via translations) with less emotion but with even greater respect. Thus, instead of a "third generation return" (Hansen 1940) there has been an "attitudinal halo-iza-tion" within large segments of all generations, albeit unaccompanied by increased use. Such a negative relationship between use rates and attitudinal positiveness over time was not foreseen by most earlier studies of language maintenance or language shift in immigrant contact settings. In the United States this development is an aspect of the continued and growing affective functioning of increasingly marginal ethnicity. In the absence of basic economic, geographic, cultural, or psychological separation be-tween most ethnics and American core society, ethnic mother tongues survive longest at two extremes: the highly formal (the ritual-symbolic) and the highly intimate (the expressive-emotive). At these extremes they remain available to successive genera-tions as reminders of ethnicity, and when needed, as reaffirmers of ethnicity.

At the level of overt behavioral implementation of maintenance or shift, most lan-guage reinforcement efforts – though much weakened by ideological and numerical attrition – continue along the traditional lines of information programs, religio-ethnic schools, periodic publications, broadcasts, cultural activities, etc. However, even in connection with language reinforcement efforts the transition to more marginal ethnicity and to more restricted language maintenance is evident. Thus, taking the field of ethnic periodic publications as an example, we note concomitant and continued shifts from more frequent to less frequent publications as well as shifts from all-mother-tongue, to mixed, to all-English publications. The process of de-ethnization has also brought with it a few novel avenues of reinforcement. As even the more "exotic" ethnic mother tongues (i.e., mother tongues not usually considered among the major carriers of European civilization and, therefore, most frequently associated with foreign ethnicity in the minds of average Americans) have ceased to be primarily associated with immigrant disadvantages or with full-blown religio-ethnic distinctiveness, these have been increasingly introduced as languages of study and research at the university, college, and public high school levels. Although bilingual public schools such as those that existed before the First World War have hardly ever been reintroduced, and althought the bilingual college (or monolingual non-English college) which passed from the American scene at about the same time has also hardly ever been reintroduced, both are increasingly viewed as "experimental" possibilities on the part of non-ethnic (rather than ethnic) authorities. Seemingly, massive displacement has greater inhibitory impact on language planning efforts than it does on language reinforcement efforts. The latter are essentially conservative and seem to require less in the way of highly specialized leadership. The former are essentially modificatory and dependent upon expert linguistic advice in concert with compliance producing or persuasive authority. Thus archaic or rustic orthographic, lexical, and structural features continue to characterize most non-English mother tongues spoken in the United States and interference proceeds apace, both because planning and enforcing authorities are lacking and because the old find it more difficult to adopt conscious and systematic innovations.

Vocal advocates of language shift have practically disappeared, although institutional support for shift still exists along quiet but pervasive lines. Religious bodies have been particularly persistent in de-ethnicizing parishes and Anglifying church activities as they have gained in institutional autonomy and centralization. The Roman Catholic Church has been most active along these lines whereas Churches in which non-English languages are ritually protected (e.g., the Byzantine Rite Catholic and Eastern Orthodox Churches) have, by comparison, remained relatively conservative. In general, religion has more quickly and more successfully disassociated itself from ethnicity and arrived at independent legitimization in the United States than has the use of non-English mother tongues.

As for the cognitive aspects of language response, the marginalization of ethnicity has resulted in greater cognitive dissociation between ethnic identification and language maintenance. Far from being viewed as components of groupness (whether in the sense of resultant or contributing factors), non-English mother tongues are increasingly viewed in terms of non-ethnic cultural or non-ethnic practical considerations. At the same time, knowledge of language history, literature, and synchronic variants has remained rare.

The foregoing must not, however, be hastily accepted as constituting paradigms for the progress of language maintenance or language shift in all possible immigrant-based contact settings. It may be applicable only to those settings characterized by sharply unequal power configurations, by incorporation as the type of control, by marked plurality and recent immigration as the plurality pattern, by intermediate stratification and substantial mobility within the social structure, and by widespread mutual legitimization of acculturation and de-ethnization as accompaniments of urbanization, industrialization, mass culture, and ever-widening social participation (Schermerhorn 1963). In general, we know (or suspect) much more about the dynamics of language maintenance and language shift in the American immigrant contact situation than we do about these processes in settings involving indigenous populations utilizing more equally "official" languages (e.g., Riksmaal-Landsmaal, Spanish-Guarani, Schwyzertütsch-Romansh, etc.). This imbalance has resulted in a skewing of conclusions and concepts among students of language maintenance and language shift.

If these findings have general significance it is primarily in their revealing that language shift may be accompanied by a heightening of certain attitudinal, cognitive, and overt implementational responses to languages that are being displaced. In general, ethnicity and culture maintenance appear to be much more stable phenomena than language maintenance. On the one hand, most immigrants become bilingual (i.e., English displaces the hitherto exclusive use of their mother tongue in certain kinds of interactions) much before they embark on de-ethnization or seriously contemplate the possibility of bi-culturism. On the other hand, marginal but yet functional ethnicity lingers on (and is transmitted via English) long after the ethnic mother tongue becomes substantially dormant or is completely lost. Curiously enough, the lingering of marginal ethnicity prompts and supports respect, interest, and nostalgia for the ethnic mother tongue, causing language loyalists to entertain renewed hopes for revitalization even though displacement is far advanced. Thus the very resultants of deep-reaching socio-cultural change carry with them seeds of further change and of reversal.

QUESTIONS AND INTERPRETATIONS

The foregoing findings invite comments and interpretations. Why has this state of affairs come into being? How is it to be understood, both in terms of American life and in terms of even wider relevance? Certainly it is not enough to say that too few have cared or that many have cared too little, since that too needs to be explained and since history records numerous instances of decisive impact of the few upon the many – in the domain of language, no less than in others.

In the planning stage of this study, the investigators were impressed with the tremendous spread of "input variance" relevant to the question uppermost in our minds. The socio-cultural worlds of carriers of non-English languages in the United States reveal many and important differences: old immigrants and new immigrants, prestige languages and non-prestige languages, peasants and intellectuals, rurality and urbanness, religious reinforcement and nationalistic reinforcement, traditional ethnic roots and modern high culture roots, social mobility and its absence. It seemed only logical that the status of language maintenance efforts in the United States would vary significantly from one language to another, and that this variation, considered as a dependent or consequent variable, could be related to the tremendous variation in the cultural-linguistic carriers of language maintenance, considered as an independent or antecedent variable. Although this approach has revealed some moderately important and consistent relationships, these have been fewer than expected, and directionally uniform. Thus, upon concluding our study, we must be more impressed with the paucity of "output variance", particularly in long-range terms, and with the tremendous power of the intervening contextual variable to which all non-English speaking cultural-linguistic groups in the United States have been exposed: American nationalism.

The American Dream and the American Experience. — The alchemists of old sought a universal solvent, an elixir, that could transmute all manner of baser metals into a single desired one. American nationalism may be viewed as such a solvent, although whether the cultural ingredients upon which it has acted were in any sense baser than the product that it has produced will always be open to question. Indeed, the solvent has not really been entirely effective as a solvent. Nevertheless, it *has* been a catalyst, and it *has* dissolved the basic ingredients of functional bilingualism: the desire and ability to maintain an intact and different way of life. It is this realization which has prompted us to suggest that the preservation and revitalization of America's non-English language resources (even for the purpose of cultural bilingualism) requires, first and foremost, several planned modifications in the goals and processes of American society.

American nationalism has been described as an extreme form of western European nationalism in that it is particularly non-ethnic and essentially ideological in nature (Kohn 1961 [a]). Even the ethnicity of the early English-speaking settlers, who imparted to American nationalism ingredients of content and of direction that it has never lost, was strongly colored by the growing de-ethnization and ideologization of British life in the 17th and 18th centuries. There were, as there are today, Englishmen, Scotsmen, Welshmen, and Irishmen – and several regional varieties of each – but there was also (and, for many, primarily) Great Britain,[1] a supra-ethnic entity which increasingly involved all of the foregoing in supra-ethnic problems and processes (Kohn 1940). The supra-ethnic political struggles and the supra-ethnic religious struggles that had convulsed the British Isles for generations before the colonization of New England not only led to this colonization but also stamped it with a view of ethnicity as an aspect of social structure which was different from that of New France, New Spain, or New Amsterdam. The problems of religious diversity and of political participation were so much greater that the importance of purely ethnic manifesta-

---

[1] The terms "Britain" and "British" were originally derived from regionally delimited ethnic and linguistic entities in northern France and southern England. Their successive semantic metamorphoses, culminating in "Great Britain", are themselves products of centuries of de-ethnization and ideologization.

tions in society paled by comparison. The ancient links between ethnicity and religion that existed in most other parts of Europe had already been weakened to the point that these were never fully re-established by British settlers in the New World. The relationships between man and God, between man and state, and between man and environment were formulated increasingly in non-ethnic terms. Even the term "Englishman" had political and ideological rather than ethnic connotations. Thus, a supra-ethnic outlook was transplanted, usually at a purely subconscious level. Later, as rivalries developed with colonists of non-British origin, with other colonial powers, with the mother country, and with the Old World itself, supra-ethnicity became a conscious value and a rally cry. By then it had already become a fact of life, even though not fully a way of life.

From the early supra-ethnic beginnings of American nationalism, the American Dream contained two recognizable components: those of process and those of promise. The components of process guaranteed personal freedom (and, therefore, political democracy and the separation of Church and State) as well as the determining use of reason (rather than ascribed status) in guiding public affairs. The components of promise held forth vistas of happiness in human affairs, limitless individual and collective advancement, and social inclusiveness in community affairs. In a very basic sense, each of these ingredients is supra-ethnic if not anti-ethnic. America offered initially and officially that which many today, all over the world, take to be the goals of all social evolution: freedom of physical, intellectual, and emotional movement in constantly expanding social, economic, and cultural spheres. American nationalism came to stand for all that was modern, good, reasonable, inclusive, and participationist in human relations. America has made good the promise of its nationalism for many millions and with dramatic rapidity.

The American Dream is crucial to language maintenance outcomes not only because of the importance of *primum mobile*. It is also crucial because, on the one hand, it has failed to answer certain questions of a substantive nature, and, on the other, most of our non-English speaking immigrants lacked any substantial counter-dream. In implying that freedom, equality, capacity, participation, and reason were sufficient guides to human behavior, it did not provide the substantive cultural ingredients of national life that both ethnicity and religion provide. In merely requiring an affirmation of its processes and promises it more quickly disarmed non-English speakers whose ethnicity had been transmuted and elaborated in consciously creative directions. In offering so much and seeming to ask so little in return, it overpowered the masses of immigrants whose primordial ethnicity was still largely intact and, therefore, still largely innocent of ideology. The overpowering nature of American nationalism is also an indication that it can be as uncompromising and as conformity-producing as the nationalisms known elsewhere throughout the world.

If is frequently claimed that Americanism processes and promises *require* cultural pluralism for their maturation and protection. Be this as it may, it is doubtless true that cultural pluralism was never explicitly "covered" by the formulators of the American Dream, nor has it been consciously and fully desired by the millions who subsequently subscribed to the Dream. Indeed, the prime factor leading most immigrants to our shores was the American Dream itself and its implicity contract and not any dream of cultural pluralism (Bruner 1956; Lerner 1958; Mead 1956). Not only was cultural pluralism a highly unlikely dream for most immigrants prior to their immigration, it was a rarely articulated or accepted dream after arrival. In most cases, ethnicity and language maintenance lived in America as they had in Europe: on a primarily traditional and non-ideological plane. Even when they crumbled or changed, they most commonly did so on a non-ideological basis. By and large, their carriers were conscious only of the American Dream, which is supra-ethnic in content. It is a Dream in which the Queen's English is no more than a "vehicle of communication" for the pursuit of perfection in human affairs, constant individual and collective advancement, and social inclusiveness in community processes. It is a vision which has spread round the world and excited envy, admiration, or both in distant places. Like most visions, it implies more than it specifies. The fact that it has emasculated both levels of functional ethnicity (upon one or another of which language maintenance has always relied), without at the same time providing for structural assimilation in more primary relationships (Gordon 1964), cannot clearly be used to its discredit – since it neither promised to maintain the former nor to attain the latter. That primordial ethnicity could not fully maintain itself under the impact of this Dream, and that ethnicity cannot fully and quickly disappear in a new world animated by this Dream alone, are as much due to the nature of ethnicity as to the Dream itself.

Ethnicity and Language Maintenance. — Ethnicity designates a constellation of primordial awarenesses, sentiments, and attachments by means of which man has traditionally recognized the discriminanda that relate him to some other men while distinguishing him from others. Blood ties, geographic proximity, common customs and beliefs – these constitute primitive principles of human organization that are still very much in evidence throughout the world. So basic are they in socialization and in subsequent experience that they frequently appear as "givens" in nature. Even when man progresses to more complex and more abstract bases of social grouping (religion, ideology, the nation, the profession, even "mankind"), the earlier principles of interaction remain recognizable in his behavior and from time to time proclaim their dominance. Both levels of human organization seem to be required for meeting different personal and societal needs in the modern world. However, the kind and proportion of behavior actually guided by primordial considerations and the kind and proportion guided by considerations of a larger scale vary from country to country, from group to group, from person to person, and from occasion to occasion. Language may affect human behavior either through its more primitive, primordial or through its more modern, larger-scale involvements.

The folk-urban continuum (Redfield 1947, 1953) has been referred to in several of the foregoing chapters not because it is presumed that villages, cities and states are totally different environments, but because it casts light upon continuity and discontinuity in primordial behaviors when these are introduced into more modern political and social contexts (Geertz 1963). The fact that there are more naunces than clearcut polarities in the rural-urban continuum (particularly when the continuum is viewed in historical and cross-cultural perspective [Benet 1963]) does not make the transition from predominantly rural to predominantly urban settings any smoother for those whose lot it is to quickly go from one to another. Under these circumstances, even without extirpation and transplantation, ethnicity and its various primordial components change in content, in saliency, and in relevance to daily life (Bruner 1961; Lewis 1952). There is no doubt that the mass of immigrants of the 1880-1920 period (upon whom language maintenance in the United States still largely depends in almost every case except Spanish and, perhaps, Ukrainian) hailed from far more rural, more homogeneous, more traditional, more ethnic contexts than those that they entered in the United States. There is no doubt that their language behavior was usually imbedded in ethnicity rather than in ideology. Finally, there is no doubt that language maintenance required (and usually did not find) a new foundation when its potential carriers came to feel at home in the American environment.

In its encounter with a non-traditional, secular world in which social interaction and social grouping are rationalized by forces emanating from progress and efficiency, justice and equality, nation and world, the ethnicity of underdeveloped and undermobilized populations has responded in two quite different ways. In many instances it has been symbolically elaborated and elevated to a higher order principle with claims for competitive legitimacy in the modern world of ideas and conscious loyalties. In other instances it has merely regrouped or restructured itself, changing in content, saliency, and part-whole articulation, but remaining far closer to the little tradition level from which it stems than to any modern Weltanschauung. While both of these transformations of old world ethnicity were attempted by immigrants to the United States, various circumstances conspired to make the latter approach much more common and much more acceptable than the former.

The relatively few intellectuals and political activists who sought to raise the ethnicity of rank-and-file immigrants to the level of religion, ideology, and nationalism by no means dismally failed. Indeed, given the difficulties they faced they were remarkably successful. They frequently united hitherto separated, particularistic ethnic populations into groups conscious of common nationality. They provided the energy and directing force that led many of the major formal organizations and undertakings of immigrants on American shores. They both pointed out and helped create Great Traditions in literature, history, and ideology which at least temporarily lifted their followers out of complete reliance on primordial ethnicity, provided them with pride in their heritage, and helped counteract feelings of insecurity vis-à-vis the accomplishments of American civilization. However, in the main and in the long run, they were unsuccessful and their fate may best be described as an alienation of the dedicated. They succeeded far better in foisting an identity between ethnicity and nationalism on the general, de-ethnicized American public (which reacted in typical early second-generation horror)[2] than they did in gaining acceptance of this same identity among their own co-ethnics. Their symbolic transmutations of everyday ethnic life probably led as many co-ethnics and their children to even more universalized, less ethnically delimited or rationalized interests in language, literature, and justice than to the kind of cultural-national self-definitions that these elites originally had in mind. In the last analysis they failed to permanently mobilized a sufficiently large proportion of their more primordially oriented co-ethnics, who were orientated in much more mundane directions. As a result, very little of language maintenance in the United States currently remains (or ever has been) under nationalistic ideological auspices.

Most immigrants to the United States, until comparatively recent times, may best be viewed as underdeveloped ethnic populations whose mobilization into modern life occurred under the aegis of the American Dream, the American city, and the American state (Steward 1951). They accepted the ideal norms of the new society round about them with relative and accelerating ease. In contrast to the relative disadvantage and lack of mobility that they had known in their own homelands they perceived and experienced rapid and marked improvements in their new homes (Shuval 1963). They eagerly accepted those values and norms that were required to maximize the benefits for which they had come. However, it is important for us to realize that their little traditions, though severely dislocated and weakened, showed an amazing capacity to regroup and even to innovate under these circumstances.

Although the ethnicity of immigrants to the United States did not become as ideologized or modernized as ethnic elites had hoped, it did move in that direction in the form of conscious organizational-associational activity. Indeed, as the ethnicity of daily life increasingly weakened its organized associational transmutations appeared in bold and abnormal relief (Anderson and Anderson 1959/60). The churches, the organizations, the schools grew pari passu with the retreat of primordial ethnicity in the home and the neighborhood. The new expressions of ethnicity were well suited for urban, modern existence but they were also entities in themselves and had goals and needs of their own. They carried language maintenance as best they could and for as long as it served their own purposes. If the result has been markedly negative insofar as attaining or retaining functional bilingualism is concerned, it has been somewhat more positive with respect to other aspects of primordial ethnicity. Above all, the new instrumentalities preserve a new kind of ethnicity, simultaneously more conscious and more marginal than the old, but seemingly more capable of endurance in the American environment (or in other modern contexts). It is in this sense that ethnicity

---

[2]   Only rarely and comparatively lately have there been glimmers of recognition that behavioral ethnicity is essentially non-ideological and, therefore, that it poses no ideological threat to American nationalism. For this very reason ethnicity has always been far less of a danger to unity and loyalty in the United States (whether to American substantive ideology or to American procedural ideology) than the openly divisive and organizationally active ideologized forces that the United States has always recognized as legitimate: organized self-interest in economic, religious, and political pursuits.

in the United States is not merely a vestigial remains but also a new creation on behalf of a kind of group solidarity and consciousness not provided for in the American Dream. In America, as elsewhere in today's world, circumstances bring about a modernization of ethnicity rather than its complete displacement. Whereas the majority of human interactions are governed by involvement, participation, and creativity on a larger scale of human organization, earlier, more primordial levels are still needed and still exist. It is not only non-Western intellectuals who currently vacillate between tradition and modernity (Shils 1961); it is not only non-Western peoples who currently alternate between emulation and solidarity in search of a more adequate great tradition (Orans 1959); most modern Americans and most modern Europeans do so as well. There are limits to the ability of larger-scale and more modern bonds and principles to solve the longings of mankind. The primordial and the modern show a capacity to co-exist side by side, to adjust to each other, and to stimulate each other.

The supra-ethnicity of the American Dream could not have found a better instrument for the enfeeblement of primordial ethnic particularities (including the displacement of ethnic languages) than the frenetic and polyglot American metropolis and the American "ways of life" which developed in it (Benet 1963; Bruner 1961). In these inauspicious surroundings the maintenance of ethnic languages became more conscious than it had ever been before, but without either a great tradition or a little tradition to maintain it. That it drew more strength from the latter than from the former seems quite natural under the circumstances of its carriers. Only in the case of two colonial languages – French and German – was a somewhat de-cthnicized and prestigeful great tradition available to buttress language maintenance among both intellectuals and common folk.[3] In connection with other languages, there was rarely any awareness or conviction that anything outstanding had been achieved nor the sophistication or experience needed to differentiate between assertive transmutations of ethnicity and more purely creative transmutations on firmer ethnic foundations. The latter were rediscovered – selectively to be sure – by second and third generations. However, this came to pass only after the second generation had revolted against the irrationally all-encompassing claims of atomized ethnicity and after the remnants of primordial ethnicity were too feeble to seriously address similar claims to the third.[4]

[3]   This is generally overlooked in discussions of the maintenance of the major colonial languages in the United States. These have benefited not only from priority, numerical resources, concentration of settlement, prestige, and homeland reinforcements, but from the fact that Americans did not continually identify the great traditions of these languages with foreign nationalism.

[4]   Generational designations are still employed too sweepingly and generational processes described too grossly in most discussions of American immigrant phenomena. Each generation passes through childhood, adolescence, maturity, and old age. It is unlikely that its ethnic attitudes and behaviors or its relationships with its "older generation" remain invariant during its life-span. Furthermore, the second generation whose adolescence occurred during the 1920's and 1930's was probably quite different from the second generation whose adolescence corresponded with the 1950's and 1960's, if only because their American environments, their ethnic communities, and their respective "older genera-

Under the impact of American ideology and American mass culture, language maintenance turned for support first to the one and then to the other. The ideology closest to it was the religion with which it had been intimately associated on its home grounds. Indeed, as a result of centuries of co-existence, primordial ethnicity and religion had completely interpenetrated each other. At times each had come to the other's rescue (Jakobson 1945). Each had formed the other; each had changed the other. What better ally, then, for language maintenance in America than religion? Immigrant religions both courted and supported language maintenance, and religion was protected in American nationalism. Indeed, what other real ally was there?

Religion and Language Maintenance. — Ethnic romanticists seem to view ethnicity in much the same way as religious mystics view religion: something pure, direct, unaltered, and unanalyzable. On the other hand, folk-immigrants, prior to arrival in the United States, may be said to have behaved as if their ethnicity were their religion. Each daily act, no matter how mundane, was within the pale of sanctity and colored by its hue. Subsequently, after varying exposure to modern American life, many immigrants came to behave as if their religion were their ethnicity. Religion came to be substituted for ethnicity and to preserve those remnants of primordial ethnicity that were amenable to it. Such preservation was rarely sufficient for the purposes of functional language maintenance.

As religiously-committed American historians look back upon the language issues that convulsed their Churches at one time or another, it strikes many of them that the linguistic particularism under which their predecessors labored were particularly misguided. How could anything as universal, as timeless, and as ultimate as religious truth ever have appeared to be inextricably dependent upon a particular vernacular (or even upon a particular sacred tongue)? The fact that religions have rendered various languages holy or have declared them to be particularly appropriate for the expression and preservation of religious attachments is conveniently overlooked when the advancement of religion – which may be distinguished from the advancement of religiosity – dictates that the bonds with particular languages need to be sundered. The Lord giveth and the Lord taketh away, in languages as in all else, and in sacred languages almost as much as in vernaculars.

Not only are the historical bonds between language and religions frequently overlooked in examining the particular bonds that existed during earlier stages of immigration to the United States, but the specific benefits to the Churches accruing from these bonds are generally ignored. Frequently, no effort is made to indicate the light in which the maintenance of particular vernaculars was viewed in former days, namely as a form of ethnic traditionalism firmly associated with religious traditionalism and,

---

tions" were much different at these two points in time. Indeed, whereas native-born children of mixed parentage classically have been grouped together with the second generation in census studies (as well as in others), it may now be more appropriate to group them with the third, in view of the accelerated pace of acculturation. All of these matters remain to be studied.

therefore, conducive to religious loyalty. Rather than a factor which strengthened immigrant Churches as organizations and institutions at a time when they were particularly weak, language maintenance is now preferably viewed as a temporary device of an established Church seeking to safeguard the faith of childish and unruly immigrants susceptible to the wickedness of the great city and to the blandishments of competing creeds. It is in this vein that a recent study recognizes "the immigrant phase" of the Catholic Church as one in "which the primary challenge was to guard the faith of Catholics and to defend the Church against calumnies" (Deedy 1963):

Looking back now, one of the curiosities of those years is the absence from the Catholic press of any strong notion of solidatiry in faith or in patriotism. Catholic readers were first Irish or German or Slovak, then Catholic.... Catholic publications played party to this folly by catering to the nostalgias, culture, and nationalism of the particular immigrant group served.... There was frequently cause to wonder whether a given publication was first Catholic or first Irish, German, French, and so on.

Obviously, language maintenance presented a very special problem to the Roman Catholic Church. In contrast to the national Protestant Churches which dealt with immigrants of a single ethnic origin, and unlike the Greek Catholic and Eastern Orthodox Churches that had long ago become decentralized along separate national lines, the Roman Catholic Church in America was simultaneously Irish, Anglified, "Americanist", and centralized. Whereas the other immigrant Churches lacked de-ethnicized, English-speaking American roots, the Roman Catholic Church as a result of over a century of effort had already developed such roots by the time masses of non-English speaking Catholics arrived. Horrified by the "regressive" centrifugal prospects of re-ethnization, the Catholic hierarchy in America may well have become (and remained) the second major organized de-ethnicizing and Anglifying force in the United States, next to the American public school system. What appeared to be at issue was not merely the hard-won beachhead of American respectability (for a Church that had been recurringly exposed to anti-papism and knownothingism), not only the loyalty of younger, English-speaking parishioners, but the very structural unity and authority of the Church itself, as various ethnic groups sought the kinds of parish government, the kinds of parish organizations, the kinds of religious services, the kinds of religiously sanctioned and sanctified ethnic practices that were in keeping with *their* particular Catholic traditions. No wonder, then, that a policy of strenuous resistance was developed in connection with language maintenance and other manifestations of ethnic particularism. Mass immigration was still in high gear when this policy of resistance culminated in Pope Leo XIII's encyclical of January 22, 1899, *Testem Benevolentiae*, "which praised the spirit and the progress of the Church in America, but which deplored the 'contentions which have arisen ... to the no slight detriment of peace'" (Deedy 1963). The promulgation of this encyclical is correctly taken as ushering in the "post-immigration period" (even though mass immigration continued for another generation) in that ethnic parishes, like the ethnic press, "came tightly within the orbit of church authority". The apostolic letter "had the effect of dropping a blanket of silence" and of producing "a speedy metamorphosis", such that the 20th century was entered in a spirit "subdued and reserved, if not completely docile", a spirit conducive to a "truly American church, indeed" (Deedy 1963). Several of our studies reveal the lengths to which various Catholic and non-Catholic ethnic groups went in their lack of docility on behalf of ethnic and linguistic continuity. Nevertheless, from that day to our own, language maintenance in the United States has not been able to look upon organized religion as a dependable source of support.

Basically, the retreat of American religious bodies from the arena of language maintenance is due to much more pervasive factors than a papal encyclical which influenced only Roman rite Catholics at best. By the same token, recent actions of the Ecumenical Council permitting the use of vernaculars in the mass and in other Roman Catholic religious rituals can hardly be expected to materially strengthen language maintenance. The separation of religion from life as a result of secularization, ritualization, and organizational primacy is what is most fundamentally involved in this retreat. Indeed, the forces leading to the de-ethnization of formerly ethnic religions in the United States are quite similar to those that have affected ethnic organizations, ethnic schools, and "Ethnic ideologies". All continue to retain remnants of ethnicity, and these remnants function as bulwarks of ethnicity, and of language maintenance for the first generation which can fill them out and join them together via memories and sentiments, if not via overt behaviors. However, they cannot function as such for subsequent generations, in whose case they serve rather to smooth the path to further de-ethnization and to successively more selective, and more marginal, and reformed ethnicity.

Mass Culture and Language Maintenance. – As ethnicity has become increasingly unable to support language maintenance, and as religion has grown increasingly unwilling to do so, the needs, values, and institutions of American society have been pointed out and appealed to on its behalf. Is it not good to know several languages? Is it not important? Does it not contribute to success in life? Does it not contribute to the national welfare? Should it not be publicly supported? These appeals all involve the utilitarianization of behavior and, as a result, they are, themselves, atraditional and supra-ethnic. That knowledge must be useful is an American bias of long standing. If bilingualism can be proved to be both good and useful, then we shall obviously "do something about it". If language maintenance can be made out to be concretely useful to the country and to the man in the street, it may yet be accorded a place of honor within American mass culture. However, there is a basic antithesis between ethnicity and mass culture.

Mass culture produces (or induces) both conformity and fluidity. On the one hand, it manufactures, popularizes, and distributes products – including cultural products – for a mass market. In this sense it is dependent upon standardization of products and homogenization of tastes and is, therefore, diametrically opposed to both particularism and traditionalism. However, once having replaced the old with the new, it establishes a cycle of replacement, both as a psychological principle and as a factor of the economy. Thus, tastes and behaviors are not merely widely homogenized. They are also rendered more fluid, more responsive to fashionability and obsolescence, and therefore more widely homogeneous even with a constantly changing repertoire or inventory. While social differentiations based on nativity, religion, age, sex, and class do not disappear – indeed, they become the best predictors of life style variables (Wilensky 1964) – behavior becomes more widely uniform and more widely changeable within and across these lines of differentiation, particularly as rich societies become richer and as the impact of abundance becomes more visible. Thus it is that the conformity-producing and the change-producing aspects of American mass culture are related to each other, and are in concerted opposition to the rooted particularism of primordial ethnicity. Mass culture has effectively reduced the hold of either behavioral or structural ethnicity, in the United States and elsewhere, as the two have come into greater contact. This has usually led to the further erosion of ethnically-based language maintenance among those for whom no other firm basis for language maintenance has existed. Incongruities between structure and culture in American life are undeniable. Nevertheless, they may well represent a transitional stage on the road to a more congruent alignment via mass culture and affluence. Both structural lag and growing accommodation are evident today.

The inroads of mass culture on ethnicity become clear to us, first of all, in connection with our consideration of the transmittal of language maintenance within the family. They become additionally apparent in connection with participationism in the American dream and in metropolitan life. The adolescent period appears to be the juncture at which the impact of mass culture on ethnically-based language maintenance is most clearly felt. In traditional society the problem of adolescent transition is significantly attenuated. There is far greater continuity and identity between the values, behaviors, and skills of the family and those of the larger society. Indeed, there is frequently no marked transition from the one to the other. Youth movements arose in modern Europe primarily as a result of the problems of middle-class youth faced by the barriers of social and economic dislocation in entering an increasingly non-familial type of society. In their case the values, behaviors, and skills required by society seemed particularly unclear or non-continuous with those of the family. This has been much less so for either lower-class or upper-class youth. Until comparatively recently there was little mass culture in Europe which could provide a transitional buffer between the experienced ethnic patterns of the family and the uncertain patterns of adult life outside the family. As a result, adolescent youth movements arose and middle-class adolescence was quite properly viewed as a sociological and political phenomenon rather than a psychological one, as it has long appeared to be in the United States. Here, an adolescent culture has developed, relying completely on mass culture as a non-institutional transition between family patterns of values, behaviors, and skills and those of middle-class society or the oncoming family of procreation. The adolescent of ethnic origin was particularly caught up by American mass culture, for in his case the discontinuity between family and society was most marked.

Indeed, the facts of life were such that in the United States ethnic society itself (to the extent that is existed) became decidedly and increasingly discontinuous with the ethnic family. To whatever extent it could, given the impact of metropolitan life, the family most frequently attempted to cling to ethnic traditions in a primordial, holistic manner. However, ethnic society (the ethnic Church, the ethnic organization, the ethnic school) tended increasingly toward organizational structure, toward ritualized ideology and pragmatic ethnicity, i.e., toward discrete, useful, and organizationally-dominated expressions of marginal ethnicity. The family's store of daily, holistic ethnicity actually became largely unnecessary for entry into ethnic society. At the same time, ethnicity traditionally made no provision for age homogeneous groups, whether adolescent or other. Thus the ethnic adolescent came to view his family's values, behaviors, and skills as doubly malfunctional: malfunctional for a role in ethnic society and malfunctional for a role in general society. Faced by conflicting total claims, the usual result was revolt on the one hand and a headlong pursuit of mass culture on the other.[5]

However, as was true with respect to American urbanization and American nationalism, mass culture need not be viewed entirely as a debilitating factor in language maintenance. It also contains shreds of reinforcement. Adolescents grow up and mass culture becomes less exclusively dominant the more they find a place for themselves in adult society. The ethnic ex-adolescent comes to derive certain stabilizing satisfactions from marginal ethnicity, particularly in a society built upon the shifting sands of mass culture. Just as over-acceptance of ethnicity in childhood led to its over-rejection in adolescence, so over-rejection, in turn, is frequently followed by re-evaluation and by ideological and behavioral selectivity. Thus de-ethnization and re-ethnization follow upon each other, perhaps in cycles of decreasing intensity, while the ubiquity of mass culture tends to render both processes meaningful. Of course, the re-ethnization of the adult second generation (which may actually be more responsible for that of the third than has usually been appreciated) is manifestly insufficient for language maintenance on an ethnic base. Indeed, de-ethnicized language maintenance must, of necessity, be far different from that which we have emphasized here. It must derive its impetus from the American Dream and from American mass culture, instead of directly or indirectly from ethnicity. If this were to be accomplished, language maintenance not only would be much changed (and therefore possibly much more attractive to ethnics), but it might contribute to the reformulation of its new-found protectors as well.

REFERENCES

Anderson, R. T., and Anderson, G., "Voluntary Associations and Urbanization: A Diachronic Analysis", *American Journal of Sociology*, 65 (1959/60), 265-273.

[5] The less frequent revolt among recent second-generation adolescents might, therefore, well be attributable to a three-way lessening of distance between the ethnic family and general society, between the ethnic family and ethnic society, and between ethnic society and general society.

Banks, A. S., and Textor, R. B., *A Cross-Polity Survey* (Cambridge, M.I.T. Press, 1963).

Benet, F., "Sociology Uncertain: The Ideology of the Rural-Urban Continuum", *Comparative Studies in Society and History*, 6 (1963), 1-23.

Brault, G. J., "Some Misconceptions about Teaching American Ethnic Children Their Mother Tongue", *Modern Language Journal*, 48 (1964), 67-71 (in press).

Bruner, E. M., "Primary Group Experience and the Process of Acculturation", *American Anthropologist*, 58 (1956), 605-623.

——, "Urbanization and Ethnic Identity in North Sumatra", *American Anthropologist*, 63 (1961), 508-521.

Deedy, J. G., Jr., "The Catholic Press: The Why and Wherefore", in *The Religious Press in America*, Martin E. Marty, *et al.* (New York, Holt, Rinehard and Winston, 1963).

Fishman, J. A., and Hayden, R. G., "The Impact of Exposure to Ethnic Mother Tongues on Foreign Language Teachers in American High Schools and Colleges", in J. A. Fishman, *et al.*, *Language Loyalty in the United States* (New York, Yeshiva University, 1964), Chapter 13. (Mimeo.) Also *Modern Language Journal*, 48 (1964), 262-274.

Geertz, C., "The Integrative Revolution: Primordial and Civil Politics in the New States", in his *Old Societies and New States* (New York, Free Press, 1963), pp. 106-157.

Gordon, M., *Assimilation in American Life* (New York, Oxford University Press, 1964).

Hansen, M., *The Immigrant in American History* (Cambridge, Mass., Harvard University Press, 1946).

Hughes, E. C., "Race Relations and the Sociological Imagination", *American Sociological Review*, 28 (1963), 879-890.

Jakobson, R., "The Beginnings of National Self-Determination in Europe", *Review of Politics*, 7 (1945), 29-42.

Kohn, H., "Genesis of English Nationalism", *Journal of the History of Ideas*, 1 (1940), 69-94.

——, *American Nationalism* (New York, Collier, 1961) (a).

——, *The Idea of Nationalism: A Study in Its Origin and Background* (New York, Macmillan, 1961) (b).

Lerner, D., *The Passing of Traditional Society* (Glencoe, Ill., Free Press, 1958).

Lewis, O., "Urbanization Without Breakdown: A Case Study", *Scientific Monthly*, 75 (1952), 31-41.

Mead, Margaret, *New Lives for Old* (New York, Morrow, 1956).

Orans, M., "A Tribe in Search of a Great Tradition; The Emulation-Solidarity Conflict", *Man in India*, 39 (1959), 108-114.

Redfield, R., "The Folk Society", *American Journal of Sociology*, 42 (1947), 293-308.

——, "The Natural History of the Folk Society", *Social Forces*, 31 (1953), 224-228.

Schermerhorn, R. A., "Toward a General Theory of Minority Groups". Paper presented at the 58th Annual Meeting of the American Sociological Association. Los Angeles, August 28, 1963.

Shils, E., *The Intellectual Between Tradition and Modernity: The Indian Situation* (= *Comparative Studies in Society and History*, 1961, Supplement I).

Shuval, Judith T., *Immigrants on the Threshold* (New York, Atherton, 1963).

Steward, J. H., "Levels of Socio-Cultural Integration: An Operational Concept", *Southwestern Journal of Anthropology*, 7 (1951), 374-390.

Usesm, J., "Notes on the Sociological Study of Language", *SSRC Items*, 17 (1963), 29-31.

Wilensky, H. L., "Mass Society and Mass Culture", *American Sociological Review*, 29 (1964), 173-197.

APPENDICES

A. METHODOLOGICAL NOTES

While the foregoing studies have not sought to introduce methodological innovations with respect to data gathering or data analysis, their authors have made every effort to preserve commonly accepted methodological standards with respect to representativeness, reliability, and validity. The original reports of the Language Resources Project (Fishman 1964) contain more detailed accounts of these efforts which will only be briefly summarized at this point.

INSTRUMENT CONSTRUCTION

Most of the findings reported in Chapter 3 through 8 are based upon specially constructed questionnaire and interview schedules. Each data-gathering instrument was pretested and revised before being put to use. In many instances two or more revisions were undertaken before the "final form" stage was reached. The project staff, a board of consultants, special consultants with expert knowledge in a particular substantive field, and representatives of various ethnic organizations or groups served as critics or as try-out subjects for the purpose of revising and improving preliminary versions of data-gathering instruments.

DATA GATHERING

1. *Enumerating the universe of study.* – Prior to the Language Resources Study there existed no exhaustive enumeration of the periodic publications, radio programs, schools, parishes, and cultural organizations of American ethnic groups. Such an enumeration was of importance to us for two reasons. First of all, we were interested in determining the *number* of units in each of these categories. Secondly, we were interested in *contacting* all or a sample of these units in order to obtain data from them concerning their language maintenance efforts and attitudes. In order to accomplish either of these goals it was first necessary to arrive at a definition of the ethnic universe for each topic of study. One or the other of the following criteria was employed in this connection:

a. *Self-definition.* Units that defined themselves as serving or being affiliated with a particular ethnic clientele were accepted as such. On this basis a small number of "missionary" units (conducted under non-ethnic central auspices) were accepted when it appeared that they represented an organized ethnic clientele rather than only an outside attempt to reach such a clientele. On the other hand, a number of non-English periodic publications, radio broadcasts, and schools were not accepted when they appeared to be under non-ethnic educational auspices. Professional publications of language teachers, language instruction programs sponsored by universities or school systems, and several schools offering intensive language programs (usually in French) were eliminated on this basis. Thus, the crucial criterion was self-definition with respect to an existing ethnic population rather than language of operation. Lists of units defined in this way were obtained through extensive field visits, and via a perusal of the publications and records of ethnic groups and organizations.

b. *Authoritative listing.* In a few topical areas ethnic and non-ethnic authorities have prepared periodic lists of ethnic units in one or another category of operation. These listings were accepted, subject to revision on the basis of more recent information pertaining to new units, discontinuation of old units, and erroneous listing of units that corresponded to no ascertainable ethnic clientele.

As a result of the two criteria employed, three categories of ethnic units were obtained.

i. Ethnic by self-definition *and* authoritative listing.

ii. Ethnic by self-definintion only. These units were usually too new or too small to be listed by authoritative sources. In some instances their names had been Americanized and, as a result, authoritative sources had prematurely assumed a de-ethnization of their membership or purpose.

iii. Ethnic by authoritative listing only. These units were usually marginally ethnic in membership or purpose but continued to be regarded as ethnic by central bodies.

The above criteria do not attempt to delimit ethnicity substantively since the variation in overt ethnic behaviors and in ethnic beliefs and sentiments constituted one of our primary parameters of study. As a result, language maintenance has been studied among units that consider themselves to be ethnic or that are so considered by central coordinating, sponsoring, or record-keeping bodies, rather than only (more narrowly) among units practicing language maintenance, interested in language maintenance, or (even more broadly) consciously serving foreign-stock populations or their offspring.

The process of enumerating the universe of study was enormously difficult and time consuming. We can only claim moderate success in this connection. Central agencies tend to prolong the apparent ethnicity of certain units and to ignore that of others for reasons of internal organizational policy rather than for reasons more germane to the nature of our study. Self-definitions tend to be variously influenced by concurrent styles and atmospheres. It is virtually impossible to obtain self-definitions from all units, particularly those that are unaffiliated with larger bodies. It is difficult to estimate the number of non-self-defined and non-listed ethnic units in various categories.

Greater accuracy and exhaustiveness of enumeration would have required a more permanent social-bookkeeping apparatus, such as those maintained by governmental units. If the ethnic press, radio, schools, parishes, and organizations are to be more adequately studied in the future, their enumeration must be recognized as being within the pale of necessary public information, as is current social bookkeeping on agriculture, commerce, industry, and education.

Obtaining data from the enumerated universe. – In all instances, non-respondents were followed up by several of the following methods: reminders (by mail, by telephone, by visit), replacement copies of original questionnaires, briefer versions of the original questionnaires, brief inquiries as to whether the unit was still in existence, interviewing of non-respondents. In connection with most topics of study it was possible to determine whether respondents and non-1espondents differed in important respects. The following information may be of interest:

Topic	% Responding	Checks on the Representativesness of Respondents
a. Press	64%	A comparison of "long form" and "short form" respondents revealed no significant differences in regional distribution or frequency of publication. A comparison of self-responding and interviewed respondents showed no significant difference in overall language positiveness. (Trend data on the number of publications and on their circulation, 1910-1960, are based on published "authoritative" listings. A 1960 LRP census, conducted to check on the current adequacy of these listings, revealed that they tend to overlook smaller, non-advertising publications.)
b. Radio	18%	A comparison between questionnaire respondents and non-respondents revealed no significant differences in regional or community size distribution. (Trend data on the number of stations and average hours/week of broadcasting per language, 1956 and 1960, are based on published "authoritative" listings. A 1960 LRP census, conducted to check on the current adequacy of these listings, revealed that they tend to under-report smaller stations and less common languages.)
c. Schools	50%	The correlation between total *number* of questionnaires distributed to schools of various

ethnic groups and the total *per cent* of replies is .25, indicating that groups sponsoring large numbers of schools are not seriously overrepresented among the respondents. The correlation (across ethnic groups) between the total *per cent* of schools replying and the total *per cent* offering mother-tongue instruction is .17 (if the extremely small Dutch and Serbian groups are discounted the above correlation shrinks to —.05), indicating that respondents are not characterized by "positive response" bias. The correlation (across ethnic groups) between the *per cent* of schools offering mother-tongue instruction among "Long form" respondents and the *per cent* of those offering such instruction among "short form" respondents is .75, indicating a basic language maintenance similarity between these two groups.

d. Mother Tongue Teachers   25%

A comparison between the schools of responding and non-responding teachers revealed that the schools do not differ significantly in enrollment or in regional distribution.

e. Ethnic Parishes   40% (83% for a brief questionnaire on intermarriage)

A comparison between responding and non-responding parishes revealed no significant differences in regional distribution or size of "place".

f. Cultural Organizations   35%

The correlation between *per cent* of replies and *number* of questionnaires distributed, across ethnic groups, is .45, indicating a tendency for ethnic groups supporting more organizations to reply more frequently. However, the correlation between *per cent* of replies and *per cent* of language maintenance "positives", across ethnic groups, is —.01, indicating no positive response bias. A brief form distributed to all ethnic organization in one major city revealed a similar *rate* of interest in language maintenance among cultural and non-cultural organizations. (An analysis of data on ethnic fraternal societies provided by an "authoritative listing" supported several distinctions between language maintenance "positives" and "negatives" derived from our questionnaire data. "Negatives" were found to be older, larger, and wealthier organizations in both instances. On the basis of "authoritative listing" data on ethnic fraternal societies, non-respondents to the questionnaire appear to be weaker in terms of membership and finances rather than more frequently "negative" or "positive".[1])

g. Cultural and   27%   Foreign-born leaders are underrepresented
    Organizational   among the respondents. Interviews with foreign-
    Leaders   born non-respondents revealed that age, questionnaire rejection, and English facility[2] (rather than pervasive language maintenance attitudes or behaviors) were the primary differences between respondents and non-respondents.

The foregoing checks on representativeness of respondents are reassuring with respect to a few of the most obvious parameters of doubt. More elaborate checks were beyond the budget or the time available to us. In addition, more elaborate checks would presuppose greater concensus concerning the definition of the includible universes and greater certainty concerning the exhaustive enumeration of the units constituting these universes. Finally, it should be observed that cooperation with social research was a novel experience for many of our respondents. Our response rates must be evaluated from the point of view of the nature of data gathering in the particular universes studied rather than from any more detached point of view.

DATA ANALYSIS AND INTERPRETATION

1. *Statistical analysis.* – Inferential statistics have not been employed in presenting the data of this volume although probability values were available to the investigators in all cases. These values were used by the investigators for initial orientation purposes in approaching the relationships and differences encountered in the data. Two factors militated against any more formal use of inferential statistics. On the one hand, the nature of the study design and the resultant data are such that the overall delineation and the directional consistency of findings from various sources is of much greater

[1] The study of the impact of ethnicity on foreign language teachers in American high schools and colleges (Hayden and Fishman 1964) also utilized a comparison between LRP data distributions and "authoritative listing" distributions to check on the representativeness of respondents. Once again the two independent distributions agreed closely.
[2] Prospective respondents were informed that all LRP questionaires could be answered in any language. Nevertheless very few non-English replies were received, and no requests for non-English versions of questionnaires were received although considerable correspondence was conducted in languages other than English.

moment than the reliability or precision of any one finding in itself. Historical data, questionnaire replies, interview materials, detailed field observations, content analyses of printed materials, and "informed" impressions have all been intertwined in a manner not congenial to formal inferential analysis.

2. *Analyses of replies to open-ended questions.* – Most data-gathering instruments employed some open-ended questions. The categories for analyzing data obtained in response to these questions were initially formulated at the same time that the questions themselves were suggested for use in try-out instruments. Ultimately these categories were further refined, formally defined, and coded after inspecting the raw data obtained. All coding of replies to open-ended questions was spot-checked by an independent reader to determine reliability of coding. Categories were redefined and re-analyses undertaken whenever inter-reader reliability dropped below 90%.

3. *Response reliability and validity.* – As is usually the case, the investigators had both objective and subjective clues to reliability. The construction of try-out forms and the revision of these forms was intended to reduce respondent misinterpretations and resistances. Finally, the consistency of most findings, both within a study and between studies, whether in respect to particular categories or units or in respect to particular ethnic groups, afforded further evidence. All indications are that the reliability of the questionnaire and interview data presented is well within the range of "fair to good". The proportions of non-response may serve as partial clues in this connection. In general, behavioral questions seem to have elicited more widespread replies than did attitudinal questions. Questions calling for factual replies were rarely avoided where the necessary data were available (with the exception of financial questions). At times adherents of language maintenance seemed to reply at greater length than did its opponents. On the other hand, adherents sometimes revealed a greater tendency to suspect the motives of the investigators. While the investigators sought to adopt a neutral role or position in connection with language maintenance, they were not always considered in this light. Given the fact that ours is an initial study in a hitherto little studied field, the overall impression of validity derived from our data is both substantial and reassuring. Nevertheless, the need for more conceptually integrated, more subtle, and more detailed inquires in the future remains clear.

U.S. CENSUS DATA ON MOTHER TONGUE

U.S. Census data on mother tongue must be the starting point for most studies of language maintenance in the United States. Unfortunately, the Bureau of the Census has not always collected data on mother tongues in as consistent or detailed a fashion as serious students would welcome. The basic variations are of two kinds: (a) variations in *languages* separately reported, reported in combination, or not reported at all, and (b) variations in *populations* from which mother tongue data were obtained.

Language variations. – The Bureau of the Census has most consistently reported mother tongue data pertaining to the major European languages. Prior to 1960, Arabic was the only non-European language for which separate figures were reported. In 1960, Chinese and Japanese were added. Other non-European languages are presumably subsumed under the "all other (languages)" heading, so that these are not separately identifiable. (The Bureau's plans to issue a report giving details on smaller languages, including those of Asia and Africa, have not as yet been implemented owing to budgetary limitations.)

In some cases the Bureau has also followed the custom of subsuming numerically "minor" European languages under more frequently reported languages to which they are linguistically or culturally related.[3] In other cases, numerically "minor" languages have been indistinguishably included under the "all other" category.[4] Finally, languages which have only recently received independent recognition have only very recently been accorded separate listing (e.g., Ukrainian is not listed until 1930 although the major influx of Ukrainian speakers came early enough to warrant listing in 1920). Since these variations and inconsistencies usually involve numerically minor mother-tongue groups, they do not introduce a great amount of error into trend analyses with respect to the major mother-tongue groups. The Bureau does have much unpublished data on claimants of the numerically small but strategically important languages grouped in the "all other" category. It is a great pity that budgetary limitations have thus far precluded the publication of these data.

Population Variations. – A more serious roadblock to trend studies is the variation, from one census to another, in the populations from which mother-tongue data were obtained.

It will be noted in Chapter 2 that the foreign born have been included in *all* mother-tongue censuses whereas the native born of native parentage have only been included on *one* occasion. This variation is due to the fact that *the Bureau of the Census has not been interested in language maintenance per se as much as it has been in the ethnic composition of the American population.* Mother-tongue data are viewed as providing needed refinement of "country of origin" data, which necessarily obscure many ethnic groups not in control of their own nation-states.[5] On the other hand, the student of language maintenance is *most* interested in that very nativity group which

---

[3]   For 1910 and 1920: Celtic is included under English, Frisian under Dutch, Hebrew under Yiddish, Lettish under Lithuanian, Syrian under Arabic, and Estonian and Lappish under Finnish.

For 1930: Lappish is included under Finnish.

For 1960: Flemish is under Dutch, Serbian and Croation are combined into Serbo-Croatian, Celtic is under English, and Breton is under French.

[4]   For 1940: Icelandic, Ruthenian, Bulgarian, Lettish, Wendish, Estonian, Turkish, and Albanian, all shown separately in 1930, were reclassified under "all other".

For 1960: Armenian, which was shown separately in 1940, was reclassified under "all other".

[5]   For a discussion of some of the difficulties in using language data in this connection see N. B. Ryder, "The Interpretation of Origin Statistics", *Canadian Journal of Economics and Political Science*, 21 (1955), 466-479.

interests the Bureau of the Census *least*, namely, the native born of native parentage. It is particularly unfortunate that 1960 Census data on mother tongue deal with the foreign born only, thus abandoning the excellent 1940 precedent of reporting on three generations and returning to the most limited pattern of all – that of 1930. The senior author opposed this decision and still considers it to be one of the most foolish steps imaginable from the point of view of the current national need for more and better language data. Hopefully, a more enlightened policy will be followed in 1970, or, preferably, in a special language facility census that might be conducted in the interim.

Another variation in population occurred in 1960 when, for the first time, mother-tongue data were gathered and undistinguishably reported on non-whites as well as whites. This variation is less likely to affect trend studies except in connection with the relatively useless "all other (languages)" category, since (with the reclassification of Mexicans as Whites in 1930) relatively few non-whites in the United States are likely to report European mother tongues.

Mother Tongue Data as an Index of Language Maintenance. – For the student of language maintenance and other socio-linguistic topics the U.S. Census data on mother tongue represent a valuable source. Nevertheless, this is not the same as saying that these data really meet the serious student's needs.

To begin with, the student of language maintenance is most frequently concerned with *current language utilization and facility* rather than with *early childhood exposure alone.* It is certainly unwise to arrive at firm conclusions concering current language status from even the most reliable mother-tongue data. Most Americans claiming non-English mother tongues have also learned English. In many cases these individuals – even among the foreign born – utilize English more intensively and in more areas of their life-space than they do their own mother tongues. In many cases, particularly among the native-born claimants of non-English mother tongues, the mother tongue may have become quite dormant and may be utilized rarely, if at all. Mother-tongue data without supplemental information concerning current language facility and use mask distinctions running a gamut from active and constant non-English monolingualism to active and constant English monolingualism. Thus mother-tongue data cannot substitute for data on current language facility and use. Unfortunately, however, it must also be pointed out that mother-tongue data also possess certain weaknesses as mother-tongue data. The first such weakness lies in their dependence on self-report. There are a number of indications that many individuals with non-English mother tongues do not report them at all or do not report them accurately. This is a by-product of Americanization and assimilation pressures stemming both from without and from within the non-English language communities. The incidence of non-report increases as the social-cultural prestige of a particular mother tongue and the concentration of its speakers decreases. As a result of these pressures many individuals (even among the foreign born) claim English as their mother tongue or claim a more prestigeful cognate or geographically proximal language. There is additional confounding stemming from self-reporting individuals who were bilingual from their earliest years. The Census makes no provision for such individuals and has either encouraged them to report a single language, assigned their double response to that language most frequently claimed by their countrymen, or included them under the "all other" category.

Finally, there is some question as to the very definition of mother tongue. This definition has fluctuated slightly from one census to the other. In 1940, mother tongue was defined as "the principal language spoken in the home of the person in his earliest childhood". In 1960, when only the foreign born were queried on mother tongue, the question was phrased as follows: "What language was spoken in his home before he came to the United States?" The 1940 emphasis on "principal language" and on "earliest childhood" is not presented in the 1960 formulation.[6] This variation may heighten the tendency to report more prestigeful languages among individuals coming from areas where more than one language was widely known or where a prestige language was utilized by elite groups. However, the reformulation of the mother-tongue question in the 1960 Census has made it less likely that foreign-born individuals from non-English speaking countries would claim English as their mother tongue. This fact, as well as the inclusion of non-whites in the mother tongue census for the first time, accounts for much of the drop in the percentage of foreign born claiming English as their mother tongue – from 22.6% in 1940 to 19% in 1960.

The above recitation of limitations inherent in U.S. Census data on mother tongue is not intended to rule out the utility of these data. They remain the most useful periodically collected governmental data available to the student of language maintenance in the United States. If these limitations are recognized the data can still be cautiously worked with on a comparative and on a time-trend basis. The correction factor of 1.4 for 1960 mother tongue data reported by the Bureau of the Census indicates that these data are somewhat more reliable than age by sex, color or race, residence in 1955, and year moved into present house – all of these being topics of considerable interest to population experts and frequently studied by them. Nativity and parentage as well as country of origin have the same correction factor as mother tongue. Most other items (e.g., state of birth, school enrollment, employment status, etc.) have correction factors that range from 0.8 to to 1.0. Nevertheless, much more consistent, more exhaustive, and more revealing mother-tongue data are obviously needed. These could be provided by the Bureau of the Census if sufficient interest in such data was expressed by academic and lay leaders.

---

[6] For a further discussion of differences in definition of mother tongue in various U.S. censuses see Clyde Kisser, "Cultural Pluralism", in J.J. Spengler and O.D. Duncan, *Demographic Analysis* (Glencoe, Free Press, 1956). Before 1940 the definition used was almost identical to that used in 1960, even though the second generation was also included in the scope of the mother-tongue data collected. Natives of foreign or mixed parentage were frequently classified as of the language of customary speech in the homes of their immigrant parents prior to immigration.

BIBLIOGRAPHY

Fishman, J. A., *et al.*, *Language Loyalty in the United States* (New York, Yeshiva University, 1964), three volumes. (Mimeographed.)

Hayden, R. G., and Fishman, J. A., "The Impact of Exposure to Ethnic Mother Tongues on Foreign Language Teachers in American High Schools and Colleges", in Fishman, *et al.*, Chapter 13, and *Modern Language Journal*, 48 (1964), 262-274.

B. LANGUAGE MAINTENANCE AND LANGUAGE SHIFT
AS A FIELD OF INQUIRY
(*A definition of the field and suggestions for its further development*)

JOSHUA A. FISHMAN

The study of language maintenance and language shift is concerned with the relationship between change or stability in habitual language use, on the one hand, and ongoing psychological, social or cultural processes, on the other hand, when populations differing in language are in contact with each other. That languages (or language variants) *sometimes* replace each other, among *some* speakers, particularly in *certain* types or domains of language behavior, under *some* conditions of intergroup contact, has long aroused curiosity and comment (46).[1] However, it is only in quite recent years that this topic has been recognized as a field of systematic inquiry among professional students of language behavior.[2] It is suggested here that the three major topical subdivisions of this field are: (a) habitual language use at more than one point in time or space under conditions of intergroup contact; (b) antecedent, concurrent or consequent psychological, social and cultural processes and their relationship to stability or change in habitual language use; and (c) behavior toward language in the contact setting, including directed maintenance or shift efforts. It is the purpose of this paper to discuss each of these three topical subdivisions briefly, to indicate their current stage of development, and to offer suggestions for their further development.

---

[1] E.g. "Everything is Greek, when it is more shameful to be ignorant of Latin" (Juvenal *Satires*, Sat. VI, 1.187) and "... Jews that had married wives of Ashdod, and could not speak in the Jews' language, but according to the language of each people" (Nehemiah, 13 : 23-24) to mention only two classical Western references.

[2] Anthropologists, historians, linguists, sociologists and psychologists have recognized and studied many phenomena related to language maintenance and language shift in their pursuit of other topics such as culture change and acculturation, nationalism, language interference, intergroup relations, second language learning and bilingualism. However, only rarely and recently has such interest led to a definition and formulation of this field of study in its own right. Among earlier partial efforts to do so one must mention those to be found in the huge "auslandsdeutsche Volksforschung" and "sprachwissenschaftliche Minderheitenforschung" literatures which continued from the latter part of the 19th century into World War II days (see e.g. 27, 53, 57, 63, 65, 75, 81), the 1953 Conference of Anthropologists and Linguists, and the exemplary work of Uriel Weinreich (87, 88) and Einar Haugen (36, 38). My indebtedness to the last two investigators is quite evident. Some of the earlier terms proposed for the phenomena here referred to have been spracherhaltung (53), language persistence (72), language replacement (62), language shift (62), language retention (36) and language displacement (38). The terminology here proposed (language maintenance and language shift), although somewhat more cumbersome than that previously proposed, may have the advantage of more clearly indicating that several simultaneous processes and outcomes require our attention.

1.0 HABITUAL LANGUAGE USE AT MORE THAN ONE POINT IN TIME OR SPACE UNDER CONDITIONS OF INTERGROUP CONTACT

The basic datum of the study of language maintenance and language shift is that two linguistically distinguishable[3] populations are in contact and that there are demonstrable consequences of this contact with respect to habitual language use. The consequences that are of *primary* concern to the student of language maintenance and language shift are *not* interference phenomena per se[4] but rather, degrees of maintenance or displacement in conjunction with several sources and domains of variance in language behavior. Thus, the very first requirement of inquiry in this field is a conceptualization of variance in language behavior whereby language maintenance and language shift can be accurately and appropriately ascertained. In the course of their labors linguists, psychologists, anthropologists and other specialists have developed a large number of quantitative and qualitative characterizations of variance in language behavior. By choosing from among them and adding to them judiciously, it may be possible to arrive at provocative insights into more sociolinguistic concerns as well. Whether those aspects of variance in language behavior that are currently conceived of as *qualitative* can be rendered ultimately commensurable with those that are currently conceived of as *quantitative* is a difficult problem which cannot now be answered definitely. As a result, these aspects may well be treated separately here.

1.1 DEGREE OF BILINGUALISM

For the student of language maintenance and language shift the *quantification* of habitual language use is related to the much older question of ascertaining *degree of bilingualism*. This question, in turn, has been tackled by a great number of investigators from different disciplines, each being concerned with a somewhat different nuance. Linguists have been most concerned with the analysis of bilingualism from the point of view of *switching or interference*. The measures that they have proposed from their disciplinary point of departure distinguish between phonological, lexical and grammatical proficiency and intactness.[5] At the other extreme stand educators who are

---

[3] Linguistic distinctions may be recognized at any level, e.g. between different languages (English and German in the American Midwest, or French and Flemish in Belgium), between different regional variants of a single language ("southern" and "non-southern" in Washington, D.C.), between different social-class variants of a single regional variant (middle class and lower class in New York City), etc. Only the first level, above, is of direct concern in this paper, although most of the topics considered may well be applicable to the other levels as well. Thus, the study of language maintenance and language shift may be of some interest to students of social dialectology.

[4] Weinreich makes this point very strongly: "Whereas interference, even in its socio-cultural setting, is a problem in which considerations of linguistic structure enter, the matter of language shifts is entirely extra-structural" (88, pp. 106-107). My own position is represented by the italicized *primary* above, and is discussed briefly in sections 1.1 and 3.4 below. It *does* seem to me that certain interference phenomena may well be of concern to us in connection with several aspects of the study of language maintenance and language shift.

[5] Thus, Haugen suggests, "distinct tests ... on each of the levels of phonemics, grammar, and basic

concerned with bilingualism in terms of *total performance contrasts* in very complex contexts (the school, even the society).[6] Psychologists have usually studied degrees of bilingualism in terms of speed, automaticity, or habit strength.[7] Sociologists have relied upon relative frequencies of use in different settings.[8] Thus, since a great number of different bilingualism scores or quotients are already available, the student of language maintenance and language shift must decide which, if any, are appropriate to his own concerns. If particular *sensitivities* to language behavior or if particular *organized approaches* to the data of habitual language use characterize the field of language maintenance and language shift, these must be brought into play in evaluating the methods suggested by scholars from other disciplines who have approached the quantification of bilingualism with other sensitivities or points of view.

1.11 *The need for a combination of interrelated measures*

It would seem that the linguist's concern with interference and switching is a necessary ingredient of the study of language maintenance and language shift, if only to answer the question "*which* language is being used". This question may be easier to answer in some cases than in others (e.g., it may be easier to answer in connection with encoding than in connection with inner speech; it may be easier to answer in connection with writing than in connection with speaking; it may be easier to answer in connection with formal and technical communication than in connection with intimate communication) for the "density" of interference and switching varies for the same individual from occasion to occasion and from situation to situation. Although interference and switching are lawful behaviors, there are advanced cases of language shift in which even linguists will be hard pressed to determine the answer to "which language is being used", particularly if a single supra-level answer is required.

Similarly, concern with relative proficiency, relative ease or automaticity, and relative frequency of language use in a contact situation are also necessarily of concern to the student of language maintenance and language shift, for these too are indications of whether or to what degree conservation or change are operative. However, these factors also vary from occasion to occasion and from situation to situation. Thus, in conclusion, the contribution that the student of language maintenance and

---

lexicon" (38, p. 76), with several further differentiations within these levels, some of which are indicated below. Mackey goes even further and suggests that separate measures are also required at the semantic and stylistic levels (66).

[6] Among the most recent measures are those of Herschel T. Manuel which seek to enable "educators to compare the achievement of a student in one language with his achievement in another" (68). It is typical of educational concerns to be more interested in determining the "overall" extent of bilingualism than in describing it in terms of quantified componential analysis.

[7] A convenient review of modern psychological approaches to the measurement of bilingualism is contained in (61), in which Wallace Lambert discusses his own studies as well as those of others.

[8] See, e.g., Hayden (39), John E. Hofman (43, 44) and Nahirny and Fishman (71). Perhaps the most influential examples of this approach are found in the work of Moses N. H. Hoffman (42) and Seth Arsenian (2).

language shift can make to the measurement of bilingualism, is precisely his awareness (a) that *various* measures are needed if the social realities of multilingual settings are to be reflected and (b) that these measures *can* be *organized* in terms of relatively *general variance considerations*. Of the many approaches to variance in language use that are possible the following have greatest appeal to the present writer:

a. *Media variance*: *Written*, *read* and *spoken* language. Degree of maintenance and shift may be quite different in these very different media.[9] Where literacy has been attained prior to interaction with an "other tongue", reading or writing in the mother tongue may resist shift longer than speaking. Where literacy is attained subsequent to (or as a result of) such interaction the reverse may hold true.

b. *Role variance*: Degree of maintenance and shift may be quite different in connection with *inner speech* (in which ego is both source and target), *comprehension* (decoding, in which ego is the target), and *production* (encoding, in which ego is the source). Where language shift is unconscious or resisted, inner speech may be most resistant to interference, switching and disuse of the mother tongue. Where language shift is conscious and desired other roles may be more resistive.

c. *Situational*[10] *variance*: *formal, semi-formal, informal, intimate*, etc., whether in accord with the distinctions recognized by Joos (52), Labov (58) or others who have recognized the greater redundancy and predictability of certain situations in comparison with others. Where language shift is unconscious or resisted more intimate situations may be most resistive of mother tongue interference, switching or disuse. The reverse may be true where language shift is conscious and desired.[11]

d. *Domain variance*, which will be discussed separately in section 1.2.

[9] Writing and reading are here differentiated as separate media primarily because each is capable of independent productive and receptive use. In general, the formal dimensions presented here make use of more distinctions than may be necessary in any one multilingual setting. Both empirical and theoretical considerations must ultimately be involved in selecting the dimensions most appropriate for the analysis of a particular setting.

[10] "Situation" and "setting" are frequently used interchangeably in the socio-linguistic literature. In this paper "setting" is intended to be the broader and more multifaceted concept. Thus, an exhaustive consideration of a multilingual "setting" would require attention to language choice data, sociocultural process data, data on attitudinal, emotional, cognitive and overt behaviors toward language, etc. "Situation" is reserved for use in characterizing certain features of communication at the time of communication.

[11] I am indebted to the work of many others for this tripartite division into media, role and situational sources of variance. Floyd Lounsbury suggested this particular *nomenclature* when I presented him with my dissatisfaction at referring to these distinctions in terms of "levels", "aspects", "modes" or other commonly used and insufficiently denotative designations. The distinctions themselves have a long history. They are obviously related to the distinctions between "receiving and sending bilinguals", "oral and visual bilinguals", and "close and distant bilinguals" suggested by Mary Haas (62, p. 42); to the distinctions between "mode of use" (speaking vs. writing and reading) suggested by Weinreich (88, p. 75); to the discussion of comprehension, production, frequency distortions and levels of style provided by Haugen (38, p. 85), and to the distinction between "internal functions" and "external functions" made by Mackey (66, pp. 55 and 63). Similar or related distinctions have certainly also been made by others.

1.2 LOCATION OF BILINGUALISM: THE DOMAINS OF LANGUAGE BEHAVIOR

The qualitative aspects of bilingualism are most easily illustrated in connection with the *location* of language maintenance and language shift in terms of *domains* of language behavior.[12] What is of concern to us here is the most parsimonious and fruitful designation of the occasions on which one language (variant, dialect, style, etc.) is habitually employed rather than (or in addition to) another. Thus far this topic has been of systematic concern only to a very few linguists, anthropologists and sociologists. Their interest has not yet led to the construction of measuring or recording instruments of wide applicability in contact settings that appear to be very different one from another. One of the major difficulties in this connection is that there is little consensus concerning the definition and classification of the domains of language behavior in bilingual communities.[13]

a. More than thirty years ago Schmidt-Rohr differentiated nine domains of language (81), namely: the family, the playground and the street, the school (subdivided into language of instruction, subject of instruction, and language of recess and entertainment), the church, literature, the press, the military, the courts, and the governmental bureaucracy (verwaltung).[14] Schmidt-Rohr also deserves recognition in connection with his claim that each domain had to be studied separately and a total inter-domain configuration presented if various "types" of bilingualism were to be differentiated and understood. Some subsequent students of language maintenance and language shift have required a more differentiated set of domains (17). Others have been satisfied with a much more abbreviated set.[15] Still others have required greater differentia-

[12] Haugen, Weinreich and Mackey all refer to "functions" of language rather than to "domains". However, in recent years, Jakobson, Hymes, Sebeok, Weir and other linguists and anthropologists have popularized the term "functions" in quite a different connection. As a result, it seems preferable to revert to the term "domain" (probably first advanced by Schmidt-Rohr, 81, p. 179) in an attempt to avoid confusion.

[13] The most extended recent discussions of the location of bilingualism pertinent to the study of language maintenance and language shift are those of Weinrich, Haugen and Mackey. Weinreich concludes that "a general survey of language functions in the bilingual communities of the world is not yet available" (88, p. 87). Haugen concludes that it is "necessary to devise subtler measures ... to draw a full profile of the speaker's activities and assign measures of language, function and skill for both languages" (38, p. 95). Mackey's theoretical cross-classification of external "functions" according to a set of "contacts" and "variables" (66) is referred to at various points throughout this section.

[14] Within a year of his original publication, Schmidt-Rohr felt it necessary to release a revised second edition. The major differences between the two are recognizable in the intense nazification and racialization of terms and interpretations as well as in the panegyric to National Socialism in the introduction and appendix to the second edition. A revised and somewhat improved statement of his domains appeared a few years later, together with a self-report questionnaire for use by auslandsdeutsche (82).

[15] Mackey recommended only five domains (66): home, community, school, mass media and correspondence, thus combining a media aspect with four domains mentioned above. At this time there is no empirical evidence concerning the adequacy of these particular domains. Both Barker (5) and Carroll Barber (3), in their studies of acculturating populations (Spanish American or Yaqui Indian) in Arizona, restricted themselves to four domains: familial (intimate), informal, formal and intergroup. In Barber's analysis the formal domain is limited to religious-ceremonial activities, while the inter-group domain is limited to economic, legal, and recreational activities. A similar consolidation or restriction in domains and activities is evident in J. Wm. Frey's analysis (26) of Amish "triple talk"

tion *within* particular domains. Domains such as these, regardless of their particular designation or number[16] are oriented toward *institutional contexts* or toward *socio-ecological co-occurrences*. They attempt to designate the major clusters of interaction situations that occur in particular multilingual settings. Domains such as these help us understand that *language choice* (41) and *topic* (16b), appropriate though they may be for analyses of individual language behavior at the level of face-to-face encounters, are themselves related to wide-spread socio-cultural regularities. Language choices, cumulated over many individuals and many choice instances, become transformed into the processes of *language maintenance* or *language shift*. Furthermore, if many individuals (or sub-groups) tend to handle topic *x* in language X, this may well be because this topic pertains to a domain in which that language is "dominant" for their society or for their sub-group. Certainly it is a far different social interaction when topic *x* is discussed in language Y *although it pertains to a domain in which language X is dominant*, than when the same topic is discussed by the same interlocutors in the language most commonly employed in that domain. By recognizing the existence of domains it becomes possible to contrast the language of topics for particular sub-populations with the language of domains for larger populations.

b. The appropriate designation and definition of domains of language behavior obviously calls for considerable insight into the socio-cultural dynamics of particular multilingual setting at particular periods in their history. Schmidt-Rohr's domains reflect multilingual settings in which a large number of socio-ecological co-occurrences, even those that pertain to governmental functions, are theoretically permissible to all of the languages present, or, at least, to multilingual settings in which such permissiveness is sought by a sizable number of interested parties. Quite different domains might be appropriate if one were to study habitual language use among children in these very same settings. Certainly, immigrant-host contexts, in which only the language of the host society is recognized for governmental functions, would require other and perhaps fewer domains, particularly if younger generations constantly leave the immigrant society and enter the host society. Finally, the domains of language behavior may differ from setting to setting not only in terms of number and designation but also in terms of level. One approach to the interrelationship between domains of language behavior defined at a societal-institutional level and domains defined at a

---

where three domains – home, school and church – suffice. It is quite obvious that Barker and Barber have formulated their domains at a more psychological level, whereas Frey's, like Schmidt-Rohr's, are along more ecological-institutional lines. The relationships between different domain levels such as these may enable us to investigate bilingualism and language maintenance or shift in newer and more stimulating ways (25).

[16] We can safely reject the implication still encountered in certain discussions of domains (14, 80) that there might be an invariant set of domains applicable to all multilingual settings. If language behavior is related to sociocultural organization, as is now widely accepted, then different kinds of multilingual settings should benefit from analyses in terms of different domains of language use, whether defined intuitively, theoretically, or empirically. Obviously the work-sphere domain, overlooked by Schmidt-Rohr, will be an appropriate domain for the analysis of many multi-lingual settings.

socio-psychological level (the latter being similar to the situational analyses discussed earlier) will be presented in our discussion of the *dominance configuration*, below.

c. The "governmental administration" domain is a social nexus which brings people together primarily for a certain *cluster of purposes*. Furthermore, it brings them together *primarily* within a certain set of status, role and environment co-occurrences. Although it is possible for them to communicate about many things, given these purposes and surroundings, the topical variety is actually quire small in certain media (e.g., written communication) and in certain situations (e.g., formal communication), and is noticeably skewed in the direction of *domain purpose* in almost all domains. Thus, a domain is a socio-cultural construct abstracted from topics of communication, relationships and interactions between communicators and locales of communication in accord with the institutions of a society and the spheres of activity of a culture in such a way that individual behavior and social patterns can be distinguished from each other and yet related to each other.[17] The domain is a higher order of abstraction or summarization which arrives out of a consideration of the socio-cultural patterning which surrounds language choices that transpire at the intra-psychic and socio-psychological levels. Of the many factors contributing to and subsumed under the domain concept some are more important and more accessible to careful measurement than others. One of these, topic, will only be referred to in passing in this paper (however, see 25). Another, role-relations, will be discussed in some detail.

d. In many studies of multilingual behavior the family domain has proved to be a very curcial one. Multilingualism often begins in the family and depends upon it for encouragement if not for protection. In other cases, multilingualism withdraws into the family domain after it has been displaced from other domains in which it was previously encountered. Little wonder then that many investigators, beginning with Braunshausen several years ago (6), have differentiated *within* the family domain in terms of "speakers". However, two different approaches have been followed in connection with such differentiation. Braunshausen (and, much more recently, Mackey, 66) have merely specified separate family "members": father, mother, children, domestic, governess and tutor, etc. Gross, on the other hand, has specified dyads within the family (31): grandfather to grandmother, grandmother to grandfather, grandfather to father, grandmother to father, grandfather to mother, grandmother to mother, grandfather to child, grandmother to child, father to mother, mother to father, etc. The difference between these two approaches is quite considerable. Not only does the second approach recognize that interacting members of a family (as well as the participants in most other domains of language behavior) are *hearers* as well as *speakers* (i.e., that there may be a distinction between multilingual *comprehension* and multilingual *production*), but it also recognizes that their language behavior may be

[17]   In contrast to "domains of language behavior" the functions of language (9, 47, 48) stand closer to socio-psychological analysis for they abstract their constituents primarily in terms of purposive-motivational considerations. The proposed functions have been advanced to help answer the questions "why did he speak and say it the way he did when he did?" The proposed domains are oriented more toward socio-ecological purpose than toward individual purpose.

more than merely a matter of individual preference or facility but also a matter of *role-relations*.[18] In certain societies particular behaviors (including language behaviors) are *expected* (if not required) of *particular individuals vis-a-vis each other*. Whether role-relations are fully reducible to situational styles for the purpose of describing habitual language choice in particular multilingual settings is a matter for future empirical determination.

The family domain is hardly unique with respect to its differentiability into role-relations. Each domain can be differentiated into role-relations that are specifically crucial or typical of it in particular societies at particular times. The religious domain (in those societies where religion can be differentiated from folkways more generally) may reveal such role-relations as cleric-cleric, cleric-parishioner, parishioner-cleric, and parishioner-parishioner. Similarly, pupil-teacher, buyer-seller, employer-employee, judge-petitioner, all refer to specific role-relations in other domains. It would certainly seem desirable to describe and analyze language use or language choice in a particular multilingual setting in terms of the crucial role-relations within the specific domains considered to be most revealing for that setting. The distinction between own-group-interlocutor and other-group-interlocutor may also be provided for in this way.[19]

The above considerations are sufficient to indicate that the student of language maintenance and language shift obviously requires a highly complex sort of evidence on habitual language use. Indeed, we can barely begin to approximate data collection and analysis in accord with all possible interactions between the several characteristics of language use mentioned thus far. However, only when our data will correspond more closely to complex models of language use will it become possible for students of language maintenance and language shift to derive valid and refined *dominance configurations* capable of representing the direction or drift of changes in bilingualism over time.

1.21 *The domains of language behavior and the compound-coordinate distinction*

If the concept of *domains of language behavior* proves to be a fruitful and manageable one (given future empirical attempts to render it more rigorously useful) it may also

[18] Unfortunately, the term *role* is currently employed in several somewhat different ways, e.g., "role in society" (mayor, untouchable, bank president), "role relation" vis-a-vis particular others (husband-wife, father-child, teacher-pupil), "occasional role" (chairman, host, spokesman), and "momentary role" (initiator of a communication, respondent, listener). It is in this last sense that the term "role" was previously used in connection with "role variance" above, while it is in the sense of "role relation": that the term "role" is now employed in our discussion of differentiations within the domains of language behavior. A less confusing terminology would certainly be helpful but would require the introduction of neologisms which would inevitably be confusing to all but their proud innovator.

[19] These remarks are not intended to imply that *all* role-relation differences are necessarily related to language-choice differences. This almost certainly is *not* the case. Just which role-relation differences *are* related to language-choice differences (and under what circumstances) is a matter for empirical determination within each multilingual setting as well as at different points in time within the same setting. This observation also applies to the variety of "social occasions" and "encounters" discussed by Goffman, only some of which may need to be retained (particularly for more traditional societies) once more general parameters such as those presented here have been studied adequately.

yield beneficial results in connection with other areas of research on bilingualism, e.g., in connection with the distinction between *coordinate* and *compound* bilingualism (16a, p. 140). The latter distinction arose out of an awareness (mentioned by several investigators over the years) that there are "at least two major types of bilingual functioning",[20] one (the compound type) being "characteristic of bilingualism acquired by a child who grows up in a home where two languages are spoken more or less interchangeably by the same people and in the same situations" and the other (the coordinate) being "typical of the 'true' bilingual, who has learned to speak one language with his parents, for example, and the other language in school and at work. The total situations, both external and emotional, and the total behaviors occurring when one language is being used will differ from those occurring with the other".[21] From our previous discussion of domains of language behavior it is clear that these two types of bilingual functioning have been distinguished[22] on the bases of some awareness, however rudimentary, that *bilinguals vary with respect to the number and overlap of domains in which they habitually employ each of their languages*. However, this is true not only initially, in the acquisition of bilingualism (with which the compound-coordinate distinction is primarily concerned) but also subsequently, *throughout* life. Initially coordinate bilinguals may become exposed to widespread bilingualism in which both languages are used rather freely over a larger set of overlapping domains (Table I). Similarly compound bilinguals may become exposed to a more compartmentalized environment, in which each language is assigned to very specific and non-overlapping domains.

Going one step further it appeares that the domain concept may facilitate a number of worthwhile contributions to the understanding of the compound-coordinate distinction in conjunction with language maintenance and language shift per se. Thus, domain analysis may help organize and clarify the previously unstructured awareness that language maintenance and language shift proceed quite unevenly across the several sources and domains of variance in habitual language use. Certain domains may well appear to be more maintenance-prone than others (e.g., the family domain in comparison to the occupational domain) across all multilingual settings characterized by urbanization and economic development, regardless of whether immigrant-

[20]   See Weinreich (88, pp. 9-10, 35 and 81-82) for several other early examples of the "two types of bilingualism" school of thought, many of which are quite similar to the coordinate-compound distinction. Still other early examples are found in the work of Schmidt-Rohr (81) and Swadesh (86a), and, most recently, in that of Vildomec (86b).

[21]   There continues to be a culture-bound suspicion that the latter type of bilingualism is not only "truer" but also inherently "healthier". See, e.g., Jakobson (62, p. 44) and Hymes (47, p. 43) to the effect that if the roles and settings of languages are not kept distinct "there may be personality difficulties" (47) and "even pathological results" (62). Schmidt-Rohr, Geissler and others working under much greater political-ethnocentric influence considered compound bilingualism to be the cause of "*racial*" degeneration and to lead to loss of depth, clarity and uniqueness in the *individual* (27, 33, 64, 81).

[22]   It is generally recognized that the labels coordinate and compound identify the extremes of a continuum of neurological organization and psychological functioning although for the sake of simplicity they are usually treated as if they pertained to a dichotomy.

TABLE I

Initial Type of Bilingual Acquisition and Subsequent Domain Overlap Type

Bilingual Acquisition Type	Domain Overlap Type	
	Overlapping Domains	Non-Overlapping Domains
Compound ("Interdependent" or fused)	Transitional bilingualism: the older second generation. The "high school French" tourist who remains abroad somewhat longer than he expected to.	"Cultural bilingualism": the bilingualism of the "indirect method" classroom whereby one language is learned through another but retained in separate domains.
Coordinate ("Independent")	Widespread bilingualism without social cleavage: the purported goal of "responsible" French-Canadians. The "direct method" classroom.	One sided bingualism or marked and stable social distinctions, such that only one group in a contact situation is bilingual or such that only particular domains are open or appropriate to particular languages.

host or co-indigenous populations are involved. Under the impact of these same socio-cultural processes other domains (e.g., religion) may be found to be strongly maintenance oriented during the early stages of interaction and strongly shift oriented once an authoritative decision is reached that their organizational base can be better secured via shift. Certain interactions between domains and other sources of variance may remain protective of contextually "disadvantaged" languages, even when language shift has advanced so far that a given domain as such has been engulfed. On the other hand, if a strict domain separation becomes institutionalized such that each language is associated with a number of important but distinct domains, bilingualism may well become both universal and stabilized even though an entire population consists of bilinguals interacting with other bilinguals. Finally, in conjunction with language maintenance and language shift among American immigrant groups the interaction between domain analysis and the compound-coordinate distinction may prove to be particularly edifying. Thus, as suggested by Table II, most late 19th and early 20th century immigrants to America from Eastern and Southern Europe began as compound bilinguals with each language assigned to separate and minimally overlapping domains. With the passage of time (involving increased interaction with English speaking Americans, social mobility, and acculturation with respect to other-than-language behaviors as well) their bilingualism became characterized, first, by far greater domain overlap (and by far greater interference) and then by progressively greater coordinate functioning. Finally, language displacement advanced so far that the mother tongue remained only in a few restricted and non-overlapping domains. Indeed, in some cases, compound bilingualism once more became the rule, except that the ethnic mother tongue came to be utilized via English (rather than vice-versa, as

TABLE II

Type of Bilingual Functioning and Domain Overlap During Successive States of Immigrant Acculturation

Bilingual Functioning Type	Domain Overlap Type	
	Overlapping Domains	Non-Overlapping Domains
Compound ("Interdependent" or fused)	2. Second Stage: More immigrants know more English and therefore can speak to each other either in mother tongue or in English (still mediated by the mother tongue) in several domains of behavior. Increased interference.	1. Initial Stage: The immigrant learns English via his mother tongue. English is used only in those few domains (work sphere, governmental sphere) in which mother tongue cannot be used. Minimal interference. Only a few immigrants know a little English.
Coordinate ("Independent")	3. Third Stage: The languages function independently of each other. The number of bilinguals is at its maximum. Domain overlap is at its maximum. The second generation during childhood. Stabilized interference.	4. Fourth Stage: English has displaced the mother tongue from all but the most private or restricted domains. Interference declines. In most cases both languages function independently; in others the mother tongue is mediated by English (reverse direction of Stage 1, but same type).

was the case in early immigrant days). Thus, the domain concept has helped place the compound-coordinate distinction in socio-cultural perspective, in much the same way as it may serve the entire area of language choice (25).

1.3 THE DOMINANCE CONFIGURATION

Sections 1.1 and 1.2, above, clearly indicate the need for basic tools of a complex and sophisticated sort. Precise measurement of *degree of maintenance or shift* will be possible only when more diversified measures of degree of bilingualism (including attention to media, role, and situational variance) are at hand. Precise measurement of *domains of maintenance or shift* will be possible only after concerted attention is given to the construction of instruments that are based upon a careful consideration of the various domains of language behavior mentioned in a scattered international literature. The availability of such instruments will also facilitate work in several related fields of study, such as the success of intensive second-language learning programs, accurate current language facility censuses, applied "language reinforcement" efforts, etc. Given such instruments, the inter-correlations between the several components of variance in degree of bilingualism will become amenable to study, as will the variation of such inter-correlations with age or with varying degrees of language ability, opportunity and motivation. The relationship between maintenance or displacement in the various domains of language will also become subject to scrutiny.[23] Speculation concerning the relationship between shifts in degree and direction of bilingualism and shifts in the domains of bilingualism will finally become subject to investigation.[24] Finally, out of all of the foregoing, it will become possible to speak much more meaningfully about the *dominance configurations* of bilinguals and of changes in these configurations in language maintenance-language shift contexts.[25]

1.31

Weinreich reintroduced the concept of *dominance configuration* as a result of his well founded dissatisfaction with the current practice of "tagging two languages in contact as respectively 'upper' and 'lower' at any cost" (88, p. 98). He correctly observes that "the difficulty of ranking two mother-tongue groups in hierarchical order is aggravated by the need to rank functions of the languages as well", but adds, in conclusion, that "it is therefore expedient, perhaps, to restrict the term *dominant* to languages in contact situations where the difference in mother-tongues is coupled with a significant difference in social status" (88, p. 98). For the purpose of studying language maintenance or language shift, this last recommendation would seem to be questionable on two counts. On the one hand it jumps from the *individual* to the *group or societal* level of analysis, whereas both the study of bilingualism and of language maintenance or language shift frequently require a determination of language dominance in the individual per se. On the other hand, it jumps from *language* to *non-language* criteria, whereas both of the aforementioned fields of inquiry usually require a determination of language dominance (or of change in dominance) based on language use alone.[26]

[23] Students of acculturation have asked whether there are "orders of structured activities which are "pillars" of a culture in the sense that effects on contact in these orders ramify widely into other orders of the culture. (If so) ... are they the same orders in different cultures or do they vary from culture to culture? Are there "carrier" activities in the contact situation which though relatively unaffected by contact themselves, nevertheless set up indirect effects on other sets of structured activities?" (Dohrenwend and Smith, 14, p. 37). These questions have very precise parallels in the study of language maintenance and language shift. Our ability to answer them will depend on our ability to specify the domains of language appropriately and to intercorrelate degrees of shift in the several domains.

[24] For a recent study conducted essentially along these lines see that of Joan Rubin (77). The growth of bilingualism in Paraguay seems to be due to a clearcut domain difference such that each language controls several crucial domains. As a result, monolinguals find it more and more necessary to learn the "other tongue", whether it be Spanish or Guarani. Rubin considers Paraguay to have "the highest degree of bilingualism in the world" due to the mutually exclusive domain pattern which has developed there.

[25] The question of dominance (or direction) of bilingualism arises less frequently today in the United States (or in other acculturated immigrant setting) where English (or another officially established language) may be assumed to be dominant and uniformally "available" in various bilingual contexts so that degree and location considerations do not apply to *it* nearly as much as they do to the immigrant languages. This situation must *not* be assumed to be universally the case in multilingual contact settings.

[26] If one mixes language and non-language criteria the relations between them cannot be examined.

For our purposes the dominance configuration constitutes an attempt ro represent the condition or direction of language maintenance and language shift in such a way as to recognize a multiplicity of considerations that are presumably incommensurable. "The dominance of a language for a bilingual individual can only be interpreted as a specific configuration or syndrome of characteristics on which the language is rated" (88, p. 79). Weinreich proposes seven characteristics on the basis of which dominance configurations may be constituted (in conjunction with the study of language interference): (a) relative proficiency, (b) mode of use,[27] (c) order of learning, (d) emotional involvement, (e) usefulness in communication, (f) function in social advance, and (g) literary-cultural value.[28] From the point of view of coordinated investigation into language maintenance or language shift several of these characteristics would seem to be of uncertain value. Thus, item (a) above would seem to be further analyzable into several components as has already been suggested in sections 1.1 and 1.2. Characteristic (b) certainly appears to be important and has already been referred to in section 1.1. Item (c) as well as items (e) through (g) appear to be antecedents, concurrents or consequences of language contact situations rather than aspects of degree or direction of bilingualism per se. As such they deserve to be considered in the second and third topical subdivisions of the study of language maintenance or language shift (see sections 2 and 3 below) rather than entered into the dominance configuration per se. Characteristic (d) is also of this latter variety and may properly be conceived of as the resultant of many experiences and values including those pertaining to characteristics (e) through (g) above. Thus, although global determinations of the "linguistic dominance of bilinguals", such as Lambert's (59), may well be both premature and insufficiently revealing from the point of view of the study of language maintenance and language shift, the particular configurational pattern suggested by Weinreich also would seem to require substantial revision.

1.32

Table III is primarily intended as an impressionistic summary of one possible approach to determining a dominance configuration based upon several *domains* of language behavior and *sources of variance* in language behavior specified earlier in our discussion. The types of language use data favored by linguists, psychologists and educators have been set aside temporarily in favor of grosser "frequency of use" data. However, of

---

As for individual and societal assessments of dominance, although both are clearly possible, it is likely that they would not correspond. Thus, a societal assessment of dominance would probably concentrate upon language use in institutional-organizationsl settings. These may actually account for a smaller percentage of interaction situations and, therefore, may be less important than non-institutionalized settings.

[27] Weinreich uses this term to refer to visual (writing, reading) exposure as contrasted with aural-vocal exposure. This is equivalent to my term "media variance" in section 1.1 above.

[28] In an earlier discussion (87) Weinreich presented a much different approach to the dominance configuration, more similar in many respects to that of Schmidt-Rohr, but with certain quantitative (rather than entirely qualitative) features.

TABLE III

Yiddish-English Maintenance and Shift in the United States: 1940-1960

Comparisons for Immigrant Generation "Secularists" Arriving Prior to World War I (First language shown is most frequently used; Second language shown is increasing in Use)

Sources of Variance			Domains of Language Behavior					
Media	Role	Situational	Family	Neighborhood		Mass Med.	Jew. Orgs.	Occup.
				Friends	Acquaints			
Speaking	Inner[a]	Formal	X[b]	X	X	X	X	X
		Informal	Y, E	Y, E	Y, E	E, E	Y, E	E, E
		Intimate	Y, E	Y, E	Y, E	E, E	Y, E	E, E
	Comp.	Formal	X	X	E, E	E, E	Y, E	E, E
		Informal	E, E	E, E	E, E	E, E	Y, E	E, E
		Intimate	Y, E	Y, E	X	X	X	X
	Prod.	Formal	X	X	E, E	X	Y, E	E, E
		Informal	E, E	E, E	E, E	X	Y, E	E, E
		Intimate	Y, E	Y, E	E, E	X	X	X
Reading	Comp.	Formal	Y, E	X	X	X	Y, E	X
		Informal	Y, E	X	X	X	Y, E	X
		Intimate	E, E	X	X	X	X	X
	Prod.[c]	Formal	Y, E	X	X	Y, E	Y, E	X
		Informal	Y, E	X	X	Y, E	Y, E	X
		Intimate	E, E	X	X	E, E	X	X
Writing	Prod.	Formal	X	X	X	X	Y, E	X
		Informal	E, E	E, E	X	X	Y, E	X
		Intimate	E, E	E, E	X	X	X	X

[a] For "speaking–inner–" combinations the domains imply topics as well as contexts. In all other instances they imply contexts alone.

[b] X = not applicable or no entry.

[c] For "reading–production" combinations the distinction between "family" and "mass media" domains is also a distinction between reading to others and reading to oneself.

primary interest at this time are the suggested parameters rather than the data approximations offered. An inspection of this Table reveals several general characteristics of the dominance configurations: (a) the dominance configuration summarizes multilingual language use data for a particular population studied at two points in time or space; (b) a complete cross-tabulation of all theoretically possible sources and domains of variance in language behavior does not actually obtain. In some instances, logical difficulties arise. In others, co-occurrences are logically possible but either necessarily rare or rare for the particular populations under study; (c) each cell in the dominance configuration summarizes detailed process data pertaining to the particular role-relations most pertinent to it and the topical/social encounter-range discovered; (d) the domains of language behavior that figure in a particular dominance configuration are selected for their utility (or promise) in conjunction with a particular multilingual setting at a particular time; (e) an exhaustive analysis of the data of dominance configurations may well require sophisticated pattern analyses or other mathematical techniques which do not necessarily assume equal weight and simple addativity for each entry in each cell;[29] (f) a much more refined presentation of language maintenance or language shift becomes possible than that which is provided by means of traditional mother tongue census statistics (54, 72);[30] (g) the integrative summary nature of the dominance configuration may obviate the proliferation of atomized findings although it can be based upon refined details; (h) finally, the dominance configuration does not preclude the combining or collapsing of domains or of sources of variance in language choice whenever simpler patterns are recognizable (e.g., "public" vs. "private" sphere or formal vs. informal situations).

1.33

All in all, the dominance configuration represents a great and difficult challenge to students of bilingualism and of language maintenance or language change. As is the case with most new integrative tools and concepts, its major problems and major promises still lie ahead. It is possible that serious problems of configurational analysis will arise in connection with it as they have in other areas in which syndromes of incommensurables are encountered.[31] However, the substantive challenges pertaining

[29] Disregarding this stricture an inspection of Table III prompts the following observations: (i) There is no cell in which the use of Yiddish is currently increasing in the studied population; (ii) reading is the most retentive area of media variance; (iii) inner speech is the most retentive area of role variance; (iv) formal usage is the most retentive area of situational variance; (v) the organizational context is the most retentive area of domain variance whereas the occupational context is the least retentive. All in all, this dominance configuration leaves one with the impression of greatest retention of Yiddish in circumstances that are either most intensely personal or most ritually symbolic.

[30] For a comparison of census data, dominance configuration data, and detailed role-process data dealing with related phenomena, see (24), in which the relationship between these several approaches is examined.

[31] Other problems of a technical measurement or recording nature can be anticipated, although no attempt will be made to discuss them at this time: the independence or independent importance of all of the measures provided for by the dominance configuration; individual vs. group forms; the need to disguise or insulate questions on language use ("One can gain the confidence of a bilingual by getting him to talk about the things he is interested in much more easily than by asking him searching questions about his language", 37, p. 21); provision for multi-lingual contact situations in contrast with "mere" bilingual situations; and the acceptability of self-report data (such as Ruth Johnston's, 48, 50), as contrasted with observed or demonstrated language use data. (Psychology and sociology have a greater tradition of self-report data, e.g. in the measurement of attitudes or preferences, although self-reports sometimes show little correlation with observed or demonstrated behavior. Nevertheless self-report data continue to be considered important in these disciplines, at least as a level of behavior noteworthy in itself. The relationship *between* self-reports of habitual language use in given domains

to the dominance configuration may well be more intriguing and unprecedented. Since domain analysis and the dominance configuration merely seek to provide a systematic approach to descriptive parameters some investigators will undoubtedly wish to utilize them in connection with *other formal features of communication than code-variety*. Thus, the study of "sociolinguistic variants" (i.e., of those linguistic alternations regarded as "free" or "optional" variants *within* a code) may gain somewhat from the greater socio-cultural context derivable via domain analysis and the dominance configuration. Other investigators might seek to establish cross-cultural and diachronic language-and-culture files in order to investigate the relationship between changes in language behavior (including changes in language choice) and other processes of socio-cultural change. In this connection, the dominance configuration may facilitate comparisons between settings (or between historical periods) of roughly similar domain structure. Still other investigators, more centrally concerned with multilingualism and with language maintenance or language shift, may well become interested in using this approach for the purpose of combining or refining the typologies and stages that have long been suggested by various investigators.[32] Ultimately, a relatively uniform but flexible analytic scheme such as that described here may enable us to arrive at valid generalizations concerning (a) the kinds of multilingual settings in which one or another configuration of variance in language choice obtains and (b) the language maintenance and language shift consequences of particular configurations of dominance or variance.

2.0 PSYCHOLOGICAL, SOCIAL AND CULTURAL PROCESSES RELATED TO STABILITY OR CHANGE IN HABITUAL LANGUAGE USE UNDER CONDITIONS OF INTERGROUP CONTACT

The second major topical subdivision of the study of language maintenance and language shift deals with the psychological, social and cultural processes associated with habitual language use under conditions of intergroup contact. Under certain conditions of interaction the relative incidence and configuration of bilingualism stabilizes

---

or sources of variance *and* the observations of field workers *or* the productions of Ss themselves have yet to be studied.) Finally, it may be anticipated that the larger the populations, and the more complex the societies involved, the more difficult will be the sampling problems encountered by dominance configuration analysis.

[32] Thus, the patterns yielded by the dominance configuration should enable us to either confirm or significantly revise Kloss's intuitive five fold classification of patterns of language use in multilingual settings (54): (i) only the given language is used for all communication purposes; (ii) the given language is used alongside another for all purposes; (iii) the given language is used only in correspondence and reading – alone or alongside another language also used for these same purposes; (iv) the given language is used only for business purposes, particularly with foreigners; (v) the given language is used only for advanced educational or scientific pursuits. Similarly, Carman's recent ten-stage analysis of language shift among immigrants settling in Kansas (10) may gain in precision and in recognizable relevance to earlier formulations of immigrant language shift phenomena when subject to dominance configuration and domain analysis.

and remains fairly constant over time within each interacting group. However, under other circumstances an "other tongue" may continue to gain speakers to the end that bilingualism initially increases and then decreases as the erstwhile "other tongue" gradually becomes the predominant language of the old and the mother tongue of the young. The second subdivision of the study of language maintenance and language shift seeks to determine the circumstances that distinguish between such obviously different conditions of interaction as well as the processes whereby either condition is transformed into the other. The processes pertaining to this topical subdivision may be conceived of either as antecedent, concurrent (contextual), or consequent variables, depending on the design of particular studies. Their major common characteristic is that they are primarily *outside* of the language domain per se.

Although it is currently impossible to specify in advance an invariant list of psychological, social and cultural processes or variables that might be of universal importance for an understanding of language maintenance or language shift, it may nevertheless be instructive to note those that have been mentioned by scholars who have devoted greatest attention to this topic thus far. Weinreich discusses the following ten "socio-cultural divisions" in some detail: geographic obstacles or facilitations,[33] indigenousness, cultural or ethnic group membership, religion, race, sex, age, social status, occupation, and rural vs. urban residence (88, pp. 89-97). Haugen also lists many of these same categories and, in addition, family, neighborhood, political affiliation (including nationality and citizenship) and education (38, p. 91). Mackey's list of external functions specifies several "variables" that may presumably modify language use: duration of contact, frequency of contact and "pressures" of contact derived from "economic, administrative, cultural, political, military, historical, religious or demographic" sources (66, p. 61-63).

Underlying (or overlying) psychological, social and cultural *processes* are less fully listed or discussed by any of the above scholars than are demographic *groupings* or institutional *categories* per se. The result of such reliance on disjointed categories has been that no broadly applicable or dynamic theories, concepts or findings have been derived from most earlier studies. Indeed, the study of language maintenance and language shift currently lacks either a close relationship to theories of socio-cultural change more generally or to theories of intergroup relations more specifically. Just as an understanding of social-behavior-through-language must depend upon a more general theory of society so the understanding of language maintenance and language shift must depend on a more general theory of socio-cultural contact and socio-cultural change.

2.1 THE PAUCITY OF CROSS-CULTURAL AND DIACHRONIC REGULARITIES

It would seem that since we are concerned with the possibility of stability or change in

[33] Weinrech points out that geographic obstacles (mountains, deserts, etc.) or facilitations (rivers, trade routes, etc.) in the path of group contact have frequently influenced group interaction and, therefore, language contact, including language maintenance and shift.

language behavior on the one hand, we must be equally concerned with all of the forces contributing to stability or to change in human behavior more generally, on the other. Thus the selection of psychological, social and cultural variables for the study of language maintenance and language shift may well be guided not only by impressions of what seem to be the most relevant processes in a particular contact situation but also by more general theories of personal, social and cultural change. This is not to imply that all forces leading to *change* in other-than-language behaviors *necessarily* also lead to language *shift*. Indeed, whether or not this is the case (or, put more precisely, a determination of the circumstances under which language and non-language behaviors change concurrently, consecutively or independently) constitutes one of the major intellectual challenges currently facing this field of inquiry. If this challenge is to be met, it will be necessary for the study of language maintenance and language shift to be conducted within the context of studies of intergroup contacts that attend to important other-than-language processes as well: urbanization (ruralization), industrialization (or its abandonment), nationalism (or de-ethnization), nativism (or cosmopolitanization), religious revitalization (or secularization), etc.

Our current state of generalizeable knowledge in the area of language maintenance and language shift is insufficient for the positing of relationships of cross-cultural or diachronic validity. Indeed, many of the most popularly cited factors purportedly influencing maintenance and shift have actually been found to "cut both ways" in different contexts or to have no general significance when viewed in broader perspective. Thus, Kloss illustrates that no uniform consequences for language maintenance or language shift are derivable from (a) absence or presence of higher education in the mother tongue,[34] (b) larger or smaller numbers of speakers, (c) greater or lesser between-group similarity, and (d) positive or hostile attitudes of the majority toward the minority (55, pp. 210-212). The presence of so many ambivalent factors is a clear indication that complex interactions between partially contributory factors (rather than a single overpowering factor) must frequently be involved and that a *typology of contact situations* may be required before greater regularity among such factors can be recognized.

Although debunking represents a rather primitive level of scientific development it may be a necessary stage on the path to greater maturity. Although we *cannot* currently formulate universally applicable regularities in our area of inquiry we *can* indicate that several earlier attempts along these lines fall somewhat short of their mark:

---

[34]   The realization that higher education (even when it is in the mother tongue) can be a two-edged sword represents a recent partial change in Kloss's thinking relative to his own earlier position (53) and that of von Pritzvald (75), Kuhn (57) and many others impressed with auslandsdeutsche phenomena in Slavic or other "underdeveloped" areas. On the other hand, Kloss continues to list "affiliation with denominations fostering parochial schools" among the six factors favorable to language maintenance for "normal, non-insulated" minority groups in the United States (55, pp. 206-209). Perhaps this should be taken as a *separation* rather than as an *education* variable.

2.11 *A few questionable generalizations*

a. *Language maintenance is a function of intactness of group membership or group loyalty, particularly of such ideologized expressions of group loyalty as nationalism.* Among the evidence pointing to the need for refining or justifying this view is that which reveals that the Guayqueries of Venezuela preserved their groupness by preserving their property relations while giving up their language and religion (45), that lower caste groups in India pursue Sanskritization (emulation) rather than solidarity as a means of intact group mobility (73), that "the Raetoromans, like the Italian Swiss, cultivate the fullest possible loyalty to their language without aspiring to such nationalistic goals as political independence" (88, p. 100), that the "Yiddishist movement in Eastern Europe before and after World War I similarly concentrated on a language program rather than on political organization" (88, p. 100); that second and third generation Americans frequently maintain "cultural (refinement) bilingualism" after ethnic group loyalty disappears at any functional level (20); that many auslandsdeutsche maintained their self-identification as Germans in the midst of Polish or Ukrainian majorities, long after completely giving up their German mother tongue (57); that language loyalty is low in many newly developing and highly nationalistic African states (8, 85);[35] that the aristocracy in Czarist Russia (and elites in several other countries at various other times) preferred a language other than their national vernacular without changing their national identity or loyalty, etc. Thus, it would seem, on the one hand, that language maintenance has continued under various and highly different forms of group membership, some of which have involved significant changes in traditional social relationships and in pre-established role-relations. On the other hand, it appears that group loyalty can be similarly (if not more) ubiquitous, continuing both with and without language maintenance. The American readiness to use language as an index of acculturation may, in itself, be

[35] The nationalism of modern developing countries seems to be much more characterized by *nationism* than by the nationalistic elaboration of ethnicity per se. It is much more concerned with the political and economic conditions of *nationhood* than with the internal, substantive content of *peoplehood*. The political and administrative limits of the new nations are now usually defined in advance of their formation rather than in the process of their formation. The new nations are less frequently formed as the result of the "painful but glorious" unification of former particularistics who have groped to define the language, the history, the customs, and the missions that unite them and set them apart from others. They are formed along supra-ethnic lines that normally follow colonial demarcations which depended on the fortunes of conquest and on the skills of treaty-making. Political and economic self-determination are much more prominent considerations in the new nations than is cultural self-determination of the pre- and post-World War I variety. Political leadership is much more evident than cultural leadership. The Western experience has typically been that industrialization preceded urbanization and that (particularly in Eastern Europe) nationalism preceded nationism and that the first set of phenomena preceded the second. In the new nations, the reverse sequences seems to be more common, and this may be among the major socio-cultural determinants de-emphasizing language issues in connection with local or regional languages, on the one hand, and which favor the continued use of supraregional and colonial languages, on the other. Indeed, it may be that language concerns are most noticeable today only where we find socio-cultural conflicts in which the likelihood of complete political separatism is highly problematic (Canada, Belgium, India, e.g.). This may partially explain the greater prevalence of language issues in southern Asia than in Africa.

quite culture-bound (78). Hymes' observation that "some languages do not enjoy the status of a symbol crucial to group identity" (47, p. 30) and Weinreich's observation that "the connection (between language maintenance and group maintenance) is thus at least flexible and cannot be taken entirely for granted" (88, p. 100) really represent important intellectual challenges to the study of language maintenance and language shift. We very much need a more refined understanding of the circumstances under which *behaviors toward language* and *behaviors toward the group* are related to each other in *particular* ways. We can recognize today that the pre-World War II views of many German students of language maintenance and language shift (as to whether language and language consciousness create – or are derived from – race, peoplehood and consciousness of kind) where too simplified and too colored by then – current political considerations. However, the fact remains that the relationship between language-saliency and group-saliency is almost as speculative today as it was at that time. Nevertheless, it does seem clear that a language undergoing massive displacement is not only retained in different degrees and in different domains by various sub-groups but that it is retained most fully by increasingly atypical sub-populations as displacement progresses.

b. *Urban dwellers are more inclined to shift; rural dwellers (more conservative and more isolated) are less inclined to shift.* This is one of the most reasonable and best documented generalizations in the study of language maintenance and language shift.[36] Nevertheless, it runs counter to the first mentioned generalization, above, in that *consciousness* of ethnicity and the *espousal* of nationalism have been primarily urban phenomena. Language revival movements, language loyalty movements, and organized language maintenance efforts have commonly originated and had their greatest impact in the cities. Intelligentsia and middle class elements, both of which are almost exclusively urban, have frequently been the prime movers of language maintenance in those societies which possess both rural and urban populations. Indeed, urban groups have been "prime movers", organizers or mobilizers more generally, that is in connection with other-than-language matters as well as in connection with language behavior and behavior toward language. Thus, whereas small rural groups may have been more successful in establishing relatively self-contained communities which reveal language maintenance through the preservation of traditional interaction patterns and social structures, urban groups, exposed to interaction in more fragmented and specialized networks, reveal more conscious, organized and novel attempts to preserve, revive or change their traditional language. The urban environment does facilitate change. However, the *direction of such change* has not always favored language shift at the expense of language maintenance. *When* it has favored the one and *when* the other (and when urban-inspired language shift has actually signified a return to a

---

[36] See, e.g., the reports of the American Council of Learned Societies (1), Carman (10), Geissler (27), Gerullis (28), Haugen (36), Hofman (44), Kloss (55), Kuhn (57), Pihlblad (74), Smith (84), Willems (90), etc. However, note Fishman's and Hofman's distinction between rural-urban differences in connection with between-group as contrasted with within-group language maintenance differentials (19).

languishing ancestral language), represents a further challenge to this field of study.[37]

c. *The more prestigeful language displaces the less prestigeful language.* Our earlier discussions of *sources of variance* and *domains of language behavior* may have prepared us for the realization that language prestige is not a unit trait or tag that can be associated with a given language under all circumstances. Indeed, our earlier discussions were necessary precisely *because* the prestige of languages can vary noticeably from one context to another and from one point of view to another. It is for this very reason that Weinreich recommends that "as a technical term ... 'prestige' had better be restricted to a language's value in social advance, or dispensed with altogether as too imprecise" (88, p. 79). However, even this limitation does not solve all of our problems since social advance itself is relative to various membership and reference groups. Advance in family and neighborhood standing may require a different language than advance in occupational or governmental standing. The fact that an overall hierarchy of reference groups may exist does not mean that the top-most reference group will be dominant in each face-to-face situation.[38]

It may be precisely because "prestige" obscure so many different considerations and has been used with so many different connotations[39] that the relationship between prestige data and language maintenance or language shift data has been rather more uneven than might otherwise be expected. Thus, whereas Hall claims that "It is hard to think of any modern instance in which an entire speech community is under pressure to learn a sub-standard variety of a second language" (34, p. 19), it is really not very hard to do so: A Low German dialect displaced Lithuanian in East Prussia before World War I, although many Lithuanians there were highly conversant with Standard German (28, p. 61). Unstandardized Schwyzertütsch is replacing Romansh, although several generations of Raetoromans have known Standard German as well (87, pp. 284-286). Standard German completely displaced Danish in a trilingual area of Schleswig, but it was itself then increasingly displaced by the local Low German dialect (83). Obviously, Schwyzertütsch maintains itself quite successfully in com-

---

[37] The related over-generalization that the upper and middle classes are more inclined to shift than are the lower classes requires no separate extended consideration here in view of the above remarks. (See e.g. H. A. Miller's claim that "when languages have given way ... it has been the intellectual class that has yielded while the simple, uneducated class has clung to its language" 6, p. 60). Like both of the previously mentioned over-generalizations this one is derived from over-reliance on data from a particular kind (or kinds) of language contact setting(s). Even within the "immigrant case" differences are encoutered in this connection. Thus while Willems reports that among German speakers in Brazil the middle and upper classes were more retentive (90), I have concluded from several studies of immigrants in the United States that the lower classes have been more retentive (22). It is obvious that these two immigrant contexts differ in many respects, particularly in connection with status differentials between the immigrant and indigenous populations.

[38] Herman makes this quite clear in his discussion of (a) conditions under which "background factors" will or will not dominate over "immediate situation factors" with respect to language choice, and of (b) conditions in which "immediate situation factors" will or will not dominate over "personal factors" (41). His paper is definitely among the more stimulating attempts to provide social-psychological theory for this area of study at the level of *individual language choice.*

[39] E.g., usefulness in communication, literary-cultural merit, emotional significance, overall respect, overall popularity, etc.

petition with Standard German; Landsmaal achieved considerable success (into the 1930's, at the very least) in competition with Dano-Norwegian; Yiddish won speakers and adherants among Russified, Polonized and Germanized Jewish elites in Eastern Europe before and after World War I; Castillian speaking workers settling in more industrialized Catalonia tend to shift to Catalan (although those settling in the Basque country do *not* tend to shift to Basque); etc. Indeed, the entire process whereby a few classical languages were displaced by "lowly" vernaculars and whereby some of the latter, in turn, were later displaced by still other and even "less prestigeful" vernaculars (13; the latter vernaculars are still frequently referred to as "dialects", e.g., Yiddish, Ukrainian, Byelo-Russian, Flemish, Afrikaans, Macedonian, to mention only European derivatives) indicates that the prestige notion is easily discredited unless serious qualifications and contextual redefinitions are attempted. This too may be an appropriate task for the study of language maintenance and language shift.[40]

All in all we will be hard put to find a single conclusion in this field of study that is not subject to question in the light of cross-cultural and diachronic study. This is not due to the fact that earlier conclusions are necessarily erroneous. It is simply due to the fact that they normally pertain to a very limited set of parameters and circumstances and that neither the original investigators nor their subsequent critics have been in a good position to state just what these were or are. A partial rectification of this state of affairs might obtain if the world-wide literature on language maintenenance and language shift could be subjected to secondary analysis on the basis of an advanced and uniform theoretical model. Under such circumstances, indeed, parameter estimation rather than merely hypotheses testing alone might finally become possible in this field of study.

2.2. TOWARD MORE GENERAL THEORY AND A MORE INCLUSIVE COMPARATIVE APPROACH

a. When two groups are in contact they (and, therefore, the languages that "represent" them to each other) are differentially involved in the crucial socio-cultural processes that characterize their interaction. These processes serve to increase or decrease interaction between the populations or sub-populations in question, to either detach them from or to confirm them in their accustomed sources of authority, to either lead

---

[40] In general, the phenomenological validity of the "prestige" concept is so widespread (i.e. speakers so commonly regard their language as appropriately prestigeful for *their* purposes) and the objective determination of the concept so difficult that the former level may be a better one to investigate than the latter. The fact that Hasidim in Williamsburg regard Yiddish as more appropriate for most of their purposes than either English, Hebrew or Hungarian, needs to be examined from the point of view of their values, goals and social organization rather than from any "more objective" point of view of language prestige. A differentiation of areas in which speakers perceive language "prestige" to be operative is contained in Laura Nader's "A note on attitudes and the use of language", *Anthrop. Ling.*, 4 (1962), no. 6, 24-29, and in Charles A. Ferguson's "Myths about Arabic", *Monograph Series on Language and Linguistics* (Georgetown University), 12 (1960), 75-82.

them to influence others or to be particularly receptive to influence from others, to either emphasize or minimize their own groupness and its various manifestations, to either rise or fall in relative power or control over their own and each other's welfare, to either view with positiveness or negativeness the drift of the interaction between them and to react toward this drift on the basis of such views. We must look to these engulfing socio-cultural processes and, particularly, to indices of individual and group involvement in them, in our efforts to explain the direction or rate of language maintenance and language shift.

However, after having appropriately selected and specified one or more variables from among the endless subleties that make up the "process" of socio-cultural change, it may still be found that their cross-cultural and diachronic study reveals inconsistent results. The "same" process (e.g. "urbanization", as measured by constant indices such as those selected and cross-culturally applied by Reissman, 76) may result in language shift *away* from hitherto traditional language in some cases, in language shift *back* to traditional languages in other cases, while revealing significantly unaltered maintenance of the status quo in still others. Under such circumstances a typology of contact situations might serve to control or regularize a number of group or contextual characteristics, in the manner of moderator variables, and, by so doing, reveal greater order in the data.

We all have an intuitive impression that the "American immigrant case" (24) is different from the "Brazilian immigrant case" (90); that the "Spanish conquest case" (7, 15) is different from the "Anglo-American conquest case" (12, 32); that the "immigrant case" in general is different from the "conquest case" in general; that the "Yiddish speaking immigrant to America case" (23) is different from the "German speaking immigrant to America case" (55), etc. The question remains how best to systematize these intuitive impressions, i.e., what variables or attributes to utilize in order that contact situations might be classified in accord with the differences between them that we sense to exist. In the terms of R. A. Schermerhorn's recently formulated typology (80) the "American immigrant case" immediately prior to World War I would be characterized as revealing (i) sharply unequal *power configurations* between non-English speaking immigrants and English-speaking "old Americans"; (ii) incorporation (rather than extrusion or colonization) as the *type of control* exercised by American core-society over the immigrants; (iii) marked plurality and recent immigration (rather than duality, intermediate plurality without recent immigration, or any other of a continuum of patterns) as the plurality pattern; (iv) intermediate stratification and substantial mobility within the *stratification pattern*; (v) widespread *mutual* legitimization of acculturation and de-ethnization as the *interpretation of contact* in philosophical or group-image terms; and (vi) growing industrialization, mass culture and social participation as *major social forces*.[41]

[41]   The inclusion of "major social forces" in Schermerhorn's typology carries one step beyond my own convictions that socio-cultural processes should be treated as variables rather than as classificatory attributes. Nevertheless Schermerhorn's approach does not preclude the study of degrees of any

Given the above typological framework it has proved possible to summarize the current status of language maintenance and language shift among pre-World War I immigrants in terms of a very few *pre-contact factors*, *host factors*, and *product factors* (24). Unfortunately, Schermerhorn's typology for intergroup contacts is so recent that it has not yet been widely tested on either practical or theoretical grounds, whether in conjunction with language maintenance and language shift or in conjunction with other topics in the area of intergroup relations. However, it may be expected that any typology based upon six parameters, each with several subdivisions, is likely to be somewhat unwieldy and require simplification.

At the opposite extreme of complexity from Schermerhorn's typology is one which is derivable from reviews of the extensive literature on auslandsdeutschtum (57a, 57b).[42] One of the major differentiations among German settlers seems to have been the *original legitimization and concentration of their settlements*. A three way break is recognizable here: *Stammsiedlungen* (settlements founded as a result of official invitation and assistance from non-German governments), *Tochtersiedlungen* (settlements founded by those who left the earlier Stammsiedlungen and who settled elsewhere as *groups*, but without governmental invitation or assistance), and *Einsiedlungen* (the inmigration of German individuals or of small, occupationally homogeneous groups into non-German communities). Another related distinction is that between the relative "cultural development" of the settlers and their hosts. During the decade before the second world war the two most frequently recognized co-occurrences were (a) *Einsiedlungen* of "culturally more mature" Germans living in the midst of a "culturally less developed" population, as opposed to (b) *Stamm* and *Tochtersiedlungen* of "culturally younger" Germans surrounded by a "more mature, nation-oriented" population. Thus, although only two diagonal cells of a theoretically complete two-by-two typology are extensively discussed, it is possible to find examples of the remaining cells as well. Even when limited to the two co-occurrences mentioned above very interesting and consistent differences appear both in rate and in stages of language shift and acculturation.[43] The implications of this rough typology and of the regulari-

---

particular major social force, taken as an independent variable, in conjunction with his overall typological approach.

[42] Kuhn seems to have developed the typology of German sprachinseln further than any of his contemporaries. He provides typologies according to (i) origin and colonization type, (ii) surroundings and (iii) period of settlement and age. In all, he discusses 15 characteristics of German sprachinseln, most of which are applicable to all types.

[43] In the case of Einsiedlungen of "culturally more mature" Germans the following progression of rough stages appears: (i) "other tongue" for communication with non-Germans, (ii) "other tongue" for communication with other German immigrants, (iii) "other tongue" for family communication, (iv) "other tongue" for internal speech, (v) national de-identification, (vi) ethnic-religious de-identification, (vii) intermarriage. In the case of *Stamm-* and *Tochtersiedlungen* of "culturally younger" Germans the following stages are most frequently differentiated: (i) national de-identification, (ii) ethnic de-identification, (iii) "other tongue" for communication with non-Germans *and* for internal speech, (iv) "other tongue" for communication with other Germans *and* with family, (v) religious de-identification and intermarriage. An overarching Protestant-Catholic difference (Catholics being more likely to experience rapid umvolkung) is also repeatedly stressed (30, 57a, 57b, 65).

ties that it has suggested deserve consideration in connection with quire different intergroup contact settings.[44]

c. Although the study of language maintenance or language shift *need* not be limited to the comparison of separate cases it is nevertheless undeniably true that the comparative method is quite central to inquiry within this topic area. Certainly the comparative method is indispensible in our pursuit of cross-cultural and diachronic regularities. Assuming that a relatively uniform set of appropriate socio-cultural process-measures could be selected and applied and assuming that a recognizably superior typology of contact situations were available it would then become possible to study:

(i) The same language group in two separate interaction contexts that are judged to be highly similar (with respect to primary socio-cultural process(es) and contact type), e.g., two separate German *Stammsiedlungen* in rural Poland.

(ii) The same language group in two separate interaction contexts judged to be quite dissimilar (with respect to major socio-cultural process(es) and contact type), e.g., one German-Swiss community in contact with Swiss Raetoromans and another German-Swiss community in Cincinnati, Ohio.

(iii) Different language groups in two separate interaction contexts judged to be highly similar (with respect to major socio-cultural process(es) and contact type), e.g., a Polish speaking and a Slovak speaking community, both of rural origin, in Cincinnati, Ohio.

(iv) Different language groups in two separate interaction contexts judged to be quite dissimilar (with respect to major socio-cultural process(es) and contact type), e.g., a German *Stammsiedlung* in rural Poland and a Slovak community in Cincinnati, Ohio.

Thus, by judiciously contrasting groups, socio-cultural processes and types of contact situations (*not* necessarily taken two at a time, if higher level interaction designs prove to be feasible) it should become possible to more meaningfully apportion the variance in language maintenance or language shift outcomes. Furthermore, the greater our insight with respect to socio-cultural processes and the more appropriate our typology of intergroup contact situations, the more possible it becomes to meaningfully assemble and analyze language maintenance and language shift files. Such files would permit both cross-cultural and diachronic analyses, of primary as well as of secondary sources, based upon comparable data, collected and organized in accord with uniform sets of socio-cultural processes and contact categories. This state of affairs is still far off but it is the goal toward which we may well attempt to move within this second topical subdivision of the study of language maintenance and language shift, once more basic methodological and conceptual questions reach a somewhat more advanced level of clarification.

[44] Yet another typology of contact settings may be derived from Weinreich's paper on bilingualism in India (89) in which exposure to contact, group size, functional importance of languages, and linguistic diversity are the major classificatory topics.

3.0 BEHAVIOR TOWARD LANGUAGE IN THE CONTACT SETTING

The third (and final) major topical subdivision of the study of language maintenance and language shift is concerned with *behavior toward language* (rather than with language behavior or behavior through language), particularly, with more focused and conscious behaviors on behalf of either maintenance or shift per se. Strictly speaking this subdivision may properly be considered as a subtopic under 2.0, above. However, it is of such central significance to this entire field of inquiry that it may appropriately receive separate recognition. Three major categories of behaviors toward language are discernible within this topical subdivision:

3.1 ATTITUDINAL-AFFECTIVE BEHAVIORS

We know all too little about language oriented attitudes and emotions (running the gamut from language loyalty – of which language nationalism is only one expression – to language antipathy – of which language betrayal is only one expression) as distinguished from attitudes and emotions toward the "typical" speakers of particular language variants. The features of language that are considered attractive or unattractive, proper or improper, distinctive or common-place, have largely remained unstudied. However, in multilingual settings, particularly in those in which a *variety* of "social types" are associated with *each* language that is in fairly widespread use, languages per se (rather than merely the customs, values and cultural contributions of their modal speakers) are reacted to as "beautiful" or "ugly", "musical" or "harsh", "rich" or "poor", etc. Generally speaking, these are language stereotypes (17). However, the absence or presence of a "kernel of truth" (or of verifiability itself) is entirely unrelated to the mobilizing power of such views.

The manifold possible relationships between language attitudes and language use also remain largely unstudied at the present time. Although Lambert reports a positive relationship between success in school-based second language learning and favorable attitudes toward the second language and its speakers (60), this finding need not be paralleled in all natural multilingual contact settings. Thus, Ruth Johnston reports a very low correlation between subjective and objective (external) assimilation in the language area (50). Many older Polish immigrants in Australia identified strongly with English, although they hardly spoke or understood it several years after their resettlement. On the other hand, many young immigrants spoke English faultlessly and yet identified strongly with Polish, although they spoke it very poorly (49). Similarly, in summarizing his findings concerning current language maintenance among pre-World War I arrivals in the United States coming from rural Eastern and Southern European backgrounds, Fishman reports a negative relationship over time between *use rates* and *attitudinal positiveness* (24). This finding was not predictable from most earlier studies of language maintenance or language shift in immigrant or non-immigrant settings. We are quite far from knowing whether its explanation in American contextual terms (i.e., in terms of the greater acceptability of marginal rather than of either primordial or ideologized ethnicity) would also apply to other settings in which similar developments might obtain.

3.2 OVERT BEHAVIORAL IMPLEMENTATION OF ATTITUDES, FEELINGS AND BELIEFS

Both language reinforcement ("language movements") and language planning may be subsumed under this heading. Language reinforcement may proceed along voluntary as well as along official routes and encompasses organizational protection, statutory protection, agitation and creative production. As for language planning, it has not always been recognized that much (if not most) of its activity (standardization, regularization, simplification, purification, amplification, hybridization, etc.) occurs in the context of language maintenance or language shift (21).

The possible relationships between language reinforcement (or language planning), on the one hand, and the waxing or waning of actual language use (or of other socio-cultural processes) are largely unknown at this time. Data from the American immigrant case imply that a number of unexpected relationships may obtain in that novel reinforcements may be introduced as actual language use diminishes.

Advocates of languages that are undergoing displacement are often much more exposed to (and identified with) the values and methods of their linguistic competitors than were their less exposed (and less threatened) predecessors. As a result, they are more likely to adopt organized protective and publicity measures from more "advantaged" co-territorial (other-tongue) models to serve language maintenance purposes. The introduction of a few ethnically infused languages into the curricula of American high schools, colleges and universities represents just such a recent innovation on behalf of mother-tongue maintenance – and an even more de-ethnicized one than was the innovative establishment of ethnic group schools, cultural organizations and camps prior to World War I.[45] In contrast, the normal processes of controlled *language change* and the more aroused processes of conscious *language planning* may require more than "last ditch" ingenuity. However, to what extent reinforcement and planning are differently balanced given varying degrees of displacement or augmentation is currently unknown but worthy of study.

3.3 COGNITIVE ASPECTS OF LANGUAGE RESPONSE

Constantly flitting between the above two categories and overlapping partially with the one, with the other, or with both are such matters as: *consciousness* of mother tongue (or other tongue) as an entity separate from folkways more generally; *knowledge*

[45] Similar phenomena have occurred previously in American history with the de-ethnication of the mother tongues of German and Scandinavian immigrants (36, 55).

of synchronic variants, language history and literature; and *perceptions of language as a component of "groupness"*. We have little systematic information concerning the circumstances under which language consciousness, language knowledge and language-related groupness-perceptions do or do not enter into reference group behavior in contact situations. As a result, it is difficult to say at this time whether or when language maintenance and language shift are ideologically mediated as distinguished from their more obvious situational and instrumental determinants discussed thus far. We recognize very gross long-term contrasts in this connection, namely, that there were periods and regions when language "was in no way regarded as a political or cultural factor, still less as an object of political or cultural struggle" (56, p. 6); that there were other periods and regions marked by a sharp increase in such regard, so that language became a principle "in the name of which people ... (rallied) themselves and their fellow speakers consciously and explicitly to resist changes in either the functions of their language (as a result of a language shift) or in the structure or vocabulary (as a consequence of interference) (88, p. 99)",[46] and that there currently seems to be less of this than previously, particularly if we compare African with European nation-building. However, gross differentiations such as these are patently insufficient to enable us to clarify the conditions under which language becomes a prominent component in *perceptions* of "own-groupness" and "other groupness". This topic (language-related groupness-perception) is, of course, closely related to one previously mentioned, namely, the role of language in group membership and in group functioning (see section 2.11a, above). In the American immigrant case we have seen a growing dissociation between self-perceived ethnic identification and language maintenance. Far from being viewed as necessary components of groupness (whether in the sense of resultants or contributors) non-English mother tongues appear to be viewed increasingly in terms of non-ethnic *cultural* or non-ethnic *practical* considerations (24, 71). At the same time, some form of ethnic self-identification is frequently still reported by many of those who no longer claim any facility at all in their ethnic mother tongues, implying that in the American immigrant case some kind of ethnicity usually appears to be a much more stable phenomenon than does language maintenance (29). Most immigrants became bilingual much before they embarked on de-ethnization or seriously contemplated the possibility of bi-culturism. However, there were obviously exceptions to this process, both in the United States and in other contact settings. We certainly do not seem to be in a position to indicate the underlying regularities in this subtle area of inquiry at the present time.

We know very little about the interactions *among* the three components of behavior toward language or about the interaction *between* any of these components and the larger psychological, social and cultural processes discussed earlier. Rather than

---

[46] The implication of this quotation is that language loyalty is necessarily or primarily defensive in nature; however, perceived threat (or advantage) may be reacted to agressively as well. Thus, language loyalty may seek to expand the permissible or required domains of one's language, i.e., to *insist on changes* rather than merely to resist them.

being a "natural", omnipresent condition, either in monolingual or in multilingual settings, heightened and integrated behaviors toward language may be related to somewhat rare and advanced symbolic and ideological extensions of primordial ethnicity. Such extensions may well require a particular form of culture and a particular group of custodians for their preservation and further development. Nevertheless, neither of these desiderata need have invariable consequences for behavior toward language. Even where heightened and integrated behaviors toward language are culturally present they will not be equally operative in all situations or among all population sub-groups. Furthermore, even where they are culturally present they need not be uniformly related to other symbolically elaborated forms of behavior. Thus, this area remains the most unsystematized topical sub-division of the study of language maintenance and language shift. Perhaps it can be clarified in the future as a result of concomitant clarification and constant interrelation in connection with the two other major sub-divisions within this field of inquiry.

3.4 INTERFERENCE AND SWITCHING

Within the topical subdivision of behavior toward language we once again meet the topic of interference and switching, first introduced in section 1.1, above. The absence or presence of interference and switching can have cognitive, affective and overt implementational consequences for language maintenance and language shift. Certainly, both interference and switching are related to type and location of bilingualism, on the one hand, and to socio-cultural processes and contact types, on the other hand. Moreover, within this topical subdivision it is appropriate to stress that where attitudes and awarenesses concerning purism obtain, interference is sometimes viewed as *an imperfection* – not in the speaker or in his productions but *in the language itself*.[47] At the opposite pole, there are multilingual contact situations in which conscious, purposive interference obtains. In these instances speakers attempt to incorporate into their language usage as many elements or features as possible from another language including (in very advanced cases) interference in stress patterns, intonation, and *denkformen*.[48] In either case (i.e., when interference occurs although it is considered undesirable, or when interference occurs and is considered desirable) inter-

[47] Negative attitudes toward mother tongues viewed by their speakers as suffering from excessive interference are revealed by such designations as gemixste pickles and die schonste lengvitch (in referring to American-German); Yankee-Dutch (Netherlandish); Yankee-Yiddish and Yinglish (Yiddish); Minnesota-Norwegian (Norwegian); Finglish (Finnish); etc., to mention instances only from the American immigrant scene. A common international designation is "jargon", this term (or an equivalent) sometimes being accepted as the official name of vernaculars (rather than being restricted to makeshift languages alone). It may very well be that languages or styles revealing considerable stable interference are particularly likely to develop when more substantial language shift is inhibited although group interaction is very substantial.
[48] There have been many proposed "language reforms" along such lines; see, e.g., the proposal of Elias Moles (70) in connection with American English.

ference is not always considered to be all of one piece. Certain occurrences are considered to be more acceptable, excusable, permissible, necessary than others. In either case it can become a factor in hastening language shift, particularly since bilinguals tend to interpret interference in each of the languages known to them quite differently. Finally, at a point when language shift is appreciably advanced, certain sounds and forms of the language undergoing displacement may become so difficult for the average speaker (while errors in connection with them become so stigmatized among purists) that this in itself may accelerate further shift. All in all, recognition of interference, attitudes toward interference, and the behavioral consequences of interference represent interesting and important topics within the field of language maintenance and language shift.

4.0 SUMMARY AND CONCLUSIONS

Various language maintenance and language shift phenomena have long been of interest to scholars and to laymen. Several sub-topics within this area have undisputed relevance to the daily concerns and joys of millions. Others, of more theoretical interest, are closely related to topics of recognized concern to linguists, anthropologists, sociologists, psychologists, political scientists, educators, etc. Culture contact and language contact will always be with us, and out of these contacts will come modifications in habitual language behavior as well as attempts to restrain or channel such modifications. Whether (or when) language habits change more or less quickly than others, whether (or when) language loyalties are more or less powerful than others, indeed, whether (or when) men can live in a supraethnic tomorrow without strong links (linguistic and non-linguistic) to their ethnic yesterday and today – these are questions to which there are currently no definitive answers. However, interest in social-psychological aspects of language behavior is currently growing (whether under that name or under the name of socio-linguistics, anthropo-linguistics, ethno-linguistics, the ethnography of speaking, the ethnography of communication, the sociology of language, or some other designation). In most instances, there is some recognition of language maintenance and language shift as a crucial topic within the field of social behavior through language. This growing interest will undoubtedly contribute answers to many of the currently unanswerable questions within this field of inquiry.

Three major subdivisions of the study of language maintenance and language shift have been suggested. The first deals with the precise establishment of habitual language use in a contact situation. This requires instruments, not yet available, for the measurement of *degree of bilingualism* and of *location of bilingualism* along sociologically relevant dimensions. Degree of bilingualism, hitherto recognizable in terms of automaticity, proficiency and code-intactness at the phonetic, lexical and grammatical levels, must also be investigated with respect to situational variance, role variance and media variance. *Location of bilingualism* requires investigation with respect to variance in appropriately designated domains of language, each domain being abstracted from patterned role relations, social occasions, encounters, topics and/or other lower order phenomena. The complex relationships between the several components of degree of bilingualism and location of bilingualism may be represented by a *dominance configuration* which, in turn, may or may not be reducible to a single index of direction of bilingualism. The drift of language maintenance or language shift may be established by diachronic measures pertaining to some or all of the above factors.

The second major topical subdivision of the study of language maintenance and language shift deals with psychological, social and cultural processes that are associated with ascertained changes in habitual language use. No simple conceptual systematization of these processes is currently available although several preliminary typologies of "contact situations" exist and require further refinement in cross-cultural perspective.

The third (and final) major subdivision of the study of language maintenance and language shift pertains to behavior toward language, including (but not limited to) more focused and conscious behaviors on behalf of maintenance or shift. Three major sub-topics within this topic are recognizable: attitudinal-affective behaviors (loyalty, antipathy, etc.), overt behavioral implementation (control or regulation of habitual language use via reinforcement, planning, prohibition, etc.), and (overlapping partially with each of the two foregoing sub-topics) cognitive behaviors (language consciousness, language knowledge, language-related group-perceptions, etc.).

The exhaustive study of language maintenance and language shift ultimately involves the diachronic and synchronic interrelation of the above three topical subdivisions along conceptual lines. In terms of systematic inquiry the field as such is still in its infancy. Since the basic instruments required for the establishment of degree and direction of language maintenance or language shift are still lacking, that would seem to be a most important area for concentrated and sophisticated attention in the near future. In addition, once such instruments are available, it would seem to be of great importance to undertake the cross-cultural (comparative) study of language maintenance and language shift guided by consistent theoretical considerations. The current writer hopes to engage in both of these undertakings in the years ahead.[49]

[49] This Appendix was written during the 1963-64 academic year, after the completion of the Language Resources Project and of all of the reports directly related to it. It represents a re-evaluation of the work completed by that project and a perspective on future research. It was stimulated by my interaction with the Fellows of the Center for Advanced Study in the Behavioral Sciences in whose company I spent that delightful year. I wish to express my sincere thanks to the following friends and colleagues for their many helpful comments on earlier drafts of this paper: Susan Ervin, John J. Gumperz, Einar Haugen, John E. Hofman, Wallace E. Lambert, Vladimir C. Nahirny, Leonard Savitz, Thomas A. Sebeok, M. Brewster Smith, and Uriel Weinreich.

REFERENCES

1. American Council of Learned Societies, Conference on Non-English Speech in the United States. *Bulletin*, 1942, no. 34.

2. Arsenian, Seth, *Bilingualism and Mental Development* (New York, Columbia University Teachers College, 1937).

3. Barber, Carroll, "Trilingualism in Pascua; Social Functions of Language in an Arizona Yaqui Village", M.A. Thesis, University of Arizona, 1952.

4. Barker, George C., "The social functions of language", *Etc.*, 2 (1945), 228-234.

5. Barker George C., "Social functions of language in a Mexican-American Community", *Acta Americana*, 5 (1947), 185-202.

6. Braunshausen, Nicolas, "Le bilinguisme et la famille", in *Le Bilinguisme et l'Education* (Geneva-Luxemburg, Bureau International d'Education, 1928).

7. Bright, William, "Animals of acculturation in the California Indian languages", *University of California Publications in Linguistics*, 4 (1960), no. 4, 215-246.

8. Brosnahan, L. F., "Some aspects of the linguistic situation in tropical Africa", *Lingua*, 12 (1963), 54-65.

9. Buhler, Karl, *Sprachtheorie* (Jena, Gustav Fischer, 1934).

10. Carman, J. Neale, Personal communication regarding a forthcoming second volume of *Foreign-Language Units of Kansas; Historical Atlas and Statistics* (Lawrence, Univ. of Kansas Press, 1962).

11. Chambers, W. W., "Language and nationality in German pre-Romantic and romantic thought", *Modern Language Review*, 41 (1946), 382-392.

12. Cook, S. F., "The conflict between the California Indian and white civilization", *Ibero-Americana*, 21 (1943), 1-194; 22, 1-55; 23, 1-115; 24, 1-29.

13. Deutsch, Karl W., "The trend of European nationalism – The language aspect", *American Political Science Review*, 36 (1942), 533-541.

14. Dohrenwend, Bruce P., and Robert J. Smith, "Toward a Theory of acculturation", *Southwest J. of Anthrop.*, 18 (1962), 30-39.

15. Dozier, Edward P., "Resistance to acculturation and assimilation in an Indian pueblo", *American Anthropologist*, 53 (1951), 56-66.

16a. Ervin, Susan M., and Charles E. Osgood, "Second language learning and bilingualism", *J. of Abnorm. and Soc. Psychol.*, 49 (1954). Supplement, 139-146.

16b. Ervin, Susan M., "An analysis of the interaction of language, topic and listener", *American Anthropologist*, 66 (1964), Part 2, 86-102.

17. Fishman, Joshua A., "The process and function of social stereotyping", *J. Soc. Psychol.*, 43 (1956), 27-64.

18. Fishman, Joshua A., et al., *Language Loyalty in the United States* (New York, Yeshiva University, 1964). (Mimeographed report in three volumes prepared for the Language Research Section, U.S. Office of Education.)

19. Fishman, Joshua A., and John E. Hofman, "Mother tongue and nativity in the American population", in Fishman, J. A., et al., *Language Loyalty in the United States*, Chapter 2.

20. Fishman, Joshua A., and Vladimir C. Nahirny, "The ethnic group school in the United States", in Fishman, J. A., et al., *Language Loyalty in the United States*, Chapter 6. (Also, *Sociology of Education*, 37, 1964, 306-317.)

21. Fishman, Joshua A., "Planned reinforcement of language maintenance in the United States; suggestions for the conservation of a neglected national resource", in this volume, Chapter 14, pp. 369-391.

22. Fishman, Joshua A., "Language maintenance in a supra-ethnic age; summary and conclusions", in this volume, Chapter 15, pp. 392-411.

23. Fishman, Joshua A., "Language Maintenance and language shift in certain urban immigrant environments: The case of Yiddish in the United States", *Europa Ethnica* (in press).

24. Fishman, Joshua A., "Language maintenance and language shift: The American Immigrant Case', *Sociologus* (in press).

25. Fishman, Joshua A., "Domains of language choice in multilingual settings", *Linguistique* (in press).

26. Frey, J. William, "Amish 'triple talk'", *American Speech*, 20 (1945), 85-98.
27. Geissler, Heinrich, *Zweisprachigkeit deutscher Kinder im Ausland* (Stuttgart, Kohlhammer, 1938).
28. Gerullis, Georg, "Muttersprache und Zweisprachigkeit in einem preussisch-litauischen Dorf", *Studi Baltici*, 2 (1932), 59-67.
29. Glazer, Nathan, and Daniel P. Moynihan, *Beyond the Melting Pot* (Cambridge, M.I.T. and Harvard Univ. Press, 1963).
30. Grentrup, Theodor, *Religion und Muttersprache* (Münster, Aschendorffsche Verlagsbuchhandlung, 1932).
31. Gross, Feliks, "Language and value changes among the Arapho", *Intern. J. of Amer. Ling.*, 17 (1951), 10-17.
32. Gulick, John, "Language and passive resistance among the eastern Cherokees", *Ethnohistory*, 5 (1958), 60-81.
33. Guntert, Hermann, "Neue Zeit – neues Ziel", *Wörter und Sachen*, 19 (1938), (n.s. 1), 1-11.
34. Hall, Robert A., Jr., "Bilingualism and applied linguistics", *Zeitschrift für Phonetik und allgegemeine Sprachwissenschaft*, 6 (1952), 13-30.
35. Hansen, Marcus L., *The Immigrant in American History*. Arthur M. Schlesinger, ed. (Cambridge, Harvard Univ. Press, 1940).
36. Haugen, Einar, *The Norwegian Language in America*, 2 volumes (Philadelphia, Univ. of Pennsylvania Press, 1953).
37. Haugen, Einar, "Some pleasures and problems of bilingual research", *International Journal of American Linguistics*, 20 (1954), 116-122.
38. Haugen, Einar, *Bilingualism in the Americas: A Bibliography and Research Guide* (= *Publication Number 26 of the American Dialect Society*) (University, Alabama, Univ. of Alabama Press, 1956).
39. Hayden, Robert G., "Some community dynamics of language maintenance", in this volume, Chapter 8, pp. 190-205.
40. Hayden, Robert G., and Joshua A., Fishman, "The impact of exposure to ethnic mother tongue on foreign language teachers in American high schools and colleges", in Fishman, J. A., et al., *Language Loyalty in the United States*, Chapter 13. (Also in *Modern Language Journal*, 48, 1964, 262-274.)
41. Herman, Simon N., "Explorations in the social-psychology of language choice", *Human Relations*, 14 (1961), 149-164.
42. Hoffman, Moses, N. H., *The Measurement of Bilingual Background* (New York, Columbia University Teachers College, 1934).
43. Hofman, John E., "Mother tongue retentiveness in ethnic parishes", in this volume, Chapter 6, pp. 127-155.
44. Hofman, John E., "The language transition in some Lutheran denominations", in Fishman, J. A., et al., *Language Loyalty in America*, Chapter 10.
45. Hohenthal, W. D., and Thomas McCorkle, "The problem of aboriginal persistance", *Southwestern Journal of Anthropology*, 11 (1955), 288-300.
46. Homeyer, Helen, "Some observations on bilingualism and language shift in Italy from the sixth to the third century B.C.", *Word*, 13 (1957), 415-440.
47. Hymes, Dell H., "The ethnography of speaking", in Gladwin, T. and W. C. Sturtevand (eds.), *Anthropology and Human Behavior* (Washington, D.C., Anthropology Society of Washington, 1962), pp. 13-53.
48. Jakobson, Roman, "Closing statement: linguistics and poetics", in Sebeok, T. A. (ed.), *Style in Language* (New York, Technology Press of M.I.T. and Wiley, 1960), pp. 350-377.
49. Johnston, Ruth, "Factors in the Assimilation of Selected Groups of Polish Post-War Immigrants in Western Australia". Unpublished Ph.D. Dissertation, University of Western Australia (Perth), 1963.
50. Johnston, Ruth, "A new approach to the meaning of assimilation", *Human Relations*, 16 (1963), 295-298.
51. Jones, Frank E., and Wallace E. Lambert, "Attitudes toward immigrants in a Canadian community", *Public Opinion Quarterly*, 23 (1959), 538-546.
52. Joos, Martin, "The isolation of styles", *Monograph Series on Languages and Linguistics, Institute of Languages and Linguistics*, Georgetown University, 12 (1959). (Section IV: "Trends in Modern Linguistic Theory"), 107-113.

53. Kloss, Heinz, "Spracherhaltung", *Archiv für Politik und Geschichte*, 8 (1927), 456-462.
54. Kloss, Heinz, "Sprachtabellen als Grundlage für Sprachstatistik, Sprachenkarten und für eine allgemeine Sociologie der Sprachgemeinschaften", *Vierteljahrschrift für Politik und Geschichte*, 1 (1929), (7), 103-117.
55. Kloss, Heinz, "German-American language maintenance efforts", in this volume, Chapter 9, pp. 206-252.
56. Kohn, Hans, *The Idea of Nationalism; A Study of Its Origins and Background* (New York, MacMillan, 1944).
57a. Kuhn, Walter, *Die Jungen Deutschen Sprachinseln in Galizien; Ein Beitrag zur Methode der Sprachinselforschung* (Münster, Aschendorffsche Verlagsbuchhandlung, 1930).
57b. Kuhn, Walter, *Deutsche Sprachinsel-Forschung* (Plauen, Günther Wolff, 1934).
58. Labov, William, "Phonological indices of stratification". Paper presented at the Annual Meeting of the Amer. Anthrop. Assoc., San Francisco, Nov. 22, 1963.
58. Labov, William, "Phonological correlates of social stratification", *American Anthropologist*, 66 (1964), Part 2, 164-176.
60. Lambert, Wallace E., R. C. Gardner, H. C. Barick, and K. Tunstall, "Attitudinal and cognitive aspects of intensive study of a second language", *J. of Abnorm. and Soc. Psychol.*, 66 (1963), 358-368.
61. Lambert, Wallace E., "Psychological approaches to the study of language. Part II: On second-language learning and bilingualism", *Modern Language Journal*, 47 (1963), 114-121.
62. Lévi-Strauss, Claude, Roman Jakobson, C. F. Voegelin and Thomas A. Sebeok, *Results of the conference of anthropologists and linguists. Memoirs* (= Supplement to *International Journal of American Linguistics*, 1953, 19, no. 2).
63. Loesch, Karl C. von, "Eingedeutschte, Entdeutschte und Renegaten", in *Volk unter Völkern, Bücher des Deutschtums*, Band I, Karl C. von Loesch, ed. (Breslau, Ferdinand Hirt, 1925).
64. Loesch, Karl C. von, "Volkstümer und Sprachwechsel", *Wörter und Sachen*, 17 (1936), 153-163.
65. Mackensen, Lutz, "Heimat, Kolonie, Umvolk", *Folk*, 1 (1937), 24-55.
66. Mackey, Wm. F., "The description of bilingualism", *Can. J. of Linguistics*, 7 (1962), 51-85.
67. Mak, Wilhelm, "Zweisprachigkeit und Mischmundart in Oberschlesien", *Schlesisches Jahrbuch für deutsche Kulturarbeit*, 7 (1935), 41-52.
68. Manuel, Herschel T., *The Preparation and Evaluation of Inter-language Testing Materials* (Austin, Univ. of Texas, 1963). (A mimeographed report of Cooperative Research Project Number 681.)
69. Miller, Herbert A., *Races, Nations and Classes* (Chicago, Lippincott, 1924).
70. Molee, Elias, *Plea for an American Language or Germanic-English* (Chicago, Anderson, 1888).
71. Nahirny, Vladimir C., and Joshua A. Fishman, "Organizational interest in language maintenance", in this volume, Chapter 7, pp. 156-189.
72. Nelson, Lowry, "Speaking of tongues", *Amer. J. of Sociol.*, 54 (1948), 202-210.
73. Orans, Martin, "A tribe in search of a great tradition. The emulation-solidarity conflict", *Man in India*, 39, 2, 108-114.
74. Pihlblad, C. Terence, "The Kansas Swedes", *Southwestern Social Science Quarterly*, 13 (1932), 34-47.
75. Pritzwald, Kurt Stegmann von, "Sprachwissenschaftliche Minderheitenforschung", *Wörter und Sachen*, 19 (1938), (n.s. 1), 52-72.
76. Reissman, Leonard, "The Urban Process". Unpublished paper presented at the Seminar on Elites, Ideologies and Social Change, Center for Advanced Study in the Behavioral Sciences, December, 1963.
77. Rubin, Joan, "Stability and Change in a bilingual Paraguayan Community". Paper presented at the Meeting of the American Anthropological Association, November 21, 1963, San Francisco, Calif.
78. Samora, Julian, and Wm. N. Deane, "Language usage as a possible index of acculturation", *Sociology and Social Research*, 40 (1956), 307-311.
79. Sapir, Edward, "Language", *Encyclopedia of the Social Sciences*, 9 (1933), 155-169.
80. Schermerhorn, Richard A., "Toward a general theory of minority groups". Paper presented at the 58th Annual Meeting, Amer. Sociol. Assoc., Los Angeles, California, August 28, 1963.
81. Schmidt-Rohr, Georg, *Mutter Sprache* (Jena, Eugen Diederichs Verlag, 1933). (Title of first edition: *Die Sprache als Bildnerin der Völker*, Munich, 1932.)

82. Schmidt-Rohr, Georg, "Zur Frage der Zweisprachigkeit", *Deutsche Arbeit*, 36 (1936), 408-411 and 443-444.

83. Selk, Paul, *Die sprachlichen Verhältnisse im deutschdänischen Sprachgebiet südlich der Grenze* (Flensburg, Verlag Heimat und Erbe, 1937). (*Ergänzungsband*: 1940.)

84. Smith, Christina A., *Mental Testing of Hebridean Children in Gaelic and English* (London, 1948). (Not personally examined.)

85. Spencer, John (ed.), *Language in Africa* (Cambridge, Cambridge University Press, 1963).

86a. Swadesh, Morris, "Observations of pattern impact on the phonetics of bilinguals", in Spier, Leslie, A. Irving Hollowell, and Stanley S. Newman (eds.), *Language Culture and Personality; Essays in Memory of Edward Sapir* (Menasha, Sapir Memorial Publication Fund, 1941).

86b. Vildomec, Veroboj, *Multilingualism* (Leyden, Sijthoff, 1963).

87. Weinreich, Uriel, "Research Problems in Bilingualism, with Special Reference to Switzerland". Unpublished Ph.D. Dissertation, Columbia University, 1951.

88. Weinreich, Uriel, *Languages in Contact* (New York, Linguistic Circle of New York, 1953).

89. Weinreich, Uriel, "Functional aspects of Indian bilingualism", *Word*, 13 (1953), 203-233.

90. Willems, Emilio, "Linguistic changes in German-Brazilian Communities", *Acta Americana*, 1 (1943), 448-463.

NAME INDEX*

Note: In this index the following code is used: 10*n* indicates that the name is to be found in a footnote on p. 10; 10*t* indicates that the name is in a table on p. 10.

* Prepared by Helene K. Marer.

SUBJECT INDEX*

Note: In this index the following code is used: 10*n* indicates that the material is to be found in a footnote on page 10; 10*f* designates material in a figure; and 10*t* shows that the material is in a table.

* Prepared by Helene K. Marer.